W9-BBZ-471

3 9042 09000700 0

WITHDRAWN

# CALIFORNIA

*Road Trip*

STUART THORNTON

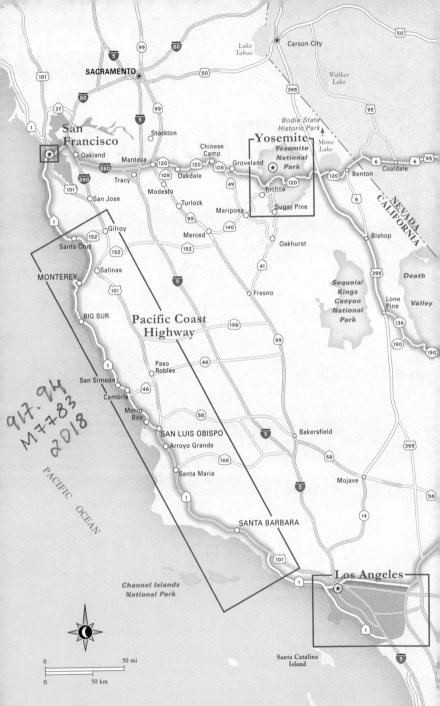

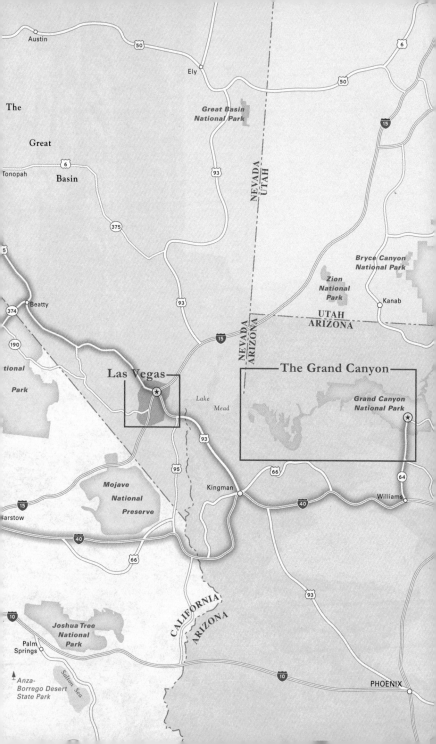

# CONTENTS

# DISCOVER
# the California Road Trip

San Francisco, Yosemite, Los Angeles, Las Vegas, and the Grand Canyon. Each is like no other place on earth. You can experience all of them in a 14-day road trip, with each stop roughly a day's drive from the next. You'll drive through a landscape that encompasses the best of the American West: modern skyscrapers and sandy beaches, granite peaks and towering trees, flat deserts and steep-sided canyons.

It's a landscape filled with overwhelming natural beauty and wide-open space. In Yosemite, waterfalls feather down faces of granite. At the Grand Canyon, layers of colorful geologic history travel back in time millions of years. Along the Pacific Coast, cliff sides tumble dramatically into the ocean.

This is nature at its most primal, but it's just a few hours away from the cosmopolitan pleasures of America's most distinctive cities. Whether it's the sunlight shimmering on the Golden Gate Bridge or the stripes of the rainbow flag, San Francisco is as proud of its colorful character as it is of its reputation as a culinary capital. Sprawling Los Angeles is a source of both world-class culture and amusement park fun. Las Vegas feels more like a mirage than a city, with its neon flashing against the otherwise dark desert sky.

Choose your own pace. Let your interests determine your routes and itineraries. Ride a cable car or hike to Half Dome. Stroll the Hollywood Walk of Fame or explore the Magic Kingdom. Descend deep into the Grand Canyon or dance until dawn in Sin City. Or just lie on the beach and soak up the sun. No matter who you are or what you're into, this road trip is for you.

# PLANNING YOUR TRIP

## Where to Go

### San Francisco

Located on a hilly peninsula between San Francisco Bay and the Pacific Ocean, San Francisco is one of the most beautiful cities in the world. Add in a renowned **food scene, world-class museums,** a healthy **arts culture,** and iconic attractions like the **Golden Gate Bridge** and **Alcatraz Island** for a mandatory stop on any serious road trip.

### Yosemite

Wander amid **sequoia groves, granite peaks,** and **mountain lakes.** See national treasures like **Half Dome** and **El Capitan.** Yosemite National Park showcases the stunning Sierra Nevada at its rugged best.

### Las Vegas

Rising out of the desert like a high-tech oasis, Las Vegas is an adult playground of **casinos, bars, buffets, over-the-top shows,** and **plush hotels.** Dig a little deeper to find fine food, a flourishing arts scene, and local hangouts in the shadows of **the Strip.**

### The Grand Canyon

A mile-deep slice into the **Kaibab Plateau,** the Grand Canyon defies easy description. Stare in awe at the colorful layers from the canyon's edge—or descend deep into the canyon to meet its creator: the mighty **Colorado River.**

### Los Angeles

Los Angeles is a massive mix of Southern California beach town, Hollywood dream factory, and 21st-century metropolis. Unmissable attractions include **world-class art,** a beach scene that begs for some time in the **sand and surf,** and an **amusement park** devoted to a cartoon mouse.

### Pacific Coast Highway

Stunning coastal views will fill your windshield as you drive along the stretch of the **Pacific Coast Highway** that connects Los Angeles and San Francisco. The winding roadway hits its peak passing through the mountains of **Big Sur,** dramatically perched above the ocean. Seaside sights include **Santa Barbara Mission, Hearst Castle,** the **Monterey Bay Aquarium,** and the **Santa Cruz Boardwalk.**

## Know Before You Go

### High Season

The West's best feature is its all-season appeal. That said, this trip is best in the **summer** and **early fall,** when CA-120 through Yosemite will most likely be open, although Las Vegas and the Grand Canyon will be quite warm. It's possible to bypass CA-120 in the **winter** and **spring** by taking a different route, but it will add hours and miles to the trip. Be aware that summer brings the most visitors, which will not only add to the crowds at attractions along the way, but also add to the traffic on the highways. Plan a little extra time to get from place to place.

The easiest places to **fly** into are **San Francisco, Los Angeles,** and **Las Vegas.** If you're flying into San Francisco, you can avoid some of the hassle of San Francisco International Airport (SFO) by flying into nearby **Oakland** or **San Jose.** Similarly, Los Angeles offers several suburban airports, including **Burbank, Long Beach,** and **Ontario,** which are typically less congested than Los Angeles International Airport (LAX). For more details, see page 419.

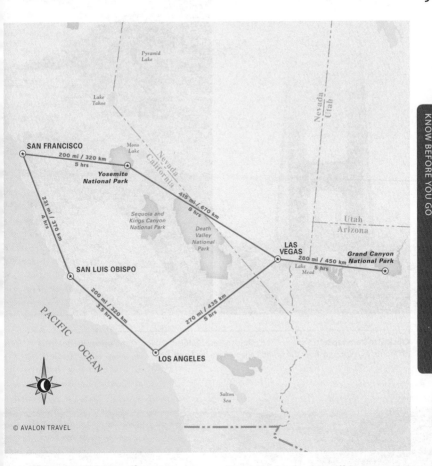

© AVALON TRAVEL

## Advance Reservations

Book **hotels** and **rental cars** in advance for the best rates and availability, especially in the summer, which is high season for travel. If you plan to rent a car in one city and return it in another (for example, rent the car in San Francisco and return it in Los Angeles), you should expect to pay an additional fee, which can be quite high.

High-season travelers should also plan ahead for the **big-name attractions.** If you have your heart set on visiting **Alcatraz** in San Francisco or the **Hearst Castle** in San Simeon, purchase tickets at least two weeks in advance. You'll save money buying advance tickets for **Disneyland** online as well. Reservations are essential at **campgrounds** in Yosemite, the Grand Canyon, and along Big Sur. If you plan to stay at the historic **Majestic Yosemite Hotel** or dine in its restaurant, make reservations as far in advance as possible.

## What to Pack

Bring **layered clothing.** Expect desert heat in Las Vegas and the Grand Canyon in the summer, but also be prepared for cooler temperatures. Summer fog is likely along the California coast, and is pretty much guaranteed in San Francisco, making the air damp and chilly. No matter what, use **sunscreen;** that cold fog doesn't

**Clockwise from top left:** San Francisco's Golden Gate Bridge in the fog; stand-up paddle boarding off Monterey's Cannery Row; the Grand Canyon from the South Rim.

stop the rays from burning unwary beachcombers.

Coming to the United States from abroad? You'll need your **passport** and possibly a **visa.**

## Driving Tips

Both **San Francisco** and especially **Los Angeles** suffer from serious **traffic congestion.** Avoid driving in or through San Francisco during rush hour traffic, typically weekdays 7am-9am and 4pm-6pm, though serious congestion can occur at other times. In Los Angeles, rush hour can stretch all the way from 5am to 10am and from 3pm to 7pm. Of course, special events can create traffic jams in both cities on weekends. To view current traffic conditions in the San Francisco Bay Area, visit **www.511.org.** For Los Angeles, go to **www.trafficinfo.lacity.org** for a city map showing current traffic information. Though not as notorious as San Francisco or Los Angeles, **Las Vegas** has its own traffic problems, especially on Thursday and Friday evenings. The **Nevada Department of Transportation** (www.nvroads.com) has information on current road conditions.

Because it's located in the high-altitude Sierra Nevada, **access to Yosemite** is dependent on the weather and the seasons. Two of the most traveled roads in the park, **Tioga Road** and **Glacier Point Road,** are typically **closed November-early June.** In recent years, **forest fires** have occurred in the park and surrounding areas, limiting access in the summer and fall as well. Check for road conditions and closures online at www.nps.gov/yose.

Fires and landslides can also impede a drive along the **Pacific Coast Highway,** especially through **Big Sur.** Visit the **Caltrans website** (www.dot.ca.gov) for highway conditions throughout California.

Expect **high summer temperatures** on the drive between Yosemite and Las Vegas, especially if you take the route through Death Valley, where blazing hot temperatures of 120°F or more can occur. Heat can also be a problem on the routes to and from the Grand Canyon. Make sure your car has sufficient **engine coolant** and working **air-conditioning,** and take along plenty of **drinking water.** You may also encounter **thunderstorms** in this area July-mid-September, which can lead to road flooding. Contact the **Nevada Department of Transportation** (877/687-6237, www.nvroads.com) and **Arizona Department of Transportation** (www.az511.gov) for each state's road conditions.

**Cell phone reception** is limited or non-existent in large sections of Yosemite, along the desert route to and from Las Vegas, and along the Pacific Coast Highway through Big Sur.

# HIT THE ROAD

## The 14-Day Best of the West

You can hit the top destinations in 14 days by driving in a rough loop. The day-by-day route below begins in San Francisco, but you can just as easily start in Los Angeles or Las Vegas if that works better for you. For detailed driving directions for each leg of this road trip, see *Getting There* at the beginning of each chapter. All mileage and driving times are approximate.

### Days 1-2
#### SAN FRANCISCO

It's easy to fill two days with fun in San Francisco. On the first day, visit the foodie-friendly **Ferry Building,** then walk 1.5 miles down the **Embarcadero** to the ferry that will take you out to **Alcatraz.** For dinner, indulge in Vietnamese fare at **The Slanted Door** or the old-school elegance of **Tadich Grill.**

On your second day, head west to **Golden Gate Park,** where you can explore the art of the **de Young Museum** or the animals at the **California Academy of Sciences.** Visit the **Japanese Tea Garden** for tea and a snack before leaving the park. Spend the afternoon at the **San Francisco Museum of Modern Art** before dining at its touted on-site restaurant **In Situ.**

Rest your head at the tech-savvy **Hotel Zetta,** homey **Golden Gate Hotel,** or **Hotel G** with its three dining and drinking establishments. For more suggestions on how to spend your time in San Francisco, see page 36.

### Day 3
#### DRIVING FROM SAN FRANCISCO TO YOSEMITE
200 mi / 320 km / 5 hrs

Grab a coffee from **Blue Bottle Café** to wake up for the drive to Yosemite. Leave San Francisco at 8am to reach Yosemite by noon. The drive to the **Big Oak Flat entrance** takes at least four hours; however, traffic, especially in summer and on weekends, can make it much longer.

### Days 4-5
#### YOSEMITE

Explore **Yosemite Valley** to see iconic attractions like **Half Dome** and **El Capitan.** Make reservations ahead of time to spend the night in the comfort of the **Majestic Yosemite Hotel** or in the mountain air at the park's **Tuolumne Meadows Campground,** which is only open in the summer. On the second day, plan a hike to **Tuolumne Meadows** or head to the more remote, less-visited **Hetch Hetchy** region, where worthwhile hikes include the **Wapama Falls Trail.**

### Day 6
#### DRIVING FROM YOSEMITE TO LAS VEGAS
415 mi / 670 km / 8 hrs

You have a long drive ahead of you, so fuel up with a stop at the **Whoa Nellie Deli** just east of the park's Tioga Pass entrance or at the **Silver Lake Resort Café** on the June Lake Loop.

For most of the year, the best route is via **Tioga Pass** (if you're traveling in winter or spring, check to make sure that it's open before heading out). The **Nevada route** is the most direct: the 415-mile drive to Las Vegas takes 7 hours, 45 minutes. Follow **CA-120 East** to US-6 in Benton. Take **US-6 East** to Coaldale, where it shares the road with **US-95 South** to **Tonopah,** which makes a good

# Best Views

A stunning view can make you feel like the king or queen of the world. It can also give you a different perspective on the place you are visiting.

## San Francisco

- **Twin Peaks:** At almost 1,000 feet high, Twin Peaks is San Francisco's second-highest point. It offers fine views of the city's rows of residences and the downtown buildings that protrude into the sky like jagged crystals (page 61).

- **The Starlight Room:** When the sun goes down, take in the lights and buildings of San Francisco from this lounge located 21 stories up (page 49).

## Yosemite

- **Glacier Point:** At 7,214 feet high, Glacier Point has one of the best overall views of Yosemite Valley, including Half Dome and Yosemite Falls (page 110).

- **Olmsted Point:** Off Tioga Road, this easy-to-access viewpoint showcases lesser-known features in the park, including Tenaya Canyon and Clouds Rest (page 121).

- **Columbia Rock:** A short and steep hike pays big dividends on this two-mile round-trip route, with stunning views of Yosemite Valley (page 104).

## Las Vegas

- **Mandarin Bar:** For unforgettable views of the Las Vegas Strip, visit this sleek, upscale bar on the 23rd floor of the Mandarin Oriental (page 189).

- **Stratosphere Tower:** The thrill rides on the observation deck are hair-raising, but head to the 107th floor and its namesake 107 Sky Lounge for a quieter view—with cocktails (page 176).

- **High Roller:** The world's highest observation wheel allows riders to see the candy-colored lights of the Strip from above (page 162).

## Grand Canyon

- **Yavapai Observation Station:** Hanging off the Grand Canyon's South Rim, the station's geological exhibits put that first glimpse of the canyon into context (page 222).

- **Mather Point:** Near the park entrance, the most-visited viewpoint in the Grand Canyon is this classic panorama (page 221).

## Los Angeles

- **The Getty Center:** On a clear day, the views from this state-of-the-art museum take in the entire Los Angeles skyline sprawling west to the Pacific (page 279).

- **Ace Hotel's Rooftop Bar:** Feel like a star at this rooftop bar and deck located atop the hip downtown hotel (page 300).

- **High:** Survey the wildly entertaining Venice Boardwalk from above—with a cocktail in hand from the rooftop lounge of Hotel Erwin (page 305).

## Pacific Coast Highway

- **Cone Peak Trail:** Every step of the four-mile round-trip hike is worth it for the stellar views of the Big Sur coastline (page 379).

- **McWay Falls Overlook Trail:** You can't get to the cove where 80-foot high McWay Falls crashes into the sea—so make do with the superb view from an observation point in Julia Pfeiffer Burns State Park (page 375).

**Clockwise from top left:** Golden Gate Park's de Young Museum; a diver in the California Academy of Science's Philippine Coral Reef Exhibit; the Grand Canyon Railway.

stopover. It's then a 210-mile straight shot on US-95 South to Vegas.

The **California route** is more scenic. It's only a few miles farther but 45 minutes longer, traversing Mammoth Lakes, Bishop, and Lone Pine. East of Lone Pine, **CA-136** becomes **CA-190,** which winds through Death Valley. A right turn onto the Daylight Pass Road leads to the Nevada border and **CA-374** just before **Beatty,** which makes a good place to stop. From Beatty, **US-95** leads southeast to Las Vegas.

## Day 7
### LAS VEGAS

The glitz of the **Las Vegas Strip** makes it a surreal stopover between the natural wonders of Yosemite and the Grand Canyon. Fortify yourself with a rich but right Croque Madame from famed chef Thomas Keller's **Bouchon** at **The Venetian.** Strip off the dust and sweat of the road with a decadent pool party at **The Palms.** Watch the sun set from the 550-foot-tall **High Roller** observation wheel and then get some creative comfort food at **Culinary Dropout** or go upscale at **Rose. Rabbit. Lie.** Indulge yourself with a stay at the lux **Mandarin Oriental Las Vegas.** For more suggestions on how to spend your time in Las Vegas, see page 145.

## Day 8
### DRIVING FROM LAS VEGAS TO THE GRAND CANYON
### 280 mi / 450 km / 5 hrs

The 280-mile drive to the Grand Canyon takes about five hours. Head south on **US-93,** breezing over the new Hoover Dam Bypass, and stop over in **Kingman, Arizona.** Then take **I-40 East** to **Williams** (115 miles) and overnight at the **Grand Canyon Railway Hotel.**

## Day 9
### THE GRAND CANYON

Enjoy a break from your car by taking the **Grand Canyon Railway** from **Williams** to **Grand Canyon National Park.** Enjoy the views from the **Rim Trail** or descend into the canyon on the **Bright Angel Trail.** Get an appetizer or a drink at the historic **El Tovar Hotel** before taking the train back to **Williams.** For dinner, indulge in a prime cut of meat from **Rod's Steak House.**

## Day 10
### DRIVING FROM THE GRAND CANYON TO LOS ANGELES
### 500 mi / 805 km / 8 hrs

After a good night's sleep, head out for Los Angeles. The 494-mile drive to Los Angeles takes 7-8 hours. Take **I-40 West** to Barstow. From Barstow, take **I-15 South,** then take **I-10 West** into the heart of L.A. Be prepared to slow down when you hit the L.A. traffic, which may extend your driving time exponentially.

## Days 11-12
### LOS ANGELES

After appreciating the natural wonder of the Grand Canyon, it's time to appreciate the achievements of civilization in Los Angeles. On your first day, see the **Space Shuttle** *Endeavour* at the **California Science Center** or view the artistic masterpieces at **The Getty Center.** For a night in the heart of downtown, stay at the **Ace Hotel** and enjoy dinner at its downstairs restaurant, **L.A. Chapter.**

On your second day, give your mind a rest and hit the beach. Choose the **Santa Monica Pier** for its beachside amusement park, **Venice Beach** for its lively boardwalk, or **Malibu** for its famous surf. For dinner, plan on fresh seafood at **Neptune's Net,** then sleep by the sea at the **Hotel Erwin** in Venice Beach. Kids (and kids at heart) might prefer a full day and night at the **Disneyland Resort.** For more suggestions on how to spend your time in Los Angeles, see page 267.

**Clockwise from top left:** Big Sur; the Grand Canyon from Bright Angel Trail; Carmel's Point Lobos State Reserve.

## Days 13-14
### DRIVING FROM LOS ANGELES TO SAN FRANCISCO
**500 mi / 805 km / 8 hrs**

This scenic route runs almost 500 miles and can easily take 8 hours to drive. While it's possible to make the drive in one long day, this is one stretch that you won't want to rush. Planning on two days allows you to take in some of the many fine attractions along the way. Alternate between **US-101 North** and **CA-1** (which are sometimes the same road) depending upon where you want to stop and linger. For a quicker drive, take the inland route **I-5,** which is just around 380 miles and takes about six hours—but you'll miss the most scenic sections of the California coast.

### PACIFIC COAST HIGHWAY

The most difficult part of this journey along PCH is deciding which of its many fine attractions deserve a stop. On the first day, soak up surf culture in **Ventura** or experience fine living in **Santa Barbara,** with its regal **Santa Barbara Mission. San Luis Obispo** is around the midway point and makes a good place to spend the night. On the second day, choose between **Hearst Castle** in San Simeon, the scenic coastal drive through **Big Sur,** or **Monterey,** with its world-class **aquarium,** on your way back to San Francisco. If you allow 3-4 days for this drive, you can see them all. Stay longer depending on where your interests lie. For specific suggestions on where to stop along the coast, see page 330.

# San Francisco, Yosemite, and Los Angeles

In just **six days,** you can experience California's most famous cities and its biggest natural attraction. But you'll be doing a lot of driving. Make it a full **seven**

**days** and you have enough time for the state's best coastal drive along Big Sur. If you have more time than that, it's well worth adding another day to each of the main stops. Mileage and driving times are approximate.

## Day 1
### SAN FRANCISCO

Spend your San Francisco day in **Golden Gate Park.** Indulge your artistic side at the **de Young Museum** or learn more about our world at the nearby **California Academy of Sciences.** Unwind with a walk through the park's **Japanese Tea Garden.** Then make your way to the **Golden Gate Bridge,** one of the world's most famous photo-ops. End your day with a meal at one of the city's culinary stars—or grab an authentic burrito at a local taqueria, which may be just as tasty. You won't have as many dining options once you make it to Yosemite. For more suggestions on how to spend your time in San Francisco, see page 36.

## Day 2
### DRIVING FROM SAN FRANCISCO TO YOSEMITE
**200 mi / 320 km / 5 hrs**

With a head full of art and science and a belly full of gourmet food, head to Yosemite. Leave San Francisco at 8am to reach Yosemite by noon. The drive to the **Big Oak Flat entrance** takes at least four hours; however, traffic, especially in summer and on weekends, can make it much longer.

## Day 3
### YOSEMITE

Spend a day touring around **Yosemite Valley,** seeing **Half Dome, El Capitan,** and **Yosemite Falls.** If you want to break a sweat, hike the 5.4-mile round-trip **Mist Trail.** Spend a night under the stars at one of the park's campgrounds or enjoy a night indoors at the classic **Majestic Yosemite Hotel** (just be sure to make reservations well in advance), or head out

# Best Hikes

the Grand Canyon's Bright Angel Trail from above

## San Francisco

* **Lands End Trail:** This trail in the Golden Gate National Recreation Area is rife with beaches and littered with shipwrecks (page 60).

* **Twin Peaks:** The reward exceeds the work on this short 0.5-mile hike up to the city's second-highest point, with its 360-degree view (page 61).

## Yosemite

* **Mist Trail:** This classic hike passes through refreshing waterfall spray from Vernal and Nevada Falls (page 105).

* **Wapama Falls Trail:** Explore the isolated grandeur of Yosemite's Hetch Hetchy region on this five-mile round-trip hike (page 115).

* **Columbia Rock Trail:** This two-mile round-trip trail out of Yosemite Valley gets you to a precariously perched rock that takes in the park's finest features (page 104).

## Grand Canyon

* **Rim Trail:** An easy 13-mile hike, this all-day trail showcases the grandeur of the Grand Canyon's South Rim (page 224).

* **Bright Angel Trail:** Experience one of the country's finest adventures on this 9.5-mile trail descending into the immensity of the Grand Canyon (page 225).

## Los Angeles

* **Hollyridge Trail:** This strenuous hike within Griffith Park leads to a unique view of the city from behind one of its best-known landmarks: the Hollywood sign (page 273).

## Pacific Coast Highway

* **Bishop Peak Trail:** This four-mile round-trip hike on 1,546-foot volcanic Bishop Peak offers superb views of the Pacific Coast far below (page 356).

* **Ewoldsen Trail:** This 4.5-mile round-trip hike in Julia Pfeiffer Burns State Park showcases Big Sur's best assets: towering redwoods and gorgeous coastline (page 379).

* **Ridge Trail and Panorama Trail Loop:** Big Sur's finest coastal trail is an eight-mile loop that takes in bluffs, ridges, and a secluded beach (page 379).

**Clockwise from top left:** Malibu's Getty Villa; Hollywood Walk of Fame; Las Vegas' High Roller observation wheel at night.

of the park to splurge at the **Rush Creek Lodge,** located 1.5 miles from Yosemite's Big Oak Flat entrance.

## Day 4
### DRIVING FROM YOSEMITE TO LOS ANGELES
**300 mi / 480 km / 6 hrs**

Exit the park via its southern entrance and go south on **CA-41.** The majority of the trip will be spent on **CA-99 South** before using **I-5 South, CA-170 South,** and **US-101 South** as you get closer to the city.

## Day 5
### LOS ANGELES

You've been to the mountains; now it's time for the beach! Experience the best of Southern California beach culture at the chaotic but entertaining **Venice Boardwalk** or the **Santa Monica Pier.** If time allows, head inland a few miles to stroll the **Hollywood Walk of Fame** and snap a pic at **TCL Chinese Theatre.** Of course, some people would give all of that up for a day at **Disneyland** (you know who you are). For more suggestions on how to spend your time in Los Angeles, see page 267.

## Days 6-7
### DRIVING FROM LOS ANGELES TO SAN FRANCISCO
**500 mi / 805 km / 8 hrs**

You can make this drive in one long day if you make only a few stops (such as getting lunch midway in San Luis Obispo), but it's better to break it up over two days and enjoy the coast. On the first day, stop in **Santa Barbara** for lunch at one of the great restaurants off **State Street.** Continue on to **San Luis Obispo** to spend the night.

On the second day, plan on stopping for a tour of **Hearst Castle** in **San Simeon,** then driving up PCH through **Big Sur** on the way back to San Francisco. (If you really need to get from Los Angeles to San Francisco in one day, it's quicker to take **I-5,** which takes around six hours.)

---

# Los Angeles, Las Vegas, and the Grand Canyon

In just **four days,** you can experience two major American cities and the West's most famous natural attraction. But you'll be doing a lot of driving. With a full **seven days,** you can add a day to each place to experience them more fully.

## Day 1
### LOS ANGELES

If you have just one day in **Los Angeles,** don't try to do it all; you'll end up spending most of your time on the freeway. Instead, focus in on the part of town that interests you the most. Movie fanatics should go to **Hollywood** to wander the **Walk of Fame.** Outdoors lovers should target one of the beach towns (**Malibu, Santa Monica,** or **Venice Beach**) to enjoy the sun and sand. Families will most likely want to head to the house of the mouse (better known as **Disneyland**). For more suggestions on how to spend your time in Los Angeles, see page 267.

## Day 2
### DRIVING FROM LOS ANGELES TO LAS VEGAS
**270 mi / 435 km / 5 hrs**

Take **I-10 East** out of Los Angeles, and then use **I-15 North** for the majority of your drive.

### LAS VEGAS

You've only got one night in **Las Vegas,** so spoil yourself. Stroll the Strip, popping into casinos like the **Cosmopolitan, Bellagio,** and **Caesars Palace** for food, drinks, a show, gambling—or all of the above. End your night at the **Mandarin Bar,** with its glittering view of the Strip.

# Stretch Your Legs

Quick roadside pullovers recharge your batteries and fight road weariness. The California Road Trip loop is flush with worthwhile roadside attractions, from stunning waterfalls to an alien-themed convenience store.

### San Francisco to Yosemite
The **Knights Ferry Covered Bridge** (page 94) is the longest covered bridge west of the Mississippi.

### Yosemite to Las Vegas
Ever wonder what it would be like to live upside down? Satisfy your curiosity at the **Upside-Down House** (page 142). Let your conspiracy theories run wild at the **Area 51 Alien Travel Center** (page 142). **Last Stop Arizona** (page 142) also celebrates life on other planets.

### Los Angeles to Grand Canyon
Let the Los Angeles freeways thin out while spending an hour at the quirky **Watts Towers** (page 271). Arizona's **Historic Route 66 Museum** (page 205) tells the story of the celebrated roadway.

Big Sur's McWay Falls

### Grand Canyon to Los Angeles
You're not hallucinating: The giant golf ball teed up in the desert is called the **Golf Ball House** (page 265).

### Los Angeles to San Francisco
The kitschy **Madonna Inn** (page 354) is the mother ship of roadside motels, while the appeal of **McWay Falls** (page 375), plunging 80 feet down into the Pacific, is more sublime.

For more suggestions on how to spend your time in Las Vegas, see page 145.

## Day 3
### DRIVING FROM LAS VEGAS TO THE GRAND CANYON
**280 mi / 450 km / 5 hrs**
This desert drive follows **US-93 South** and **I-40 East** to the Arizona town of **Williams.** From there, take **AZ-64 North** to the **South Rim** of the **Grand Canyon.**

### THE GRAND CANYON
Walk along the park's **Rim Trail** for outstanding, accessible views of the canyon. In **Grand Canyon Village,** stop into the **Hopi House** to see Native American art and the **Lookout Studio,** where you can use telescopes set up on the outdoor terrace to get better views of canyon features. Dip into the canyon on the **Bright Angel Trail.** Get a meal and spend the night at the **El Tovar Hotel,** the national park's most elegant lodging option.

## Day 4
### DRIVING FROM THE GRAND CANYON TO LOS ANGELES
**500 mi / 805 km / 8 hrs**
The eight-hour trek from the Grand Canyon to Los Angeles is a grueling desert drive. Take **I-40 West** to Barstow. From Barstow, take **I-15 South,** then take **I-10 West** into the heart of L.A. Be prepared to slow down when you hit the L.A. traffic.

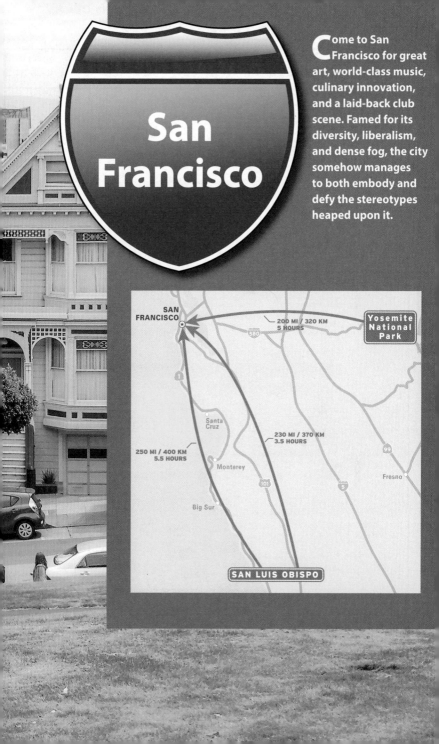

# San Francisco

Come to San Francisco for great art, world-class music, culinary innovation, and a laid-back club scene. Famed for its diversity, liberalism, and dense fog, the city somehow manages to both embody and defy the stereotypes heaped upon it.

SAN FRANCISCO

200 MI / 320 KM
5 HOURS

580

Yosemite National Park

1

Santa Cruz

230 MI / 370 KM
3.5 HOURS

99

250 MI / 400 KM
5.5 HOURS

Monterey

101

5

Fresno

Big Sur

SAN LUIS OBISPO

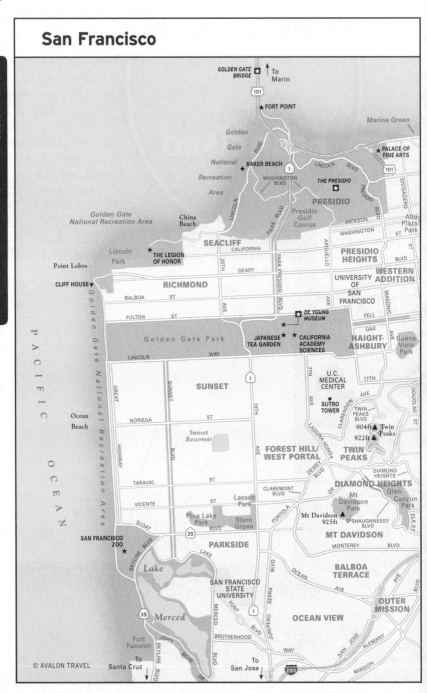

# San Francisco

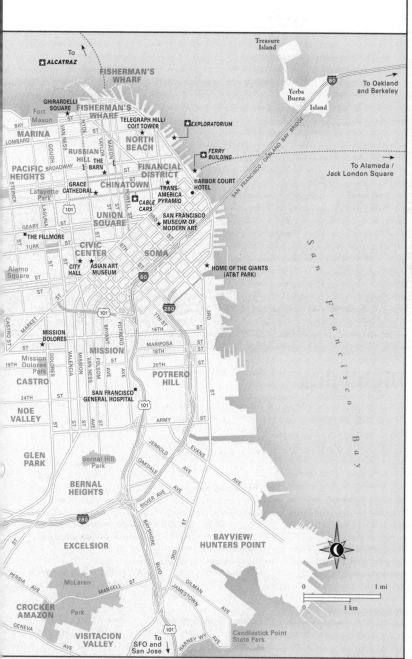

# Highlights

★ **Cable Cars:** Get a taste of free-spirited San Francisco—not to mention great views of Alcatraz and the Bay—via open-air public transit (page 30).

★ **Ferry Building:** The 1898 Ferry Building has been renovated and reimagined as the foodie mecca of San Francisco. The Tuesday and Saturday farmers market is not to be missed (page 32).

★ **Exploratorium:** The exhibits at this innovative and interactive science museum are meant to be touched, heard, and felt (page 35).

★ **Alcatraz:** Spend the day in prison—at the famous former maximum-security penitentiary in the middle of the Bay (page 35).

★ **The Presidio:** The original 1776 El Presidio de San Francisco is now a national park. Tour the historic buildings that formerly housed a military hospital, barracks, and fort—all amid a peaceful and verdant setting (page 39).

★ **Golden Gate Bridge:** Nothing beats the view from one of the most famous and fascinating bridges in the country. Pick a fogless day for a stroll or bike ride across the 1.7-mile span (page 41).

★ **de Young Museum:** The de Young is the showpiece of Golden Gate Park. A mixed collection of media and regions is highlighted by the 360-degree view from the museum's tower (page 43).

★ **San Francisco Museum of Modern Art:** After a massive renovation, SFMOMA showcases some of modern art's greatest hits and features the largest space dedicated to photographic art in the country (page 33)

**S**an Francisco perches restlessly on an uneven spit of land overlooking the Bay on one side and the Pacific Ocean on the other.

Street-corner protests and leather stores are certainly part of the landscape, but farmers markets and friendly communities also abound. English blends with languages from around the world in an occasionally frustrating, often joyful cacophony. Those who've chosen to live here often refuse to live anyplace else, despite the infamous cost of housing and the occasional violent earthquake. Don't call it "San Fran," or worse, "Frisco," or you'll be pegged as a tourist. To locals, this is The City, and that's that.

# Getting to San Francisco

## From Los Angeles
### The Coastal Route

The **Pacific Coast Highway (CA-1)** from Los Angeles to San Francisco is one of America's iconic drives. This coastal route has a lot to see and do, but it's not the fastest route between the two cities. It runs almost **500 miles** and can easily take **eight hours** or longer, depending on traffic. It's worth the extra time to experience the gorgeous coastal scenery, which includes Santa Barbara, Big Sur, and Monterey. The highway is long, narrow, and winding; in winter rockslides and mudslides may close the road entirely. Always check **Caltrans** (www.dot. ca.gov) for highway traffic conditions before starting your journey.

From Los Angeles, take **US-101 North** (past Oxnard, US-101 also follows CA-1). At Gaviota, US-101 turns inland toward Buellton and Santa Maria before rejoining CA-1 again at Pismo Beach. At San Luis Obispo, US-101 and CA-1 split again: CA-1 continues west along the Big Sur coast; US-101 moves inland through Paso Robles up toward Salinas, Gilroy, and San Jose. Note that US-101 is a more direct route to San Francisco. CA-1, while scenic, is longer and often clogged with traffic in Santa Cruz, where it meets **CA-17.**

### Stopping in San Luis Obispo

It's easier to enjoy the drive by dividing it up over two days and spending a night somewhere along the coast. Right off both CA-1 and US-101, the city of **San Luis Obispo** is close to halfway between the two cities, which makes it an ideal place to stop. It takes three hours to make the 201-mile drive from Los Angeles if traffic isn't bad. The additional 232 miles to San Francisco takes four hours or more. An affordable motel right off the highway is the **Peach Tree Inn** (2001 Monterey St., 800/227-6396, http:// peachtreeinn.com, $89-300). For a wilder experience, stay at popular tourist attraction **The Madonna Inn** (10 Madonna Rd., 805/543-3000, www.madonnainn.com, $210-490), which offers the **Gold Rush Steak House** for dinner and the **Copper Café & Pastry Shop** for breakfast. **Novo** (726 Higuera St., 805/543-3986, www. novorestaurant.com, 11am-close Mon.-Sat., 10am-2pm Sun., $16-32) has a truly international menu and outdoor dining on decks overlooking San Luis Obispo Creek. For something fast, the **Firestone Grill** (1001 Higuera St., 805/783-1001, www.firestonegrill.com, 11am-10pm Sun.-Wed., 11am-11pm Thurs.-Sat., $5-18) is known for its tasty tri-tip sandwich. For complete information on San Luis Obispo, see page 354.

### The Interior Route

A faster but much less interesting driving route is **I-5** from Los Angeles to San Francisco. It takes about **six hours** if the traffic is cooperating. On holiday

# Best Hotels

★ **Golden Gate Hotel:** This bed-and-breakfast-like hotel has nice, moderate rooms in a narrow building right by Union Square (page 74).

★ **Hotel G:** It comes on like an unassuming cool kid that impresses with understated style (page 75).

★ **Phoenix Hotel:** The Phoenix Hotel is popular with touring rock bands, which may be a plus to some and a minus to others. You don't have to be a rock star to enjoy this casual hotel's expansive pool deck (page 75).

★ **Hotel Triton:** Hotel Triton reflects the city's independent spirit with vibrant rooms, including suites designed by pop culture figures like Jerry Garcia (page 76).

★ **Hotel Zetta:** In the SOMA neighborhood, this hotel embraces the region's tech-savvy side. Each room comes equipped with a gaggle of gadgets (page 76).

★ **Harbor Court Hotel:** You can't beat the location—just a block from the Ferry Building, with a nighttime view of the Bay Bridge lights (page 77).

★ **Marina Motel:** This moderately priced motel in the Marina District has something most accommodations in the city don't have: individual parking garages for guests (page 78).

★ **The Metro Hotel:** This family-owned hotel near Haight Ashbury has clean, comfy rooms for some of the better rates within city limits (page 81)

---

weekends, the drive time can increase to 10 hours. From Los Angeles, most freeways lead or merge onto I-5 North and ascend to higher elevations before crossing the **Tejon Pass** over the Tehachapi Mountains. This section of the highway, nicknamed **the Grapevine,** can close in winter due to snow and ice (and sometimes in summer due to wildfires). November-March, tule fog (thick, ground-level fog) can also seriously impede driving conditions and reduce visibility to a crawl. After the Grapevine, the highway narrows to two lanes and is mostly straight and flat, not particularly scenic, and filled with trucks and highway patrol cars that can slow traffic considerably. Stay on I-5 for the first 308 miles, before diverting onto **I-580 West** (toward Tracy and San Francisco) for 62 miles. At that point, connect to **I-80 West.** Follow signs for San Francisco for the next 45-50 miles to cross the **Bay Bridge** (toll $6) into the city. Always check **Caltrans** (www.dot.ca.gov) for highway traffic conditions before starting your journey.

## From Yosemite

The drive from Yosemite to San Francisco involves lots of time on small highways that frequently pass orchards, farms, and sprawling valley towns. The drive of roughly **200 miles** can take four hours if traffic is on your side, but plan on **five hours.** The trip may require navigating heavy traffic in and out of Yosemite National Park (especially on weekends), the annual closure of **Tioga Pass** (a.k.a. **CA-120**), twists and turns on mountain roads, and traffic in the Central Valley and greater Bay Area.

### Summer

In summer, park roads and surrounding freeways are open, but they are also heavily trafficked. From Yosemite, exit the park via the **Big Oak Flat entrance** on **CA-120 West** to Manteca. Follow CA-120 West for about 100 miles as it merges with **CA-49** and **CA-108.** Near Manteca, CA-120 merges into I-5. Take **I-5 South** for about two miles, then take **I-205 West** for 14 miles to **I-580 West.** In

## Best Restaurants

★ **Yank Sing:** Sample dim sum by choosing from wheeled carts full of dumplings, pot stickers, spring rolls, and more (page 63).

★ **Brenda's French Soul Food:** Start the day with a hearty New Orleans-style breakfast like crawfish beignets at this Tenderloin eatery (page 63).

★ **Michael Mina:** The celebrity chef dishes out upscale cuisine, including a Maine lobster pot pie, at his namesake restaurant (page 64).

★ **The Cavalier:** Experience what upscale British pub food tastes like. Start with the golden fried lamb riblets (page 65).

★ **Tadich Grill:** After 160 years, the Tadich Grill is still serving an extensive

menu that includes sensational Italian seafood stew (page 65).

★ **Tony's Pizza Napoletana:** This North Beach pizzeria employs seven different kinds of ovens to cook its unique pies (page 68).

★ **Swan Oyster Depot:** Locals and visitors line up every day to get inside this tiny restaurant that serves seafood lunches (page 70).

★ **Jardinière:** Chef Traci Des Jardins combines French and California dining elements in this upscale restaurant (page 71).

★ **Tartine Bakery:** Lines snake out the door all day long, but the fresh baked goods and sandwiches are worth the wait (page 72).

---

about 45 miles, I-580 merges with **I-80 West** onto the **Bay Bridge** (toll $6) and into San Francisco.

### Winter

Many Yosemite park roads are closed in winter. **Tioga Pass** and **CA-120**—the east-west access through the park—are closed from the end of September until May or June. In addition, CA-120 west and north through the park and to San Francisco can also be closed due to snow. Chains can be required on park roads at any time. If traveling from Yosemite September-May, your surest access is **CA-140** and the **Arch Rock entrance.** From this entrance, follow **CA-140 West** to Merced. In Merced, merge onto **CA-99 North** to Manteca. At Manteca, merge onto **CA-120 West,** then continue the summer route to I-5, I-205, I-580, and I-80 into San Francisco.

### From Big Sur

En route to San Francisco from the south, many visitors divert from **US-101**

to **CA-1** to enjoy the narrow, twisting, two-lane, cliff-carved track to Big Sur. The drive is breathtaking both because of its beauty and because of its dangers. The **170-mile** drive can be as little as **3-4 hours** long, continuing on CA-1 from Big Sur through Monterey and Santa Cruz and up to San Francisco. Compared to US-101, CA-1 adds a few miles to your trip along with another 20 to 30 minutes of driving.

If it's a busy summer weekend, consider heading inland to US-101 north of Big Sur to avoid traffic delays. This is also a good idea during October, when traffic backs up on CA-1 around Half Moon Bay due to its Art & Pumpkin Festival. Head out of the Big Sur Valley for 49 miles on **CA-1 North,** then exit onto **CA-156 East,** which connects with US-101 North 6.5 miles later. Continue for 97 miles through San Jose and up into San Francisco.

### By Air, Train, or Bus

It's easy to fly into the San Francisco Bay Area. There are three major airports. Among them, you should be able to find a flight that fits your schedule. **San Francisco International Airport** (SFO, www.flysfo.com) is 13 miles south. **Oakland Airport** (OAK, www.oaklandairport.com) is 11 miles east of the city, but requires crossing the Bay, either via the Bay Bridge or public transit. **Mineta San José Airport** (SJC, www.flysanjose.com) is the farthest away, roughly 47 miles to the south. These last two airports are less than an hour away by car, with car rentals available. Some San Francisco hotels offer complimentary airport shuttles as well.

Several public and private transportation options can get you into San Francisco. **Bay Area Rapid Transit** (BART, www.bart.gov) connects directly with SFO's international terminal; an airport shuttle connects Oakland airport to the nearest station. **Caltrain** (www.caltrain.com, tickets $3.75-13.75) is a good option from San Jose; an airport shuttle connects to the train station. **Millbrae Station** is where the BART and Caltrain systems connect; it's designed to transfer from one line to the other.

**Amtrak** (www.amtrak.com) does not run directly into San Francisco, but you can ride to San Jose, Oakland, or Emeryville Stations, then take a connecting bus to San Francisco. **Greyhound** (200 Folsom St., 415/495-1569, www.greyhound.com, 5:30am-1:30am daily) offers bus service to San Francisco from all over the country.

# Sights

## Union Square and Downtown
### ★ Cable Cars

Perhaps the most recognizable symbol of San Francisco is the **cable car** (www.sfcablecar.com), originally conceived by Andrew Smith Hallidie as a safer alternative for traveling the steep, often slick hills of San Francisco. The cable cars ran as regular mass transit from 1873 into the 1940s, when buses and electric streetcars began to dominate the landscape. Dedicated citizens, especially "Cable Car Lady" Friedel Klussmann, saved the cable car system from extinction, and the cable cars have become a rolling national landmark.

Today you can ride the cable cars from one tourist destination to another for $5 per ride. A full day "passport" ticket ($13, also grants access to streetcars and buses) is totally worth it if you want to run around the city all day. Cable car routes can take you up Nob Hill from the Financial District, or from Union Square along Powell Street, through Chinatown, and out to Fisherman's Wharf. Take a seat, or grab one of the exterior poles and hang on! Cable cars have open-air seating only, making for a chilly ride on foggy days.

The cars get stuffed to capacity with tourists on weekends and with local commuters at rush hours. Expect to wait an hour or more for a ride from any of the turnaround points on a weekend or holiday. But a ride on a cable car from Union Square down to the Wharf is more than worth the wait. The views from the hills down to the bay inspire wonder even in lifetime residents. To learn a bit more, make a stop at the **Cable Car Museum** (1201 Mason St., 415/474-1887, www.cablecarmuseum.org, 10am-6pm daily Apr.-Oct., 10am-5pm daily Nov.-Mar., free), the home and nerve center of the entire fleet. Here a sweet little museum depicts the life and times of the cable cars while an elevated platform overlooks the engines, winding wheels, and thick steel cable that keeps the cars humming. You can even glimpse the 1873 tunnels that snake beneath the city.

### Grace Cathedral

Local icon **Grace Cathedral** (1100

# Union Square and Nob Hill

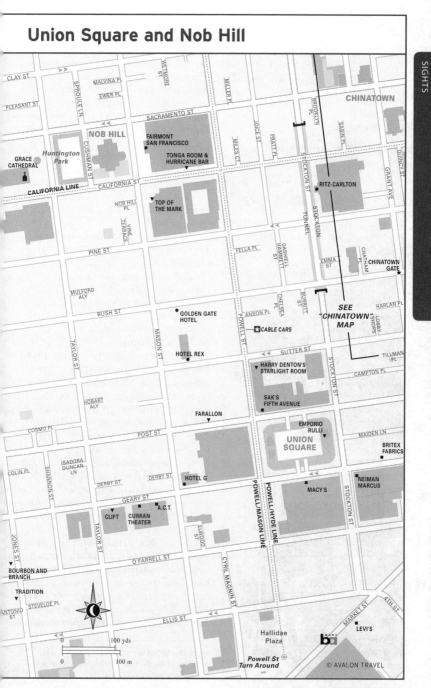

CLAY ST

PLEASANT ST

SPROULE LN

MALVINA PL

EWER PL

WETMORE ST

SACRAMENTO ST

MILLER PL

JOICE ST

PRATT PL

BROOKLYN PL

SABIN PL

**CHINATOWN**

QUINCY ST

NOB HILL

GRACE CATHEDRAL

Huntington Park

CUSHMAN ST

FAIRMONT SAN FRANCISCO

TONGA ROOM & HURRICANE BAR

STOCKTON ST

RITZ-CARLTON

GRANT AVE

**CALIFORNIA LINE** CALIFORNIA ST

NOB HILL PL

VINE TERRACE

TOP OF THE MARK

STOCKTON

TUNNEL

PINE ST

FELLA PL

DASHIELL HAMMETT

EMMA ST

CHATHAM PL

CHINATOWN GATE

MULFORD ALY

BUSH ST

MASON ST

GOLDEN GATE HOTEL

POWELL ST

ANSON PL

CHELSEA

BURRITT ST

HARLAN PL

SEE CHINATOWN MAP

LOBBY SHOPS

TAYLOR ST

HOTEL REX

CABLE CARS

SUTTER ST

STOCKTON ST

TILLMAN PL

HARRY DENTON'S STARLIGHT ROOM

CAMPTON PL

HOBART ALY

COSMO PL

POST ST

SAK'S FIFTH AVENUE

FARALLON

EMPORIO RULLI

**UNION SQUARE**

MAIDEN LN

BRITEX FABRICS

ISADORA DUNCAN LN

COLIN PL

SHANNON ST

DERBY ST

DERBY ST

HOTEL G

POWELL/MASON LINE

POWELL ST

MACY'S

STOCKTON ST

NEIMAN MARCUS

JONES ST

GEARY ST

CLIFT

CURRAN THEATER

A.C.T.

TAYLOR ST

ELWOOD ST

POWELL/HYDE LINE

BOURBON AND BRANCH

TRADITION

O'FARRELL ST

CYRIL MAGNIN ST

ANTONIO ST

STEVELOE PL

ELLIS ST

0      100 yds

0      100 m

Hallidae Plaza

Powell St Turn Around

MARKET ST

4TH ST

bars

LEVI'S

© AVALON TRAVEL

California St., 415/749-6300, www.gracecathedral.org, 7am-6pm Thurs., 8am-6pm Fri.-Wed., 8am-4pm holidays) is many things to many people. The French Gothic-style edifice, completed in 1964, attracts architecture and Beaux-Arts lovers by the thousands with its facade, stained glass, and furnishings. The labyrinths—replicas of the Chartres Cathedral labyrinth in France—appeal to meditative walkers seeking spiritual solace. Concerts featuring world music, sacred music, and modern classical ensembles draw audiences from around the Bay Area and farther afield.

The 1.5-hour **Grace Cathedral Grand Tour** (www.gracecathedral.org, $25) includes a walk up 94 steps to the top of the cathedral's South Tower. Download the GraceGuide app for information about the structure's architecture, history, and art.

### ★ Ferry Building

Restored to its former glory, the 1898 **San Francisco Ferry Building** (1 Ferry Bldg., 415/983-8030, www.ferrybuildingmarketplace.com, 10am-7pm Mon.-Fri., 8am-6pm Sat., 11am-5pm Sun., check with businesses for individual hours) stands at the edge of the Bay, its 230-foot-tall clock tower serving as a beacon to both land and water traffic. Photos and interpretive plaques just inside the main lobby describe its history. Free **walking tours** (www.sfcityguides.org) of the building are offered one day a week.

Inside, it's all about the food. Permanent shops provide top-tier artisanal food and drink, with local favorites like Cowgirl Creamery, Blue Bottle Café, and Acme Bread Company, while a few quick-and-easy restaurants offer reasonable meals. The famous **Farmers Market**

---

**From top to bottom:** the Ferry Building; a remnant of the Presidio's military past; an iconic San Francisco cable car.

# Financial District and Soma

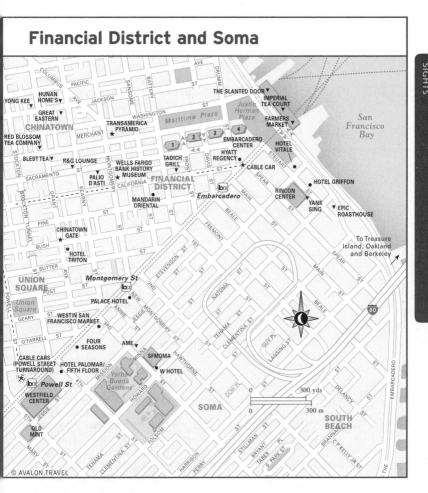

(415/291-3276, www.cuesa.org/markets, 10am-2pm Tues. and Thurs., 8am-2pm Sat.) draws crowds shopping for produce out front.

On the water side of the Ferry Building, boats come and go from Sausalito, Tiburon, Larkspur, Vallejo, and Alameda each day. Check with the **Blue and Gewold Fleet** (www.blue-andgoldfleet.com), **Golden Gate Ferry** (www.goldengateferry.org), and **San Francisco Bay Ferry** (http://sanfrancis-cobayferry.com) for information about service, times, and fares.

## ★ San Francisco Museum of Modern Art

After a massive three-year renovation, the **San Francisco Museum of Modern Art** (SFMOMA, 151 3rd St., 415/357-4000, www.sfmoma.org, 10am-5pm Sun.-Tues. and Fri., 10am-9pm Thurs., 10am-8pm Sat. summer, 10am-9pm Thurs., 10am-5pm Fri.-Tues. winter, $25 adults, $22 seniors, $22 young adult 19-24, chil-dren under 18 free) reopened in 2016 with three times as much gallery space. Modern classics on display include major works by Roy Lichtenstein, Georgia

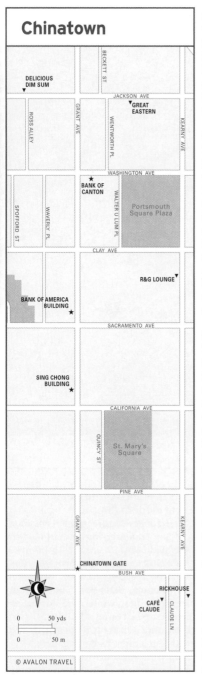

**Chinatown**

O'Keefe, Jackson Pollock, and Andy Warhol. The 3rd-floor Pritzker Center for Photography is the largest space dedicated to photographic art in the country. Enjoy views of the building's stunning design by walking across the 5th floor's Oculus Bridge, or get a breath of fresh air on the 3rd-floor sculpture terrace.

### Contemporary Jewish Museum

The local favorite **Contemporary Jewish Museum** (736 Mission St., 415/655-7800, www.thecjm.org, 11am-5pm Fri.-Tues., 11am-8pm Thurs., $14 adults, $12 seniors and students, children 18 and under free) curates superb temporary exhibits on pop culture. Recent subjects include filmmaker Stanley Kubrick, Bay Area music promoter Bill Graham, and singer Amy Winehouse. The museum's sleek building is part historic power station and part blue steel structure that spells out the Hebrew word *chai*, meaning life.

## Chinatown

The massive Chinese migration to California began almost as soon as the news of easy gold in the mountain streams made it to East Asia. And despite rampant prejudice, the Chinese not only stayed, but persevered and eventually prospered. Many never made it to the gold fields, preferring instead to remain in bustling San Francisco to open shops and begin the business of commerce in their new home. They carved out a thriving community at the border of **Portsmouth Square,** then center of the young city, which became known as Chinatown. Along with much of San Francisco, the neighborhood was destroyed in the 1906 earthquake and fire.

Today visitors see the post-1906 visitor-friendly Chinatown that was built after the quake, particularly if they enter through the **Chinatown Gate** (Grant Ave. and Bush St.) at the edge of Union Square. In this historic neighborhood, beautiful Asian architecture mixes with more mundane blocky city buildings to create a unique skyline. Small alleyways wend between the touristy commercial corridors, creating an intimate atmosphere.

## North Beach and Fisherman's Wharf

North Beach has long served as the Little Italy of San Francisco, a fact still reflected in the restaurants in the neighborhood. North Beach truly made its mark in the 1950s when it was, for a brief time, home to many writers in the Beat Generation, including Jack Kerouac, Gary Snyder, and Allen Ginsburg.

### Coit Tower

Built in 1933 as a monument to benefactor Lillie Hitchcock Coit's beloved firefighters, **Coit Tower** (1 Telegraph Hill Blvd., 415/249-0995, http://sfrecpark. org, 10am-6pm daily May-Oct., 10am-5pm daily Nov.-Apr., entrance free) has beautified the city just as Coit intended. Inside the art deco tower, the walls are covered in the restored frescos painted in 1934 depicting city and California life during the Great Depression. For a fee ($8 adults, $5 seniors and youth, $2 children 5-11, children under 5 free), you can ride the elevator to the top, where on a clear day, you can see the whole city and bay. Part of what makes Coit Tower special is the walk up to it. Rather than contributing to the acute congestion in the area, consider taking public transit to the area and walking up Telegraph Hill Boulevard through Pioneer Park to the tower, and descend down either the Filbert or Greenwich steps toward the Embarcadero. It's long and steep, but there's no other way to see the lovely little cottages and gardens of the beautiful and quaint Telegraph Hill.

### Lombard Street

You've no doubt seen it in movies: **Lombard Street** (Lombard St., one way from Hyde St. to Leavenworth St.), otherwise known as "the crookedest street in the world." The section of the street that visitors flock to spans only one block, from Hyde Street at the top to Leavenworth Street at the bottom. However, the line of cars waiting their turn to drive bumper-to-bumper can be just as legendary as its 27 percent grade. Bypass the car and take the hill by foot. The unobstructed vistas of San Francisco Bay, Alcatraz Island, Fisherman's Wharf, Coit Tower, and the city are reason enough to add this walk to your itinerary, as are the brick steps, manicured hydrangeas, and tony residences that line the roadway. To avoid traffic jams, drive the road in the early morning or at night during the summer.

### ★ Exploratorium

Lauded both as "one of the world's most important science museums" and "a mad scientist's penny arcade," the **Exploratorium** (Pier 15, 415/528-4444, www.exploratorium.edu, 10am-5pm Tues.-Sun. and Fri.-Sun., 10am-6pm Thurs. only, $25 seniors and youth 13-17, $20 children 4-12, children under 4 free) houses 150 playful exhibits on physics, motion, perception, and the senses that utilize its stunning location. Make a reservation ($15) to walk blindly (and bravely) into the Tactile Dome, a lightless space where you can "see" your way only by reaching out and touching the environment around you. Exploratorium "After Dark" targets adults 18 and over (6pm-10pm Thurs., $15). Its location between the Ferry Building and Fisherman's Wharf makes a crowd-free trip impossible, especially on the weekends.

### ★ Alcatraz

Going to **Alcatraz** (www.nps.gov/alcatraz), one of the most famous landmarks in the city, feels a bit like going to purgatory; this military fortress-turned-maximum-security prison, nicknamed "The Rock," has little warmth or welcome on its craggy, forbidding shores. While it still belonged to the military, the fortress became a prison in the 19th

# Two Days in San Francisco

San Francisco may only be roughly seven miles long and seven miles wide, but it packs in historic neighborhoods, one of the West Coast's most iconic landmarks, and dozens of stomach-dropping inclines within its small area. Exploring all its hills and valleys takes some planning.

## Day 1

Start your day at the **Ferry Building.** Graze from the many vendors, including **Blue Bottle Café, Cowgirl Creamery,** and **Acme Bread Company,** then walk two blocks to **Yank Sing** for a dim sum lunch. Catch the Muni F line (Steuart St. and Market St., $2) to Jefferson Street and take a stroll along **Fisherman's Wharf.** Stop into the **Musée Mécanique** to play a few coin-operated antique arcade games. Near Pier 39, catch the ferry to **Alcatraz**—be sure to buy your tickets well in advance. Alcatraz will fill your mind with amazing stories from the legendary island prison.

After you escape from Alcatraz, take the N Judah line ($2) to 9th Avenue and Irving Street, then follow 9th Avenue north into **Golden Gate Park,** where you can delve into art at the fabulous **de Young Museum** or science at the **California Academy of Sciences.** Stroll the scenic **Japanese Tea Gardens** and get a snack at the Tea House.

Catch a cab to North Beach and **Tony's**

**Pizza Napoletana** to get some real sustenance directly from one of its seven pizza ovens. Now you are ready to enjoy the talented performers, silly jokes, and gravity-defying hats of the long-running theater production *Beach Blanket Babylon.* If theater is not your thing, see some live music at the **Great American Music Hall**.

## Day 2

Fortify yourself for a day of sightseeing with a hearty breakfast at **Brenda's French Soul Food,** then drive or take a cab out to the **Land's End Trail,** where you can investigate the ruins of the former Sutro Baths and get views of the city's rocky coastline. Then head back to **Crissy Field** for views of the **Golden Gate Bridge.**

Walk to the adjacent Marina District for oysters at **Swan Oyster Depot** or sushi at **Ace Wasabi's.** Venture back downtown to wander the streets of **Chinatown** and adjacent **North Beach.** Browse through **City Lights,** the legendary Beat Generation bookstore. Wind down with a cocktail at **Vesuvio,** a colorful bar and former Beat writer hangout located nextdoor.

Head to the bustling Mission District, stopping first for a drink at the rooftop bar **El Techo de Lolinda** or **Trick Dog.** Then enjoy dinner at **Tartine Manufactory** or **Ichi Sushi.**

century to house Civil War prisoners. The isolation of the island in the bay, the frigid waters, and the nasty currents surrounding Alcatraz made it a perfect spot to keep prisoners contained, with little hope of escape and near-certain death if the attempt were ever made. In 1934, after the military closed down its prison and handed the island over to the Department of Justice, construction began to turn Alcatraz into a new style of prison ready to house a new style of prisoner: Depression-era gangsters. A few of the honored guests of this maximum-security penitentiary were Al Capone, George "Machine Gun" Kelly, and Robert Stroud, "the Birdman of Alcatraz." The prison closed in 1963, and in 1964 and 1969 occupations were staged by Indians of All Tribes, an exercise that eventually led to the privilege of self-determination for North America's original inhabitants.

Visit the island on tours offered by **Alcatraz Cruises** (Pier 33, 415/981-7625, www.alcatrazcruises.com, adults $37 and up, seniors $35 and up, children $24 and up, check website for times and prices), departing from Pier 33. Options include the **Day Tour, Night Tour, Behind the Scenes Tour,** and the **Alcatraz and Angel Island Tour.** Tours typically sell out, especially on weekends, so reserve tickets at least two weeks in advance.

### Fisherman's Wharf

Welcome to **Fisherman's Wharf** (Beach St. from Powell St. to Van Ness Ave., backs onto Bay St., www.fishermanswharf.org), the tourist mecca of San Francisco! While warehouses, stacks of crab pots, and a fleet of fishing vessels let you know this is still a working wharf, it is also where visitors come and snap photos. Reachable by the Muni F line and the Hyde-Powell cable car, the Wharf sprawls along the waterfront and inland several blocks.

Be prepared to push through a sea of humanity to buy souvenirs, eat seafood, and enjoy fun pieces of San Francisco's heritage, like the **Musée Mécanique** (Pier 45, Fishermen's Wharf, 415/346-2000, www.museemechaniquesf.com, 10am-8pm daily, free), a strange collection of over 300 working coin-operated machines from the 1800s to today. Machines include a 3-D picture show of San Francisco after the catastrophic 1906 earthquake and fire, along with more modern favorites like Ms. Pac-Man.

### Ghirardelli Square

**Ghirardelli Square** (900 North Point St., www.ghirardellisq.com, winter 10am-6pm Sun.-Thurs., 10am-9pm Fri.-Sat.), pronounced "GEAR-ah-DEL-ee," began its life as a chocolate factory in 1852, but has since reinvented itself as an upscale shopping, dining, and living compound. The **Ghirardelli Chocolate Manufactory** (900 North Point St., 415/474-3938, www.ghirardellisq.com, 9am-11pm Sun.-Thurs., 9am-midnight Fri.-Sat.) anchors the corner of the square. Here you can

**From top to bottom:** Musée Mécanique; the Palace of Fine Arts; Tadich Grill, said to be San Francisco's oldest restaurant.

# North Beach and Fisherman's Wharf

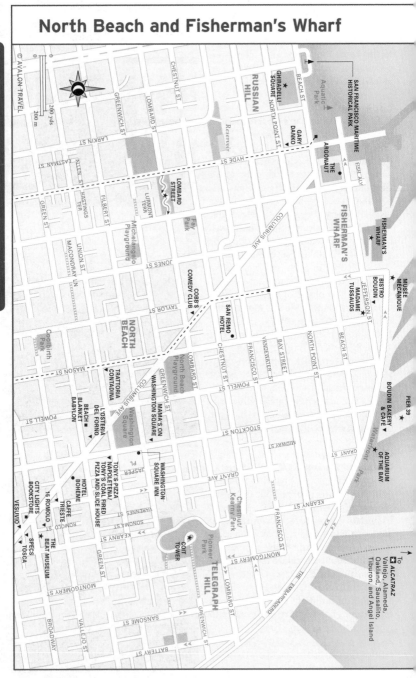

© AVALON TRAVEL

0    200 yds
0    200 m

RUSSIAN HILL

GHIRARDELLI SQUARE

BEACH ST

Aquatic Park

SAN FRANCISCO MARITIME HISTORICAL PARK

GARY DANKO

THE ARGONAUT

FISH ALY

CHESTNUT ST

LOMBARD ST

NORTH POINT ST

GREENWICH ST

HYDE ST

Reservoir

COLUMBUS AVE

FISHERMAN'S WHARF

FISHERMAN'S WHARF ★

LOMBARD STREET

LURMONT TERR

Fay Park

Michelangelo Playground

MUSÉE MÉCANIQUE ★

BISTRO BOUDIN ▼

MADAME TUSSAUDS ▼

JEFFERSON ST

LARKIN ST

EASTMAN ST

ALLEN ST

HASTINGS TER

FILBERT ST

GREEN ST

UNION ST

MACONDRAY LN

JONES ST

TAYLOR ST

COBB'S COMEDY CLUB ★

SAN REMO HOTEL ●

NORTH BEACH

CHESTNUT ST

FRANCISCO ST

VANDEWATER ST

BAY STREET

NORTH POINT ST

BEACH ST

BOUDIN BAKERY & CAFÉ ▼

PIER 39

AQUARIUM OF THE BAY ★

Waterfront Park

MASON ST

Croillirth Park

TRATTORIA CONTADINA ▼

L'OSTERIA DEL FORNO ▼

BEACH BLANKET BABYLON ■

POWELL ST

GREENWICH ST

LOMBARD ST

North Beach Playground

COLUMBUS AVE

Washington Square

MAMA'S ON WASHINGTON SQUARE ▼

POWELL ST

STOCKTON ST

MIDWAY ST

GRANT AVE

CITY LIGHTS BOOKSTORE ●

VESUVIO ▼

15 ROMOLO ▼

CAFFÈ TRIESTE ●

HOTEL BOHÈME ●

THE BEAT MUSEUM ▼

SPECS ▼

TOSCA ▼

ROMOLO ST

SONOMA ST

VARENNES ST

JASPER PL

WASHINGTON SQUARE INN ●

TONY'S PIZZA NAPOLETANA/ TONY'S COAL FIRED PIZZA AND SLICE HOUSE ▼

KEARNY ST

GREEN ST

MONTGOMERY ST

Pioneer Park

COIT TOWER ★

TELEGRAPH HILL

Chestnut/ Kearny Park

FRANCISCO ST

LOMBARD ST

GREENWICH ST

MONTGOMERY ST

SANSOME ST

VALLEJO ST

BROADWAY

BATTERY ST

THE EMBARCADERO

Waterfront Park

To ✈ ALCATRAZ
Vallejo, Alameda,
Oakland, Sausalito,
Tiburon, and Angel Island

browse the rambling shop and pick up truffles, wafers, candies, and sauces for all your friends back home. Finally, get in line at the ice cream counter to order a hot fudge sundae. Once you've finished gorging on chocolate, wander out into the square to enjoy more shopping and an unbelievably swank condo complex overlooking the bay.

### San Francisco Maritime National Historical Park

The real gem of the Wharf is the **San Francisco Maritime National Historical Park** (415/561-7000, www.nps.gov/safr), which spreads from the base of Van Ness to Pier 45. At the **visitors center** (499 Jefferson St., 415/447-5000, 9:30am-5pm daily), not only will rangers help you make the most of your visit, but you can also get lost in the labyrinthine museum that houses an immense Fresnel lighthouse lens and engaging displays that recount San Francisco's history. For $5 you can climb aboard the historic ships at permanent dock across the street at the **Hyde Street Pier.** The shiniest jewel of the collection is the 1886 square-rigged *Balclutha*, a three-masted schooner that recalls times gone by, complete with excellent historical exhibits below deck. There are also several steamboats, including the workhorse ferry paddle wheeler *Eureka* and a cool old steam tugboat called the *Eppleton Hall*. Farther down, at Pier 45, World War II buffs can feel the claustrophobia of the submarine **USS Pampanito** (415/775-1943, www.maritime.org, 9am-close daily, $20 adults, $12 seniors, $10 children 6-12, children under 6 free) or the expansiveness of the Liberty ship **SS Jeremiah O'Brien** (415/544-0100, www.ssjeremiahobrien.org, 9am-4pm daily, $20 adults, $10 seniors and children 5-16, children under 5 free).

The 1939 art deco **Aquatic Bathhouse Building** (900 Beach St., 415/561-7100, www.nps.gov/safr, 10am-4pm daily, adults $5, children free), built in 1939, houses the Maritime Museum, where you can see a number of rotating exhibits alongside its brilliant WPA murals.

## Marina and Pacific Heights

The Marina and Pacific Heights are wealthy neighborhoods, with a couple of yacht harbors, plenty of open space, great dining, and shopping that only gets better as you go up the hill.

### Palace of Fine Arts

The **Palace of Fine Arts** (3301 Lyon St.) was originally meant to be nothing but a temporary structure—part of the Panama-Pacific International Exposition in 1915. But the lovely building designed by Bernard Maybeck won the hearts of San Franciscans, and a fund was started to preserve the palace beyond the exposition. Through the first half of the 20th century, efforts could not keep it from crumbling, but in the 1960s and 1970s, serious rebuilding work took place, and today the Palace of Fine Arts stands proud, strong, and beautiful. It houses the **Palace of Fine Arts Theatre** (415/563-6504, www.palaceoffinearts.org), which hosts events nearly every day, from beauty pageants to conferences to children's musical theater performances.

### ★ The Presidio

It seems strange to think of progressive, peace-loving San Francisco as a town with a long military history, yet it is nowhere more evident than at **The Presidio** (Montgomery St. and Lincoln Blvd., 415/561-4323, www.nps.gov/prsf, visitors center 10am-5pm daily, trails dawn-dusk daily, free). This sweeping stretch of land running along the San Francisco Headlands down to the Golden Gate Bridge has been a military installation since 1776, when the Spanish created their El Presidio del San Francisco fort on the site. In 1846, the U.S. Army took over the site (peacefully), and in 1848 the American Presidio military installation formally opened. The Presidio had a role in every Pacific-related war from the

# Marina and Pacific Heights

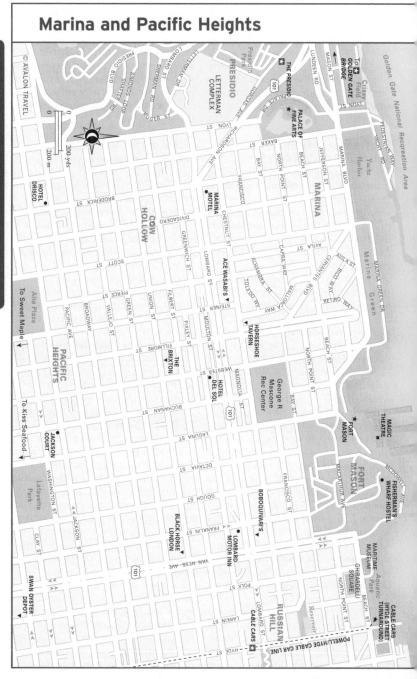

SAN FRANCISCO

## Side Trip to Muir Woods

Giant coast redwoods are located not far outside San Francisco's city limits. Some of the finest examples of these towering trees can be found at **Muir Woods National Monument** (1 Muir Woods Rd., 415-388-2596, www.nps.gov/muwo, 8am-sunset daily, $10). More than six miles of trails wind through the lush forest and cross verdant creeks. Begin your exploration at the **Muir Woods Visitors Center** (1 Muir Woods Rd., 415-388-2595, from 8am daily, closing time varies). In addition to maps, information, and advice about hiking, you'll also find a few amenities.

First-time visitors should follow the wheelchair- and stroller-accessible **Main Trail Loop** (1 mile), an easy and flat walk with an accompanying interpretive brochure that identifies and describes the flora and fauna. Serious hikers can continue the loop on the **Hillside Trail** for an elevated view of the valley. Take the **Muir Woods Shuttle** (www.marintransit.org) to avoid challenging parking and congestion, especially in summer.

After your hike, fill up on a hearty lunch of British comfort food at **The Pelican Inn** (10 Pacific Way, Muir Beach, 415-386-6000, www.pelicaninn.com, 11:30am-9pm Mon.-Fri., 8am-9pm Sat.-Sun., $15-30). Dark wood and a long trestle table give a proper Old English feel to the dimly lit dining room. It's just a short drive from the restaurant to lovely **Muir Beach** (www.nps.gov/goga, sunrise-sunset daily), perfect for wildlife-watching and beachcombing.

End the day with oysters and drinks at the Farley Bar at **Cavallo Point Lodge** (601 Murray Circle, Fort Baker, Sausalito, 415-339-4750, www.cavallopoint.com, 11am-11pm Sun.-Thurs., 11am-midnight Fri.-Sat., $12-56). Snag a blanket and a seat on the porch to watch the fog roll in over the Golden Gate Bridge.

### Getting There

Take **US-101 North** out of the city and over the Golden Gate Bridge. Once on the north side of the Bay, take the **Stinson Beach/CA-1 exit.** On CA-1, also named the **Shoreline Highway,** follow the road under the freeway and proceed until the road splits at a T junction at the light. Turn left, continuing on Shoreline Highway for 2.5 miles. At the intersection with **Panoramic Highway,** make a sharp right turn and continue climbing uphill. At the junction of Panoramic Highway and **Muir Woods Road,** turn left and follow the road 1.5 twisty miles down to the Muir Woods parking lots on the right.

---

Civil War through Desert Storm. It was abandoned by the military and became a national park in 1994.

To orient yourself among the more than 800 buildings that make up the Presidio, start at the **William Penn Mott Jr. Presidio Visitor Center** (Bldg. 210, Lincoln Blvd., 415/561-4323, 10am-5pm daily), where exhibits include a model of the grounds. You can also explore the pioneering aviation area **Crissy Field** (www.parksconservancy.org), Civil War-era fortifications at **Fort Point** (415/556-1693, 10am-5pm Thurs.-Mon. summer, 10am-5pm Fri.-Sun. winter), and the **Walt Disney Family Museum** (104 Montgomery St., 415/345-6800, www.waltdisney.org, 10am-6pm Wed.-Mon., $30 adults, $25 seniors and students, $20 children 6-17), founded by Disney's daughter to examine the animator's life and work. Other highlights include art installations by Andy Goldsworthy, who works with natural materials. The most renowned is *Spire*, a sculpture that rises 90 feet into the air, utilizing 35 cypress tree trunks.

### ★ Golden Gate Bridge

People come from the world over to see and walk the **Golden Gate Bridge** (U.S. 101/Hwy. 1 at Lincoln Blvd., 415/921-5858, www.goldengatebridge.com, southbound cars $7.75, pedestrians free). A marvel of human engineering constructed in 1936 and 1937, the suspension bridge spans the narrow "gate" from which the Pacific Ocean enters the San Francisco Bay. Pedestrians are allowed on the **east sidewalk** (5am-9pm daily mid-Mar.-Oct., 5am-6:30pm daily Nov.-mid-Mar.). On a clear day, the whole bay, Marin Headlands, and city skyline are visible. Cyclists are allowed on both sidewalks (check the website for times), but as the scenery is stunning, be aware of pedestrians and cyclists not keeping their eyes on where they are going.

The Golden Gate National Parks Conservancy has quit offering its Golden Gate Bridge Tours, but the nonprofit **City Guides** (415/557-4266, www.sfcityguides. org) leads bridge walks twice a week. Check the website for days and times.

## Civic Center and Hayes Valley

The Civic Center functions as the heart of San Francisco. Not only is the seat of government here, but so are venerable high-culture institutions: the War Memorial Opera House and Davies Symphony Hall, home of the world-famous San Francisco Symphony. As the Civic Center melts into Hayes Valley, you'll find fabulous hotels and restaurants serving both the city's politicos and the well-heeled.

### City Hall

Look at San Francisco's **City Hall** (1 Dr. Carlton B. Goodlett Pl., 415/554-6079, www.sfgov.org, 8am-8pm Mon.-Fri., free) and you'll think you've somehow been transported to Europe. The stately Beaux-Arts building with the gilded dome is the pride of the city and houses the mayor's office and much of the city's government. Enjoy walking through the parklike square in front of City Hall (though this area can get a bit sketchy after dark). Inside you'll find a combination of historical grandeur and modern accessibility and convenience as you tour the Arthur Brown Jr.-designed edifice.

### Asian Art Museum

Across from City Hall is the **Asian Art Museum** (200 Larkin St., 415/581-3500, www.asianart.org, 10am-5pm Sat.-Tues. and Thurs., 5pm-9pm Fri. summer, 10am-5pm Tues.-Wed. and Fri.-Sun., 5pm-9pm Thurs. winter $15 adults, $10 seniors and children 13-17, children under 12 free), with enormous Ionic columns. Inside you'll have an amazing window into the Asian cultures that have shaped and defined San Francisco and the Bay Area. The 2nd and 3rd floors of this intense museum are packed with great art from all across Asia, including a Chinese gilded Buddha dating from AD 338. The breadth and diversity of Asian culture may stagger you; the museum's displays come from Japan and Vietnam, Buddhist Tibet, and ancient China. Special exhibitions cost extra—check the website to see what will be displayed on the ground-floor galleries when you're in town. The curators regularly rotate items from the permanent collection, so you'll probably encounter new beauty every time you visit.

### Alamo Square

At this area's far western edge sits **Alamo Square** (Hayes St. and Steiner St.), possibly the most photographed neighborhood in San Francisco. Among its stately Victorians are the famous **"painted ladies,"** a row of brilliantly painted and immaculately maintained homes. From the adjacent Alamo Square Park, the ladies provide a picturesque foreground for views of the Civic Center and downtown.

## Mission and Castro

Castro is the heart of gay San Francisco, complete with nightlife, festivals, and LGBT community activism. With its mix of Latino immigrants, working artists, and hipsters, the Mission is a neighborhood bursting at the seams with idiosyncratic energy. Changing from block to block, the zone manages to be blue-collar, edgy, and gentrified all at once.

While the heart of the neighborhood is still Latin American, with delicious burritos and *pupusas* around every corner, it is also the go-to neighborhood for the tech economy, with luxury condos, pricey boutiques, and international restaurants in a city famous for its food.

## Mission Dolores

**Mission Dolores** (3321 16th St., 415/621-8203, www.missiondolores.org, 9am-4:30pm daily May-Oct., 9am-4pm daily Nov.-Apr., donation $7 adults, $5 seniors and students), formally named Mission San Francisco de Asís, was founded in 1776. Today the mission is the oldest intact building in the city, having survived the 1906 earthquake and fire, the 1989 Loma Prieta quake, and more than 200 years of use. You can attend Roman Catholic services here each Saturday, or you can visit the Old Mission Museum and the Basilica, which house artifacts from the Native Americans and Spanish of the 18th century. The beauty and grandeur of the mission recall the heyday of the Spanish empire in California, as important to the history of the state as it is today.

## Golden Gate Park and the Haight

The neighborhood surrounding the intersection of Haight and Ashbury Streets (known locally as "the Haight") is best known for the wave of countercultural energy that broke out in the 1960s. Haight Street terminates at the entrance to San Francisco's gem—Golden Gate Park.

## Golden Gate Park

Dominating the western half of San Francisco, **Golden Gate Park** (main entrance at Stanyan St. at Fell St., McLaren Lodge Visitors Center at John F. Kennedy Dr., 415/831-2700, www.golden-gate-park.com, http://sfrecpark.org) is one of the city's most enduring treasures. Its 1,000-plus acres include lakes, forests, formal gardens, windmills, museums, a buffalo pasture, and plenty of activities. Enjoy free concerts in the summer, hike in near solitude in the winter, or spend a day wandering and exploring scores of sights.

## ★ de Young Museum

The **de Young Museum** (50 Hagiwara Tea Garden Dr., 415/750-3600, http://deyoung.famsf.org, 9:30am-5:15pm Tues.-Thurs. and Sat.-Sun., 9:30am-8:30pm Fri. summer, 9:30am-5:15pm Tues.-Sun. winter, $15 adults, $10 seniors, $6 students, children 17 and under free) is staggering in its size and breadth: You'll see everything from pre-Columbian art to 17th-century ladies' gowns. View paintings, sculpture, textiles, ceramics, "contemporary crafts" from all over the world, and rotating exhibits that range from King Tut to the exquisite Jean Paul Gaultier collection. Competing with all of that is the building itself.

The museum's modern exterior is wrapped in perforated copper, while the interior incorporates pockets of manicured gardens. Poking out of the park's canopy is a twisted tower that offers a spectacular 360-degree view of the city and the bay. Entrance to the tower, lily pond, and art garden is free. Surrounded by sphinxes and draping wisteria, you can enjoy an art-filled picnic lunch.

## California Academy of Sciences

A triumph of the sustainable scientific principles it exhibits, the **California Academy of Sciences** (55 Music Concourse Dr., 415/379-8000, www.calacademy.org; 9:30am-5pm Mon.-Sat., 11am-5pm Sun., $36 adults, $31 seniors, students, and children 12-17, $26 children 4-11) drips with ecological perfection. From the grass-covered roof to the underground **aquarium,** visitors can explore every part of the universe. Wander through a steamy endangered **rainforest** contained inside a giant glass bubble, or travel through an all-digital outer space

# Civic Center, Hayes Valley, Mission, and Castro

in the high-tech **planetarium.** More studious nature lovers can spend days examining every inch of the **Natural History Museum,** including favorite exhibits like the 87-foot-long blue whale skeleton. The Academy of Sciences takes pains to make itself kid-friendly, with interactive exhibits, thousands of live animals, and endless opportunities for learning. On **Thursday nights** (6pm-10pm, $15), the academy is an adults-only zone, where DJs play music and the café serves cocktails by some of the city's most renowned mixologists.

### Japanese Tea Garden

The **Japanese Tea Garden** (75 Hagiwara Tea Garden Dr., 415/752-4227, http://japaneseteagardensf.com, 9am-6pm daily Mar.-Oct., 9am-4:45pm daily Nov.-Feb., $8 adults, $6 seniors and children 12-17, $2 children 5-11, children under 5 free) is a haven of peace and tranquility that's a local favorite within the park, particularly in the spring. The planting and design of the garden began in 1894 for the California Exposition. Today the flourishing garden displays a wealth of beautiful flora, including stunning examples of rare Chinese and Japanese plants, some quite old. As you stroll along the paths, you'll come upon sculptures, bridges, ponds, and even traditional *tsukubai* (a tea ceremony sink). Take one of the docent-led tours and conclude your visit with tea and a fortune cookie at the tea house. Free admission is available on Monday, Wednesday, and Friday before 10am.

### San Francisco Botanical Garden

Take a bucolic walk in the middle of Golden Gate Park by visiting the **San Francisco Botanical Garden** (1199 9th Ave. at Lincoln Way, 415/661-1316, www.sfbotanicalgarden.org, 7:30am-6pm mid Mar.-Sept., 7:30am-5pm Oct.-Nov., 7:30am-4pm Nov.-Jan., 7:30am-5pm Feb.-mid Mar., $8 adults, $6 students and seniors, $2 children 5-11, children under 5

The Legion of Honor

and city residents with ID free). The 55-acre gardens are home to more than 8,000 species of plants from around the world, and include a California Natives garden and a shady redwood forest. Fountains, ponds, meadows, and lawns are interwoven with the flowers and trees to create a peaceful, serene setting in the middle of the crowded city.

### Conservatory of Flowers
For a trip to San Francisco's Victorian past, step inside the steamy **Conservatory of Flowers** (100 John F. Kennedy Dr., 415/831-2090, www.conservatoryofflowers.org, 10am-6:30pm Tues.-Sun., $8 adults, $5 students and seniors, $2 children 5-11, children under 5 free). Built in 1878, the striking wood and glass greenhouse is home to more than 1,700 plant species that spill out of containers, twine around rainforest trees, climb trellises reaching the roof, and rim deep ponds where eight-foot lily pads float serenely on still waters. Surrounded by the exotic flora illuminated only by natural light, it's easy to transport yourself to the heyday of colonialism when the study of botany was in its first bloom. Plus, it's one of the best places to explore on a rainy day. Strollers are not permitted inside; wheelchairs and power chairs are allowed.

### The Legion of Honor
A beautiful museum in a town filled with beauty, the **Legion of Honor** (100 34th Ave. at Clement St., 415/750-3600, http://legionofhonor.famsf.org, 9:30am-5:15pm Tues.-Sun., $15 adults, $10 seniors, $6 students and ages 13-16, children under 16 free) sits on its lonely promontory in Lincoln Park, overlooking the Golden Gate. A gift to the city from philanthropist Alma Spreckels in 1924, this French Beaux-Arts-style building was built to honor the memory of California soldiers who died in World War I. From its beginning, the Legion of Honor was a museum dedicated to bringing European art to the population of San Francisco. Today visitors can view gorgeous collections of European paintings, sculpture, decorative arts, ancient artifacts from around the Mediterranean, thousands of paper drawings by great artists, and much more. Special exhibitions come from the Legion's own collections and museums of the world.

# Entertainment and Events

## Nightlife
San Francisco isn't a see-and-be-seen kind of town. You'll find gay clubs, vintage dance clubs, Goth clubs, and the occasional underground burner rave, mixed in with neighborhood watering holes.

Several bus services can ferry your party from club to club. Many of these offer VIP entrance to clubs and will stop wherever you want to go. **Think Escape** (800/823-7249, www.thinkescape.com)

# Golden Gate Park

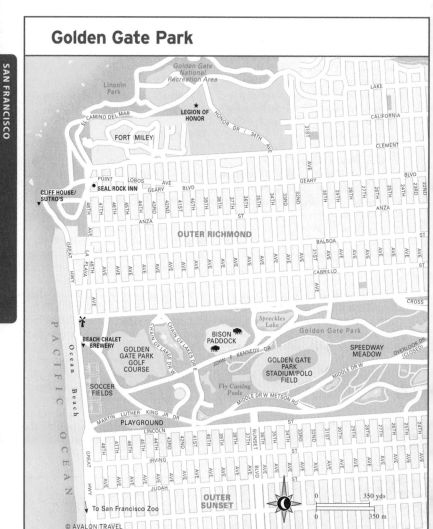

has buses and limos with drivers and guides to get you to the hottest spots with ease.

## Union Square and Nob Hill

These ritzy areas are better known for their shopping than their nightlife, but a few bars hang in there, plying weary shoppers with good drinks. Most tend toward the upscale. Some inhabit upper floors of the major hotels, like the **Tonga Room and Hurricane Bar** (950 Mason St., 415/772-5278, www.fairmont.com, www.tongaroom.com, 5pm-11:30pm Wed.-Thurs. and Sun., 5pm-12:30am Fri.-Sat.), where an over-the-top tiki theme adds a whimsical touch to the stately Fairmont Hotel on Nob Hill. Enjoy the tropical atmosphere with a fruity rum drink topped with a classic paper umbrella.

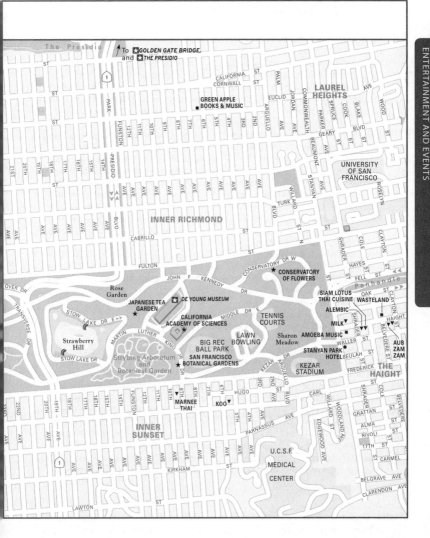

Be prepared for the bar's virtual tropical storms that roll in every once in a while.

Part live-music venue, part elegant bar, **Top of the Mark** (InterContinental Mark Hopkins, 999 California St., 415/392-3434, www.intercontinentalmarkhopkins.com, 4:30pm-11:30pm Mon.-Thurs., 4:30pm-12:30am Fri.-Sat., 5pm-11:30pm Sun.) has something for every discerning taste in nighttime entertainment. Since World War II, the views at the top of the InterContinental Mark Hopkins Hotel have drawn visitors to see the city lights. Live bands play almost every night of the week. The dress code is business casual or better and is enforced, so leave the jeans in your room. Have a top-shelf martini, and let your toes tap along.

**Harry Denton's Starlight Room** (450 Powell St., 21st Fl., 415/395-8595, www.

# ◆ Side Trip to Wine Country

For oenophiles, no trip to California is complete without an excursion to the state's renowned wine country. Though the main draw is sampling wines at their source, Napa and Sonoma Valleys offer multiple ways to spoil yourself, including spas, fine hotels, revered restaurants, and understated natural beauty. Both are less than 100 miles north of San Francisco, about an hour's drive if traffic is light.

The city of Napa is located on the southern end of Napa Valley, with a scenic downtown perched on the Napa River. For an introduction to the area's vibrant food and wine scene, visit the **Oxbow Public Market** (610 and 644 1st St., 707/226-6529, www.oxbowpublicmarket. com, 9am-8pm Tues., 9am-7pm Wed.-Mon.), which has food vendors, produce markets, and cafés.

A multitude of vineyards are strung along the Silverado Trail and CA-29, two roads that head north out of the city of Napa and into serious wine country. Grape vines braid the scenic valley as you drive through the towns of Rutherford, St. Helena, and Calistoga. **Grgich Hills Winery** (1829 St. Helena Hwy., Rutherford, 800/532-3057, www.grgich.com, 9:30am-4:30pm daily, tasting $25) is the winery that put Napa Valley on the map with a win at the Paris Wine Tasting of 1976. It's still known for its chardonnay. **Mumm** (8445 Silverado Trail, Rutherford, 800/686-6272, www.mummnapa. com, 10am-6pm daily, tasting $20-35) produces sparkling wines worth a taste

even for wine purists. **Clos Pegase** (1060 Dunaweal Ln., Calistoga, 707/942-4981, www.clospegase.com, 10:30am-5pm daily, tasting $20-30) mixes in some culture with its wine, with over 100 artworks on the grounds, including sculptor Henry Moore's *Mother Earth* and a painting by Francis Bacon.

There is a range of options for staying overnight (and sleeping off an afternoon of wine tasting). One of the more luxurious is **Auberge du Soleil** (180 Rutherford Hill Rd., St. Helena, 707/963-1211, www.aubergedusoleil.com, $875-5,200). Less expensive options include St. Helena's **El Bonita Motel** (195 Main St./CA-29, 800/541-3284, www.elbonita. com, $140-320), which is within walking distance of the historic downtown and has a 1950s motel charm, and Calistoga's **Dr. Wilkinson's Hot Springs Resort** (1507 Lincoln Ave., 707/942-4102, www. drwilkinson.com, $229-350), with an on-site spa.

## Getting There

To reach CA-29, the central conduit that runs north into the valley from the city of Napa, from San Francisco, take **US-101 North** across the Golden Gate Bridge to Novato. In Novato, take the exit for **CA-37 East** to Napa. CA-37 skirts the tip of the San Pablo Bay and runs all the way to Vallejo. From Vallejo, take **CA-29 (Sonoma Blvd.) North** for seven miles until you reach downtown Napa. CA-29 will take you as far north as Calistoga.

starlightroomsf.com, 6pm-midnight Tues.-Thurs., 5pm-2am Fri.-Sat., Sun. drag shows 11:30am and 2pm, cover charge up to $20) brings the flamboyant side of San Francisco downtown. Enjoy a cocktail in the early evening or a nightcap and dessert after the theater in this truly old-school nightclub. Dress in your best to match the glitzy red-and-gold decor and mirrors. Whoop it up at the "Sunday's a Drag" shows. Reservations are recommended.

South of the Union Square area in the sketchy Tenderloin neighborhood, brave souls can find a gem: **The Royale** (800 Post St., 415/441-4099, www.the-royalesf.com, 4pm-midnight Sun.-Wed., 4pm-2am Thurs.-Sat.) isn't a typical watering hole by any city's standards, but its intense focus on art fits perfectly with the endlessly eclectic ethos of San Francisco. Local artists exhibit their work in Café Royale on a monthly basis, and a wide range of entertainment is available, from DJs and live jazz to "The Mildly Intoxicated Spelling Bee." The primary intoxicants are lesser known microbrews and small-batch beers. Also in the Tenderloin, **Tradition** (411 Jones St., 415/474-2284, http://tradbar.com, 6pm-2am Mon.-Sat.) is a two-level bar that takes its cocktails seriously. Eight themed drink menus zero in on cocktail traditions from English pub to tiki. This neighborhood can get dicey after dark; keep your wits (and your valuables) close.

## Financial District and SoMa

All those high-powered business suit-clad executive types working in the Financial District need places to drink too. One of these is the **Royal Exchange** (301 Sacramento St., 415/956-1710, http://royalexchange.com, 11am-11pm Mon.-Fri.). This classic pub-style bar has a green-painted exterior, big windows overlooking the street, and a long, narrow barroom. The Royal Exchange serves a full lunch and dinner menu, a small wine list, and a full complement of top-shelf spirits. But most of all, the Exchange serves beer. With 73 taps pouring out 32 different types of beer, the only problem will be choosing one. This businesspeople's watering hole is open to the public only on weekdays; on weekends it hosts private parties.

In SoMa (South of Market), upscale wine bars have become an evening institution. Among the trendiest you'll find is **District** (216 Townsend St., 415/896-2120, www.districtsf.com, 4pm-close Mon.-Fri., 5pm-2am Sat.). A perfect example of its kind, District features bare brick walls, simple wooden furniture, and a big U-shaped bar at the center of the room with wine glasses hanging above it. While you can get a cocktail or even a beer, the point of coming to District is to sip the finest wines from California, Europe, and beyond. With more than 40 wines available by the glass each night, it's easy to find a favorite, or enjoy a flight of three similar wines to compare. While you can't quite get a full dinner at District, you will find a lovely lounge menu filled with small portions of delicacies to enhance your tasting experience (and perhaps soak up some of the alcohol).

Secret passwords, a hidden library, and an art deco vibe make **Bourbon and Branch** (505 Jones St., 415/346-1735, www.bourbonandbranch.com, 6pm-2am daily, reservations suggested) a must for lovers of the brown stuff. Tucked behind a nameless brown door, this resurrected 1920s-era speakeasy evokes its Prohibition-era past with passwords and secret passages. A business-class elite sips rare bourbon and scotch in dark secluded booths, while those without reservations step into the hidden library.

The **Rickhouse** (246 Kearney St., 415/398-2827, www.rickhousebar. com, 5pm-2am Mon., 3pm-2am Tues.-Fri., 6pm-2am Sat.) feels like a country shack plopped down in the midst of the Financial District. The artisanal cocktail bar draws in the city's plentiful young urban hipsters. It's dimly lit, the walls and floors are wood, and stacks of barrels and old bottles line the mantle. There's also live music on Saturday and Monday nights.

It's dark, it's dank, and it's very Goth. The **Cat Club** (1190 Folsom St., 415/703-8965, www.sfcatclub.com, 9pm-3am Tues.-Sun., cover charge) gets pretty energetic on 1980s dance nights, but it's still a great place to go after you've donned your best down-rent black attire and painted your face deathly pale, especially on Goth-industrial-electronica nights. In fact, there's no dress code at the Cat Club, unlike many local nightspots, which makes it great for travelers who live in their jeans. You'll find a friendly crowd, decent bartenders, strong drinks, and easy access to smoking areas. Each of the two rooms has its own DJ, which somehow works perfectly even though they're only a wall apart from each other. Check the website to find the right party night for you, and expect the crowd to heat up after 11pm.

**Monarch** (101 6th St., 415/284-9774, www.monarchsf.com, 5:30pm-2am Tues.-Fri., 8pm-2am Sat.-Sun.) is aiming to be a one-stop after-dark venue. Upstairs is a Victorian-inspired cocktail lounge, while the downstairs club hosts international and local DJs. You might also catch offbeat performers like acrobats twirling from the ceilings.

**AsiaSF** (201 9th St., 415/255-2742, www.asiasf.com, 7:15pm-11pm Sun. and Wed.-Thurs., 7:15pm-2am Fri., 5pm-2am Sat., cover charge) is famous for its transgender performers and servers, "The Ladies of AsiaSF." Weekend reservations for dinner and a show include free admission to the dance floor downstairs.

## North Beach and Fisherman's Wharf

Jack Kerouac loved **Vesuvio** (255 Columbus Ave., 415/362-3370, www.vesuvio.com, 8am-2am Mon.-Fri., 6am-2am Sat.-Sun.), which is why it's probably North Beach's most famous saloon. This cozy, eclectic bi-level hideout is an easy place to spend the afternoon with a pint of Anchor Steam. Its eclectic decor includes tables decorated with tarot cards.

Almost across the street from Vesuvio is one of the oldest and most celebrated bars in the city. **Tosca** (242 Columbus Ave., 415/986-9651, http://toscacafesf.com, 5pm-2am Tues.-Sun.) has an unpretentious yet glam 1940s style. Hunter S. Thompson once tended bar here when the owner was out at the dentist. The jukebox plays grand opera to the patrons clustered in the big red booths. Locals love the lack of trendiness, the classic cocktails, the occasional star sightings, and the chicken marsala.

Dress up for a night out at **15 Romolo** (15 Romolo Pl., 415/398-1359, www.15romolo.com, 5pm-2am Mon.-Fri., 11:30am-2am Sat.-Sun.). You'll have to hike up the steep little alley (Fresno St. crosses Romolo Pl., which can be hard to

find) to this hotel bar. You'll love the creative cocktails, edgy jukebox music, and often mellow crowd. The bar is smallish and can get crowded on the weekend, so come on a weeknight if you prefer a quiet drink.

Known for its colorful clientele and cluttered decor, **Specs** (12 William Saroyan Pl., 415/421-4112, 4pm-2am daily, cash only) is a dive bar located in a North Beach alley. Its full name is the Specs' Twelve Adler Museum Café.

## Marina and Pacific Heights

Marina and Pacific Heights denizens enjoy a good glass of vino. The **Bacchus Wine Bar** (1954 Hyde St., 415/928-2633, www.bacchussf.com, 5:30pm-midnight daily) is a tiny local watering hole that offers an array of wines, sake cocktails, and craft beers.

The Marina District's Chestnut Street is known for its high-end restaurants and swanky clientele. The **Horseshoe Tavern** (2024 Chestnut St., 415/346-1430, 10am-2am daily) is a place for people to let their hair down, shoot pool, and drink without pretension.

Get to really know your fellow beer drinkers at the tiny **Black Horse London Pub** (1514 Union St., 415/928-2414, www.blackhorselondon.com, 5pm-midnight Mon.-Thurs., 2pm-midnight Fri., 11am-midnight Sat.-Sun., cash only), which can accommodate just nine people. Bottles of beer are served from a claw-foot bathtub located behind the bar.

Clubs in the Marina are all about the trendy and the spendy. The **Hi-Fi Lounge** (2125 Lombard St., 415/345-8663, www.maximumproductions.com, 8pm-2am Wed.-Sat., cover charge Fri.-Sat.) personifies the fun that can be had in smaller San Francisco venues. This one-floor wonder with a tiny dance floor gets incredibly crowded. Yet even the locals have a good time when they come out to the Hi-Fi. The decor is funky and fun, and the patrons are young and affluent. Most visitors find the staff friendly and the bartenders attentive. Come early to get decent parking. On Thursday and Friday, early birds get $1 draft beer.

## Civic Center and Hayes Valley

Hayes Valley bleeds into Lower Haight (Haight St. between Divisadero St. and Octavia Blvd.) and supplies most of the neighborhood bars. For proof that the independent spirit of the Haight lives on in spite of encroaching commercialism, stop in and have a drink at the **Toronado** (547 Haight St., 415/863-2276, www.toronado.com, 11:30am-2am daily), a grimy cathedral to superb beer. This dimly lit haven with a metal- and punk rock-heavy jukebox maintains one of the finest beer selections in the nation, with a changing roster of several dozen microbrews on tap, including Russian River Brewing Company's Pliny the Elder, one of the most sought after beers in the state.

If you'd rather drink a cocktail than a beer, head over to **Smuggler's Cove** (650 Gough St., 415/869-1900, http://smugglerscovesf.com, 5pm-1:15am daily). The drink menu includes 70 cocktails and an impressive number of rare rums.

## Mission

These neighborhoods seem to hold a whole city's worth of bars. The Mission still has plenty of no-frills bars, many with a Latino theme. And, of course, men seeking men flock to the Castro's endless array of gay bars. For lesbians, the Mission might be a better bet.

**Trick Dog** (3010 20th St., 415/471-2999, www.trickdogbar.com, 3pm-2am daily) is shaking up the city's cocktail scene. Named after city landmarks, the drinks use unexpected ingredients like dandelion, lychee, or horseradish (thankfully not all at the same time). The small food menu includes thrice-cooked fries, Scotch eggs, and a standout kale salad.

Expect to hear some old-school vinyl from a lo-fi record player in the dimly lit **Royal Cuckoo** (3202 Mission St., http://royalcuckoo.com, 4pm-2am Mon.-Thurs.,

3pm-2am Fri.-Sun.). There's also live music played on a vintage Hammond B3 organ Wednesday-Sunday. The cocktail list includes variations on the classics, including a sour old-fashioned.

Excellent draft beers, tasty barbecue plates, and a motorcycle-inclined crowd give **Zeitgeist** (199 Valencia St., 415/255-7505, 9am-2am daily) a punk-rock edge. This Mission favorite, though, endears itself to all sorts, thanks to its spacious outdoor beer garden, 40 beers on tap, and popular Bloody Marys.

Get a sweeping view of the city with superb South American cocktails at ★ **El Techo de Lolinda** (2518 Mission St., 415/550-6970, http://eltechosf.com, 4pm-10:30pm Mon.-Thurs., 4pm-12:30am Fri., 11pm-12:30am Sat., 11am-10:30pm Sun.), a rooftop bar associated with the Argentinean steak house Lolinda. The bar serves pitchers of margaritas, glasses of *caipirinhas* (a Brazilian cocktail resembling a mojito), and the best Cuba Libre I've ever had. (I know it's a simple drink, but this version is transcendent.) The small food menu includes superb snacks like empanadas, ceviche, and a variety of skewers.

## Golden Gate Park and the Haight

Haight Street crowds head out in droves to the **Alembic** (1725 Haight St., 415/666-0822, www.alembicbar.com, 4pm-midnight Mon.-Fri., 2pm-midnight Sat.-Sun.) for artisanal cocktails laced with American spirits. On par with the whiskey and bourbon menu is the cuisine: Wash down the pork belly sliders or chicken liver mousse with a Sazerac.

**Hobson's Choice** (1601 Haight St., 415/621-5859, www.hobsonschoice.com, 2pm-2am Mon.-Fri., noon-2am Sat.-Sun.) claims the largest selection of rums in the country. Try your rum in everything from a Brazilian *caipirinha* to a Cuban mojito, or in one of Hobson's famous rum punches.

Featured in an episode of Anthony Bourdain's travel show *No Reservations*,

**Aub Zam Zam** (1633 Haight St., 415/861-2545, 3pm-2am Mon.-Fri., 1pm-2am Sat.-Sun.) is an old-school bar with an Arabian feel. Zam Zam doesn't take credit cards, but it does have an Arabian mural behind the U-shaped bar, where an interesting mix of locals and visitors congregate for the cheap drinks.

The **Beach Chalet Brewery** (1000 Great Hwy., 415/386-8439, www.beachchalet.com, 9am-11pm Mon.-Thurs., 9am-midnight Fri., 8am-midnight Sat., 8am-11pm Sun.) is an attractive brewpub and restaurant directly across the street from Ocean Beach. Sip a pale ale while watching the sunset, and check out the historical murals downstairs.

## Gay and Lesbian

San Francisco's gay nightlife has earned a worldwide rep for both the quantity and quality of options. In fact, the gay club scene totally outdoes the straight club scene for frolicsome, fabulous fun. While the city's queer nightlife caters more to gay men than to lesbians, there's plenty of space available for partiers of all persuasions. For a more comprehensive list of San Francisco's queer bars and clubs, visit http://sanfrancisco.gaycities.com/bars.

You'll have no trouble finding a gay bar in the Castro. One of the best is called simply **Q Bar** (456 Castro St., 415/864-2877, www.qbarsf.com, 4pm-2am Mon.-Fri., 2pm-2am Sat.-Sun.). Just look for the red neon "Bar" sign set in steel out front. Inside, expect to find the fabulous red decor known as "retro-glam," delicious top-shelf cocktails, and thrumming beats spun by popular DJs almost every night of the week. Unlike many Castro establishments, the Q Bar caters to pretty much everybody: gay men, gay women, and gay-friendly straight folks. You'll find a coat check and adequate restroom facilities, and the strength of the drinks will make you want to take off your jacket and stay awhile.

Looking for a stylin' gay bar turned club, Castro style? Head for **Badlands** (4121 18th St., 415/626-9320, www.sfbadlands.com, 2pm-2am daily). This Castro icon was once an old-school bar with pool tables on the floor and license plates on the walls. Now you'll find an always-crowded dance floor, au courant peppy pop music, ever-changing video screens, gay men out for a good time, and straight women who count themselves as regulars at this friendly establishment, which attracts a youngish but mixed-age crowd. The dance floor gets packed and hot, especially on weekend nights. There's a coat check on the bottom level.

**The Lookout** (3600 16th St., 415/431-0306, www.lookoutsf.com, 3:30pm-2am Mon.-Fri., 12:30pm-2am Sat.-Sun., cover charge) gets its name and much of its rep from its balcony overlooking the iconic Castro neighborhood. Get up there for some primo people-watching as you sip your industrial-strength alcoholic concoctions and nibble on surprisingly edible bar snacks and pizza. Special events come with a cover charge.

Yes, there's a Western-themed gay bar in San Francisco. **The Cinch Saloon** (1723 Polk St., 415/776-4162, http://cinchsf.com, 9am-2am Mon.-Fri., 6am-2am Sat.-Sun.) has a laid-back (no pun intended), friendly, male-oriented vibe that's all but lost in the once gay, now gentrified Polk Street hood. Expect fewer females and strong drinks to go with the unpretentious decor and atmosphere.

## Live Music

In the late 1960s, **The Fillmore** (1805 Geary Blvd., 415/346-6000, www.thefillmore.com, prices vary) became legendary for performances by rock acts like the Grateful Dead, Jefferson Airplane, and Carlos Santana. These days, all sorts of national touring acts stop by, sometimes for multiple nights. The Fillmore is also known for its distinctive poster art: Attendees to certain sold-out shows are given commemorative posters.

With its marble columns and ornate balconies, the **Great American Music Hall**

(859 O'Farrell St., 415/885-0750, www. slimspresents.com, prices vary) is one of the nicest places to see a nationally touring act in the city, with bragging for shows by Arcade Fire and the legendary Patti Smith.

The beautiful **Warfield** (982 Market St., 415/345-0900, http://thewarfieldtheatre.com) books all sorts of acts, from John Prine to the Wu-Tang Clan. Choose from limited table seating on the lowest level (mostly by reservation), reserved seats in the balconies, or open standing in the orchestra below the stage.

The **Boom Boom Room** (1601 Fillmore St., 415/673-8040, www.boomboomblues. com, 4pm-2am Sun. and Tues.-Thurs., 4pm-3am Fri.-Sat.) has kept it real in the Fillmore for more than two decades. Today you'll find the latest in a legacy of live blues, boogie, groove, soul, and funk music in this fun, divey joint.

On the other side of town, **Biscuits and Blues** (401 Mason St., 415/292-2583, www.biscuitsandblues.com, hours and days vary) is a local musicians' favorite. Headliners have included Joe Louis Walker, Jimmy Thackery, and Jim Kimo. Dinner is served nightly and features a surprisingly varied and upscale menu.

Bringing jazz to the high culture of Hayes Valley is **SFJazz Center** (201 Franklin St., 866/920-5299, http://sfjazz. org, hours vary Tues.-Sun.), a stunning 35,000-square-foot space with state-of-the-art acoustics. It's designed to feel like a small club, thanks to steep seating that brings the large audience close to the performers, and has drawn major acts such as Herbie Hancock and the Afro-Cuban All Stars.

## Comedy

San Francisco's oldest comedy club, the **Punch Line** (444 Battery St., 415/397-7573, www.punchlinecomedyclub.com, shows 7:30pm, 8pm, 9:45pm, 10:15pm Tues.-Sun., cover varies) is an elegant and intimate venue that earned its top-notch reputation with stellar headliners such as Ellen DeGeneres and Dave Chappelle. An on-site bar keeps the audience primed.

**Cobb's Comedy Club** (915 Columbus Ave., 415/928-4320, www.cobbscomedy.com, shows 7:30pm, 8pm, 9:45pm, 10:15pm Thurs.-Sun., cover varies, two-drink minimum) has played host to star comedians such as Louis CK, Sarah Silverman, and Margaret Cho since 1982. The 425-seat venue offers a full dinner menu and a bar to slake your thirst. Be sure to check your show's start time—some comics don't follow the usual Cobb's schedule.

## The Arts
### Theater

San Francisco may not be known as a big theater town, but it does boast a number of small and large theaters. A great way to grab last-minute theater tickets (or for music or dance shows) is to walk right up to **Union Square TIX** (Union Square, 415/433-7827, www.tixbayarea.com, 8am-6pm Sun.-Thurs., 8am-5pm Fri.-Sat.) for same-day, half-price, no-refund tickets to all kinds of shows across the city. TIX also sells half-price tickets to same-day shows online—check the website at 11am daily for up-to-date deals. If you really, really need to see a major musical while you're in San Francisco, check out the three venues where big Broadway productions land when they come to town: the Orpheum and Golden Gate Theatres (www.shnsf.com), and the Curran Theatre (www.sfcurran.com).

Just up from Union Square, the traditional San Francisco theater district continues to entertain crowds. The **American Conservatory Theater** (A.C.T., 415 Geary St., 415/749-2228, www.act-sf.org, shows Tues.-Sun., $25-115) puts on a season filled with big-name, big-budget productions, such as high-production-value musicals, American classics by the likes of Sam Shepard and Somerset Maugham, and intriguing new works. Discount parking is available with a ticket stub from A.C.T. at the Mason-O'Farrell garage around the corner.

The **Curran Theatre** (445 Geary St., 888/746-1799, www.sfcurran.com, $49-285), next door to A.C.T., has a state-of-the-art stage for classic, high-budget musicals, such as *Les Misérables*, *Phantom of the Opera*, and *Chicago*. Expect to pay a premium for tickets to these productions, which can sometimes run for months or even years. Check the schedule for current shows.

There's one live show that's always different, yet it's been running continuously since 1974. It's *Beach Blanket Babylon* (678 Green St., 415/421-4222, www.beachblanketbabylon.com, shows Wed.-Sun., $25-155), which mocks pop culture and continuously evolves to take advantage of tabloid treasures. Although minors are welcome at the Sunday matinees, evening shows are restricted to attendees 21 and over.

Located in the seedy Mid-Market area, both the **Orpheum Theatre** (1192 Market St., 888/746-1799, www.shnsf.com, $50-200) and the **Golden Gate Theatre** (1 Taylor St., 888/746-1799, www.shnsf.com, $50-200) run touring productions of popular Broadway musicals.

### Classical Music and Opera

Right around the Civic Center, culture takes a turn for the upscale. This is the neighborhood where the ultra-rich and not-so-rich classics lovers come to enjoy a night out. Acoustically renovated in 1992, **Davies Symphony Hall** (201 Van Ness Ave., 415/864-6000, www.sfsymphony.org) is home to Michael Tilson Thomas's world-renowned San Francisco Symphony. Loyal patrons flock to performances that range from the classic to the avant-garde. Whether you want to hear Mozart and Mahler or classic rock blended with major symphony orchestra, the San Francisco Symphony does it.

The **War Memorial Opera House** (301 Van Ness Ave., 415/621-6600, www.sfwmpac.org), a Beaux-Arts-style building designed by Coit Tower and City Hall architect Arthur Brown Jr., houses the **San Francisco Opera** (415/864-3330, http://sfopera.com) and **San Francisco Ballet** (415/861-5600, www.sfballet.org). Tours are available (415/552-8338, 10am-2pm Mon., $5-7).

### Cinema

The **Castro Theatre** (429 Castro St., 415/621-6120, www.castrotheatre.com, $9-12) is a grand movie palace from the 1920s that has enchanted San Francisco audiences for almost a century. The Castro Theatre hosts everything from revival double features (from black-and-white through 1980s classics) to musical movie sing-alongs, live shows, and even the occasional book signing. The Castro also screens current releases and documentaries about queer life in San Francisco and beyond. Once inside, be sure to admire the lavish interior decor. If you get to your seat early, you're likely to be rewarded with a performance of the Mighty Wurlitzer pipe organ before the show.

For a more modern and upscale moviegoing experience, go to the **Sundance Kabuki** (1881 Post St., www.sundance-cinemas.com/kabuki.html, $12.50-16). The "amenity fee" pays for reserved seating, film shorts rather than commercials, and bamboo decor. The Kabuki has eight screens, all of which show mostly big blockbuster Hollywood films, plus a smattering of independents and the occasional filmed opera performance. The Over 21 shows are in the two theaters connected to full bars.

### Festivals and Events

San Francisco is host to numerous events year-round. Following are some of the biggest that are worth planning a trip around.

During the **Chinese New Year Parade** (Chinatown, www.chineseparade.com, Feb.), Chinatown celebrates the lunar new year with a parade of costumed dancers, floats, and firecrackers.

Join rowdy, costumed revelers for **Bay to Breakers** (Embarcadero to Great Highway, www.baytobreakers.com, May), a 12K run/walk/stumble across the city through Golden Gate Park to a massive street party at Ocean Beach.

One of the year's biggest parades is the **San Francisco LGBT Pride Parade and Celebration** (Market St., www.sf-pride.org, June). Hundreds of thousands of people of all orientations take to the streets for this quintessentially San Franciscan party-cum-social justice movement.

Golden Gate Park is host to two wildly popular summer music festivals. **Outside Lands** (www.sfoutsidelands.com, Aug.) is a three-day music festival that floods the park with revelers, food trucks, and hundreds of bands. Headliners have included Radiohead, LCD Soundsystem, Kanye West, Metallica, Neil Young, and Elton John. The park barely recovers in time for **Hardly Strictly Bluegrass** (www.hardlystrictlybluegrass.com, late Sept. or early Oct.), a free music festival celebrating a wide variety of bluegrass sounds, from Lucinda Williams and Emmylou Harris to Ryan Adams and Yo La Tengo.

# Shopping

## Union Square

For the biggest variety of department stores and high-end international designers, plus a few select boutiques, locals and visitors alike flock to **Union Square** (bounded by Geary St., Stockton St., Post St., and Powell St.). The shopping area includes more than just the square proper: More designer and brand-name stores cluster for several blocks in all directions.

The big guys anchor Union Square. **Macy's** (170 O'Farrell St., 415/397-3333, www.macys.com, 10am-9pm Mon.-Sat., 11am-8pm Sun.) has two immense locations, one for women's clothing and

another for the men's store and housewares. **Neiman Marcus** (150 Stockton St., 415/362-3900, www.neimanmarcus.com, 10am-7pm Mon.-Sat. noon-6pm, Sun.) is a favorite among high-budget shoppers, and **Saks Fifth Avenue** (384 Post St., 415/986-4300, www.saksfifthavenue.com, 10am-7pm Mon.-Wed., 10am-8pm Thurs.-Sat., noon-7pm Sun.) adds a touch of New York style to funky-but-wealthy San Francisco.

**Levi's** (815 Market St., 415/501-0100, www.levi.com, 9am-9pm Mon.-Sat., 10am-8pm Sun.) may be a household name, but this three-floor fashion emporium offers incredible customization services while featuring new music and emerging art. Levi's got its start outfitting gold miners in 1849, so it's literally a San Francisco tradition.

The bones of fashion can be found at **Britex Fabrics** (146 Geary St., 415/392-2910, www.britexfabrics.com, 10am-6pm Mon.-Sat.), which draws designers, quilters, DIYers, and costume geeks from all over the Bay Area to its legendary monument to fabric. If you're into any sort of textile crafting, a visit to Britex has the qualities of a religious experience. All four floors are crammed floor to ceiling with bolts of fabric, swaths of lace, and rolls of ribbon. From $1-per-yard grosgrain ribbons to $95-per-yard French silk jacquard and $125-per-yard Italian wool coating, Britex has it all.

## North Beach

One of the most famous independent bookshops in a city known for its literary bent is ★ **City Lights** (261 Columbus Ave., 415/362-8193, www.citylights.com, 10am-midnight daily). It opened in 1953 as an all-paperback bookstore with a decidedly Beat aesthetic, focused on selling modern literary fiction and progressive political tomes. As the Beats flocked to San Francisco and to City Lights, the shop put on another hat—that of publisher. Allen Ginsberg's *Howl* was published by the erstwhile independent, which never looked back. Today City Lights continues to sell and publish the best of cutting-edge fiction and nonfiction.

## Marina and Pacific Heights

The shopping is good in the tony Marina and its elegant neighbor Pacific Heights. **Chestnut and Union Streets** cater to the Marina's young and affluent residents with plenty of clothing boutiques and makeup outlets. Make a stop at **Books Inc.** (2251 Chestnut St., 415/931-3633, www.booksinc.net, 9am-10pm Mon.-Sat., 9am-9pm Sun.), one of the best bookstores in the city. You'll find everything from fiction to travel, as well as a great selection of magazines. **Fillmore Street** is the other major shopping corridor. It's funkier than its younger neighbors in the Marina, probably because of its proximity to Japantown and the Fillmore.

## Hayes Valley

In Hayes Valley, adjacent to the Civic Center, shopping goes uptown, but the unique scent of counterculture creativity still permeates. This is a fun neighborhood to get your stroll on, checking out the art galleries and peeking into the boutiques for clothing and upscale housewares, and then stopping at one of the lovely cafés for a restorative bite to eat.

**Ver Unica** (437B Hayes St. and 526 Hayes St., 415/621-6259, 11am-7pm Mon.-Sat., noon-6pm Sun.) is a vintage boutique that attracts locals and celebrities with high-quality men's and women's clothing and accessories dating from the 1920s to the 1980s, along with a small selection of new apparel by up-and-coming designers.

Paolo Iantorno's boutique **Paolo Shoes** (524 Hayes St., 415/552-4580, http://paoloshoes.com, 11am-7pm Mon.-Sat., 11am-6pm Sun.) showcases his collection of handcrafted shoes, for which all leather and textiles are conscientiously selected and then inspected to ensure top quality.

You can hardly walk 10 feet without passing a sweet shop selling macarons. The original is **Miette** (449 Octavia St., 415/626-6221, www.miette.com, 11am-7pm daily), a cheery European-inspired candy shop, sister store to the Ferry Plaza bakery (415/837-0300). From double-salted licorice to handmade English toffee, the quality confections include imports from England, Italy, and France.

## Mission

In a city known for its quirky style, the Mission was the last neighborhood with a funky, easy-on-the-wallet shopping district. Sadly, the days are gone when you could buy cool vintage clothes by the pound, but **Valencia Street** is still the most vibrant and diverse neighborhood for shoppers in the city.

The **Bell Jar** (3187 16th St., 415/626-1749, https://belljarsf.com, 11am-7pm Mon.-Sat., noon-6pm Sun.) has everything you need to make you and your home into stylish trendsetters of the 21st century, from dresses and jewelry to art books and soaps.

Author Dave Eggers's tongue-in-cheek storefront at **826 Valencia** (826 Valencia St., 415/642-5905, www.826valencia.org, noon-6pm daily) doubles as a pirate supply shop and youth literacy center. While you'll find plenty of pirate booty, you'll also find a good stock of literary magazines and books. Almost next door, **Paxton Gate** (824 Valencia St., 415/824-1872, www.paxtongate.com, 11am-7pm Sun.-Wed., 11am-8pm Thurs.-Sat.) takes the typical gift shop to a new level with taxidermy. This quirky spot is surprisingly cheery, with garden supplies, books, and candles filling the cases in addition to the fossilized creatures.

## Haight-Ashbury

The **Haight-Ashbury shopping district** isn't what it used to be, but if you're willing to poke around a bit, you can still find a few bargains in the remaining thrift shops. One relic of the 1960s counterculture still thrives on the Haight: head shops.

Music has always been a part of the Haight. To this day you'll find homeless folks pounding out rhythms on *doumbeks* and congas on the sidewalks and on Hippy Hill in the park. Located in an old bowling alley, **Amoeba** (1855 Haight St., 415/831-1200, www.amoeba.com, 11am-8pm daily) is a larger-than-life record store that promotes every type of music imaginable. Amoeba's staff, many of whom are musicians themselves, are among the most knowledgeable in the business.

The award-winning **Booksmith** (1644 Haight St., 800/493-7323, www.booksmith.com, 10am-10pm Mon.-Sat., 10am-8pm Sun.) boasts a helpful and informed staff, a fabulous magazine collection, and Northern California's preeminent calendar of readings by internationally renowned authors.

Originally a vaudeville theater, the capacious **Wasteland** (1660 Haight St., 415/863-3150, www.shopwasteland.com, 11am-8pm Mon.-Sat., 11am-7pm Sun.) has a traffic-stopping art nouveau facade, a distinctive assortment of vintage hippie and rock-star threads, and a glamour-punk staff.

# Sports and Recreation

## Beaches
### Ocean Beach

San Francisco boasts of being a city that has everything, and it certainly comes close. This massive urban wonderland even claims several genuine sand beaches within its city limits. No doubt the biggest and most famous of these is **Ocean Beach** (Great Hwy., parking at Sloat Blvd., Golden Gate Park, and the Cliff House, www.parksconservancy.org). This four-mile stretch of sand forms the breakwater for the Pacific Ocean along the whole west side of the city. Because it's so large, you're likely to find a spot to

sit down and maybe even a parking place along the beach, except perhaps on that rarest of occasions in San Francisco—a sunny, warm day. Don't go out for an ocean swim at Ocean Beach: Extremely dangerous rip currents cause fatalities every year.

It may be hard to believe that you can surf in San Francisco, but Ocean Beach has a series of beach breaks that are good in the fall and monstrous in the winter. It's not for beginners, and even accomplished surfers can find it difficult to paddle out. Five blocks from the beach, **Aqua Surf Shop** (3847 Judah St., 415/242-9283, www.aquasurfshop.com, 10am-5:30pm Sun.-Tues., 10am-7pm Wed.-Sat., surfboard rentals $25-35 per day, wetsuits $15 per day) rents shortboards, longboards, and the very necessary 4/3 wetsuit.

### Aquatic Park

The beach at **Aquatic Park** (Beach St. and Hyde St., www.nps.gov/safr) sits at the west end of the Fisherman's Wharf tourist area. This makes Aquatic Park incredibly convenient for visitors who want to grab a picnic on the Wharf to enjoy down on the beach. It was built in the late 1930s as a bathhouse catering to wealthy San Franciscans, and today, swimming remains one of Aquatic Park's main attractions: Triathletes and hard-core swimmers brave the frigid waters to swim for miles in the protected cove. More sedate visitors can find a seat and enjoy a cup of coffee, a newspaper, and some people-watching.

### Baker Beach

**Baker Beach** (Golden Gate Point and the Presidio, www.parksconservancy.org) is best known for its scenery, and that doesn't just mean the lovely views of the Golden Gate Bridge. Baker is San Francisco's own clothing-optional (that is, nude) beach. But don't worry, plenty of the denizens of Baker Beach wear clothes while flying kites, playing volleyball and Frisbee, and even just strolling on the beach. Because Baker is much smaller than Ocean Beach, it gets crowded in the summer. Whether you choose to sunbathe nude or not, don't try to swim here. The currents get seriously strong and dangerous because it's so close to the Golden Gate.

## Parks
### Golden Gate Park

The largest park in San Francisco is **Golden Gate Park** (main entrance at Stanyan St. and Fell St., McLaren Lodge Visitors Center at John F. Kennedy Dr., 415/831-2700, www.golden-gate-park. com). In addition to housing popular sights like the **Academy of Sciences,** the **de Young,** and the **Japanese Tea Garden,** Golden Gate Park is San Francisco's unofficial playground. There are three botanical gardens, a **children's playground** (Martin Luther King Jr. Dr. and Bowling Green Dr.), tennis courts, and a golf course. **Stow Lake** (415/386-2531, http:// stowlakeboathouse.com, 10am-6pm daily, $22-38 per hour) offers paddleboats for rent, and the park even has its own bison paddock. Weekends find the park filled with locals inline skating, biking, hiking, and even Lindy Hopping. John F. Kennedy Drive east of Transverse Drive is closed to motorists every Saturday April-September and Sunday year-round for pedestrian-friendly fun.

### Crissy Field

**Crissy Field** (Marina Blvd. and Baker St., 415/561-4700, www.parksconservancy. org), with its beaches, restored wetlands, and wide promenade, is the playground of the **Presidio** (415/561-4323, www.nps.gov/prsf, free). It's part of the Golden Gate National Recreation Area and is dedicated to environmental education. At the **Crissy Field Center** (1199 E. Beach, 415/561-7690, 8:30am-4:30pm daily) you'll find a list of classes, seminars, and fun hands-on activities for all ages. Many of these include walks out into the marsh and the Presidio.

### Lands End

The **Lands End Trail** (Merrie Way, 415/561-4700, www.nps.gov/goga) is part of the Golden Gate National Recreation Area. Rising above rugged cliffs and beaches, Lands End feels wild, but the three-mile trail, which runs from El Camino Del Mar near the Legion of Honor to the ruins of the Sutro Baths, is perfect for any hiking enthusiast. For a longer adventure, there are plenty of auxiliary trails to explore that lead down to little beaches. Be sure to look out for the remains of three shipwrecks on the rocks of Point Lobos at low tide. Grab a cup of hot chocolate at the stunning **Lands End Lookout visitors center** (680 Point Lobos Ave., 415/426-5240, www.parksconservancy.org, 9am-5pm daily) when your hike is finished.

### Mission Dolores Park

If you're looking for a park where the most strenuous activity is people-watching, then head to **Mission Dolores Park** (Dolores St. and 19th St., 415/554-9521, http://sfrecpark.org). Usually called Dolores Park, it's a favorite of Castro and Mission District denizens. Bring a beach blanket to sprawl on the lawn and a picnic lunch supplied by one of the excellent nearby eateries. On weekends, music festivals and cultural events often spring up at Dolores Park.

## Biking

In other places, bicycling is a sport or a mode of transportation. In San Francisco, bicycling is a religion. Some might say that the high church of this religion is the **San Francisco Bike Coalition** (415/431-2453, www.sfbike.org). In addition to providing workshops and hosting events, the Bike Coalition is an excellent resource for anyone who wants to cycle through the city. Check out its website for tips, maps, and rules of the road.

Newcomers to biking in the city may want to start off gently, with a guided tour that avoids areas with dangerous

# Twin Peaks

Twin Peaks rises up from the center of San Francisco and is the second-highest point in the city. Twin Peaks divides the city between north and south, catching the fog bank that rolls in from the Golden Gate and providing a habitat for lots of wild birds and insects, including the endangered mission blue butterfly.

While you barely need to get out of your car to enjoy the stunning 360-degree views of the city from the peaks, the best way to enjoy the view is to take a hike. To scale the less traveled South Peak, start at the pullout on the road below the parking lot. You'll climb a steep set of stairs up to the top of the South Peak in less than 0.2 mile. Stop and marvel at human industry: the communications tower that's the massive eyesore just over the peak. Carefully cross the road to access the red-rock stairway up to the North Peak. It's only 0.25 mile, but as with the South Peak, those stairs seem to go straight up! It's worth it when you look out across the Golden Gate to Mount Tamalpais in the north and Mount Diablo in the east.

If you're seeking an amazing view along with your exercise, head to Twin Peaks on a sunny day. If the fog is in, as so often happens in the summertime, you'll have trouble seeing five feet in front of you. Don't expect a verdant paradise—the grass doesn't stay green long in the spring, so most visitors get to see the dried-out brush that characterizes much of the Bay Area in the summertime and fall.

## Getting There

Drive west up **Market Street** (eventually turning into **Portola Drive**) and turn right onto **Twin Peaks Boulevard** and past the parade of tour buses to the parking lot past the North Peak. Parking is free, and Twin Peaks is open year-round.

traffic. **Blazing Saddles** (2715 Hyde St., 415/202-8888, www.blazingsaddles. com, $8-15 per hour) rents bikes and offers tips on where to go. There are five locations, most in the Fisherman's Wharf area. If you prefer the safety of a group, take the guided tour (10am daily, three hours, adult $55, child $35, reservations required) through San Francisco and across the Golden Gate Bridge into Marin County. One of the most popular treks is the easy and flat nine-mile ride across the **Golden Gate Bridge** and back. This is a great way to see the bridge and the bay for the first time, and it takes only an hour or two to complete. Another option is to ride across the bridge and into the town of Sausalito (8 miles) or Tiburon (16 miles), enjoy an afternoon and dinner, and then ride the ferry back into the city (bikes are allowed on board).

Another easy and low-stress option is the paved paths of **Golden Gate Park** (main entrance at Stanyan St. and Fell St., McLaren Lodge Visitors Center at John F. Kennedy Dr., 415/831-2700, www.golden-gate-park.com) and the **Presidio** (Montgomery St. and Lincoln Blvd., 415/561-4323, www.nps.gov/prsf). A bike makes a perfect mode of transportation to explore the various museums and attractions of these two large parks, and you can spend all day and never have to worry about finding parking. At the entrance of Golden Gate Park, **Golden Gate Tours & Bike Rentals** (1816 Haight St., 415/922-4537, www.goldengateparkbikerental.com, 9:30am-6:30pm daily, $8-15 per hour, $30-60 per day) has a kiosk. Another choice is **Golden Gate Park Bike and Skate** (3038 Fulton St., 415/922-4537, http://goldengatepark-bikeandskate.com, 9:30am-6:30pm daily, $5-15 per hour, $15-75 per day), located just north of the park on Fulton near the de Young Museum.

## Whale-Watching

With day-trip access to the marine sanctuary off the Farallon Islands,

## Go Wild on the Farallon Islands

On one of those rare clear San Francisco days, you might catch a glimpse of something far offshore in the distance. It's not a pirate ship or an ocean-based optical illusion. It's the **Farallon Islands,** a series of jagged islets and rocks 28 miles west of the Golden Gate Bridge.

At certain times, humans have attempted to make a living on these harsh rocky outcroppings. In the 1800s, Russians hunted the Farallons' marine mammals for their pelts and blubber. Following the Gold Rush, two rival companies harvested murre eggs on the Farallons to feed nearby San Francisco's growing population.

Now the islands have literally gone to the birds. The islands have been set aside as a national wildlife refuge, allowing the region's bird populations to flourish. The Farallons are home to the largest colony of western gulls in the world and has half the world's ashy storm petrels.

But this wild archipelago is also known for its robust population of great white sharks that circle the islands looking for seal and sea lion snacks. The exploits of a group of great white shark researchers on the island were detailed in Susan Carey's gripping 2005 book *The Devil's Teeth*.

Nature lovers who want to see the Farallons' wildlife up close can book an all-day boat trip through **San Francisco Whale Tours** (415/706-7364, www. sanfranciscowhaletours.com) or **SF Bay Whale Watching** (415/331-6267, www. sfbaywhalewatching.com). Don't fall overboard.

whale-watching is a year-round activity in San Francisco. **San Francisco Whale Tours** (Pier 39, Dock B, 415/706-7364, www.sanfranciscowhaletours.com, tours daily, $60-89, advance purchase required) offers six-hour trips out to the Farallons almost every Saturday and Sunday, with almost-guaranteed whale sightings on each trip. Shorter whale-watching trips along the coastline run on weekdays, and 90-minute quickie trips out to see slightly smaller local wildlife, including elephant seals and sea lions, also go out daily. Children ages 3-15 are welcome on boat tours (for reduced rates), and kids often love the chance to spot whales, sea lions, and pelicans. Children under age three are not permitted for safety reasons.

### Spectator Sports

Lovers of the big leagues will find fun in San Francisco. Major League Baseball's **San Francisco Giants** (http://sanfrancisco.giants.mlb.com), winners of the 2014 World Series, play at **AT&T Park** (24 Willie Mays Plaza, 3rd St. and King St.,

415/972-2000). Come out to enjoy the game, the food, and the views at San Francisco's ballpark. Giants games take place on weekdays and weekends, both day and night. It's not hard to snag last-minute tickets to a regular-season game. Check out the gourmet restaurants that ring the stadium; it wouldn't be San Francisco without top-tier cuisine.

The National Football League's **San Francisco 49ers** (www.49ers.com) left behind their longtime home at Candlestick Park in 2014 and now play at **Levi's Stadium** (4900 Marie P. DeBartolo Way, at Tasman Ave., 415/464-9377, www.levisstadium.com) in Santa Clara, 45 minutes south of the city.

## Food

From near and far, people come to San Francisco to eat. Some of the greatest culinary innovations in the world come out of the kitchens in the city. The only problem is to narrow down the choices for dinner tonight.

## Union Square and Nob Hill

### California Cuisine

Make reservations in advance if you want to dine at San Francisco legend **Farallon** (450 Post St., 415/956-6969, www.far-allonrestaurant.com, 5:30pm-9:30pm Mon.-Thurs., 5:30pm-10pm Fri.-Sat., 5:30pm-9pm Sun., $27-65). Dark, cave-like rooms are decorated in an under-the-sea theme complete with the unique Jellyfish Bar. The cuisine, on the other hand, is out of this world. Chef Mark Franz has made Farallon a 20-year fad that just keeps gaining ground. The major culinary theme, seafood, dominates the pricey-but-worth-it menu.

### Chinese

It may not be in Chinatown, but the dim sum at ★ **Yank Sing** (101 Spear St., 415/781-1111, www.yanksing.com, 11am-3pm Mon.-Fri., 10am-4pm Sat.-Sun., $4-11) is second to none. They even won a prestigious James Beard Award in 2009. The family owns and operates both this restaurant and its sister location (49 Stevenson St., 415/541-4949), and now the third generation is training to take over. Expect traditional steamed pork buns, shrimp dumplings, and egg custard tarts. Note that it's open for lunch only.

### French

Tucked away in a tiny alley that looks like it might have been transported from Saint-Michel in Paris, **Café Claude** (7 Claude Ln., 415/392-3505, www.cafe-claude.com, 11:30am-10:30pm Mon.-Sat., 5:30pm-10:30pm Sun., $21-28) serves classic brasserie cuisine to French expatriates and Americans alike. Much French is spoken here, but the simple food tastes fantastic in any language. Café Claude is open for lunch through dinner (dinner only on Sun.), serving an attractive post-lunch menu for weary shoppers looking for sustenance at 3 or 4pm. In the evening it can get crowded, but reservations aren't strictly necessary if you're willing to order a classic French cocktail or a glass of wine and enjoy the bustling atmosphere and live music (on weekends) for a few minutes.

### Thai

Located in the Parc 55 Wyndham Hotel, **Kin Khao** (55 Cyril Magnin St., 415/362-7456, http://kinkhao.com, 11:30am-2pm and 5:30pm-10pm Sun.-Thurs., 11:30am-2pm and 5:30pm-11pm Fri.-Sat., $10-25) offers cuisine far beyond peanut sauces, with dishes like caramelized pork belly, vegetables in a sour curry broth, and green curry with rabbit meatballs. The curries are made from scratch, and the seafood is never frozen.

Just outside of the Union Square area, **Lers Ros Thai** (730 Larkin St., 415/931-6917, http://lersros.com, 11am-midnight daily, $9-18) is a great place to expand your knowledge of Thai cuisine. Daily specials might include stir-fried alligator or venison, while specialties include shredded green papaya salads, garlic quail, and stir-fried pork belly. Bring a handkerchief to mop up the sweat caused by these spicy dishes! Other locations are in Hayes Valley (307 Hayes St., 415/874-9661, 11am-11pm daily) and the Mission District (3189 16th St., 415/923-8983, 11:30am-10pm Sun.-Thurs., 11:30am-11pm Fri.-Sat.).

### Breakfast

Even on a weekday morning, there will be a line out the door of ★ **Brenda's French Soul Food** (652 Polk St., 415/345-8100, http://frenchsoulfood.com, 8am-3pm Mon.-Tues., 8am-10pm Wed.-Sat., 8am-8pm Sun., $12-17). People come in droves to this Tenderloin eatery for its delectable and filling New Orleans-style breakfasts. Unique offerings include crawfish beignets, an Andouille sausage omelet, and beef cutlet and grits. Entrées like chicken étouffée and red beans and rice top the dinner menu.

### Bakeries and Cafés

**Blue Bottle Café** (66 Mint Plaza,

415/495-3394, www.bluebottlecoffee.net, 7am-7pm daily, $5-10), a popular local chain with multiple locations around the city, takes its equipment seriously. Whether you care about the big copper thing that made your mocha or not, you can get a good cup of joe and a small if somewhat pretentious meal at the Mint Plaza, which is Blue Bottle's only café with a full food program. Other locations can be found at the Ferry Building (1 Ferry Bldg., Ste. 7 and Kiosk #4 at Ste. 56), Market Square (1355 Market St.), Pacific Heights (2453 Fillmore St.), and Hayes Valley (315 Linden St.). Expect a line.

## Financial District and SoMa
### California Cuisine
★ **Michael Mina** (252 California St., 415/397-9222, www.michaelmina.net, 11:30am-2pm and 6pm-9pm Mon.-Thurs., 11:30am-2pm and 5:30pm-10pm Fri., 5:30pm-10pm Sat.-Sun., $135-195) finds the celebrity chef using Japanese ingredients and French influences to create bold California entrées. This sleek, upscale restaurant with attentive service is where Mina showcases his signature dishes, including his ahi tuna tartare and his Maine lobster pot pie, an inventive take where the lobster, lobster cream sauce, and vegetables are ladled over a flaky pastry crust. With the only dinner options available being the five-course menu and the eight-course chef's tasting menu, expect to spend some money.

### International
Located in the San Francisco Museum of Modern Art, **In Situ** (151 3rd St., 415/941-6050, http://insitu.sfmoma.org, 11am-3:30pm Mon.-Tues., 11am-3:30pm and 5pm-9pm Thurs.-Sun., $12-28) is almost an art piece unto itself. The concept behind the dining room and lounge: Chef Corey Lee re-creates popular dishes from fine restaurants around the world. The à la carte menu of mostly small plates features the stories of the chefs behind the

a hearty breakfast at Brenda's French Soul Food

creations, immersing diners in their creative process. Reservations for the dining room are recommended, but if you can't get in, opt for the 29-seat lounge.

### Gastropub
★ **The Cavalier** (360 Jessie St., 415/321-6000, http://thecavaliersf.com, 7am-10pm Mon.-Wed., 7am-11pm Thurs.-Fri., 10am-11pm Sat., 10am-9pm Sun., $16-34) serves a California take on upscale British pub food. The restaurant is decorated like a British hunting lodge, with mounted game heads on the walls. A stuffed fox named Floyd reclines on a bookcase in the back. As for the food, it is inventive, tasty, sometimes rich, and surprisingly well priced. The golden-fried lamb scrumpets are worth the trip, while other entrées include classics like fish-and-chips and meat pies.

### Seafood
It's easy to see why the ★ **Tadich Grill** (240 California St., 415/391-1849, www.

tadichgrill.com, 11am-9:30pm Mon.-Fri., 11:30am-9:30pm Sat., $15-38), claiming to be the oldest restaurant in the city, has been around for over 160 years. Sit at the long wooden bar, which stretches from the front door back to the kitchen, and enjoy the attentive service by the white-jacketed waitstaff. The food is classic and hearty, and the seafood-heavy menu has 75 entrées, including a dozen daily specials. One of the standouts is the restaurant's delectable seafood cioppino, which might just be the best version of this Italian-American stew out there.

### Steak
**Alexander's Steakhouse** (448 Brannan St., 415/495-1111, www.alexanderssteakhouse.com, 5:30pm-9pm Mon.-Thurs., 5:30pm-10pm Fri., 5pm-10pm Sat., 5pm-9pm Sun., $48-190) describes itself as "where East meets beef." It's true: The presentation at Alexander's looks like something you'd see on *Iron Chef*, and the prices of the *wagyu* beef look like the monthly payment on a small Japanese car. This white-tablecloth steak house is the antithesis of a bargain, but the food, including the steaks, is more imaginative than most, and the elegant dining experience will make you feel special as your wallet quietly bleeds out.

### Italian
For fine Italian-influenced cuisine, make a reservation at **Quince** (470 Pacific Ave., 415/775-8500, www.quincerestaurant.com, 5:30pm-9:30pm Mon.-Thurs., 5pm-9:30pm Fri.-Sat., $210-250). Chef-owner Michael Tusk blends culinary aesthetics to create his own unique style of cuisine. There are three options: the single extended tasting menu, the abbreviated seasonal tasting menu, or ordering à la carte from the salon menu.

### Japanese
Forget your notions of the plain-Jane sushi bar; **Ozumo** (161 Steuart St., 415/882-1333, www.ozumosanfrancisco.

com, 11:30am-2pm and 5:30pm-10:30pm Mon.-Thurs., 11:30am-2pm and 5:30pm-11pm Fri., 5:30pm-11pm Sat., 5:30pm-10pm Sun., $28-46) takes Japanese cuisine upscale, San Francisco-style. Order some classic *nigiri*, tempura battered dishes, or a big chunk of meat off the traditional *robata* grill. High-quality sake lines the shelves above the bar and along the walls. For non-imbibers, choose from a selection of premium teas. If you're a night owl, enjoy a late dinner on weekends and drinks in the lounge nightly.

## Vietnamese

Probably the single most famous Asian restaurant in a city filled with eateries of all types is **The Slanted Door** (1 Ferry Plaza, Ste. 3, 415/861-8032, www.slanteddoor.com, 11am-2:30pm and 5:30pm-10pm Mon.-Sat., 11:30am-3pm and 5:30pm-10pm Sun., $11-45). Owner Charles Phan, along with more than 20 family members and the rest of his staff, pride themselves on welcoming service and top-quality food. Organic local ingredients get used in both traditional and innovative Vietnamese cuisine, creating a unique dining experience. Even experienced foodies remark that they've never had green papaya salad, glass noodles, or shaking beef like this before. The light afternoon-tea menu (2:30pm-4:30pm daily) can be the perfect pick-me-up for weary travelers who need some sustenance to get them through the long afternoon until dinner, and Vietnamese coffee is the ultimate Southeast Asian caffeine experience.

## Bakeries and Cafés

One of the Ferry Building mainstays, the **Acme Bread Company** (1 Ferry Plaza, Ste. 15, 415/288-2978, http://acmebread.com, 7am-7:30pm Mon.-Fri., 8am-7pm Sat.-Sun.) remains true to its name. You can buy bread here, but not sandwiches, croissants, or pastries. All the bread that Acme sells is made with fresh organic

ingredients in traditional style; the baguettes are traditionally French, so they start to go stale after only 4-6 hours. Eat fast!

The motto of **Café Venue** (67 5th St., 415/546-1144, www.cafevenue.com, 7am-3:30pm Mon.-Fri., 8am-2:30pm Sat., $6-10) is "real food, fast and fresh." This simple strategy is clearly working: On weekdays, you can expect a long line of local workers grabbing a salad or a sandwich for lunch. The warm chicken pesto sandwich is a highlight.

## Farmers Markets

While farmers markets litter the landscape in just about every California town, the **Ferry Plaza Farmers Market** (1 Ferry Plaza, 415/291-3276, www.ferrybuildingmarketplace.com, 10am-2pm Tues. and Thurs., 8am-2pm Sat.) is special. At the granddaddy of Bay Area farmers markets, you'll find a wonderful array of produce, cooked foods, and even locally raised meats and locally caught seafood. Expect to see the freshest fruits and veggies from local growers, grass-fed beef from Marin County, and seasonal seafood pulled from the Pacific beyond the Golden Gate. Granted, you'll pay for the privilege of purchasing from this market—if you're seeking bargain produce, you'll be better served at one of the weekly suburban farmers markets. Even locals flock downtown to the Ferry Building on Saturday mornings, especially in the summer when the variety of California's agricultural bounty becomes staggering.

## Chinatown
### Chinese Banquets

Banquet restaurants offer tasty meat, seafood, and veggie dishes along with rice, soups, and appetizers, all served family-style. Tables are often round, with a lazy Susan in the middle to facilitate the passing of communal serving bowls around the table. In the city, most banquet Chinese restaurants have at least a few dishes that will feel familiar to the American palate, and menus often have English translations.

The **R&G Lounge** (631 Kearny St., 415/982-7877, www.rnglounge.com, 11am-9:30pm daily, $12-40, reservations suggested) takes traditional Chinese American cuisine to the next level. The menu is divided by colors that represent the five elements, according to Chinese tradition and folklore. In addition to old favorites like moo shu pork, chow mein, and lemon chicken, you'll find spicy Szechuan and Mongolian dishes and an array of house specialties. Salt-and-pepper Dungeness crab, served whole on a plate, is the R&G signature dish, though many of the other seafood dishes are just as special. Expect your seafood to be fresh since it comes right out of the tank in the dining room. California-cuisine mores have made their way into the R&G Lounge in the form of some innovative dishes and haute cuisine presentations. This is a great place to enjoy Chinatown cuisine in an American-friendly setting.

**Dim Sum**

The Chinese culinary tradition of dim sum is translated as "touch the heart," meaning "order to your heart's content" in Cantonese. In practical terms, it's a light meal composed of small bites of a wide range of dishes. Americans tend to eat dim sum at lunchtime, though it can just as easily be dinner or even Sunday brunch. In a proper dim sum restaurant, you do not order anything or see a menu. Instead, you sip your oolong and sit back as servers push steam trays out of the kitchen one after the other. Servers and trays make their way around the tables; you pick out what you'd like to try as it passes, and enough of that dish for everyone at your table is placed before you.

One of the many great dim sum places in Chinatown is the **Great Eastern** (649 Jackson St., 415/986-2500, www. greateasternrestaurant.net, 10am-11pm Mon.-Fri., 9am-11pm Sat.-Sun., $15-25),

which serves its dim sum menu 10am-2:30pm daily. It's not a standard dim sum place; instead of the steam carts, you'll get a menu and a list. You must write down everything you want on your list and hand it to your waiter, and your choices will be brought out to you, so family style is undoubtedly the way to go here. Make reservations or you may wait 30-60 minutes for a table. This restaurant jams up fast, right from the moment it opens, especially on weekends. The good news is that most of the folks crowding into Great Eastern are locals. You know what that means.

Ordering dim sum at **Delicious Dim Sum** (752 Jackson St., 415/781-0721, 7am-6pm Thurs.-Tues., $3) may pose challenges. The signs are not in English, and they don't take credit cards. Also, there is only one table inside so you'll probably be getting your dim sum to go. The inexpensive dim sum, with popular pork buns and shrimp and cilantro dumplings, among other options, is worth rising to the challenge.

# North Beach and Fisherman's Wharf
## California Cuisine

San Francisco culinary celebrity Gary Danko has a number of restaurants, but the finest is the one that bears his name. **Gary Danko** (800 North Point St., 415/749-2060, www.garydanko.com, 5:30pm-10pm daily, prix fixe $87-124) offers the best of Danko's California cuisine, from the signature horseradish-crusted salmon medallions to the array of delectable fowl dishes. The herbs and veggies come from Danko's own farm in Napa. Choose 3-5 courses. Make reservations in advance to get a table, and dress up for your sojourn in the elegant white-tablecloth dining room.

## Italian

North Beach is San Francisco's own version of Little Italy. Poke around and find one of the local favorite mom-and-pop pizza joints, or try a bigger, more upscale Italian eatery.

Want a genuine world-champion pizza while you're in town? Tony Gemignani, winner of 11 World Pizza Champion awards, can hook you up. ★ **Tony's Pizza Napoletana** (1570 Stockton St., 415/835-9888, www.tonyspizzanapoletana.com, noon-10pm Mon., noon-11pm Wed.-Sun., $15-30) has seven different pizza ovens that cook by wood, coal, gas, or electric power. You can get a classic American pie loaded with pepperoni, a California-style pie with quail eggs and chorizo, or a Sicilian pizza smothered in meat and garlic. The chef's special Neapolitan-style pizza margherita is a simple-sounding pizza made to perfection. The wood-fired atmosphere of this temple to the pie includes marble-topped tables, dark woods, and white linen napkins stuck into old tomato cans. The long full bar dominates the front dining room, so grab a fancy bottle of wine or a cocktail to go with that champion pizza. For a slice to go, head next door to **Tony's Coal-Fired Pizza and Slice House** (1556 Stockton St., 11:30am-8pm Tues., 11:30am-11pm Wed.-Sun., $3-6).

**Trattoria Contadina** (1800 Mason St., 415/982-5728, www.trattoriacontadina.com, 5pm-9pm Mon.-Thurs., 5pm-9:30pm Fri., 4pm-9:30pm Sat.-Sun., $18-35) presents mouthwatering Italian fare in a fun, eclectic dining room. Dozens of framed photos line the walls, and fresh ingredients stock the kitchen in this San Francisco take on the classic Italian trattoria. Menu items include veal, spaghetti, and gnocchi. Kids are welcome, and vegetarians will find good meatless choices on the menu.

A teensy neighborhood place, **L'Osteria del Forno** (519 Columbus Ave., 415/982-1124, www.losteriadelforno.com, 11:30am-10pm Sun.-Mon. and Wed.-Thurs., 11:30am-10:30pm Fri.-Sat., $6-19) serves up a small menu to match its small dining room and small tables and small (but full) bar. The delectable northern

tasty lamb riblets at The Cavalier

Italian-style pizzas and pastas paired with artisanal cocktails go a long way toward warming up frozen, fog-drenched visitors from the Wharf and the beach. Locals love L'Osteria, which means it's next to impossible to get a table at lunchtime or dinnertime, and doubly impossible on weekends. Your best bet is to drop by during the off-hours; L'Osteria stays open all afternoon and makes a perfect haven for travelers who find themselves in need of a late lunch.

### Greek

In the Greek fishing village of Kokkari, wild game and seafood hold a special place in the local mythology. At **Kokkari Estiatorio** (200 Jackson St., 415/981-0983, www.kokkari.com, 11:30am-2:30pm and 5:30pm-10pm Mon.-Thurs., 11:30am-2:30pm and 5:30pm-11pm Fri., 5pm-11pm Sat., 5pm-10pm Sun., $22-49), patrons enjoy Mediterranean delicacies made with fresh California ingredients amid rustic elegance, feasting on such classic dishes as crispy zucchini cakes, moussaka, and grilled lamb chops.

### Steak House

A New York stage actress wanted a classic steak house in San Francisco, and so **Harris' Restaurant** (2100 Van Ness Ave., 415/673-1888, www.harrisrestaurant. com, 5:30pm-close Mon.-Fri., 5pm-close Sat.-Sun., $49-198) came to be. The fare runs to traditional steaks and prime rib as well as upscale features, with a Kobe *wagyu* beef and surf-and-turf featuring a whole Maine lobster. Music lovers can catch live jazz in the lounge most evenings.

### Breakfast

Smack-dab in the middle of North Beach, **Mama's on Washington Square** (1701 Stockton St., 415/362-6421, www. mamas-sf.com, 8am-3pm daily, $8-10) is perched right across from the green lawn of Washington Square. This more that 50-year-old institution is the perfect place to fuel up on gourmet omelets, freshly baked breads that include a delectable cinnamon brioche, and daily specials like crab Benedict before a day of sightseeing. Arrive early, or be prepared to wait . . . and wait.

### Bakeries and Cafés

Widely recognized as the first espresso coffeehouse on the West Coast, family-owned **Caffé Trieste** (601 Vallejo St., 415/392-6739, www.caffetrieste.com, 6:30am-11pm daily, cash only) first opened its doors in 1956. It became a hangout for Beat writers in the 1950s and 1960s and was where Francis Ford Coppola penned the screenplay for his classic film *The Godfather* in the 1970s. Sip a cappuccino, munch on Italian pastries, and enjoy frequent concerts at this treasured North Beach institution. There are now four locations, from Berkeley to Monterey.

Serving some of the most famous sourdough in the city, the **Boudin Bakery &**

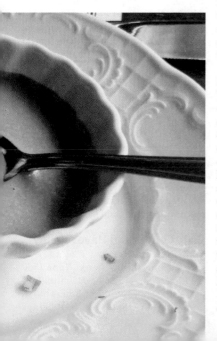

Café (Pier 39, Space 5-Q, 415/421-0185, www.boudinbakery.com, 7:30am-9pm daily, $6-8) is a Pier 39 institution. Grab a loaf of bread to take with you, or order in one of the Boudin classics. Nothing draws tourists like the fragrant clam chowder in a bread bowl, but if you prefer, you can try another soup, a signature sandwich, or even a fresh salad. For a more upscale dining experience with the same great breads, try **Bistro Boudin** (160 Jefferson St., 415/351-5561, 11:30am-10pm Sun.-Thurs., 11:30am-10:30pm Fri.-Sat., $13-38).

## Marina and Pacific Heights
### New American
**The Brixton** (2140 Union St., 415/409-1114, www.brixtonsf.com, 11am-midnight daily, entrées $13-23) might have rock posters on the wall and loud music blaring overheard, but that doesn't mean you shouldn't try the food. The dinner menu goes late into the night and includes items like half a chicken and a tasty burger. The appetizer menu, including a chorizo clam dish and a crab cake plate, is worth grazing, and the "Tacos of the Day" can sate smaller appetites.

### Seafood
Anytime you come to the tiny ★ **Swan Oyster Depot** (1517 Polk St., 415/673-1101, 10:30am-5:30pm Mon.-Sat., $10-25, cash only), there will be a line out the door. With limited stools at a long marble bar, Swan, which opened in 1912, is an old-school seafood place that serves fresh seafood salads, seafood cocktails, and clam chowder, the only hot item on the menu. The seafood is so fresh that you pass it resting on ice while waiting for your barstool.

### Steak House
The Marina is a great place to find a big thick steak. One famed San Francisco steak house, **Boboquivari's** (1450 Lombard St., 415/441-8880, www.boboquivaris.com, 5pm-11pm daily, $23-150) prides itself on its dry-aged beef and fresh seafood. In season, enjoy whole Dungeness crab. But most of all, enjoy "The Steak," thickly cut and simply prepared to enhance the flavor of the beef. The 49-ounce porterhouse costs a pretty penny: $150.

### Japanese
With rolls named after rock acts U2 and Elvis, it's no surprise that **Ace Wasabi's** (3339 Steiner St., 415/567-4903, www.acewasabisf.com, 5:30pm-10pm Mon.-Wed., 5:30pm-10:30pm Thurs., 5:30pm-11pm Fri.-Sat., 5pm-10pm Sun., $6-18 per item) advertises itself as a "rock 'n' roll sushi" joint. Some of the fish is flown in from Tokyo's Tsukiji Fish Market, and the menu includes unusual offerings like tuna tostadas.

If you're in Pacific Heights, give **Kiss Seafood** (1700 Laguna St., 415/474-2866, 5:30pm-9:30pm Wed.-Sat., $38-78) a try. This tiny restaurant (12 seats total) boasts some of the freshest fish in town, which is no mean feat in San Francisco. The lone chef prepares all the fish himself, possibly due to the tiny size of the place. If you're up for sashimi, you'll be in raw-fish heaven. Round off your meal with a glass of chilled premium sake. Reservations are a good idea.

### Breakfast
**Sweet Maple** (2101 Sutter St., 415/655-9169, www.sweetmaplesf.com, 8am-3pm daily, $11-22) takes breakfast to the next level. The varied menu takes eggs in new directions with morning pizzas, egg tacos, and creations including a *wagyu* sliders Benedict. Wash it down with a morning cocktail. It's all served in an airy space with orchids and hanging lamps.

## Civic Center and Hayes Valley
### California Cuisine
Housed in a former bank, **Nopa** (560 Divisadero St., 415/864-8643, http://nopasf.com, 6pm-midnight Sun.-Thurs., 6pm-1am Fri.-Sat., $16-32) brings

together the neighborhood that the restaurant is named after with a whimsical mural by a local artist, a communal table, and a crowd as diverse as the surrounding area. A creative and inexpensive menu offers soul-satisfying dishes and keeps tables full into the wee hours. The cocktails are legendary.

**State Bird Provisions** (1529 Fillmore St., 415/795-1272, http://statebirdsf.com, 5:30pm-10pm Sun.-Thurs., 5:30pm-11pm Fri.-Sat., $14-22) burst onto the San Francisco dining scene in a big way, winning two James Beard Awards (Best New Restaurant in the Whole of the USA in 2013 and the Best Chef in the West in 2015). Part of the unique menu is devoted to "Pancakes and Toast," with items like a beef tongue and horseradish buckwheat pancake. Of course, they also serve the state bird (quail) with provisions.

### French

★ **Jardinière** (300 Grove St., 415/861-5555, www.jardiniere.com, 5pm-close daily, $25-95) was the first restaurant opened by local celebrity chef Traci Des Jardins. The bar and dining room blend into one another and feature stunning art deco decor. The ever-changing menu is a masterpiece of French California cuisine, and Des Jardins has long supported the sustainable restaurant movement. Eating at Jardinière is not only a treat for the senses, it is also a way to support the best of trends in San Francisco restaurants. Make reservations if you're trying to catch dinner before a show.

**Absinthe** (398 Hayes St., 415/551-1590, www.absinthe.com, 11:30am-11pm Mon.-Wed., 11:30am-midnight Thurs.-Fri., 11am-midnight Sat., 11am-10pm Sun., $15-37) takes its name from the notorious "green fairy" drink made of liquor and wormwood. Absinthe indeed does serve absinthe, including locally made St. George Spirits Absinthe Verte. It also serves upscale French bistro fare, including what may be the best french fries in the city. The French theme carries on into the decor as well, so expect the look of a Parisian brasserie or perhaps a café in Nice, with retro-modern furniture and classic prints on the walls. The bar is open until 2am on Thursday, Friday, and Saturday, so if you want drinks or dessert after a show at the Opera or Davies Hall, just walk around the corner.

### German

**Suppenküche** (525 Laguna St., 415/252-9289, www.suppenkuche.com, 5pm-10pm Mon.-Sat., 10am-2:30pm and 5pm-10pm Sun., $12.50-20) brings a taste of Bavaria to the Bay Area. The beer list is a great place to start, since you can enjoy a wealth of classic German brews on tap and in bottles, plus a few Belgians thrown in for variety. For dinner, expect German classics with a focus on Bavarian cuisine. Spaetzle, pork, sausage—you name it, they've got it, and it will harden your arteries right up. They now serve a Sunday brunch that's almost as heavy as its dinners. Suppenküche also has a **Biergarten** (424 Octavia St., 415/252-9289, http://biergartensf.com, 3pm-9pm Mon.-Sat., 1pm-7pm Sun. summer, 2pm-8pm Mon.-Sat., 1pm-7pm Sun. winter), two blocks away.

## Mission and Castro
### Mexican

Much of the rich heritage of the Mission District is Latino, thus leading to the Mission being *the* place to find a good taco or burrito. **Farolito Taqueria** (2950 24th St., 415/641-0758, www.elfarolito-inc.com, 10am-1:30am Mon.-Thurs. and Sun., 10am-2:30am Fri.-Sat., $10) has found favor with the picky locals who have dozens of taqueria options within a few blocks. It seems that every regular has a different favorite: the burritos, the enchiladas, the quesadillas. Whatever your pleasure, you'll find a tasty version of it at Farolito. A totally casual spot, you order at the counter and sit at picnic-style tables to chow down on the properly greasy Mexican fare. (Don't confuse this

Farolito with the taqueria with the same name on Mission Street.)

## Seafood

For great seafood in a lower-key atmosphere, locals eschew the tourist traps on the Wharf and head for the **Anchor Oyster Bar** (579 Castro St., 415/431-3990, www.anchoroysterbar.com, 11:30am-10pm Mon.-Sat., 4pm-9:30pm Sun., $14-39) in the Castro. The raw bar features different ways to have oysters, including an oyster *soju* shot. The dining room serves seafood, including local favorite Dungeness crab. Service is friendly, as befits a neighborhood spot, and it sees fewer large crowds. This doesn't diminish its quality, and it makes for a great spot to get a delicious meal before heading out to the local clubs for a late night out.

## Italian

Sometimes even the most dedicated culinary explorer needs a break from the endless fancy food of San Francisco. When the time is right for a plain ol' pizza, head for **Little Star Pizza** (400 Valencia St., 415/551-7827, www.littlestarpizza.com, 5pm-10pm Mon.-Tues., noon-10pm Wed.-Thurs. and Sun., noon-11pm Fri.-Sat., $12-23). A jewel of the Mission District, this pizzeria specializes in Chicago-style deep-dish pies, but also serves thin-crust pizzas for devotees of the New York style. Once you've found the all-black building and taken a seat inside the casual eatery, grab a beer or a cocktail from the bar if you have to wait for a table. Pick one of Little Star's specialty pizzas, or create your own variation from the toppings they offer. Can't get enough of Little Star? They've got a second location in the city (846 Divisadero St., 415/441-1118).

**Delfina** (3621 18th St., 415/552-4055, www.delfinasf.com, 5pm-9:30pm Mon.-Thurs., 4pm-10:30pm Fri., 3pm-10:30pm Sat., 3pm-9:30pm Sun., $10-32) gives Italian cuisine a hearty California twist. From the antipasti to the entrées, the dishes speak of local farms and ranches,

fresh seasonal produce, and the best Italian American taste that money can buy. With both a charming, warm indoor dining room and an outdoor garden patio, there's plenty of seating at this lovely restaurant.

## Korean

Owned and operated by three brothers, **Namu Gaji** (499 Dolores St., 415/431-6268, www.namusf.com, 5:30pm-10pm Tues., 11:30am-3pm and 5:30pm-10pm Wed.-Thurs., 11:30am-3pm and 5:30pm-10:30pm Fri., 10:30am-4pm and 5pm-10:30pm Sat., 10:30am-4pm and 5pm-10pm Sun., $13-21) presents a new take on Korean food. One standout dish is the *okonomiyaki*, a pan-fried entrée made with kimchee and oysters. The adventurous can try beef tongue, while the less courageous might opt for salmon or a burger.

## Sushi

**Ichi Sushi & Ni Bar** (3369 Mission St., 415/525-4750, http://ichisushi.com, 5:30pm-10pm Mon.-Tues., 11:30am-2pm and 5:30pm-10pm Wed.-Thurs., 11:30am-2pm and 5:30pm-11pm Fri., 11am-2:30pm and 5:30pm-11pm Sat., 11am-2:30pm and 5:30pm-9:30pm Sun., $4.50-14.50) started out as a Bernal Heights food stall and evolved into a sleek restaurant. The emphasis is on sustainable sashimi. There are also rolls, a unique cold ramen with pesto, and some perfectly golden-brown chicken wings. Get good deals on appetizers and drinks at the bar's happy hour (5:30pm-6:30pm Mon.-Fri.).

### Bakeries and Cafés

A line snakes into the ★ **Tartine Bakery** (600 Guerrero St., 415/487-2600, www.tartinebakery.com, 8am-7pm Mon., 7:30am-7pm Tues.-Wed., 7:30am-8pm Thurs.-Fri., 8am-8pm Sat.-Sun.) almost all day long. You might think that there's an impromptu rock show or a book signing by a prominent author, but the eatery's baked goods, breads, and sandwiches are the stars. A slab of the transcendent quiche made with crème fraîche, Niman smoked ham, and organic produce is an inspired way to start the day, especially if you are planning on burning some serious calories. Meanwhile, there is nothing quite like a piece of Passion Fruit Lime Bavarian Rectangle, a cake that somehow manages to be both rich in flavor and light as air. Its latest endeavor is **Tartine Manufactory** (595 Alabama St., 7:30am-5pm and 5:30pm-10pm Mon.-Fri., 8am-5pm and 5:30pm-10pm Sat.-Sun.), a big industrial building with a bread baking operation, a coffee bar, a bar, and a café serving breakfast, lunch, and dinner.

You can also satisfy your sweet tooth at **Bi-Rite Creamery & Bakeshop** (3692 18th St., 415/626-5600, http://biritecreamery.com, 11am-10pm daily). The ice cream is made by hand with organic milk, cream, and eggs; inventive flavors include honey lavender, salted caramel, and white chocolate raspberry swirl. Pick up a scoop to enjoy at nearby Mission Dolores Park. They also have a location at 550 Divisadero (415/551-7900, 9am-9pm daily).

## Golden Gate Park and the Haight
### California Cuisine
One of the most famous restaurant locations on the San Francisco coast is the **Cliff House.** The high-end eatery inhabiting the famed facade is **Sutro's** (1090 Point Lobos Ave., 415/386-3330, www.cliffhouse.com, 11:30am-9:30pm Mon.-Sat., 11am-9:30pm Sun., $25-39). The appetizers and entrées are mainly seafood in somewhat snooty preparations. Although the cuisine is expensive and fancy, in all honesty it's not the best in the city. What *is* amazing are the views from the floor-to-ceiling windows out over the vast expanse of the Pacific Ocean. These views make Sutro's a perfect spot to enjoy a romantic dinner while watching the sun set over the sea.

The Cliff House also houses the more casual **Bistro** (1090 Point Lobos Ave., 415/386-3330, www.cliffhouse.com, 9am-3:30pm and 4:15pm-9:30pm Mon.-Sat., 8:30am-3:30pm and 4:15pm-9:30pm Sun., $15-30).

### Japanese
Sushi restaurants are immensely popular in these residential neighborhoods. **Koo** (408 Irving St., 415/731-7077, www.sushikoo.com, 5:30pm-10pm Tues.-Thurs., 5:30pm-10:30pm Fri.-Sat., 5pm-9:30pm Sun., $30-50) is a favorite in the Sunset. While sushi purists are happy with the selection of *nigiri* and sashimi, lovers of fusion and experimentation will enjoy the small plates and unusual rolls created to delight diners. Complementing the Japanese cuisine is a small but scrumptious list of premium sakes. Only the cheap stuff is served hot, as high-quality sake is always chilled.

### Thai
Dining in the Haight? Check out the flavorful dishes at **Siam Lotus Thai Cuisine** (1705 Haight St., 415/933-8031, noon-4pm and 5pm-9pm Mon. and Thurs., 5pm-9pm Wed., noon-4pm and 5pm-9:30pm Fri., noon-9:30pm Sat., noon-9pm Sun., $7-13). You'll find a rainbow of curries, pad thai, and all sorts of Thai meat, poultry, and vegetarian dishes. Look to the lunch specials for bargains, and to the Thai iced tea for a lunchtime pick-me-up. Locals enjoy the casually romantic ambience, and visitors make special trips down to the Haight just to dine here.

### Vietnamese
**Thanh Long** (4101 Judah St., 415/665-1146, http://thanhlongsf.com, 5pm-9pm Tues.-Thurs. and Sun., 5pm-9:30pm Fri.-Sat., $20-30) was the first family-owned Vietnamese restaurant in San Francisco. Since the early 1970s, Thanh Long has been serving one of the best preparations of local Dungeness crab in the city: roasted crab with garlic noodles. This

isn't a $5 pho joint, so expect white tablecloths and higher prices at this stately small restaurant in the outer Sunset neighborhood. Fans include actors Harrison Ford and Danny Glover.

# Accommodations

Both the cheapest and the most expensive places tend to be in Union Square and downtown. Cheaper digs can be had in the neighborhoods surrounding Fisherman's Wharf. You'll find the most character in small boutique hotels, but plenty of big chain hotels have at least one location in town. Valet parking and overnight garage parking can be expensive. Check to see if your hotel has a "parking package" that includes this expense.

## Union Square and Nob Hill

In and around Union Square and Nob Hill, you'll find approximately a zillion hotels. As a rule, those closest to the top of the Hill or to Union Square proper are the most expensive. For a one- or two-block walk away from the center, you get more personality and a genuine San Francisco experience for less money and less prestige. There are few inexpensive options in these areas. Hostels are located to the southwest, closer to the gritty Tenderloin neighborhood, where safety becomes an issue after dark.

### $150-250

One of the best deals in town is at the ★ **Golden Gate Hotel** (775 Bush St., 415/392-3702, www.goldengatehotel. com, $150-225), centrally located between Union Square and the top of Nob Hill. This narrow yellow building has 25 rooms decorated with antiques, giving it a bed-and-breakfast feel. The cheapest option is a room with a shared bath

**From top to bottom:** the Metro Hotel near San Francisco's Golden Gate Park; the colorful pool deck at the Phoenix Hotel; Hotel Zetta

down the hall, though there are rooms with their own baths. The Golden Gate serves a fine continental breakfast with fresh croissants.

Despite its location in the seedier Tenderloin neighborhood—or perhaps because of it—the ★ **Phoenix Hotel** (601 Eddy St., 415/776-1380, www.phoenixsf. com, $229-329) has serious rock-and-roll cred. A former motor lodge, the Phoenix has hosted a who's who of rock music, including the Red Hot Chili Peppers, Debbie Harry, and Sublime. When a Kurt Cobain letter was found mocking his wedding vows to Courtney Love, it was written on Phoenix letterhead. The main draw is the large deck with an in-laid, heated pool that has a mosaic on the bottom. Palm trees rising overhead make the Phoenix feels like it's a beachside oasis rather than sited in a gritty urban neighborhood. At night, the sounds of the surrounding Tenderloin remind you of the hotel's true location, but most guests don't come here to catch up on their sleep.

### Over $250

★ **Hotel G** (386 Geary St., 877/828-4478, http://hotelgsanfrancisco.com, $279-499) comes on like an unassuming cool kid that impresses with understated style. The rooms in this boutique hotel are all simple, clean, and serene with accouterments like smart TVs, Nespresso coffeemakers, Tivoli clock radios, and comfy beds with denim headboards (a nod to Levi's San Francisco roots). The lower-level rooms have bathrooms with subway-tiled floors and showers, while the upper-floor bathrooms utilize marble flooring and shower walls. Choose a room on the 8th floor if you enjoy rooms with high ceilings. There's also three drinking and dining establishments within the building: the **Klyde Café & Wine Bar,** the **398 Brasserie,** and the difficult-to-find speakeasy craft cocktail and oyster bar **Benjamin Cooper.** Best of all, your room will feel like a homey apartment or studio even though the hotel is located just a block from bustling Union Square.

Just blocks from Union Square, **Hotel Rex** (562 Sutter St., 415/433-4434, www. jdvhotels.com/rex, $250-300) is an ideal writer's retreat. The spacious guest rooms all have wooden writing desks and are decorated with the work of local artists. The downstairs Library Bar is a fine place to sip a cocktail or glass of wine while browsing its shelves of hardback books. Live jazz acts perform on Friday.

A San Francisco legend, the **Clift** (495 Geary St., 415/775-4700, www.morgan-shotelgroup.com, $269-2,100) has a lobby worth walking into, whether you're a guest of the hotel or not. The high-ceilinged, gray industrial space is devoted to modern art, including a Salvador Dalí coffee table. By contrast, the big Philippe Starck-designed guest rooms are almost Spartan in their simplicity, with colors meant to mimic the city skyline. Stop in for a drink at the **Redwood Room,** done in brown leather and popular with a younger crowd. **The Velvet Room** serves breakfast and dinner. The Clift is perfectly located for theatergoers, and the square is an easy walk away.

Certain names just mean luxury in the hotel world. The **Fairmont San Francisco** (950 Mason St., 415/772-5000, www. fairmont.com, $499-4,999) is among the best of these. With a rich history, above-and-beyond service, and spectacular views, the Fairmont makes any stay in the city memorable. Check online for package specials, including "Room with a Vroom," which includes parking, starting at $299 when available. While onsite, head downstairs for a Mai Tai at the Tonga Room & Hurricane Bar.

The **Ritz-Carlton** (600 Stockton St., 415/296-7465, www.ritzcarlton.com, $399-1,000) provides patrons with ultimate pampering. From the high-thread-count sheets to the five-star dining room and the full-service spa, guests at the Ritz all but drown in sumptuous amenities. Even the "standard" guest rooms are exceptional, but if you've got the bread, spring for the Club Floors, where they'll give you an iPod, a personal concierge, and possibly the kitchen sink if you ask for it.

## Financial District and SoMa

Top business execs make it their, well, business to stay near the towering offices of the Financial District, down by the water on the Embarcadero, or in SoMa. Thus, most of the lodgings in these areas cater to the expense-account set. The big-name chain hotels run expensive; book one if you're traveling on an unlimited company credit card. Otherwise, look for smaller boutique and indie accommodations that won't tear your wallet to bits.

### $150-250

For something small but upscale, check out **Hotel Griffon** (155 Steuart St., 800/321-2201, www.hotelgriffon.com, $230-500), a boutique business hotel with a prime vacation locale on the Embarcadero, just feet from the Ferry Building. The Griffon offers business and leisure packages to suit any traveler's needs. Although they're pricey, the best guest rooms have views of the Bay Bridge and Treasure Island.

### Over $250

Entering the bright lobby exploding with color, you'll realize the ★ **Hotel Triton** (342 Grant Ave., 844/808-0290, www.hoteltriton.com, $389-529) celebrates San Francisco's independent spirit. The rooms are wallpapered with text from Jack Kerouac's *On the Road*, while copies of Allen Ginsberg's *Howl* take the place of the Gideon Bibles found in most other hotels across the country. There are three specialty suites, including one designed by musician Jerry Garcia. The Häagen-Dazs "Sweet Suite" comes stocked with a fridge of the gourmet ice creams. The environmentally friendly practices developed at the Triton are being adopted by sister hotels all over the world. Guest rooms are small but comfortable and well stocked with ecofriendly amenities and bath products.

★ **Hotel Zetta** (55 5th St., 415/543-8555, www.viceroryhotelgroup.com/en/zetta, $299-1,214) embraces San Francisco's reputation as a technology hub. The ultra-modern rooms are equipped with a gaggle of gadgets, including a G-Link station for mobile devices and a device that streams content from your smartphone onto the large flat-screen TVs. There are also espresso machines and a large butcher-block desk for those who need to get work done. The hotel's common rooms are more playful, with shuffleboard, a pool table, and an oversize game of Jenga. Recycled art throughout the building includes chandeliers made of old eyeglasses, located in the lobby. The upscale on-site restaurant **The Cavalier** features British-meets-California cuisine.

**Hotel Vitale** (8 Mission St., 888/890-8688, www.hotelvitale.com, $309-900) professes to restore guests' vitality with its lovely guest rooms and exclusive spa, complete with rooftop hot soaking tubs and a yoga studio. Many of the good-size guest rooms also have private deep soaking tubs. The Vitale's **Americano Restaurant** serves Italian fare.

**Le Méridien San Francisco** (333 Battery St., 415/296-2900, www.starwoodhotels.com, $362-843) stands tall in the Embarcadero Center, convenient to shopping, dining, and cable car lines. This expensive luxury hotel pampers guests with Frette sheets, down duvets, and stellar views. Expect nightly turndown service and 24-hour room service. A pedestrian bridge connects the hotel to the Federal Reserve Building.

For a true San Francisco hotel experience, book a room at the famous **Hotel Palomar** (12 4th St., 415/348-1111, www.hotelpalomar-sf.com, $268-549). You'll find every amenity imaginable, from extra-long beds for taller guests to in-room spa services and temporary pet goldfish.

Get drinks and dinner at the on-site restaurant **Dirty Habit,** which names *Project Runway* finalist Melissa Fleis as a "muse and collaborator." Join a wellness ambassador for a group run on weekday mornings at 7am or borrow one of the hotel's complimentary bikes to tool around town.

## North Beach and Fisherman's Wharf

Perhaps it's odd, but the tourist mecca of San Francisco is not a district of a zillion hotels. Most of the major hostelries sit down nearer to Union Square. But you can stay near the Wharf or in North Beach if you choose; you'll find plenty of chain motels here, plus a few select boutique hotels in all price ranges.

### Under $150

The unexpected **Fisherman's Wharf Hostel** (Fort Mason, Bldg. 240, 415/771-7277, www.sfhostels.com/fishermanswharf, dorm $44-60, private room $120-170) sits in bucolic Fort Mason, far from the problems that plague other SF hostels but within walking distance of frenetic downtown. The best amenities (aside from the free parking, free continental breakfast, and no curfews or chores) are the sweeping lawns, mature trees, and the views of Alcatraz and the Bay.

The **San Remo Hotel** (2237 Mason St., 800/352-7366, www.sanremohotel.com, $99-179) is one of the best bargains in the city. The blocky old yellow building has been around since just after the 1906 earthquake, offering inexpensive guest rooms to budget-minded travelers. One of the reasons for the rock bottom pricing is the baths: You don't get your own. Four shared baths with shower facilities located in the hallways are available to guests day and night. The guest rooms boast the simplest of furnishings and decorations as well as clean, white-painted walls and ceilings. Some rooms have their own sinks, all have either double beds or two twin beds, and none have telephones or TVs, so this might not be the best choice of lodgings for large media-addicted families. Couples on a romantic vacation can rent the Penthouse, a lovely room for two with lots of windows and a rooftop terrace boasting views of North Beach and the Bay.

### $150-250

Located in a quieter section of the Embarcadero, the ★ **Harbor Court Hotel** (165 Steuart St., 415/882-1300, www.harborcourthotel.com, $219-430) is housed in an attractive brick building just a block from the Ferry Building. Spring for a harbor-view room to watch ships passing by during the day and the pulsing lights of the Bay Bridge after dark. Modern touches include iPod docks and flat-screen TVs. Guests can get a day pass to the adjacent Embarcadero YMCA, which has a gym, a spa, and a swimming pool.

**Hotel Bohème** (444 Columbus Ave., 415/433-9111, www.hotelboheme.com, $194-320) offers comfort, history, and culture at a pleasantly low price for San Francisco. Guest rooms are small but comfortable, Wi-Fi is free, and the spirit of the 1950s bohemian Beats lives on. The warmly colored and gently lit guest rooms are particularly welcoming to solo travelers and couples, with their retro brass beds covered by postmodern geometric spreads. All guest rooms have private baths, and the double-queen room can sleep up to four people for an additional charge.

The **Washington Square Inn** (1660 Stockton St., 415/981-4220, www.wsisf.com, $209-359) doesn't look like a typical California B&B. With its city-practical architecture and canopy out on the sidewalk, it's more a small, elegant hotel. The inn offers 15 guest rooms with private baths, elegant appointments, and fine linens. Some guest rooms have spa bathtubs, and others have views of Coit Tower and Grace Cathedral. Only the larger guest rooms and junior suites are spacious; the standard guest rooms are "cozy" in the European urban style. Amenities include a generous continental breakfast brought to your room daily, afternoon tea, a flat-screen TV in every guest room, and free Wi-Fi. To stay at the Washington Square Inn is to get a true sense of the beauty and style of San Francisco.

### Over $250

For a luxurious stay in the city, save up for a room at **The Argonaut** (495 Jefferson St., 800/790-1415, www.argonauthotel.com, $249-849). With stunning Bay views from its prime Fisherman's Wharf location, in-room spa services, and a yoga channel, The Argonaut is all San Francisco. The rooms feature exposed brick walls and nautical-inspired decor. Guest rooms range from cozy standards to upscale suites with separate bedrooms and whirlpool tubs. The SF Maritime National Historical Park's visitors center and interactive museum is located in the same building as The Argonaut.

## Marina and Pacific Heights

These areas are close enough to Fisherman's Wharf to walk there for dinner, and the lodgings are far more affordable than downtown digs.

### $150-250

Staying at the ★ **Marina Motel** (2576 Lombard St., 415/921-9406 or 800/346-6118, www.marinamotel.com, $209-349) feels like you have your own apartment in the fancy Marina District. This European-styled motor lodge features rooms above little garages where you can park your car. More than half the rooms have small kitchens with a stove, fridge, microwave, and dishes for taking a break from eating out. Though the Marina Motel was built in the 1930s, the rooms are updated with modern amenities, including sometimes-working Wi-Fi and TVs with cable. With major attractions like the Exploratorium and the Palace of Fine Arts within walking distance, this reasonably priced motel is a great place to

Harbor Court Hotel

hunker down for a few days and see the nearby sights. Reserve a room away from Lombard Street if you are a light sleeper.

Pack the car and bring the kids to the **Hotel del Sol** (3100 Webster St., 877/433-5765, www.thehoteldelsol.com, $230-340). This unique hotel-motel embraces its origins as a 1950s motor lodge, with the guest rooms decorated in bright, bold colors with whimsical accents, a heated courtyard pool, palm trees, hammocks, and parking for $25 a night, which is a deal in this city. The Marina locale offers trendy cafés, restaurants, bars, and shopping within walking distance, as well as access to major attractions.

Another Pacific Heights jewel, the **Jackson Court** (2198 Jackson St., 415/929-7670, www.jacksoncourt.com, $219-255) presents a lovely brick facade in the exclusive neighborhood. The 10-room inn offers comfortable, uniquely decorated queen rooms and a luscious continental breakfast each morning.

The exterior and interior amenities

of the **Hotel Majestic** (1500 Sutter St., 415/441-1100, www.thehotelmajestic.org, $200-448) evoke the grandeur of early 20th-century San Francisco. It is said that one of the former hotel owner's daughters haunts the Edwardian-style 1902 building, which boasts antique furnishings and decorative items from England and France. Cozy guest rooms, junior suites, and one-bedroom suites are available. The on-site **Cafe Majestic** serves breakfast and dinner, with a focus on local, healthful ingredients.

## Over $250

Tucked in with the money-laden mansions of Pacific Heights, **Hotel Drisco** (2901 Pacific Ave., 800/634-7277, www.hoteldrisco.com, $379-949) offers elegance to discerning visitors. Away from the frenzied pace and noise of downtown, at the Drisco you get quiet, comfy guest rooms with overstuffed furniture, breakfast with a latte, and a glass of wine in the evening. Families and larger parties can look into the hotel's suite with two bedrooms and two baths. They also have a morning car service to downtown on weekdays.

The stately **Queen Anne Hotel** (1590 Sutter St., 800/227-3970, www.queen-anne.com, $249-305) brings the elegance of downtown San Francisco out to Pacific Heights. Sumptuous fabrics and rich colors in the guest rooms and common areas add to the feeling of decadence and luxury in this boutique hotel. Small, moderate guest rooms offer attractive accommodations on a budget, while superior rooms and suites are more upscale. Continental breakfast is included, as are high-end services such as courtesy car service in the morning and afternoon tea and sherry.

The **Lombard Motor Inn** (1475 Lombard St., 415/441-6000, www.lombardmotorinn.com, $262-285) has the standard-issue amenities: reasonable-size guest rooms, flat-screen TVs, Internet, free parking, and location, location,

location. Of course, the location means there's plenty of nighttime noise pouring in through the windows, especially on weekends.

The aptly named **Inn at the Presidio** (42 Moraga Ave., 415/800-7356, www.innatthepresidio.com, $295-450) is just minutes from the heart of the city, but its location in the Presidio's green space makes it feel a world away. The inn offers immediate access to the national park's hiking trails and cultural attractions along with panoramic views of the Bay and Alcatraz in the distance. Most of the rooms are within a former housing unit for bachelor officers. While the inn is modernized, it nods to its past with military decorations on the lobby's walls. Continental breakfast is served in the former mess hall. Suites are spacious for the city, including a bedroom with an adjoining room, a pullout sofa, and a gas fireplace. The nearby four-bedroom **Funston House** is available for large groups.

## Civic Center and Hayes Valley
You'll find a few reasonably priced accommodations and classic inns in the Civic Center and Hayes Valley areas.

### Under $150
Take a step back into an older San Francisco at the **Chateau Tivoli** (1057 Steiner St., 800/228-1647, www.chateau-tivoli.com, $150-300). The over-the-top colorful exterior matches perfectly with the American Renaissance interior decor. Each unique guest room and suite showcases an exquisite style evocative of the Victorian era. Some furnishings come from the estates of the Vanderbilts and J. Paul Getty. Most guest rooms have private baths, although the two least expensive share a bath.

Located in Hayes Valley a few blocks from the Opera House, the **Inn at the Opera** (333 Fulton St., 888/298-7198, www.shellhospitality.com, $179-323) promises to have guests ready for a swanky night of San Francisco culture.

the Inn at the Presidio

Clothes-pressing services count among the inn's many amenities. French interior styling in the guest rooms and suites that once impressed visiting opera stars now welcomes guests from all over the world. The on-site restaurant **Plaj** serves Scandinavian fare.

## Golden Gate Park and the Haight

Accommodations around Golden Gate Park are surprisingly reasonable. Leaning toward Victorian and Edwardian inns, most lodgings are in the middle price range for well above average guest rooms and services. However, getting downtown from the quiet residential spots can be a trek; ask at your inn about car services, cabs, and the nearest bus lines.

Out on the ocean side of the park, motor inns of varying quality cluster on the Great Highway. They've got the advantages of more space, low rates, and free parking, but they range from drab all the way down to seedy; choose carefully.

### Under $150

Just west of the Haight-Ashbury neighborhood, ★ **The Metro Hotel** (319 Divisadero St., 415/861-5364, www.metrohotelsf.com, $107-182) is one of the best priced lodging options in the city. It's a huge plus that the rooms in this wonderful three-story building are also clean and comfy. Some units have bay windows that bulge out over the bustling Divisadero Street below, but don't worry, street noise is near nonexistent due to triple-paned windows. Enjoy the tranquil courtyard garden out back or pepper the friendly, 24-hour-staffed front desk with questions. The only real negative here for discerning budget travelers is the lack of designated parking.

### $150-250

The **Stanyan Park Hotel** (750 Stanyan St., 415/751-1000, www.stanyanpark.com, $179-284) graces the Upper Haight across the street from Golden Gate Park. This renovated 1904-1905 building, listed on the National Register of Historic Places, shows off its Victorian heritage both inside and out. Guest rooms can be small but are elegantly decorated. Multiple-room suites are available. Ask for a room overlooking the park. A stay includes a morning continental breakfast and a late afternoon wine and cheese reception.

To say the **Seal Rock Inn** (545 Point Lobos Ave., 888/732-5762, www.sealrockinn.com, $170-217) is near Golden Gate Park pushes even the fluid San Francisco neighborhood boundaries. In fact, this pretty place perches near the tip of Land's End, only a short walk from the Pacific Ocean. All guest rooms at the Seal Rock Inn have ocean views, private baths, free parking, and free Wi-Fi. With longer stays in mind, the Seal Rock offers rooms with kitchenettes (two-day minimum stay to use the kitchen part of the room; weird but true). You can call and ask for a fireplace room that faces the Seal Rocks, so you can stay warm and toasty while training your binoculars on a popular mating spot for local sea lions. The restaurant downstairs serves breakfast and lunch; on Sunday you'll be competing with brunch-loving locals for a table.

## Transportation and Services

### Air

**San Francisco International Airport** (SFO, 800/435-9736, www.flysfo.com) is actually about 12 miles south of the city center, near the town of Millbrae. You can easily get a taxi, Lyft, Uber, or other ground transportation into the heart of the city from the airport. BART is available from SFO's international terminal, but Caltrain is only accessible via a BART connection from SFO. Some San Francisco hotels offer complimentary shuttles from the airport as well. You can also rent a car here.

As one of the 30 busiest airports in the world, SFO has long check-in and security lines much of the time and dreadful overcrowding on major travel holidays. Plan to arrive at the airport two hours prior to departure for domestic flights and three hours prior to an international flight.

### Train and Bus

Amtrak does not run directly into San Francisco. You can ride into the San Jose, Oakland, or Emeryville stations and then take a connecting bus into San Francisco.

**Greyhound** (200 Folsom St., 415/495-1569, www.greyhound.com, 5:30am-1am daily) offers bus service to San Francisco from all over the country.

### Car

The **Bay Bridge** (toll $6) links I-80 to San Francisco from the east, and the **Golden Gate Bridge** (toll $7.75) connects CA-1 from the north. From the south, US-101 and I-280 snake up the peninsula and

BART station

into the city. Be sure to get a detailed map and good directions to drive into San Francisco—the freeway interchanges, especially surrounding the east side of the Bay Bridge, can be confusing, and the traffic congestion is legendary. For traffic updates and route planning, visit **511. org** (www.511.org).

If you have your car with you, try to get a room at a hotel with a parking lot and either free parking or a parking package for the length of your stay.

### Car Rental
All the major car rental agencies have a presence at the **San Francisco Airport** (SFO, 800/435-9736, www.flysfo.com). In addition, most reputable hotels can offer or recommend a car rental. Rates tend to run $50-100 per day and $200-550 per week (including taxes and fees), with discounts for weekly and longer rentals.

### Parking
Parking a car in San Francisco can easily

cost $50 per day or more. Most downtown and Union Square hotels do not include free parking with your room. Expect to pay $35-65 per night for parking, which may not include in-and-out privileges.

Street parking meters cost up to $2 per hour, often go late into the night, and charge during the weekends. At least many now take credit cards. Unmetered street parking spots are as rare as unicorns and often require residential permits for stays longer than two hours during the day. Lots and garages fill up quickly, especially during special events.

## Muni
The **Muni** (www.sfmta.com, $2.75 adults, $1.35 youth and seniors, children under 4 free) transit system can get you where you want to go as long as time isn't a concern. Bus and train tickets can be purchased from any Muni driver; underground trains have ticket machines at the entrance. Exact change is required, except on the cable cars, where drivers can make change for up to $20. See the website for a route map, tickets, and schedules.

### BART
Bay Area Rapid Transit, or **BART** (www. bart.gov, fees vary), is the Bay Area's late-coming answer to major metropolitan underground railways like Chicago's L trains and New York's subway system. Sadly, there's only one arterial line through the city. However, service directly from San Francisco Airport into the city runs daily, as does service to Oakland Airport, the cities of Oakland and Berkeley, and many other East Bay destinations. BART connects to the Caltrain system and San Francisco Airport in Millbrae. See the website for route maps, schedules (BART usually runs on time), and fare information.

To buy tickets, use the vending machines found in every BART station. If you plan to ride more than once, you can add money to a single ticket and then keep that ticket and reuse it for each ride.

## Caltrain

This traditional commuter rail line runs along the peninsula into Silicon Valley, from San Francisco to San Jose, with limited continuing service to Gilroy. **Caltrain** (www.caltrain.com, one-way $3.75-13.75) Baby Bullet trains can get you from San Jose to San Francisco in an hour during commuting hours. Extra trains are often added for San Francisco Giants, San Francisco 49ers, and San Jose Sharks games.

You must purchase a ticket in advance at the vending machines found in all stations. The main Caltrain station in San Francisco is at the corner of 4th and King Streets, within walking distance of AT&T Park and Moscone Center.

## Taxis and Ride Shares

Ride-sharing drivers abound in the Bay Area. Download the apps for **Lyft** (www.lyft.com) or **Uber** (www.uber.com) on your smartphone and secure a ride. You'll find some taxis scooting around all the major tourist areas of the city. If you have trouble hailing a cab, try **City Wide Dispatch** (415/920-0700).

## Tours

**San Francisco City Guides** (415/557-4266, www.sfcityguides.org, free) is a team of enthusiastic San Francisco tour guides who want to show you more about their beloved city. Opt to learn about San Francisco sights like Fort Mason and Fisherman's Wharf, or choose a walk where you'll hear about the local locales used by famed director Alfred Hitchcock in his films, including *Vertigo*. Visit the website for a complete schedule of the current month's offerings.

One of the most popular walking tour companies in the city is **Foot** (415/793-5378, www.foottours.com, $20-40 pp). Foot was founded by stand-up comedian Robert Mac and hires comics to act as guides for its many different tours around San Francisco. The two-hour "San Francisco in a Nutshell" tour offers a funny look at the basics of city landmarks and history, and the three-hour "Whole Shebang" is a comprehensive if speedy look at Chinatown, Nob Hill, and North Beach. For visitors who are back for the second or third time, check out the more in-depth neighborhood tours that take in Chinatown, the Castro, or the Haight. You can even hit "Full Exposure," a look at the rise of 18-and-up entertainment in North Beach. Tour departure points vary, so check the website for more information about your specific tour and about packages of more than one tour in a day or two.

For an inside look at the culinary delights of Chinatown, sign up for a spot on **"I Can't Believe I Ate My Way Through Chinatown"** (650/355-9657, www.wokwiz.com, $90 pp). This three-hour bonanza will take you first for a classic Chinese breakfast, then out into the streets of Chinatown for a narrated tour around Chinatown's food markets, apothecaries, and tea shops. You'll finish up with lunch at one of Chef Shirley's favorite hole-in-the-wall dim sum places. For folks who just want the tour and lunch, or the tour alone, check out the standard "Wok Wiz Daily Tour" ($50 pp with lunch, $35 pp).

The **Chinatown Ghost Tour** (888/440-7976, www.sfchinatownghosttours.com, 7:30pm-9:30pm Fri.-Sat., $48 adults) delves into the neighborhood's mysticism and rich histpory. The whole thing burned down more than a century ago, and it was rebuilt in exactly the same spot, complete with countless narrow alleyways. This tour will take you into these alleys after the sun sets, when the spirits are said to appear on the streets. You'll start out at Four Seas Restaurant (731 Grant Ave.) and follow your loquacious guide along the avenues and side streets of Chinatown. As you stroll, your guide will tell you the stories of the neighborhood spirits, spooks, and ancestors.

The curious get to learn about the deities worshipped by devout Chinese to this day, along with the folklore that permeates what was until recently a closed and secretive culture. Then you head into a former gambling den where a magician will attempt to conjure the soul of a long-dead gambler.

## Tourist Information

The main San Francisco **Visitor Information Center** (900 Market St., 415/391-2000, www.sftravel.com, 9am-5pm Mon.-Fri., 9am-3pm Sat.-Sun. May-Oct., 9am-5pm Mon.-Fri., 9am-3pm Sat. Nov.-Apr.) can give you information about attractions and hotels, and discounted tickets for various museums and attractions. The Market Street location (just below Hallidie Plaza at Powell St.) has brochures in 14 different languages and a few useful coupons.

## Medical Services

The **San Francisco Police Department** (766 Vallejo St., 415/553-0123, http://sanfranciscopolice.org) is headquartered in Chinatown, on Vallejo Street between Powell and Stockton Streets. For life-threatening emergencies or to report a crime in progress, dial 911.

San Francisco boasts a large number of full-service hospitals. The **UCSF Medical Center at Mount Zion** (1600 Divisadero St., 415/567-6600, www.ucsfhealth.org) is renowned for its research and advances in cancer treatments and other important medical breakthroughs. The main hospital is at the corner of Divisadero and Geary Streets. Right downtown, **St. Francis Memorial Hospital** (900 Hyde St., 877/649-7525, www.saintfrancismemorial.org), at the corner of Hyde and Bush Streets, has an emergency department.

# Yosemite

With its giant granite rock faces, jagged peaks, and thundering waterfalls, Yosemite National Park inspires millions of road trippers.

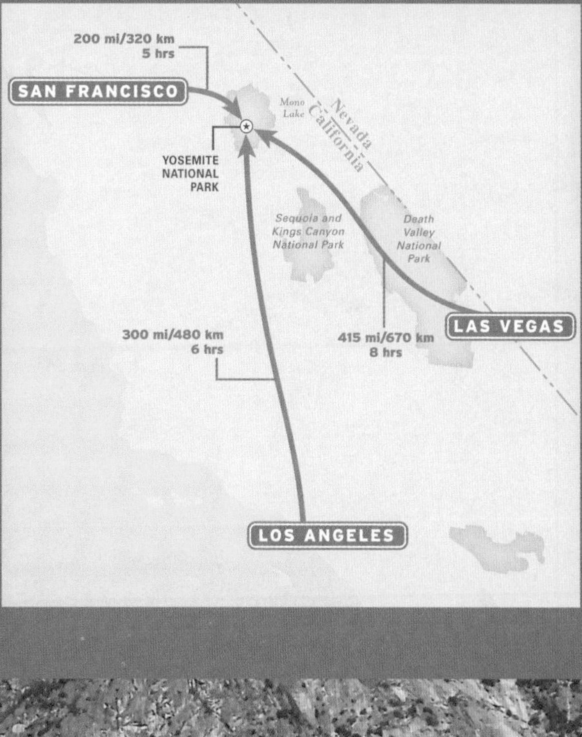

200 mi/320 km
5 hrs

SAN FRANCISCO

Mono Lake

Nevada
California

YOSEMITE NATIONAL PARK

Sequoia and Kings Canyon National Park

Death Valley National Park

LAS VEGAS

300 mi/480 km
6 hrs

415 mi/670 km
8 hrs

LOS ANGELES

# Yosemite National Park

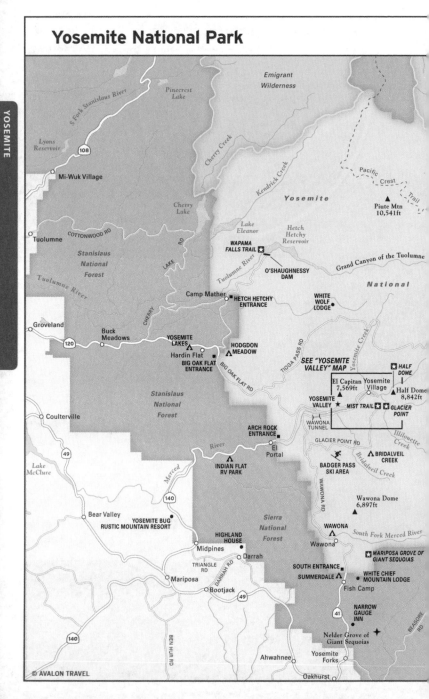

Emigrant Wilderness

Pinecrest Lake

S Fork Stanislaus River

Lyons Reservoir

108

Mi-Wuk Village

Cherry Creek

Yosemite

Piute Mtn 10,541ft

Pacific Crest Trail

Kendrick Creek

COTTONWOOD RD

Tuolumne

Cherry Lake

Lake Eleanor

Hetch Hetchy Reservoir

LAKE RD

Stanislaus National Forest

WAPAMA FALLS TRAIL

Tuolumne River

O'SHAUGHNESSY DAM

Grand Canyon of the Tuolumne

National

Tuolumne River

CHERRY

Camp Mather

HETCH HETCHY ENTRANCE

WHITE WOLF LODGE

Groveland

120

Buck Meadows

YOSEMITE LAKES

HODGDON MEADOW

TIOGA PASS RD

SEE "YOSEMITE VALLEY" MAP

Yosemite Creek

HALF DOME

Hardin Flat

BIG OAK FLAT ENTRANCE

BIG OAK FLAT RD

El Capitan 7,569ft

Yosemite Village

Coulterville

Stanislaus National Forest

YOSEMITE VALLEY

Half Dome 8,842ft

MIST TRAIL

GLACIER POINT

49

ARCH ROCK ENTRANCE

River

Merced River

El Portal

WAWONA TUNNEL

GLACIER POINT RD

Illilouette Creek

Lake McClure

INDIAN FLAT RV PARK

140

BRIDALVEIL CREEK

Bridalveil Creek

BADGER PASS SKI AREA

Bear Valley

YOSEMITE BUG RUSTIC MOUNTAIN RESORT

WAWONA RD

Wawona Dome 6,897ft

HIGHLAND HOUSE

Sierra National Forest

WAWONA

South Fork Merced River

Midpines

Darrah

Wawona

TRIANGLE RD

DARRAH RD

MARIPOSA GROVE OF GIANT SEQUOIAS

Mariposa

SOUTH ENTRANCE

WHITE CHIEF MOUNTAIN LODGE

Bootjack

SUMMERDALE

Fish Camp

49

NARROW GAUGE INN

140

BEN HUR RD

41

BEASORE RD

Nelder Grove of Giant Sequoias

Ahwahnee

Yosemite Forks

© AVALON TRAVEL

Oakhurst

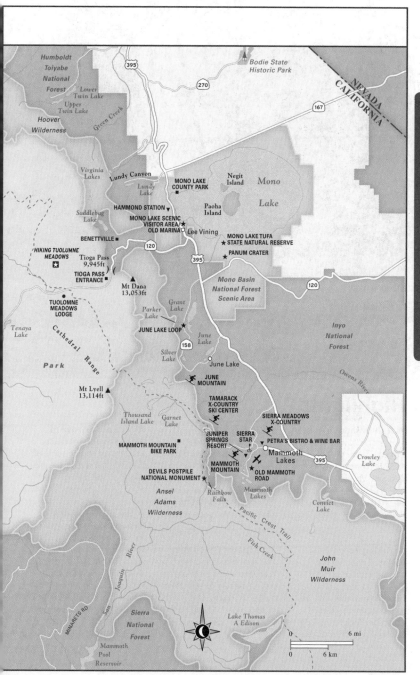

Bachelor and Three Graces

# Highlights

★ **Half Dome:** Yosemite's most iconic natural feature is a giant granite bust of rock 4,737 feet above the floor of Yosemite Valley. See it from below or make the strenuous 14- to 16-mile round-trip hike to the top (page 100).

★ **Hiking Yosemite Valley:** Get out of the car and explore some of California's best alpine trails from the one-mile hike up to the stunning views of Columbia Rock to the iconic Mist Trail, which takes you to two waterfalls, whose spray is the source of the eponymous mist (page 101).

★ **Glacier Point:** This viewpoint, located 3,214 feet above the valley floor, is the best place to take in Yosemite Valley's full grandeur, with a panorama that includes Half Dome and Yosemite Falls (page 110).

★ **Wapama Falls Trail:** This five-mile round-trip hike is an ideal way to explore the natural beauty of less crowded Hetch Hetchy, with views of two waterfalls and Kolana Rock (page 115).

★ **Mariposa Grove of Giant Sequoias:** Wander in amazement among some of the largest and oldest living things on earth (page 119).

★ **Hiking in Tuolumne Meadows:** Whether you are hiking through the wild-flower-dotted meadow or opting to climb to one of the region's scenic lakes, there are a dizzying number of hiking options from Tuolumne Meadows, which is only open late spring-fall (page 122).

**N**aturalist John Muir noted that "no temple made with hands can compete with Yosemite."

Located in the Sierra Nevada, Yosemite is home to California's most iconic natural sights: polished granite knobs, jagged peaks, waterfalls that can trickle in ribbons or rush like torrents. It was the preservation of this landscape by President Abraham Lincoln in 1864 that paved the way for the country's national park system.

The park's best-known sights are located in Yosemite Valley: the giant rock wall of El Capitan, the granite bust of Half Dome, and North America's highest waterfall, Yosemite Falls. During the summer, the valley is crowded with visitors gawking at such stunning natural beauty. Even the most jaded individual will look past the crowds in amazement when wandering below the towering canyon walls.

Beyond the crowds, the park's more remote sections beckon those seeking (relative) solitude. In Glacier Point you can get the best view of Yosemite Valley, while in Mariposa Grove you can walk among the rust-colored spires of giant sequoias. Only accessible by car from spring to fall, Tuolumne Meadows is a large, high-elevation field dotted with mirrored lakes that reflect the scenery. The least-visited Hetch Hetchy region has granite outcroppings and waterfalls comparable to what you can see in the valley, but without the heavy crowds.

It's worth exploring the foothill and mountain towns surrounding the park for their own unique characters, from the gold rush vibe of Groveland to the peaceful high desert of Mono Lake. With plenty of restaurant and hotel options, these communities make ideal bases for visiting the park and stocking up on supplies.

# Getting to Yosemite

Almost all the most popular sights, attractions, and trailheads are accessible by road. The **Arch Rock entrance** to the west of the park is accessed via **CA-140**. The **Big Oak Flat entrance** is accessed via **CA-120** from the north; it's about another 45 minutes to Yosemite Valley from there. Both entrances provide access to **Tioga Pass Road** via **Big Oak Flat Road.** Tioga Pass reconnects to CA-120 at the **Tioga Pass entrance** on the east side of the park. Tioga Pass closes in November or December each year and reopens in the spring, usually in May or June. Yosemite's **South entrance** is accessed via **CA-41** from Oakhurst. **Wawona Road** leads from the South entrance through Wawona and into Yosemite Valley. **Glacier Point Road** is reached from Wawona Road and allows access to the Yosemite Ski & Snowboard Area (formerly Badger Pass). The more remote **Hetch Hetchy entrance** of the park is reached by taking CA-120 out of Groveland east for 23 miles and then taking a left onto Evergreen Road for 8.2 miles. In the town of Camp Mather, take a right onto **Hetch Hetchy Road,** which heads to the park's Hetch Hetchy entrance. In winter, chains can be required on any road at any time, so check with the **National Park Service** (209/372-0200, www.nps.gov/yose) for **current road conditions.**

## From San Francisco

Yosemite is approximately **200 miles** east of San Francisco. The drive takes roughly **five hours** as motorists navigate urban traffic getting out of the city and its surrounding suburbs and continue along some two-lane highways on the way to the park.

The **Big Oak Flat entrance** is the closest to San Francisco, accessed via **CA-120 East.** Begin by taking **I-80 East** out of the city and over the Bay Bridge. Continue on **I-580 East** for 46 miles before turning off

# Best Hotels & Campgrounds

★ **Majestic Yosemite Hotel:** With its rock facade and superb Yosemite Valley views, this luxury hotel is a quintessential national parks property (page 107).

★ **Big Trees Lodge:** Relax on a large veranda and take in the mountain air at this historic park hotel in Wawona near the Mariposa Grove of Big Trees (page 120).

★ **Yosemite Bug Rustic Mountain Resort:** For those on a budget, this sprawling complex of hostel dorms, tent cabins, private bedrooms, and guest houses is just 26 miles from Yosemite Valley (page 110).

★ **Rush Creek Lodge:** The newest resort in the Yosemite area is less than two miles from the park's Big Oak Flat entrance and has a saltwater pool, game room for kids, and a tavern (page 118).

★ **Far Meadow Base Camp Cabins:** Rent an off-the-grid A-frame or log cabin located on 22 serene acres 45 minutes from the park's South entrance (page 120).

★ **Summerdale Campground:** This small U.S. Forest Service campground with roomy, idyllic campsites on a creek is a mere 1.5 miles from the park's South entrance (page 121).

★ **Tuolumne Meadows Campground:** This sprawling campground provides access to Yosemite's stunning high country. Best of all, you can head out on a hike to Elizabeth Lake right from your campsite (page 131).

★ **High Sierra Camps:** Enjoy tent cabins in the park's backcountry without having to hike in supplies. A night's stay includes breakfast and dinner (page 132).

on **I-205 East** toward Tracy and Stockton. Follow I-205 East for 14.5 miles before hopping on **I-5 North** for just a mile. Merge onto **CA-120 East** for six miles and then take **CA-99 North** for less than two miles before reconnecting with **CA-120 East.** The road will climb up into the Sierra Nevada and pass scenic towns, including **Groveland,** on the way to the park's **Big Oak Flat entrance.** Within the park, Big Oak Flat Road continues into Yosemite Valley. Time your drive for weekdays or early mornings to avoid traffic and crowds. From the Big Oak Flat entrance, it's about another 45 minutes to Yosemite Valley.

The **Arch Rock entrance** is another option. From San Francisco, take **I-580 East** to **I-205 East.** In Manteca, take **CA-99 South** for 56 miles to Merced. In Merced, turn right onto **CA-140 East.** CA-140 will take you right to the Arch Rock entrance.

## From Los Angeles

Getting from Los Angeles to Yosemite National Park involves driving roughly **300 miles** (about **six hours**) along two of the state's biggest highways. Take **US-101 North,** then **CA-170 North,** and finally **I-5 North,** following signs for Sacramento. Continue for 83 miles on I-5, then get on **CA-99 North** for 132 miles, passing through Bakersfield and Fresno. Merge onto **CA-41 North** and continue for 62 miles, passing through the city of Oakhurst, which is a good place to stock up on supplies. After the community of Fish Camp, CA-41 enters the park at its **South entrance.** In the park, the highway becomes Wawona Road. You can reach Yosemite Valley from the South entrance in about one hour.

## From Las Vegas

If there's any chance **Tioga Pass** will be closed (and between October and May,

## Best Restaurants

★ **Majestic Yosemite Hotel Dining Room:** Treat yourself to a meal within the historic hotel's fine restaurant, with its floor-to-ceiling windows and magnificent high-beamed ceiling (page 106).

★ **Big Trees Lodge Dining Room:** Enjoy hearty meaty entrées or healthier fare in a dining room with lots of windows and big tree-inspired hanging lamps (page 120).

★ **High Country Health Foods & Cafe:** This Mariposa health food store serves up smoothies and creative sandwiches. Dine in the nice dining area or take it to go for a picnic in the park (page 107).

★ **Whoa Nellie Deli:** Yes, this is a restaurant within a gas station mini-mart, but how many convenience stores serve lobster taquitos and sashimi (page 128)?

★ **Silver Lake Resort Café:** Located in June Lake, this tiny diner's hearty breakfasts make it an essential stop for those on Yosemite's eastern side (page 128).

that's likely), call the **National Park Service** at 209/372-0200 for the latest weather and road report. If the pass is open, you have your choice of two direct routes from Las Vegas to Yosemite. If that road is closed, you have no choice but to bypass Tioga Pass via a longer route through central California.

### Via Tioga Pass: Nevada Route

Driving over Tioga Pass from Nevada into the park is only an option when Tioga Pass Road is open, usually June-October. To begin this eight-hour drive, head out of Las Vegas on **US-95 North** and stay on this highway through the desert for 250 miles. Then turn west on **US-6 West** in Tonopah. Continue for 40 miles and then turn right on **CA-120 West.** The highway will merge into **US-395** just south of Mono Lake. Utilize US-395 North/CA-120 West for a couple of miles before turning left on **Tioga Pass Road,** which heads into the park via the **Tioga Pass entrance.** Be sure to fill up your car's tank at the Tioga Gas Mart (and fill your belly at Whoa Nellie Deli) before entering the park.

### Stopping in Tonopah

Tonopah is a natural crossroads that rewards travelers with colorful mining history and one of the darkest starry skies in the country.

Tonopah's few restaurants specialize in American versions of Mexican fare. Tequila, beer, and spice lovers will revel in the cheesy chile rellenos at **El Marques** (348 N. Main St., 775/482-3885, 11am-9pm Tues.-Sun., $10-20). If you're in a hurry but still jonesing for Mexican, hit the pick-up window at **Cisco's Restaurant** (10am-8:30pm Mon.-Sat., $10-15), which has burgers, pizza, and tacos. How about a beer and some barbecue? **Tonopah Brewing Co.** (315 S. Main St., 775/482-2000, www.tonopahbrewing.com, 11am-9pm daily, $9-27) is your stop. Taste its on-site brewed beers in pint or pitcher form along with some delicious barbecued meats, including ribs cooked for at least seven hours.

The owners have faithfully restored the **Mizpah Hotel** (100 N. Main St., 775/482-3030, $100-165), the "Grand Lady of Tonopah" with claw-foot tubs, wrought-iron bedsteads, and lots of carmine accents. You can dine on-site at the casual **Pittman Café** (6am-10pm daily, $10-15). Next door, the guest rooms at **Jim Butler Motel** (100 S. Main St., 775/482-3577, $80-100) are bright and inviting, with wood furniture and faux hearths. Some guest

## Stretch Your Legs

Driving from San Francisco to Yosemite via CA-120, most people have no idea that there is a minor engineering marvel just a few miles off the highway. Just east of Oakdale is the **Knights Ferry Covered Bridge** (Knights Ferry Recreation Area, 17968 Covered Bridge Rd., Oakdale, 209/881-3517, 6am-sunset daily, $5), which is said to be the longest covered bridge west of the Mississippi. Built in 1864, this 330-foot bridge, spanning the Stanislaus River, was considered an example of state-of-the-art engineering at the time. Though you cannot drive across it, the bridge is open to pedestrians. To reach the bridge, head east out of Oakdale on CA-108/120 for 11 miles. Take a left on Kennedy Road and then, after 0.5 mile, take a left on Sonora Road. After 0.5 mile, take a right on Covered Bridge Road, and the attraction will appear soon.

rooms have fridges and microwaves; all have free Wi-Fi.

### Via Tioga Pass: California Route

When Tioga Pass is open, travelers can get to Yosemite from Las Vegas with some time on US-395, one of the most scenic highways in the state. Only a few miles farther but 45 minutes longer (roughly nine hours total), it is a far **more scenic route** that includes a drive through Death Valley National Park. If it is during the summer months, Death Valley can be extremely hot, so make sure your vehicle's fluids are topped off and your air conditioner is working. The route begins by taking **US-95 North** out of Las Vegas for 117 miles. At the town of Beatty, take a left, heading southwest on **NV-374.** In just nine miles you pass the Death Valley National Park boundary. After entering **Death Valley National Park,** the road becomes **Daylight Pass Road.** Turn left to head south on **Scotty's Castle Road** within the park; after 0.5 mile take a right on **CA-190 West** and follow the road for 68 miles, at which point it becomes **CA-136.** After 17.5 miles, take a right on scenic **US-395 North** for 123 miles as it passes by the towns of Lone Pine, Big Pine, Bishop, and Mammoth Lakes. Just south of the town of Lee Vining, **US-395 North** connects with **CA-120 West,** also known as **Tioga Pass Road,** which heads into the park.

### Stopping in Bishop

A 4.5-hour drive from Las Vegas, Bishop is a great place to spend the night on this route. From Bishop, it's a scenic 1.5-hour drive to the park's Tioga Pass entrance. The small town in the Owens Valley, between the Sierra Nevada and the White Mountains, is a world-class destination for climbing, bouldering, and hiking. Outdoor enthusiasts may want to linger here for a few days before heading onward to the park.

The volcanic tablelands north of town are known for the **Happy Boulders** and **Sad Boulders,** with over 2,000 opportunities for climbers. In the winter, you can camp for cheap at the nearby **Pleasant Valley Pit** (760/872-5000, www.blm.gov, $2), a primitive campground located in an old rock quarry. The Owens River provides opportunities for floating, and the landscape is dotted with many artesian wells that double as swimming holes during the summer. The helpful people at the **Bishop Chamber of Commerce** (760/873-8403, www.bishopvisitor.com) can give directions to these sites and provide other assistance.

**The Hostel California** (213 Academy Ave., 760/399-6316, www.thehostelcalifornia.com, dorm beds $25-35, private rooms $60-170) offers cheap accommodations and communal living. Amenities include a shared kitchen, outdoor hangout space, and free use of bikes to tool around town. Downtown, right on Bishop Creek, the **Creekside Inn** (725 Main St., 760/872-3044, www.bishopcreeksideinn. com, $125-225) offers free laundry, a hot breakfast buffet, a pool, and a hot tub.

Next door to the Creekside Inn, customers line up at the wildly popular **Erick Schat's Bakkery** (763 N. Main St., 760/873-7156, www.erickschatsbakery. com, 6am-6pm Sun.-Thurs., 6am-7pm Fri., under $10) for baked goods, sandwiches, and its famed chili cheese bread. Across the street is **Holy Smoke BBQ** (772 N. Main St., 760/872-4227, www. holysmoketexasstylebbq.com, 11am-9pm Wed.-Mon., $7-17), where weary travelers chomp down on tasty barbecue sandwiches or "redneck tacos," a slab of cornbread topped with barbecued meat and coleslaw.

### Bypassing Tioga Pass

If Tioga Pass is closed, the only way to reach Yosemite from Las Vegas is an ugly **8- to 10-hour, 500-mile** ordeal. Take **I-15 South** from Las Vegas and continue for 160 miles to Barstow. In Barstow, get on **CA-58 West** for 126 miles to Bakersfield, where you'll merge onto **CA-99 North.** Stay on CA-99 North for 107 miles before turning onto **CA-41 North.** Follow CA-41 North for 62 miles to the park's **South entrance.**

### Stopping in Bakersfield

While far from a tourist destination, Bakersfield is at least a diversion on the otherwise dreary winter Yosemite-Las Vegas route.

While there are plenty of chain hotels, travelers looking for more personality in their lodgings will have to look a little harder. The search pays off at the **Padre Hotel** (1702 18th St., 661/427-4900, www.thepadrehotel.com, $109-299), rescued and restored to its 1930s grandeur with a Spanish colonial exterior and sleek rooms with modern furniture. Dine at the Belvedere Room or get a cup of coffee at the Farmacy Café. There are also two

bars: Brimstone and Prairie Fire, a rooftop bar on the 2nd floor. Sound walls and thick insulation ensure a peaceful rest.

One well-regarded chain hotel off CA-99 is the **Hampton Inn & Suites Bakersfield North-Airport** (8818 Spectrum Park Way, 661/391-0600, www. hamptoninn.com, $104-119). Besides its convenient location, its pluses include a free hot breakfast, an outdoor pool, and a fitness room for getting some exercise after a day crammed in the car.

It's tough to decide among the Caribbean-style chicken, steak, and seafood at **Mama Roomba** (1814 Eye St., 661/322-6262, www.mamaroomba.com, 11am-10pm Mon.-Fri., 5pm-10pm Sat., $10-15). Both the calamari and the tri-tip are good bets. They also serve beer, wine, and cocktails to tamp down your road rage after hours in the car. A bit more highbrow, **Uricchio's Trattoria** (1400 17th St., 661/326-8870, 11am-2pm and 5pm-9pm Mon.-Thurs., 11am-2pm and 5pm-10pm Fri., 5pm-10pm Sat., $14-27) serves the best lasagna in town. The lobster ravioli in clam sauce is no slouch either.

## By Train or Bus
### Train

**Amtrak** (324 W. 24th St., Merced, 209/722-6862, reservations 800/872-7245, www.amtrak.com) has a station in Merced, an hour away from the park. You can take the train there and then take the **Amtrak Thruway Service bus** ($15 one-way) to locations in Yosemite Valley, including Yosemite Valley Lodge, Majestic Yosemite Hotel, Half Dome Village, Crane Flat, and the Yosemite Visitors Center. The bus schedule changes seasonally but runs all year. It is about a 2.5-hour bus ride from Merced to the park. The bus also goes to White Wolf and Tuolumne Meadows during the summer months (daily service July-Aug., weekends only June and Sept.).

### Bus

The **Yosemite Area Regional Transit**

System (YARTS, 877/989-2787, www. yarts.com, $13) operates daily buses from Merced to Yosemite. They also have seasonal buses taking passengers from towns along CA-120 (Sonora, Jamestown, and Groveland) to the park. In the summer months, an Eastern Sierra service connects Mammoth Lakes, June Lake, and Lee Vining to the park as well.

Starline Tours (800/959-3131, www. starlinetours.com, $131-804) offers bus tours of Yosemite departing from and returning to San Francisco. Options include one very long day tour, as well as two-day and three-day tours.

# Visiting the Park

## Entrances

Yosemite National Park is accessible via five park entrances: Big Oak Flat, Arch Rock, South, Tioga Pass, and Hetch Hetchy. The Arch Rock entrance (CA-140) and the Big Oak Flat entrance (CA-120 West) are usually open year-round. The Tioga Pass entrance (CA-120 East) is just a few miles from Tuolumne Meadows and is the eastern access to Yosemite from US-395. Tioga Road closes in November or December each year and reopens in the spring, usually in May or June. The Hetch Hetchy entrance in the northwest part of the park is only open during daylight hours. The South entrance is open year-round.

## Park Passes and Fees

The park entrance fee includes entry and parking for up to seven days. The cost is $30 per car and $20 per motorcycle. The entrance fee is $15 per person for those entering by bus, bike, or on foot, also good for seven days. A one-year pass for an automobile to Yosemite is available for $60.

The National Park Service offers several annual passes for frequent park visitors. The America the Beautiful Pass allows access to all the national parks for a year for $80; the Senior Pass (age 62 or older) costs only $80 for lifetime access to the parks. To purchase passes, inquire at the entrance station or at one of the visitors centers in the park.

## Visitors Centers

The Yosemite Valley Visitors Center (Yosemite Village, 209/372-0200, 9am-5pm daily year-round) is a great place to get information upon arriving in the park. At the staffed information desk, rangers can give you information about everything from trails to the upcoming weather. An exhibit hall offers insight into the park's natural and human history. The Yosemite Museum (west end of Yosemite Village, 209/372-0304, 9am-5pm daily year-round) is the place to learn about the area's native Miwok and Paiute people.

Stop in at the Valley Wilderness Center (Yosemite Village, 209/372-0745, 8am-5pm daily May-Oct.) if you are planning a multiday backpacking hike. You can pick up your wilderness permit, bear canister, map, and backcountry information here. You can also secure wilderness permits at the Tuolumne Meadows Wilderness Center (off Tioga Rd., 8 miles west of Tioga Pass and 2 miles east of Tuolumne Meadows Visitors Center, 209/372-0309, 8am-4:30pm daily late May-Oct. 14).

Visitors entering the park's South entrance can get information while viewing the paintings of Thomas Hill at the Wawona Visitors Center at Hill's Studio (Big Trees Lodge, 209/375-9531, 8:30am-5pm daily May-Sept.). The Big Oak Flat Information Station (209/379-1899, 8am-5pm daily Apr.-Oct.) is to the right after passing through the Big Oak Flat entrance. It has information, wilderness permits, and a gift shop. The Tuolumne Meadows Visitors Center (Tioga Rd., west of the Tuolumne Meadows Campground, 209/372-0263, hours vary, late June-early Sept.) is housed in a small building where you can get info along with a great map and guide to Tuolumne Meadows for $4.

# Changing Names

In 2016, Yosemite National Park switched park concessionaires from Delaware North to Aramark. Unfortunately, Delaware North trademarked the names of a handful of park properties and held onto the names during a contract dispute with the new concessionaire. What this means for visitors is that longtime hotels like The Ahwahnee have new, possibly temporary names. The dispute is in the courts, but eventually the parks hope that the landmarks may revert back to their former names. Below are the old names and current names.

- **Yosemite Lodge at The Falls** is now **Yosemite Valley Lodge**

- **The Ahwahnee** is now **The Majestic Yosemite Hotel**

- **Curry Village** is now **Half Dome Village**

- **Wawona Hotel** is now **Big Trees Lodge**

- **Badger Pass** is now **Yosemite Ski & Snowboard Area**

## Reservations

### Accommodations

All the lodges, hotels, and cabin-tent clusters in Yosemite are run by the same booking agency. Contact the **Yosemite Park concessionaire** (inside U.S. 888/413-8869, outside the U.S. 602/278-8888, www.yosemitepark.com) to make reservations. Coming to Yosemite in the summer high season? Try to make reservations 6-9 months in advance, especially if you have a specific lodging preference. If you wait until the week before your trip, you may find the park sold out or end up in a tent cabin at Curry when you wanted a suite at the Majestic Yosemite Hotel.

For more accommodations options, try the communities outside Yosemite:

- **El Portal** (CA-140): 3 miles from the Arch Rock entrance

- **Mariposa** (CA-140): 40 miles from the South entrance

- **Groveland** (CA-120): 26 miles from the Big Oak Flat entrance

- **Fish Camp** (CA-41): 2 miles from the South entrance

- **Lee Vining** (US-395): 13 miles from the Tioga Pass (eastern) entrance

- **Mammoth Lakes** (US-395): 40 miles from the Tioga Pass (eastern) entrance

### Campgrounds

Inside the park, you'll find 13 designated campgrounds and the High Sierra Camps. Seven of those designated campgrounds are on the reservation system. For any Yosemite National Park campground, make reservations early! All the major campgrounds fill up spring-fall, and reservations can be difficult to come by. Consider making your Yosemite campground reservation at least five months in advance to get the campsite you want. Make reservations through the **National Park Service** (877/444-6777, www.recreation.gov). Campgrounds outside the park boundaries are often less expensive and require less advance notice.

## Information and Services

Published bi-weekly in summer and monthly in spring, fall, and winter, *Yosemite Guide* provides information about the park's places and services. Most important, it includes a detailed schedule of all classes, events, and programs in the park. You'll receive your copy when you enter the park at any of the entrance stations. Download a PDF version online at www.nps.gov/yose/planyourvisit/guide.htm.

## Banking and Post Offices

**ATMs** are available throughout Yosemite Valley: in Yosemite Village at the Art and Education Center within the Village Store, in Yosemite Valley Lodge, and in Half Dome Village's gift and grocery store. Outside the valley, ATMs are located in the Wawona store and the Tuolumne Meadows grocery store.

Several post offices provide **mailing services** in Yosemite. Look for a **post office** in **Yosemite Village** (9017 Village Dr., 209-372-4475, www.usps.com, 8:30am-5pm Mon.-Fri., 10am-noon Sat.), inside **Yosemite Valley Lodge** (9015 Lodge Dr., 209/372-4853, www.usps.com, 12:30pm-2:45pm Mon.-Fri.), in **El Portal** (5508 Foresta Rd., 209/379-2311, www.usps.com, 8:30am-1pm and 1:30pm-3pm Mon.-Fri.), and in **Tuolumne Meadows** (14000 CA-120 E., 209/372-4475, 9am-5pm Mon.-Fri., 9am-noon Sat.).

## Gas Stations and Car Repairs

Limited seasonal gas is available up at Tuolumne Meadows just past the visitors center on Tioga Pass. There's also gas within the park at the **Crane Flat Gas Station** (8028 Big Flat Rd.), which is located at the junction of Tioga Pass Road and Big Oak Flat Road on CA-120, just 17 miles from the valley. The Wawona area has a **Wawona Gas Station** (8310 Wawona Rd.) near the park's South entrance. If your car breaks down, you can take it to the **Village Garage** (9002 Village Dr., 209/372-8320, 8am-5pm daily, towing 24 hours). Expect to pay a high premium for towing and repairs.

## Groceries and Laundry

Laundry facilities are available at the **Housekeeping Camp** inside the Half Dome Village complex (8am-10pm daily). Within the Yosemite Village, the **Village Store** (8am-10pm daily) has a surprisingly large grocery section with fresh meat, produce, ice, wood, and unexpected specialty items including brown rice pasta and noodle bowls. Limited-stock, expensive grocery stores in Half Dome Village are the **Gift and Grocery** (8am-10pm daily) and the **Housekeeping Camp Grocery** (8am-8pm daily). In Wawona, the **Pioneer Gift & Grocery** (8am-6pm daily) sells some groceries, wine, and souvenirs. For a better selection of goods and much lower prices, you're better off shopping outside the park. Stock up on healthy foodstuffs at Mariposa's **High Country Health Foods & Café** (5186 CA-49, Mariposa, 209/966-5111, www.highcountryhealthfoods.com, 8am-7pm Mon.-Sat., 9am-5pm Sun.). Also in Mariposa, the **Pioneer Market** (5034 Coakley Cir., Mariposa, 209/742-6100, www.pioneersupermarket.com, 7am-9pm daily) has groceries along with a deli and meat counter.

## Internet and Phone Service

Limited **Internet access** is available in a few spots in Yosemite Valley. The Majestic Yosemite Hotel and the Big Trees Lodge provide Wi-Fi to guests only, while Yosemite Valley Lodge offers wireless access for a $6 fee. Internet kiosks in Degnan's Café can be rented at a rate of $1 for three minutes. Guests who stay in Half Dome Village can access the Internet in the Half Dome Village Lounge. Meanwhile, the Mariposa County Library in the Valley Village also has free Wi-Fi (though donations are appreciated) along with three computers with Internet access that visitors can use.

Most **cell phones** will have no coverage in most areas of the park. Phones with AT&T and Verizon plans will work in some parts of Yosemite Valley.

## Emergency Services

For any emergencies within the park, **dial 911.** In Yosemite Village, the **Yosemite Medical Clinic** (9000 Ahwahnee Cir.,

209/372-4637, 9am-7pm daily summer, 9am-5pm Mon.-Fri. winter) has urgent and primary care along with emergency services through an ambulance that is available 24-7.

## Getting Around
### Parking
During busy days, it becomes wholly apparent that Yosemite Valley has more cars than parking spaces. It is recommended to come into the park before 10am and find a space in one of the three big parking lots (the **Yosemite Village Parking Lot,** the **Yosemite Falls Parking Area,** and the **Half Dome Parking Area**) and then utilize the free shuttle bus to travel to different attractions and trails.

### Shuttle Services
Yosemite runs an extensive network of shuttles in different areas of the park. One of the most-used travels through the **Yosemite Valley** (7am-10pm daily year-round, free). The **El Capitan Shuttle** (9am-5pm daily mid-June-Oct., free) also runs around certain parts of Yosemite Valley during the summer season. There are also seasonal Wawona to Yosemite Valley shuttles and seasonal Tuolumne Meadows shuttles.

### Bus Tours
Learn about Yosemite's natural and cultural history by taking a guided bus tour. The popular **Yosemite Valley Tour** (888/413-8869, www.travelyosemite.com, 10am, 11am, noon, 1pm, 2pm, 3pm daily summer, 10am and 2pm daily fall-spring, summer $35 adults, $32 seniors, $25 children; $29 winter adults, $28 seniors, $20 children) is a two-hour trip around the park's valley section. There's also the four-hour-long **Glacier Point Tour** (888/413-8869, www.travelyosemite.com, 8:30am and 1:30pm daily late May-early Nov., round-trip $49 adults, $44 seniors, $35 children 5-12, children under 5 free) and the eight-hour **Yosemite Valley to Tuolumne Meadows Hikers Bus** (209/372-1240, www.travelyosemite.com, 8:20am daily early summer-fall, pricing varies).

# Yosemite Valley

The first place most people go when they reach the park is the floor of Yosemite Valley (CA-140, Arch Rock entrance). From the valley floor, you can check out the visitors center, the theater, galleries, museums, hotels, and outdoor historical exhibits. Numerous pullouts from the main road invite photographers to capture the beauty of the valley and its many easily visible natural wonders. It's the most visited place in Yosemite, and many hikes, ranging from easy to difficult, begin in the valley.

## Sights
### Valley Visitors Center
After the scenic turnouts through the park, your first stop in Yosemite Valley should be the **Yosemite Valley Visitors Center** (Yosemite Village, off Northside Dr., 209/372-0200, www.nps.gov/yose, 9am-5pm daily, hours vary by season). Here you'll find the ranger station as well as an intricate interpretive museum describing the geological and human history of Yosemite. The visitors center also shows two films on Yosemite every half hour 9:30am-4:30pm. Separate buildings house the **Yosemite History Museum** (9am-5pm daily) and the **Ansel Adams Gallery** (650/692-3285, http://anseladams.com, 9am-5pm daily). This is also where you'll find the all-important public restrooms.

A short, flat walk from the visitors center takes you down to the re-created Miwok Native American village. The village includes all different types of structures, including those of the later Miwoks who incorporated European architecture into their building techniques. You can walk right into the homes and public buildings of this nearly lost culture. One of the most fascinating parts of this reconstruction is the evolution of construction techniques—as nonnative settlers infiltrated the area, building

# One Day in Yosemite

The sights, waterfalls, and hikes here are enough to fill a lifetime, but try to squeeze as much as you can into one day.

## Morning

Arrive at Yosemite National Park through the Arch Rock entrance (CA-140), only 11 miles from Yosemite Valley. Stop at **Bridalveil Fall** for a photo op, then continue on to the Valley Visitors Center, where you'll leave your car for the day. At the visitors center, check for any open campsites or tent cabins at Half Dome Village, and confirm your reservations for dinner later at the Majestic Yosemite Hotel. Explore **Yosemite Village,** stopping for picnic supplies and water, then board the Valley Shuttle Bus. The shuttle provides a great free tour of the park, with multiple points to hop on and off.

## Afternoon

Choose one of the valley's stellar day hikes (tip: not Half Dome). Take the Valley Shuttle Bus to Happy Isles (shuttle stop 16) and the trailhead for the strenuous **Mist Trail.** This hike is best done in spring when the waterfalls are at their peak, but it's still gorgeous at any time of year. Hike to the Vernal Fall Footbridge (1-2 hours round-trip) and gaze at the Merced River as it spills over Vernal Fall. Hardier souls can continue on the strenuous trail to the top of Vernal Fall (3 hours round-trip) and enjoy a picnic lunch soaking in the stellar views of the valley below. Return via the John Muir Trail back to the Happy Isles trailhead and the Valley Shuttle. A shorter option is the steep two-mile round-trip hike up the **Columbia Rock Trail** to stunning views of the valley and its granite rock formations.

## Evening

With all that hiking, you probably built up an appetite. Fortunately, you have reservations at the **Majestic Yosemite Hotel Dining Room.** Change out of your shorts and hiking shoes (and maybe grab a shower at Half Dome Village), and then catch the Valley Shuttle to the Majestic Yosemite Hotel (shuttle stop 3). Grab a drink in the bar and spend some time enjoying the verdant grounds and stellar views of this historic building. After dinner, take the shuttle back to Yosemite Village, where your car awaits, and immediately start planning your return.

## Extending Your Stay

If you have more time to spend in the park, you can easily fill two or three days just exploring **Yosemite Valley,** with an excursion to **Glacier Point.** With a week, add the **Tuolumne** (summer only), **Hetch Hetchy,** and **Wawona** sections of the park.

---

cabins and larger structures, the Miwok took note. They examined these buildings and incorporated pieces that they saw as improvements.

### El Capitan

The first natural stone monument you encounter as you enter the valley is **El Capitan** (Northside Rd., west of El Capitan Bridge). Formed of Cretaceous granite that's actually named for this formation, this granite monolith was created by millions of years of glacial action. The 3,000-foot craggy rock face is accessible in two ways: You can take a long hike west from the Upper Yosemite Fall and up the back side of the formation, or you can grab your climbing gear and scale the face. El Cap boasts a reputation as one of the world's seminal big-face climbs.

### ★ Half Dome

At the far end of the valley, perhaps the most recognizable feature in Yosemite rests high above the valley floor. Ansel Adams's famed photographs of **Half Dome,** visible from most of the valley floor, made it known to hikers and photo-lovers the world round. Scientists believe that Half Dome was never a whole dome; in fact, it still towers 4,737 feet above the valley floor in its original formation. This piece of a narrow granite ridge was polished to its smooth shape by glaciers tens of millions of years ago, giving it the fallacious appearance of half a dome. A Yosemite guidebook from 1868 (not a Moon guidebook!) proclaimed that "the summit of Half Dome will never be trodden by human feet." This statement was proven false just seven years later by George Anderson's first ascent in 1875. Now it is climbed by hundreds of people every summer.

### Bridalveil Fall

Coming before the main lodge, parking, and visitors center complex, **Bridalveil Fall** (Southside Dr. past Tunnel View) makes a great first stop. It is many visitors' introduction to Yosemite's numerous water features. Although the 620-foot-high falls cascade down the granite walls year-round, their fine mist sprays strongest in spring. Expect to get wet! Reach it by following a 0.5-mile round-trip trail—more of a pleasant walk than a hike. You can also get a fine view of Bridalveil Fall from afar at Tunnel View, a viewpoint at the east end of Wawona Tunnel along Wawona Road.

### Yosemite Falls

You must hike to see most of the falls, but the 2,425-foot high **Yosemite Falls** are visible from the valley floor near Yosemite Valley Lodge. Actually three separate waterfalls, Yosemite Falls join together to create one of the highest waterfalls in the world. The best time to see a serious gush of water is the spring, when the snowmelt swells the river above and creates the beautiful cascade that makes these falls so famous. If you visit during the fall or winter, you'll see a trickle of water slowly spill down the rock faces like sand falling in an hourglass; it's also possible you'll see no water at all.

### Mirror Lake

Still and perfect **Mirror Lake** (shuttle stop 17) reflects the already spectacular views of Tenaya Canyon and the ubiquitous Half Dome. Walk or bike a gentle mile into the park from Yosemite Valley to reach it. Visit in spring or early summer because the lake gradually dries out, often existing as a meadow in the late summer and fall.

### Tunnel View

At the east end of the Wawona Tunnel is one of the best photo-ops of the Yosemite Valley. **Tunnel View** perfectly frames Bridalveil Fall cascading in the right-hand corner. It's so stunning, people may mistake it as a photographer's backdrop in your photos. From the CA-41/CA-140 intersection, head south out of the valley on CA-41 for 1.6 miles to reach the viewpoint parking lot.

## Recreation
### ★ Hiking

Yosemite Valley is the perfect place to take a day hike. Although the hikes described here provide a good sample of what's available, plenty of other trails wind through this gorgeous area. Hiking maps are available at the **Yosemite Valley Visitors Center** (Northside Dr., Yosemite Valley Village). Read your map carefully and ask the rangers for advice about which trail is best for you. Many people love the valley trails, so you won't be hiking alone, especially in high season. One way to avoid crowds during the summer is to take advantage of more hours of daylight by heading out for a hike early in the morning or around dinnertime.

### Lower Yosemite Fall Loop

**Distance:** 1 mile round-trip
**Duration:** 20 minutes
**Elevation gain:** little
**Effort:** easy
**Trailhead:** shuttle stop 6

If you are in Yosemite Valley Village and want a gentle walk with a great view, take

YOSEMITE VALLEY

YOSEMITE

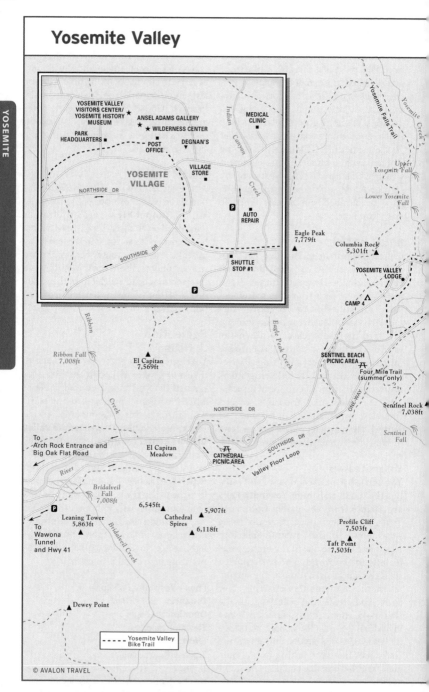

# Yosemite Valley

YOSEMITE VALLEY
VISITORS CENTER/
YOSEMITE HISTORY
MUSEUM ★    ANSEL ADAMS GALLERY
★ ★ WILDERNESS CENTER

PARK
HEADQUARTERS ■

MEDICAL
CLINIC

POST
OFFICE    DEGNAN'S ▽

YOSEMITE
VILLAGE

VILLAGE
STORE ■

Indian Canyon

Creek

NORTHSIDE DR

SOUTHSIDE DR

P

AUTO
REPAIR ■

SHUTTLE
STOP #1

P

Yosemite Falls Trail

Yosemite Creek

Upper
Yosemite Fall

Lower Yosemite
Fall

Eagle Peak
7,779ft ▲

Columbia Rock
5,301ft ▲

YOSEMITE VALLEY
LODGE

CAMP 4 ⌂

Ribbon Creek

Ribbon Fall
7,008ft ▒

El Capitan
7,569ft ▲

Eagle Peak Creek

SENTINEL BEACH
PICNIC AREA ⊼

Four Mile Trail
(summer only)

Sentinel Rock ▲
7,038ft

Sentinel
Fall

NORTHSIDE DR

ONE WAY

To
Arch Rock Entrance and
Big Oak Flat Road

El Capitan
Meadow

⊼
CATHEDRAL
PICNIC AREA

SOUTHSIDE DR

Valley Floor Loop

River

Bridalveil
Fall
7,008ft

P

Leaning Tower
5,863ft ▲

6,545ft ▲    ▲ 5,907ft

Cathedral
Spires

▲ 6,118ft

Profile Cliff
7,503ft ▲

To
Wawona
Tunnel
and Hwy 41

Bridalveil Creek

Taft Point
7,503ft ▲

▲ Dewey Point

----    Yosemite Valley
        Bike Trail

© AVALON TRAVEL

▲ Yosemite Point
6,936ft

Snow
Creek Falls

▲ Basket Dome

▲ North Dome
7,542ft

Royal Arch Creek

Royal Arch Cascade

**SEE DETAIL**
**YOSEMITE VILLAGE**

Tenaya Creek

▲ Ahwiyah Point
6,922ft

▲ Washington Column
5,912ft

Royal Arches

★ MIRROR LAKE

▲ Half Dome
8,836ft

**THE MAJESTIC YOSEMITE**

**NORTH PINES**

▲ HOUSEKEEPING CAMP

**LOWER PINES**

**YOSEMITE VALLEY STABLE**

Mirror Lake

(RESTRICTED VEHICLE ACCESS)

■ SENTINEL BRIDGE
CHAPEL

**STONEMAN BRIDGE**

**HALF DOME VILLAGE**

**UPPER PINES**

Staircase Falls

▲ Union Point
6,314ft

**CAMPGROUND RESERVATION OFFICE**

Glacier Point
7,214ft

**HAPPY ISLES NATURE CENTER**

★ GLACIER POINT

Pohono Trail

▲ Grizzly Peak
6,219ft

▲ Mt Broderick
6,706ft

★ MIST TRAIL
Vernal Fall
5,044ft

Emerald Pool

▲ Liberty Cap
7,076ft

Mist Trail

Silver Apron

(horse trail only)

Clark Point ▲

John Muir Trail

Nevada Fall
5,907ft

▲ Sentinel Dome
8,122ft

Panorama Trail

To
★ HALF DOME

Sentinel Creek

GLACIER POINT RD
(CLOSED NOVEMBER TO MAY)

Illilouette Creek

Panorama Trail

Illilouette Fall

Pothole Meadows

Illilouette Ridge

| 0 | | 0.5 mi |
| 0 | | 0.5 km |

the one-mile **Lower Yosemite Fall Loop.** This paved path winds between fields of boulders to a bridge where you can peer up to enjoy wondrous views of both Upper and Lower Yosemite Falls, complete with lots of cooling spray! Hike this trail in the springtime or early summer, when the flow of the falls is at its peak. This easy trail works well for families with kids who love the water.

## Cook's Meadow Loop
**Distance:** 1 mile round-trip
**Duration:** 30 minutes
**Elevation gain:** none
**Effort:** easy
**Trailhead:** Yosemite Valley Visitors Center (shuttle stops 5 and 9)

Quintessential Yosemite Valley views are visible along the **Cook's Meadow Loop,** a one-mile walk through the heart of the valley. Perhaps the most famous is the view of Half Dome from the Sentinel Bridge, which was captured in the iconic photography of Ansel Adams. Farther on, you can gaze up at the Royal Arches and Glacier Point.

## Mirror Lake Loop
**Distance:** 7 miles round-trip
**Duration:** 2-3 hours
**Elevation gain:** 100 feet
**Effort:** easy to moderate
**Trailhead:** Mirror Lake Junction (shuttle stop 17)

From the shuttle stop, a one-mile, wheelchair-accessible paved road leads to **Mirror Lake,** the shallow body of water that gives this trail that follows its name. Exhibits around the lake discuss the ongoing natural process that is drying the lake out and will eventually transform it into a meadow. From this pool, the connected footpath make a five-mile loop around the lake, following Tenaya Creek, crossing two bridges, and offering great views of Half-Dome.

## Valley Floor Loop
**Distance:** full loop 11.5 miles round-trip; half loop 7.2 miles round-trip
**Duration:** full loop 5-7 hours; half loop 2.5-3.5 hours
**Elevation gain:** little
**Effort:** moderate
**Trailhead:** Lower Yosemite Fall (shuttle stop 6), then head west on the bike path until you see the trail signs

The **Valley Floor Loop** is a great way to see all the most beautiful parts of the Yosemite Valley while escaping the crowds on the roads. The full loop is 11.5 miles along the path of old wagon roads and historic trails through meadows and forests, and takes most of a day to hike. But it's worth it. For visitors who want a mid-length hike, the half loop runs 7.2 miles. Cross the El Capitan Bridge to start back toward Yosemite Village. To complete the whole loop, hike past the bridge and continue west toward Bridalveil Fall. The route is not entirely clear on the trail map, so it's a good idea to talk to the rangers at the visitors center before your hike to avoid getting lost.

## Upper Yosemite Fall
**Distance:** 7 miles round-trip
**Duration:** 6-8 hours
**Elevation gain:** 2,700 feet
**Effort:** strenuous
**Trailhead:** Camp 4 (shuttle stop 7 and El Capitan shuttle stop E2)

One of the more challenging hikes in Yosemite Valley, the trek up to **Upper Yosemite Fall** is also one of the most satisfying. Take the shuttle to the trailhead rather than walking up from Lower Yosemite Fall. The trail gets steep, climbing 2,700 vertical feet in three miles to reach the top of America's tallest waterfall. Your efforts will be rewarded by some of the most astonishing aerial views to be found anywhere in the world. Look down over the fall and out over the valley, with its grassy meadows so far below. Plan on spending all day on this hike. Bring plenty of water and snacks to replenish your energy for the tricky climb down.

## ★ Columbia Rock Trail
**Distance:** 2 miles round-trip

**Duration:** 2-3 hours
**Elevation gain:** 1,000 feet
**Effort:** strenuous
**Trailhead:** Camp 4 (shuttle stop 7 and El Capitan shuttle stop E2)

To get a commanding view of the valley with a short but steep hike, opt for the **Columbia Rock Trail.** The trail climbs 1,000 feet via many steep, stone stair switchbacks over the course of one mile. Its destination is Columbia Rock, a stone ledge with minimal handrails that offers stunning views of the valley below and Half Dome, which towers in the distance like a giant hooded figure. Continue on another 0.5 mile to Upper Yosemite Fall for more amazing views.

★ Mist Trail

**Distance:** 5.4 miles round-trip
**Duration:** 5-6 hours
**Elevation gain:** 2,000 feet
**Effort:** strenuous
**Trailhead:** Happy Isles Nature Center (shuttle stop 16)

Starting at the Happy Isles Nature Center, the **Mist Trail** takes you first to Vernal Fall, then on to Nevada Fall. The first mile of the hike is on a paved path to the Vernal Fall Footbridge. It then rises over much steep, slick granite, including 600 stairsteps to the top of Vernal Fall, offering a unique perspective on the 317-foot waterfall. The trail then undergoes some rocky switchbacks on its way to the top of the 594-foot-high Nevada Fall. Take a lightweight parka, since this aptly named trail drenches intrepid visitors in the spring and early summer months.

**Half Dome**

**Distance:** 14-16 miles round-trip
**Duration:** 10-12 hours
**Elevation gain:** 4,800 feet
**Effort:** strenuous
**Trailhead:** Happy Isles Nature Center (shuttle stop 16)

Perhaps the most famous—and potentially dangerous—climb in Yosemite Valley takes you to the top of the monumental granite **Half Dome.** With a 4,800-foot ascent, this arduous, all-day hike is not for children, the elderly, or the out-of-shape. Attempt this climb only late May-early October (weather permitting), when the cables are up to help climbers keep their balance and pull themselves the steep final 400 feet to the top of the dome. Once you reach the top, you'll find a restful expanse of stone on which to sit and rest and enjoy the scenery. Only 300 people per day are allowed to take this hike. The first step is before you even go to the park: secure a permit ($12.50-14.50), distributed by lottery on-line at www.recreation.gov, or by calling 877/444-6777. There's also the chance of securing a last-minute permit by lottery two days prior to the hiking date. Bring along a pack with water, food, and essentials for safety.

## Cycling

Cycling is a great way to get out of the car and off the crowded roads, but still explore Yosemite Valley at a quicker pace. The valley includes 12 miles of paved, mostly flat trails. You can bring your own bikes, or rent from **bike stands** (8am-7pm daily spring-fall, $12.50 per hour, $30.50 per day) at Yosemite Valley Lodge or Half Dome Village. Get a bike trail map while you're there.

## Rock Climbing

The rock climbing at Yosemite is some of the best in the world. **El Capitan,** the face of **Half Dome,** and **Sentinel Dome** in the high country are challenges that draw climbers from all over. If you plan to climb one of these monuments, check with the Yosemite park rangers and the Mountaineering School well in advance of your planned climb for necessary information and permits.

Many of the spectacular ascents are not beginner climbs. If you try to scale El Capitan for your first climb ever, you'll fail, or worse. The right place to start is the **Yosemite Mountaineering School**

(209/372-8344, www.yosemitepark.com, $143-167), where you can get one-on-one guided climbing experience. You'll find rock climbing lessons every morning at 8:30am as well as guided climbs out of Yosemite Valley and Tuolumne Meadows. In addition to guided hikes and backpacking trips, there are cross-country skiing lessons and treks in winter.

## Entertainment and Events
### Theater
The **Valley Visitors Center Auditorium** (Yosemite Village Visitors Center, Northside Dr., www.yosemiteconservancy.org, live theater tickets $10 adults, children 12 and under free) in the heart of Yosemite Village acts as home to the Yosemite Theater. For an evening of indoor entertainment, check the copy of *Yosemite Guide* you received at the gate for a list of what shows are playing during your visit. You may see Ranger Shelton Johnson portray a buffalo soldier, or the extravagantly bearded actor Lee Stetson portray John Muir, as he has since 1983.

### Photography and Art Classes
The unbelievable scenery of Yosemite inspires visitors young and old to create images to take home with them. Knowing this, Yosemite offers art and photography classes to help people catch hold of their inner Ansel Adams. In the summertime, art classes are offered for a nominal fee out of the **Yosemite Art Center** (Yosemite Village, next to the Yosemite Village Store, 209/372-4207, www.yosemiteconservancy.org, 10am-2pm Mon.-Sat. late Mar.-Oct., $15). Check the *Yosemite Guide* for a list of classes during your visit. You must bring your own art supplies, chair or cushion to sit on, and walking shoes (you'll take a brief walk out to a good location to see the scenery). If you don't have supplies, you can buy them at the Village Store just before class. Also check the *Guide* for guided tours of the **Ansel Adams Gallery** in the village.

### Guided Tours
A wide variety of hikes and tours are available, led by various park staff. Some include ranger-led walks and evening programs, such as "Starry Skies over Yosemite." There are also group hikes, guided bus tours, and full-moon bike rides available for visitors. See the *Yosemite Guide* or www.yosemitepark.com for more information and a schedule of events.

### Festivals and Events
A few annual events are designed to draw visitors back to the park during the less crowded winter months.

**The Grand Grape Celebration** (Nov.-early Dec., www.travelyosemite.com) puts the focus on wine, with celebrated winemakers highlighting rare releases, wine aficionados leading tasting seminars, and a five-course dinner paired with wines (the wines are chosen first, of course!).

Since 1927, the Majestic Yosemite Hotel has been decorated like an 18th-century English manor for the holiday season. The accompanying seven-course **Bracebridge Dinner** (mid-Dec., www.travelyosemite.com) includes a program of Christmas carols and other entertainment.

For over 30 years, some of the state's most acclaimed chefs have descended on the historic Majestic Yosemite Hotel for **Taste of Yosemite** (mid-Jan.-early Feb., www.travelyosemite.com), a multiple-week foodie fest that includes culinary demonstrations, tastings, and five-course dinners.

## Food
### Inside the Park
The ★ **Majestic Yosemite Hotel Dining Room** (Majestic Yosemite Hotel, 209/372-1489, www.travelyosemite.com, 7am-10am, 11:30am-3pm, and 5:30pm-9pm Mon.-Sat., 7am-3pm and 5:30pm-9pm Sun., $12-21) enjoys a reputation for fine cuisine that stretches back to the 1920s.

The grand dining room features expansive 34-foot-high ceilings, wrought-iron chandeliers, and a stellar valley view. The restaurant serves three meals daily, but dinner is a highlight, with California cuisine that mirrors top-tier San Francisco restaurants (with a price tag to match). Reservations are recommended for all meals, though it's possible to walk in for breakfast and lunch. Dinner requires "resort casual" attire.

At the other side of the valley, you can enjoy a spectacular view of Yosemite Falls at the **Mountain Room Restaurant** (Yosemite Valley Lodge, 209/372-1281, www.travelyosemite.com, 5pm-10pm Mon.-Sat., 9am-1pm and 5pm-10pm Sun., $17-38), part of Yosemite Valley Lodge. The glass atrium lets every guest at every table take in the view of the 2,424-foot falls. The menu runs to American food, and drinks are available from the full bar. They now do Sunday brunch as well. A casual bar menu is available at the **Mountain Room Lounge** (4:30pm-11pm Mon.-Fri., noon-11pm Sat.-Sun.) immediately across from the restaurant. Enjoy the patio in the summer and the fireplace in the winter. In the same building, the **Yosemite Valley Food Court** (6:30am-8pm daily, $7-15) offers cafeteria food with less atmosphere but reasonable prices.

For more casual dining, head to Yosemite Village for **Degnan's Loft** (www.travelyosemite.com, 5pm-9pm daily May-Sept.) for hot pizza, soups, and appetizers, and **Degnan's Delicatessen** (7am-5pm daily) for an array of sandwiches, salads, and other take-away munchies. Behind the Village Store, the **Village Grill Deck** (11am-6pm daily) serves fast-food hamburgers, salads, and sandwiches.

In Half Dome Village, options include **Pizza Deck** (summer daily 11am-10pm, fall and winter hours vary), **Half Dome Village Pavilion** (7am-10am and 5:30pm-8:30pm daily late Mar.-late Oct.), and

**Meadow Grill** (11am-8pm daily Apr.-mid Sept.), a coffee shop and bar.

## Outside the Park
An hour west of the Yosemite Valley, the ★ **High Country Health Foods & Café** (5186 CA-49, Mariposa, 209/966-5111, www.highcountryhealthfoods.com, store 8am-7pm Mon.-Sat., 9am-5pm Sun., café 8am-4pm Mon.-Sat., 9am-4pm Sun., $6-10) is a great place to stock up on tasty sandwiches, revitalizing smoothies, and healthy produce. If you get the Midpines sandwich, a flavorful smoked chicken and feta cheese concoction, there is a chance you'll eat it all in the nice café setting before ever making it to the park.

With big windows looking out over the gold rush town of Mariposa, **Savoury's Restaurant** (5034 CA-140, Mariposa, 209/966-7677, http://savouryrestaurant.com, 5pm-9:30pm daily summer, 5pm-close Thurs.-Tues. winter, $15-31) is a fine place for supper and a cocktail. The steak-heavy menu also includes seafood, pasta, and salad.

## Accommodations
### Inside the Park
Almost all of the lodging in Yosemite National Park is run by hospitality management company Aramark. There are a limited number of places to stay within the park's boundaries. If you would like to stay in the park during the summer high season, make **reservations** as early as possible—as much as **a year in advance**—by calling 888/413-8869 if in the United States or 602/278-8888 if outside the country. Another option is to do it all online at www.travelyosemite.com. Also book a year in advance for Christmas and holiday weekends. Spring reservations can be just as competitive during wet years that promise prime waterfall viewing.

If you're looking for luxury among the trees and rocks, check in to the ★ **Majestic Yosemite Hotel** (formerly the Ahwahnee Hotel, inside U.S.

888/413-8869, outside the U.S. 602/278-8888, www.travelyosemite.com, $482-1,178). Built as a luxury hotel in the early 20th century, it lives up to its reputation with soaring ceilings in the common rooms, a gorgeous stone facade, and striking stone fireplaces. Guest rooms, whether in the hotel or in the individual cottages, drip sumptuous appointments. The theme is Native American, and you'll find intricate, multicolored geometric and zoomorphic designs on linens, furniture, and pillows. Rooms with king beds invite romance for couples, while those with two doubles are perfect for families. Many have views of the valley, while a limited number include balconies and decks.

**Yosemite Valley Lodge** (formerly Yosemite Lodge at the Falls, inside U.S. 888/413-8869, outside the U.S. 602/278-8888, www.travelyosemite.com, $258-278), situated near Yosemite Village on the valley floor, has a location perfect for touring all over the park. The motel-style rooms are light and pretty, with polished wood furniture. Environmentally friendly features include energy-saving lighting and floors made from recycled products. Families should opt for the aptly named Family Rooms with one king bed and a bunk bed. Enjoy the heated pool in the summertime and the free shuttle transportation up to the Yosemite Ski & Snowboard Area (formerly Badger Pass) in winter. The amphitheater at the middle of the lodge runs nature programs and movies all year. The lodge has a post office, an ATM, and plenty of food options, and it is central to the Yosemite shuttle system.

**Half Dome Village** (formerly Curry Village, inside U.S. 888/413-8869, outside the U.S. 602/278-8888, www.travelyosemite.com, $141-353) offers some of the oldest lodgings in the park. Locally

**From top to bottom:** Yosemite Valley Lodge; Big Trees Lodge; the pool deck at Rush Creek Lodge.

called Camp Curry, this sprawling array of wood-sided and tent cabins was originally created in 1899 to provide affordable lodgings so that people of modest means could afford to visit and enjoy the wonders of Yosemite. At Half Dome Village, you can rent a hard-walled cabin or a tent cabin, with or without heat and with or without a private bath, depending on your budget and your needs. The tent cabins, the most affordable option, are small, fitting cot beds and a small dresser on the wood floor. Bear-proof lockers sit outside each tent cabin. Wood cabins have one or two double beds and electricity, but little else. The cabins with private baths are heated and boast daily maid service, but no TVs or phones. All cabins have an outdoor deck or patio for taking in the mountain air. Another option is a room in the Stoneman Cottage, a rustic motel with private bathrooms. With its perfect location on the valley floor, a swimming pool in the summer, and an ice skating rink in the winter, Camp Curry makes an inexpensive vacation at Yosemite a joyful reality.

Want to camp, but don't want to schlep all the gear into the park? Book a tent cabin at **Housekeeping Camp** (inside U.S. 888/413-8869, outside the U.S. 602/278-8888, www.travelyosemite.com, $106). Located on the banks of the Merced River, Housekeeping Camp has its own sandy river beach for playing and sunbathing. Cabins have cement walls, white canvas roofs, and a white canvas curtain that separates the bedroom from the covered patio that doubles as a dining room. Every cabin has a double bed plus a bunk bed (can also add two cots per unit), a bear-proof food container, and an outdoor fire ring. You can bring your own linens, or rent a "bed pack" (no towels) for $2.50 per night. No maid service is provided, but you won't miss it as you sit outside watching the sun set over Yosemite Valley.

## Outside the Park: CA-140

You can't miss the **River Rock Inn** (4993 7th St., Mariposa, 209/966-5793, www.riverrockmariposa.com, $139-179) with its vivid orange-and-purple exterior in the heart of Mariposa. What was once a rundown 1940s motor lodge is now a quirky, fun motel with uniquely decorated rooms that make the most of the space with modern Pottery Barn-esque wrought-iron and wood styling. Have no fear: The colors become softer as you step through the door of your reasonably priced guest room. Four suites provide enough space for families, while the other five rooms sleep couples in comfort. Guests also enjoy a comprehensive continental breakfast before heading out. The River Rock is a 45-minute drive from the Arch Rock entrance to Yosemite, and at the southern end of the long chain of Gold Country towns, making it a great base of operations for an outdoorsy, Western-style California vacation.

If you prefer cozy seclusion to large lodge-style hotels, stay at the **Highland House** (3125 Wild Dove Ln., 559/250-0059, www.highlandhouseinn.com, $139-169), 11 miles outside Mariposa to the west of Yosemite. The house is set deep in the forest far from town, providing endless peace and quiet. This tiny B&B has only three guest rooms, each uniquely decorated in soft colors and warm, inviting styles. All rooms have down comforters, sparkling clean bathtubs and showers, and TVs with hundreds of cable channels. There's also a game room with a pool table if you're feeling competitive. The morning breakfast leaves guests well fed.

On the western edge of Mariposa, the **Best Western Plus Yosemite Way Station** ($219-229) has all you'll need for a night before venturing into the park. It's walking distance to Mariposa's restaurants, while the rooms have refrigerators and microwaves for leftovers. Adjacent to the swimming pool and hot tub is a small fitness room and, most important for those on long road trips, a coin-operated laundry. Fuel up with the motel's hot breakfast buffet.

## Camping
### Inside the Park
In Yosemite Valley, the campgrounds at **Upper Pines** (inside U.S. 877/444-6777, outside the U.S. 518/885-3639, www.recreation.gov, year-round, reservations required all year, $26), **Lower Pines** (inside U.S. 877/444-6777, outside the U.S. 518/885-3639, www.recreation.gov, Mar.-Oct., reservations required, $26), and **North Pines** (inside U.S. 877/444-6777, outside the U.S. 518/885-3639, www.recreation.gov, Apr.-Sept., reservations required, $26) allow trailers and RVs, and you can bring your dog with you. Camp Curry offers plenty of food options within walking distance, and showers are available nearby.

How many campgrounds are listed on the National Register of Historic Places? Not many, and **Camp 4** (near Yosemite Valley Lodge, 35 campsites, year-round, $6) has that distinction due to its importance to the sport of rock climbing. Patagonia founder Yvon Chouinard began his business career by selling climbing gear here. You'll find showers nearby and lots of food and groceries at Yosemite Valley Lodge. It's not possible to make reservations, so all sites are first-come, first-served. The campground fills up quickly, especially spring-fall. FYI: No RVs or trailers are allowed at these sites.

### Outside the Park: CA-140
A hostel with a 10-person hot tub and a cedar sauna? The ★ **Yosemite Bug Rustic Mountain Resort** (6979 CA-140, Midpines, 866/826-7108, www.yosemite-bug.com, dorm beds $34, tent cabins $75, private rooms with shared baths $135, private rooms with baths $175) has that and more. Options begin at basic hostel-style dorm rooms and go up to uniquely decorated private bedrooms, including one with a steampunk theme and

another with a psychedelic vibe. There are also tent cabins and two guesthouses: The **Barn Studio** ($150-195), with room for four people, and the **Starlite House** ($260-340), with room for 5-9. The hub of the property is the mountain lodge café, serving three meals a day and California beers on tap. The grilled rib-eye dinner is perfect after a long day of hiking.

RVers aiming for the Arch Rock entrance flock to the **Indian Flat RV Park** (9988 CA-140, 209/379-2339, www.indianflatrvpark.com, tent sites $30, RV sites $42-48, tent cabins $129-139, cottages $169-289, pet fee $5). This park is a full-service low-end resort, with everything from minimal-hookup RV sites through tent cabins and a couple of cabins with kitchenettes and cable TV. Showers are available here, even for passers-through who aren't staying at Indian Flat. The lodge next door has extended an invitation to all Indian Flat campers to make use of its outdoor pool. Because Indian Flat is relatively small (25 RV sites, 25 tent sites), reservations are strongly recommended. You can make your booking up to a year in advance, and this kind of planning is a really good idea for summertime Yosemite visitors.

# Glacier Point

The best view of Yosemite Valley may not be from the valley floor. To get a different look at the familiar formations and falls, drive up Glacier Point Road to Glacier Point. The vista down into Yosemite Valley is anything but ordinary. Glacier Point Road stays open all year to allow access to the Yosemite Ski & Snowboard Area.

## Sights
### ★ Glacier Point
Located at the top of Yosemite Valley's south wall, **Glacier Point** offers what is arguably the best view within the whole park. At 7,214 feet high, the spot looks

down on the valley floor 3,214 feet below, with stunning views of iconic features like Half Dome and Yosemite Falls. It's easy to get to the lookout area, which is wheelchair-accessible and includes an amphitheater, snack stand, gift shop, and restrooms. The road to Glacier Point is open late May-October or November, except when storms make it temporarily impassable. During winter, experienced cross-country skiers can ski 10.5 miles in to the viewpoint.

## Recreation
### Hiking

If you love the thrill of heights, head up Glacier Point Road and take a hike up to or along one of the spectacular (and slightly scary) granite cliffs. Hikes in this area run from quite easy to rigorous; many of the cliff-side trails aren't appropriate for children.

### Sentinel Dome

**Distance:** 2 miles round-trip
**Duration:** 2 hours
**Elevation gain:** 400 feet
**Effort:** moderate
**Trailhead:** Sentinel Dome-Taft Point Trailhead

The two-mile round-trip hike up **Sentinel Dome** makes for a surprisingly easy walk; the only steep part runs right up the dome at the end of the trail. You can do this hike in two hours, and you'll find views at the top to make the effort and high elevation (more than 8,000 feet at the top) more than worthwhile. On a clear day, you can see from Yosemite Valley to the High Sierra and all the way out to Mount Diablo in the Bay Area to the west. Bring a camera! Be careful; there are no guardrails or walls to protect you from the long drop along the side of the trail and at the top of the dome.

### Taft Point and the Fissures

**Distance:** 2 miles round-trip
**Duration:** 2 hours
**Elevation gain:** 200 feet
**Effort:** moderate
**Trailhead:** Sentinel Dome-Taft Point Trailhead

It doesn't take long to reach the magnificent vista point at **Taft Point and the Fissures.** This two-mile round-trip hike takes you along some of Yosemite's unusual rock formations, the Fissures, and continues through lovely woods to Taft Point. This precarious precipice boasts not a single stone wall, but only a rickety set of guardrails to keep visitors from plummeting 2,000 feet down to the nearest patch of flat ground. Thrill seekers enjoy challenging themselves to get right up to the edge of the cliff and peer down. The elevation change from the trailhead to the point is only about 200 feet, even though you are hiking at an elevation of 3,500 feet above the valley floor.

### Four Mile Trail

**Distance:** 9.6 miles round-trip; 4.8 miles one-way
**Duration:** 6-8 hours round-trip; 3-4 hours one-way
**Elevation gain:** 3,200 feet
**Effort:** round-trip strenuous; one-way moderate
**Trailhead:** Four Mile Trailhead (Southside Dr. in Yosemite Valley)

For the most spectacular view of *all* of Yosemite Falls anywhere in the park, take the **Four Mile Trail** that connects Glacier Point to Yosemite Valley. The easiest way to take this hike is to start at the top, from Glacier Point, and hike down to the valley. You can then catch a ride on the Glacier Point Tour Bus (buy tickets in advance!) back up to your car. The steep climb up the trail from the valley on the round-trip version can be much harder on your legs and lungs, but it affords an ascending series of views of Yosemite Falls and Yosemite Valley that grow more spectacular with each switchback.

### Ostrander Lake

**Distance:** 11.4 miles round-trip
**Duration:** 8-10 hours
**Elevation gain:** 1,600 feet
**Effort:** strenuous
**Trailhead:** Ostrander Lake Trailhead (1.3 miles east of the Bridalveil Creek Campground turnoff)

For a longer high-elevation hike, take

the 11.4-mile walk to **Ostrander Lake** and back. (You can cross-country ski to the lake in the winter and stay overnight at the local ski hut.) This trek can take all day at a relaxed pace. In June and July, wildflowers bloom all along the trail. You can also still see the remnants of a 1987 fire and the regrowth in the decades since. The lake itself is a lovely patch of shining clear water surrounded by granite boulders and picturesque pine trees. Start up the trail in the morning, packing a picnic lunch to enjoy beside the serene water. Bring bug repellent; the still waters of the lake are mosquito heaven.

## Skiing and Snowshoeing

Downhill skiing at **Yosemite Ski & Snowboard Area** (formerly Badger Pass, Glacier Point Rd., 5 miles from Wawona, 209/372-1000, www.travelyosemite.com, 9am-4pm daily mid-Dec.-Apr., prices vary) is another favorite wintertime activity at Yosemite. This was the first downhill ski area created in California. Today, it's the perfect resort for families and groups who want a relaxed day or three of moderate skiing. With plenty of beginner runs and classes, Yosemite has helped thousands of kids (and adults!) learn to ski and snowboard as friends and family look on from the sundecks at the lodge. There are enough intermediate runs to make it interesting for mid-level skiers, and a terrain park for ripping boarders. Double-black-diamond skiers may find Yosemite Ski too tame for their tastes since there are just a few advanced runs. But everyone agrees that the prices are reasonable, and the focus is on friendliness and learning rather than showing off and extreme skiing.

Yosemite has 90 miles of marked cross-country ski trails and 25 miles of groomed track. In fact, many places in Yosemite are accessible in winter only by cross-country skis or snowshoes. Check out the **Yosemite Cross-Country Center**

the Yosemite Bug Rustic Mountain Resort

& Ski School (www.travelyosemite.com) for classes, rentals, and guided cross-country ski and snowshoeing tours. If you're looking for a fun day out in the snow, the groomed tracks from Yosemite Ski & Snowboard Area to Glacier Point run 21 miles and are frequented by day skiers. You'll see fewer other skiers on the backcountry trails, which can also be traversed in a single day by a reasonably strong skier. For the hard-core XC skier who wants a serious skiing experience, check out the overnight and multiday tours; hiring a guide for these trips is recommended for most skiers.

Even if you're not up for hard-core skiing, you can get out and enjoy the snow-covered landscapes of wintertime Yosemite. Snowshoeing requires no experience and only minimal fitness to get started. "If you can walk, you can snowshoe," claims Yosemite's own website. You can rent snowshoes at several locations in Yosemite and acquire trail maps from the rental centers.

## Food

During winter, the Yosemite Ski & Snowboard Area has a fast-food grill and the **Snowflake Room** (11am-4pm winter weekends and holidays), which serve hot dogs, nachos, soda, and beer.

## Accommodations

If you're planning an extended stay with friends or family, consider renting a condo or house with a full kitchen, privacy, and the comforts of home. You can find these at the **Yosemite West Condominiums** (559/642-2211, www.yosemitewestreservations.com, $195-505). The modular buildings can be divided into a number of separate units—or not—if you want enough space for a big crowd. The studio and loft condos sleep 2-6 people and have full kitchens and access to all complex amenities. Luxury suites are one-bedroom apartments with full kitchens, pool tables, and all sorts of other amenities. Two- and three-bedroom apartments sleep 6-10 people.

### Camping

For a picturesque Yosemite camping experience, check out **Bridalveil Creek Campground** (Glacier Point Rd., 8 miles east of Wawona Rd., July-early Sept., 110 campsites, $18, $30 stock camp, $50 group). The campground sits at 7,200 feet elevation and has a creek running around its perimeter. It's not possible to make reservations for the regular sites, which are all first-come, first-served. The campground fills up quickly, especially spring-fall. You can reserve one of three horse sites if you're traveling with your mount or two group camps by calling 877/444-6777; the group campsites also can be secured at www.recreation.gov. RVs are welcome.

# Hetch Hetchy

Naturalist and wilderness activist John Muir noted that Hetch Hetchy Valley was once "a wonderfully exact counterpart of the great Yosemite." Perhaps the most disputed valley in all California, Hetch Hetchy today is a reservoir that supplies much of the San Francisco Bay Area with drinking water. Many environmental activists see the reservoir's existence as an affront and lobby continuously to have O'Shaughnessy Dam torn down and the valley returned to its former state of natural beauty. But there is plenty of beauty in this northwest corner of the park, including the Half Dome-like bump of Kolana Rock and two waterfalls that spill down 1,000-foot cliff faces. Experience the grandeur of the Sierra Nevada without the crowds that clog up Yosemite Valley.

## Sights
### O'Shaughnessy Dam
Named for its chief engineer, **O'Shaughnessy Dam** is a 430-foot concrete dam that diverts the Tuolumne River into the 117-billion-gallon Hetch Hetchy Reservoir. The spot had long been considered for a possible dam. The 1906 San Francisco earthquake established a need for a substantial water supply for San Francisco, leading to the Raker Act in 1913, which authorized construction of the dam. The first phase was completed 1923, with a second wave of building that raised the height of the structure lasting until 1938. Today, the reservoir's water flows 167 miles to the Bay Area without any pumps; gravity does all the work.

The O'Shaughnessy Dam is easily accessible and has a small parking lot just feet away. Walk out onto the structure to see Kolana Rock and Wapama Falls in the distance and imagine what Hetch Hetchy Valley looked like before human engineering intervened.

## Recreation
### Hiking
The relatively low elevation of Hetch Hetchy means that snow thaws sooner, allowing for hiking year-round, though July and August can be very hot. The

Hetch Hetchy

287 miles of hiking trails in the Hetch Hetchy watershed include a range of options, from the 2.8-mile Lookout Point Trail to the 29-mile Hetch Hetchy-Lake Vernon Loop.

### Lookout Point Trail
**Distance:** 2.8 miles round-trip
**Duration:** 1.5 hours
**Elevation gain:** 500 feet
**Effort:** moderate
**Trailhead:** just past the Hetch Hetchy entrance station

The **Lookout Point Trail** climbs steadily up to a rock slab with a 260-degree view of the Hetch Hetchy Reservoir, the O'Shaughnessy Dam, and Wapama Falls below. You can also see the Central Valley to the west if it's not too hazy. Expect plentiful wildflowers in early spring.

### ★ Wapama Falls Trail
**Distance:** 5 miles round-trip
**Duration:** 2 hours
**Elevation gain:** 200 feet
**Effort:** moderate
**Trailhead:** O'Shaughnessy Dam

The **Wapama Falls Trail** is an ideal introduction to the Hetch Hetchy area. The hike begins by crossing O'Shaughnessy Dam. After passing through a tunnel blasted into the rock, the trail hugs the rim of the reservoir, offering fine views of Kolana Rock. Along the way, you'll probably see some burned tree trunks left over from the 2013 Rim Fire, the third-largest wildfire in California history. In spring, expect a profusion of wildflowers along the way. Eventually, the trail gets rockier, with some rock steps, before reaching wooden bridges over Falls Creek and the impressive view of Wapama Falls spilling over a giant rock face. Be careful crossing the four bridges, which can be slippery when the creek is rushing.

### Backpacking
To head out into the backcountry from Hetch Hetchy, secure a free **wilderness permit** from the Hetch Hetchy entrance station, where you can also rent a **bear canister** ($5 per week with a credit card deposit) for backcountry food storage. One of the most popular multiday excursions is the **Hetch Hetchy-Lake Vernon Loop** (29 miles, strenuous), which goes northeast of the Hetch Hetchy Reservoir. The first four miles head up and out of the valley on the old Lake Eleanor Road. The trail carries on to scenic Lake Vernon before heading to Rancheria Falls and then back along the north side of the reservoir.

### Swimming
On a hot day, a dip in the Hetch Hetchy Reservoir looks tempting, but resist the urge: entering the water is illegal. Instead, head to **Rainbow Pool** (CA-120 at South Fork Tuolumne River Bridge, east of the Rim of the World Viewpoint, www.fs.usda.gov), a U.S. Forest Service day-use area located between Groveland and the Big Oak Flat entrance to the park (11 miles west of the Big Oak Flat

# Hetch Hetchy

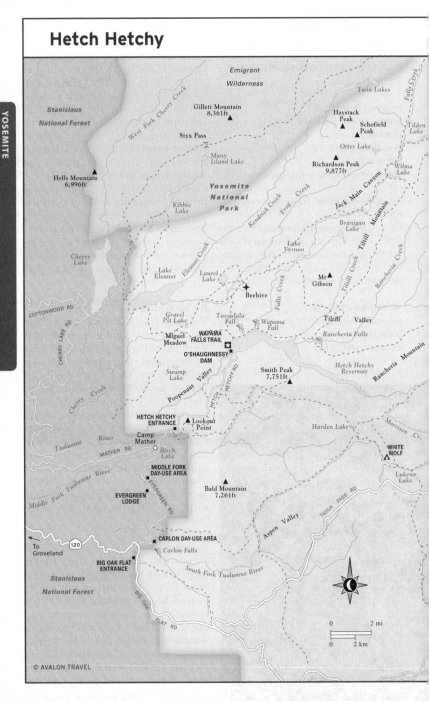

entrance). This was once a toll stop for stagecoaches, where a resort flourished before burning down in 1858. Today, all that remains from those days are some brackets and drill holes within the riverside rocks. The real attraction is a waterfall that spills into a deep, pooled section of the Tuolumne River. It's a favorite spot for locals. Watch in awe as kids jump off a 20-foot ledge into the pool below—or try it yourself.

## Food
### Outside the Park
There are no dining options within the Hetch Hetchy region of the park. The closest place to get a bite is at the **Evergreen Lodge** (33160 Evergreen Rd., 209/379-2606, www.evergreenlodge.com, 7am-10:30am, noon-3pm, and 5:30pm-10pm daily summer, 7am-10:30am, noon-3pm, and 5pm-9pm daily winter, closed Jan.-mid-Feb., dinner $18-28), just 1.5 miles from the park's Hetch Hetchy entrance. Dine inside in the dining room or the tavern or outdoors on the front porch or the heated patio.

Craving authentic Mexican food? **Cocina Michoacana** (18730 Main St., Groveland, 209/962-6651, 10am-9pm daily, $10.50-14) in Groveland is the place for tacos, burritos, and chimichangas. Try the chicken fajitas, which are served in a hot skillet. The dining room is narrow and the kitchen is small, so expect a wait on the weekend.

The **Iron Door Saloon** (18761 Main St., Groveland, 209/962-6244, 7am-9pm daily, $8-12) claims to be California's oldest bar. Whether or not that's true, it delivers serious gold rush-era ambience, from the bullet holes in its walls to the old pictures of Hetch Hetchy before the dam was constructed. Entertainment includes live bands on weekends and watching folks trying to get their dollar bills to

**From top to bottom:** the O'Shaughnessy Dam; a bridge on the Wapama Falls Trail; Groveland's Iron Door Saloon.

stick to the high ceiling. As for the food, the menu includes burgers, onion rings, fish-and-chips, and an all-you-can-eat soup and salad bar.

## Accommodations
### Outside the Park

Just a mile and a half from Yosemite's Big Oak Flat entrance, the 20-acre ★ **Rush Creek Lodge** (34001 CA-120, 209/379-2373, www.rushcreeklodge.com, $390-515) is an ideal place to unwind after exploring the park. The superb deck beckons with a saltwater pool, two large soaking tubs, lounge chairs, fire pits, and a Ping-Pong table. Children will love the adjacent game room, while adults can imbibe in the lounge or tavern, which frequently hosts live music. The on-site restaurant has a wood-fired oven used for s'mores roasting in the evenings. The rooms in both the main lodge and the 16 hillside villas are rustic with a modern twist. All have a balcony or porch to take in the mountain air.

Just one mile from Yosemite's Hetch Hetchy entrance, the **Evergreen Lodge** (33160 Evergreen Rd., 209/379-2606, www.evergreenlodge.com, camping $100-135, cabins and cottages $260-455) has different lodging options scattered across its 22 acres of pine-shaded land. For camping, don't even pack your gear, as you'll arrive to an already set-up mesh-topped tent outfitted with foam mattresses and toiletries. Even the cabins for budget-conscious visitors have Sirius satellite radios, Keurig coffeemakers, and mini fridges. Enjoy a dip in the pool or hot tub after a hike. Head out to the main lodge for a meal or walk to the tavern for a drink and live entertainment.

Most lodging options can be found in Groveland, a scenic mountain town right on CA-120 just 26 miles from the park entrance. **Hotel Charlotte** (18736 Main St., Groveland, 209/962-6455, www.hotelcharlotte.com, $129-249) has been hosting visitors since way back in 1921. The starting rooms are cozy (small) but

go up to deluxe suites and master suites. No matter what room you are in, you'll get to indulge in a complimentary breakfast buffet in the morning. For larger groups, the hotel also has vacation rentals ($259-299) available that can accommodate up to 11 people in a gated community located 10 minutes from Groveland.

## Camping
### Outside the Park: CA-120

To camp in Big Oak Flat along CA-120 near Groveland, try the Thousand Trails RV campground at **Yosemite Lakes RV Resort** (31191 Harden Flat Rd., 877/570-2267, www.1000trails.com, tents $90, RVs $137) if you are in a pinch. This sprawling campground has more than 250 RV sites with full hookups, 130 tent sites, a few dozen cabins, tent cabins, yurts, and a 12-bed hostel. This is not a great campground, but there are frequent openings on summer weekends, which will put you close to the northern section of Yosemite.

---

# Wawona

The small town-like area of Wawona (Wawona Rd./CA-41, 1.5 hours from Yosemite Valley) is only a few miles from the South entrance of Yosemite. The historic Big Trees Lodge (formerly Wawona Hotel) was built in 1917 and also houses a popular restaurant as well as a store.

## Sights
### Pioneer Yosemite History Center

The first thing you'll see at the **Pioneer Yosemite History Center** (trail from Wawona information station, open daily) is a big open barn housing an array of vehicles used for over a century in Yosemite. These conveyances range from big cushiony carriages for rich tourists to oil wagons once used in an ill-conceived attempt to control mosquitoes on the ponds. Continuing, walk under the Vermont-style covered bridge to the main museum area. This rambling, not-overcrowded stretch of land contains many of the original structures built in the park, most over 100 years ago. Most were moved from various remote locations. Informative placards describe the history of Yosemite National Park through its structures, from the military shacks used by soldiers who were the first park rangers to the homes of early settlers, presided over by stoic pioneer women. There's also a tiny rock building that was used as a jail and a morgue. Check your *Yosemite Guide* for living-history programs and live demonstrations held at the museum.

### ★ Mariposa Grove of Giant Sequoias

One of three groves of these rare, majestic trees in Yosemite, the **Mariposa Grove** (Wawona Rd./CA-41) offers the easiest access. The trail winds between the rust-colored spires of the giant sequoias and past rounds as big as dinner tables. Highlights in the Lower Grove include the Grizzly Giant with its impressive girth and the California Tunnel Tree, with a doorway through its trunk that you can walk through. Between May and October, the **Big Trees Tram Tour** (9:30am-5pm daily) departs every half hour from the Mariposa Grove Gift Shop. The one-hour and 15-minute ride meanders through the grove, complete with an audio tour describing the botany of the trees, their history, and more. The **Mariposa Grove Museum** (Upper Mariposa Grove, 10am-4pm daily May-Sept.) offers still more information. Parking is limited; it's best to take the free shuttle to the grove from Wawona or Yosemite Valley, especially in high season, to cut down on auto traffic.

## Recreation
### Hiking

It's not quite as popular or as crowded as Yosemite Valley, but the hikes near Wawona in southern Yosemite can be just as scenic and lovely.

### Wawona Meadow Loop
**Distance:** 3.5-mile loop or extended 5-mile loop
**Duration:** 1.5-2.5 hours
**Elevation gain:** none for 3.5-mile loop; 500 feet for 5-mile loop
**Effort:** easy
**Trailhead:** Big Trees Lodge

Start with the **Wawona Meadow Loop,** a flat and shockingly uncrowded 3.5-mile sweep around the lovely Wawona meadow and somewhat incongruous nine-hole golf course. Begin by taking the paved road across from the Wawona Golf Course and then turn left on the marked trail. This wide path was once fully paved, and is still bikeable, but the pavement has eroded over the years and now you'll find much dirt and tree detritus. Best in late spring when the wildflowers are blooming in profusion, this trail takes about two hours to navigate. If you'd like a longer trip, you can extend this walk to five miles (with about 500 feet elevation change) by taking the detour at the south end of the meadow.

### Chilnualna Fall
**Distance:** 8.2 miles round-trip
**Duration:** 5 hours
**Elevation gain:** 2,300 feet
**Effort:** strenuous
**Trailhead:** Chilnualna Falls Parking Area

The hard-core hike along this trail to **Chilnualna Fall** offers tantalizing views of the cascades few visitors ever see. Sadly, there's no dedicated viewing area, so you'll need to peek through the trees. The trail runs all the way up to the top of the falls. Be careful to avoid the stream during spring and summer high flow—it can be dangerous. Plan 4-6 hours for the 2,300-foot ascent, and bring water, snacks, and a trail map.

### Horseback Riding

You'll find more horses than mules at **Big Trees Stable** (Pioneer Yosemite History Center, Wawona Rd., 209/375-6502, www.travelyosemite.com, rides depart 8am, 10am, and 2pm daily June-Sept.,

$65), and more visitors, too; reservations are strongly encouraged. From Wawona, you can take a sedate two-hour ride around the historic wagon trail running into the area.

## Entertainment and Events

It's worth making an evening trip out to Wawona to listen to the delightful piano music and singing of legendary Tom Bopp. He plays vintage camp music (and requests, and whatever else strikes his fancy) in the **Piano Lounge at the Big Trees Lodge** (209/372-8243) Tuesday-Saturday 5:30pm-9:30pm. Older visitors especially love his old-style performance and familiar songs, but everyone enjoys the music and entertainment he provides. Even if you're just waiting for a table at the restaurant, stop in to say hello and make a request.

## Food

The ★ **Big Trees Lodge Dining Room** (Big Trees Lodge, 209/375-1425, www.travelyosemite.com, 7am-10am, 11am-3pm, and 5pm-9pm daily, $20-32) serves upscale but homey California cuisine in an old-timey dining room with lots of windows. Check out the kitschy but cool redwood lamps hanging overhead. The menu offers options for both vegetarians (onion gratiné) and devout carnivores (pot roast, grilled filet). Reservations are recommended for groups of six or more. All other seating is first-come, first-served, but while you wait for your table you can enjoy drinks and live piano music by local legend Tom Bopp. There's a weekly outdoor barbecue on Saturday evenings during the summer.

## Accommodations
### Inside the Park

Near the South entrance of the park, the gleaming white ★ **Big Trees Lodge** (formerly Wawona Hotel, 888/413-8867, www.travelyosemite.com, $132-195), with its wide verandas, is reminiscent of a 19th-century riverboat. The interior matches the exterior, with furnishings in period style, private baths—and no TVs or telephones. Rooms with shared baths are also available for budget travelers. Dating back to 1879, this Yosemite institution has hosted Presidents Ulysses S. Grant and Theodore Roosevelt.

### Outside the Park: CA-41

To soak in the tranquil beauty of the mountains, stay in one of the handsome ★ **Far Meadow Base Camp Cabins** (Beasore Rd., between Jone's Store and Globe Rock, 310/455-2425 or 866/687-9358, www.boutique-homes.com, $250-275 plus $100 cleaning fee, 3-night minimum). The two A-frames and one log cabin are perched on a 20-acre spread with woods and meadows, just a 45-minute drive from the park's South entrance. These structures are fully off the grid, equipped with solar power, well water, and satellite Internet access. Each cabin sleeps 2-4 people and is equipped with a kitchen and bath.

Near the South entrance to Yosemite on CA-41, the **Narrow Gauge Inn** (48571 CA-41, Fish Camp, 559/683-7720, www.narrowgaugeinn.com, $209-379) recalls the large lodges inside the park, in miniature. This charming 26-room mountain inn offers one- and two-bed guest rooms done in wood paneling, light colors, and white linens or vintage-style quilts. Each room has its own outdoor table and chairs to encourage relaxing outside with a drink on gorgeous summer days and evenings. The restaurant and common rooms feature antique oil lamps, stonework, and crackling fireplaces. Step outside your door and you're in the magnificent High Sierra pine forest. A few more steps take you to the Yosemite Mountain Sugar Pine Railroad, the narrow-gauge steam train from which the inn takes its name.

Just outside the South entrance, the **Tenaya Lodge** (1122 CA-41, 888/514-2167, www.tenayalodge.com, $359-835) offers plush lodge-style accommodations. Guest rooms are styled with rich fabrics in bold colors and modern wall art that evokes the woods and vistas of Yosemite. The beds are comfortable, the baths attractive, and the views forest-filled. Take advantage of the dining room, which offers three meals a day, a full-service spa, two indoor pools, and three outdoor pools.

## Camping
### Inside the Park
You can camp year-round at lovely forested **Wawona** (1 mile north of Wawona, 209/375-9535 or 877/444-6777, www.recreation.gov, reservations required Apr.-Sept., 93 sites, $26 family, $30 stock camp, $50 group). Several of the sites are perched right on the South Fork of the Merced River. RVs are welcome, though there are no hookups on-site. Two sites can accommodate horses. Most services (including showers) can't be found closer than Yosemite Valley.

### Outside the Park: CA-41
Just 1.5 miles from the park's South entrance, idyllic ★ **Summerdale Campground** (CA-41, Fish Camp, 559/642-3212 or 877/444-6777, www.recreation.gov, May-Sept., $30) is alongside the refreshing waters of Big Creek. Each of the 30 roomy campsites has a campfire ring and a picnic table, while water spigots and vault toilets are nearby. Between the campsites and the highway, a trail leads to a small waterfall and pool.

# Tioga Pass and Tuolumne Meadows

Tioga Pass, a.k.a. CA-120, is Yosemite's own "road less traveled." The pass (as locals call it) crosses Yosemite from west to east, leading from the populous west edge of the park out toward Mono Lake in the east. To get to Tioga Pass from Yosemite Valley, take Northside Road to Big Oak Flat Road to the CA-120 junction and turn east. Its elevation and

location lead to annual winter closures, so don't expect to be able to get across the park November-May. Along the pass, you'll find a number of developed campgrounds, plus a few natural wonders that many visitors to Yosemite never see.

## Sights
### Olmsted Point
**Olmsted Point** (road marker T24, Tioga Rd., 30 miles east of the Crane Flat turnoff) offers sweeping views of Tenaya Canyon, the mass of granite known as Clouds Rest, and the northern side of Half Dome, which, from this vantage point, looks like a giant helmet. Seeing them requires little effort. Turn your vehicle off Tioga Road into the parking area and then climb onto the large rock formation to the south. This spot is named after landscape architect Frederick Law Olmsted Jr., who worked as a planner in Yosemite National Park.

### Tenaya Lake
Right off Tioga Road is **Tenaya Lake** (Tioga Rd., 2 miles east of Olmsted), a natural gem nearly a mile long and framed by granite peaks. The body of water was formed by the action of Tenaya Glacier. Both are named for a local Native American chief. It's a popular place for swimming, fishing, and boating. The northeastern side of the lake has a beach with picnic tables and restrooms.

### Tuolumne Meadows
Once you're out of the valley and driving along Tioga Pass, you're ready to come upon **Tuolumne Meadows** (about 10 miles from the eastern edge of the park, accessible by road summer only). After miles of soaring rugged mountains, these serene alpine meadows almost come as a surprise. They are brilliant green and dotted with wildflowers in spring, gradually turning to golden orange as fall approaches. The waving grasses support a variety of wildlife, including yellow-bellied marmots. You may see moraines

and boulders left behind by long-gone glaciers. Stop the car and get out for a quiet, contemplative walk through the meadows. Tuolumne Meadows is also a base camp for high-country backpacking.

## Recreation
### ★ Hiking
For smaller crowds along the trails, take one or more of the many scenic hikes along Tioga Pass. However, they don't call it "the high country" for nothing; the altitude *starts* at 8,500 feet and goes higher on many trails. If you're not in great shape, or if you have breathing problems, take the altitude into account when deciding which trails to explore.

### Tuolumne Grove of Giant Sequoias
**Distance:** 2.5 miles round-trip
**Duration:** 1.5-2.5 hours
**Elevation gain:** 400 feet
**Effort:** easy
**Trailhead:** Tuolumne Grove Parking Lot, at the junction of Tioga Pass Rd. and Old Big Oak Flat Rd.

If you're aching to see some giant trees, but you were put off by the parking problems at Mariposa Grove, try the **Tuolumne Grove of Giant Sequoias.** This 2.5-mile round-trip hike takes you down about 400 feet into the grove, which contains more than 20 mature giant sequoias, including one that you can walk through. (You do have to climb back up the hill to get to your car.) While you'll likely see other visitors, the smaller crowds make this grove an attractive alternative to Mariposa, especially in high season.

### Olmsted Point
**Distance:** 0.25 mile round-trip
**Duration:** 15-30 minutes
**Elevation gain:** 100 feet
**Effort:** easy
**Trailhead:** Olmsted Point Parking Lot, 1-2 miles west of Tenaya Lake on Tioga Rd.

This trail exists to show off the amazing views from **Olmsted Point:** Clouds Rest in all its underrated grandeur, with Half

Tenaya Lake

## 🧭 Side Trip to Sequoia and Kings Canyon

If you can't get enough of towering trees, majestic mountain peaks, and steep canyons, continue onward to **Sequoia and Kings Canyon National Park** (559/565-3341, www.nps.gov/seki, 7-day vehicle pass $30, foot or bicycle $15), two parks adjacent to one another in the southern section of the Sierra Nevada.

The oft-quoted John Muir called the 8,200-foot-deep Kings Canyon "a rival to Yosemite," but it also makes a good complement. The only accessible area of the canyon itself is **Cedar Grove,** which includes strolls like the 0.6-mile walk to **Roaring River Falls** and longer hikes like the 8-mile round-trip hike to **Mist Falls.** In **Grant Grove,** a 2-mile round-trip walk leads to the **General Grant Tree,** one of the world's largest trees. Stay overnight at the **John Muir Lodge** (86728 Hwy. 180, Kings Canyon National Park, 877/436-9615, www.visitsequoia. com, $95-212).

South of Kings Canyon, Sequoia National Park has plenty of its namesake trees. Head to the **Giant Forest** to see the 275-foot-tall **General Sherman Tree.** Nearby **Moro Rock** offers a view of the national park from an impressive granite dome. It's accessible by a short but steep 0.3-mile hike that ascends 300 vertical feet. Stay overnight at the **Wuksachi Lodge** (64740 Wuksachi Way, Sequoia National Park, 888/252-5757, www.visitsequoia.com, $215-273).

### Getting There

Sequoia and Kings Canyon National Parks are just 2.5 hours' drive from Yosemite's South entrance. Head out of Yosemite's South entrance on **CA-41 South** toward Fresno for roughly 60 miles. In Fresno, turn on **CA-180 West** toward Mendota and Kings Canyon, and then merge onto **CA-180 East.** Follow the road for roughly 50 miles until it enters Kings Canyon National Park at the **Big Stump entrance.**

Dome peeking out behind it. The short walk is perfect for non-athletes. At the trailhead parking lot, several large glacial errata boulders draw almost as much attention as the point itself.

### Tenaya Lake

**Distance:** 2.5 miles round-trip
**Duration:** 1-2 hours
**Elevation gain:** none
**Effort:** easy
**Trailhead:** 20 miles west of the park's Tioga Pass (eastern) entrance, along Tioga Pass Rd., with parking lots at either end of the lake

The loop trail to **Tenaya Lake** offers an easy walk, sunny beaches, and possibly the most picturesque views in all of Yosemite. The trail around the lake runs about 2.5 miles. The only difficult part is fording the outlet stream at the west end of the lake, because the water gets chilly and can be high in the spring and early summer. If the rest of your group is sick of hiking and scenery, you can leave them

on the beach while you take this easy one- to two-hour stroll. Just remember the mosquito repellent!

### May Lake
**Distance:** 2.5 miles round-trip
**Duration:** 1.5-2.5 hours
**Elevation gain:** 400 feet
**Effort:** moderate
**Trailhead:** May Lake Parking Lot, 1 mile southwest of Tenaya Lake on Tioga Pass Rd.

**May Lake** sits peacefully at the base of the sloping granite of Mount Hoffman. While the hike to and from May Lake is only 2.5 miles, there's a steady, steep 400-foot climb from the trailhead up to the lake. One of Yosemite's High Sierra Camps perches here. For truly hard-core hikers, a trail leads from the lake up another 2,000 vertical feet and six miles round-trip to the top of Mount Hoffman.

### Elizabeth Lake
**Distance:** 4.6 miles round-trip
**Duration:** 4-5 hours
**Elevation gain:** 1,000 feet
**Effort:** moderate
**Trailhead:** back side of the Tuolumne Meadows Campground

Originating at the Tuolumne Meadows Campground's horse camp, the trail to **Elizabeth Lake** starts with a real climb through a boulder-strewn forest. Don't give up: The path levels out after 1,000 vertical feet, meandering along a little creek and through a meadow. The destination is a picturesque subalpine lake with an impressive mountain wall as a backdrop. The 10,823-foot horn of Unicorn Peak tops the northernmost edge of the rocky ridge. Hop into the chilly water to cool off before returning down the same trail.

### Gaylor Lakes and Granite Lakes
**Distance:** 3-6 miles round-trip

**From top to bottom:** Tioga Pass Road on the way to Tuolumne Meadows; Elizabeth Lake; Lembert Dome

**Duration:** 3-6 hours
**Elevation gain:** 700-1,000 feet
**Effort:** moderate
**Trailhead:** parking lot just west of the Tioga Pass entrance station, on the north side of the road

If you're willing to tackle longer, steeper treks, you will find an amazing array of small scenic lakes within reach of Tioga Pass. **Gaylor Lakes** starts high (almost 10,000 feet elevation) and climbs a steep 600 vertical feet up the pass to the Gaylor Lakes valley. Once you're in the valley, you can wander at will around the lovely Granite Lakes, stopping to admire the views out to the mountains surrounding Tuolumne Meadows. You can also visit the abandoned 1870s mine site above Upper Gaylor Lake. It's one of Yosemite's less crowded hikes.

### North Dome

**Distance:** 8.8 miles round-trip
**Duration:** 4-6 hours
**Elevation loss:** 560 feet
**Effort:** moderate
**Trailhead:** Porcupine Creek Lot

For a different look at a classic Yosemite landmark, take the **North Dome** trail through the woods and out to the dome, which sits right across the valley from Half Dome. You'll hike almost nine miles round-trip, with a few hills thrown in. But getting to stare right into the face of Half Dome at eye level, and to see Clouds Rest beyond it, is worth the effort.

### Cathedral Lakes

**Distance:** 8 miles round-trip
**Duration:** 4-6 hours
**Elevation gain:** 1,000 feet
**Effort:** moderate
**Trailhead:** Tuolumne Meadows Visitors Center, part of the John Muir Trail

If you can't get enough of Yosemite's granite-framed alpine lakes, take the long walk out to one or both of the **Cathedral Lakes.** Starting at ever-popular Tuolumne Meadows, you'll climb about 800 vertical feet over 3-4 miles, depending on which lake you choose. The picture-perfect lakes show off the dramatic rocky peaks above, surrounding evergreens, and crystalline waters of Yosemite at their best. Bring water, munchies, and a camera!

### Glen Aulin Trail

**Distance:** 12 miles round-trip
**Duration:** 6-8 hours
**Elevation gain:** 800 feet
**Effort:** strenuous
**Trailhead:** Tuolumne Stables, Soda Springs

The **Glen Aulin Trail** to Tuolumne Fall and White Cascade is part of the John Muir Trail. Several of its forks branch off to pretty little lakes. There are some steep and rocky areas on the trail, but if you've got the lungs for it, you'll be rewarded by fabulous views of the Tuolumne River alternately pooling and cascading right beside the trail. This hike gets crowded in the high season. In the hot summertime, many hikers trade dusty jeans for swimsuits and cool off in the pools at the base of both White Cascade and Tuolumne Fall. If you want to spend the night, enter the High Sierra Camp lottery; if you win, you can arrange to stay at the Glen Aulin camp. If you do this, you can take your hike a few miles farther, downstream to California Fall, Le Conte Fall, and finally Waterwheel Fall.

### Lembert Dome

**Distance:** 2.8 miles round-trip
**Duration:** 2-3 hours
**Elevation gain:** 850 feet
**Effort:** moderate
**Trailhead:** Dog Lake Trailhead

**Lembert Dome** rises like a giant shark's fin from Tuolumne Meadows. Seeing this granite dome, you may be inspired to climb it for views of the meadow. From the trailhead, follow the signs to Dog Lake before taking a left at a trail junction toward the dome. Follow the marked path to avoid exposed sections that are dangerous due to steep drops. The last section of the hike involves a steep ascent. This is a fine vantage point to take in the rising or setting sun.

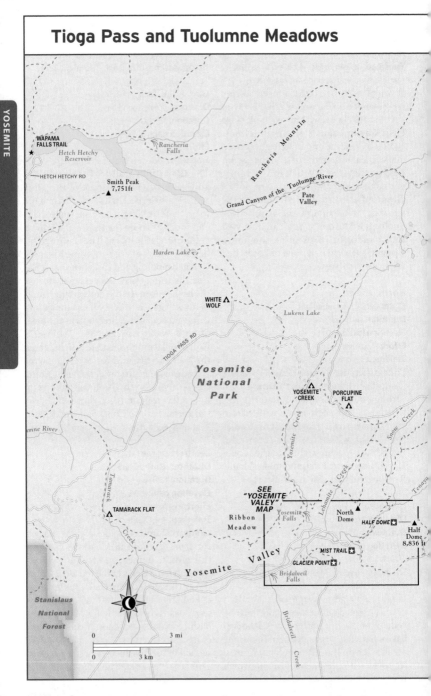

# Tioga Pass and Tuolumne Meadows

YOSEMITE

WAPAMA FALLS TRAIL ★
Hetch Hetchy Reservoir
HETCH HETCHY RD
Smith Peak ▲ 7,751ft

*Rancheria Falls*

Rancheria Mountain

Grand Canyon of the Tuolumne River

Pate Valley

Harden Lake

WHITE WOLF ⊼

*Lukens Lake*

TIOGA PASS RD

*Yosemite National Park*

YOSEMITE CREEK ⊼   PORCUPINE FLAT ⊼

*Yosemite Creek*

*Snow Creek*

*Tenaya*

umne River

Tamarack Creek

TAMARACK FLAT ⊼

**SEE "YOSEMITE VALLEY" MAP**

*Lehamite Creek*

North Dome ▲

HALF DOME ✪ ▲ Half Dome 8,836 ft

Ribbon Meadow

*Yosemite Falls*

Yosemite Valley

MIST TRAIL ✪

GLACIER POINT ✪

*Bridalveil Falls*

*Stanislaus National Forest*

*Bridalveil Creek*

0   3 mi
0   3 km

Pettit Peak
10,788ft

Virginia
Lake

Roosevelt
Lake

Saddlebag Lake

Gardisky
Lake

Mt Conness
12,590ft

To
Lee Vining

120

Pacific Crest Trail

Conness Creek

Waterwheel
Falls

Young Lakes

Ragged
Peak

Gaylor
Peak
11,004ft

Ellery
Lake

Tuolumne River

Delaney Creek

Granite
Lakes

Tioga
Lake

GLEN AULIN
HIGH SIERRA
CAMP

Gaylor Lakes

TIOGA PASS
ENTRANCE

Tuolumne
Meadows

Dog Lake

Dana Meadows

Tuolumne Peak
10,845ft

Pothole
Dome

Lembert
Dome

Dana Fork

Fairview
Dome

TUOLUMNE
MEADOWS
LODGE

TIOGA PASS RD

Medlicott
Dome

TUOLUMNE
MEADOWS
WILDERNESS
CENTER

TUOLUMNE
MEADOWS

Lyell Fork

Mt Hoffmann
10,850ft

May Lake

Cathedral Peak
10,940ft

Elizabeth Lake

Lyell Canyon

Kuna Crest

MAY LAKE
HIGH SIERRA
CAMP

Cathedral
Lakes

John Muir Trail

Unicorn Peak

Rafferty Creek

Tenaya
Lake

Tresidder
Peak

Echo Peaks

Johnson Peak

OLMSTED
POINT

SUNRISE
HIGH SIERRA
CAMP

Sunrise
Lakes

Cathedral Range

Potter
Point

Pacific Crest Trail

Evelyn
Lake

Amelia
Earhart
Peak

John Muir Trail

Creek

Emeric
Lake

Fletcher Creek

VOGELSANG
HIGH SIERRA
CAMP

Ireland Lake

Donohue
Peak
12,023ft

Tenaya Canyon

Clouds Rest
9,926ft

Vogelsang
Peak

Bernice
Lake

Donohue
Pass

Babcock
Lake

Lewis Creek

Merced River

MERCED LAKE
HIGH SIERRA CAMP

Mt Florence
12,561ft

Mt Maclure

Mt Lyell
13,114ft

Ansel Adams

Wilderness

© AVALON TRAVEL

## Food
### Inside the Park
Food options in this area of the park are limited.

The **Tuolumne Meadows Lodge Dining Room** (Tuolumne Meadows Lodge, 209/372-8413, www.travelyosemite.com, 7am-9am and 5:45pm-8pm daily mid-June-mid-Sept., $10-28), located along the Tuolumne River, is open for breakfast and dinner. Breakfast options are limited, while dinner is more varied and can include steak, trout, a burger, or beef stew. Reservations are necessary for dinner.

The **White Wolf Lodge Dining Room** (White Wolf Lodge, www.travelyosemite.com, 7:30am-9:30am and 6pm-8pm daily mid-June-mid-Sept., $29 adults, $26 seniors, $10 children) serves up one main item each night with a few sides in a wooden building on the grounds. Dinner reservations are required.

The **Tuolumne Meadows Grill** is located in the tent-like store and serves basic fare, including burgers, hot dogs, and breakfast items.

### Outside the Park
#### Lee Vining
For a unique dining experience, stop in for a tank of gas and a meal at the ★ **Whoa Nellie Deli** (22 Vista Point Dr., CA-120 and US-395, 760/647-1088, www.whoanelliedeli.com, 7am-9pm daily Apr.-Nov., $8-12) at the Tioga Gas Mart. What other gas station deli counter serves tasty sashimi, lobster taquitos, or fish tacos with mango salsa and ginger coleslaw? This dinner menu also includes lighter fare like sandwiches. The hearty morning breakfast menu includes a grilled ribeye steak and eggs. Expect to wait in line to order at the counter, then some more to pick up food. The rowdy cooks sometimes provide impromptu dinner entertainment. Seating, both indoor and out, is at a premium during high-traffic mealtimes. Heaven help you if you arrive at the same time as a tour bus.

If you're looking for Wild West atmosphere and good spicy sauce, have dinner at **Bodie Mike's Barbecue** (51357 US-395, 760/647-6432, 11:30am-10pm daily summer, $7-25). Use your fingers to dig into barbecued ribs, chicken, beef, brisket, and more. A rustic atmosphere with rough-looking wood, red-checked tablecloths, and local patrons in cowboy boots completes your dining experience. Just don't expect the fastest service in the world. At the back of the dining room you'll find a small, dark bar populated by local characters.

The **Mono Market** (51303 US-395, 760/647-1010, www.leeviningmarket.com, 7am-10pm daily summer, 7:30am-8pm daily winter) is a great place to pick up breakfast or lunch on the go. An array of breakfast sandwiches, pastries, and wraps are made fresh daily. Messier napkin-requisite entrées can be carried out for lunch or dinner.

#### June Lake
Locals love the hearty breakfasts at the ★ **Silver Lake Resort Café** (6957 CA-158, 760/648-7525, http://silverlakeresort.net, 7am-2pm daily, $6-12), a classic home-style restaurant. There are just six tables and six seats at the bar, and lots of folks waiting to get in on summer mornings. Wake up with three-egg omelets, scrambles, breakfast burritos, and specials including steak and eggs. Lunch includes a beef burger, a buffalo meat burger, and some stacked sandwiches. Get ready to shop for a wider-waisted wardrobe!

Yet another reason to love June Lake is the **June Lake Brewery** (131 S. Crawford Ave., 858/668-6340, www.junelakebrewing.com, tasting room 11am-8pm Sun.-Thurs., 11am-9pm Fri.-Sat. summer, noon-8pm Sun.-Thurs., noon-9pm Fri.-Sat. winter). The tasting room serves pale ales, brown ales, and a porter, among others. The beams, bar, tables, and benches are made from sections of a Jeffrey pine tree that once stood 120 feet tall. Usually parked nearby, food truck **Ohanas 395** (http://ohanas395.com, noon-6pm daily) serves up Hawaiian tacos and plate lunches.

## Mammoth Lakes

Plenty of dining options cluster in Mammoth Lakes. You can get your fast-food cheeseburger and your chain double-latte here, but why would you, with so many more interesting choices?

**Petra's Bistro & Wine Bar** (6080 Minaret Rd., 760/934-3500, 5pm-9pm Tues.-Sun., $18-34) brings a bit of the California wine country all the way out to Mammoth Lakes. The menu changes seasonally, designed to please the palate and complement the wine list, an eclectic mix of vintages that highlight the best of California with a few European and South American options. The by-the-glass offerings change each night. Your server will happily cork your half-finished bottle to take home for tomorrow. Two dining rooms and a wine bar divide up the seating nicely. The atmosphere is romantic without being cave-dark. Reservations are a good idea during high season.

**Roberto's Mexican Cafe** (271 Old Mammoth Rd., 760/934-3667, http://robertoscafe.com, 11am-close daily, $11-30) serves classic California-Mexican food (chile rellenos, enchiladas, burritos, and so on) in large quantities perfect for skiers and boarders famished after a long day on the slopes (check out the huge three-combo platter). For a quiet meal, stay downstairs in the main dining room. To join in with a livelier crowd, head upstairs to the bar, which serves the full restaurant menu. Even the stoutest of drinkers should beware Roberto's lethal margaritas.

## Accommodations
### Inside the Park

In the high country, **Tuolumne Meadows Lodge** (inside U.S. 888/413-8869, outside the U.S. 602/278-8888, www.travelyosemite.com, mid-June-mid-Sept., $135) offers rustic lodgings and good food in a gorgeous subalpine meadow setting. Expect no electricity, no private baths, and no other plush amenities. What you will find are small, charming wood-frame tent cabins that sleep up to four, central bath and hot shower facilities, and a dining room. The tent cabins have beds and wood-burning stoves. The location is perfect for starting or finishing a backcountry trip through the high country.

The rustic **White Wolf Lodge** (inside U.S. 888/413-8869, outside the U.S. 602/278-8888, www.travelyosemite.com, mid-June-mid-Sept., $135-155) sits back in the trees off Tioga Pass. Amenities are few, but breathtaking scenery is everywhere. With only 28 cabins, it's a good place to get away from the crowds. You can rent either the standard wood-platform tent cabin with use of central bath and shower facilities, or a solid-wall cabin with a private bath, limited electricity, and daily maid service. All cabins and tent cabins include linens and towels.

### Outside the Park
#### Lee Vining

Located a few miles outside Yosemite's eastern Tioga Pass entrance, Lee Vining offers no-frills motels and lodges on the shores of eerily still Mono Lake.

Rent clean, comfortable, affordable lodgings at **Murphey's Motel** (51493 US-395, 760/647-6316 or 800/334-6316, www.murpheysyosemite.com, $80-175). Open all year, this motel provides one or two queen beds with cozy comforters, TVs, tables and chairs, and everything you need for a pleasant stay. Its central location in downtown Lee Vining makes dining, shopping, and trips to the visitors center and chamber of commerce convenient.

At the intersection of CA-120 and US-395, stay at the comfortable and affordable **Lake View Lodge** (51285 US-395, 800/990-6614, www.lakeviewlodgeyosemite.com, rooms $149-179, cottages $164-299). This aptly named lodge offers both motel rooms and cottages.

## Lee Vining

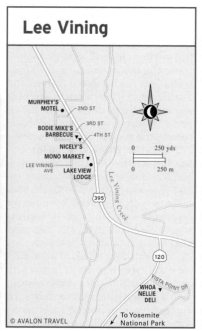

MURPHEY'S MOTEL
2ND ST
3RD ST
BODIE MIKE'S BARBECUE
4TH ST
NICELY'S
MONO MARKET
LEE VINING AVE
LAKE VIEW LODGE
0   250 yds
0   250 m
Lee Vining Creek
395
120
WHOA NELLIE DELI
VISTA POINT DR
To Yosemite National Park
© AVALON TRAVEL

The cottages can be rented in the summer only, but the motel rooms are available all year. Whether you choose a basic room for only a night or two, or larger accommodations with a kitchen for more than three days, you'll enjoy the simple country-style decor, the outdoor porches, and the views of Mono Lake. All rooms have TVs with cable, and Internet access is available. Pick up supplies at the local market for a picnic on the lawns of the lodge, or enjoy one of the nearby restaurants in Lee Vining.

### June Lake

June Lake is just 20 miles from Yosemite's eastern gate and a 30-minute drive to Tuolumne Meadows. It's off the June Lake Loop, a roadway off US-395 that's open in the summer months. A sage-scented town with fantastic mountain views, June Lake makes a fine base of operations to explore Yosemite as well as Eastern Sierra treasures, including **Bodie State Historic Park** and **Mono Lake.**

In the winter, **June Mountain** (888/586-3686, www.junemountain.com) has seven lifts that give skiers and riders access to the slopes. Summer means trout fishing, swimming, hiking, and backpacking. The mountain setting is so nice you may never want to leave.

★ **Fern Creek Lodge** (4628 CA-158, 760/648-7722, www.ferncreeklodge.com, $125-400) is the oldest year-round resort in June Lake. Its cabins are strung along a U-shaped driveway and include an old 1930s schoolhouse. Even the rustic cabins have modern conveniences like cable TV, Wi-Fi, and microwaves; all units have full kitchens. The rooms are decorated with playful fishing decor, which is no surprise since anglers flock to the area. The outdoor fireplace in the lodge's courtyard hosts barbecues, while the on-site store sells supplies.

Don't be surprised if you find yourself browsing homes for sale at June Lake's local real estate office. That was the effect it had on Hollywood celebrities like Buster Keaton, Charlie Chaplin, and Jimmy Durante. Frank Capra (director of 1946's *It's a Wonderful Life*) was so smitten with the area that he bought a cabin here. Remnants of this era can be seen at the **Heidelberg Inn** (2635 CA-158, 760/648-7781, www.heidelberginnresort.com, $179-289). Its lobby is decorated with photos of the Hollywood stars who used to hang out here. It also features a four-sided fireplace with a stuffed eight-foot California grizzly bear on top. Every unit has a bedroom, a living room, and a kitchen. Even if you don't stay at the Heidelberg, visit its lobby, which is a monument to the resort's past glory.

### Mammoth Lakes

Farther south, Mammoth Lakes offers a larger concentration of options if you are willing to drive 45 minutes from the park's eastern Tioga Pass entrance. Accommodations at Mammoth run from motels and inns to luxurious ski condos with full kitchens.

# June Lake

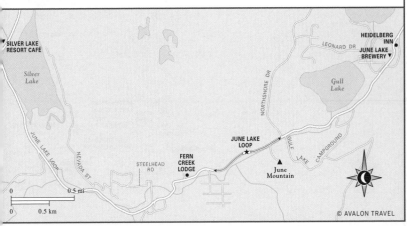

Economy rooms at the **Innsbruck Lodge** (913 Forest Trail, 760/934-3035, www.innsbrucklodge.com, $85-245) offer a queen bed, table and chairs, and access to the motel's whirlpool tub and lobby with stone fireplace at super-reasonable nightly rates. Other rooms can sleep 2-6, and some include kitchenettes. The quiet North Village location sits on the ski area shuttle route for easy access to the local slopes.

It's not cheap, but the **Juniper Springs Resort** (4000 Meridian Blvd., 800/626-6684, www.juniperspringsmammoth. com, $150-600) has absolutely every luxury amenity you could want to make your mountain getaway complete. Condos come in studio, one-bedroom, two-bedroom, three-bedroom, and townhouse sizes, sleeping up to eight people. The interiors boast stunning appointments, from snow-white down comforters to granite-topped kitchen counters to 60-inch flat-screen TVs. Baths include deep soaking tubs, perfect to relax aching muscles privately after a long day on the slopes. The resort also features heated pools year-round and three outdoor heated spas. Juniper Springs is close to local golfing and the Mammoth Mountain bike park.

## Camping
### Inside the Park

Yosemite visitors who favor the high country tend to prefer to camp rather than to stay in a lodge. Accordingly, most of Yosemite's campgrounds are north of the valley, away from the largest tourist crowds (excluding the High Sierra Camps, which are also up north).

★ **Tuolumne Meadows Campground** (Tioga Pass Rd. at Tuolumne Meadows, 877/444-6777, www.recreation.gov, reservations advised, July-late Sept., $26 family, $30 stock camp, $50 group) hosts the largest campground in the park, with over 300 individual campsites, plus four horse sites. The campground sprawls among trees and boulders. All the sites include fire rings and picnic tables along with food lockers to keep the bears at bay. Expect Tuolumne to be crowded for the whole of its season. Tuolumne is RV-friendly and has most necessary services, including food and showers available at the Tuolumne Meadows Lodge. Half the campsites can be reserved via

# Mammoth Lakes

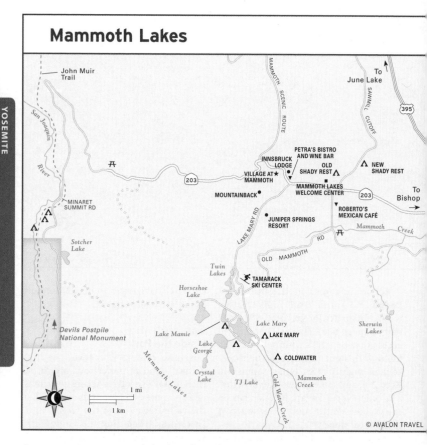

the reservation system, while the other half are first-come, first-served.

Other good-size campgrounds off Tioga Pass include **Crane Flat** (877/444-6777, www.recreation.gov, 166 campsites, RVs OK, reservations required, July-Sept., $26 family), **White Wolf** (74 campsites, no reservations, July-early Sept., $18), and **Hodgdon Meadow** (877/444-6777, www.recreation.gov, 105 campsites, reservations required mid-Apr.-mid Oct., open year-round, $26 family, $36 double, $50 group) at the west edge of the park.

If you're looking to ditch the RV traffic and crowded central visitor areas, head for **Yosemite Creek** (no reservations, $12). This tents-only campground boasts only 75 campsites on a first-come, first-served

basis July-September. There are few amenities and no on-site potable water—a good fit for campers who want to rough it. The creek flows right through the campground, perfect for cooling off on a hot day. You can even drink the water if you first treat it properly. Another no-frills option is **Tamarack Flat** (Tioga Pass Rd., 52 campsites, no reservations, late June-Sept., $12), located on Tamarack Creek, which is closer to Yosemite Valley.

The ★ **High Sierra Camps** (888/413-8869, www.travelyosemite.com, unguided trips $139-146 adults, $74-78 children, guided trips $709-1,705 adults, $94-102 children meals and lodging) at Yosemite offer far more than your average backcountry campground. Rather

# ◆ Side Trip to Death Valley

**Death Valley National Park** (760/786-3200, www.nps.gov/deva, 7-day vehicle pass $25) is a place of extremes. It's the lowest, driest, and hottest place in North America. But this park, located in the Mojave Desert, is also a place of rugged beauty, with colored badlands, impressive sand dunes, and otherworldly salt flats. It is amazing that such a place exists just four hours' drive from the waterfall-decorated granite cliffs of Yosemite.

Get the best views of the desert landscape at **Zabriskie Point,** which is breathtaking at sunrise or sunset. One of the park's most extreme places is **Badwater Basin,** the lowest point in North America at 282 feet below sea level.

To stay overnight, choose between the resort atmosphere at **Furnace Creek Inn** (Greenland Ranch Rd., 800/236-7916, www.furnacecreekresort.com, mid-Oct.-mid-May, $349-549), the motel rooms at **Furnace Creek Ranch** (CA-190, 800/236-7916, www.furnacecreekresort.com, year-round, $239-259), or the rustic

**Panamint Springs Resort** (40440 CA-190, 775/482-7680, www.panamintsprings.com, year-round, $349-539).

## Getting There

In the summer, when Tioga Pass is open, Death Valley is just a four-hour, 283-mile drive from Yosemite. Head out of the park on **CA-120 East.** After 12 miles, take **US-395 South** and continue on the scenic highway for 123 miles. Turn left to follow **CA-136 East** for 17.5 miles. Continue straight onto **CA-190 East** into the park.

In winter, when Tioga Pass is closed, it's a grueling 8.5-hour drive around the Sierra Nevada. Take **CA-41 South** out of the park's South entrance. After 62 miles, get on **CA-99 South** for another 107 miles. Then take **CA-58 East** for 58 miles. Take **Exit 167** toward Bishop and Mojave. Make a left on **CA-14** and continue for 46 miles. Get on scenic **US-395 North** for 41.5 miles before taking a right on **CA-190 Northeast,** which heads into Death Valley.

than carrying heavy packs filled with food, tents, and bedding, multiday hikers can plan to hit the High Sierra Camps, which provide tent cabins with amenities, breakfast and dinner in camp, and a box lunch to take along during the day. Choose from among the Merced Lake, Vogelsang, Glen Aulin, May Lake, and Sunrise Camp—or hike from one to the next if you get lucky. Why do you need luck? Because you can't just make a reservation to stay in a High Sierra Camp. In the fall, a lottery takes place for spots at High Sierra Camps through the following summer. You'll need to submit an application if you want to join the lottery, and even if you get a spot, there's no guarantee you'll get your preferred dates. The bottom line: If you want to experience the Yosemite backcountry, plan for a summer when you can be flexible in your dates, and start making your arrangements a year in advance.

## Outside the Park: Inyo National Forest

Out east, near US-395 and Tioga Pass, campgrounds tend to cluster in the Inyo National Forest. You can stay at **Ellery Lake** (CA-120, Upper Lee Vining Canyon, 760/873-2400, www.fs.fed.us/r5/inyo, no reservations, $21), which boasts 14 campsites perched at 9,500 feet elevation, with running water, pit toilets, and garbage cans available. Get there at dawn if you want a site on a weekend!

Another option is **Sawmill Walk-In** (Saddlebag Rd., 1.6 miles from CA-120, 760/873-2400, www.fs.fed.us/r5/inyo, June-Oct., $16). This primitive, no-reservations, hike-in campground has no water but an astonishing 9,800-foot elevation that will, after a day or two, prepare you for any high-altitude activity you want to engage in.

# Las Vegas

Las Vegas seduces the senses, indulges the appetite, and sparks the imagination. This oasis of flashing marquees, feathered showgirls, chiming slot machines, and endless buffets is a monument to fantasy.

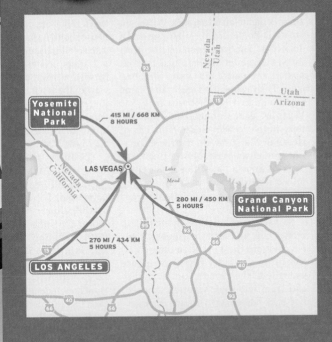

Nevada
Utah

Utah
Arizona

Yosemite National Park

415 MI / 668 KM
8 HOURS

LAS VEGAS

Lake Mead

Nevada
California

280 MI / 450 KM
5 HOURS

Grand Canyon National Park

270 MI / 434 KM
5 HOURS

LOS ANGELES

The chance at fortune has lured vacationers into the southern Nevada desert ever since the Silver State legalized gambling in 1931.

At first, the "sawdust joints"—named for the stuff spread on the floor to sop up spilled beer (and perhaps a few tears)—that popped up along downtown's Fremont Street were the center of the action, but they soon faced competition from a resort corridor blooming to the south on Highway 91. The burgeoning entertainment district reminded Los Angeles nightclub owner Billy Wilkerson of Sunset Boulevard in Hollywood, so he dubbed it "The Strip," and together with Bugsy Siegel built the Flamingo, the first upscale alternative to frontier gambling halls. Their vision left a legacy that came to define Las Vegas hotel-casinos. Las Vegas has gone through many reinventions in the decades since—from city of sleaze to Mafia haven, family destination, and upscale resort town. Today, Las Vegas is known for its fine restaurants, music festivals, and people-watching as much as its slot machines and craps tables.

So pack your stilettos, string bikini, money clip, and favorite hangover remedy and join the 35 million others who trek to Sin City every year to experience as many of the Seven Deadlies as they can cram into their vacation time. No one back home has to know you've succumbed to the city's siren song.

# Getting to Las Vegas

## From Los Angeles
Multilane highways ensure that the **270-mile, five-hour** drive from L.A. to Las Vegas is smooth, if not visually appealing.

Even mild traffic can easily add an hour or more to your trip. Take **I-10 East** past Ontario to connect to **I-15 North.** Then continue 220 miles through Victorville, Barstow, and Baker before reaching Las Vegas.

### Stopping in Calico
About two hours outside the L.A. environs, the restored boomtown of Calico is tourist-trappy but can make for a fun stop. It's just four miles off I-15 (take Exit 191 between Barstow and Yermo). The building exteriors at **Calico Ghost Town** (36600 Ghost Town Rd., Yermo, 800/86-CALICO—800/862-2542, 9am-5pm daily, $8 adults, $5 children 6-15, children under 6 free) are restored to their 1880s appearance, and they now house shops, restaurants, and attractions. The small museum, located in an original adobe building, contains original furnishings and gives a thorough overview of the town and its mining history. Pretend you're back in the Wild West: Pan for gold, ride a horse, tour the town by rail, tour a mine, and trick your eyes at the Mystery Shack (all cost extra).

The dining options stick to the ghost-town theme. At **Calico House Restaurant** (760/254-1970, 8am-5pm Sun.-Fri., 8am-7:30pm Sat., $10-20), the meat is smoked, the chili simmers all day, and Western art adorns the walls. **Lil's Saloon** (760/254-2610, 11am-5pm Mon.-Fri., 9am-5pm Sat.-Sun., $8-15) is full of Western ephemera—roulette wheels, a manual cash register, and gun collections. Munchies, including pizza, hot dogs, and giant pretzels, dominate the menu.

There's really no reason to visit the ghost town for more than a couple of hours, but overnight guests can bed down in a 4-person **cabin** (800/862-2542, www.sbcountyparks.com, $40), 6-person **mini bunkhouse** ($100), or 12- to 20-person **bunkhouse** ($80). There are 265 **camping sites** ($30-35, $25-30 seniors) for tents and RVs with full and partial hookups.

# Highlights

★ **Caesars Palace:** Caesars Palace carries on the Roman Empire's regality and decadence with over-the-top excess (page 150).

★ **Fremont Street Experience:** Part music video, part history lesson, the six-minute shows are a four-block-long, 12-million-diode, 550,000-watt burst of sensory overload (page 164).

★ **Gondola Rides:** Just like the real Grand Canal, only cleaner, The Venetian's waterway meanders along the Strip, with gondoliers providing the soundtrack (page 161).

★ **Secret Garden and Dolphin Habitat:** At The Mirage's twin habitats, the tigers, lions, and leopards can be seen playing impromptu games, while the bottlenose dolphins never resist the spotlight (page 162).

★ **High Roller:** The world's largest observation wheel overwhelms the senses with driving music, videos, and unmatched views of the Strip (page 162).

★ **Mob Museum:** Explore what some old-timers still refer to as "the good old days," when wise guys ran the town, meting out their own brand of justice (page 167).

★ **Las Vegas Springs Preserve:** The city's birthplace, these natural springs now display the area's geological, anthropological, and cultural history along with what may be its future: water-conserving "green" initiatives (page 167).

★ **Atomic Testing Museum:** Visit a fallout shelter and measure your body's radioactivity at this museum that traces the military, political, and cultural significance of the bomb (page 168).

★ *LOVE:* Cirque du Soleil's magical mystery tour features artistry, acrobatics, and Beatles music in a surreal examination of the Fab Four's legacy (page 172).

## Best Hotels

★ **Wynn:** No castles, no pyramids. Opting for class over kitsch, substance over splash, the Wynn is a worthy heir to "Old Vegas" joints (page 147).

★ **Harrah's:** It may seem middle-of-the-road, but its location puts it in the middle of the action (page 150).

★ **Bellagio:** All the romance of Italy manifests through dancing fountains, lazy gondola rides, intimate bistros, and—in case the spirit moves you—a wedding chapel (page 154).

★ **Cosmopolitan:** Part Museum of Modern Art, part *Cabaret* Kit Kat Klub, this center-Strip resort blends visual overload with sensuous swank (page 155).

★ **Aria:** The centerpiece of City Center makes no concessions to old-school Sin City, choosing an urban feel accentuated by marble, steel, glass, and silk (page 156).

★ **Mandalay Bay:** Let the conscientious staff and serene elegance of this end-of-the-Strip hotel take you away from Vegas's pounding hip-hop and clanging slot machines (page 159).

★ **Golden Nugget:** A Strip-style resort in the otherwise staid downtown district, the Nugget features a waterslide surrounded by a shark-filled aquarium (page 161).

★ **Mandarin Oriental:** Splurge for environmentally friendly luxury at this LEED-certified hotel (page 189).

## From the Grand Canyon
### From the West Rim

The good news is that the West Rim is the closest canyon point to Las Vegas—only about **120 miles,** or **2.5 hours,** even with the big detour south around the White Hills. The bad news is there's almost nothing to see along the way. If you parked and rode the shuttle from Meadview, take **Pierce Ferry Road** 39 miles down past Dolan Springs, Arizona, and pick up **US-93 North** for another 76 miles to Las Vegas.

### From the South Rim

The South Rim is roughly **280 miles** or **5 hours** from Las Vegas. Take **US-180/ AZ-64 South** for 55 miles to **Williams,** then **I-40 West** for 116 miles to **Kingman.** Here you'll connect with **US-93 North** for the final 100 miles of the journey to Las Vegas. Most summer weekends, you'll find the route crowded but manageable, unless there's an accident.

### Stopping in Kingman

Proving ground for the manifest destiny of the United States, training ground for World War II heroes, and playground for the postwar middle class, Kingman preserves and proudly displays this heritage at several well-curated museums, such as the Historic Route 66 Museum and the Mohave Museum of History and Arts.

The best restaurant for miles in any direction is **Mattina's Ristorante Italiano** (318 E. Oak St., 928/753-7504, 5pm-10pm Tues.-Sat., $13-25), where you can get perfectly prepared Italian food. It's difficult to pass up the lobster ravioli or the creamy fettuccini alfredo. Don't leave without trying the tiramisu or the key lime pie.

With a checkerboard floor, Formica tables, a long counter, and a comfort-food menu, **Rutherford's 66 Family Diner** (2011 E. Andy Devine Ave., 928/377-1660, 6am-9pm Sun.-Thurs., 6am-10pm Fri.-Sat., $8-16) is a 1950s diner straight out of Central Casting. Skillet breakfasts and

# Best Restaurants

★ **The Egg & I:** You can order something other than eggs—but given the name, why would you (page 182)?

★ **Mon Ami Gabi:** Order the baked gruyère and a baguette and channel your inner Hemingway for a traditional French bistro experience (page 186).

★ **RM Seafood:** Soft lines and brushed metal accents evoke a glittering sea, while the menu reflects Chef Rick Moonen's advocacy of sustainable fishing practices (page 186).

★ **Rose. Rabbit. Lie.:** Order six or eight

small plates per couple, and let the sultry torch singers and rousing dancers play on as you nosh the night away (page 187).

★ **Le Thai:** The best of Las Vegas's impressive roster of Thai restaurants boasts playful interpretations of traditional cuisine in a trendy yet unpretentious atmosphere (page 187).

★ **Phat Phrank's:** The no-frills presentation keeps the focus on the food: California- and New Mexico-inspired variations of traditional Mexican fare (page 188).

steak and meatloaf sandwiches will have you waxing nostalgic.

There are several affordable basic hotels on Andy Devine Avenue (Route 66) in Kingman's downtown area, some of them with retro road-trip neon signs and Route 66 themes. The Hollywood-themed **El Trovatore Motel** (1440 E. Andy Devine Ave., 928/692-6520, $56-76) boasts that Marilyn Monroe, James Dean, and Clark Gable all slept there. One of only a handful of prewar motels left in town, the motel retains its art deco sign and architecture. Rooms, which command views of the Hualapai Mountains, are utilitarian, with king or queen beds, a microwave, and a fridge. Pets are welcome.

The small, affordable **Hill Top Motel** (1901 E. Andy Devine Ave., 928/753-2198, www.hilltopmotelaz.com, $47-55) beckons Route 66 road-trippers with a 1950s-era neon sign even cooler than El Trovatore's. The motel maintains its nostalgic charms despite the addition of a swimming pool and in-room refrigerators and microwaves. Although it's located in the city center, the motel's guest rooms still overlook the mountains and are set back from the main streets, making use of block walls to deflect city noise.

## From the North Rim

From the North Rim, it's a **5.5-hour, 280-mile** drive to Vegas. This route may appeal to canyon lovers, as it takes drivers through Utah's Zion National Park for another opportunity to view nature's handiwork with stone, wind, and water. Only attempt this route during good weather; AZ-67 is subject to closure early November-late May, and all facilities at the North Rim are closed mid-October-mid-May. From the North Rim, take **AZ-67 North** for 44 miles to **Jacob Lake** and head east on **US-89A** for 15 miles to **Fredonia.** Then take **AZ-389 West,** which becomes **UT-59 North,** for 55 miles to **Hurricane,** Utah. There pick up **UT-9 West** for 11 miles to **US-15 South.** From there it's 125 miles to Las Vegas.

## Stopping in Overton

Crossing into Nevada and approaching Glendale, look for the Overton exit. Twelve miles off the highway, Overton is a compact agricultural community whose downtown is strung along several blocks of NV-169, also known as Moapa Valley Boulevard and Main Street. Overton offers two strong lunch options. **Sugars Home Plate** (309 S. Moapa Valley Blvd., 702/397-8084, 7am-9pm

# Las Vegas

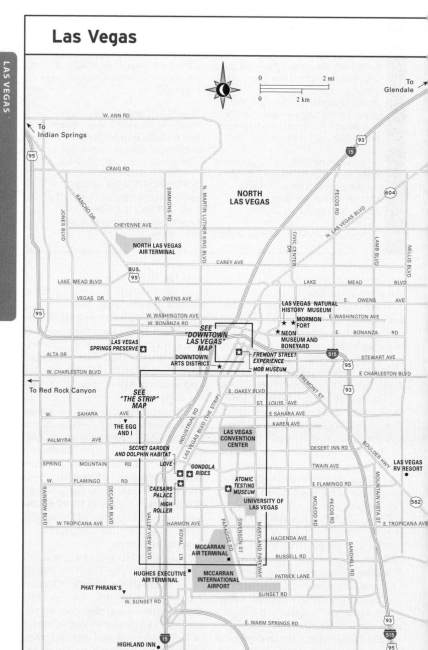

© AVALON TRAVEL

Tues.-Sun., $9-25) serves $7.50 bacon and eggs, $8-10 burgers—including the Sugar Burger, a cheeseburger with Polish sausage—and homemade pie. There's also a sports bar with bar-top video poker and sports memorabilia. Just a block away, **Inside Scoop** (395 S. Moapa Valley Blvd., 702/397-2055, 11am-8pm Mon.-Sat., 11am-7pm Sun., $10-25) has filling sandwiches and 30-plus ice cream flavors. The baked potatoes come with whatever toppings you can imagine.

The **Plaza Motel** (207 Moapa Valley Blvd., 702/397-2414, $50-60) provides basic guest rooms and a jumping-off point for visits to Valley of Fire State Park.

## From Yosemite

If there's any chance that **Tioga Pass** might be closed, which generally happens October-May, check with the **National Park Service** (209/372-0200, www.nps. gov/yose) for the latest **road conditions.** If the pass is open, you have your choice of two fairly direct routes to Las Vegas; both start by heading on **CA-120 East** through the pass to Mono Lake. If the pass is closed, prepare for a tedious **8- to 10-hour** trip through central California: **CA-41 South** to Fresno, **CA-99 South** to Bakersfield, and then **CA-58 East** to Barstow.

### Via Tioga Pass: Nevada Route

The quickest route covers **415 miles,** with a typical driving time of **8 hours.** Follow **CA-120 East** to **Benton,** California (3 hours, 15 minutes). Take **US-6 East** to **Coaldale,** Nevada (35 minutes), where it shares the road with **US-95 South** for another 40 minutes to **Tonopah.** It's then a 210-mile, 3.5-hour straight shot on **US-95** to Las Vegas.

### Stopping in Tonopah

Tonopah is a natural crossroads that rewards travelers with colorful mining history and one of the darkest starry skies in the country. Its restaurants specialize in old-fashioned American food and Mexican fare. The salsa seals the deal at **El Marquez** (348 N. Main St., 775/482-3885, 11am-9pm Tues.-Sun., $10-20), where the enchiladas and cheesy chiles rellenos rule. If you're in a hurry but still jonesing for Mexican, hit the drive-through at **Cisco's Restaurant** (10am-8:30pm Mon.-Sat., $10-15), which has burgers, pizza, and ribs as well. How about a beer and some barbecue? **Tonopah Brewing Co.** (315 S. Main St., 775/482-2000, www.tonopahbrewing.com, 11am-9pm daily, $9-27) is your stop. Taste its on-site brewed beers in pint or pitcher form along with some delicious barbecued meats, including ribs cooked for at least seven hours.

The owners have faithfully restored the **Mizpah Hotel** (100 N. Main St., 775/482-3030, $100-165), the "Grand Lady of Tonopah," with claw-foot tubs, wrought-iron bedsteads, and lots of carmine accents. You can dine on-site at the casual **Pittman Café** (6am-10pm daily, $10-15). Next door, the guest rooms at **Jim Butler Motel** (100 S. Main St., 775/482-3577, $80-100) are bright and inviting, with wood furniture and faux hearths. Some guest rooms have fridges and microwaves; all have free Wi-Fi.

### Via Tioga Pass: California Route

Only a few miles farther but 45 minutes longer, an arguably more scenic route—taking **US-395 South** from CA-120, rather than continuing on to US-6—traverses Mammoth Lakes, Bishop, and Lone Pine, California, and includes views of Mount Whitney and the possibility of an overnight stay at Death Valley National Park. Follow **CA-120 East** to **US-395 South.** At Lone Pine, California, take **CA-136 East.** This becomes **CA-190 West,** which winds through Death Valley. A left turn onto the **Daylight Pass Road** leads to the Nevada border and **NV-374 North** just before **Beatty.** From Beatty, **US-95 South** leads 117 miles to Las Vegas.

## Stretch Your Legs

Ever wonder what it would be like to live upside down? Satisfy your curiosity at the **Upside-Down House** (Yosemite-Las Vegas Dr., corner of 1st Ave. and Matley Ave., Lee Vining, 760/647-6461, 10am-4pm Thurs.-Tues., Memorial Day-mid-Sept., $2), just a block off US-395 outside Yosemite National Park. Inspired by the children's stories "Upside Down Land" and "The Upsidedownians," the small wooden cabin features a bed, a rug, and furniture on the ceiling.

The infamous Area 51 is the focus of conspiracy theories about UFOs. Capitalizing on its location just south of the secret military installation, the **Area 51 Alien Travel Center** (Yosemite-Las Vegas Dr., 2711 E. US-95, Amargosa Valley, 775/372-5678) sells all sorts of extraterrestrial-influenced merchandise. Painted fluorescent yellow, it's hard to miss. (This being Nevada, there's also a brothel out back.)

**Last Stop Arizona** (Yosemite-Las Vegas Dr., 20606 N. US-93, White Hills, 928/767-4911, www.arizonalaststop.com, gift store 6:30am-8pm daily, restaurant 7am-6pm daily) also celebrates life on other planets. Pose for a photo in an alien cutout display and fill up your tank with "Uranus" gas. There's also a diner and a quirky gift shop, which doubles as a source of Powerball lottery tickets.

### Stopping in Beatty

Once a center of Nevada mining, Beatty is a microcosm of Western history, serving at various times as a Shoshone settlement, a ranching center, and a railway hub.

The meals at ★ **KC's Outpost** (100 E. Main St., 775/553-9175, 10am-10pm daily, $8-12) use homemade bread and meats roasted on-site. The Old West charm includes a lively barroom separate from the dining room and a faux jail cell where your darling desperados can burn off some car-trip energy.

The laundry room and small pool and spa at **Death Valley Inn** (651 US 95 S., 775/553-9400, $80-100) are welcome amenities greeting road-weary travelers. There's also a 39-space RV park—all pull-throughs with 50-amp hookups. Originally serving defense contractor employees at the Nevada Test Site and Area 51, the **Atomic Inn** (350 S. 1st St., 775/553-2250, $70-80) has standard guest rooms, with lots of golds and honey-blond wood furniture and paneling.

### Bypassing Tioga Pass

If Tioga Pass is closed—ugh. The only way to Las Vegas is an ugly **8- to 10-hour,** 500-mile ordeal. Take **CA-41 South** 95 miles to **Fresno** (2.5 hours), then follow **CA-99 South** to **Bakersfield** (1 hour 45 minutes). Continue on **CA-58 East** to **Barstow** (2 hours 15 minutes) before catching **US-95 North** to Las Vegas (2.5 hours).

### Stopping in Bakersfield

While far from a tourist destination, Bakersfield is at least a diversion on the otherwise dreary winter Yosemite-Las Vegas route.

You wouldn't think cabbage could form the basis for a hearty and satisfying meal. But you'd be proven wrong if you visit **Bit of Germany** (1901 Flower St., 661/325-8874, 11am-2pm and 5pm-8pm Mon.-Sat., $10-15). Stuffed, rolled, or shredded into a salad, the cabbage puts Bit of Germany "head" and shoulders above any other German joint in town. It offers a solid selection of Bavarian beers, and the wurst (brat, knack, and weiss) is among the best.

More highbrow, **Uricchio's Trattoria** (1400 17th St., 661/326-8870, 11am-2pm and 5pm-9pm Mon.-Thurs., 11am-2pm and 5pm-10pm Fri., 5pm-10pm Sat., $15-30) serves the best chicken *piccata*; seafood fans can't go wrong with the diver scallops or orange roughy almandine.

Skip the chains and treat yourself to lodgings with character. With eight stories of Spanish colonial revival architecture, the **Padre Hotel** (1702 18th St., 888/443-3387, $129-199) has been faithfully restored to its 1930s grandeur. But the rooms are strictly 21st century, with sleek furniture and plush textiles. Kick off your shoes, soak in a chromatherapy spa tub, then snuggle into a fine down comforter to guarantee a fine night's rest. Or bust a move in the hotel's 5th-floor Prospect Lounge.

A few blocks west, the guest rooms at **Hotel Rosedale** (2400 Camino Del Rio Ct., 661/327-0681, $79-149) lure guests with their springy umber, burnt orange, and green decor. The oversize pool is surrounded by plenty of shade and shrubbery. A small playground will keep little tykes busy, while an arcade ensures older children don't lose their video-game dexterity while on vacation.

## By Air and Bus
### Air
More than 900 planes arrive or depart **McCarran International Airport** (LAS, 5757 Wayne Newton Blvd., 702/261-5211, www.mccarran.com) every day, making it the sixth busiest in the country and 19th in the world. Terminal 1 hosts domestic flights, while Terminal 3 has domestic and international flights.

About 40 percent of the runway traffic at McCarran belongs to **Southwest Airlines,** by far the largest carrier serving Las Vegas. Other major players include **United, Delta, American,** and **Spirit.** The number of airlines keeps fares competitive. Given that Las Vegas is one of the world's top tourist destinations, it's best to make your reservations as early as possible. Last-minute deals are few and far between, and you'll pay through the nose to fly to Vegas on a whim.

United and Virgin offer round-trip **flights from San Francisco** for as low as $170-220, when booked well in advance. Flight time is 1.5 hours. **Flights from Los Angeles** (LAX or Long Beach) are available on Spirit and JetBlue for as low as $175-200, even at the last minute. Virgin, Delta, and United will do the job for $230 or so. Flight time is 70 minutes.

McCarran Airport provides easy transfers to the Las Vegas Strip using **shuttle vans, buses,** and **rental cars.** Limousines are available curbside for larger groups. A **taxi ride** from the airport to the Strip (15 minutes) or downtown (20 minutes) runs no more than $25. A $2 surcharge is assessed for pickups from the airport, and there is a $3 credit card processing fee. It's cheaper and often faster to take the surface streets from the airport to your destination rather than the freeway, which is several miles longer.

### Bus
Las Vegas City Area Transit **buses** serve the airport. **Route 108** runs north from McCarran on Swenson Street, and the closest it comes to Las Vegas Boulevard is the corner of Paradise Road and West Sahara Avenue, but you can connect with the **Las Vegas Monorail** at several stops. If you're headed downtown, stay on the bus to the end of its 45-minute line. Alternately, grab the Route 109 bus, which runs east of the 108 up Maryland Parkway. To get to the Strip, you have to transfer at the large cross streets onto westbound buses that cross the Strip. The northbound 109 stops at Tropicana Avenue, Flamingo Road, Desert Inn Road, Sahara Avenue, and Charleston Boulevard. Route 109 also ends up at the Downtown Transportation Center. Bus fare is $2, with passes of varying duration available. Travel time is 20-35 minutes, depending on how far north your hotel is located.

**Gray Line** is one of several companies that will ferry you via airport shuttle to your Strip ($12 round-trip) or downtown ($16 round-trip) hotel. All have ticket kiosks inside the terminals, most near the baggage claim. These shuttles run continuously, leaving about every 15 minutes. You don't need reservations from the airport, but you will need reservations from your hotel to return to the airport.

The **Greyhound station** (200 S. Main St., 702/383-9792, www.greyhound.com) is on the south side of the Plaza Hotel. Buses arrive and depart frequently throughout the day and night to and from all points in North America, and they are a reasonable alternative to driving or flying.

Five of six buses originating at the **San Francisco station** (200 Folsom St., 415/495-1569) arrive in Las Vegas each day after 12- to 17-hour slogs through California and Nevada. Tickets can be had for as little as $27, if booked well in advance, purchased online and without the possibility of a refund. Last-minute tickets with the same stipulations are $50-60, and standard rates are 25-50 percent higher.

Eight to ten Greyhounds arrive from the **Los Angeles terminal** (1716 E. 7th St., 213/629-8401) each day. Travel time can be as little as five hours, with a single stop in either San Bernardino or Barstow. Rates are a reasonable $15-30, with some as low as $6 when purchased well ahead of time.

**Megabus** (Patsaouras Transit Plaza, One Gateway Plaza, Los Angeles, 877/462-6342) runs four buses a day from Los Angeles for $28-30 per person. It delivers passengers to the Regional Transportation Center's South Strip Transfer Terminal. Those heading to the Strip or downtown can catch the "Deuce" double-decker bus at Bay 14. It runs 24 hours a day, seven days a week, and the next one will be there in less than 15 minutes.

# Orientation

Las Vegas Boulevard South—better known as the Strip—is the city's focal point, with 14 of the 25 largest hotels in the world welcoming gamblers and hedonists from around the world. Six of the world's 10 biggest hostelries line a four-mile north-south stretch between Tropicana and Sahara Avenues. Running parallel to I-15, this is what most folks think of when someone says "Vegas."

Major east-west thoroughfares include Tropicana Avenue, Harmon Avenue, Flamingo Road, Spring Mountain Road, Desert Inn Road, and Sahara Avenue. Koval Lane and Paradise Road parallel the Strip to the east, while Frank Sinatra Drive does likewise to the west, giving a tour of the loading docks and employee parking lots of some of the world's most famous resorts.

I-15 also mirrors the Strip to the east, as both continue north-northeast through **downtown** and its casino and arts districts. Main Street juts due south at Charleston Boulevard and joins Las Vegas Boulevard at the Stratosphere. The Strip and I-15 continue parallel southeast and south out of town.

# Casinos

## Upper Strip

Ranging from Spring Mountain Road to the Stratosphere, the **Upper Strip** is known for its throwback swagger, but has something for everyone. Visitors can opt for world-class art, celebrity chef creations, midway games, stand-up comedy—and friendly rates at old standby casinos.

### Stratosphere Casino, Hotel, and Tower

**Restaurants:** Top of the World, McCalls, Nunzio's Pizzeria, Fellini's, Stratosphere Buffet, Roxy's Diner, Mookies, Tower Creamery, Starbucks, McDonald's,

## Two Days in Las Vegas

### Day 1

Pick a hotel based on your taste and budget. We suggest **The Linq,** close to the High Roller observation wheel, fine dining, hip watering holes, and rocking live music venues.

Get your gambling fix for a few hours before heading across the street for brunch at The Mirage's **Cravings Buffet.** It operates on a familiar theory, with separate stations highlighting different cuisines. After the gorge-fest, you'll be ready for a nap, and you'll need it. This is Vegas; no early nights for you!

Couples should start the evening off with a romantic dinner at Paris's **Mon Ami Gabi.** For a more modest meal, the eponymous offering at The Venetian's **B&B Burger & Beer** hits the spot. If you only have time for one show, make it *LOVE* at The Mirage. The show is a loose biography of the Beatles' creative journey, told by tumblers, roller skaters, clowns, and the characters from John, Paul, George, and Ringo's songs—Eleanor Rigby, Lucy in the Sky, and Sgt. Pepper.

### Day 2

Celebrate the kitsch and class of vintage Vegas. Head downtown to stock up on Elvis sideburns and Sammy Davis Jr. sunglasses before loading up on eggs Benedict and 1970s flair at the **Peppermill Restaurant & Fireside Lounge.** While it's daylight, make your way to the **Neon Museum and Boneyard,** the final resting place of some of Las Vegas's iconic signage. And while you're in the neighborhood, witness the rise and fall of the Mafia in Las Vegas at the **Mob Museum.**

Back at the hotel, change into your glad rags and beat it over to the Tuscany's **Copa Room.** Order up a neat bourbon and watch Sinatra try to make it through a rendition of "Luck Be a Lady" while Dino and Sammy heckle and cut up from the wings in *The Rat Pack Is Back.* Then get out there and gamble into the wee hours! For a chance to rub elbows with celebrities, head over to **XS** at the Wynn. Expect celebrity DJs, a major party, and steep prices.

---

El Nopal Mexican Grill, Wok Vegas, Chicago Hot Dog Construction Co.

**Entertainment:** *MJ Live, Spy Escape & Evasion, World's Greatest Rock Show,* L.A. Comedy Club

**Attractions:** SkyJump, Top of the Tower thrill rides, Elation Pool, Radius Pool, Observation Deck, Roni Josef Spa, Tower Shops, Fitness Center

**Nightlife:** Margarita Bay, Sin City Hops, Air Bar, CBar, 107 Sky Lounge

It's altitude with attitude at this 1,149-foot-tall exclamation point on the north end of the Strip. The **Stratosphere Tower** (2000 Las Vegas Blvd. S., 702/380-7777, www.stratospherehotel.com, $103-146) is the brainchild of entrepreneur, politician, and professional poker player Bob Stupak. Daredevils will delight in the 40-mph quasi-freefall at SkyJump, along with the other vertigo-inducing thrill rides on the tower's observation deck. The more faint-of-heart may want to steer clear not only of the rides but

also the resort's double-decker elevators, which launch guests to the top of the tower at 1,400 feet per minute. But even acrophobes should conquer their fears long enough to enjoy the views from the restaurant and bars more than 100 floors up, where the **Chapel in the Clouds** can also ensure a heavenly beginning to married life.

If the thrill rides on the observation deck aren't your style, get a rush of gambling action on the nearly 100,000-square-foot ground-floor casino. Or perhaps the two swimming pools (one is tops-optional) and the dozen bars and restaurants are more your speed.

Spot-on impersonators and elaborate choreography make the Stratosphere's two tribute shows among the best in town. Each night, one of two Michael Jackson impersonators takes the stage at *MJ Live* (daily 7pm, $61-90), backed

LAS VEGAS

# Las Vegas Strip

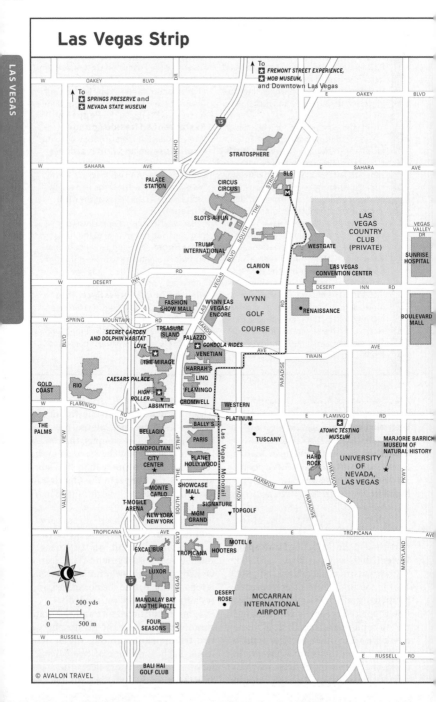

To ⭐ FREMONT STREET EXPERIENCE, ⭐ MOB MUSEUM, and Downtown Las Vegas

To ⭐ SPRINGS PRESERVE and ⭐ NEVADA STATE MUSEUM

STRATOSPHERE

W OAKEY BLVD DR E OAKEY BLVD

W SAHARA AVE E SAHARA AVE

SLS

PALACE STATION

CIRCUS CIRCUS

LAS VEGAS COUNTRY CLUB (PRIVATE)

VEGAS VALLEY DR

SLOTS-A-FUN

WESTGATE

SUNRISE HOSPITAL

TRUMP INTERNATIONAL

CLARION

LAS VEGAS CONVENTION CENTER

W DESERT INN RD E DESERT INN RD

FASHION SHOW MALL

WYNN LAS VEGAS/ ENCORE

WYNN GOLF COURSE

RENAISSANCE

BOULEVARD MALL

W SPRING MOUNTAIN RD

SECRET GARDEN AND DOLPHIN HABITAT

TREASURE ISLAND

PALAZZO

LOVE

THE MIRAGE

GONDOLA RIDES

VENETIAN

SANDS AVE

TWAIN AVE

CAESARS PALACE

HARRAH'S

LINQ

GOLD COAST

RIO

HIGH ROLLER

FLAMINGO

PARADISE

W FLAMINGO RD

ABSINTHE

CROMWELL

WESTERN

E FLAMINGO RD

THE PALMS

BELLAGIO

PLATINUM

ATOMIC TESTING MUSEUM

BALLY'S

TUSCANY

MARJORIE BARRICK MUSEUM OF NATURAL HISTORY

COSMOPOLITAN

PARIS

CITY CENTER

PLANET HOLLYWOOD

HARD ROCK

UNIVERSITY OF NEVADA, LAS VEGAS

PKWY

MONTE CARLO

SHOWCASE MALL

HARMON AVE

T-MOBILE ARENA

SIGNATURE

TOPGOLF

NEW YORK NEW YORK

MGM GRAND

SWENSON ST

W TROPICANA AVE E TROPICANA AVE

EXCALIBUR

TROPICANA

MOTEL 6

HOOTERS

MARYLAND

LUXOR

MANDALAY BAY AND THE HOTEL

DESERT ROSE

MCCARRAN INTERNATIONAL AIRPORT

FOUR SEASONS

0 500 yds
0 500 m

W RUSSELL RD E RUSSELL RD

BALI HAI GOLF CLUB

© AVALON TRAVEL

by a full cast of dancers, a live band, and a dazzling array of lighting effects in the Stratosphere Theater. Similarly, *World's Greatest Rock Show* (Tues.-Sun., $35-45) captures classic artists' sounds and mannerisms, with doppelgangers of Van Halen, Journey, Bruce Springsteen, Kiss, and other arena rock gods.

**Roxy's Diner** (daily 24 hours, $10-15) is a trip back to the malt shop for comfort food, red vinyl booths, checkered floors, and wisecracking waitstaff.

## Lucky Dragon

**Restaurants:** Pearl Ocean, Phoenix, Cha Garden, Dragon's Alley, Bao Now
**Attractions:** Sothys Spa
**Nightlife:** Pagoda Bar, Atrium Bar

Swathed in red for good fortune and surrounding a pagoda-shaped bar, the 27,000-square-foot casino floor at the **Lucky Dragon** (300 W. Sahara Ave., www.luckydragonlv.com, 702/889-2018, $108-228) spreads Eastern-style games such as pai gow and baccarat, with only the occasional blackjack table sprinkled in.

Strip views and dainty, intimate tables and chairs resembling porcelain teacups set just the right mood for sampling the modern and adventurous Chinese fare at **Phoenix** (5pm-10pm Mon.-Fri., 5pm-11pm Sat.-Sun., $28-40). Dare you order the deer tendon or sea cucumber?

The Lucky Dragon's rooms are largish at 415 square feet, with complimentary water and tea. The decor is airy and light; the cherry blossom murals over the bed add to the relaxing atmosphere.

## SLS

**Restaurants:** Katsuya, Bazaar Meat, Cleo, Umami Burger, 800 Degrees, Northside Café & Chinese Kitchen, The Perq
**Entertainment:** The Foundry, Sayers Club
**Attractions:** Foxtail Pool
**Nightlife:** Foxtail, Center Bar, Monkey Bar, W Living Room

On the site of the legendary Sahara Casino, **SLS** (2535 Las Vegas Blvd. S., 702/761-7000, www.slslasvegas.com, $139-249) draws 21st-century Frank and Sammy wannabes and the rest of the swanky sophisticate set. It's Rat Pack cool, filtered through modern hipsterism.

Two towers offer standard rooms of 325-360 square feet, with suites measuring up to a spacious 730 square feet. All standard accommodations boast 55-inch televisions, minibars and snacks at no extra charge, soft pastel accents, and 310-thread-count sheets atop BeautyRest mattresses. A third tower is the independent **W Hotel**, where guests in the European-accented rooms enjoy their own entrance, pool, and spa.

Chef Jose Andres doesn't want guests at **Bazaar Meat** (Sun.-Thurs. 5:30pm-10pm, Fri.-Sat. 5:30pm-11pm, $65-140) ordering a huge bone-in rib eye, rack of lamb, or inch-thick tuna steak. He wants you to try them all. His Spanish-influenced meat-centric dishes are meant to be shared. The restaurant's decor reinforces that aim with long communal tables, open cooking stations, and a small gaming area.

**Sayers Club** (Thurs.-Sat. 10pm-2am) bills itself as a live-music venue. There's plenty of live indie pop, folk, and psychobilly bands on weekends, but with lots of open space and an industrial-warehouse feel, it's a natural environment for DJs. The go-go cages, platforms, and poles seem imported en masse from the Sayers' original location on L.A.'s Hollywood Boulevard.

## Wynn Las Vegas/Encore

**Restaurants:** Andrea's, Costa Di Mare, Country Club, Lakeside Seafood, Mizumi, Sinatra, SW Steakhouse, Tableau, Wing Lei, The Buffet, Allegro, La Cave, Drugstore Café, Jardin, Red 8 Asian Bistro, Wazuzu, Terrace Point Cafe
**Entertainment:** Le Rêve, Encore Theater
**Attractions:** Lake of Dreams, Wynn Golf Course, Esplanade shopping, Wynn Salon and Spa, Encore Salon and Spa, fitness center, pools
**Nightlife:** Surrender, Intrigue, Encore Beach Club, Eastside Lounge, Lobby Bar, Players Bar, Parasol Up, Parasol Down, Tower Suite Bar, Encore Players Lounge

An eponymous monument to indulgence, ★ **Wynn** (3131 Las Vegas Blvd. S., 702/770-7000 or 888/320-9966, www.wynnlasvegas.com, $200-450) is mogul Steve Wynn's $2.5 billion invitation to wallow in the good life. Gaze at Wynn's art, one of the best and most valuable private collections in the world. The appropriately named **Encore** is next door. The twins' opulence is matched with casino areas awash in red—carpet, tapestries, and neon. Although guests come to explore the privileges of wealth, they can also experience the wonders of nature without the inconvenience of bugs and dirt. Lush plants, waterfalls, lakes, and mountains dominate the pristine landscape. Plans call for further growth with the construction of **Paradise Park**, a 20-acre sandy lagoon and waterfront entertainment complex. The lake will be big enough for waterskiing and non-motorized boating, while bars, boutiques, ice cream stands, and nightly fireworks will tempt beachcombers.

In addition to the gourmet offerings, don't miss the dim sum and Hong Kong barbecue at **Red 8 Asian Bistro** (11:30am-midnight Sun.-Thurs., 11:30am-1am Fri.-Sat., $20-40). Then party to excess at **XS** ($20-50) where Skrillex, David Guetta, or some other world-class DJ is likely to be spinning this weekend.

The formal sophistication belies the hotels' location on the site of the old Desert Inn, with the unselfconscious swagger Frank, Dino, and Sammy brought to the joint. Both towers boast some of the biggest guest rooms and suites on the Strip, with the usual (although better-quality) amenities, including 55-inch TVs, and a few extra touches, like remote-controlled drapes, lights, and air-conditioning. Wynn's guest rooms are appointed in wheat, honey, and other creatively named shades of beige. Encore's all-suite accommodations are more colorful, with the color scheme running toward dark chocolate and cream.

## Center Strip

The **Center Strip** is between Harmon Avenue and Spring Mountain Road. The casinos are packed tight, and though the sidewalks can become masses of humanity on weekend nights, all the temptations are within walking distance.

### The Venetian

**Restaurants:** AquaKnox, B&B Burger & Beer, B&B Ristorante, Bouchon, Bouchon Bakery, Café Presse, Chica, Delmonico Steakhouse, Grand Lux Café, Juice Farm, Noodle Asia, Public House, Sugarcane, Yardbird, Zio Gelato, Buddy V's Ristorante, Canaletto, Canonita, Carlo's Bakery, Casanova, Cocolini, Lobster ME, Mercato Della Perscheria, Otto Enoteca Pizzeria, Tao Asian Bistro, Coffee Bean and Tea Leaf, Trattoria Reggiano, Zeffirino, Food Court
**Entertainment:** *Human Nature Juke Box*
**Attractions:** Madame Tussauds Las Vegas, gondola rides, Streetmosphere, Grand Canal Shoppes
**Nightlife:** Tao Nightclub, Bellini Bar, The Dorsey, Sin City Brewing Co., Rockhouse, Fat Tuesday

**The Venetian** (3355 Las Vegas Blvd. S., 702/414-1000 or 866/659-9643, www.venetian.com, $209-349) comes close to capturing the elegance of Venice. An elaborate faux-Renaissance ceiling fresco greets visitors in the hotel lobby, and the sensual treats just keep coming. A life-size streetscape—with replicas of the Bridge of Sighs, Doge's Palace, the Grand Canal, and other treasures—gives the impression that the best of the Queen of the Adriatic has been transplanted in toto. Tranquil rides in authentic **gondolas** with serenading pilots are perfect for relaxing after a hectic session in the 120,000-square-foot casino. Canalside, buskers entertain the guests in the **Streetmosphere** (St. Mark's Square, noon-6pm daily on the hour, free), and the **Grand Canal Shoppes** (10am-11pm Sun.-Thurs., 10am-midnight Fri.-Sat.) entice strollers, window-shoppers, and serious spenders.

World-class DJs, A-list celebrities, and wall-to-wall hardbodies pack **Tao Nightclub** (10:30pm-5am Thurs.-Sat.) at the end of each week to groove to thumping house and hip-hop. Reservations and advance tickets are recommended, as this is one of the hottest party spots in town, with a powerful light and sound system, two dance rooms, and open architecture. Scattered throughout, bathing beauties luxuriate, covered (more or less) only by rose petals.

After you've shopped till you're ready to drop, **Madame Tussauds Las Vegas** (10am-8pm Sun.-Thurs., 10am-9pm Fri.-Sat., adults $30, ages 4-12 $20, under age 4 free) invites stargazers for hands-on experiences with their favorite entertainers, superheroes, and athletes.

Fine dining options abound. Try the lobster ravioli or traditional pizza and pasta dishes in the bistro setting of **Trattoria Reggiano** (10am-midnight daily, $20-30). Or step away from the Italian theme and go French at Thomas Keller's **Bouchon** (702/414-6200, 7am-1pm and 5pm-10pm Mon.-Thurs., 7am-2pm and 5pm-10pm Sat.-Sun., $30-65). Try the sensational croque madame sandwich with its rich Mornay sauce, or climb a tower of French fries to recover from a night in Sin City. The luxe setting features high ceilings, wood columns, and tile floors.

The Venetian spares no expense in the hotel department. Its 4,027 suites are tastefully appointed with plum accents and Italian (of course) marble, and at 650 square feet, they're big. They include sunken living rooms and Roman tubs.

### The Palazzo

**Restaurants:** Carnevino, Coffee Bean and Tea Leaf, Cut, Grand Lux Café, Hong Kong Café, Illy Coffee, Juice Farm, Lagasse's Stadium, Lavo, Morels Steakhouse & Bistro, Café Presse, Grimaldi's Pizzeria, Sushisamba, Table 10

**Entertainment:** *Baz—Star Crossed Love*

**Attractions:** Grand Canal Shoppes, Atrium Waterfall

**Nightlife:** Fusion Latin Mixology Bar, Laguna Champagne Bar, Lavo Lounge, Double Helix Wine and Whiskey Bar

An 80-foot domed skylight illuminates a faux-ice sculpture, bronze columns, and lush landscaping surrounding the lobby at **The Palazzo** (3325 Las Vegas Blvd. S., 702/607-7777 or 866/263-3001, www.palazzo.com, $239-349). Motel 6 this ain't. A big chunk of the 100,000-square-foot casino is smoke-free, embodying the casino's efforts toward energy efficiency and environmentally friendly design.

The Palazzo is a gourmand's dream, with a handful of four-star establishments dominated, as you would expect, by Italian influences. **Carnevino** (5pm-11pm daily, $40-75) is light and bright, with snootiness kept to a minimum, especially during the Taverna lunch (noon-midnight daily, $20-40). That does not mean chef Mario Batali skimps on quality. He selects the best cuts and refrains from overwhelming them in preparation. Wine shares top billing in the restaurant's name, so you know the cellar is excellent.

Accommodations are all suites, measuring even larger than The Venetian's, with Roman tubs, sunken living rooms, and sumptuous beds that would make it tough to leave the room if not for the lure of the Strip.

### The Mirage

**Restaurants:** Tom Colicchio's Heritage Steak, Fin, Otoro, Portofino, Cravings Buffet, Carnegie Delicatessen, Paradise Café, Samba, Pantry, LVB Burger, Stack, Paradise Café, California Pizza Kitchen, Blizz Frozen Yogurt, The Roasted Bean

**Entertainment:** *LOVE*, Terry Fator, Boys II Men, Aces of Comedy

**Attractions:** Secret Garden and Dolphin Habitat, Aquarium, Mirage Volcano, Atrium

**Nightlife:** 1 Oak, Rhumbar, The Still, The Sports Bar, Lobby Bar, Parlor Cocktail Lounge, Heritage Steak Lounge, Stack Lounge, Otoro Lounge, Portofino Lounge

**The Mirage** (3400 Las Vegas Blvd. S., 702/791-7111 or 800/627-6667, www.mirage.com, $140-300) was the first "understated" megaresort, starting a trend that brought Vegas full circle to the mature pursuits it was built on—gourmet dining, lavish production shows, hip music, and hard liquor. This Bali Hai-themed paradise lets guests bask in the wonders of nature alongside the sophistication and pampering of resort life. More an oasis than a mirage, the hotel greets visitors with exotic bamboo, orchids, banana trees, secluded grottoes, and peaceful lagoons. Dolphins, white tigers, stingrays, sharks, and a volcano provide livelier sights.

The Mirage's guest rooms have tasteful appointments and some of the most comfortable, down-comforter beds in town. The standard 396-square-foot rooms emit a modern and relaxing feel in golds, blacks, and splashes of tangerine, mauve, and ruby.

Bump and grind at **1 Oak** (10:30pm-4am Wed., Fri., Sat.), an urban space with lots of hip-hop and gritty, socially aware artwork. Two separate rooms have bars, DJs, and crowded dance floors. With dark walls and sparse lighting, it's a sinful, sexy venue for the beautiful people to congregate.

The Mirage commands performances by the world's top headliners, but Cirque du Soleil's Beatles show *LOVE* packs 'em in every night for a celebration of the Fab Four's music.

### Harrah's

**Restaurants:** Ruth's Chris Steak House, Flavors the Buffet, Oyster Bar, Ben & Jerry's, Toby Keith's I Love This Bar & Grill, Fulton Street Food Hall, Starbucks
**Entertainment:** *Tenors of Rock*, *Menopause the Musical*, Ralphie May, Mac King Comedy Magic, Big Elvis, *X Country*
**Nightlife:** Carnaval Court, Numb Bar, Piano Bar, Signature Bar

Adjacent to the happening Linq, ★ **Harrah's** (3475 Las Vegas Blvd. S., 800/214-9110, www.caesars.com/harrahs-las-vegas, $115-201) suddenly finds itself on the cutting edge of the Las Vegas party scene. The venerable property has taken a few baby steps toward hipsterism, booking edgy comedian **Ralphie May**, the topless *X Country* revue, and the raunchy *Menopause, the*

*Musical.* Still, conservative habits are hard to break, and **Mac King's** family-friendly comedy magic show remains one of the best afternoon offerings in town.

**Carnaval Court,** outside on the Strip's sidewalk, capitalizes on the street-party atmosphere with live bands and juggling bartenders. Just inside, Vegas icon **Big Elvis** (2pm, 3:30pm, and 5pm Mon., Wed., and Fri., free) performs in the **Piano Bar,** which invites aspiring singers to the karaoke stage Monday through Wednesday evenings, and dueling twin sister keyboardists take over each night at 9pm. The country superstar lends his name and unapologetic patriotism to **Toby Keith's I Love This Bar & Grill** (11:30am-2am Sun.-Thurs., 11:30am-3am Fri.-Sat., $15-25). Try the fried bologna sandwich.

For the best experience, book a room in the remodeled (2016) and renamed Valley Tower. Its 600 rooms and 72 suites feature subtle blues and grays along with traditional Harrah's purple in geometric designs and artwork throughout. Backlighted vanities, big windows, and modern lights and fixtures add to the sleek design.

### ★ Caesars Palace

**Restaurants:** Bacchanal Buffet, Gordon Ramsay Hell's Kitchen, Gordon Ramsay Pub & Grill, Restaurant Guy Savoy, Brioche by Guy Savoy, Stripside Café & Bar, Beijing Noodle No. 9, Mesa Grill, Old Homestead Steakhouse, Rao's, Mr. Chow, Searsucker, Nobu, Payard Patisserie & Bistro, Café Americano, Forum Food Court (Smashburger, Phillips Seafood Express, Earl of Sandwich, Tiger Wok & Ramen, Difara Pizza, La Gloria, Romaine Empire), Starbucks
**Entertainment:** Absinthe
**Attractions:** *Fall of Atlantis*, aquarium, Appian Way Shops, Forum Shops
**Nightlife:** Omnia, Fizz, Cleopatra's Barge, Spanish Steps, Numb Bar, Alto Bar, Lobby Bar, Vista Lounge, Montecristo Cigar Bar

The Roman Empire probably would look a lot like Las Vegas had it survived this long. **Caesars Palace** (3570 Las Vegas Blvd. S., 866/227-5938, www.caesars.com, $175-300) has incorporated all of ancient

Rome's decadence while adding a few thousand slot machines. Caesars opened with great fanfare in 1966 and has ruled the Strip ever since. Like the empire, it continues to expand and innovate, now boasting 3,348 guest rooms in six towers and 140,000 square feet of gaming space accented with marble, fountains, gilding, and royal reds. Wander the grounds searching for reproductions of some of the world's most famous statuary, including Michelangelo's *David*.

**Cleopatra's Barge** (7pm-2am Tues.-Weds., 8pm-3am Thurs.-Sat.), a floating lounge, attracts the full spectrum of the 21-and-over crowd for late-night bacchanalia. Local rockers and pop-choral fusionists are the current house bands, with occasional forays from touring groups taking the stage for acoustic performances in the intimate, 170-seat venue.

Guests luxuriate in the **Garden of the Gods Pool Oasis**, with each of several distinct water-and-sun shrines catering to a different proclivity. Gamblers can play at a swim-up blackjack table at Fortuna; beach bunnies can flaunt it toplessly at Venus; tanners can roast in peace at Apollo; kids can frolic at Temple; and the wealthy can splurge on cabanas at Bacchus. What, no aqueduct?

All roads lead to the **Forum Shops** (10am-11pm Sun.-Thurs., 10am-midnight Fri.-Sat.), a collection of famous designer stores, specialty boutiques, and restaurants. An hour here can do some serious damage to your bankroll. You'll also find the *Fall of Atlantis* show (hourly 11am-11pm Sun.-Thurs., 11am-11pm Fri.-Sat., free), a multisensory, multimedia depiction of the gods' wrath.

Caesars is the center of the world for celebrity chefs, with culinary all-stars lending their names to multiple eateries. Epicureans (and fans of the F-word, we presume) eagerly await the opening of **Gordon Ramsay Hell's Kitchen** in late 2017 or early 2018. In the meantime, guests can get their British on at **Gordon Ramsay Pub & Grill** (11am-11pm Sun.-Thurs., 11am-midnight Fri.-Sat., $25-40). Sip a Guinness while munching on shepherd's pie, bangers and mash, and fish-and-chips among the iconic red phone booths straight out of *Doctor Who*.

With so many guest rooms in six towers, it seems Caesars is always renovating somewhere. Most newer guest rooms are done in tan, wood, and marble. Ask for a south-facing room in the Augustus or Octavius tower to get commanding vistas of both the Bellagio fountains and the Strip.

### The Linq

**Restaurants:** Guy Fieri's Vegas Kitchen and Bar, Chayo Mexican Kitchen & Tequila Bar, Hash House a Go Go, Nook Café, Off the Strip
**Entertainment:** Mat Franco's *Magic Reinvented*, Frank Marino's *Divas Las Vegas*
**Attractions:** High Roller, VR Adventures, Auto Collection, Club Tattoo, Brooklyn Bowl
**Nightlife:** 3535, Catalyst, O'Shea's, Tag Lounge and Bar

Rooms at **The Linq** (3535 Las Vegas Blvd. S., 800/634-6441, www.caesars.com/linq, $99-249), are sleek, stylish, and smallish, at 250-350 square feet. Pewter and chrome are accented with eggplant, orange, or aqua murals depicting vintage Vegas in all its neon glory. Other amenities include marble countertops, 47-inch flat-screen TVs, and iPod docks. But the hotel is really just a way to stay close to all the Gen X-focused boutiques, bars, and restaurants in the adjacent outdoor promenade.

The high point of this pedestrian-friendly plaza is the **High Roller** ($22-32, age 4-12 $9-19), the highest observation wheel in the world, but there's plenty more to warrant a stop. **Brooklyn Bowl** (5pm-1am Sat.-Thurs., 5pm-2am Fri., $15-25) has you covered on eat, drink, and be merry, combining tenpin excitement with dozens of beer taps, delectable finger foods, and live entertainment. The spicy diablo shrimp highlights the modern fare at **Chayo Mexican Kitchen & Tequila Bar** (9am-midnight Sun.-Thurs.,

9am-3am Fri.-Sat., $16-28), but the menu takes a back seat to the tequila-fueled party. There's a mechanical bull in the middle of the dining room, for goodness sake. Patio seating puts diners and drinkers in prime people-watching territory. Vegas icon and local favorite **O'Shea's** (24 hours daily) brings back the lowbrow frivolity of the kegger party with cheap drafts, heated beer pong matches, and a rockin' jam band that keeps the festivities raging well into the wee hours.

*America's Got Talent* winner **Mat Franco** (7pm Thurs.-Mon., 4pm Sat., $48-88) combines jaw-dropping production illusions with how'd-he-do-that close-up tricks. His easygoing banter and anything-to-please attitude ensure it's never the same show twice.

## Flamingo

**Restaurants:** Center Cut Steakhouse, Paradise Garden Buffet, Jimmy Buffett's Margaritaville, Carlos N Charlie's, Beach Club Bar & Grill, Club Cappuccino, Café Express Food Court (Bonanno's Pizza, Johnny Rockets, L.A. Subs, Pan Asian Express)

**Entertainment:** Donny & Marie, Piff the Magic Dragon, *Legends in Concert, X Burlesque*

**Attractions:** Wildlife Habitat

**Nightlife:** It's 5 O'Clock Somewhere Bar, Garden Bar, Bugsy's Bar

Named for Virginia "Flamingo" Hill, the girlfriend of Benjamin "don't call me Bugsy" Siegel, the **Flamingo** (3555 Las Vegas Blvd. S., 702/733-3111, www.caesars.com/flamingo-las-vegas, $109-219) has at turns embraced and shunned its gangster ties, which stretch back to the 1960s. After Bugsy's (sorry, Mr. Siegel's) Flamingo business practices ran afoul of the Cosa Nostra and led to his untimely end, Meyer Lansky took over. Mob ties continued to dog the property until Hilton Hotels bought the Flamingo in 1970, giving the joint the legitimacy it needed. Today, its art deco architecture and pink-and-orange neon conjure images of aging Mafiosi lounging by the pool in a Vegas where the mob era is remembered almost fondly. At the

**Flamingo Wildlife Habitat** (8am-dusk daily, free), ibis, pelicans, turtles, koi fish, and, of course, Chilean flamingos luxuriate amid riparian plants and meandering streams.

Guests can search for their lost shaker of salt at **Jimmy Buffett's Margaritaville** (702/733-3302, 8am-1am Sun.-Thurs., 8am-2am Fri.-Sat., $20-30).

**Piff the Magic Dragon** (8pm, days vary, $69) performs mind-boggling card tricks with deadpan delivery and the help of adorable Chihuahua Mr. Piffles. Most of the humor is family-friendly, but the venue recommends audience members be age 13 and over.

The Flamingo transformed many of its guest rooms into Fab Rooms in 2012, but the older Go Rooms are actually more modern, dressed in swanky mahogany and white. The rooms are only 350 square feet but boast high-end entertainment systems and 42-inch TVs, vintage art prints, padded leather headboards, and all the other Vegas-sational accoutrements. Fab Rooms are more boldly decorated, incorporating swatches of hot pink.

## Rio

**Restaurants:** VooDoo Steakhouse, Carnival World & Seafood Buffets, Royal India Bistro, Wine Cellar & Tasting Room, KJ Dim Sum & Seafood, All-American Bar & Grille, Hash House a Go Go, Pho Da Nang Vietnamese Kitchen, Guy Fieri's El Burro Borracho, Sports Deli, Smashburger

**Entertainment:** Penn & Teller, Chippendales, *X Rocks*

**Attractions:** VooDoo Beach, VooDoo Zip Line, Kiss by Monster Mini Golf, Masquerade Village, Count's Tattoo Company

**Nightlife:** VooDoo Rooftop Nightclub & Lounge, IBar, Flirt Lounge, Masquerade Bar, Purple Zebra Daiquiri Bar

This Carnival-inspired resort of more than 2,500 all-suite accommodations just off the Strip keeps the party going with terrific buffets, beautiful people-magnet bars, and steamy shows. "Bevertainers" at the **Rio** (3700 W. Flamingo Rd.,

866/983-4279, www.caesars.com/rio-las-vegas, $99-199) take breaks from schlepping cocktails by jumping on mini stages scattered throughout the casino to belt out tunes or shimmy to the music. Dancers and other performers may materialize at your slot machine to take your mind off your losses.

While topless dancers and hard rock are the premise of every strip club in town, the focus at *X Rocks* (10pm Thurs.-Sat., $48-73, 18 and over) is on the music, costumes, choreography, and props, rather than the flesh (yeah, right!). Comedian John Bizarre yuks it up between routines. Rio has an equal-opportunity policy when it comes to titillation, with the famous **Chippendales** (8:30pm and 10:30pm daily, $60-70) flashing pecs and crooning ballads. There's more beefcake at **Flirt Lounge** (6:30pm-midnight Sun.-Thurs., 6:30pm-1am Fri.-Sat.) in the form of easy-on-the-eyes waiters.

Rio suites measure about 600 square feet. The hotel's center-Strip location and room-tall windows provide middle-of-the-action sights. A dressing area separate from the bathroom makes night-on-the-town preparations easy.

**VooDoo Beach** is a complex comprising four pools, a maze of waterfalls, cabanas, and more. Kids are welcome everywhere but Voo Pool, which attracts the over-21 crowd with a bar, spa treatment tables, and topless bathing.

## Lower Strip

The **Lower Strip**—roughly between the "Welcome to Fabulous Las Vegas" sign and Harmon Avenue—is a living city timeline. The Tropicana is here, providing a link to the mobbed-up city of the 1960s and 1970s. Camelot-themed Excalibur, completed in 1990, and the Egyptian-inspired Luxor, which opened in 1993, serve as prime examples from the city's hesitant foray into becoming a

**Top to bottom:** Caesars Palace; Bellagio Conservatory; Paris Las Vegas.

"family" destination in the early 1990s. Across from the Tropicana, the emerald-tinted MGM Grand opened in 1993 as a salute to *The Wizard of Oz*. City Center puts the mega in megaresort—condos, boutique hotels, trendy shopping, a huge casino, and a sprawling dining and entertainment district—and cemented the city's biggest-is-best trend. The Lower Strip seems made for budget-conscious families. Rooms are often cheaper than mid-Strip, and there are plenty of kid-friendly attractions (even a roller coaster).

## The Palms

**Restaurants:** Nove Italiano, Alizé, 24 Seven Café, Bistro Buffet, Café 6, Hooters, The Eatery (Earl of Sandwich, McDonalds, Panda Express, Nathan's Famous, Famous Famiglia Pizzeria, Blizz Frozen Yogurt, Chronic Tacos, Coffee Bean and Tea Leaf)
**Entertainment:** Pearl Theater, Brendan Theater
**Nightlife:** Rojo, Tonic, Moon, Rain

The expression "party like a rock star" could have been invented for **The Palms** (4321 W. Flamingo Rd., 866/942-7777, www.palms.com, $110-175). Penthouse views, uninhibited pool parties, lavish theme suites, and starring roles in several televised parties have brought notoriety and stars to the clubs, concert venue, and recording studio. The 2,500-seat **Pearl Concert Theater** regularly hosts rock concerts.

Andre Rochat's **Alizé** (5:30pm daily, $60-90) is the quintessential French restaurant: authentic fare, a cognac cellar, snooty clientele, sophisticated decor, and top-of-the-world views.

The Palms' Fantasy Tower houses the fantasy suites, where you can choose from rooms with bowling lanes, erotic rotating beds, pool tables, basketball courts, and more. The original Ivory Tower offers large guest rooms. They're sleek, with geometric shapes and custom artwork, but their best features are the feathery beds and luxurious comforters. The rejuvenating shower and "spa-inspired" stone, glass, and chrome bathrooms help get the day started. The

newest tower, Palms Place, has 599 studios and one-bedrooms with suite views, gourmet kitchens, and nearby restaurant, spa, and pool.

## Bellagio

**Restaurants:** Lago, Todd English's Olives, Yellowtail, Harvest by Roy Ellamar, Jasmine, Fix, Michael Mina, Picasso, Prime Steakhouse, Le Cirque, Noodles, The Buffet, Café Bellagio, Jean Philippe Patisserie, Starbucks, Café Gelato, Palio, Snacks, Pool Café
**Entertainment:** Cirque du Soleil's O
**Attractions:** Fountains at Bellagio, Bellagio Conservatory & Botanical Garden, Bellagio Gallery of Fine Art, public art
**Nightlife:** The Bank, Hyde, Lily Bar & Lounge, Petrossian Bar, Baccarat Bar, Pool Bar, Sports Bar Lounge

With nearly 4,000 guest rooms and suites, ★ **Bellagio** (3600 Las Vegas Blvd. S., 702/693-7111 or 888/987-6667, www.bellagio.com, $199-349) boasts a population larger than the village perched on Lake Como from which it borrows its name. To keep pace with its Italian namesake, Bellagio created an 8.5-acre lake between the hotel and Las Vegas Boulevard. The views of the lake and its **Fountains at Bellagio** (3pm-midnight Mon.-Fri., noon-midnight Sat., 11am-midnight Sun.) are free, as is the 80,000-flower aromatic fantasy at **Bellagio Conservatory & Botanical Garden** (24 hours daily). The **Bellagio Gallery of Fine Art** (10am-8pm daily, $18) would be a bargain at twice the price—you can spend an edifying day at one of the world's priciest resorts (including a cocktail and lunch) for less than $50. Even if you don't spring for gallery admission, art demands your attention throughout the hotel and casino. The 2,000 glass flower petals in Dale Chihuly's *Fiori di Como* sculpture bloom from the lobby ceiling, foreshadowing the opulent experiences to come. Masatoshi Izumi's *A Gift from the Earth*, comprising four massive basalt sculptures representing wind, fire, water, and land, dominates the hotel's main entrance.

The display of artistry continues but

the bargains end at **Via Bellagio** (10am-midnight daily), the resort's shopping district, including heavyweight retailers Armani, Prada, Chanel, Gucci, and their ilk.

Befitting Bellagio's world-class status, intriguing and expensive restaurants abound. **Michael Mina** (5:30pm-10pm Mon.-Sat., $70-100) is worth the price. Restrained decor adds to the simple elegance of the cuisine, which is mostly seafood with European and Asian influences.

Bellagio's tower rooms are the epitome of luxury, with Italian marble, oversize bathtubs, remote-controlled drapes, Egyptian-cotton sheets, and 510 square feet in which to spread out. The sage-plum and indigo-silver color schemes are refreshing changes from the goes-with-everything beige and the camouflages-all-stains paisley often found on the Strip.

## Paris Las Vegas

**Restaurants:** Burger Brasserie, Mon Ami Gabi, Martorano's, Hexx, Gordon Ramsay Steak, Eiffel Tower Restaurant, Café Belle Madeleine, La Creperie, JJ's Boulangerie, Beef Park, Café Belle Madeleine, Sekushi, La Creperie, Le Café Ile St. Louis, Le Village Buffet, Yong Kang Street

**Entertainment:** Sex Tips for Straight Women from a Gay Man, Anthony Cools

**Attractions:** Eiffel Tower

**Nightlife:** Napoleon's Lounge, Le Cabaret, Le Central, Le Bar du Sport, Gustav's, Chateau Nightclub & Rooftop

Designers used Gustav Eiffel's original drawings to ensure that the half-size tower that anchors **Paris Las Vegas** (3655 Las Vegas Blvd. S., www.caesars.com/paris-las-vegas, 877/242-6753, $149-276) conformed—down to the last cosmetic rivet—to the original. That attention to detail prevails throughout this property, which works hard to evoke the City of Light, from large-scale reproductions of the Arc de Triomphe, Champs Élysées, and Louvre to more than half a dozen French restaurants. The tower is perhaps the most romantic spot in town to view the Strip; you'll catch your breath as the elevator whisks you to the observation deck 460 feet up, then have it taken away again by the lights from one of the most famous skylines in the world. Back at street level, the cobblestone lanes and brass streetlights of **Le Boulevard** (8am-2am daily) invite shoppers into quaint shops and patisseries. The casino offers its own attractions, not the least of which is the view of the Eiffel Tower's base jutting through the ceiling. Paris is one of the first casinos to test "skill-based" gaming, which combines video poker with video games. It also offers a variation of fantasy football during the NFL season.

Entertainment veers toward the bawdy, with **Anthony Cools—The Uncensored Hypnotist** (9pm Tues. and Thurs.-Sun., $49-82) cajoling mesmerized subjects through very adult simulations. The same venue hosts the Broadway export *Sex Tips for Straight Women from a Gay Man* (7pm and 11pm, Sun.-Thurs., $39-69), in which the audience and flamboyant Dan help uptight Robyn shed her bedroom inhibitions.

You'll be wishing you had packed your beret when you order a beignet and cappuccino at **Le Café Ile St. Louis** (6pm-11pm Sun.-Thurs., 6am-midnight Fri.-Sat., $12-20). While the checkered tablecloths and streetlights scream French sidewalk café, the menu tends toward American comfort food.

Standard guest rooms in the 33-story tower are decorated in a rich earth-tone palette and have marble baths. There's nothing Left Bank bohemian about them, however. The guest rooms exude little flair or personality, but the simple, quality furnishings make it a moderately priced option. Book a Red Room if modern decor is important to you.

## Cosmopolitan

**Restaurants:** Scarpetta, Rose. Rabbit. Lie., E by Jose Andres, STK, Beauty & Exxex, Blue Ribbon Sushi Bar & Grill, China Poblano, D.O.C.G., Secret Pizza, Eggslut, Estiatorio Milos, The Henry, Holsteins, Jaleo, The

Juice Standard, Milk Bar, Momofuku, Overlook Grill, Starbucks

**Attractions:** public art

**Nightlife:** Marquee, Bond, The Chandelier, Clique, The Study, Vesper Bar

Modern art, marble bath floors, and big soaking tubs in 460-square-foot rooms evoke urban penthouse living at ★ **Cosmopolitan** (3708 Las Vegas Blvd. S., 702/698-7000, www.cosmopolitan-lasvegas.com, $220-4380). The hefty rates do nothing to harsh the NYC vibe. Because it's too cool to host production shows, the resort's entertainment schedule mixes DJs of the moment with the coolest headliners.

That nouveau riche attitude carries through to the dining and nightlife. **Rose. Rabbit. Lie.** (6pm-midnight Wed.-Sat., $80-150) is equal parts supper club, nightclub, and jazz club. Bluesy, jazzy torch singers, magicians, tap and hip-hop dancers, and a rocking sound system keep the joint jumping. If you go for dinner, order 5-6 small plates per couple. **Vesper Bar** (24 hours daily), named for James Bond's favorite martini, prides itself on serving hipster versions of classic cocktails. Possibly the best day club in town, **Marquee** (11am-sunset daily Apr.-Oct.), on the roof, brings in the beautiful people with DJs and sweet bungalow lofts. When darkness falls, the day club becomes an extension of the pulsating Marquee nightclub (10:30pm-5am Mon. and Fri.-Sat.).

## Aria

**Restaurants:** Bardot, Sage, Herringbone, Tetsu, Blossom, Jean Georges Steakhouse, BarMasa, Carbone, Jean Philippe Patisserie Javier's, Lemongrass, The Buffet, Julian Serrano Tapas, Aria Café, Five50 Pizza Bar, Bobby's Burger Palace

**Entertainment:** Cirque du Soleil's *Zarkana*

**Attractions:** public art, Crystals

**Nightlife:** Jewel, Alibi, Baccarat Lounge, High Limit Lounge, Lift Bar, Lobby Bar, Pool Bar, Sports Bar

All glass and steel, ultramodern ★ **Aria** (3730 Las Vegas Blvd. S., 702/590-7757, www.aria.com, $210-379) would look more at home in Manhattan than Las Vegas. Touch pads control the drapes, the lighting, the music, and the climate in Aria's fern- or grape-paletted guest rooms. Program the "wake up scene" before bedtime, and the room will gradually summon you from peaceful slumber at the appointed time. A traditional hotel casino, Aria shares the City Center umbrella with **Vdara,** a Euro-chic boutique hotel with no gaming.

Guests are invited to browse an extensive public art collection, with works by Maya Lin, Jenny Holzer, and Richard Long, among others. **Crystals,** a 500,000-square-foot mall, lets you splurge among hanging gardens. Restaurants fronted by Julian Serrano and Michael Mina take the place of Sbarro's and Cinnabon.

Culinary genius Masa Takayama guarantees that the bluefin at **BarMasa** (5pm-10pm Thurs.-Tues., $40-80) goes from the Sea of Japan to your spicy tuna roll in less than 24 hours.

## Hard Rock

**Restaurants:** MB Steak, Culinary Dropout, Fu Asian Kitchen, Mr. Lucky's, Nobu, Pink Taco, Oyster Bar, Fuel Café, Goose Island Pub, Pizza Forte, Juice Bar, Dunkin' Donuts

**Entertainment:** Magic Mike Live, Raiding the Rock Vault, Vinyl, Soundwaves

**Nightlife:** The Joint, Rehab Pool Party, Breathe, Vanity, Center Bar, Sidebet Draft Bar, Luxe Bar, Midway Bar

Young stars and the media-savvy 20-somethings who idolize them contribute to the frat party mojo at the **Hard Rock** (4455 Paradise Rd., www.hardrockhotel.com, 800/473-7625, $129-275). While the casino is shaped like an LP, if your music collection dates back to wax records, this probably isn't the place for you. The gaming tables and machines are located in the "record label," and the shops and restaurants are in the "grooves."

Contemporary and classic rockers regularly grace the stage at **The Joint** and party with their fans at **Rehab Pool**

**Parties** (11am-dusk Fri.-Sat.). The provocatively named **Pink Taco** (11am-10pm Sun.-Thurs., 11am-2am Fri.-Sat., $15-25) dishes up Mexican and Caribbean specialties.

The 1,500 sleek guest rooms include stocked minibars, Bose CD sound systems, and 55-inch plasma TVs, a fitting crib for wannabe rock stars.

## New York New York

**Restaurants:** Tom's Urban, Il Fornaio, Nine Fine Irishmen, Gallagher's Steakhouse, America, MGM Grand Buffet, New York Pizzeria, Chin Café & Sushi Bar, Broadway Burger Bar & Grill, Gonzalez y Gonzalez, Shake Shack, 48th and Crepe, Greenberg's Deli, Fulton's Fish Frye, Village Bakery, Times Square to Go, Nathan's Famous, Starbucks

**Entertainment:** Cirque du Soleil's *Zumanity*, Brooklyn Bridge buskers, dueling pianos, The Park

**Attractions:** Hershey's Chocolate World, Big Apple Coaster & Arcade, T-Mobile Arena

**Nightlife:** Coyote Ugly, The Bar at Times Square, Center Bar, Pour 24, Big Chill, High Limit Bar, Lobby Bar, Chocolate Bar

One look at this loving tribute to the city that never sleeps and you won't be able to fuhgedaboutit. From the city skyline outside (the skyscrapers contain the resort's hotel rooms) to laundry hanging between crowded faux brownstones indoors, **New York New York** (3790 Las Vegas Blvd. S., 702/740-6969 or 866/815-4365, www.newyorknewyork.com, $130-255) will have even grizzled Gothamites feeling like they've come home again.

The **Big Apple Coaster** (11am-11pm Sun.-Thurs., 10:30am-midnight Fri.-Sat., $15, all-day pass $26) winds its way around the resort, an experience almost as hair-raising as a New York City cab ride, which the coaster cars are painted to resemble.

Dueling pianists keep **The Bar at Times Square** (1pm-2:30am Mon.-Thurs., 11am-2:30am Fri.-Sun.) rocking into the wee hours, and the sexy bar staff at **Coyote Ugly** (6pm-3am daily) defy its name.

**The Park** takes dining, drinking, and strolling to new heights. The plaza surrounding T-Mobile Arena, where the NHL's Vegas Golden Knights and the hottest musical acts play, incorporates responsible landscaping and artistic, if man-made, shade structures.

New York New York's 2,023 guest rooms are standard size, 350-400 square feet. The roller coaster zooms around the towers, so you might want to ask for a room out of earshot.

## MGM Grand

**Restaurants:** Morimoto, Joël Robuchon, Tom Colicchio's Craftsteak, Michael Mina Pub 1842, Emeril's New Orleans Fish House, L'Atelier de Joël Robuchon, Wolfgang Puck Bar & Grill, Hakkasan, Grand Wok and Sushi Bar, Hecho En Vegas, Crush, MGM Grand Buffet, Fiamma Trattoria & Bar, Stage Deli, Tap Sports Bar, Blizz, Pieology, Avenue Café, Cabana Grill, Corner Cakes, Starbucks, Subway, Pan Asian Express, Bonanno's New York Pizzeria, Häagen-Dazs, Nathan's Famous, Original Chicken Tender, Tacos N 'Ritas, Johnny Rockets

**Entertainment:** Cirque du Soleil's *Kà*, David Copperfield, Jabbawockeez, Brad Garrett's Comedy Club, MGM Garden Arena

**Attractions:** Topgolf, Level Up, CSI: The Experience, CBS Television City Research Center

**Nightlife:** Wet Republic, Hakkasan, Whiskey Bar, Losers Bar, Centrifuge, Lobby Bar

Gamblers enter **MGM Grand** (3799 Las Vegas Blvd. S., 888/646-1203, www.mgmgrand.com, $130-250) through portals guarded by MGM's mascot, the 45-foot-tall king of the jungle. The uninitiated may feel like a gazelle on the savanna, swallowed by the 171,000-square-foot casino floor, the largest in Las Vegas. But the watering hole, MGM's 6.5-acre pool complex, is relatively predator-free. MGM capitalizes on the movie studio's greatest hits. Even the hotel's emerald facade evokes the magical city in *The Wizard of Oz.*

Boob tube fans can volunteer for studies at the **CBS Television City Research Center** (10am-8:30pm daily, free), where they can screen pilots for shows under consideration. If your favorite show happens to revolve around solving crimes, don some rubber gloves and search for clues at **CSI: The Experience** (9am-8pm daily, age 12 and up $32, not recommended for children under 12). Three crime scenes keep the experience fresh.

MGM Grand houses enough top restaurants for a week of gourmet dinners. You can take your pick of celebrity chef establishments, but **L'Atelier de Joël Robuchon** (5pm-10pm daily, $75-200) offers the most bang for the buck. Counter service overlooks kitchen preparations, adding to the anticipation.

Standard guest rooms in the Grand Tower are filled with the quality furnishings you'd expect. The West Tower guest rooms are smaller, at 350 square feet, but exude swinging style with high-tech gizmos; the 450-square-foot rooms in the Grand Tower are more traditional.

## Tropicana

**Restaurants:** Bacio Italian Cuisine, Biscayne, Chef Irvine, Beach Café, South Beach Food Court, Starbucks
**Attractions:** Xposed!

**Entertainment:** Men of the Strip, Rich Little, Laugh Factory
**Nightlife:** Tropicana Lounge, Lucky's Sports Bar, Coconut Grove Bar

When it opened at in 1959, the **Tropicana** (3801 Las Vegas Blvd. S., 702/739-2222, www.troplv.com, $140-200) was the most luxurious, most expensive resort on the Strip. It has survived several boom-and-bust cycles since then, and its decor reflects the willy-nilly expansion and refurbishment efforts through the years. Today, the rooms have bright, airy South Beach themes with plantation shutters, light wood, 42-inch plasma TVs, and garden views.

The beach chic atmosphere includes a two-acre pool complex with reclining deck chairs and swim-up blackjack. After a slow start, Las Vegas is now quite LGBTQ friendly. On summer Saturdays (noon-7pm) the pool deck hosts **Xposed!,** a gay-friendly pool party with sand volleyball, go-go dancers, and trendy DJs.

While it features hard-bodied singers

MGM Grand hotel

and dance routines by world-renowned choreographers, the sultry **Men of the Strip** (9pm Thurs.-Sun., $50-80) promises a more risqué version of the male revue. Think more bump and grind than flex and flirt. The producers note that both women and men are welcome in the audience.

### Luxor

**Restaurants:** Tender Steak & Seafood, Rice & Company, Public House, T&T Tacos & Tequila, More Buffet, Pyramid Café, Backstage Deli, Blizz, Burger Bar, Ri Ra Irish Pub, Slice of Vegas, Hussong's Cantina, Bonanno's Pizzeria, Johnny Rockets, LA Subs, Nathan's Famous, Original Chicken Tender, Starbucks
**Entertainment:** Criss Angel *Mindfreak Live*, Carrot Top, Blue Man Group, *Fantasy*
**Attractions:** *Bodies…the Exhibition*, *Titanic* artifacts
**Nightlife:** Centra, Aurora, Flight, High Bar, PlayBar

Other than its pyramid shape and name, not much remains of the Egyptian theme at the **Luxor** (3900 Las Vegas Blvd. S., 702/262-4000, www.luxor.com, $99-220). In its place are upscale and decidedly post-pharaoh nightclubs, restaurants, and shops. Many are located in the **Shoppes at Mandalay Place**, on the sky bridge between Luxor and Mandalay Bay. The huge base of the pyramid houses a cavernous 120,000-square-foot casino, while the slanted walls and twin 22-story towers contain 4,400 guest rooms. Luxor also has the largest atrium in the world, an intense light beam that is visible from space, and inclinators—elevators that move along the building's oblique angles.

**Carrot Top**'s (8pm Wed.-Mon., $50-82) rapid-fire prop comedy fills the Atrium Showroom, while in *Mindfreak Live* (7pm and 9:30pm Wed.-Sun., $72-173) Criss Angel performs his skull-crushing illusions and shares the stage with comedians, jugglers, and other specialty acts in the Luxor Theater. Angel shares the stage with the comely and talented singers and dancers in the topless *Fantasy* (10:30pm nightly, $49-66).

Staying in the pyramid makes for interesting room features, such as a slanted exterior wall. Stay on higher floors for panoramic views of the atrium below. Tower rooms are newer and more traditional in their shape, decor, and amenities.

### Mandalay Bay

**Restaurants:** Aureole, Red Square, Lupo by Wolfgang Puck, Charlie Palmer Steak, Fleur by Hubert Keller, Rick Moonen's RM Seafood, Kumi, Stripsteak, Libertine Social, Border Grill, Rx Boiler Room, Rivea, Ri Ra Irish Pub, Della's Kitchen, Hussong's Cantina, Citizens Kitchen & Bar, Slice of Vegas, Seabreeze Café, Burger Bar, Bayside Buffet, Noodle Shop, Bonanno's Pizzeria, Nathan's Famous, Pan Asian Express, Johnny Rockets, Subway
**Entertainment:** House of Blues, *Michael Jackson One*
**Attractions:** Shark Reef, Mandalay Place
**Nightlife:** Foundation Room, Light, Daylight Beach Club, Skyfall, Mizuya, Press, Minus 5 Ice Bar, Eyecandy Sound Lounge, Orchid Lounge, Evening Call, Fat Tuesday, Bikini Bar, Verandah Lounge, 1923 Bourbon Bar

The South Pacific behemoth ★ **Mandalay**

**Bay** (3950 Las Vegas Blvd. S., 877/632-7800, www.mandalaybay.com, $150-300) has one of the largest casino floors in the world at 135,000 square feet. An 11-acre paradise comprises eight pools, including a lazy river, a 1.6-million-gallon wave pool complete with a real beach made of five million pounds of sand, an adults-only dipping pool, and tops-optional sunbathing deck. You could spend your entire vacation in the pool area, gambling at the beach's three-level casino, eating at its restaurant, and loading up on sandals and bikinis at the nearby Pearl Moon boutique. The beach hosts a concert series during summer.

**House of Blues** (hours vary by event) hosts live blues, rock, and acoustic sets and a surprisingly good restaurant. It's the site of the Sunday **Gospel Brunch** (702/632-7600, 10am and 1pm Sun., $55), where a gospel choir serenades guest with contemporary spirituals as they dine on Southern delicacies like chicken and waffles, biscuits and gravy, brisket, and more.

Even at 100,000 square feet, **Mandalay Place** (10am-11pm daily), on the sky bridge between Mandalay Bay and the Luxor, is smaller and less hectic than other casino malls. It features unusual shops, such as the Guinness Store, celebrating the favorite Irish stout, and Cariloha, with clothes, accessories, and housewares made of bamboo. The shops share space with eateries and high-concept bars like **Minus 5 Ice Bar** (11am-3am daily), where barflies don parkas before entering the below-freezing (23°F) establishment. The glasses aren't just frosted; they're fashioned completely out of ice.

An urban hip-hop worldview and the King of Pop's unmatched talent guide the vignettes in *Michael Jackson One* (7pm and 9:30pm Fri.-Tues., $69-170). Michael's musical innovation and the Cirque du Soleil trademark aerial and acrobatic acts pay homage to the human spirit.

Sheathed in Indian artifacts and crafts, the **Foundation Room** (5pm-3am daily) is just as dark and mysterious as the subcontinent, with private rooms piled with overstuffed furniture, fireplaces, and thick carpets; a dining room; and several bars catering to various musical tastes.

Vegas pays tribute to Paris, Rome, New York, and Venice, so why not Moscow? Round up your comrades for caviar and vodka as well as continental favorites at **Red Square** (5pm-10pm Sun.-Thurs., 5pm-11pm Fri.-Sat., $35-50). Look for the headless Lenin statue at the entrance.

Standard guest rooms are chic and roomy (550 square feet), with warm fabrics and plush bedding. Get a north-facing room and put the floor-to-ceiling windows to use gazing the full length of the Strip. The guest rooms are big, but nothing special visually, but the baths are fit for royalty, with huge tubs and glass-walled showers. To go upscale, check out the Delano boutique hotel or book at the Four Seasons—both are part of the same complex.

# Downtown
## Binion's

**Restaurants:** Top of Binion's Steakhouse, Binion's Deli, Binion's Café, Benny's Smokin BBQ & Brews
**Entertainment:** Hypnosis Unleashed
**Nightlife:** Cowgirl Up Cantina, Whiskey Licker

Before Vegas became a resort city, it catered to inveterate gamblers, hard drinkers, and others on the fringes of society. Ah, the good old days! A gambler himself, Benny Binion put his place in the middle of downtown, a magnet for the serious player, offering high limits and few frills. **Binion's** (128 Fremont St., 702/382-1600, www.binions.com) now attracts players with occasional $1 blackjack tables and a poker room frequented by grizzled veterans. This is where the World Series of Poker began, and the quaint room still stages some wild action on its 10 tables. Players can earn $2 per hour in comps—about double what they can pull down in most rooms. A $4 maximum rake and big-screen TV add to the attraction. The little den on Fremont Street still retains the flavor of Old Vegas.

The hotel at Binion's closed in 2009, but the restaurants remain open, including the **Top of Binion's Steakhouse** (5pm-10pm daily, $40-55), famous for its Fremont Street views, aged steaks, and chicken-fried lobster appetizer.

### Golden Nugget

**Restaurants:** Vic & Anthony's, Chart House, Grotto, Lillie's Asian Cuisine, Red Sushi, Cadillac Mexican Kitchen & Tequila Bar, Buffet, The Grille, Claim Jumper, Starbucks

**Entertainment:** 52 Fridays

**Attractions:** Hand of Faith, shark tank

**Nightlife:** Rush Lounge, Gold Diggers, H2O Bar at the Tank, Claude's Bar, Ice Bar, Bar 46, Cadillac Tequila Bar, Stage Bar

The ★ **Golden Nugget** (129 E. Fremont St., 702/385-7111, www.goldennugget. com, $129-249) has been a fixture for nearly 70 years, beckoning diners and gamblers with gold leaf and a 61-pound gold nugget in the lobby. Landry's, the restaurant chain and Nugget owner since 2005, has maintained and restored the hotel's opulence, investing $300 million for casino expansion, more restaurants, and a new 500-room hotel tower. Rooms are appointed in dark wood and warm autumn hues.

If you don't feel like swimming with the sharks in the poker room, you can get up close and personal with their finned namesakes at the **Golden Nugget Pool** (9am-6pm daily, free), an outdoor pool with a three-story waterslide that takes riders through the hotel's huge aquarium, home to sharks, rays, and other exotic marine life. Bathers can also swim up to the aquarium for a face-to-face with the aquatic predators. Waterfalls and lush landscaping help make this one of the world's best hotel pools.

**Gold Diggers nightclub** (9pm-late Thurs.-Sun.) plays hip-hop, pop, and classic rock for the dancing pleasure of guests and go-go girls. Thursday is

Ladies Night, and Sunday features flashbacks to the '80s.

# Sights

## Center Strip
### Madame Tussauds Las Vegas

Ever wanted to dunk over Shaq? Party with the dudes from *The Hangover*? **Madame Tussauds Las Vegas** (3377 Las Vegas Blvd. S., 702/862-7800, www.madametussauds.com/lasvegas, 10am-8pm Sun.-Thurs., 10am-9pm Fri.-Sat., adults $30, age 4-12 $20, under age 4 free) at The Venetian gives you your chance. Unlike most other museums, Madame Tussauds encourages guests to get up close and "personal" with the world leaders, sports heroes, and pop icons immortalized in wax. Photo ops and interactive activities abound. Club Tussauds puts you in the middle of the happening club scene, with A-listers all around. Share a cocktail with Angelina Jolie; hit the dance floor with Channing Tatum; or discuss your screenplay with Will Smith.

### ★ Gondola Rides

We dare you not to sigh at the grandeur of Venice in the desert as you pass beneath quaint bridges and idyllic sidewalk cafés, your gondolier serenading you with the accompaniment of the Grand Canal's gurgling wavelets. The **indoor gondolas** (Venetian, 3355 Las Vegas Blvd. S., 702/607-3982, www.venetian. com, 10am-11pm Sun.-Thurs., 10am-midnight Fri.-Sat., $29) skirt the Grand Canal Shoppes inside The Venetian under the mall's painted-sky ceiling fresco for a half mile; **outdoor gondolas** (11am-10pm daily, weather permitting, $29) skim The Venetian's 31,000-square-foot lagoon for 12 minutes, giving riders a unique perspective on the Las Vegas Strip. Plying the waters at regular intervals, the realistic-looking gondolas seat four, but couples who don't want to share a boat can pay double.

### ★ Secret Garden and Dolphin Habitat

It's no mirage—those really are pure-white tigers lounging in their own plush resort on The Mirage casino floor. Legendary Las Vegas magicians Siegfried and Roy, who have dedicated much of their lives to preserving big cats, opened the **Secret Garden** (Mirage, 3400 Las Vegas Blvd. S., 702/791-7188, www.miragehabitat.com, 10am-6pm daily, adults $22, age 4-12 $17, under 4 free) in 1990. In addition to the milky-furred tigers, the garden is home to blue-eyed, black-striped white tigers as well as black panthers, lions, and leopards. Although caretakers don't "perform" with the animals, if your visit is well-timed you could see the cats playing, wrestling, and even swimming in their pristine waterfall-fed pools. The cubs in the specially built nursery are sure to register high on the cuteness meter.

Visit the Atlantic bottlenoses at the **Dolphin Habitat** right next door, also in the middle of The Mirage's palm trees and jungle foliage. The aquatic mammals don't perform on cue either, but they're natural hams and often interact with their visitors, nodding their heads in response to trainer questions, turning aerial somersaults, and "walking" on their tails across the water. An underwater viewing area provides an unusual perspective into the dolphins' world. Feeding times are a hoot.

Budding naturalists (age 13 and over) won't want to miss Dolphin Habitat's Trainer for a Day program ($495), which allows them to feed, swim with, and pose for photos with some of the aquatic stars while putting them through their daily regimen. Other interactive activities with the aquatic mammals include painting and yoga.

### ★ High Roller

Taller than even the London Eye, the 550-foot **High Roller** (The Linq, 3545 Las Vegas Blvd. S., 702/777-2782 or

High Roller observation wheel at The Linq

866/574-3851, www.caesars.com/linq/ high-roller, 11:30am-2:30am daily, $25-37, youth $10-20) is the highest observation wheel in the world. Two thousand LED lights dance in intricate choreography among the ride's spokes and pods. The dazzling view from 50 stories up is unparalleled. Ride at night for a perfect panorama of the famous Strip skyline. Ride at dusk for inspiring glimpses of the desert sun setting over the mountains. Forty passengers fit in each of the High Roller's 28 compartments, lessening wait time for the half-hour ride circuit. With **Happy Half Hour** tickets (noon-1am daily, age 21 and up, $52) passengers can board special bar cars and enjoy unlimited cocktails during the ride. Book online to save on tickets.

## Lower Strip
### Showcase Mall

"Mall" is an overly ambitious moniker for the **Showcase Mall** (3785 Las Vegas Blvd. S., 702/597-3117, 9am-5pm Mon.-Sat.),

a mini diversion on the Strip. The centerpiece, the original **M&M's World** (702/736-7611, www.mmsworld.com, 9am-midnight daily, free), underwent a 2010 expansion and now includes a printing station where customers can customize their bite-size treats with words and pictures. The 3,300-square-foot expansion on the third floor of the store, which originally opened in 1997, includes additional opportunities to stock up on all things M: Swarovski crystal candy dishes, a guitar, T-shirts, and purses made from authentic M&M wrappers. The addition brings the chocoholic's paradise to more than 30,000 square feet, offering keychains, coffee mugs, lunch boxes, and the addicting treats in every color imaginable. Start with a viewing of the short 3-D film, *I Lost My M in Las Vegas*. A replica of Kyle Busch's M&M-sponsored No. 18 NASCAR stock car is on the fourth floor.

As you might expect, everything inside the **Everything Coca-Cola** store (702/270-5952, 10am-11pm daily, free) is related to the iconic soft drink. The small retail outlet has collectibles, free photo ops, and a soda fountain where you can taste a dozen Coke products from around the world ($7). Look for the giant green Coke bottle facade on the Strip.

Other mall tenants include a food court, an eight-screen movie theater, Adidas, and Hard Rock Café.

### *Bodies . . . the Exhibition* and *Titanic* Artifacts

Although they are tastefully and respectfully presented, the dissected humans at ***Bodies . . . the Exhibition*** (Luxor, 3900 Las Vegas Blvd. S., 702/262-4400, www. luxor.com, 10am-10pm daily, adults $32, over age 64 $30, age 4-12 $24, under age 4 free) still have a creep factor. That uneasiness quickly gives way to wonder and interest as visitors examine 13 full-body specimens, carefully preserved to reveal bone structure and muscular, circulatory, respiratory, and other systems. Other system and organ displays drive home the importance of a healthy lifestyle, with structures showing the damage caused by overeating, alcohol consumption, and sedentary lifestyle. Perhaps the most sobering exhibit is the side-by-side comparisons of healthy and smoke-damaged lungs. A draped-off area contains fetal specimens, showing prenatal development and birth defects.

Luxor also hosts some 250 less surreal but just as poignant artifacts and reproductions commemorating the 1912 sinking of the *Titanic* (3900 Las Vegas Blvd. S., 702/262-4400, 10am-10pm daily, adults $32, over age 64 $30, ages 4-12 $24, under age 4 free). The 15-ton rusting hunk of the ship's hull is the biggest artifact on display; it not only drives home the Titanic's scale but also helps transport visitors back to that cold April morning a century ago. A replica of the *Titanic*'s grand staircase—featured prominently in the 1997 film—testifies to the ship's opulence, but it is the passengers' personal effects (a pipe, luggage, an unopened bottle of champagne) and recreated first-class and third-class cabins that provide some of the most heartbreaking discoveries. The individual stories come to life as each patron is given the identity of one of the ship's passengers. At the end of tour they find out the passenger's fate.

Luxor offers combination admission to both attractions for $42.

### Shark Reef

Just when you thought it was safe to visit Las Vegas. . . . This 1.6-million-gallon habitat proves not all the sharks in town prowl the poker rooms. **Shark Reef** (Mandalay Bay, 3950 Las Vegas Blvd. S., 702/632-4555, www.sharkreef. com, 10am-10pm daily, $25, ages 65 and over $23, ages 4-12 $19, under age 4 free) is home to 2,000 animals—almost all predators. Transparent walkthrough tubes and a sinking-ship observation deck allow terrific views, bringing visitors nearly face-to-face with some of the

most fearsome creatures in the world. Among the 15 species of sharks on display is a sand tiger shark, whose mouth is so crammed with razor-sharp teeth that it doesn't fully close. Other species include golden crocodiles, moray eels, stingrays, giant octopuses, the venomous lionfish, jellyfish, water monitors, and the fresh-from-your-nightmares eight-foot-long Komodo dragon.

Mandalay Bay guests with dive certification can dive in the 22-foot-deep shipwreck exhibit at the reef. Commune with eight-foot nurse sharks as well as reef sharks, zebra sharks, rays, sawfish, and other denizens of the deep. **Scuba excursions** (3pm daily, age 18 and over, $650) include 3-4 hours underwater, a guided aquarium tour, a video, and admission for up to four guests. Wearing chain mail is required. One tour option will prove your love runs deep: Have a reef diver present a surprise proposal at the end of a guided one-hour tour ($100). The price includes a commemorative photo.

## Downtown
### ★ Fremont Street Experience

With land at a premium and more and more tourists flocking to the opulence of the Strip, downtown Las Vegas in the last quarter of the 20th century found its lights beginning to flicker. Enter the **Fremont Street Experience** (702/678-5600, www.vegasexperience.com), an ambitious plan to transform downtown and its tacky "Glitter Gulch" reputation into a pedestrian-friendly enclave. Highlighted by a four-block-long canopy festooned with 12 million light-emitting diodes 90 feet in the air, the Fremont Street Experience is downtown's answer to the Strip's erupting volcanoes and fantastic dancing fountains. The canopy, dubbed Viva Vision, runs atop Fremont Street between North Main Street and North 4th Street.

Once an hour between dusk and 1am, the promenade goes dark and all heads

# Downtown Las Vegas

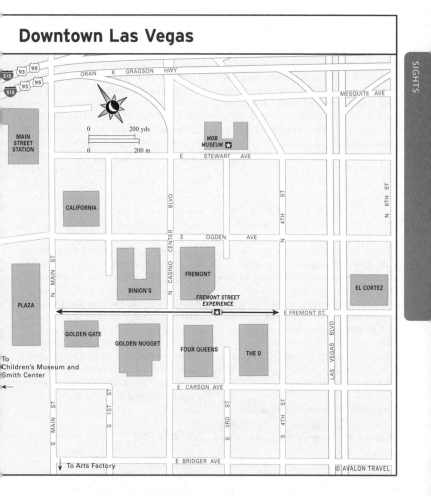

lift toward the canopy, supported by massive concrete pillars. For six minutes, visitors are enthralled by the multimedia shows that chronicle Western history, span the careers of classic rock bands, or transport viewers to fantasy worlds. Viva Vision runs several different shows daily.

Before and after the light shows, strolling buskers sing for their supper, artists create five-minute masterpieces, caricaturists airbrush souvenir portraits, and (sometimes scantily) costumed characters pose for photos. Tipping is all but mandatory ($2-5 is fair). Fremont Street hosts top musical acts, including some A-listers during big Las Vegas weekends such as National Finals Rodeo, NASCAR races, and New Year's. The adjacent Fremont East Entertainment District houses quirky eateries, clubs, and art galleries.

## Las Vegas Natural History Museum

Las Vegas boasts a volcano, a pyramid, and even a Roman coliseum, so it's little wonder that an animatronic *Tyrannosaurus rex* calls the valley home, too. Dedicated to "global life forms. . .

from the desert to the ocean, from Nevada to Africa, from prehistoric times to the present," the **Las Vegas Natural History Museum** (900 Las Vegas Blvd. N., 702/384-3466, www.lvnhm.org, 9am-4pm daily, adults $10, seniors, military, and students $8, ages 3-11 $5) is filled with rotating exhibits that belie the notion that Las Vegas culture begins and ends with neon casino signs.

Visitors to the Treasures of Egypt gallery can enter a realistic depiction of King Tut's tomb to study archaeological techniques and discover golden treasures of the pharaohs. The Wild Nevada gallery showcases the raw beauty and surprisingly varied life-forms of the Mojave Desert. Interactive exhibits also enlighten visitors on subjects such as marine life, geology, African ecosystems, and more.

The 35-foot-long T. rex and his friends (rivals? entrées?)—a triceratops, a raptor, and an ichthyosaur—greet visitors in the Prehistoric Life gallery. And by "greet" we mean a bloodcurdling roar from the T. rex, so take precautions with the little ones and the faint of heart.

## Neon Museum and Boneyard

Book a one-hour guided tour of the **Neon Museum and Boneyard** (770 Las Vegas Blvd. N., 702/387-6366, www.neonmuseum.org, 8:30am-10pm daily, adults $19-26, students, seniors, and veterans $15-22) and take a trip to Las Vegas's more recent past. The boneyard displays 200 old neon signs that were used to advertise casinos, restaurants, bars, and even a flower shop and a dry cleaner. Several have been restored to their former glory and are illuminated during the more costly nighttime tours. The boneyard is not open for self-guided exploration, but the **visitors center**, housed in the scallop-shaped lobby of the historical La Concha Motel, offers a prime example of Googie architecture and can serve as a base for a do-it-yourself tour of restored neon displayed as public art. A word of

caution: The neighborhood surrounding the museum and public neon signs is a bit sketchy after dark.

## Lied Discovery Children's Museum

Voted Best Museum in Las Vegas by readers of the local newspaper for 21 out of the last 25 years, **Lied Discovery Children's Museum** (360 Promenade Pl., 702/382-3445, www.discoverykidslv.org, summer 10am-5pm Mon.-Sat., noon-5pm Sun., winter 9am-4pm Tues.-Fri., 10am-5pm Sat., 12pm-5pm Sun., $14.50) near the Smith Center in the cultural corridor presents more than 100 interactive scientific, artistic, and life-skill activities. Children enjoy themselves so much that they forget they're learning. Among the best permanent exhibits is *It's Your Choice,* which shows kids the importance of eating right and adopting a healthy lifestyle. Exhibits show kids creative ways to explore their world: drama, cooperation, dance, and visual arts. *The Summit* is the playground jungle gym on steroids—three levels of slides, ladders, tubes, and interactive experiments. *Solve It! Mystery Town* lets junior CSI agents gather evidence and practice the scientific method.

## Mormon Fort

The tiny **Mormon Fort** (500 E. Washington Ave., 702/486-3511, http://parks.nv.gov, 8am-4:30pm Tues.-Sat., $1, under 12 free) is the oldest building in Las Vegas. The adobe remnant, constructed by Mormon missionaries in 1855, was part of their original town site, the first permanent non-native settlement in the valley, which they abandoned in 1858. It then served as a store, a barracks, and a shed on the Gass-Stewart Ranch. After that, the railroad leased the old fort to various tenants, including the Bureau of Reclamation, which stabilized and rebuilt the shed to use as a concrete-testing laboratory for Hoover Dam. In 1955 the railroad sold the old fort to the Elks, who in 1963 bulldozed the whole wooden structure (except the little remnant) into the ranch swimming pool and torched it.

Now a state park, the museum includes a visitors center, a recreation of the original fort built around the remnant, and a recreation of the little spring-fed creek that enticed the Mormons to put down roots here in the first place. A tour guide presents the history orally while display boards provide it visually. Your visit will not go unrewarded—it's immensely refreshing to see some preservation of the past in this city of the ultimate now.

### ★ Mob Museum

The **Museum of Organized Crime and Law Enforcement** (300 Stewart Ave., 702/229-2734, http://themobmuseum.org, 9am-9pm daily, $24, seniors, military, law enforcement, and teachers $18, age 11-17 $14, under age 11 free) chronicles Las Vegas's Mafia past and the cops and agents who finally ran the wiseguys out of town. The museum is inside the city's downtown post office and courthouse, appropriately the site of the 1951 Kefauver Hearing investigating organized crime.

Displays include the barber chair where Albert Anastasia was gunned down while getting a haircut, as well as an examination of the violence, ceremony, and hidden meanings behind Mafia "hits," all against a grisly background—the wall from Chicago's St. Valentine's Day Massacre that spelled the end of six members of Bugs Moran's crew and one hanger-on. *Bringing Down the Mob* displays the tools federal agents used—wiretaps, surveillance, and weapons—to clean up the town. Another section explores Hollywood's treatment of organized crime. Say hello to my little friend!

### Downtown Arts District

Centered at South Main Street and East Charleston Boulevard, the district gives art lovers a concentration of galleries to suit any taste, plus an eclectic mix of shops, eateries, and other surprises. The **Arts Factory** (107 E. Charleston Blvd., 702/383-3133, www.theartsfactory.com), a two-story redbrick industrial building, is the district's birthplace. It hosts exhibitions, drawing classes, and poetry readings. Tenants include a toy shop, a yoga studio, a roller-skate store, a *très chic* bistro, and galleries and studios belonging to artists working in every medium and genre imaginable. One downstairs space, **Jana's RedRoom** (11am-7pm Wed.-Sun. and by appointment), displays and sells canvases by local artists.

Virtually all the galleries and other paeans to urban pop culture in the district participate in Las Vegas's **First Friday** (https://ffflv.org, 5pm-11pm 1st Fri. each month) event, which includes wine receptions, pub crawls, art lessons, and plenty of exhibits. Otherwise galleries keep limited hours, so if there's something you don't want to miss, call for an appointment.

Bringing art to the masses, the nonprofit **City of the World Art Gallery** (1229 S Casino Center Blvd., 702/523-5306, www.cityoftheworldlasvegas.org, 1pm-5pm Sun. and Wed., 1pm-7pm Thurs., 11am-7pm Fri.-Sat., donation) showcases the works of dozens of local artists and offers classes for children and adults.

## Off the Strip
### ★ Las Vegas Springs Preserve

The **Las Vegas Springs Preserve** (333 S. Valley View Blvd., 702/822-7700, www.springspreserve.org, 10am-6pm daily, adults $19, students and over age 64 $17, ages 5-17 $11, free under age 5) is where Las Vegas began, at least from a Eurocentric viewpoint. More than 100 years ago, the first nonnatives in the Las Vegas Valley—Mormon missionaries from Salt Lake City—stumbled on this clear artesian spring. Of course, the native Paiute and Pueblo people knew about the springs and exploited them millennia before the Mormons arrived. You can see examples of their tools, pottery, and houses at the site, now a 180-acre monument to environmental stewardship, historical preservation, and geographic discovery. The preserve is home to lizards, rabbits, foxes, scorpions, bats, and more. The nature-minded will love the cactus, rose, and sage gardens, and there's even an occasional cooking demonstration using the desert-friendly fruits, vegetables, and herbs grown here.

Las Vegas has become a leader in water conservation, alternative energy, and other environmentally friendly policies. The results of these efforts and tips on how everyone can reduce their carbon footprint are found in the Sustainability Gallery.

### Nevada State Museum

Visitors can spend hours studying Mojave and Spring Mountains ecology, southern Nevada wildlife (both contemporary and prehistoric), and local mining and railroad history at the **Nevada State Museum** (309 S. Valley View Blvd., 702/486-5205, http://nvculture.org, 9am-5pm Tues.-Sun., $19, included in admission to the Springs Preserve, college students and ages 65 and over $17, ages 5-17 $11, under 5 free). Permanent exhibits on the 13,000-square-foot floor describe southern Nevada's role in warfare, mining, and atomic weaponry and include skeletons of a Columbian mammoth, which roamed the Nevada deserts 20,000 years ago, and the ichthyosaur, a whale-like remnant of the Triassic period. The *Nevada from Dusk to Dawn* exhibit explores the nocturnal lives of the area's animal species. Other exhibits trace the contributions of Las Vegas's gaming, marketing, and business communities.

### ★ Atomic Testing Museum

Members of the "duck and cover" generation will find plenty to spark Cold War memories at the **Atomic Testing Museum** (755 E. Flamingo Rd., 702/794-5151, www.nationalatomictestingmuseum.org, 10am-5pm Mon.-Sat., noon-5pm Sun., adults $22). Las Vegas embraced its role as ground zero in the development of the nation's atomic and nuclear deterrents after World War II. Business leaders welcomed defense contractors to town, and casinos hosted bomb-watching parties as nukes were detonated at the Nevada Test Site, a huge swath of desert 65 miles away. One ingenious marketer promoted the Miss Atomic Bomb beauty pageant in an era when patriotism overcame concerns about radiation.

The museum presents atomic history without bias, walking a fine line between appreciation of the work of nuclear scientists, politicians, and the military and the catastrophic consequences their activities and decisions could have wrought. The museum's best permanent feature is a short video in the Ground Zero Theatre, a multimedia simulation of an actual atomic explosion. The theater, a replica of an observation bunker, is rigged for motion, sound, and rushing air.

One gallery helps visitors put atomic energy milestones in historical perspective, along with the age's impact on 1950s and 1960s pop culture. Another permanent exhibit explains the effects of radiation and how it is tracked and measured. Just as relevant today are the lectures and traveling exhibits that the museum hosts.

Computer simulators, high-speed photographs, Geiger counters and other testing and safety equipment, along with first-person accounts, add to the museum's visit-worthiness.

# Entertainment

## Headliners and Production Shows

An American version of French burlesque, the Las Vegas production show has been gracing various stages around town since the late 1950s. Recently, however, these variety shows have evolved from distinct acts—a juggler, followed by a contortionist, magician, acrobat, etc.

# Grand Canyon Tours from Vegas

Nearly a dozen tour companies relay visitors from Vegas to and through the Grand Canyon via a variety of conveyances—buses, airplanes, helicopters, off-road vehicles, and rafts. Coupons and discounts for online reservation and off-season bookings are plentiful; it is not uncommon to book tours at less than half the rack rates listed here.

## Grand Canyon Tours

**Grand Canyon Tours** (702/655-6060 or 800/222-6966, www.grandcanyontours.com) packs plenty of sightseeing into its bus tours ($80-200), which can include the Grand Canyon Railway or Hualapai Ranch. Helicopter tours ($275-408) cut down the commute, leaving more time at the canyon and allow an earlier return. Choppers skim over Hoover Dam, Lake Mead, the Black Mountains, and the Strip during the 1.5-hour flight. Stops can include the Grand Canyon Skywalk, Grand Canyon West Ranch, and the canyon floor.

## Look Tours

**Look Tours** (4285 N. Rancho Dr., 702/749-5715 or 888/796-4345, www.looktours.com) also offers bus tours (6am-10pm daily, $80-115) and an overnight trip via fixed-wing aircraft ($160-309). Do-it-yourselfers can rent an SUV from Look (7am, 8am, or 9am daily, $170 pp, 2-person minimum) for a leisurely 24-hour exploration of the West Rim.

## Maverick Helicopter Tours

**Maverick Helicopter Tours** (6075 Las Vegas Blvd. S., 702/261-0007 or 888/261-4414, and 1410 Jet Stream Dr., Ste. 100, Henderson, 702/405-4300 or 888/261-4414, www.maverickhelicopter.com) shuttles its customers to the canyon via spacious, quiet Eco-Star helicopters (7am-4:30pm daily, $619) and partners with Pink Jeep Tours for a guided road tour to the West Rim followed by a slow descent to the bottom of the canyon (6am-5pm daily, $395).

## SweeTours

**SweeTours** (6363 S. Pecos Rd., Ste. 106, 702/456-9200 or 877/997-9338, http://sweetours.com) offers several packages ($169-385), which include options for travel by bus, SUV, helicopter, and boat.

---

Today, many shows incorporate these talented performers, but in the context of a connected story. The Cirque du Soleil franchise is a good example. Most other variety shows have given way to more one-dimensional, specialized productions of superstar imitators, jukebox musical revues, and striptease acts masquerading as song-and-dance programs. Most of these are large-budget, skillfully produced and presented extravaganzas, and they make for highly entertaining nights on the town.

As Las Vegas has grown more sophisticated, it has also attracted Broadway productions to compete with the superstar singers—many now signing extended-engagement mini residencies—that helped launch the town's legendary status.

Since they're so expensive to produce, the big shows are fairly reliable, and you can count on them being around for the life of this book's edition. They do change on occasion; the smaller shows come and go with some frequency, but unless a show bombs and is gone in the first few weeks, it'll usually be around for at least a year.

### Absinthe

As great as they are, the world-class singers and dancers and specialty acts featuring astounding acts of balance, athleticism, magic, striptease, and other Vaudeville- and cabaret-inspired performances aren't even the main attraction in **Absinthe** (Caesars Palace, 3570 Las Vegas Blvd. S., 800/745-3000, www.absinthevegas.com, 8pm and 10pm Wed.-Sun., $99-139). That distinction goes to The

Gazillionaire, the show's foul-mouthed, sleaze ball ringmaster, and his female counterpart.

If you go, leave your inhibitions and prudishness at home, lest you find yourself the target of the Gazillionaire's barbs. In-the-round audience configuration assures there's not a bad seat in the house, but with VIP tickets, the performers are, sometimes literally, right in your lap.

### Avengers S.T.A.T.I.O.N./ Transformers

Immerse yourself in two of today's most enduring entertainment franchises at **Avengers S.T.A.T.I.O.N./Transformers** (Treasure Island, 3300 Las Vegas Blvd. S., 702/894-7722, www.stationattraction.com, 10am-10pm daily, $34, age 4-11 $24). Train to become a Marvel Avenger at this interactive Scientific Training and Tactical Intelligence Operative Network center, full of movie props like a life-size Iron Man suit and David Banner's laboratory. Guests will be tested on their Marvel superhero knowledge with trivia questions throughout. The same creative team is developing a similar museum/experience (not yet open at press time) based on the Transformers.

### Baz—Star Crossed Love

**Baz—Star Crossed Love** (Palazzo, 3325 Las Vegas Blvd. S., 702/414-9000, www. venetian.com, 7pm Tues.-Sun., $64-86) reimagines love songs from the films of director Baz Luhrmann. Performers sing and dance their way through highlights from *Moulin Rouge, The Great Gatsby,* and *Romeo and Juliet.*

Tables placed on the stage and banquettes arranged in a semicircle give the production a theater-in-the-round feel, evoking a cabaret floor show. It's almost as if Luhrmann had this show in mind when he selected the songs that appeared in his films. Despite the movies' historical settings, the soundtracks feature contemporary pop songs rather than mood music or stereotypical musical theater standards. As a result, the songs evoking doomed love affairs play well with the show's polished choreography.

### Blue Man Group

Bald, blue, and silent (save for homemade PVC musical instruments), **Blue Man Group** (Luxor, 3900 Las Vegas Blvd. S., 702/262-4400 or 877/386-4658, www. blueman.com, 7pm and 9:30pm daily, $69-128) was one of the hottest things to hit the Strip when it debuted in 2000 after successful versions in New York, Boston, and Chicago. It continues to wow audiences with its thought-provoking, quirkily hilarious gags and percussion performances. It is part street performance, part slapstick, and all fun.

### Carrot Top

With fresh observational humor, outrageous props, and flaming orange hair, Scott Thompson stands alone as the only true full-time headlining stand-up comic in Las Vegas. He's also better known as **Carrot Top** (Luxor, 3900 Las Vegas Blvd. S., 702/262-4400 or 800/557-7428, www. luxor.com, 8pm Wed.-Mon., $55-76). His rapid-fire, stream-of-consciousness delivery ricochets from sex-aid props and poop jokes to current events, pop culture, and social injustice, making him the thinking person's class clown.

### Chippendales

With all the jiggle-and-tease shows on the Strip, **Chippendales** (Rio, 3700 W. Flamingo Rd., 702/777-7776, www.chippendales.com, 8:30pm and 10:30pm Thurs.-Sat., 8:30pm Sun.-Wed., $55-90) delivers a little gender equity. Tight jeans and rippled abs bumping and grinding with their female admirers may be the main attraction, but the choreography is more tasteful than most similar shows, and the guys really can dance. The "firefighters," "cowboys," and other manly man fantasy fodder boys dance their way through sultry and playful renditions of "It's Raining Men" and other tunes with similar themes. They occasionally stroll through the crowd flirting and lap-sitting. However, there is a hands-off policy (wink, wink).

## Circus 1903

Feats of strength, daring, comedy, and skill recall the golden age of the big top at **Circus 1903** (Paris, 3655 Las Vegas Blvd. South, 702/777-2782, 7pm Tues.-Sun., some 3pm matinees Sat.-Sun., $55-129). This circus is turn-of-the-century authentic, from its top-hatted, handlebar-mustachioed ringmaster to its precariously perched acrobats. State-of-the-art sound and lighting and comfortable theater seats are the only bow to modern production values—other than the elephants. Named Queenie and Peanut, the pachyderms are actually realistic life-sized puppets, created by the same geniuses who brought *War Horse* to the stage.

## Donny and Marie

A little bit country, a little bit rock-and-roll, **Donny and Marie Osmond** (Flamingo, 3555 Las Vegas Blvd. S., 702/733-3333, www.caesars.com, 7:30pm Tues.-Sat., $116-134) manage a bit of hip-hop and soul as well, as they hurl affectionate put-downs at each other between musical numbers. The most famous members of the talented family perform their solo hits, such as Donny's "Puppy Love" and Marie's "Paper Roses," along with perfect-harmony duets, while their faux sibling rivalry comes through with good-natured ribbing.

## Terry Fator

*America's Got Talent* champion **Terry Fator** (Mirage, 3400 Las Vegas Blvd. S., 702/792-7777, www.terryfator.com, 7:30pm Mon.-Thurs., $65-142) combines two disparate skills—ventriloquism and impersonation—to channel Elvis, Garth Brooks, Lady Gaga, and others. Backed by a live band, Fator sings and trades one-liners with his foam rubber friends. The

comedy is fresh and mostly clean, the impressions spot-on, and the ventriloquism accomplished with nary a lip quiver.

## Fear the Walking Dead

Because Las Vegas naturally will be the Armageddon of the zombie apocalypse, guests can receive their basic training at **Fear the Walking Dead** (425 Fremont St., 702/947-8342, www.vegasexperience.com, 1pm-1am Sun-Thurs., 1pm-2am Fri.-Sat., $30), in the Fremont Street Experience. Only the most intrepid and dexterous will escape the brain-eaters by negotiating this part haunted house, part escape room, part video game attraction.

## *Kà*

Cirque du Soleil's *Kà* (MGM Grand, 3799 Las Vegas Blvd. S., 702/531-3826, www.mgmgrand.com, 7pm and 9:30pm Sat.-Wed., $75-209) explores the yin and yang of life through the story of separated twins journeying to meet their shared fate. Martial arts, acrobatics, puppetry, plenty of flashy pyrotechnics, and lavish sets and costumes bring cinematic drama to the variety-show acts. Battle scenes play out on two floating, rotating platforms. The show's title was inspired by the ancient Egyptian belief of *ka*, in which every human has a spiritual duplicate.

## *Legends in Concert*

The best of the celebrity impersonator shows, *Legends in Concert* (Flamingo, 3555 Las Vegas Blvd. S., 702/777-2782, www.legendsinconcert.com, 7:30pm and 9:30pm Mon., 9:30pm Tues., 4pm and 9:30pm Wed.-Thurs., and Sat., 7:30pm Sun., $53-82), brings out the "stars" in rapid-fire succession. Madonna barely finishes striking a pose before Janis Joplin gives us another little piece of her heart. Each show features four acts; two generally rotate, while Elvis and Michael Jackson appear in almost every show.

### Le Rêve

All the spectacle we've come to expect from the creative geniuses behind Cirque du Soleil is present in the aquatic stream-of-unconsciousness *Le Rêve* (Wynn, 3131 Las Vegas Blvd. S., 702/770-9966, www.wynnlasvegas.com, 7pm and 9:30pm Fri.-Tues., $115-175). The loose concept is a romantically conflicted woman's fevered dream (*rêve* in French). Some 80 perfectly sculpted specimens of human athleticism and beauty flip, swim, dive, and show off their muscles around a huge pool/stage. More than 2,000 guests fill the theater in the round, with seats all within 50 feet; those in the first couple of rows are in the "splash zone." Clowns and acrobats complete the package.

### ★ LOVE

For Beatles fans visiting Las Vegas, all you need is *LOVE* (Mirage, 3400 Las Vegas Blvd. S., 866/983-4279, www.cirquedusoleil.com/love, 7pm and 9:30pm Thurs.-Mon., $86-196). This Cirque du Soleil-produced journey down Penny Lane features dancers, aerial acrobats, and other performers interpreting the Fab Four's lyrics and recordings. With the breathtaking visual artistry of Cirque du Soleil and a custom sound-scape using the original master tapes from Abbey Road Studios, John, Paul, George, and Ringo have never looked or sounded so good.

### Magic Mike Live

Is it hot in here, or is it just the 13 studs parading around the *Magic Mike Live* stage (Hard Rock, 4455 Paradise Rd., 800/745-3000, www.magicmikelivelasvegas.com, 7pm and 10pm Wed.-Sun., $49-139)? Based on the wildly popular movies, the show features baby oil-slathered hunks in tight jeans, tear-away T-shirts, and less strutting around a facsimile of Club Domina.

### Mystère

Celebrating the human form in all its beauty, athleticism, and grace, *Mystère* (Treasure Island, 3300 Las Vegas Blvd. S., 702/894-7722 or 800/392-1999, www.cirquedusoleil.com/mystere, 7pm and 9:30pm Sat.-Wed., $76-149) is the Cirque du Soleil production that most resembles a traditional American circus. But among the trapeze artists, feats of strength, and clowning around, Mystère also plays on other performance archetypes, including classical Greek theater, Kabuki, and surrealism. The first Cirque show in Las Vegas, *Mystère* continues to dazzle audiences with its revelations of life's mysteries.

### O

Bellagio likes to do everything bigger, better, and more extravagant, and *O* (Bellagio, 3600 Las Vegas Blvd. S., 866/983-4279, www.cirquedusoleil.com/O, 7:30pm and 9:30pm Wed.-Sun., $107-187) is no exception. This Cirque du Soleil incarnation involves a $90 million set, 80 artists, and a 1.5-million-gallon pool of water. The title comes from the French word for water, *eau*, pronounced like the letter O in English. The production involves both terrestrial and aquatic feats of human artistry, athleticism, and comedy.

### Penn & Teller

The oddball comedy magicians **Penn & Teller** (Rio, 3700 W. Flamingo Rd., 702/777-2782, www.pennandteller.com, 9pm Sat.-Wed., $77-97) have a way of making audiences feel special. Seemingly breaking the magicians' code, they reveal the preparation and sleight-of-hand involved in performing tricks. The hitch is that even when forewarned, observers still often can't catch on. And once they do, the verbose Penn and silent Teller add a wrinkle no one expects.

### Raiding the Rock Vault

Join rock archaeologists as they unearth the treasures of the 1960s, '70s, and '80s in **Raiding the Rock Vault** (Hard Rock,

4455 Paradise Rd., 800/745-3000, www.
raidingtherockvault.com, 8pm Sat.-
Wed., $69-109). Each room of the vault
brings a rock era to life, with members
of music's hit-makers—Bon Jovi, Quiet
Riot, Whitesnake, Guns N' Roses, Heart,
and more—performing the best arena
anthems.

### Tournament of Kings

Pound on the table with your goblet and
let loose a hearty "huzzah!" to cheer
your king to victory over the other na-
tions' regents at the **Tournament of Kings**
(Excalibur, 3580 Las Vegas Blvd. S.,
702/597-7600, www.excalibur.com, 6pm
and 8:30pm Sat.-Mon. and Wed.-Thurs.,
$76). Each section of the equestrian the-
ater rallies under separate banners as
their hero participates in jousts, sword
fights, riding contests, and lusty-maid
flirting at this festival hosted by King
Arthur and Merlin. A regal feast, served
medieval style (that is, without utensils),
starts with a tureen of dragon's blood (to-
mato soup). But just as the frivolity hits
its climax, an evil lord appears to wreak
havoc. Can the kings and Merlin's magic
save the day? One of the best family
shows in Las Vegas.

### Zumanity

Cirque du Soleil seems to have succumbed to the titillation craze with the
strange melding of sensuality, athleticism, and voyeurism that is **Zumanity**
(New York New York, 3790 Las Vegas
Blvd. S., www.cirquedusoleil.com/zu-
manity, 866/983-4279, 7pm and 9:30pm
Tues.-Sat., $75-145). The cabaret-style
show makes no pretense of story line,
but instead takes audience members
through a succession of sexual and
topless fantasies—cellmates, sexual
awakening, bathing beauties, ménage-
à-trois, and more for the uninhibited
over-18 crowd.

**Top to bottom:** Cirque du Soleil's *LOVE;* Cirque
du Soleil's *Kà;* Cirque du Soleil's *O.*

## Showroom and Lounge Acts

Showrooms are another Las Vegas institution, with most hotels providing live entertainment—usually magic, comedy, or tributes to the big stars who played or are playing the big rooms and theaters under the same roofs.

The Vegas lounge act is the butt of a few jokes and more than one satire, but they offer some of the best entertainment values in town—a night's entertainment for the price of a few drinks and a small cover charge. Every hotel in Las Vegas worth its salt has a lounge. These acts are listed in the free entertainment magazines and the *Las Vegas Review-Journal*'s helpful website, but unless you're familiar with the performers, it's the luck of the draw: They list only the entertainer's name, venue, and showtimes.

### The Rat Pack Is Back

Relive the golden era when Frank, Dean, Sammy, and Joey ruled the Strip with **The Rat Pack Is Back** (Tuscany, 255 E. Flamingo Rd., 702/947-5981, www.ratpackisback.com, 7:30pm Mon.-Sat., $60-66). Watch Sinatra try to make it through "Luck Be a Lady" amid the others' sophomoric antics. Frank plays right along, pretending to rule his crew with an iron fist, as the crew treats him with the mock deference the Chairman of the Board deserves.

### All Shook Up: A Tribute to the King

A swivel-hipped, curled-lip journey through his career, **All Shook Up** (Planet Hollywood, 3667 Las Vegas Blvd. S., 702/260-7200, www.vtheaterboxoffice.com, 6pm daily, $60-70) is the only all-Elvis impersonator show on the Strip. Both rotating impressionists bear a strong resemblance to the King, capturing not only his voice but also his mannerisms, as they recount Elvis's hits from rock-and-roll pioneer to movie idol. The intimate 300-seat showroom makes every seat a good one.

### Mac King Comedy Magic Show

The quality of afternoon shows in Las Vegas is spotty at best, but **Mac King Comedy Magic Show** (Harrah's, 3475 Las Vegas Blvd. S., 866/983-4279, www.mackingshow.com, 1pm and 3pm Tues.-Sat., $36-47) fits the bill for talent and affordability. King's routine is clean both technically and content-wise. With a plaid suit, good manners, and a silly grin, he cuts a nerdy figure, but his tricks and banter are skewed enough to make even the most jaded teenager laugh.

### Divas Las Vegas

Veteran female impersonator Frank Marino has been headlining on the Strip for 25 years, and he still looks good—with or without eye shadow and falsies. Marino stars as emcee Joan Rivers, leading fellow impersonators who lip-synch their way through cheeky renditions of tunes by Lady Gaga, Katy Perry, Madonna, and others in **Divas Las Vegas** (The Linq, 3535 Las Vegas Blvd. S., 702/777-2782 or 866/574-3851, www.caesars.com, 9:30pm Sat.-Thurs., $26-98).

### Gordie Brown

A terrific song stylist in his own right, **Gordie Brown** (Planet Hollywood, 3667 Las Vegas Blvd. S., 702/260-7200, www.gordiebrown.com, 7pm Tues.-Thurs. and Sat.-Sun., $59-80) is the thinking person's singing impressionist. Using his targets' peccadilloes as fodder for his song parodies, Brown pokes serious fun with a surgeon's precision. Props, mannerisms, and absurd vignettes add to the madcap fun. But make no mistake—behind the gimmicks, Brown is not only a talented impressionist but a gifted singer in his own right, no matter whose voice he uses.

### Comedy

Nearly gone are the days of top-name comedians as resident headliners. However, The Venetian (3355 Las Vegas Blvd. S., 866/641-7469, www.venetian.com) regularly books funny females for its *Lipshtick* shows (nights and times vary, $54-118), such as Lisa Lampanelli, Joy Behar, and other A-listers. The other biggies—Daniel Tosh, Jay Leno, and Ron White, among others—still make regular appearances as part of the **Aces of Comedy** (Mirage, 3400 Las Vegas Blvd. S., 702/791-7111, www.mirage.com, 7:30pm-10pm Fri.-Sat., $50-60). But most of the yuks nowadays come from the talented youngsters toiling in the comedy club trenches.

The journeymen and up-and-coming have half a dozen places to land gigs when they're in town. Among the best are **Brad Garrett's Comedy Club** (3799 Las Vegas Blvd. S., 866/740-7711, www.bradgarrettcomedy.com, 8pm daily, $43-65, plus $22 when Garrett performs) at the MGM Grand, **L.A. Comedy Club** (Stratosphere, 2000 Las Vegas Blvd. S., 702/380-7777 or 800/998-6937, www.thelacomedyclub.com, 8pm daily, 6pm and 10pm shows some nights, $47-64), **Laugh Factory** (Tropicana, 801 Las Vegas Blvd. S., 702/739-2222, www.laughfactory.com, 8:30pm and 10:30pm daily, $38-55), **Las Vegas Live** (Planet Hollywood, 3667 Las Vegas Blvd. S., 702/260-7200, www.lasvegaslivecomedyclub.com, 9pm daily, $56-67), and **Jokesters** (The D, 301 Fremont St., 702/388-2111, www.jokesterslasvegas.com, 10:30pm daily, $30-40).

### Magic

Magic shows are nearly as ubiquitous as comedy, with the more accomplished, such as Penn & Teller at Rio, Criss Angel at Luxor, and **David Copperfield** (MGM Grand, 3799 Las Vegas Blvd. S., 866/740-7711, www.davidcopperfield.com, 7pm and 9:30pm Sun.-Fri., 4pm, 7pm, and 9:30pm Sat., $78-123) playing long-term gigs in their own showrooms.

The best smaller-scale magicians also have the distinction of being kid-friendly. In addition to Mac King at Harrah's, two other clean prestidigitators have taken up residency at Planet Hollywood. Both are *America's Got Talent* alumni. **Nathan Burton Comedy Magic** (Planet Hollywood, 3663 Las Vegas Blvd. S., 866/932-1818, www.nathanburton.com, 4pm Tues., Thurs., and Sat.-Sun., $50-60) serves up epic disappearing acts, while **Murray the Magician** (Planet Hollywood, 3663 Las Vegas Blvd. S., 866/932-1818, www.murraymagic.com, 4pm Sat.-Mon. and Thurs., $60-80) mixes comedy banter with his sleight of hand.

## Live Music

Those who don't want to deal with the hassles of a trip to the Strip or whose musical tastes don't match the often-mainstream pop of the resort lounges might find a gem or two by venturing away from the neon.

The newest, best, and most convenient venue for visitors, **Brooklyn Bowl** (The Linq Promenade, 3545 Las Vegas Blvd. S., Ste. 22, 702/862-2695, www.brooklynbowl.com, 5pm-late daily) replicates its successful New York City formula with 32 lanes, comfortable couches, beer, and big-name groups sprinkled among the party band lineup. Elvis Costello, Wu-Tang Clan, Jane's Addiction, and the Psychedelic Furs are among the notables that have played the Brooklyn. Showtimes range from noon to midnight, often with several acts slated throughout the day.

The best indie bands in Las Vegas, as well as touring jammers, electropoppers, and garage bands, make it a point to play the **Bunkhouse Saloon** (124 S. 11th St., 702/982-1764, www.bunkhousedowntown.com, 5pm-1am Sun.-Mon. and Wed.-Thurs., 5pm-2am Fri.-Sat.). **Count's Vamp'd** (6750 W. Sahara Ave., 702/220-8849, www.vampdvegas.com, 11am-2am daily) books a mix of tribute bands and '80s metal icons appearing solo or with their newest project. Progressive metal and punk fans should check out **Backstage Bar & Billiards** (601 Fremont St., 702/382-2227, www.backstagebarlv.com, 8pm-3am Tues.-Sat.).

With more than 20,000 square feet of space and a 2,500-square-foot dance floor, **Stoney's Rockin' Country** (6611 Las Vegas Blvd. S., Ste. 160, 702/435-2855, http://stoneysrockincountry.com, 7pm-2am Wed.-Sat.) in the Town Square mall could almost *be* its own country. It is honky-tonk on a grand scale, with a mechanical bull and line-dancing lessons. Muddy Waters, Etta James, B. B. King, and even Mick Jagger have graced the stage at the reopened **Sand Dollar** (3355 Spring Mountain Rd., 702/485-5401, http://thesanddollarlv.com, 7pm-3am Tues.-Sun.), where blue-collar blues and smoky jazz rule. Bands start around 10pm weekends. The people your mama warned you about hang out at the never-a-cover-charge **Double Down Saloon** (4640 Paradise Rd., 702/791-5775, www.doubledownsaloon.com, 24 hours daily), drinking to excess and thrashing to the punk, ska, and psychobilly bands on stage.

## The Arts

With all the plastic and neon, it's easy to accuse Las Vegas of being a soulless, cultureless wasteland, and many have. But beyond the glitz, Las Vegas is a community. Why shouldn't the city enjoy and foster the arts?

The local performing arts are thriving, thanks to the **Smith Center for the Performing Arts** (361 Symphony Park Ave., 702/749-2012, www.thesmithcenter.com), a major cog in the revitalization of downtown. It is home to the **Las Vegas Philharmonic** (702/258-5438, http://lvphil.org) and the **Nevada Ballet Theatre** (702/243-2623, www.nevadaballet.org), and also hosts local performances and theatrical touring companies.

## Rides and Games
### Stratosphere Tower

Daredevils will delight in the vertigo-inducing thrill rides on the observation deck at the **Stratosphere Tower** (2000 Las Vegas Blvd. S., 702/383-5210, www.stratospherehotel.com, 10am-1am Sun.-Thurs., 10am-2am Fri.-Sat., $15-120).

The newest ride, Sky Jump Las Vegas, invites the daring to plunge into space for a 15-second free fall. Angled guide wires keep jumpers on target and ease them to gentle landings. This skydive without a parachute costs $120. The other rides are 100-story-high variations on traditional thrill rides: The Big Shot is a sort of 15-person reverse bungee jump; X-Scream sends riders on a gentle (at first) roll off the edge, leaving them suspended over Las Vegas Boulevard; Insanity's giant arms swing over the edge, tilting to suspend riders nearly horizontally. These attractions are $25 each, including the elevator ride to the top of the tower. Multiple-ride packages and all-day passes are available but don't include the Sky Jump.

### SlotZilla

For an up-close, high-speed view of the Fremont Street Experience canopy and the iconic casino signs, take a zoom on **SlotZilla** (425 Fremont St., 702/678-5780, www.vegasexperience.com, 1pm-1am Sun.-Thurs., 1pm-2am Fri.-Sat., $25-45), a 1,750-foot-long zip line that takes off from a the world's largest slot machine (only in Vegas, right?). Riders are launched horizontally, Superman-style, for a 40-mph slide. For the less adventurous, SlotZilla also operates a lower, slower, half-as-long version. Fly before 6pm to save $5 per ride.

### Adventuredome

Behind Circus Circus, the **Adventuredome Theme Park** (2880 Las Vegas Blvd. S., 702/794-3939, www.circuscircus.com, 10am-midnight daily summer, 10am-6pm Sun.-Thurs. and 10am-midnight Fri.-Sat. during the school year, over 48 inches tall $33, under 48 inches $19) houses two roller coasters, a 4-D motion simulator, laser beam mazes, climbing wall, miniature golf, and vertigo-inducing amusement machines—all inside a pink plastic shell. The main teen and adult attractions are the coasters—El Loco and Canyon Blaster, the only indoor double-loop, double-corkscrew coaster in the world, with speeds up to 55 mph, which is pretty rough. The five-acre fun park can host birthday parties. The all-day passes are a definite bargain over individual ride prices, but carnival games, food vendors, and special rides and games not included in the pass give parents extra chances to spend money. It's not the Magic Kingdom, but it has rides to satisfy all ages and bravery levels. Besides, Las Vegas is supposed to be the *adult* Disneyland.

### Wet 'n' Wild

With rides conjuring Las Vegas, the desert, and the Southwest, **Wet 'n' Wild** (7055 Fort Apache Rd., 702/979-1600, www.wetnwildlasvegas.com, 10:30am-8pm Sun.-Thurs., 10:30am-10pm Fri.-Sat. June-Aug. and weekends and holidays Apr., May, and Sept., $35, discounts for seniors, guests under 42 inches tall, and entrance after 4pm) provides a welcome respite from the dry heat of southern Nevada. Challenge the Royal Flush Extreme, which whisks riders through a steep pipe before swirling them around a simulated porcelain commode and down the tube. The water park boasts 12 rides of varying terror levels along with a lazy river, wave pool, and Kiddie Cove. Guests must be over 42 inches tall to enjoy all the rides.

### Cowabunga Bay

Wet 'n' Wild's competitor on the east side of town, **Cowabunga Bay** (900 Galleria Dr., Henderson, 702/850-9000, www.cowabungabayvegas.com, 11am-7pm Sun.-Thurs., 11am-10pm Fri.-Sat. June-Aug., limited days and hours Apr., May, and Sept., $40, under 48 inches $30) has nine waterslides, four pools, and the longest lazy river in the state.

### Driving Experiences

Calling all gearheads! If you're ready to take the wheel of a 600-hp stock car, check out the **Richard Petty Driving Experience** (Las Vegas Motor Speedway, 7000 Las Vegas Blvd. N., 800/237-3889, www.drivepetty.com, days and times vary, $109-3,200). The Rookie Experience ($499) lets NASCAR wannabes put the stock car through its paces for eight laps around the 1.5-mile tri-oval after extensive in-car and on-track safety training. Participants also receive a lap-by-lap breakdown of their run, transportation to and from the Strip, and a tour of the Driving Experience Race Shop. Even more intense—and more expensive— experiences, with more laps and more in-depth instruction, are available. To feel the thrill without the responsibility, opt for the three-lap ride-along ($109) in a two-seat stock car with a professional driver at the wheel.

**Exotics Racing** (6925 Speedway Blvd., Ste. C-105, 702/802-5662, www.exotics-racing.com, 7am-8pm Mon.-Fri., 8am-7pm Sat.-Sun., $300-500 for five laps), **Dream Racing** (7000 Las Vegas Blvd. N., 702/599-5199, www.dreamracing.com, $199-500 for five laps), and **Speed Vegas** (14200 Las Vegas Blvd. S., 888/341-7133, www.speedvegas.com, $39-99 per lap) offer similar pedal-to-the-metal thrills in Porsches, Ferraris, Lamborghinis, and more. All offer add-ons such as videos of your drive, passenger rates, and ride-alongs with professional drivers.

## Sports
### Golf

A world-class golfing destination, Las Vegas is chock-full of picturesque courses. All are eminently playable and fair, although the dry heat makes the greens fast and the city's valley location can make for some havoc-wreaking winds in the spring. Many Las Vegas courses, especially in recent years, have removed extraneous water-loving landscaping, opting for xeriscape and desert landscape, irrigating the fairways and greens with reclaimed water. Still, lush landscaping and tricky water holes abound. Greens fees and amenities range from affordable municipal-type courses to some of the most exclusive country clubs anywhere. The following is a selective list in each budget category. There are bargains, if you're willing to brave the scorching afternoon temperatures. Fees are exponentially higher in the early morning and evening.

The only course open to the public on the Strip is **Bali Hai** (5160 Las Vegas Blvd. S., 888/427-6678, www.balihaigolfclub.com, $149-189), next to Mandalay Bay on the south end of casino row. The South Pacific theme includes lots of lush green tropical foliage, deep azure ponds, and black volcanic outcroppings. A handful of long par-4s are fully capable of making a disaster of your scorecard even before you reach the par-3 sphincter-clenching 16th. Not only does it play to an island green, it comes with a built-in gallery where others can enjoy your discomfort while dining on Bali Hai's restaurant patio.

There's plenty of water to contend with at **Siena Golf Club** (10575 Siena Monte Ave., 702/341-9200, www.sienagolfclub.com, $85). Six small lakes, deep fairway bunkers, and desert scrub provide significant challenges off the tee, but five sets of tee boxes even things out for shorter hitters. The large, flattish greens are fair and readable. The first Las Vegas course to adopt an ecofriendly xeriscape design, **Painted Desert** (5555 Painted Mirage Rd., 702/645-2570, www.painteddesertgc.com, $45-90) uses cacti, mesquite, and other desert plants to separate its links-style fairways. The 6,323-yard, par-72 course isn't especially challenging, especially if you're straight off the tee, making it a good choice for getting back to the fundamentals. Video tips from the 18-time major winner himself play on an in-cart screen at **Bear's Best** (11111 W. Flamingo Rd., 702/804-8500, www.clubcorp.com, $129-199), a collection of Jack Nicklaus's favorite holes from

courses he designed: Castle Pines, PGA West, and more.

## Las Vegas Motor Speedway

Home to two events (March and Sept.) in the Monster Energy NASCAR Cup Series, the **Las Vegas Motor Speedway** (7000 Las Vegas Blvd. N., 702/644-4444, www.lvms.com) is a racing omniplex. In addition to the superspeedway, a 1.5-mile tri-oval for NASCAR races, the site also brings in dragsters to its quarter-mile strip; modifieds, late models, bandoleros, legends, bombers, and more to its paved oval; and off-roaders to its half-mile clay oval. There's also a motocross track and a road course. A multimillion-dollar renovation project between NASCAR Weekends in 2006 and 2007 created the Neon Garage in the speedway's infield. It brings fans up close with their favorite drivers and their crews, providing an unprecedented interactive fan experience. Neon Garage has unique and gourmet concession stands, live entertainment, and the winner's circle.

## Boxing and Mixed Martial Arts

Las Vegas retains the title as heavyweight boxing champion of the world. Nevada's legalized sports betting, its history, and the facilities at the MGM Grand Garden, Mandalay Bay Events Center, T-Mobile Arena, and other locations make it a natural for the biggest matches. For the megafights, expect to dole out big bucks to get inside the premier venues. The "cheap" seats at MGM and Mandalay Bay often cost a car payment and require the Hubble telescope to see any action. Ringside seats require a mortgage payment. Check the venues' websites for tickets.

Fight fans can find a card pretty much every month from March to October at either the Hard Rock, Sam's Town, Sunset Station, Palms, or other midsize arena or showroom. The fighters are hungry, the matches are entertaining, and the cost is low, with tickets priced $15-100. Mixed

## ◈ Side Trip to Hoover Dam

The 1,400-mile Colorado River has been carving and gouging great canyons and valleys with red sediment-laden waters for 10 million years. For 10,000 years Native Americans, the Spanish, and Mormon settlers coexisted with the fitful river, rebuilding after spring floods and withstanding the droughts that often reduced the mighty waterway to a muddy trickle in fall. But the 1905 flood convinced the Bureau of Reclamation to "reclaim" the West, primarily by building dams and canals. The most ambitious of these was Hoover Dam: 40 million cubic yards of reinforced concrete, turbines, and transmission lines.

Hoover Dam remains an engineering marvel, attracting millions of visitors each year. It makes an interesting half-day escape from the glitter of Las Vegas, only 30 miles to the north. The one-hour **Dam Tour** (every 30 minutes, 9:30am-3:30pm daily, $30 age 8 and over) offers a guided exploration of its power plant and walkways, along with admission to the visitors center. The two-hour **Power Plant Tour** ($15 adults, $12 seniors, children, and military, uniformed military and children under 4 free) focuses on the dam's construction and engineering through multimedia presentations, exhibits, docent talks, and a power plant tour.

### Getting There

The bypass bridge diverts traffic away from Hoover Dam, saving time and headaches for both drivers and dam visitors. Still, the **35-mile drive** from central Las Vegas to a parking lot at the dam will take **45 minutes** or more. From the Strip, **I-15 South** connects with I-215 southeast of the airport, and **I-215 East** takes drivers to US 93 in Henderson. Remember that US 93 shares the roadway with US 95 and I-515 till well past Henderson. Going south on **US 93,** exit at **NV-172** to the dam. Note that this route is closed on the Arizona side; drivers continuing on to the **Grand Canyon** must retrace **NV-172** to **US 93** and cross the bypass bridge. A **parking garage** ($10) is convenient to the visitors center and dam tours, but free parking is available at turnouts on both sides of the dam for those willing to walk.

martial arts also continues to grow in popularity, with MGM and Mandalay Bay hosting UFC title fights about every other month.

# Shopping

## Malls

The most upscale and most Strip-accessible of the traditional, non-casino-affiliated, indoor shopping complexes, **Fashion Show** (3200 Las Vegas Blvd. S., 702/369-8382, www.thefashionshow.com, 10am-9pm Mon.-Sat., 11am-7pm Sun.), across from the Wynn, is anchored by Saks Fifth Avenue, Dillard's, Neiman Marcus, Macy's, and Nordstrom. The mall gets its name from the 80-foot retractable runway in the Great Hall, where resident retailers put on fashion shows on weekend afternoons. Must-shop stores include Papyrus, specializing in stationery and gifts centering on paper arts and crafts, and The Lego Store, where blockheads can find specialty building sets tied to movies, video games, and television shows. Dine alfresco at a Strip-side café, shaded by "the cloud," a 128-foot-tall canopy that doubles as a projection screen.

If your wallet contains dozens of Ben Franklins, **Crystals at City Center** (3720 Las Vegas Blvd. S., 702/590-9299, www.simon.com, 10am-11pm Mon.-Thurs., 10am-midnight Fri.-Sat.) is your destination for impulse buys like a hand-woven Olimpia handbag from Bottega Veneta for her or a titanium timepiece from Porsche Design for him.

Parents can reward their children's patience with rides on cartoon animals, spaceships, and other kiddie favorites in the carpeted, clean play area at **Meadows Mall** (4300 Meadows Ln., 702/878-3331, www.meadowsmall.com, 10am-9pm Mon.-Sat., 10am-6pm Sun.). There are 140 stores and restaurants—all the usual mall denizens along with some interesting specialty shops. It's across the street from the Las Vegas Springs Preserve, so families can make a day of it. The **Boulevard Mall** (3528 S. Maryland Pkwy., 702/735-8268, www.boulevard-mall. com, 10am-9pm Mon.-Sat., 10am-6pm Sun.) is similar. It's in an older and less trendy setting, but a new facade, family attractions, and better dining are driving a comeback. Oddly, there's a large call center in the space recently vacated by the withdrawal of two anchor tenants.

A visit to **Town Square** (6605 Las Vegas Blvd. S., 702/269-5001, www.mytown-squarelasvegas.com, 10am-9pm Mon.-Thurs., 10am-10pm Fri.-Sat., 11am-8pm Sun.) is like a stroll through a favorite suburb. "Streets" wind between stores in Spanish, Moorish, and Mediterranean-style buildings. Mall stalwarts like Victoria's Secret and Abercrombie & Fitch are here, along with some unusual treats—Tommy Bahama's includes a café. Just as in a real town, the retail outlets surround a central square, which holds 13,000 square feet of mazes, tree houses, and performance stages. Around holiday time, machine-made snowflakes drift down through the trees. Nightlife ranges from laid-back wine and martini bars to rousing live entertainment and the 18-screen Rave movie theater.

Easterners and Westerners alike revel in the wares offered at **Chinatown Plaza** (4255 Spring Mountain Rd., 702/221-8448, http://lvchinatownplaza.com, 10am-10pm daily). Despite the name, Chinatown Las Vegas is a pan-Asian clearinghouse where Asians can celebrate their history and heritage while stocking up on favorite reminders of home. Meanwhile, Westerners can submerge themselves in new cultures by sampling the offerings at authentic Chinese, Thai, Vietnamese, and other Asian restaurants and strolling the plaza reading posters explaining Chinese customs. Tea sets, silk robes, Buddha statuettes, and jade carvings are of particular interest, as is the Diamond Bakery, with its elaborate wedding cakes and sublime mango mousse cake.

## Casino Plazas

Almost two-thirds of the Las Vegas Strip's $19 billion in annual casino revenue comes from non-gaming activities. Restaurants and hotel rooms are the biggest contributors, but upscale shopping plazas—many with tenants that would feel right at home on Rodeo Drive, Ginza, or the Champs-Élysées—increasingly are doing their part to put brass in casino investors' pockets.

Caesars Palace initiated the concept of Las Vegas as a shopping destination in 1992 when it unveiled the **Forum Shops** (3570 Las Vegas Blvd. S., 702/893-3807, www.caesars.com, 10am-11pm Sun.-Thurs., 10am-midnight Fri.-Sat.). Top brand luxury stores coexist with fashionable hipster boutiques amid some of the best people-watching on the Strip. A stained-glass-domed pedestrian plaza greets shoppers as they enter the 175,000-square-foot expansion from the Strip. You'll find one of only two spiral escalators in the United States. The gods come alive hourly to extract vengeance in the *Fall of Atlantis* show, and you can check out the feeding of the fish in the big saltwater aquarium twice daily.

Part shopping center, part theater in the round, the **Miracle Mile** (Planet Hollywood, 3663 Las Vegas Blvd. S., 702/866-0703, www.miraclemileshops-lv.com, 10am-11pm Sun.-Thurs., 10am-midnight Fri.-Sat.) is a delightful (or vicious, depending on your point of view) circle of shops, eateries, bars, and theaters. If your budget doesn't quite stand up to the Forum Shops, Miracle Mile could be just your speed. Low-cost shows include an Elvis tribute, the campy *Zombie Burlesque,* and family-friendly animal acts and magicians.

Las Vegas comedy icon Rita Rudner loves the **Grand Canal Shoppes** (Venetian, 3377 Las Vegas Blvd. S., 702/414-4525, www.grandcanalshoppes. com, 10am-11pm Sun.-Thurs., 10am-midnight Fri.-Sat.) because "Where else but in Vegas can you take a gondola to the Gap?" There's not really a Gap here. It would stick out like a sore thumb among the shops that line the canal among streetlamps and cobblestones under a frescoed sky. Nature gets a digital assist in the photos for sale at Peter Lik gallery, and Armani and Diane von Furstenberg compete for your shopping dollar. The "Streetmosphere" includes strolling minstrels and specialty acts, and many of these entertainers find their way to St. Mark's Square for seemingly impromptu performances.

Money attracts money, so it's no wonder Hermes, Prada, Rolex, and Loro Piana count themselves among the tenants at Steve Wynn's **Esplanade** (Wynn/Encore, 3131 Las Vegas Blvd. S., 702/770-7000, www.wynnlasvegas.com, 10am-11pm Sun.-Thurs., 10am-midnight Fri.-Sat.). Wide, curved skylights, fragrant flowers, and delicate artwork create a pleasant window-shopping experience.

Perfectly situated in the flourishing urban arts district, the **Downtown Container Park** (707 E. Fremont St., 702/359-9982, www.downtowncontainerpark.com, 11am-9pm Mon.-Thurs., 11am-10pm Fri.-Sat., 11am-8pm Sun.) packs 40 boutiques, galleries, bars, and bistros into their own shipping containers. The Dome ($9-15), an IMAX-like theater with reclining chairs, shows immersive, surround-sound video rock band performances and nature documentaries. Container Park is the centerpiece of the Fremont East District, an ambitious development aimed at reclaiming a formerly dicey area with eateries, bars, and shops.

Unless you're looking for a specific item or brand, or you're attracted to the atmosphere, attractions, architecture, or vibe of a particular Strip destination, you can't go wrong browsing the shopping center in your hotel. You'll find shops just as nice at **Le Boulevard** (Paris, 3655 Las Vegas Blvd. S., 702/946-7000, www.boulevardmall.com, 8am-2am daily), **Grand Bazaar Shops** (Bally's, 3645 Las Vegas Blvd. S., 702/967-4366 or 888/266-5687, http://grandbazaarshops.com, 10am-10pm Sun.-Thurs., 10am-11pm Fri.-Sat.), **The Linq** (3545 Las Vegas Blvd. S., 702/694-8100 or 866/328-1888, www.caesars.com, shop and restaurant hours vary), and **Mandalay Place** (Mandalay Bay, 3950 Las Vegas Blvd. S., 702/632-7777 or 877/632-7800, www.mandalaybay.com, 10am-11pm daily).

# Food

The exclusive resorts on the Strip have developed their buffets into gourmet presentations, often including delicacies such as crab legs, crème brûlée, and even caviar. Others, especially downtown, remain low-cost belly-filling options for intense gamblers and budget-conscious families. The typical buffet breakfast presents the usual fruits, juices, croissants, steam-table scrambled eggs, sausages, potatoes, and pastries. Lunch is salads and chicken, pizza, spaghetti, tacos, and more. For dinner, buffets add steamed vegetables, mashed potatoes, and several varieties of meat, including a carving table with prime rib, turkey, and pork loin.

Most major hotels still have 24-hour coffee shops (often with a graveyard or gambler's special), a top-line steak/chop/seafood house, and a buffet along with a couple restaurants offering French, Italian, Asian, or Mexican fare. Non-casino restaurants around town are also proliferating quickly. Except for the highbrow and celebrity-chef spots, menu prices, like room rates, are consistently less expensive in Las Vegas than in any other major city in the country.

## Upper Strip
### Breakfast
It's all about the hen fruit at ★ **The Egg & I** (4533 W. Sahara Ave., Ste. 5, 702/364-9686, http://theeggworks.com, 6am-3pm daily, $10-20). They serve other breakfast fare as well, of course—the banana muffins and stuffed French toast are notable—but if you don't order an omelet, you're just being stubborn. It has huge portions, fair prices, and on-top-of-it service. Go!

The retro-deco gaudiness of the neon decor and bachelor pad-esque sunken fire pit may not do wonders for a Vegas-sized headache, but the tostada omelet at the **Peppermill Restaurant & Fireside Lounge** (2985 Las Vegas Blvd. S., 702/735-7635, www.peppermilllasvegas.com, daily 24 hours, $12-20) will give it what-for. For a little less zest, try the French toast ambrosia.

### French and Continental
The pink accents at **Pamplemousse** (400 E. Sahara Ave., 702/733-2066, www.pamplemousserestaurant.com, 5pm-10pm daily, $35-56) hint at the name's meaning (grapefruit) and set the stage for romance. The cuisine is so fresh that the menu changes daily. Specialties include leg and breast of duck in cranberry-raspberry sauce and a rosemary and pistachio rack of lamb. Save room for chocolate soufflé.

### Italian
Long a hangout for the Rat Pack, athletes, presidents, and certain Sicilian "businessmen," **Piero's** (355 Convention Center Dr., 702/369.2305, http://pieroscuisine.com, 5:30pm-10pm daily, $40-60) still attracts the celebrity set with leather booths, stone fireplace, stellar service, and assurance they won't be bothered

Forum Shops, Caesars Palace

FOOD

by autograph hounds. The menu hasn't changed much since the goodfellas started coming here in the early 1980s; it's heavy (and we do mean "heavy") on the veal, breading, cheese, and sauce.

Wall frescoes put you on an Italian thoroughfare as you dine on authentic cuisine at **Fellini's** (Stratosphere, 2000 Las Vegas Blvd. S., 702/383-4859, http://fellinislv.com, 5pm-11pm Sun.-Thurs., 5pm-midnight Fri.-Sat., $28-50). Each smallish dining room has a different fresco. The food is more contemporary and Americanized than the classic Italian served at Piero's, but only food snobs could find anything to complain about.

### Steak
The perfectly cooked steaks and attentive service that once attracted Frank Sinatra, Nat "King" Cole, Natalie Wood, and Elvis are still trademarks at **Golden Steer** (308 W. Sahara Ave., 702/384-4470, www.goldensteerlasvegas.com, 4:30pm-10:30pm daily, $45-65). A gold rush

motif and 1960s swankiness still abide here, along with classics like crab cakes, big hunks of beef, and Caesar salad prepared tableside.

### Vegas Views
The 360-seat, 360-degree **Top of the World** (Stratosphere, 2000 Las Vegas Blvd. S., 702/380-7711 or 800/998-6937, www.topoftheworldlv.com, 11am-11pm daily, $50-80), on the 106th floor of Stratosphere Tower more than 800 feet above the Strip, makes a complete revolution once every 80 minutes, giving you the full city panorama during dinner. The view of Vegas defies description, and the food is a recommendable complement. Order the seafood fettuccine or surf-and-turf gnocchi with lobster and beef short rib. It's even money that you will witness (or receive) an offer of marriage during your meal. If you're the one popping the question, ask about their proposal packages.

## Center Strip
### Asian
You may pay for the setting as much as for the food at **Fin** (The Mirage, 3400 Las Vegas Blvd. S., 866/339-4566, www.mirage.com, 5pm-10pm Thurs.-Mon., $40-60). But why not? Sometimes the atmosphere is worth it, especially when you're trying to make an impression on your mate or potential significant other. The metallic-ball curtains evoke a rainstorm in a Chinese garden, setting just the right romantic mood. Still, it is difficult to pull off gourmet Chinese. While Fin's prices are not outrageous, the fare isn't much better than you could find at many midpriced restaurants; you can probably find more yum for your yuan elsewhere.

Better value can be had at **Tao Asian Bistro** (Venetian, 3377 Las Vegas Blvd. S., 702/388-8338, www.taolasvegas.com, 5pm-midnight daily, $35-50). Pan-Asian dishes—the roasted Thai Buddha chicken is our pick—and an extensive sake selection are served amid decor that is a trip through Asian history, including imperial koi ponds and a floating Buddha.

At **Wing Lei** (Wynn, 3131 Las Vegas Blvd. S., 702/770-3388, www.wynnlasvegas.com, 5:30pm-9:30pm Sun.-Thurs., 5:30pm-10pm Fri.-Sat., $50-75), French colonialism comes through in chef Ming Yu's Shanghai style. If you order one of the live seafood specialties, be prepared to part with a C-note—two if you opt for the red cod.

### Breakfast/Brunch

Bright, airy with a touch of South Beach, **Tableau** (Wynn, 3131 Las Vegas Blvd. S., 702/770-3330, www.wynnlasvegas.com, 7am-2:30pm daily, $20-25), overlooking the pools from the garden atrium, changes its menu to suit the season. Any meal is a treat here, but the salmon eggs Benedict and pineapple coconut pancakes make breakfast the most important meal of the day at Wynn.

### Buffets

At Caesars Palace's **Bacchanal Buffet** (3570 Las Vegas Blvd. S., 702/731-7928, www.caesars.com, 7:30am-10pm Mon.-Fri., 8am-10pm Sat.-Sun., $30-60, $15 wine, beer, and mimosa supplement), specialty dishes range from gourmet (smoked pork belly) to pub grub (Bacchanal sliders) and include plenty of international delicacies: curry, dim sum, crepes, and more, prepared in bustling show kitchens and with many presented small-plate style.

### French and Continental

The vanilla mousse-colored banquettes and chocolate swirl of the dark wood grain tables at **Payard Patisserie & Bistro** (Caesars Palace, 3570 Las Vegas Blvd. S., 702/731-7292 or 866/462-5982, http://payard.com, 7am-1:30pm Mon.-Thurs., 7am-3pm Fri.-Sun., $15-30, pastry counter 6am-11pm daily) foreshadow the sweet experience ahead. The bakery displaying the delightful French pastries for which François Payard is famous takes up most of the restaurant, tantalizing visitors with cakes, tarts, and petit fours. But the restaurant stands on its own, with the quiches and crepes taking best in show.

### Italian

It's no surprise that a casino named after the most romantic of Italian cities would be home to one of the best Italian restaurants around. **Canaletto** (Venetian, 3377 Las Vegas Blvd. S., 702/733-0070, www.venetian.com, 11am-11pm Sun.-Thurs., 11am-midnight Fri.-Sat., $28-40), of course, focuses on Venetian cuisine. The kitchen staff performs around the grill and rotisserie—a demonstration kitchen—creating sumptuously authentic dishes under a high vaulted ceiling. The spicy *salsiccia picante* thin-crust pizza gets our vote.

You can almost picture Old Blue Eyes himself between shows, a bourbon at his elbow, twirling linguini and holding court at **Sinatra** (Encore, 3131 Las Vegas Blvd. S., 702/770-5320 or 888/352-3463, www.wynnlasvegas.com, 5:30pm-10:30pm daily, $40-70). The Chairman's voice wafts through the speakers, and his iconic photos and awards decorate the walls while you tuck into classic Italian food tinged with chef Theo Schoenegger's special touches.

### Seafood

Submerge yourself in the cool, fluid, atmosphere at **AquaKnox** (Venetian, 3355 Las Vegas Blvd. S., 702/420-2541, http://aquaknox.net, 5:30pm-10pm daily, $40-70). Its cobalt and cerulean tableware offset by chrome, cream, and frosted glass suggest a sea-sprayed embarcadero. The fish soup is the signature entrée, but the pan-seared options—barramundi, halibut, or scallops—are the way to go. Start with the crab cake appetizer.

They serve shrimp, lobster, mussels, and more at **Oyster Bar** (Harrah's, 3475 Las Vegas Blvd. S., 702/369-5000, www.caesars.com, 11:30am-11pm Sun.-Thurs.,

11:30am-1am Fri.-Sat., $20-40). But stick with the eponymous bivalve in all its glorious forms—grilled, fried, Rockefeller, or Royale.

### Vegas Views

Bellagio's dancing fountains and the majestic Caesars Palace provide the eye candy at **Giada** (Cromwell, 3595 Las Vegas Blvd. S., 702/442-3271, www.giadadelaurentiis.com, 8am-2:30pm and 5pm-11pm daily, $45-75), opened by celebrity chef Giada De Laurentiis. If that's not enough, watch the chefs hard at work in the open kitchen.

Strip views await at **VooDoo Steakhouse** (Rio, 3700 W. Flamingo Rd., 702/777-7800, www.caesars.com, 5pm-10:30pm daily, $55-80), along with steaks with a N'awlins Creole and Cajun touch. Getting to the restaurant and the lounge requires a mini thrill ride to the top of the Rio tower in the glass elevator. The Rio contends that the restaurant is on the 51st floor and the lounge is on the 52nd floor, but they're really on the 41st and 42nd floors, respectively—Rio management dropped floors 40-49 as the number 4 has an ominous connotation in Chinese culture. Whatever floors they're on, the VooDoo double-decker provides a great view of the Strip. The food and drink are expensive and tame, but the fun is in the overlook, especially if you eat or drink outside on the decks. Diners get free entry into VooDoo nightclub.

## Lower Strip
### Asian

Soft lighting, mauve and teal accents, and intricate wooden screens provide the right balance of privacy and people-watching during your journey into the depths of Chinese cuisine at **Blossom** (Aria, 3730 Las Vegas Blvd. S., 877/230-2742, www.aria.com, 5:30pm-10:30pm daily, $50-70). Much of the menu is exotic, bold, and authentic, but there are plenty of playful American spins on traditional dishes to appeal to Western palates. Adventuresome diners receive the full benefit of chef Chi Kwun Choi's creative mastery—go for the veal cheek or *jian bo* beef. The sweet-and-sour crisp-fried flounder is a signature dish for the more cautious.

Chinese art in a Hong Kong bistro setting with fountain and lake views makes **Jasmine** (Bellagio, 3600 Las Vegas Blvd. S., 702/693-8865, www.bellagio.com, 5:30pm-10pm daily, $50-70) one of the most visually striking Chinese restaurants in town. The food is classic European-influenced Cantonese.

### Breakfast

The **Veranda** (Four Seasons, 3960 Las Vegas Blvd. S., 702/632-5121, www.fourseasons.com, 6:30am-10pm Mon.-Fri., 7am-10pm Sat.-Sun., $30-45) transforms itself from a light, airy, indoor-outdoor breakfast and lunch nook into a late dinner spot oozing with Mediterranean ambience and a check total worthy of a Four Seasons restaurant. As you might expect from the name, dining on the terrace is a favorite among well-to-do locals, especially for brunch on spring and fall weekends. Tiramisu French toast? Yes, please! Dinner here, with wine, dessert, and tip, can easily run $100 per person.

### Buffets

You're in Las Vegas so it's perfectly reasonable to drop a hundo for breakfast. Head over to Bally's **Sterling Brunch Buffet** (3645 Las Vegas Blvd. S., 702/967-7258, www.caesars.com, 9:30am-2:30pm Sun., $95-125) for the only fine dining buffet in town. All-you-can-eat lobster tails? Yes, please. Also rack of lamb, caviar, truffled potatoes, and Perrier-Jouet champagne. Waiters are standing by to present gruyere popover bread, fetch more lobster bisque and Belgian waffles, refill your glass, and refold your napkin while you're making yet another sortie through the buffet.

On the other hand, for the price of

that one brunch at Bally's, you can eat for three days at the **French Market Buffet** (The Orleans, 4500 W. Tropicana Ave., 702/365-7111, www.orleanscasino.com, 8am-9pm daily, breakfast $11, lunch $13, dinner $19-28, Sun. brunch $22, age 16 and under get $5 off; children under 43 inches are free). All-day passes are available ($30 Mon.-Thurs., $36 Fri.-Sun.).

Helical lighting fixtures evoke jellyfish and tuna, so you know the limited seafood offerings at **Wicked Spoon** (3708 Las Vegas Blvd. S., 702/698-7870, www.cosmopolitanlasvegas.com, 8am-9pm Sun.-Thurs., 8am-10pm Fri.-Sat., $28-50, $15 beer, wine, mimosa, bloody Mary supplement) are pretty good. Try the scampi and made-to-order fruits de mer soup.

## French and Continental

The steaks and seafood at ★ **Mon Ami Gabi** (Paris, 3655 Las Vegas Blvd. S., 702/944-4224, www.monamigabi.com, 7am-11pm daily, $35-55) are comparable to those at any fine Strip establishment—at about half the price. It's a bistro, so you know the crepes and other lunch specials are terrific, but you're better off coming for dinner. Try the baked goat cheese appetizer.

Though his flagship at Monte Carlo has closed, award-winning chef Andre Rochat still manages **Alizé** (The Palms, 4321 W. Flamingo Rd., 702/951-7000, http://alizelv.com, 5:30pm-10pm daily, $60-80), with its unbeatable view of the Strip. You might as well splurge on the tasting menu at $155 per person, which could include seared foie gras, roasted squab, and orange cheesecake (it's better than the soufflé); à la carte meals won't be much cheaper.

When you name your restaurant after a maestro, you're setting some pretty high standards for your food. Fortunately, **Picasso** (Bellagio, 3600 Las Vegas Blvd. S., 702/693.8865, www.bellagio.com, 5:30pm-9:30pm Wed.-Mon., $113-123) is up to the self-inflicted challenge. Because of limited seating in its cubist-inspired

dining room and a small dining time window, the restaurant has a couple of prix fixe menus. It's seriously expensive, and if you include Kobe beef, lobster, wine pairings, and a cheese course, you and a mate could easily leave several pounds heavier and $500 lighter.

## Gastropub

Shed your culinary mores and enjoy as chef Shawn McClain blurs the lines between avant-garde and comfort food at **Libertine Social** (Mandalay Bay, 3950 Las Vegas Blvd. S., 702/632-7558, www.mandalaybay.com, 5pm-10:30pm daily, $35-55). The best dishes revolve around cured meats—the prosciutto and toasted cornbread, artisanal sausages and sauerkraut. Pick one and pair it with roasted cauliflower. Start with the crab and spinach dip.

**Michael Mina Pub 1842** (MGM Grand, 3799 Las Vegas Blvd. S., 702/891-3922, www.michaelmina.net, 11:30am-10pm Thurs.-Mon., $20-35) delivers tasty burgers and barbecue. Better yet, order appetizers and sides, then share the joy of smoked salmon dip, soft pretzels and beer cheese, and oniony mac-and-cheese.

## Pizza

With lines snaking out its unmarked entrance, in a dark alleyway decorated with record covers, **Secret Pizza** (Cosmopolitan, 3708 Las Vegas Blvd. S., 3rd Fl., 11am-5am Fri.-Mon., 11am-4am Tues.-Thurs., slices $5-6) is not so secret anymore. Located next to Blue Ribbon Sushi on the Cosmopolitan's third floor, it's a great place to get a quick, greasy slice.

## Seafood

Rick Moonen is to be commended for his advocacy of sustainable seafood harvesting practices, and ★ **RM Seafood** (Mandalay Bay, 3950 Las Vegas Blvd. S., 702/632-9300, http://rmseafood.com, 11:30am-11pm daily, $45-90) practices what he preaches. You can almost hear the tide-rigging whirr and the mahogany creak in the yacht-club restaurant setting.

**Estiatorio Milos** (3708 Las Vegas Blvd. S., 877/551-7776, http://milos.ca/restaurants/las-vegas, 11:30am-3pm and 5pm-11pm Mon.-Thurs., 11:30am-3pm and 4pm-midnight Fri., 11:30am-midnight Sat., 11:30am-11pm Sun., $40-60) brings the Mediterranean to Las Vegas, with Greek-, Italian-, and Spanish-influenced presentations—think lemons, olives, and capers.

Partially housed in what looks like a modern-art latticed hornet's nest, **Mastro's Ocean Club** (Crystals and City Center, 3720 Las Vegas Blvd. S., 702/798-7115, www.mastrosrestaurants.com, 5pm-11pm daily, $60-100) is dubbed "The Treehouse." The restaurant inside offers standard top-of-the-line dishes elevated through preparation and atmosphere. The sushi menu is limited but a perfectly viable option.

### Steak

The care used by the small farms from which Tom Colicchio's **Craftsteak** (MGM Grand, 3799 Las Vegas Blvd. S., 702/891-7318, www.craftsteaklasvegas.com, 5pm-10pm Sun.-Thurs., 5pm-10:30pm Fri.-Sat., $50-75) buys its ingredients is evident in the full flavor of the excellently seasoned steaks and chops. Spacious with gold, umber, and light woodwork, Craftsteak's decor is conducive to good times with friends and family and isn't overbearing or intimidating.

### Tapas

The Cosmopolitan's reinvention of the social club takes diners' taste buds to flavor nirvana. Equal parts supper club, nightclub, and jazz club, ★ **Rose. Rabbit. Lie.** (Cosmopolitan, 3708 Las Vegas Blvd. S., 702/698-7440, www.cosmopolitanlasvegas.com, 6pm-midnight Wed.-Sat., $70-125) serves a mostly tapas-style menu. Sharing is encouraged, with about four small plates per person satisfying most appetites,

especially if you splurge on the chocolate terrarium for dessert. The supper club experience includes varied entertainment throughout the evening (mostly singers, but sometimes magicians and acrobats), but no one will blame you for focusing on the food and cocktails.

### Vegas Views

Paris's **Eiffel Tower Restaurant** (3655 Las Vegas Blvd. S., 702/948-6937, http://eiffeltowerrestaurant.com, 11:30am-3pm and 4:30pm-10:30pm Mon.-Thurs., 11:30am-3pm and 4:30pm-11pm Fri., 10am-3pm and 4:30pm-11pm Sat., 10am-3pm and 4:30pm-10:30pm Sun., $60-100) hovers 100 feet above the Strip. Your first "show" greets you when the glass elevator opens onto the organized chaos of chef Jean Joho's kitchen. Order the soufflé, have a glass of wine, and bask in the romantic piano strains as the bilingual culinary staff performs delicate French culinary feats, with Bellagio's fountains as a backdrop.

## Downtown
### Asian

A perfect little eatery for the budding Bohemia of East Fremont Street, ★ **Le Thai** (523 E. Fremont St., 702/778-0888, www.lethaivegas.com, 11am-11pm Mon.-Thurs., 11am-midnight Fri.-Sat., 4pm-10pm Sun., $10-25) attracts a diverse clientele ranging from ex-yuppies to body-art lovers. Most come for the three-color curry, and you should too. There's nothing especially daring on the menu, but the *pad prik, ga pow,* and garlic fried rice are better than what's found at many Strip restaurants that charge twice as much. Choose your spice level wisely; Le Thai does not mess around.

### Buffets

Assuming you're not a food snob, the **Garden Court Buffet** (Main Street Station, 200 N. Main St., 702/387-1896, www.mainstreetcasino.com, 7am-3pm and 4pm-9pm Mon.-Thurs., 7am-3pm and 4pm-10pm Fri.-Sun., breakfast $8, lunch $9, dinner $12-15, Fri. seafood $23-26) will satisfy your taste buds and your bank account. The fare is mostly standard, with some specialties designed to appeal to the casino's Asian and Pacific Islander target market.

At **The Buffet** (Golden Nugget, 129 E. Fremont St., 702/385-8152, www.golden-nugget.com, 7am-10pm daily, breakfast $15, lunch $16, dinner $21-28, weekend brunch $22), the food leaves nothing to be desired, with extras like an omelet station, calzone, Greek salad, and a delicate fine banana cake putting it a cut above the ordinary buffet, especially for downtown. Glass and brass accents make for peaceful digestion.

### French and Continental

**Hugo's Cellar** (Four Queens, 202 E. Fremont St., 702/385-4011, www.hugos-cellar.com, 5pm-10pm daily, $65-80) is romance from the moment each woman in your party receives her red rose until the last complimentary chocolate-covered strawberry is devoured. Probably the best gourmet room for the money, dimly lit Hugo's is located below the casino floor, in a faux wine cellar, shutting it off from the hubbub above. It is pricey, but the inclusion of sides, a mini dessert, and salad—prepared tableside with your choice of ingredients—helps ease the sticker shock. Sorbet is served between courses. The house appetizer is the Hot Rock—four meats sizzling on a lava slab; mix and match the meats with the dipping sauces.

### Italian

Decidedly uncave-like with bright lights and an earthen-tile floor, **The Grotto** (Golden Nugget, 129 E. Fremont St., 702/386-8341, www.goldennugget.com, 11:30am-10:30pm daily, $30-40) offers top-quality northern Italian-influenced sandwiches and pizza with a view of the Golden Nugget's shark tank (ask for a window table). Portions are large and the margaritas refreshing.

### Seafood

With prices as refreshing as a dip in the Gulf, **7 Mares** (2000 E. Charleston Blvd., 702/473-5522, 10am-9pm Mon.-Thurs., 10am-10pm Fri.-Sun., $14-25) authentically prepares fish and shrimp in a variety of spices and sauces for any taste.

The prime rib gets raves, but the seafood and the prices are the draw at **Second Street Grill** (Fremont, 200 Fremont St., 702/385-3232, www.fremontcasino.com, 5pm-10pm Sun. and Wed.-Thurs., 5pm-11pm Fri.-Sat., $25-40). The grill bills itself as "American contemporary with Pacific Rim influence," and the menu reflects this Asian inspiration with steaks and chops—but do yourself a favor and order the crab legs with lemon ginger butter. If you can't shake your inner landlubber, the nightly T-bone special ($30) should do the trick.

Steaks and seafood get equal billing on the menu at **Triple George** (201 N. 3rd St., 702/384-2761, www.triplegeorgegrill. com, 11am-10pm Mon.-Fri., 4pm-10pm Sat.-Sun., $25-45), but again, the char-broiled salmon and the martinis are what brings the suave crowd back for more.

### Steak

Fronted by ex-mob mouthpiece and Las Vegas mayor Oscar Goodman, **Oscar's** (Plaza, 1 S. Main St., 702/386-7227, www. oscarslv.com, 4pm-10pm daily, $40-70) is dedicated to hizzoner's favorite things in life—beef, booze, and broads. With dishes named, apparently, for former wiseguy clients—Fat Herbie, Crazy Phil, Joe Pig, etc.—you're in for an old Vegas treat, full of the scents of leather, cigars, and broiling steaks.

## Off the Strip

The congenial proprietor of ★ **Phat Phrank's** (4850 W. Sunset Rd., http:// phatphranks.com, 702/247-6528, 7am-7pm Mon.-Fri., 9am-4pm Sat., $10-15) keeps the atmosphere light and the fish tacos crispy and delicious. Try all three of the house salsas; they're all great complements to all the offerings, especially the flavorful pork burrito and *adobada torta*.

**Thai Spice** (4433 W. Flamingo Rd., 702/362-5308, www.thaispicelv.com, 11am-10pm Mon.-Thurs., 11am-10:30pm Fri., 11:30am-10:30pm Sat., $10-20) gives Le Thai a run for its baht as best Thai restaurant in town; the soups, noodle dishes, traditional curries, pad thai, and egg rolls are all well prepared. Tell your waiter how hot you want your food on a scale of 1 to 10. The big numbers peg the needle on the Scoville scale, so beware.

---

# Accommodations

Casino accommodations offer the closest thing to a sure bet as you will find in Vegas: the most convenient setting for a vacation that includes gambling, dining, drinking, and show-going. See the *Casinos* section for information on these rooms. That being said, if you don't want to expose yourself or your kids to the smoke or vices on display at casinos, or need proximity to the airport, you will find plenty of choices. Even more affordable digs can be had at smaller motels in locations close to the Strip, downtown, the convention center, the university, and other high-traffic areas.

Even with more than 150,000 rooms, Vegas sells out completely on many three-day weekends, for major sports betting events like the Super Bowl and March Madness, big local events like music festivals, the National Finals Rodeo, and NASCAR week, and over U.S. and international holidays such as Chinese New Year, Cinco De Mayo, New Year's Eve, and Valentine's Day. There are some relative quiet times, such as the three weeks before Christmas and July-August, when the mercury doesn't drop below 100°F. Finding the perfect room should not be a problem then.

If you're just coming for the weekend, keep in mind that many major hotels don't even let you check in on a Saturday night. You can stay Friday and Saturday, but not Saturday alone. It may be easier to find a room Sunday-Thursday, when there aren't as many large conventions, sporting events, or getaway visitors from Southern California. Almost all the room packages and deep discounts are only available on these days.

Most Strip hotels charge **resort fees** of $20-40 per night. These charges are not included in the quoted room rate. Many downtown hotel casinos, as well as the mid-level national chains, have not yet resorted to resort fees

## Hotels

Feel like royalty at City Center's ★ **Mandarin Oriental Las Vegas** (City Center, 3752 Las Vegas Blvd. S., 702/590-8888, www.mandarinoriental.com/lasvegas, $295-399), which looks down on the bright lights of the Strip from a peaceful remove. A master control panel in each of the modern rooms sets the atmosphere to your liking, controlling the lights, temperature, window curtains, music, and more. Once everything is set, sink into the sleek, chrome-and-jade plushness with decorations suggesting silks, pearls, Shoji screens, and other hints of the exotic East. Valet closets allow hotel staff to deliver items to your room without entering your unit. The **Mandarin Bar** (888/881-9367, 4pm-1am Sun.-Thurs., noon-2am Fri.-Sat.) on the 23rd floor offers stunning views of the city skyline and several signature martinis. And it's all environmentally friendly, or at least LEED-certified.

There's even more pampering and more Asian influence at **Nobu** (3570 Las Vegas Blvd. S., 800/727-4923, www.caesars.com, $239-319), Caesars Palace's venture into the boutique market. Reflecting the same style and attention to detail that highlight chef Nobu Matsuhisa's eponymous restaurants, the first Nobu hotel includes teak and cherry blossoms, as well as stylized dragon artwork and traditional Japanese prints. Guests are greeted with hot tea, and the nightly turndown service includes scented sleep oils and customizable bath and pillow menus. Nobu restaurant and lounge (5pm-11pm Sun.-Thurs., 5pm-midnight Fri.-Sat., $35-65) occupies the ground floor, so the indulgences can continue through the cocktail hour and mealtime.

Every guest room is a suite at the **Signature** (145 E. Harmon Ave., 702/797-6000 or 877/612-2121, www.signaturemgmgrand.com, $159-288) at MGM Grand. Even the standard Deluxe suite is a roomy 550 square feet and includes a king bed, kitchenette, and spa tub. Most of the 1,728 smoke-free guest rooms in the gleaming 40-story tower include private balconies with Strip views, and guests have access to the complimentary 24-hour fitness center, three outdoor pools, a business center, and free wireless Internet throughout

the hotel. A gourmet deli and acclaimed room service satisfy noshing needs.

Representing for many the definition of opulence, the **Four Seasons** (Mandalay Bay, 3960 Las Vegas Blvd. S., 702/632-5000, www.fourseasons.com, $199-319) entices guests with vibrant colors, lush landscaping, and an elaborate porte cochere that sets the art-deco lemonade-on-the-veranda mood that induces a stress-shedding sigh at first sight. Floor-to-ceiling windows command Strip or mountain views from atop Mandalay Bay. The **Spa** (702/632-5302), which includes a nail bar, offers treatments that relax all the senses, from aromatherapy and eucalyptus steam to menthol wraps and citrus infusions.

Farther removed from the Strip, the panoramas from the top floors of the 18-story **Berkley** (8280 Dean Martin Dr., 702/224-7400, www.theberkleylasvegas.com, $159-179) rank among the best you will find. Studio units sleep two, but families can go up to two bedrooms to

Mandarin Oriental Las Vegas

accommodate six comfortably. Fully equipped kitchens, laundry rooms, and living areas with 49-inch TVs provide a home-away-from-home experience. It's across the street from the Silverton Casino, so there is plenty of gaming action, plus dining options, and a shuttle can whisk you away to primo shopping venues. Still, you will want to rent a car to conveniently take in the whole Vegas experience.

Offering sophisticated accommodations and amenities without the hubbub of a rowdy casino, the **Renaissance** (3400 Paradise Rd., 702/784-5700, $77-189 d) has big, bright, airy standard guest rooms that come complete with triple-sheeted 300-thread-count Egyptian cotton beds with down comforters and duvets, walk-in showers, full tubs, 42-inch flat-panel TVs, a business center, and high-speed Internet. Upper-floor guest rooms overlook the Wynn golf course. The pool and whirlpool are outside, and the concierge can score show tickets and tee times.

Onyx- and burgundy-clad ★ **Envy Steakhouse** (6:30am-11am and 5pm-10pm daily, $40-70) has a few poultry and seafood entrées, but the Angus beef gets top billing.

Offering sophisticated accommodations and amenities without the hubbub of a rowdy casino, the **Renaissance** (3400 Paradise Rd., 702/784-5700, www.renaissancelasvegas.com, $77-189) has big, bright, airy standard guest rooms that come complete with triple-sheeted 300-thread-count Egyptian cotton beds with down comforters and duvets, walk-in showers, full tubs, 42-inch flat-panel TVs, a business center, and high-speed Internet. Upper-floor guest rooms overlook the Wynn golf course. The pool and whirlpool are outside, and the concierge can score show tickets and tee times. Onyx- and burgundy-clad ★ **Envy Steakhouse** (6:30am-11am and 5pm-10pm daily, $40-70) has a few poultry and seafood entrées, but the Angus beef gets top billing.

Catering to families and vacationers seeking a more "residential" stay, **Platinum** (211 E. Flamingo Rd., 702/365-5000 or 877/211-9211, www.theplatinumhotel.com, $113-194) treats both guests and the environment with kid gloves. The resort uses the latest technology to reduce its carbon footprint through such measures as low-energy lighting throughout, ecofriendly room thermostats, and motion sensors to turn lights off when restrooms are unoccupied. Guests also can use PressReader to access thousands of digital publications. Standard suites are an expansive 910 square feet of muted designer furnishings and accents, and they include all modern conveniences, such as high-speed Internet, high-fidelity sound systems, full kitchens, and oversize tubs. **Kil@watt** (6am-2pm daily, $12-20), with sleek silver decor accented with dark woods, is a feast for the eyes and the palate for breakfast and lunch.

The one- and two-bedroom condominium suites at **Desert Rose** (5051 Duke

Ellington Way, 702/739-7000 or 888/732-8099, www.shellhospitality.com, $142-249) are loaded, with new appliances and granite countertops in the kitchen as well as private balconies or patios outside. One-bedrooms are quite large, at 650 square feet, and sleep four comfortably. Rates vary widely, but depending on your needs and travel dates, you might find a deal within walking distance of several casinos and the monorail.

No two rooms are the same at the **Artisan** (1501 W. Sahara Ave., 702/214-4000, $99-179 d), located a mile northwest of the convention center. Most include playful, classic-style prints in baroque frames, dark wood, and bold colors; schemes range from burgundy to gold to emerald. The **Artisan Lounge** hosts one of the best early-night parties in town. And you can nix the tan lines at the European-style (read: topless) pool.

## Motels

There are several low-cost motels north of the Strip resorts and downtown, scattered along Las Vegas Boulevard and east of downtown along Boulder Highway. Few are recommendable. One exception is the **Downtowner** (129 N. 8th St., 702/384-1441, www.downtownerlv.com, $68-125). Its modern, minimalist rooms are sparkling white with red, gray, and black accents. The pool and lounge areas are luxuries in this neighborhood and price range, and the Downtowner even has a few cottages for rent. Another viable choice, **City Center Motel** (700 Fremont St., 702/382-4766, http://citycenterlv.com, $69-89) is near the Fremont Street Experience, an outlet mall, and the transitioning Fremont East district. Its pastel walls and busy bedspreads reveal the motel's age, but it's clean and rooms include the standard amenities: coffeemaker, mini fridge, hair dryer, etc. There's a microwave at the front desk for guest use. **Roulette Motel** (2019 Fremont St., 702/910-4637, http://roulettemotel.com, $65-85) features dark wood furnishings,

tasteful bedding, and artwork on the walls. A bit east of the downtown arts district, it may provide the best bang for the buck. Right in the middle of the arts district, the building exterior of the **Star Motel** (1418 S. 3rd St., 702/383-9770) is not much to look at, but the grounds are meticulously maintained. The lush landscaping is more in keeping with room interiors, which include wood and tile laminate flooring rather than stiff, is-it-design-or-is-it-a-stain carpeting.

Motels along the Lower Strip, from Bally's below Flamingo Avenue all the way out to the Mandalay Bay at the far south end of the Strip, are well placed to visit all the new big-brand casino resorts. Prices here are much lower than at the resorts but higher than those to the north, reflecting premium real estate costs. Those costs also all but price out independent motels, but you can take your pick of established brands like **Travelodge Las Vegas Center Strip** (3735 Las Vegas Blvd. S., 702/736-3443, www.travelodgevegasstrip.com, $59-99), which gets a top rating for its reasonable prices; location near the MGM Grand and City Center; and little extras like free continental breakfast, free parking, and a heated swimming pool.

## Hostels

It's hard to beat these places for budget accommodations. They offer rock-bottom prices for no-frills "rack rooms," singles, and doubles. Closest to the Strip, **Hostel Cat** (1236 Las Vegas Blvd. S., 702/380-6902, http://hostelcat.com, $23-40) puts the focus on group activities, organizing pub crawls, beer pong and video game tournaments, movie nights, and more. There's even a 24-hour party table where there are always interesting fellow travelers to talk to.

**Sin City Hostel** (1208 Las Vegas Blvd. S., 702/868-0222, www.sincityhostel.com, $23-26) is reserved for international, student, and out-of-state travelers only (ID required). Perfect for the starving student's budget, rates include breakfast. The hostel features a barbecue pit, a basketball court, and Wi-Fi. A recent check of Sin City's website revealed current guests included visitors from England, France, the Netherlands, and Singapore.

Six blocks east of the downtown resorts, **Las Vegas Hostel** (1322 Fremont St., 702/385-1150 or 800/550-8958, http://lasvegashostel.net, $16-51) has a swimming pool and a hot tub. The rates include a make-your-own pancake breakfast, billiards and TV room, and wireless Internet connections. The hostel also arranges trips to the Strip and visits to the Grand Canyon and other outdoorsy attractions. Or you can borrow a bike and explore the area on your own.

## RV Parking

A number of casinos have attached RV parks. Other casinos allow RVs to park overnight in their parking lots but have no facilities.

The best bet on the Strip, thanks almost exclusively to its location, the **RV Park at Circus Circus** (2880 Las Vegas Blvd. S., 702/794-3757 or 800/444-2472, www.circuscircus.com, $41-46) is big (170 spaces, all paved, including more than 70 pull-throughs), with a few grassy islands and shade trees. RVing families will appreciate the hotel/casino amenities and entertainment. The convenience store is open 24 hours daily. Ten minutes spent learning where the Industrial Road back entrance is will save hours of sitting in traffic on Las Vegas Boulevard. The free dog wash in the off-leash park is a nice touch.

Again, convenience and amenities, rather than lush surroundings, are the attraction at **Main Street Station RV Park** (200 N. Main St., 702/387-1896, $24-28). The showers and laundry have *hot* water, and the Fremont Street casinos are an easy walk away. Downtown has some sketchy areas after dark, but Main Street's security patrol is diligent, and safety is

not an issue. Highway noise and Vegas's famous flashing neon, however, may be, come bedtime.

Boulder Highway, which connects downtown with Lake Mead to the southeast, is RV park central. The cleanest and best-maintained along this road, ★ **Las Vegas RV Resort** (3890 S. Nellis Blvd., 866/846-5432, www.lasvegasrvresort.com, $33-51) has level asphalt pads and palm tree landscaping. A guard is on-site 24 hours, and the laundry, restrooms, pool area, and fitness center are spotless. **Las Vegas KOA at Sam's Town** (5225 Boulder Hwy., 702/454-8055, https://koa.com, $36-45) has nearly 300 spaces for motor homes, all with full hookups and 20-, 30-, and 50-amp power. It's mostly a paved parking lot with spacious sites, a heated (if a bit dated) pool, and a spa; the rec hall has a pool table and a kitchen. And, of course, it's near the bowling, dining, and movie theater in the casino. **Arizona Charlie's Boulder** (4445 Boulder Hwy., 702/951-5911, www.arizonacharliesboulder.com, $32) has 239 spaces and weekly rates. The clubhouse contains a large-screen TV, fitness room, and pool table. Spaces at the back are quieter and closer to the dog run but farther from the laundry room and pool area.

South of the airport, **Oasis RV Resort** (2711 W. Windmill Ln., www.oasislasvegasrvresort.com, 800/566-4707, $52-74) is directly across I-15 from the Silverton Casino. Opened in 1996, Oasis has more than 800 snug spaces with huge date palms and a cavernous 24,000-square-foot clubhouse. Each space is wide enough for a car and motor home but not much else and comes with a picnic table and patio. The foliage is plentiful and flanks an 18-hole putting course with real grass greens along with family and adult swimming pools. The resort features a full calendar of poker tournaments, movies, karaoke, and bar and restaurant specials. Wheelchair-accessible

# ◈ Southwest Side Trip

Las Vegas is located just outside the "Grand Circle"—the largest concentration of national parks and monuments in the country—making it a great base for visiting colorful canyons, inspiring geological formations, and living history. The **Grand Canyon** should be the first southwestern park on your list, but nine other national parks are within 500 miles of Glitter Gulch.

**Zion National Park** is the most accessible (160 miles from Las Vegas), a straight shot up I-15 North for 128 miles to UT-9 for the final 32-mile stretch to Zion. Zion's imposing monoliths, such as the Court of the Patriarchs, whose sandstone behemoths are named for Abraham, Isaac, and Jacob, contrast with the three serene Emerald Pools that reflect the region's features.

Continue on to **Bryce Canyon** (260 miles from Las Vegas; 72 miles from Zion), where it's easy to see why ancient Paiute people believed the narrow hoodoos were people turned to stone by angry gods. The haunting formations are the result of eons of the winds' and waters' masonry skills. From Zion, continue northeast on UT-9 for 13 miles to US-89 North for 43 miles to UT-12 East. Continue 14 miles to UT-63 South for 2 miles to the park gate.

Northeast of Bryce, **Capitol Reef National Park** (roughly 352 miles from Las Vegas; 112 miles from Bryce Canyon) is a vast network of natural bridges, domes, and cliffs created by the Waterpocket Fold, which was formed during an ancient geologic upheaval. From Bryce Canyon, take UT-63/Johns Valley Road/UT-22 North for 45 miles to UT-62 North for another 26 miles. Turn right onto Browns Lane for 3 miles. Then turn right onto UT-24 East/East 300 Street South for the final 38 miles.

Farther afield from Las Vegas are **Arches National Park** (453 miles) and **Canyonlands National Park** (465 miles). The backdrop for any self-respecting Western, Arches is home to Delicate Arch, as well as more than 2,000 other natural arches, fins, towers, and crevasses. I-15 will get you most of the way to either of these eastern Utah parks. To get to Arches, take I-15 North for 426 miles to US-191 and follow it for 27 miles to Arches Entrance Road. Canyonlands was formed by the Colorado River system, which carved out its unique buttes, mesas, and sandstone spires. It's only 26 miles from Arches: Take US-191 North for 7 miles to UT-313; continue for 15 miles to Grand View Point Road/Island in the Sky Road for 4 miles. To get to these two parks from Las Vegas, take I-15 for 243 miles to I-70 toward Denver. Follow I-70 for 182 miles, then take US-191 for 21 miles. A right turn onto UT-313 West will take you the last 19 miles to Canyonlands; it's just a little farther to Arches.

Nevada's only national park, **Great Basin** (296 miles from Las Vegas) is home to a glacier, the oldest living trees in the world (bristlecone pines), Nevada's second-highest peak (the majestic 13,000-foot Wheeler Peak), and the extensive Lehman Caves system, complete with stalagmites, stalactites, and rare shield formations. From Las Vegas, take US-93 North for 286 miles to NV-487 West for 5 miles then to NV-488 West for the final 5 miles.

Several Vegas-based tour companies offer full-day, round-trip excursions to Zion and Bryce Canyon National Parks. The professional guides at **Adventure Photo Tours** (702/889-8687 or 888/363-8687, 6am-8:30pm Tues. and Thurs. and by appointment, $239) take photographers and sightseers to both parks, serving a continental breakfast, lunch, bottled water, and snacks. **Viator** (6am-9pm Thurs., $239) offers a similar service, along with a three-day trip ($595) that includes trips to the Grand Canyon and Monument Valley.

restrooms have flush toilets and hot showers; other amenities include a laundry, a grocery store, an exercise room, and an arcade.

# Transportation and Services

## Air

More than 900 planes arrive or depart **McCarran International Airport** (LAS, 5757 Wayne Newton Blvd., 702/261-5211, www.mccarran.com) every day, making it the sixth busiest in the country and 19th in the world. Terminal 1 hosts domestic flights, while Terminal 3 has domestic and international flights.

## Bus

**Citizen Area Transit** (CAT, 702/228-7433, www.rtcsouthernnevada.com), the public bus system, is managed by the Regional Transportation Commission. CAT runs 39 routes all over the Las Vegas Valley. Fares are $6 for 2 hours, $8 for 24 hours, free under age five when riding with a guardian. Call or access the ride guide online. Bus service is pretty comprehensive, but even the express routes with fewer stops take a long time to get anywhere.

## Car

Downtown Las Vegas crowds around the junction of I-15, US 95, and US 93. I-15 runs from Los Angeles (272 miles, 4-5 hours' drive) to Salt Lake City (419 miles, 6-8 hours). US 95 meanders from Yuma, Arizona, on the Mexican border, up the western side of Nevada, through Coeur D'Alene, Idaho, all the way up to British Columbia, Canada. US 93 starts in Phoenix and hits Las Vegas 285 miles later, then merges with I-15 for a while only to fork off and shoot straight up the east side of Nevada and continue due north all the way to Alberta, Canada.

## Car Rental

Most of the large car-rental companies have desks at the **McCarran Rent-A-Car Center** (702/261-6001). Dedicated McCarran shuttles leave the main terminal from outside exit doors 10 and 11 about every five minutes bound for the Rent-A-Car Center. International airlines and a few domestic flights arrive at Terminal 3. Here, the shuttle picks up outside doors 51 through 58. Taxicabs are also available at the center.

## Monorail

The site of the SLS Casino on the north end of the Strip and the MGM Grand near the south end are connected via the **Las Vegas Monorail** (702/699-8200, 7am-midnight Mon., 7am-2am Tues.-Thurs., 7am-3am Fri.-Sun., $5, 24-hour pass $12), with stops at the SLS, Westgate, Convention Center, Harrah's/The Linq, Flamingo/Caesars Palace, Bally's/Paris, and MGM Grand. More than 30 major resorts are now within easy reach along the Strip without a car or taxi. Reaching speeds up to 50 mph, the monorail glides above traffic to cover the four-mile route in about 14 minutes. Nine trains with four air-conditioned cars each carry up to 152 riders along the elevated track running on the east side of the strip, stopping every few minutes at the stations. Tickets are available at vending machines at each station as well as at station properties.

## Limo

Offering chauffeur-driven domestic and imported sedans, shuttle buses, and SUVs in addition to stretch and superstretch limos, **Las Vegas Limousines** (702/888-4848, www.lasvegaslimo.com) can transport up to 15 people per vehicle to and from sporting events, corporate meetings, airport connections, bachelor and bachelorette parties, sightseeing tours, and more. Rates are $60 per hour for a 6-seat stretch limo, $80 and up for a 10-seat superstretch.

Presidential Limousine (702/438-5466, www.presidentiallimolv.com) charges $69 per hour for its stretch six-seater, $80 per hour for the superstretch eight-seater; both include TVs and video players, mobile phones, sparkling cider, and roses for the women. They don't include a mandatory fuel surcharge or driver gratuity. Bell Limousine (866/226-7206, www.belllimousine.com) has similar rates and fleets.

## Tours

Several companies offer the chance to see the sights of Las Vegas by bus, helicopter, airplane, or off-road vehicle. There are plenty of tour operators offering similar services. Search the Internet to find tours tailored for your needs, the best prices, and the most competent providers.

The ubiquitous Gray Line (702/739-7777 or 877/333-6556, www.graylinelasvegas.com) offers air-conditioned motor coach tours of the city by night as well as tours of Hoover Dam and the Grand Canyon. City tours (7pm Thurs.-Sat., $69) visit the major Vegas free sights: the Bellagio Fountains and Conservatory, the "Welcome to Las Vegas" sign, the Fremont Street Experience, and some of the more opulent hotels. The Hoover Dam tour ($66) includes a buffet lunch and a stop at Ethel M's chocolatier for a self-guided tour and a free sample. Travelers can add a 15-minute helicopter flight over Lake Mead and the dam ($99 extra) or a riverboat cruise on the lake ($31 extra).

To book a lake cruise directly, contact Lake Mead Cruises (866/292-9191, www.lakemeadcruises.com, noon and 2 pm daily Apr.-Oct., days and times vary Feb.-Mar. and Nov., $26 adults, $13 children 2-11, Sun. 10am champagne brunch cruise $45 adults, $19.50 children 2-11, Sun., Tues., Thurs. dinner cruise $61.50 adults, $25 children 2-11).

Vegas Tours (866/218-6877, www.vegastours.com) has a full slate of outdoor, adventure, and other tours. Some of the more unusual ones include trail rides and full-day dude ranch tours ($120-350) and a visit and tour of the Techatticup gold mine ($113-189). Tours of the Grand Canyon and other nearby state and national parks are available as well.

All Las Vegas Tours (702/233-1627 or 800/566-5868, www.alllasvegastours.com) has all the usual tours: zip-lining over the desert or between hotel towers (weight must be between 75 and 250 pounds, $30-159), tandem skydiving (age 18 and over, less than 240 pounds, $229), and ATV sand-duning (18 and over with valid driver's license, $185).

Pink Jeep Tours (702/895-6778 or 888/900-4480, www.pinkjeeptourslasvegas.com) takes visitors in rugged but cute and comfortable 10-passenger ATVs to such sites as Red Rock Canyon, Valley of Fire, and Hoover Dam.

For history, nature, and entertainment buffs looking for a more focused adventure, themed tours are on the rise in Las Vegas. Haunted Vegas Tours (702/677-6499, www.hauntedvegastours.com, 9:30pm Thurs.-Mon., $85) takes an interesting if macabre trip to the "Motel of Death," where many pseudo-celebrities have met their untimely ends. Guides dressed as undertakers take you to the Redd Foxx haunted house, a creepy old bridge, and an eerie park. The same company offers the Las Vegas Mob Tour ($85), taking visitors to the sites of Mafia hits. Guides, dressed in black pin-striped suits and fedoras, tell tales of the 1970s, when Anthony "The Ant" Spilotro ran the city, and give the scoop on the fate of casino mogul Lefty Rosenthal. A pizza party is included in both tours.

## Tourist Information

The Las Vegas Convention and Visitors Authority (LVCVA, 3150 Paradise Rd., 702/892-0711 or 877/847-4858, www.lvcva.com, 8am-5pm daily) maintains a website of special hotel deals, show tickets, and other offers at www.lasvegas.com. One of LVCVA's priorities is filling hotel rooms. You can also call the same number for convention schedules and entertainment offerings. The **Las Vegas Chamber of Commerce** (575 Symphony Park Ave., Ste. 100, 702/641-5822, www.lvchamber.com) has a bunch of travel resources and fact sheets on its website. For-profit **Vegas. com** is a good resource for up-to-the-minute show schedules and reviews.

## Medical Services

If you need the police, the fire department, or an ambulance in an emergency, **dial 911.**

The centrally located **University Medical Center** (1800 W. Charleston Blvd., at Shadow Ln., 702/383-2000) has 24-hour emergency service, with outpatient and trauma-care facilities. Hospital emergency rooms throughout the valley are open 24 hours, as are many privately run urgent care centers.

Most hotels will have lists of dentists and doctors, and the **Clark County Medical Society** (2590 E. Russell Rd., 702/739-9989, www.clarkcountymedical.org) website lists members based on specialty. You can also get a physician referral from **Desert Springs Hospital** (702/733-8800).

# The Grand Canyon

The Grand Canyon must be seen to be believed. If you see it for the first time and don't have to catch your breath, you might need to check your pulse. Take your time—this view could last forever.

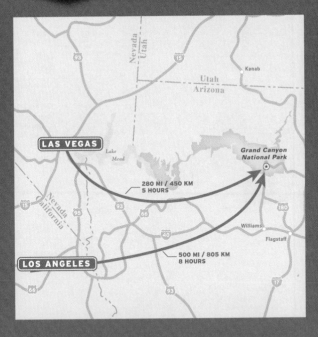

Nevada
Utah

Utah
Arizona

Kanab

**LAS VEGAS**

Lake Mead

Grand Canyon National Park

Nevada
California

280 MI / 450 KM
5 HOURS

**LOS ANGELES**

Williams

Flagstaff

500 MI / 805 KM
8 HOURS

# The Grand Canyon

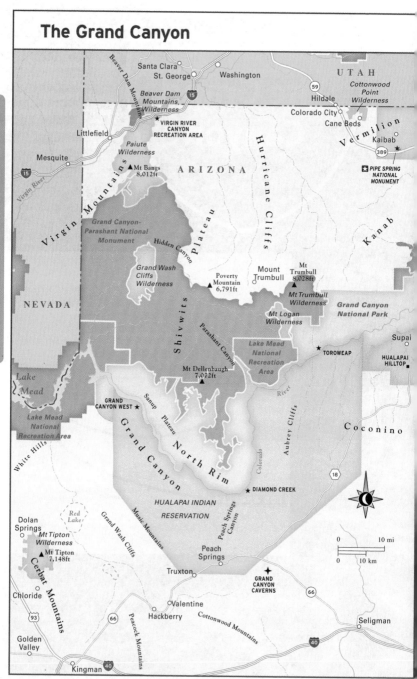

UTAH

Santa Clara
St. George
Washington
59
Cottonwood
Point
Wilderness
Beaver Dam
Mountains
Wilderness
Hildale
Colorado City
Cane Beds
Vermilion
Kaibab
Littlefield
VIRGIN RIVER
CANYON
RECREATION AREA
389
Mesquite
Paiute
Wilderness
15
ARIZONA
PIPE SPRING
NATIONAL
MONUMENT
Virgin River
Virgin Mountains
▲Mt Bangs
8,012ft
Hurricane Cliffs
Kanab
Grand Canyon-
Parashant National
Monument
Hidden Canyon
Plateau
Grand Wash
Cliffs
Wilderness
Poverty
Mountain
6,791ft
Mount
Trumbull
Mt
Trumbull
8,028ft
NEVADA
Shivwits
Mt Trumbull
Wilderness
Grand Canyon
National Park
Supai
Parashant Canyon
Mt Logan
Wilderness
Lake Mead
National
Recreation
Area
TOROWEAP
HUALAPAI
HILLTOP
Lake
Mead
▲Mt Dellenbaugh
7,072ft
River
Lake Mead
National
Recreation Area
GRAND
CANYON WEST ★
Sanup
Plateau
Aubrey Cliffs
Coconino
White Hills
Grand Canyon
North Rim
Colorado
18
DIAMOND CREEK
Dolan
Springs
Red
Lake
Grand Wash Cliffs
HUALAPAI INDIAN
RESERVATION
Peach Springs Canyon
Mt Tipton
Wilderness
▲Mt Tipton
7,148ft
Music Mountains
Peach
Springs
0        10 mi
Cerbat Mountains
Truxton
GRAND
CANYON
CAVERNS
0        10 km
Chloride
93
66
Valentine
66
Hackberry
Cottonwood Mountains
Seligman
Golden
Valley
Peacock Mountains
40
Kingman
40

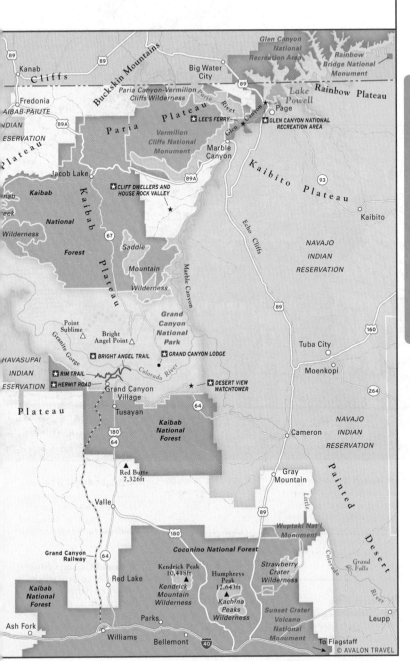

© AVALON TRAVEL

★ **Hermit Road:** Make your way west along the forested rim to the enchanting stone cottage called Hermit's Rest, stopping to see the setting sun turn the canyon walls into fleeting works of art (page 217).

★ **Desert View Watchtower:** See one of architect Mary Colter's finest accomplishments—a rock tower standing tall on the edge of the canyon (page 223).

★ **Rim Trail:** Walk along the rim on this easy, accessible trail, past historic buildings, famous lodges, and the most breathtaking views in the world (page 224).

★ **Bright Angel Trail:** Hike down the most popular trail on the South Rim, its construction based on old Native American routes (page 225).

★ **Grand Canyon Lodge:** Inside this rustic old lodge balancing on the edge of the gorge, you can sink into a chair and gaze out at the multicolored canyon (page 240).

**T**his true natural wonder of the world is waiting for you to discover it.

Even the view from one of the South Rim's easily accessible lookouts will last in your memory for a lifetime. The more adventurous can make reservations, obtain a permit, and enter the desert depths of the canyon, taking a hike, or even a mule ride, to the Colorado River, or spending a weekend trekking rim-to-rim with an overnight at the famous Phantom Ranch, deep in the canyon's inner gorge. The really brave can hire a guide and take a once-in-a-lifetime trip down the great river, riding the roiling rapids and camping on its serene beaches.

There are plenty of places to stay and eat, many of them charming and historic, on the canyon's South Rim. If you decide to go to the high, forested, and often snowy North Rim, you'll drive through a corner of the desolate Arizona Strip, which has a beauty and a history all its own.

Water-sports enthusiasts will want to make it up to the far northern reaches of the state to the Glen Canyon Recreation Area to do some waterskiing or maybe rent a houseboat, and anyone interested in the far end of America's engineering prowess will want to see Glen Canyon Dam, holding back the once-wild Colorado River.

# Getting to the Grand Canyon

The majority of Grand Canyon visitors drive here, reaching the South Rim from either Flagstaff or Williams and entering the park through the South or East entrances. The **South entrance** is usually the busiest, and during the summer, traffic is likely to be backed up somewhat. The quickest way to get to the South entrance by car is to take **AZ-64 North** from

**Williams.** It's about a 60-mile drive across a barren plain; there are a few kitschy places to stop along the way, including Bedrock City, a rather dilapidated model of the Flintstones' hometown with an RV park and a gift shop.

From **Flagstaff** take **US-180 East** through the forest past the San Francisco Peaks for about 80 miles. The road merges with **AZ-64** at Valle. To reach the East entrance, take **US-89 North** from Flagstaff to Cameron, then take **AZ-64 West** to the entrance. This longer route is recommended if you want to see portions of Navajo country on your way to the canyon, and entering through the **East entrance** will put you right at Desert View, the Desert View Watchtower, and Tusayan Museum and Ruin—sights that you'll otherwise have to travel 25 or so miles east from Grand Canyon Village to see.

## From Las Vegas
### South Rim

Las Vegas is **280 miles** from the Grand Canyon's South Rim; it's about a **five-hour drive,** quite breathtaking in some parts and quite boring and monotonous in others. Even if you get a late-morning start and make a few stops along the way, you're still likely to arrive at the park by dinnertime. Most summer weekends, you'll find the route crowded but manageable, unless there's an accident; in that case you'll likely be stuck where you are for some time. At all times of the year, you'll be surrounded by 18-wheelers barreling across the land.

The main and most direct route leaves Las Vegas on **US-93 South.** After you are free of the city, the road passes near Lake Mead and Hoover Dam and through a barren landscape of jagged rocks and creosote bushes. About 100 miles (2 hours) southeast of Vegas you'll hit **Kingman.** Here you take **I-40 East,** which replaced the old Route 66; drive 115 miles to **Williams,** where you pick up **AZ-64 North** for the 60-mile shot across empty,

# Best Hotels

★ **El Tovar:** The South Rim's most stylish and storied lodge, built in arts-and-crafts style, overlooks the canyon (page 233).

★ **Bright Angel Lodge:** This historic, rustic lodge is on the edge of Grand Canyon's bustling South Rim (page 233).

★ **Historic Cameron Trading Post and Lodge:** This travelers' crossroads has sweeping views of the Navajo Nation (page 235).

★ **Grand Canyon Hotel:** This refurbished and affordable gem is in the heart of historic Williams, gateway to the Grand Canyon (page 236).

★ **Mather Campground:** Sleep under starry skies at one of 300 campsites close to Grand Canyon Village (page 238).

★ **Grand Canyon Lodge:** This grand old hotel is perched high on the edge of the canyon's wild and forested North Rim (page 243).

★ **Phantom Ranch:** Few visit this small paradise deep in the canyon's bottomlands, but those who do never forget it (page 250).

windswept prairie to Grand Canyon National Park. If you feel like stopping overnight—and perhaps it is better to see the canyon with fresh eyes—do so in Williams, just an hour or so from the park's **South entrance.**

### West Rim

Driving from Vegas, you may also want to stop at **Grand Canyon West** and the Hualapai Reservation's **Skywalk.** This area is only **125 miles southwest** of Vegas (about a **2.5-hour drive**). However, this will add at least a full day to your trip, and the view from the South Rim is infinitely better and cheaper. Grand Canyon West charges a $43 entrance fee on top of $32 for the Skywalk, and you'll probably have to ride a shuttle bus part of the way. You can purchase tickets to the Skywalk and to any of the other attractions at Grand Canyon West when you arrive.

To reach Grand Canyon West from Las Vegas, take **US-93 South** out of the city, heading south for about 65 miles to **mile marker 42,** where you'll see the exit for Dolan Springs, Meadview City, and Pierce Ferry. Turn north onto **Pierce Ferry Road.** In about 30 miles, turn east on **Diamond Bar Road** and continue for 20 miles, with about 7 miles unpaved, to Grand Canyon West.

To continue on to the South Rim, head to Peach Springs along old **Route 66.** You can stop for the night at the Hualapai Lodge, or continue on for about an hour east on Route 66 to **Seligman.** Then head east on Route 66 to **Ash Fork,** where you can pick up **I-40 East** to **Williams,** the gateway to the South Rim. From there, head north along **AZ-64** to reach the park's **South entrance.**

## From Los Angeles

It's **500 miles** from Los Angeles to Grand Canyon's South Rim. Most of the **eight-hour** drive is along I-40, across an empty, hard landscape without much respite save the usual interstate fare. From Los Angeles, take **I-10 East** for 50 miles to reach **I-15,** which heads **northwest** out of the region toward Barstow. The driving time from L.A. to Barstow is about two hours, but it takes considerably longer on weekends and during the morning and evening rush hours. Expect snarls and delays around Barstow as well. At **Barstow,** pick up **I-40** for the remainder of the trip to Williams, Arizona (about

# Best Restaurants

★ **El Tovar Dining Room:** Enjoy locally sourced gourmet meals in a stylishly historical atmosphere on the canyon's edge (page 230).

★ **The Arizona Room:** This quiet place amid the South Rim's bustle is perfect for a lunch with a view (page 230).

★ **Bright Angel Restaurant:** This Fred Harvey-inspired eatery serves pre-hike American fare right next to the Bright Angel Trailhead (page 230).

★ **Rod's Steak House:** This institution in nearby Williams serves up Old West charm and juicy steaks (page 231).

★ **Diablo Burger:** This Flagstaff favorite serves one of the best burgers in the Southwest (page 231).

---

5 hours). At **Williams,** take **AZ-64 North** for about an hour to the **South entrance.**

About 320 miles from Los Angeles, but with 173 miles still left to go until you reach the canyon, Kingman, Arizona, sits along I-40 and offers a few good restaurants and affordable places to sleep—unless you're willing to push on for the final three hours or so to reach the rim in one shot.

## Stopping in Kingman

Kingman is located along the route to the South Rim of the Grand Canyon coming from either Las Vegas or Los Angeles. Proving ground for the manifest destiny of the United States, training ground for World War II heroes, and playground for the postwar middle class, Kingman preserves and proudly displays this heritage at several well-curated museums, such as the **Historic Route 66 Museum** (Powerhouse Visitors Center, 120 W. Andy Devine Ave., 928/753-9889, www. route66museum.net, 9am-5pm daily, $4 adults, children under 13 free) and the **Mohave Museum of History and Arts** (400 W. Beale St., 928/753-3195, www.mohave-museum.org, 9am-4:30pm Mon.-Fri., 1pm-5pm Sat., $4 adults, children under 12 free).

The best restaurant for miles is **Mattina's Ristorante Italiano** (318 E. Oak St., 928/753-7504, www.mattinas-ristorante.com, 5pm-9pm Tues.-Sat., $14-28), where you can get perfectly prepared Italian food, including outstanding beef medallions and rack of lamb. It's difficult to pass up the lobster ravioli or the creamy fettuccini alfredo. **Mr. D'z Route 66 Diner** (105 E. Andy Devine Ave., 928/718-0066, www. mrdzrt66diner.com, $9-18) serves the best burger in town, but they also have a large menu with all manner of delectable diner and road food: chili dogs, pizza, and even chicken-fried steak. Plus, breakfast is served all day. Save room for a thick shake or a root-beer float, and bring your camera: the cool old jukebox is snapshot-ready.

The **Ramblin' Rose Motel** (1001 E. Andy Devine Ave., 928/753-4747, www. ramblinrosemotel.com, $40-45) doesn't look like much, just another roadside place to park and snooze. But it's inexpensive, for one thing, and it's clean and has big, comfy beds. And you can check your email using the free wireless access, chill your soda in the mini fridge, and warm up a burrito in the microwave. You can't ask for much more for the price.

The 1950s-era neon sign of the **Hill Top Motel** (1901 E. Andy Devine Ave., 928/753-2198, $52-68) calls out to road-trippers. This small, affordable motel has standard, comfortable rooms with refrigerators and microwaves, and it offers free wireless Internet. Outside is a pool and well-kept cactus garden.

THE GRAND CANYON

# Grand Canyon Village

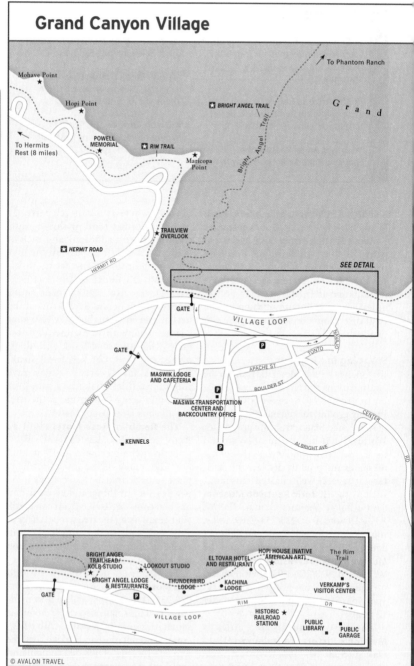

To Phantom Ranch

Mohave Point

Hopi Point

⭐ BRIGHT ANGEL TRAIL

G r a n d

POWELL MEMORIAL

⭐ RIM TRAIL

To Hermits Rest (8 miles)

Maricopa Point

Bright Angel Trail

TRAILVIEW OVERLOOK

⭐ HERMIT ROAD

HERMIT RD

SEE DETAIL

GATE

VILLAGE LOOP

NAVAJO

TONTO

GATE

P

MASWIK LODGE AND CAFETERIA

APACHE ST

ROWE WELL RD

P

BOULDER ST

MASWIK TRANSPORTATION CENTER AND BACKCOUNTRY OFFICE

CENTER RD

KENNELS

P

ALBRIGHT AVE

BRIGHT ANGEL TRAILHEAD/ KOLB STUDIO

LOOKOUT STUDIO

EL TOVAR HOTEL AND RESTAURANT

HOPI HOUSE (NATIVE AMERICAN ART)

The Rim Trail

GATE

BRIGHT ANGEL LODGE & RESTAURANTS

P

THUNDERBIRD LODGE

KACHINA LODGE

VERKAMP'S VISITOR CENTER

VILLAGE LOOP

RIM

DR

HISTORIC RAILROAD STATION

PUBLIC LIBRARY

PUBLIC GARAGE

© AVALON TRAVEL

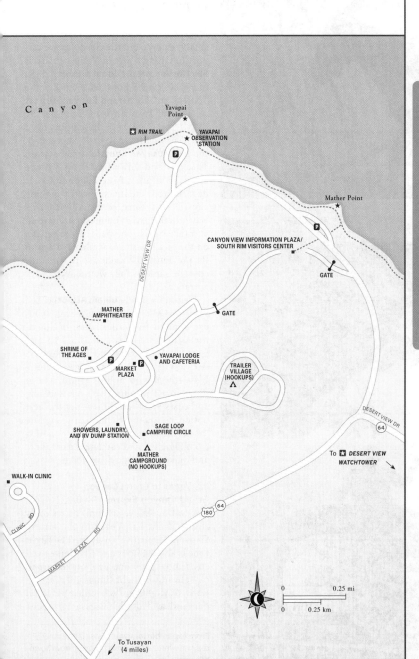

Canyon

Yavapai Point ★

★ RIM TRAIL

YAVAPAI OBSERVATION STATION ★

Mather Point ★

CANYON VIEW INFORMATION PLAZA/ SOUTH RIM VISITORS CENTER

GATE

GATE

MATHER AMPHITHEATER

SHRINE OF THE AGES

MARKET PLAZA

YAVAPAI LODGE AND CAFETERIA

TRAILER VILLAGE (HOOKUPS)

DESERT VIEW DR

DESERT VIEW DR 64

To DESERT VIEW WATCHTOWER

SHOWERS, LAUNDRY, AND RV DUMP STATION

SAGE LOOP CAMPFIRE CIRCLE

MATHER CAMPGROUND (NO HOOKUPS)

WALK-IN CLINIC

CLINIC RD

MARKET PLAZA RD

180 64

0        0.25 mi

0        0.25 km

To Tusayan (4 miles)

## By Air, Train, or Bus
### Air

Flagstaff, Tusayan, and Williams have small airports, but the closest major airport to Grand Canyon National Park is **Sky Harbor International Airport** (PHX) in Phoenix, a 3.5-hour drive south of the South Rim. The **Grand Canyon Airport** (GCN) at Tusayan, just outside the park's South entrance, has flights from Las Vegas daily. May-early September, the free **Tusayan Shuttle** runs between Tusayan and Grand Canyon Village every 20 minutes 8am-9:30pm daily. It departs from the Imax Theater, making stops along the main drag (AZ-64) on its way into the park. You must purchase an entrance pass to the park before getting on the bus. These are available at any of the previously mentioned stops, and they cost the same as they would at the park entrance.

Flagstaff's small **Pulliam Airport** (FLG, 928/556-1234, www.flagstaff.az.gov), located about five miles south of downtown, offers five flights daily to and from Sky Harbor in Phoenix through US Airways (800/428-4322 usairways.com). It's a roughly 50-minute flight, as opposed to a 2.5-hour drive from Phoenix, and costs $150-300. This is not the best option, as you must rent a car to explore the northland properly. If you are coming from Phoenix, it's best to rent a car there and make the scenic drive north.

### Las Vegas to Grand Canyon

**Grand Canyon Express** (800/222-6966, reservation@airvegas.com) offers daily flights from Las Vegas to the Grand Canyon Airport in Tusayan. The flight time is about 1 hour and 10 minutes and costs about $210 one-way. Make sure to call ahead for flight times and reservations, as flights are scheduled based on demand and don't necessarily occur

**From top to bottom:** mule rides in the inner canyon; winter at the Grand Canyon; downtown Williams.

## 🔁 Side Trip: Retro Fun on Route 66

**Seligman,** a tiny roadside settlement 87 miles east of Kingman, holds on tightly to its Route 66 heritage. There are less than 500 full-time residents and often, especially on summer weekends, twice that number of travelers. Don't be surprised to see European visitors, classic car nuts, and 60-something bikers passing through town. John Lasseter, co-director of the 2006 Disney-Pixar film *Cars*, has said that he based the movie's fictional town of Radiator Springs partly on Seligman, which, like Radiator Springs, nearly died out when it was bypassed by I-40 in the late 1970s.

Stop at **Delgadillo's Snow Cap Drive-In** (301 E. Chino Ave., 928/422-3291, $5-10), off Route 66 on the east end of town, a famous food shack dedicated to feeding, entertaining, and teasing Route 66 travelers for generations. They serve a mean chili burger, a famous "cheeseburger with cheese," hot dogs, malts, soft ice cream, and much more. Expect a wait, especially on summer week-

ends, and you will be teased, especially if you have a question that requires a serious answer. The **Roadkill Café** (502 W. Route 66, 928/422-3554, 7am-9pm daily, $8-24) is more than just a funny name; it's a popular place for buffalo burgers, steaks, and sandwiches.

There are several small, affordable, locally owned motels in Seligman. The **Supai Motel** (134 W. Chino St., 928/422-4153, www.supaimotelseligman.com, $69-82), named for the nearby Grand Canyon village inhabited by the Havasupai people, has clean and comfortable guest rooms at a fair price. The **Historic Route 66 Motel** (928/422-3204, www.route66seligmanarizona.com, $69-82) offers free wireless Internet and refrigerators in clean, comfortable guest rooms, and the **Canyon Lodge** (114 E. Chino St., 928/422-3255, www.route66canyonlodge.com, $69-82) has free wireless Internet along with refrigerators and microwaves in its themed guest rooms. They also serve a free continental breakfast.

GETTING TO THE GRAND CANYON

every day. Much more expensive but worth it if you're looking for a one-day tour of the canyon from Vegas, **Grand Canyon Airlines** offers the 9.5-hour **Grand Canyon Deluxe Tour** (866/735-9422, $344). The tour includes hotel-to-hotel service, access to the park, and a box lunch. For most people, driving from Las Vegas to the South Rim is the best option, in part because there's more to see from the ground than the air.

### Los Angeles to Grand Canyon

You can fly to the Grand Canyon Airport from **Los Angeles International Airport** (LAX), but you'll likely layover at **Sky Harbor Airport** (PHX) in Phoenix for at least an hour. Another option is to fly into Sky Harbor and rent a car there to make the 3-4 hour drive from Phoenix to the South Rim. The route from Phoenix to the South Rim along **I-17** is quite scenic, moving from the cactus-choked

desert to the high cool pines in a matter of hours.

**US Airways** (800/428-4322, www.usairways.com) and **United** (800/864-8331, www.united.com) both offer flights from LAX to Phoenix, then on to Grand Canyon Airport in Tusayan, which is about seven miles from the park's South Rim. These flights run $300-500 round-trip and can take up to five hours depending on your layover at Sky Harbor.

**US Airways** (800/428-4322, www.usairways.com) offers several daily flights from LAX to Flagstaff's small **Pulliam Airport** (FLG, 928/556-1234, www.flagstaff.az.gov), where you can rent a car or hire a shuttle to take you the remaining 1.5 hours to the park. These flights almost always have a layover of at least an hour at Phoenix's Sky Harbor Airport, so the flight from L.A. to Flagstaff and the subsequent drive to the South Rim can end up taking not too much longer than the drive straight from L.A. Expect to pay between $300 and $500 round-trip.

### Renting a Car

Most of the major car-rental companies have a presence at Flagstaff's small **Pulliam Airport** (FLG, 928/556-1234, www.flagstaff.az.gov), about five miles south of downtown. **Avis Downtown Flagstaff Car Rental** (175 W. Aspen Ave., 928/714-0713, www.avis.com, 7am-6pm Mon.-Fri., 8am-4pm Sat., 9am-1pm Sun.) is located right in the middle of all the action at the corner of Aspen Avenue and Humphreys Street. **Budget** (800/527-7000, www.budget.com) operates out of the same facility with the same hours and phone number. **Enterprise Rent-A-Car** (213 E. Route 66, 928/526-1377, www.enterprise.com, 8am-6pm Mon.-Fri., 9am-noon Sat.) is located on the eastern edges of town along I-40. If you're looking for a mythic Southwestern experience, stop by **EagleRider Flagstaff** (800 W. Route 66, 928/637-6575, www.route66rider.com, 8am-6pm daily, $159 per day, $931 per week) and rent a Harley-Davidson.

### Train

If you're coming from L.A., a trip east on the train can be a fun and romantic way to see the interior West. **Amtrak's Southwest Chief route** (800/872-7245, www.amtrak.com) departs daily from **L.A.'s Union Station,** usually around 6pm. The 10-hour overnight trip ends at **Flagstaff's downtown depot** (1 E. Route 66) at around 5am, where you can book a shuttle straight to the South Rim or take a shuttle to Williams, about an hour west of Flagstaff, and pick up the Grand Canyon Railway there, arriving in the park about 2.5 hours later. A ticket on the *Southwest Chief* to Flagstaff costs $70-291 round-trip, depending on options.

A fun, retro, and environmentally conscious way to reach the park, the **Grand Canyon Railway** (800/843-8724, www.thetrain.com, $65-220 pp round-trip) re-creates what it was like to visit the great gorge in the early 20th century. It takes about 2.5 hours to get to the South Rim depot from the station in Williams, where the **Grand Canyon Railway Hotel** (235 N. Grand Canyon Blvd., 928/635-4010, www.thetrain.com, $205-370), just beyond the train station, makes a good base, attempting as it does to match the atmosphere of the old Santa Fe Railroad Harvey House that once stood on the same ground.

A trip to and from the Grand Canyon on the old train is recommended for anyone who is interested in the heyday of train travel or the Old West—or for anyone desiring a slower-paced journey across the northland. Besides, the fewer visitors who drive their vehicles to the rim, the better. Kids especially enjoy the train trip. Comedian-fiddlers often stroll through the cars, and on some trips there's even a mock train robbery complete with bandits on horseback with blazing six-shooters.

### Bus

Flagstaff's **Greyhound bus station** (800 E. Butler Ave., 928/774-4573, www.greyhound.com) is located along industrial East Butler Avenue. The bus trip from Las Vegas to Flagstaff takes about six hours and costs $95 round-trip. From L.A., the bus trip takes about 12 hours and costs about $140.

**Arizona Shuttles** (928/226-8060, www.arizonashuttle.com) offers comfortable rides from Flagstaff to the Grand Canyon (Mar. 1-Oct. 31, round-trip $58 adults) three times daily. The shuttle departs from the Amtrak station in Flagstaff and makes stops at the Flagstaff's Pulliam Airport, the Grand Canyon Railway depot in Williams, the Imax Theater in Tusayan, and the Maswik Lodge inside the park. The whole trip takes about two hours. The company also goes to and from Phoenix's Sky Harbor Airport ($39 one-way) several times a day.

# One Day at the Grand Canyon

The ideal South Rim-only trip lasts three days and two nights. If you just have one day, about five hours or so will allow you to see all the sights on the rim and take in the sunset over the canyon. Be warned: Once you stare deep into this natural wonder, you might have trouble pulling yourself away.

## Morning

If you have just one day to see the Grand Canyon, drive to the South Rim and park your car at one of the large, free parking lots inside the national park. Hop on one of the park's free shuttles or rent a bike or walk along the **Rim Trail** and head toward Grand Canyon Village. Spend a few hours looking at the buildings and, of course, the canyon from this central, busy part of the rim. Stop in at the **Yavapai Observation Station,** check out the history of canyon tourism at the **Bright Angel Lodge,** watch a movie about the canyon at the visitors center, and have lunch at **The Arizona Room** or, better yet, **El Tovar Dining Room.**

## Afternoon

After lunch, take the shuttle along the eastern **Desert View Drive,** stopping along the way at a few of the eastern viewpoints, especially at Mary Colter's **Desert View Watchtower** on the far eastern edge of the park.

## Evening

End your day by heading all the way to the western reaches of the park to see **Hermit's Rest.** If you time it right, you'll catch a gorgeous canyon sunset from one of the western viewpoints along the way. For dinner, try **El Tovar** or one of the cafeterias before turning in early. If this is your only day at the canyon, visit Hermit's Rest first and leave the park via Desert View Drive, stopping at the Watchtower and the **Tusayan Museum and Ruin** on your way out.

## Extending Your Stay

If you're able to spend more time in the park, hit one of the **corridor trails** for a day hike below the rim. Rest up after rising out of the depths, then check the park newspaper to see what's happening at the **Shrine of the Ages,** where on most nights there's an entertaining and informative talk by a ranger.

If you include a North Rim or West Rim excursion, add at least 1-2 more days and nights. It takes at least five hours to reach the **North Rim** from the South Rim, perhaps longer if you take the daily shuttle from the south instead of your own vehicle. The **West Rim** and the **Hualapai** and **Havasupai Indian Reservations** are some 250 miles from the South Rim and a trip to these remote places should be planned separately from one to the popular South Rim.

The most important thing to remember when planning a trip to the canyon is to plan far ahead, even if, like the vast majority of visitors, you're just planning to spend time on the South Rim. Six months' advance planning is the norm, longer if you are going to ride a mule down or stay overnight at Phantom Ranch in the inner canyon.

# Visiting the Park

## Entrances

Unless you choose to ride the chugging train from Williams, there are only two ways, by road, in and out of the park's South Rim section. The vast majority of visitors to Grand Canyon National Park enter through the **South entrance** along AZ-64 from Williams. US-180 from Flagstaff meets up with AZ-64 near Valle, about 30 miles south of the South entrance; it's about 55 miles along scenic US-180 from Flagstaff to Valle. AZ-64 from Williams to the South entrance is 60 miles of flat, dry, windswept plain, dotted with a few isolated trailers, manufactured homes, and gaudy For Sale signs offering cheap "ranchland." Entering through the busy South entrance will ensure that your first look at the Grand Canyon is from **Mather Point,** one of the most iconic views of the river-molded gorge. The entrance stations are open 24 hours daily, including all holidays.

A less used but certainly no less worthy park entrance is the **East entrance,** in the park's **Desert View** section. About 25 miles east of Grand Canyon Village and all the action, this route is a good choice for those who want a more leisurely and comprehensive look at the rim, as there are quite a few stops along the way to the village that you might not otherwise get to if you enter through the South entrance. To reach the East entrance station, take US-89 for 46 miles north of Flagstaff, across a wide big-sky landscape covered in volcanic rock, pine forests, and yellow wildflowers, to Cameron, on the red-dirt Navajo Nation. Then head west on AZ-64 for about 30 miles to the entrance station.

The small, little-visited **North Rim entrance,** on AZ-67, is open around May 15-October 15.

## Park Passes and Fees

The **park entrance fee** is $30 per car and includes entry and parking for up to seven days. Payment of the entrance fee at the South Rim will be honored at the North Rim as long as you go within seven days. The entrance fee is $15 per person for those entering on foot or bicycle, and $25 per person for those entering on motorcycle, also good for seven days.

The National Park Service offers several **annual passes** for frequent park visitors, including one for $60 that allows unlimited access to Grand Canyon National Park for a year. The **America the Beautiful Pass** allows access to all the national parks for a year for $80; a lifetime version of this pass is available to seniors (age 62 or older). To purchase passes, inquire at the entrance station or one of the visitors centers in the park.

## Visitors Centers
### South Rim

**Canyon View Information Plaza** (9am-5pm daily) near Mather Point, the first overlook you pass on entering the park's main South entrance, is the perfect place to begin your visit to the park. You get there by walking the short path from the Mather Point parking lot or by hopping off the free shuttle, for which the plaza serves as a kind of central hub. Throughout the plaza there are displays on the natural and human history of the canyon and suggestions on what to do, and inside the **South Rim Visitor Center,** the park's main welcome and information center, there are displays on canyon history and science. Rangers are always on duty to answer questions, give advice, and help you plan your visit. Head to the visitors center's 200-seat theater and watch the thrilling *Grand Canyon: A Journey of Wonder,* a 20-minute orientation film that takes you on a daylong journey through the canyon and around the park and explains the basics of the canyon's natural and human histories. The movie is free and starts on the hour and half hour.

At the **National Geographic Grand Canyon Visitors Center** (Rte. 64, 928/638-2468, www.explorethecanyon. com, 8am-10pm daily Mar.-Oct., 10am-8pm daily Nov.-Feb., IMAX tickets $13 over age 10, $10 children 6-10, children under 6 free), you can purchase a park pass here, book tours, but what makes it worth a stop is its **IMAX Theater,** which shows the 35-minute movie *Grand Canyon—The Hidden Secrets* every hour at half past. Another information center, **Verkamp's Visitor Center** (8am-5pm daily), sits near El Tovar and the Hopi House in Grand Canyon Village. Verkamp's was a souvenir shop, the park's first, from 1906 to 2008. **Desert View Visitor Center and Bookstore** (9am-5pm daily), sits on Desert View Point about 25 miles east of Grand Canyon Village. It is staffed by helpful rangers and has information and displays on visiting the canyon; this is the natural place to stop for those entering the park from the quieter East entrance.

## North Rim

The **North Rim Visitor Center and Bookstore** (8am-6pm daily May-Oct.), near the Grand Canyon Lodge, has information, maps, and exhibits on North Rim science and history. The nonprofit Grand Canyon Association operates the well-stocked bookstore. Rangers offer a full program of talks and guided hikes throughout the day and night programs around the campfire. The North Rim edition of *The Pocket Map*, the free park newspaper, has an up-to-date list of topics, times, and meeting places. Try to attend at least one or two—they are typically interesting and entertaining for both kids and adults, and it tends to deepen your connection with this storied place when you learn about its natural and human history from those who know it best. For the kids, the visitors center has the usual super-fun and educational Junior Ranger program.

## Reservations
### Accommodations

To obtain a room at one of the lodges inside Grand Canyon National Park, you must book far in advance, especially if you are hoping to visit during the busy summer season. Reservations for all of the lodges on the South Rim, including Phantom Ranch and Trailer Village, are handled by **Xanterra Parks & Resorts** (303/297-2757, www.grandcanyonlodges. com). If at first it seems like you're not going to get the room you want, keep trying right up until you arrive. Call every day and check; if you are diligent, you can take advantage of cancellations. Reservations for the North Rim's only in-park accommodations, at **Grand Canyon Lodge** (928/638-2611 or 888/297-2757, www.grandcanyonlodgenorth.com), are handled separately. Some of the towns

outside the South Rim area of the park offer more accommodations options:

**Tusayan** (AZ-64): 1.5 miles (5 minutes) from Grand Canyon National Park South entrance; 7 miles from Grand Canyon Village

**Williams** (I-40): 54 miles (1 hour) from Grand Canyon National Park South entrance; 60 miles from Grand Canyon Village

**Flagstaff** (I-40): 73.5 miles (1.5 hours) from Grand Canyon National Park South entrance; 79 miles from Grand Canyon Village

### Campgrounds

There are two campgrounds at the South Rim. You can reserve a spot only at **Mather Campground** in Grand Canyon Village. The more rustic and undeveloped **Desert View Campground** is first-come, first-served. Spots at the **North Rim Campground** can be reserved as well. Contact the **National Recreation Reservation Service** (877/444-6777, www.recreation.gov) to reserve a spot up to six months before your trip.

### Mule Rides

Mule rides are popular at the park's busy South Rim, so they book up quickly. Luckily, you can book up to 13 months in advance through **Xanterra Parks & Resorts** (inside U.S. 888/297-2757, outside the U.S. 303/297-2757, www.grand-canyonlodges.com). To book a mule ride on the North Rim, contact **Canyon Trail Rides** (435/679-8665, www.canyonrides. com, May 15-Oct. 15).

### River Trips

A once-in-a-lifetime trip down the mighty Colorado River through the heart of the gorge takes a good deal of advance planning and booking. Book a tour or at least start the process at least 12-18 months in advance of your preferred departure date. The best place to start is the **Grand Canyon River Outfitters Association** (www.gcroa.org), a nonprofit group of about 16 licensed river outfitters, all of them monitored and approved by the National Park Service, each with a good safety record and similar rates. After you decide what kind of trip you want, the website links to the individual outfitters for booking. **O.A.R.S.** (800/346-6277, www.oars.com) is one highly recommended outfitter. Most of the companies offer trips between 3 and 18 days, and have a variety of boat styles. Choose two or three companies, call them up, and talk to someone live to make sure that you like the spirit of the tour. River trips are very social; you'll be spending a lot of time with your fellow boaters. Ask about previous trips so you can get a sense of the atmosphere and how many people are typically on a trip.

## Seasons

At about 7,000 feet elevation, the South Rim has a temperate climate: warm in the summer months, cool in fall, and cold in the winter. It snows in the deep winter and often rains in the late afternoon in late summer. Summer is the park's busiest season—and it is *very* busy—four or five million visitors from all over the world will be your companions, which isn't as bad as some make it out to be. People-watching and hobnobbing with fellow visitors from the far corners of the globe become legitimate enterprises if you're so inclined. During the summer months (May-Sept.), temperatures often exceed 110°F in the inner canyon, which has a desert climate, but average 75-85°F up on the forested rims. There's no reason for anybody to hike deep into the canyon in summer. It's not fun, and it is potentially deadly. It is better to plan a marathon trek in the fall.

Fall is light-jacket cool on the South Rim and warm but not hot in the inner canyon, where high temperatures during October range 80-90°F, making hiking much more pleasant than it is during the infernal summer months. October or November are the last months of the year

that a rim-to-rim hike from the North Rim is possible, as rim services shut down by the end of October, and the only road to the rim is closed by late November, and often before that, due to winter snowstorms. It's quite cold on the North Rim during October, but on the South Rim it's usually clear, cool, and pleasant during the day and snuggle-up chilly at night. A winter visit to the South Rim has its own charms. There is usually snow on the rim January-March, contrasting beautifully with the red, pink, and dusty green canyon colors. The crowds are thin and more laid-back than in the busy summer months. It is, however, quite cold, even during the day, and you may not want to stand and stare too long at the windy, bone-chilling viewpoints.

## Information and Services

As you enter the South Rim, you'll get a copy of *The Pocket Map,* a newsprint publication that is indispensable. It's pretty comprehensive and will likely answer many of your questions. A **North Rim edition** is passed out at the North Rim entrance.

If you're driving to the park, note that the last place to fill up with gas is in **Tusayan,** seven miles from the park. The only in-park gas station is 26 miles east of the central park at **Desert View.** The park operates a public garage near the rail depot (8am-noon and 1pm-5pm daily), where you can fix relatively minor car issues.

The **Canyon Village Market and General Store** (7am-9pm daily), inside the park at **Market Plaza,** sells a variety of groceries, camping supplies, and clothing. **Chase Bank** has an ATM at Market Plaza and a bank branch that's open 9am-5pm weekdays. Market Plaza also has a **post office** (9am-4:30pm Mon.-Fri., 11am-1pm Sat.).

The **Camper Services Building** at Mather Campground has a **laundry** and **showers** (6am-11pm daily, last load in at 9:45pm).

For 24-hour medical services within the park, **dial 911.**

The national parks, including Grand Canyon, stopped selling bottled water some time ago, so don't forget to bring along an easy-to-carry receptacle to refill at the water fountains situated throughout the park. A **water bottle, Camelback, or canteen** is required gear for a visit. You are going to get thirsty in the high, dry air along the rim. You might even take along a cooler with cold water and other drinks, which you can leave in your car and revisit as the need arises.

## Getting Around
### Shuttles

The park operates an excellent free shuttle service with comfortable buses fueled by compressed natural gas. It's best to park your car for the duration of your visit and use the shuttle. It's nearly impossible to find parking at the various sights, and traffic through the park is not always easy to navigate—there are a lot of one-way routes and oblivious pedestrians that can lead to needless frustration. Make sure you pick up a copy of the free park newspaper, *The Pocket Map,* which has a map of the various shuttle routes and stops.

Pretty much anywhere you want to go in the park a shuttle will get you there, and you rarely have to wait more than 10 minutes at any stop. That being said, there is no shuttle that goes all the way to the Tusayan Museum and Ruin or the Watchtower near the East entrance. Shuttle drivers are a good source of information about the park. They are generally friendly and knowledgeable, and a few of them are genuinely entertaining. The shuttle conveniently runs from around sunup until about 9pm, and drivers always know the expected sunrise and sundown times and seem to be intent on getting people to the best overlooks to view these two popular daily park events.

### Bicycle

Whether you're staying in the park or just visiting for the day, consider bringing your bike along. You can park at the **South Rim Backcountry Information Center parking lot** and ride your bike all around the park from there using the paved **Tuyasan Greenway Trail.** Every hotel, restaurant, store, and sight has a bike rack; don't forget your bike lock. If you get tired, park shuttles have racks that fit 2-3 bikes. Remember, though, that the shuttles take a lot longer because they make many stops. There's a good map of all the in-park bike routes in the free *Pocket Map* guide, and the staff at **Bright Angel Bicycles and Café** (928/814-8704, www.bikegrandcanyon.com, 6am-8pm daily Apr.-Nov., 7am-7pm daily Dec.-Mar.), right next to the **Grand Canyon Visitor Center** near the South entrance and Mather Point, can answer your questions.

## Tours
### Bus Tours

Xanterra, the park's main concessionaire, offers in-park **Motorcoach Tours** (888/297-2757, ww.grandcanyonlodges.com, $22-65). Sunrise tours are available, and longer drives to the eastern and western reaches of the park are offered. This is a comfortable, educational, and entertaining way to see the park, and odds are you will come away with a few new friends—possibly even a new email pal from abroad.

Only pay for a tour if you like being around a lot of other people and listening to mildly entertaining banter from the tour guides for hours at a time. It's easy to see and learn about everything the park has to offer without spending extra money on a tour, as it is in most national parks, and the highly informed and friendly rangers hanging around the South Rim's sites offer the same information that you'll get on an expensive tour, but for free.

Reservations are recommended, and

it's a good idea to make reservations at least three days in advance. Book trips at least a week ahead of time during the busy summer season. To book a tour last-minute, head to the Xanterra desk at the Bright Angel Lodge.

### Airplane and Helicopter Tours

Several companies offer helicopter tours of the canyon of varying lengths. One of the better operators is **Maverick Helicopters** (888/261-4414, www.maverickhelicopter.com, $264 for 45-minute flyover, $399 and up for 3.5-hour tour from Las Vegas). Though not ideal from the environmentalist point of view, a helicopter flight over the canyon is an exciting, rare experience, well worth the rather high price—a chance to take some rare photos from a condor's perspective. Maverick and other plane and helicopter tour operators operate out of **Grand Canyon Airport** (www.grandcanyonairport.org), along AZ-64 in Tusayan. All prefer reservations.

# The South Rim

The reality of the Grand Canyon is often suspect even to those standing on its rim. "For a time it is too much like a scale model or an optical illusion," wrote Joseph Wood Krutch, a great observer and writer of the Southwest. The canyon appears at first, Krutch added, "a man-made diorama trying to fool the eye." It is *too big* to be immediately comprehended, especially to those visitors used to the gaudy, lesser wonders of the human-made world.

Once you accept its size and understand that a river full of dry rocks and sand carved this mile-deep, multicolored canyon into the Colorado Plateau, the awesome power and wonder of it all is bound to leave you breathless and wondering what you've been doing with your life. If there are any sacred places in the natural world, this is surely one. The layers of primordial earth that compose this deep rock labyrinth tell the history of the planet—a geology textbook for new gods. And it is a story in which humans appear only briefly, if at all.

Never hospitable, the canyon has nonetheless had a history of human occupation for around 5,000 years, though the settlements have been small and usually seasonal. It was one of the last regions of North America to be explored and mapped. The first expedition through, led by the one-armed genius John Wesley Powell, was completed at the comparatively late date of 1869. John Hance, the first Anglo to reside at the canyon, explored its depths in the 1880s and built trails based on ancient Native American routes. A few other tough loners tried to develop mining operations here but soon found out that guiding avant-garde canyon tourists was the only sure financial bet in the canyonlands. It took another 20 years or so and the coming of the railroad before it became possible for the average American visitor to see the Grand Canyon.

Though impressive, statistics don't do the canyon justice. It is some 277 river miles long, beginning just below Lee's Ferry on the north and ending somewhere around the Grand Wash Cliffs in northwestern Arizona. It is 18 miles across at its widest point and an average of 10 miles across from the South to the North Rim. It is a mile deep on average; the highest point on the rim, the north's Point Imperial, rises nearly 9,000 feet above the river. Its towers, buttes, and mesas, formed by the falling away of layers undercut by the river's incessant carving, are red and pink, dull brown, and green-tipped, though these basic hues are altered and enhanced by the setting and rising of the sun and changes in the light.

It is folly, though, to try too hard to describe and boost the Grand Canyon. Perhaps the most poetic words ever spoken about the Grand Canyon, profound for their obvious simplicity, came from

## The Canyon and the Railroad

Musing on the Grand Canyon in 1902, John Muir lamented that, thanks to the railroad, "children and tender, pulpy people as well as storm-seasoned travelers" could now see the wonders of the West, including the Grand Canyon, with relative ease. It has always been easy for storm-seasoned travelers to begrudge us tender, pulpy types a good view—as if all the people who visit the canyon every year couldn't fit in its deep mazes and be fairly out of sight. Muir came to a similar conclusion after actually seeing the railway approach the chasm: "I was glad to discover that in the presence of such stupendous scenery they are nothing," he wrote. "The locomotives and trains are mere beetles and caterpillars, and the noise they make is as little disturbing as the hooting of an owl in the lonely woods."

It wasn't until the Santa Fe Railroad reached the South Rim of the Grand Canyon in 1901 that the great chasm's now-famous tourist trade really got going. Prior to that, travelers faced an all-day stagecoach ride from Flagstaff at a cost of $20, a high price to pay for sore bones and cramped quarters.

For half a century or more, the Santa Fe line from Williams took millions of tourists to the edge of the canyon. The railroad's main concessionaire, the Fred Harvey Company, enlisted the considerable talents of arts-and-crafts designer and architect Mary Colter to build lodges, lookouts, galleries, and stores on the South Rim that still stand today, now considered to be some of the finest architectural accomplishments in the entire national parks system. Harvey's dedication to simple elegance and Colter's interest in and understanding of Pueblo Indian architecture and lifeways created an artful human stamp on the rim that nearly lives up to the breathtaking canyon it serves.

The American love affair with the automobile, the rising mythology of the go-West road trip, and finally the interstate highway killed train travel to Grand Canyon National Park by the late 1960s. In the 1990s, however, entrepreneurs revived the railroad as an excursion and tourist line. Today, the Grand Canyon Railway carries more than 250,000 passengers to the South Rim every year, which has significantly reduced polluting automobile traffic in the cramped park.

Teddy Roosevelt, speaking on the South Rim in 1903. "Leave it as it is," he said. "You cannot improve on it; not a bit."

## Driving Tours
### ★ Hermit Road

March-November the park's free shuttle goes all the way to architect and Southwestern-design queen Mary Colter's **Hermit's Rest,** about seven miles from the village along the park's western scenic drive called the Hermit Road. It takes approximately two hours to complete the loop, stopping at eight viewpoints along the way. On the return route buses stop only at Mohave and Hopi Points. The Hermit Road viewpoints are some of the best in the park for viewing the sunsets. To make it in time for these dramatic solar performances, catch the bus at least an hour before sunset. There is often a long wait at the **Hermit's Rest Transfer Stop** just west of the Bright Angel Lodge. The bus drivers generally know the times of sunrise and sunset. The route is open to cars beginning in December, when you can drive to most of the viewpoints and stare at your leisure.

Each of the Hermit Road lookouts provides a slightly different perspective on the canyon, whether it be a strange unnoticed outcropping or a brief view of the white-tipped river rapids far, far below. The first stop along the route is the **Trailview Overlook,** from which you can see the Bright Angel Trail twisting down into the canyon and across the plateau to overlook the Colorado River.

The next major stop along the route is **Maricopa Point,** which provides a vast, mostly unobstructed view of the canyon all the way to the river. The point is on a promontory that juts out into the canyon over 100 feet. To the west you can see the rusted remains of the Orphan Mine, first opened in 1893 as a source of copper and silver—and, for a few busy years during the height of the Cold War, uranium. Consider taking the 10- to 15-minute hike along the Rim Trail west past the fenced-off Orphan Mine and through the piney rim world to the next viewing area, **Powell Point.** Here stands a memorial to the one-armed explorer and writer John Wesley Powell, who led the first and second river expeditions through the canyon in 1869 and 1871. The memorial is a flat-topped pyramid, which you can ascend and stand tall over the canyon. You can't see the river from here, but the views of the western reaches of the gorge are pretty good, and this is a strong candidate for a sunset-viewing vantage point.

About a quarter of a mile along the Rim Trail from Powell Point is **Hopi Point,** which offers sweeping, open views of the western canyon. As a result, it is the most popular west-end point for viewing the sun dropping red and orange in the west. North from here, across the canyon, look for the famous mesas named after Egyptian gods—Isis Temple, off to the northeast, and the Temple of Osiris, to the northwest. The next viewpoint heading west is **Mohave Point,** from which you can see the Colorado River and a few white-tipped rapids. Also visible from here are the 3,000-foot red-and-green cliffs that surround a deep side canyon, appropriately named **The Abyss.** Right below the viewpoint you can see the red-rock mesa called the Alligator. The last viewpoint before Hermit's Rest is **Pima Point,** a wide-open view to the west and the east, from which you can see the winding Colorado River and the Hermit Trail twisting down into the depths of the canyon.

view of the South Rim

### Desert View Drive

One more Mary Colter construction—arguably her greatest—and a Puebloan ruin are located along Desert View Drive, the 25-mile eastern scenic drive from the village. The viewpoints along this drive, which one ranger called the "quiet side of the South Rim," gradually become more desertlike and are typically less crowded. The free shuttle goes only as far as **Yaki Point,** a great place to watch the sunrise and near the popular South Kaibab Trailhead. Yaki Point is at the end of a 1.5-mile side road 2 miles east of AZ-64. The area is closed to private vehicles. Along Desert View Drive, make sure not to miss the essential **Grandview Point,** where the original canyon lodge once stood long ago. From here the rough Grandview Trail leads below the rim. The viewpoint sits at 7,400 feet, about 12 miles east of the village and then a mile on a side road. It's considered one of the grandest views of them all, hence the name; the canyon spreads out willingly from here, and the sunrise in the east hits it all strong and happy. To the east, look for the 7,844-foot monument called the Sinking Ship, and to the north below look for Horseshoe Mesa. This is a heavily wooded area, so for the best view hike a bit down the Grandview Trail. The steep and narrow trail is tough, but if you're prepared to hike, you can descend three miles to Horseshoe Mesa.

**Moran Point,** east of Grandview, is just eight miles south of Cape Royal (as the condor flies) on the North Rim and offers some impressive views of the canyon and the river. The point is named for the great painter of the canyon, Thomas Moran, whose brave attempts to capture the gorge on canvas helped create the buzz that led to the canyon's federal protection. Directly below the left side of the point you'll see Hance Rapid, one of the largest on the Colorado. It's three miles away, but if you're quiet you might be able to hear the rushing and roaring. Farther on the Desert View Drive you'll come to **Lipan Point,** with its wide-open vistas and the best view of the river from the South Rim. At Desert View, from the top of the Watchtower, you'll be able to catch a faraway glimpse of sacred Navajo Mountain near the Utah-Arizona border, the most distant point visible from within the park.

### Sights

Though you wouldn't want to make a habit of it, you could spend a few happy hours at **Grand Canyon Village Historical District** with your back to the canyon. Then again, this small assemblage of hotels, restaurants, gift shops, and lookouts offers some of the best viewpoints from which to gaze comfortably at all that multicolored splendor. Here is a perfect vantage from which to spot the strip of greenery just below the rim called **Indian Garden,** and follow with your eyes—or even your feet—the famous **Bright Angel Trail** as it twists improbably down the rim's rock face. You can also see some of

the most interesting and evocative buildings in the state, all of them registered National Historic Landmarks.

## Bright Angel Lodge

The village's central hub of activity, rustic **Bright Angel Lodge** was designed in 1935 by Mary Colter to replace the old Bright Angel Hotel, which was built by John Hance in the 1890s, and the Bright Angel Camp tent-city near the trail of the same name. Originally meant to attract more middle-class tourists to the park, the lodge is still a romantic and comfortable place to stay, resembling a rough-hewn hunting lodge constructed of materials found nearby.

In a room off the lobby there's a small museum with fascinating exhibits about Fred Harvey, Colter, and the early years of Southwestern tourism. You'll see Colter's "geologic fireplace," a 10-foot-high re-creation of the canyon's varied strata. The stones were collected from the inner canyon by a geologist and then loaded on the backs of mules for the journey out. The fireplace's strata appear exactly like those stacked throughout the canyon walls, equaling a couple of billion years of earth-building from bottom to rim. The lodge includes a collection of small cabins just to the west of the main building. The cabin closest to the rim was once the home of **Bucky O'Neill**, an early canyon resident and prospector who died while fighting with Teddy Roosevelt's Rough Riders in Cuba.

## El Tovar

Just east of the lodge is **El Tovar,** the South Rim's first great hotel and the picture of haute-wilderness style. Designed in 1905 by Charles Whittlesey for the Santa Fe Railroad, El Tovar has the look of a Swiss chalet and a log-house interior, watched over by the wall-hung heads of elk and buffalo; it is at once rustic, cozy, and elegant. This Harvey Company jewel has hosted dozens of rich and famous canyon visitors over the years, including George Bernard Shaw and Presidents Teddy Roosevelt and William Howard Taft. On the rim side, a gazebo stands near the edge. While it is a wonderfully romantic building up close, El Tovar looks even more picturesque from a few of the viewpoints along the Hermit Road, and you can really get a good idea of just how close the lodge is to the rim by seeing it from far away. Inside you'll find two gift shops and a cozy lounge where you can have a drink or two while looking at the canyon. El Tovar's restaurant is the best in the park, and it's quite pleasant to sink into one of the arts-and-crafts leather chairs in the rustic, dark-wood lobby.

## Hopi House

A few steps from the front porch of El Tovar is Colter's **Hopi House,** designed and built in 1905 as if it sat not at the edge of the Grand Canyon but on the edge of Hopi's Third Mesa. Hopi workers used local materials to build this unique gift shop and Native American arts museum. The Fred Harvey Company even hired the famous Hopi-Tewa potter Nampeyo to live here with her family while demonstrating her artistic talents and Hopi lifeways to tourists. This is one of the best places in the region for viewing and buying Hopi, Navajo, and Pueblo art (though most of the art is quite expensive), and there are even items made by Nampeyo's descendants on view and for sale here.

## Lookout Studio

Mary Colter also designed the **Lookout Studio,** west of the Bright Angel Lodge, a little stacked-stone watch house that seems to be a mysterious extension of the rim itself. The stone patio juts out over the canyon and is a popular place for picture taking. The Lookout was built in 1914 exactly for that purpose—to provide a comfortable but "indigenous" building and deck from which visitors could gaze at and photograph the canyon. It was fitted with high-powered telescopes and soon became one of the most popular snapshot scenes on the rim. It still is today, and on many days you'll be standing elbow to elbow with camera-carrying tourists clicking away. As she did with her other buildings on the rim, Colter designed the Lookout to be a kind of amalgam of Native American ruins and backcountry pioneer utilitarianism. Her formula of using found and indigenous materials, stacked haphazardly, works wonderfully. When it was first built, the little stone hovel was so "authentic" that it even had weeds growing out of the roof. Inside, where you'll find books and canyon souvenirs, the studio looks much as it did when it first opened. The jutting stone patio is still one of the best places from which to view the canyon.

## Kolb Studio

Built in 1904 right on the canyon's rim, **Kolb Studio** is significant not so much for its design but for the human story that went on inside. It was the home and studio of the famous Kolb Brothers, pioneer canyon photographers, moviemakers, river rafters, and entrepreneurs. Inside there's a gift shop, a gallery, and a display about the brothers, who, in 1912, rode the length of the Colorado in a boat with a movie camera rolling. The journey resulted in a classic book of exploration and river running, Emery Kolb's 1914 *Through the Grand Canyon from Wyoming to Mexico*. The Kolb Brothers were some of the first entrepreneurs at the canyon. Around 1902 they set up a photography studio in a cave near the rim and later moved it to this house. After a falling-out between the brothers, the younger Emery Kolb stayed on at the canyon until his death in 1976, showing daily the film of their epic river trip to several generations of canyon visitors.

## The Viewpoints

While the canyon's unrelenting vastness tends to blur the eyes into forgetting the details, viewing the gorge from many different points seems to cure this; however, there are 19 named viewpoints along the South Rim Road, from the easternmost Desert View to the westernmost Hermit's Rest. Is it necessary, or even a good idea, to see them all? No, not really. For many it's difficult to pick out the various named buttes, mesas, side canyons, drainages, and other features that rise and fall and undulate throughout the gorge, and one viewpoint ends up looking not that different from the next.

The best way to see the canyon viewpoints is to park your car and walk along the **Rim Trail.** Attempts to visit each viewpoint tend to speed up your visit and make you miss the subtleties of the different views. Consider really getting to know a few select viewpoints rather than trying to quickly and superficially hit each one. Any of the viewpoints along the **Hermit Road** and **Desert View Drive** are candidates for a long love affair. The views from just outside **El Tovar** or the **Bright Angel Lodge,** right in the middle of all the bustling village action, are as gorgeous as any others, and it can be fun and illuminating to watch people's reactions to what they're seeing.

There isn't a bad view of the canyon, but if you have limited time, ask a ranger at Canyon View Information Plaza or Yavapai Observation Station what their favorite viewpoint is and why. The shuttle bus drivers are also great sources of information and opinions. Try to see at least one sunset or sunrise at one of the developed viewpoints. The canyon's colors and details can seem monotonous after the initial thrill wears off (if it ever does), but the sun splashing and dancing at different strengths and angles against the multihued buttes and sheer, shadowy walls makes it all new again.

## Mather Point

As most South Rim visitors enter through the park's South entrance, it's no surprise that the most visited viewpoint in the park is the first one along that route—**Mather Point,** named for the first

National Park Service director, Stephen T. Mather. While crowded, Mather Point offers a typically astounding view of the canyon and is probably the mind's-eye view that most casual visitors take away. It can get busy, especially in the summer. If you're going to the park's main visitors center (and you should), park near here and walk the short paved path to the **Canyon View Information Plaza.** At Mather Point you can walk out onto two railed-off jutting rocks to feel like you're hovering on the edge of an abyss, but you may have to stand in line to get right up to the edge. A good way to see this part of the park is to leave your car at the large parking area at Mather (which is often full, of course) and then walk a short way along the Rim Trail west to **Yavapai Point** and the **Yavapai Observation Station,** the best place to learn about the canyon's geology and get more than a passing understanding of what you're gazing at. It's a good idea to check out the informative displays on canyon geology here before

you hit any of the other viewpoints (unless you are coming in from the East entrance).

### Yavapai Observation Station

First opened in 1928, **Yavapai Observation Station and Geology Museum** (8am-8pm daily summer, 8am-6pm daily winter, free) is the best place in the park to learn about the canyon's geology. This limestone-and-pine museum and bookstore is a must-visit for visitors interested in learning about what they're seeing. The building itself is of interest. Designed by architect Herbert Maier, the stacked-stone structure, like Colter's buildings, merges with the rim itself to appear a foregone and inevitable part of the landscape. The site for the station, which was originally called the Yavapai Trailside Museum, was handpicked by canyon geologists as the best for viewing the various strata and receiving a rim-side lesson on the region's geologic past and present. Inside the building

Hopi House

you'll find displays about canyon geology. Particularly helpful is the huge topographic relief map of the canyon—a giant's-eye view that really helps you discern what you're seeing once you turn into an ant outside on the rim.

## Hermit's Rest

The final stop on the Hermit Road is the enchanting gift shop and rest house called **Hermit's Rest.** As you walk up a path through a stacked-boulder entranceway, from which hangs an old mission bell, the little stone cabin comes into view. It looks as if some lonely hermit stacked rock upon rock until something haphazard but cozy rose from the rim—a structure from the realm of fairy tales. Inside, the huge, yawning fireplace, tall and deep enough to be a room itself, dominates the warm, rustic front room, where there are a few chairs chopped out of stumps, a Navajo blanket or two splashing color against the gray stone, and elegant lantern-lamps hanging from

the stones. Outside, the views of the canyon and down the Hermit Trail are spectacular, but something about that little rock shelter makes it hard to leave.

## Tusayan Museum and Ruin

The **Tusayan Museum and Ruin** (9am-5pm daily, free) has a small but interesting exhibit on the canyon's early human settlers. The museum is located near an 800-year-old Ancestral Puebloan ruin with a self-guided trail and regularly scheduled ranger walks. Since the free shuttle doesn't extend this far east, you have to drive to the museum and ruin; it's about 3 miles west of Desert View and 22 miles east of the village. It's worth the drive, though, especially if you're going to be heading to the Desert View section anyway (which you should). There are several interesting displays on the history of human life in the region. While the canyonlands haven't been exactly hospitable to humans over the eons, the oldest artifacts found in the Grand Canyon date back about 12,000 years. They include little stick-built animal fetishes and other mysterious hints at what life was once like on the rim and inside the canyon. Imagine living along the rim, walking every day to the great gorge, tossing an offering of cornmeal into the abyss, and wondering what your hidden canyon gods were going to provide you with next.

## ★ Desert View Watchtower

What is perhaps the most mysterious and thrilling of Colter's canyon creations, the **Desert View Watchtower** is an artful homage to smaller Ancestral Puebloan-built towers found at Hovenweep National Monument and elsewhere in the Four Corners region, the exact purpose of which is still unknown.

You reach the tower's high, windy deck by climbing the twisting, steep steps winding around the open middle, past walls painted with visions of Hopi lore and religion by Hopi artist Fred Kabotie. Pick up *The Watchtower Guide* free in the gift shop on the bottom floor for interpretations of the figures and symbols. From the top of the Watchtower, the South Rim's highest viewpoint, the whole arid expanse opens up, and you feel something like a lucky survivor at the edge of existence, even among the crowds. Such is the evocative power, the rough-edged romanticism, of Colter's vision.

## Recreation
### Hiking

Something about a well-built trail twisting deep into an unknown territory can spur even the most habitually sedentary canyon visitor to begin an epic trudge. This phenomenon is responsible for both the best and worst of the South Rim's busy recreation life. It is not uncommon to see hikers a mile or more below the rim picking along in high heels and sauntering blithely in flip-flops, not a drop of water between them. It's best to go to the canyon prepared to hike, with proper footwear and plenty of water and snacks. You'll probably want to hike a little, and since there's no such thing as an easy hike into the Grand Canyon, going in prepared, even if it's just for a few miles, will make your hike a pleasure rather than a chore. Also, remember that there aren't any loop hikes here: If you hike in a mile—and that can happen surprisingly quickly—you also must hike out (up) a mile, at an oxygen-depleted altitude of 6,000-7,000 feet.

### ★ Rim Trail

**Distance:** 12.8 miles one-way
**Duration:** all day
**Elevation gain:** about 200 feet
**Effort:** easy
**Trailhead:** Grand Canyon Village east to South Kaibab Trailhead or west to Hermit's Rest

If you can manage a 13-mile, relatively easy walk at an altitude of around 7,000 feet, the **Rim Trail** provides the single best way to see all of the South Rim. The trail, paved for most of its length, runs

the entrance to Hermit's Rest

from the South Kaibab Trailhead area on the east, through the village, and all the way to Hermit's Rest, hitting every major point of interest and beauty along the way. The path gets a little tough as it rises a bit past the Bright Angel Trailhead just west of the village. The trail becomes a thin dirt single-track between Powell Point and Monument Creek Vista, but it never gets too difficult. It would be considered an easy, scenic walk by just about anybody, kids included. But perhaps the best thing about the Rim Trail is that you don't have to hike the whole 13 miles—far from it. There are at least 16 shuttle stops along the way, and you can hop on and off the trail at your pleasure. Dogs are allowed on the Rim Trail with a leash, but you can't take them on the shuttle buses.

Few will want to hike the entire 13 miles, of course. Such an epic walk would in fact require twice the miles, as the trail is not a loop but a ribbon stretched out flat along the rim from west to east. It's better to pick out a relatively short stretch to walk, starting from the village and ending back there after turning around. Toward the west, try walking the roughly 2.2-mile stretch from the village to Hopi Point. This would be an ideal hike toward the end of the day, as Hopi Point is a famed spot for viewing the sunset. You could then hike back by flashlight or take the free shuttle bus. Eastward, hike the Rim Trail from the village to Yavapai Point, a distance of about 2 miles one-way. This route will take you past stunning views of the canyon to the Yavapai Observation Station.

### ★ Bright Angel Trail

**Distance:** 1.5-9.6 miles one-way
**Duration:** a few hours to overnight
**Elevation gain:** 4,380 feet
**Effort:** moderate to difficult
**Trailhead:** Grand Canyon Village, just west of Bright Angel Lodge

Hiking down the **Bright Angel Trail,** you quickly leave behind the piney rim and enter a sharp and arid landscape, twisting down and around switchbacks on a path that is sometimes all rock underfoot. Step aside for the many mule trains that use this route, and watch for the droppings, which are everywhere. Because this trail is so steep, it doesn't take long for the rim to look far away, and you soon feel like you are deep within a chasm and those rim-top people are mere ants scurrying about.

The Bright Angel Trail is the most popular trail in the canyon owing in part to its starting just to the west of the Bright Angel Lodge in the village center. It's considered by park staff to be the "safest" trail because it has two rest houses with water. The Bright Angel was once the only easily accessible corridor trail from the South Rim.

Many South Rim visitors choose to walk down Bright Angel a bit just to get a feeling of what it's like to be below the rim. If you want to do something a little more structured, the 3-mile round-trip hike to the **Mile-and-a-Half Resthouse** is

# Hiking the Grand Canyon the Easy Way

One of the first things you notice while journeying through the inner canyon is the advanced age of many of your fellow hikers. It is not uncommon to see men and women in their 70s and 80s hiking along at a good clip, packs on their backs and big smiles on their faces.

At the same time, all over the South Rim you'll see warning signs about overexertion, each featuring a buff young man in incredible shape suffering from heatstroke or exhaustion, with the warning that most of the people who die in the canyon—and people die every year—are people like him. You need not be a wilderness expert or marathon runner to enjoy even a long, 27-mile, rim-to-rim hike through the inner canyon. Don't let your fears hold you back from what is often a life-changing trip.

There are several strategies that can make a canyon hike much easier than a forced march with a 30-pound pack of gear on your back. First of all, don't go in the summer; wait until September or October, when it's cooler, though still quite warm, in the inner canyon. Second, try your best to book a cabin or a dorm room at Phantom Ranch rather than camping. That way, you'll need less equipment, you'll have all or most of your food taken care of, and there will be a shower and a beer waiting for you upon your arrival. Also, for about $75 you can hire a mule to carry up to 30 pounds of gear for you, so all you have to bring is a day pack with water and snacks. This way, instead of suffering while you descend and ascend the trail, you'll be able to better enjoy the magnificence of this wonder of the world.

a good introduction to the steep, twisting trail. A little farther on is **Three-Mile Resthouse,** a 6-mile round-trip hike. Both rest houses have water seasonally. One of the best day hikes from the South Rim is the 9-mile round-trip to beautiful **Indian Garden,** a cool and green oasis in the arid inner canyon. This is a rather punishing day hike, not recommended in the summer. The same goes for the 12-mile round-trip trudge down to **Plateau Point,** from which you can see the Colorado River winding through the inner gorge.

### South Kaibab Trail

**Distance:** 1.5-7 miles one-way
**Duration:** several hours to all day
**Elevation gain:** 4,780 feet
**Effort:** moderate to difficult
**Trailhead:** near Yaki Point

Steep but relatively short, the 7-mile **South Kaibab Trail** provides the quickest, most direct South Rim route to and from the river. It's popular with day hikers and those looking for the quickest way into the gorge, and many consider

it superior to the often-crowded Bright Angel Trail. The trailhead is located a few miles east of the village near Yaki Point; take the shuttle bus on the Kaibab Trail Route. The 1.8-mile round-trip hike to **Ooh Aah Point** has great views of the canyon from steep switchbacks. **Cedar Ridge** is a 3-mile round-trip hike down the trail, well worth it for the views of O'Neill Butte and Vishnu Temple. There's no water anywhere along the trail, and there's no shade to speak of. Bighorn sheep have been known to haunt this trail, and you might feel akin to those dexterous beasts while hiking the rocky ridgeline, which seems unbearably steep in a few places, especially on the way back up. If you are interested in a longer haul, the 6-mile round-trip hike to **Skeleton Point,** from which you can see the Colorado River, is probably as far along this trail as you'll want to go in one day, though in summer you might want to reconsider descending so far. Deer and California condors are also regularly seen along the South Kaibab Trail.

## Hermit Trail to Dripping Springs

**Distance:** 6.2 miles round-trip
**Duration:** 5-6 hours
**Elevation gain:** 1,400 feet
**Effort:** moderate
**Trailhead:** just west of Hermit's Rest

Built by the Santa Fe Railroad as a challenge to the fee-charging keeper of the Bright Angel Trail, the **Hermit Trail** just past Hermit's Rest leads to some less visited areas of the canyon. This trail isn't maintained with the same energy as the well-traveled corridor trails, and it has no potable water. You could take the Hermit Trail 10 miles deep into the canyon to the river, where Fred Harvey built the first below-rim camp for tourists, complete with a tramway from the rim, the ruins of which are still visible. But such a trudge should be left only to fully geared experts. Not so the 6.2 mile round-trip hike to the secluded and green **Dripping Springs,** which is one of the best day hikes in the canyon for midlevel to expert hikers. Start out on the Hermit Trail's steep, rocky, almost stair-like switchbacks, and then look for the **Dripping Springs Trailhead** after about 1.5 miles, once you reach a more level section dominated by piñon pine and juniper. Veer left on the trail, which begins to rise a bit and leads along a ridgeline across Hermit Basin; the views are so awe-inspiring and so unobstructed that it's difficult to keep your eyes on the skinny trail. Continue west once you come to the junction with the Boucher Trail, after about 1 mile, then it's about 0.5 mile up a side canyon to the cool and shady rock overhang known as Dripping Springs. And it really does drip: A shock of fernlike greenery creeps off the rock overhang, trickling cold, clean spring water at a steady pace into a small collecting pool. Get your head wet, have a picnic, and kick back in this out-of-way, hard-won oasis. But don't stay too long. The hike up is nothing to take lightly: The switchbacks are punishing, and the end, as it always does when one is hiking up a trail in the Grand Canyon, seems to get farther away as your legs begin to gain fatigue-weight. There's no water on the trail, so make sure to bring enough along and conserve it.

## Grandview Trail

**Distance:** 8.4 miles to the river
**Duration:** a few hours to overnight
**Elevation gain:** 4,792 feet
**Effort:** difficult
**Trailhead:** Grandview Point, 12 miles east of Grand Canyon Village

A steep, rocky, and largely unmaintained route built first to serve a copper mine at Horseshoe Mesa and then to entice tourists below the forested rim, the **Grandview Trail** should be left to midlevel hikers and above. Though you can take the trail all the way to the river and Hance Rapid, more than 8 miles in, for day hikers the 6.4-mile round-trip trek to Horseshoe Mesa and the mine's ruins is probably as far as you'll want to go. This trail is definitely not safe for winter hiking. Hiking back up, you won't soon forget the steep slab-rock and cobblestone switchbacks, and hiking down will likely take longer than planned as the steepest parts of the route are quite technical and require heads-up attention. Park staff are not exactly quick to recommend this route to casual hikers. Don't be surprised if you meet a ranger hanging out along the trail about 1.5 miles in, who may tell you to turn around if they don't think you have the proper gear or enough water to continue on.

## Biking

Riding bikes in the national parks seems to get easier and more popular every year, and the Grand Canyon is no exception to the trend. It's now possible to ride from outside the park near Tusayan to the visitors center, and then on across the park to Hermit's Rest, on either paved trails or roads closed to cars. This long round-trip ride, starting and ending about 6.5 miles outside the park at the **Tusayan Greenway** trailhead, is about 32 miles. It's probably not for everyone, but it's also not that difficult. The easy paved trails undulate across the park, so you're never too far away from a gentle downhill.

Bikes are not allowed on the Rim Trail except for a 2.8-mile section called the **Hermit Road Greenway Trail.** The paved trail begins at Monument Creek Vista along the Hermit Road and ends close to Hermit's Rest. This is about as close as you can get to the rim on a bike, and it's a fun and beautiful stretch of trail highly recommended to bicyclists. To get to the very edge of the rim, you have to park your bike and walk a bit, but never far, and there are bike racks at each developed viewpoint.

While the main park roads are open to bikes, they don't have wide shoulders or bike lanes, so it's best to stick to the Greenway Trail. The exception is **Hermit Road,** which is closed to cars during peak season. Seven miles one-way between the village and the western end of the park at Hermit's Rest, the Hermit Road is the best and most popular bikeway on the South Rim. The only traffic you'll have to deal with on this rolling ride of tough ups and fun downs is the occasional shuttle bus. Just pull over and let them pass.

The free *Pocket Map* includes a map of bike routes around the park.

**Bright Angel Bicycles and Café** (928/814-8704, www.bikegrandcanyon. com, 6am-8pm daily Apr.-Nov., 7am-7pm daily Dec.-Mar., $12 per hour, $30 for 5 hours, $40 for 24 hours) rents comfortable, easy-to-ride bikes as well as safety equipment and trailers for the tots. They also offer guided bike tours of the South Rim's sights ($40 adults, $32 children under 17). The friendly staff members are quick to offer suggestions about the best places to ride. The little café serves excellent coffee and sells premade sandwiches and other snacks. Bright Angel Bicycles is located right next to the **Grand Canyon Visitors Center** near the South entrance and Mather Point.

The **Tusayan Bike Trails** are a series of

view from the Hermit Trail

single-track trails and old mining and logging roads organized into several easy to moderate loop trails for mountain bikers near the park's South entrance. The trails wind through a forest of pine, juniper, and piñon. The longest loop is just over 11 miles, and the shortest is just under 4 miles. There's a map at the beginning of the trails that shows the various loops. Pick up the trails on the west side of AZ-64 north of Tusayan, about 1 mile south of the park entrance.

## Lectures and Programs

Every day the park offers numerous ranger-guided hikes and nature walks, as well as lectures and discussions on the animals, human history, and geology of the canyon, at various spots around the park; check at the visitors center or on the park's website for specific programs.

Most nights during the summer, there's a typically fascinating evening ranger program at the **McKee Amphitheater.** This varied program of lectures and night

walks, on subjects ranging from astronomy to the Colorado River to "Surviving the Apocalypse at the Grand Canyon," is usually popular, so it's best to plan ahead. You must get a ticket to secure a spot, starting at 7:30pm at the Shrine of the Ages venue near the park headquarters for an 8:30pm program. The amphitheater is just east of the Shrine of the Ages and across the road from Canyon Village Market Plaza, 1.4 miles east of the village. Other times of the year ranger programs are held daily and nightly at Shrine of the Ages and elsewhere around the park, and they are always free.

## Shopping

There are more than 16 places to buy gifts, books, souvenirs, supplies, and Native American arts and crafts at the South Rim. Nearly every lodge has a substantial gift shop in its lobby, as do Hermit's Rest, Kolb Studio, Lookout Studio, and the Desert View Watchtower.

For books, the best place to go is **Books & More** at the Canyon View Information Plaza, operated by the nonprofit Grand Canyon Association. You'll find books about canyon science and history for both adults and children. All the gift shops have a small book section, most of them selling the same selection of popular canyon-related titles published by the GCA. If you're in need of camping and hiking supplies to buy or rent—including top-of-the-line footwear, clothes, and backpacks—try the general store at the **Canyon Village Market Plaza.** Here you'll also find groceries, toiletries, produce, alcoholic beverages, and "I hiked the Grand Canyon" T-shirts.

Whether you're a semiserious collector or a first-time dabbler, the best place on the South Rim to find high-quality Native American arts and crafts is Mary Colter's **Hopi House.** Shop here for baskets, overlay jewelry, sand paintings, kachina dolls, and other regional treasures. Don't expect to find too many great deals—most of the best pieces are priced accordingly.

## Food
### Inside the Park

★ **El Tovar Dining Room** (928/638-2631, ext. 6432, www.grandcanyonlodges. com, 6:30am-11am, 11:30am-2pm, and 5pm-10pm daily, $17-35, reservations required) truly carries on the Fred Harvey Company traditions on which it was founded more than 100 years ago. A serious, competent staff serves fresh, creative, locally inspired dishes in a cozy, mural-clad dining room that has not been significantly altered from the way it looked back when Teddy Roosevelt and Zane Grey ate here. The wine, entrées, and desserts are all top-notch and would be appreciated anywhere in the world—but they always seem to be that much more tasty with the sun going down over the canyon. Pay attention to the specials, which usually feature some in-season local edible; they are always the best thing to eat within several hundred miles in any direction. If you only have one nice dinner planned for your trip, choose El Tovar over The Arizona Room. El Tovar has greater historical and aesthetic interest and is not that much more expensive than The Arizona Room.

★ **The Arizona Room** (928/638-2631, www.grandcanyonlodges.com, 11:30am-3pm and 4:30pm-10pm daily Mar.-Dec., $14-32), next to the Bright Angel Lodge, serves Southwestern-inspired steak, prime rib, fish, and chicken dishes in a stylish but still casual atmosphere. There's a full bar, and the steaks are excellent—hand-cut and cooked just right with unexpected sauces and marinades. The Arizona Room is closed for dinner in January and February and closes to the lunch crowd November-February.

★ **Bright Angel Restaurant** (928/638-2631, www.grandcanyonlodges.com, 6:30am-10pm daily, $9-22), just off the Bright Angel Lodge's lobby, is a perfect place for a big, hearty breakfast before a day hike below the rim. It serves all the standard, rib-sticking dishes amid decorations and ephemera recalling the Fred Harvey heyday. At lunch there's stew, chili, salads, sandwiches, and burgers, and for dinner there's steak, pasta, and fish dishes called "Bright Angel Traditions," along with a few offerings from The Arizona Room's menu. Nearby is the **Bright Angel Fountain** (11am-5pm daily in season), which serves hot dogs, ice cream, and other quick treats.

**Maswik Food Court** (928/638-2631, www.grandcanyonlodges.com, 6am-10pm daily, $5-15) is an ideal place for a quick, filling, and delicious meal. You can find just about everything—burgers, salads, country-style mashed potatoes, french fries, sandwiches, prime rib, chili, and soft-serve ice cream, to name just a few of the dozens of offerings. Just grab a tray and pick your favorite dish, and you'll be eating in a matter of a few minutes.

**Yavapai Lodge Restaurant** (www.visitgrandcanyon.com, 6am-10pm daily, $10-20) has decent food in a cafeteria setting where you order from a computer. Sandwiches, both hot and cold, dominate the limited menu.

### Outside the Park
#### Tusayan

Nobody would go to Tusayan specifically to eat, but it makes for a decent stop if you're hungry. A lot of tour buses stop here, so you might find yourself crowded into waiting for a table at some places, especially during the summer high season. Better to eat in the park or in Flagstaff or Williams, both of which have many charming and delicious local restaurants worth seeking out. It's only about an hour's drive to either place, so you might be better off having a snack and skipping Tusayan altogether.

**Sophie's Mexican Kitchen** (110 Hwy. 64, Grand Canyon Village Shops, 928/638-4654, 10am-9pm daily, $10-15) is a great option for vegetarians, including vegans—and anyone who likes Mexican food. You'll find a fun, festive atmosphere here. It's a popular place with delicious margaritas and good fajitas, chimichangas, and the like.

If you're craving pizza after a long day exploring the canyon, try **We Cook Pizza & Pasta** (125 E. Rte. 64, 928/638-2278, www.wecookpizzaandpasta.com, 11am-10pm daily Mar.-Oct., 11am-8pm daily Nov.-Feb., $10-30) for an excellent, high-piled pizza pie. It calls to you just as you enter Tusayan coming from the park. The pizza, served in slices or whole pies, is pretty good considering the locale, and they have a big salad bar with all the fixings, plus beer and wine. It's a casual place, with picnic tables and an often harried staff. It gets really busy in here during the high summer season.

**The Coronado Room** (74 Rte. 64, 928/638-2681, 5pm-10pm daily, $15-25) inside the Grand Canyon Squire Inn serves tasty steaks, seafood, pasta, and Southwestern-inspired dishes.

### Williams

A northland institution with some of the best steaks in the region, ★ **Rod's Steak House** (301 E. Route 66, 928/635-2671, www.rods-steakhouse.com, 11am-9:30pm Mon.-Sat., $12-25) has been operating at the same site since 1946. The food is excellent, the staff is friendly and professional, and the menus are shaped like steers.

The **Pine Country Restaurant** (107 N. Grand Canyon Blvd., 928/635-9718, http://pinecountryrestaurant.com, 6:30am-9:30pm daily, $5-10) is a family-style place that serves diner-style food and homemade pies. Check out the beautiful paintings of the Grand Canyon on the walls.

**Cruiser's Route 66 Bar & Grill** (233 W. Route 66, 928/635-2445, www.cruisers66.com, 7am-10:30am and 11am-close daily, $7-15) offers a diverse menu, with superior barbecue ribs, burgers, fajitas, pulled-pork sandwiches, and homemade chili. They have a full bar and offer live music most nights. During the summer evenings, the patio is lively and fun.

For something a bit more upscale and romantic, try the **Red Raven Restaurant** (135 W. Route 66, 928/635-4980, www.redravenrestaurant.com, 11am-2pm and 5pm-close daily, $11-25), a charming little place along Route 66 with big windows looking out on the bustling sidewalk and the tourists strolling by. It serves delicious and inventive dishes: steak wraps, Guinness stew, tasty lamb, sweet potato fries, and Southwest egg rolls, to name just a few. The restaurant also has a deep beer list with selections mainly from Arizona and Colorado, and a good wine selection heavy on Italy and California. Make a reservation for dinner.

The vegetarian's best bet this side of downtown Flagstaff is the **Dara Thai Café** (145 W. Route 66, 928/635-2201, 11am-2pm and 5pm-9pm Mon.-Sat., $5-10), an agreeable little spot in the Grand Canyon Hotel. They serve a variety of fresh and flavorful Thai favorites and offer quite a few meat-free dishes.

### Flagstaff

For the best burgers in the northland, head to ★ **Diablo Burger** (20 N. Leroux St. #112, 928/774-3274, www.diabloburger.com, 11am-9pm Sun.-Wed., 11am-10pm Thurs.-Sat., $10-13), which serves a small but stellar menu of beef raised locally on the plains around Flagstaff. All the finely crafted creations, such as the "Cheech" (guacamole, jalapeños, and spicy cheese) or the "Vitamin B" (bleu cheese with bacon and a beet) come on Diablo's branded English muffin-style buns alongside a mess of Belgian fries. They also have a terrific veggie burger.

**Brandy's Restaurant and Bakery** (1500 E. Cedar Ave. #40, 928/779-2187, www.brandysrestaurant.com, 6:30am-3pm daily, $6-10) often wins the Best Breakfast honors from readers of the local newspaper, and those readers know what they're talking about. The homemade breads and bagels make everything else taste better.

Try the Eggs Brandy, two poached eggs on a homemade bagel smothered in hollandaise sauce. For lunch there are crave-worthy sandwiches (Brandy's Reubens are some of the best in the business), burgers, and salads. They also serve beer, wine, and mimosas.

**Josephine's Modern American Bistro** (503 N. Humphreys St., 928/779-3400, www.josephinesrestaurant.com, 11:30am-2pm and 5pm-9pm Mon.-Fri., 11:30am-2pm and 5pm-9pm Sat., 9am-2pm Sun., $10-30) offers a creative fusion of tastes for lunch and dinner, such as the roasted pepper and hummus grilled-cheese sandwich and the chile relleno with sun-dried cranberry guacamole, from a cozy historic home near downtown. This is one of the best places in town for brunch.

**Charly's Pub and Grill** (23 N. Leroux St., 928/779-1919, www.weatherfordhotel.com, 8am-10pm daily, $11-26), inside the Weatherford Hotel, serves Navajo tacos, enchiladas, burritos, and a host of other regional favorites for breakfast, lunch, and dinner. Its Navajo taco, a regional delicacy featuring fry bread smothered in chili and beans, might be the best off the reservation. Try it for breakfast topped with a couple of fried eggs. Charly's also has more conventional but appetizing bar-and-grill food such as hot, high-piled sandwiches, juicy burgers, steaks, and prime rib.

**Brix Restaurant & Wine Bar** (413 N. San Francisco St., 928/213-1021, http://brixflagstaff.com, 5pm-close Tues.-Sun., $18-36) operates out of a historic building a few blocks north of downtown and serves creative and memorable food using regional ingredients. The menu here changes often based on what's new at Arizona's small farms, ranches, and dairies. The New American cuisine that results is typically spectacular. They also have fine selections of wine, a slew of creative cocktails, and desserts that should not be missed.

The **Tinderbox Kitchen** (34 S. San Francisco St., 928/226-8400, www.tinderboxkitchen.com, 5pm-10pm daily, $18-26) in the Southside District serves a revolving menu of gourmet takes on familiar American favorites and has an elegant lounge (4pm-close daily) where you can wait for your table with a martini. The chef uses seasonal ingredients, and there's always something new and exciting here—like venison served with bleu cheese grits, bacon creamed corn, or jalapeño mac-and-cheese. It's one of those places where the chef is limited only by ingredients and imagination, and the chef here is lacking in neither.

For the best sandwiches in the northland, head to **Crystal Creek Sandwich Company** (1051 S. Milton Rd., 928/774-9373, http://crystalcreeksandwiches.com, 9am-9pm daily, $5-8). A Flagstaff institution, this casual order-at-the-counter joint serves high-piled delights on fresh bread and has a pool table too. Grab a couple of big sandwiches to go, and head out into the pines for a picnic—the perfect way to spend a day in Flagstaff.

The **Morning Glory Café** (115 S. San Francisco St., 928/774-3705, http://morningglorycafeflagstaff.com, 10am-2:30pm Tues.-Fri., 9am-2:30pm Sat.-Sun., $8-11) serves natural, tasty vegetarian eats from a cozy little spot on San Francisco Street. Try the hemp burger for lunch, and don't miss the blue corn pancakes for breakfast. With local art on the walls, free wireless Internet, and friendly service, this is an ideal place to get to know the laid-back Flagstaff vibe. There are a lot of vegan and gluten-free options here. They don't take credit cards, so bring some cash.

**Macy's European Coffee House** (14 S. Beaver St., 928/774-2243, www.macyscoffee.net, 6am-8pm daily, $5-10), south of the tracks, is the best place to get coffee and a quick vegetarian bite to eat, or just hang out and watch the locals file in and out.

## Accommodations

The park's lodging rates are audited annually and compare favorably to those offered outside the park, but you can sometimes find excellent deals at one of several gateway towns around canyon country. Using one of these places as a base for a visit to the canyon makes sense if you're planning on touring the whole of the canyonlands and not just the park.

### Inside the Park

There are six lodges within Grand Canyon National Park at the South Rim, most of them operated by Xanterra (www.grandcanyonlodges.com).

A stay at ★ **El Tovar** (303/297-2757, www.grandcanyonlodges.com, $217-263 standard room, $442-538 suite), more than 100 years old and one of the most distinctive and memorable hotels in the state, would be the secondary highlight—after the gorge itself—of any trip to the South Rim. The log-and-stone National Historic Landmark, standing about 20 feet from the rim, has 78 rooms and suites. The hotel's restaurant serves some of the best food in Arizona for breakfast, lunch, and dinner, and there's a comfortable cocktail lounge off the lobby with a window on the canyon. A mezzanine sitting area overlooks the log-cabin lobby, and a gift shop sells Native American arts and crafts as well as canyon souvenirs. If you're looking to splurge on something truly exceptional, there's a honeymoon suite overlooking the canyon.

When first built in the 1930s, the ★ **Bright Angel Lodge** (303/297-2757, www.grandcanyonlodges.com, $95-210) was meant to serve the middle-class travelers then being lured by the Santa Fe Railroad, and it's still affordable and comfortable while retaining a rustic character that fits perfectly with the wild canyon just outside. Lodge rooms don't have TVs, and most have only one bed. The utilitarian "hikers" rooms have refrigerators and share several private showers, which have lockable doors and just enough room to dress. Bright Angel is the place to sleep before hiking into the canyon; you just roll out of bed onto the Bright Angel Trail. The lodge's cabins just west of the main building have private baths, TVs, and sitting rooms. Drinking and dining options include a small bar and coffeehouse, a Harvey House diner, and a restaurant with big windows framing the canyon.

Standing along the rim between El Tovar and Bright Angel, the **Kachina Lodge** (303/297-2757, www.grandcanyonlodges.com, $225 for regular room, $243 for room facing the canyon), offers basic, comfortable rooms with TVs, safes, private baths, and refrigerators. There's not a lot of character, but its location and modern comforts make the Kachina an ideal place for families to stay. The **Thunderbird Lodge** (303/297-2757, www.grandcanyonlodges.com, $225 for regular room, $243 for room facing the canyon) is in the same area and has similar offerings. Both properties have some rooms facing the canyon.

**Maswik Lodge** (303/297-2757, www.grandcanyonlodges.com, $215) is located on the west side of the village about 0.25 mile from the rim. The hotel has a cafeteria-style restaurant that serves just about everything you'd want and a sports bar with a large-screen TV. The rooms are motel-style basic but clean and comfortable, with TVs, private baths, and refrigerators, but there's no elevator. In spring 2018, the lodge's two-story south section was torn down to make way for a new building. The project is expected to take two years, so you may want to think twice before booking here, as there's likely to be construction noise and parking hassles.

About five miles from the park entrance on the road to Canyon Village Market Plaza, **Yavapai Lodge** (11 Yavapai Lodge Rd., 928/638-4001 or 877/404-4611, www.visitgrandcanyon.com, $150-200) is basic but clean and comfortable. The East Section has clean and comfortable rooms with air-conditioning, refrigerators, and TVs, and the King Family Room is a great option for families, with a king bed and twin bunk beds. The West Section, a retro motel-style structure, lacks air-conditioning but has pet rooms for an extra $25.

## Outside the Park
### Tusayan

Most of Tusayan's accommodations are of the chain variety. Though they are clean and comfortable, few of them have any character to speak of, and most are rather overpriced for what you get. Staying in either Flagstaff or Williams is a better choice if you're looking for an independent hotel or motel with some local color, and you can definitely find better deals in those gateways.

Before you reach Tusayan you'll pass through Valle, a tiny spot not far off AZ-64, where you'll find one of the better deals in the whole canyon region. The **Red Lake Campground and Hostel** (8850 N. Rte. 64, 928/635-4753, $20 pp per night), where you can rent a bed in a shared room, is a basic but reasonably comfortable place sitting lonely on the grasslands next to a gas station; it has shared bathrooms with showers, a common room with a kitchen and a TV, and an RV park ($25) with hookups. If you're going super-budget, you can't beat this place, and it's only about 45 minutes from the park's south gate.

The **Red Feather Lodge** (300 Rte. 64, 928/638-2414, www.redfeatherlodge.com, $172-205), though more basic than some of the other places in Tusayan, is a comfortable, affordable place to stay with a pool, hot tub, and clean rooms in separate hotel and motel complexes.

The **Grand Hotel** (149 Rte. 64, 928/638-3333, www.grandcanyongrandhotel. com, $200-400), resembling a kind of Western-themed ski lodge, has clean and comfortable rooms and a pool, hot tub, fitness center, and beautiful lobby. One of the more luxurious places to stay in

Bright Angel Lodge

the region, with prices to match, the hotel also has a large saloon and steak house.

The **Best Western Grand Canyon Squire Inn** (74 Rte. 64, 928/638-2681, www.grandcanyonsquire.com, $188-289) has a fitness center, pool and spa, salon, game room, bowling alley, and myriad other amenities—so many that it may be difficult to get out of the hotel to enjoy the natural sights.

### Cameron

About 50 miles north of Flagstaff along US-89, near the junction with AZ-64 (the route to the park's east gate), the more than 100-year-old ★ **Historic Cameron Trading Post and Lodge** (800/338-7385, www.camerontradingpost.com, $79-199) is only about a 30-minute drive from the Desert View area of the park, a good place to start your tour. Starting from the east entrance, you'll see the canyon gradually becoming grand. Before you reach the park, the Little Colorado drops some 2,000 feet through the arid, scrubby land,

cutting through gray rock on the way to its marriage with the big river and creating the **Little Colorado Gorge.** Stop here and get a barrier-free glimpse at this lesser chasm to prime yourself for what is to come. There are usually a few booths set up selling Navajo arts and crafts and a lot of touristy souvenirs at two developed pull-offs along the road.

The Cameron Lodge is a charming and affordable place to stay, and a perfect base for a visit to the Grand Canyon. It has a good **restaurant** (6am-9:30pm daily summer, 7am-9pm daily winter, $6-15) serving American and Navajo food, including excellent beef stew, heaping Navajo tacos, chili, and burgers. There's also an art gallery, a visitors center, a huge trading post/gift shop, and an RV park ($35 full hookups, no bathroom or showers). A small grocery store has packaged sandwiches, chips, and sodas. The rooms are decorated with a southwestern Native American style and are clean and comfortable, some with views of the Little Colorado River and the old 1911 suspension bridge that spans the stream just outside the lodge. There are single-bed rooms, rooms with two beds, and a few suites that are perfect for families. The stone-and-wood buildings and the garden patio, laid out with stacked sandstone bricks with picnic tables and redstone walkways below the open-corridor rooms, create a cozy, history-soaked setting and make the lodge a memorable place to stay. The vast, empty red plains of the Navajo Reservation spread out all around and create a lonely, isolated atmosphere, especially at night, but the rooms have cable TV and free wireless Internet, so you can be connected and entertained even way out here.

If you're visiting in the winter, the lodge drops its prices significantly during this less crowded touring season. In January and February, you can get one of the single-bed rooms for about $79.

## Williams

Williams has some of the most affordable independent accommodations in the Grand Canyon region, as well as several chain hotels.

It's difficult to find a better deal than the clean and basic **El Rancho Motel** (617 E. Route 66, 928/635-2552 or 800/228-2370, $94-112), an independently owned, retro motel on Route 66 with few frills save comfort, friendliness, and a heated pool open in season.

The **Canyon Country Inn** (442 W. Route 66, 928/635-2349, www.thecanyon-countryinn.com, $89-115) is an enchanting little place, home to a whole mob of stuffed bears and right in the heart of Williams's charming historic district. Its country-Victorian decor is not for everyone, but it's a comfortable and friendly place to stay while exploring the canyon country.

The **Grand Canyon Railway Hotel** (235 N. Grand Canyon Blvd., 928/635-4010, www.thetrain.com, $205-370) stands now where Williams's old Harvey House once stood. It has a heated indoor pool, two restaurants, a lounge, a hot tub, a workout room, and a huge gift shop. The hotel serves riders on the Grand Canyon Railway and offers the highest-end accommodations in Williams.

The original ★ **Grand Canyon Hotel** (145 W. Route 66, 928/635-1419, www.thegrandcanyonhotel.com, $74-168) opened in 1891, even before the railroad arrived and made Grand Canyon tourism something not just the rich could do. New owners refurbished and reopened the charming old redbrick hotel in Williams's historic downtown in 2005, and now it's an affordable, friendly place to stay with a lot of character and a bit of an international flavor. Spartan single-bed rooms go for $74 a night with a shared bathroom, and individually named and eclectically decorated double rooms with private baths are $87 a night—some of the most distinctive and affordable accommodations in the region. There are no televisions in the rooms. Several larger rooms with private baths and other amenities go for $104-168. There are also hostel rooms for $33-38.

The **Red Garter Bed & Bakery** (137 W. Railroad Ave., 928/635-1484, www.red-garter.com, $175-199) makes much of its original and longtime use as a brothel (which, like many similar places throughout Arizona's rural regions, didn't finally close until the 1940s), where the town's lonely, uncouth miners, lumberjacks, railway workers, and cowboys met with unlucky women, ever euphemized as "soiled doves," in rooms called "cribs." The 1897 frontier-Victorian stone building, with its wide, arching entranceway, has been beautifully restored with a lot of authentic charm, without skimping on the comforts—like big brass beds for the nighttime and delightful homemade baked goods, juice, and coffee in the morning. Famously, this place is haunted by some poor unquiet, regretful soul, so you might want to bring your night-light along.

The **Lodge on Route 66** (200 E. Route 66, 877/563-4366, http://thelodgeonroute66.com, $129-200) has stylish rooms with sleep-inducing pillow-top mattresses; it has a few civilized two-room suites with kitchenettes, dining areas, and fireplaces—perfect for a family that's not necessarily on a budget. The motor court-style grounds, right along the Mother Road, of course, feature a romantic cabana with comfortable seats and an outdoor fireplace. Pets are not allowed.

## Flagstaff

Flagstaff, 79 miles southeast of the park's main South entrance, was the park's first gateway town, and it's still in many ways the best. The home of Northern Arizona University is a fun, laid-back college town with a railroad and Route 66 history. To reach the Grand Canyon from Flagstaff, take US-180 northwest for about 1.5 hours, and there you are. The route is absolutely the most scenic of all the approaches to the canyon (with apologies to desert rats who prefer the eastern Desert View approach), passing through Coconino National Forest and beneath the San Francisco Peaks.

Historic hotels downtown offer both good value and a unique experience. East Flagstaff, as you enter along Route 66, has a large number of small hotels and motels, including chains and several old-school motor inns. It lacks the charm of downtown but is an acceptable place to stay if you're just passing through. If you're a budget traveler, try the hostels in the Historic Southside District.

The **Grand Canyon International Hostel** (19 S. San Francisco St., 888/442-2696, www.grandcanyonhostel.com, $27-78) is a clean and friendly place to stay on the cheap, located in an old 1930s building in the Southside, in which you're likely to meet some lasting friends, many of them foreign tourists tramping around the Colorado Plateau. The hostel offers bunk-style sleeping arrangements and private rooms, mostly shared bathrooms, a self-serve kitchen, wireless Internet, free breakfast, and a chance to join in on tours of the region. It's a rustic but cozy and welcoming hippie-home-style place to stay. The same folks operate the **Motel DuBeau** (19 W. Phoenix St., 800/398-7112, www.modubeau.com, $27-85), a clean and charming hostel-inn with a small dorm and eight private rooms. They offer a free breakfast, wireless Internet, and a friendly atmosphere. Make sure to spend some time at Nomad's Global Lounge kicking back a few cold ones with your new friends.

The **Weatherford Hotel** (23 N. Leroux St., 928/779-1919, www.weatherfordhotel.com, $80-175) is one of two historic hotels downtown. It's basic but romantic, and feels as if you're stepping back in time when you head off to bed. There are no TVs or phones in most of the rooms, the cheapest of which share a bathroom. While the whole place is a little creaky,

the location and the history make this a fun place to rest. With live music at the hotel's two pubs and the odd wedding or private party in the historic ballroom, the Weatherford can sometimes get a bit noisy. It's not for those looking for the tranquility of the surrounding pine forest.

The **Hotel Monte Vista** (100 N. San Francisco St., 928/779-6971 or 800/545-3068, www.hotelmontevista.com, $140-160 Apr. 15-Nov. 5, $50-175 Nov. 6-Apr. 14), the other historic downtown hotel, is a retro-swanky, redbrick high-rise, built in 1927, that once served high-class and famous travelers heading west on the Santa Fe Railroad. These days it offers rooms that have historic charm but are still comfortable and convenient, with cable TV and private bathrooms. There's a divey cocktail lounge and sleek coffee bar off the lobby, and, as with many of the grand old railroad hotels, there are lots of tales to be heard about the Hollywood greats who stayed here and the restless ghosts who stayed behind.

**The Inn at 410 Bed and Breakfast** (410 N. Leroux St., 928/774-0088 or 800/774-2008, www.inn410.com, $185-325) has eight artfully decorated rooms in a classic old home on a quiet, tree-lined street just off downtown. This is a wonderful little place, with so much detail and stylishness. Breakfasts are interesting and filling, often with a Southwestern tinge, and tea is served every afternoon. You certainly can't go wrong here. Booking far in advance, especially for a weekend stay, is a must.

The stately **England House Bed and Breakfast** (614 W. Santa Fe Ave., 928/214-7350 or 877/214-7350, www.englandhousebandb.com, $139-209) is located in a quiet residential neighborhood near downtown at the base of Mars Hill, where sits the famous Lowell Observatory. This beautiful old Victorian has been sumptuously restored, and its rooms are booked most weekends. If you're just passing through, the innkeepers are happy to show you around, after which you will probably make a reservation for some far future date. They pay as much attention to their breakfasts here as they do to details of the decor. This is one of the best little inns in the region.

The same can be said of the **Aspen Inn Bed and Breakfast** (218 N. Elden St., 928/773-0295 or 800/999-4110, $139-209), an inviting arts-and-crafts-style B&B a few blocks from downtown. Wyatt Earp's cousin, C. B. Wilson, built the house in 1912, and these days it offers four comfortable rooms with televisions, wireless Internet, and all the other comforts, plus a delicious breakfast and friendly atmosphere.

The sprawling **Little America** (2515 E. Butler Ave., 928/779-7900, http://flagstaff.littleamerica.com, $219-239) is a huge hotel complex on 500 acres near the University of Northern Arizona and popular with visiting parents. It has a pool, several restaurants, pine-studded grounds, and hundreds of rooms and suites.

## Camping
### Inside the Park

★ **Mather Campground** (877/444-6777, www.recreation.gov, $18 Mar.-Nov., $15 Dec.-Feb.) takes reservations up to six months ahead for the March-November 20 peak season and thereafter operates on a first-come, first-served basis. Located near the village and offering more than 300 basic campsites with grills and fire pits, the campground typically fills up by about noon during the summer busy season. It has restrooms with showers and coin-operated laundry machines. The campground is open to tents and trailers but has no hookups and is closed to RVs longer than 30 feet. Even if you aren't an experienced camper, a stay at Mather is a fun and inexpensive alternative to sleeping indoors. Despite its large size and crowds, the campground gets pretty quiet at night. Even in summer, the night takes on a bit of a chill, making a campfire not

exactly necessary but not out of the question. Bring your own wood or buy it at the store nearby. A large, clean restroom and shower facility is within walking distance from most sites, and they even have blow-dryers. Everything is coin operated, and there's an office on-site that gives change. Consider bringing bikes along, especially for the kids. The village is about a 15-minute walk from the campground on forested, paved trails, or you can take the free tram from a stop nearby. Pets are allowed but must be kept on a leash, and they're not allowed on shuttle buses.

About 25 miles east of the village, near the park's East entrance, is **Desert View Campground** (first-come, first-served, May-mid-Oct. depending on weather, $12), with 50 sites for tents and small trailers only, with no hookups. There's a restroom with no showers and only two faucets with running water. Each site has a grill but little else. Pets are allowed but must be kept on a leash.

If you're in a rolling mansion, try **Trailer Village** (888/297-2757, www.xanterra.com, $45) next to Mather Campground, near the village, where you'll find hookups for trailers up to 50 feet long.

# The North Rim

Standing at Bright Angel Point on the Grand Canyon's North Rim, crowded together with several other gazers as if stranded on a jetty over a wide, hazy sea, blurred evergreens growing atop great jagged rock spines banded with white and red, someone whispers, "It looks pretty much the same as the other rim."

It's not true—far from it—but the comment brings up the main point about the North Rim: Should you go? Only about 10 percent of canyon visitors make the trip to the North Rim, which is significantly less developed than the South; there aren't many activities other than gazing, unless you are a hiker and a backcountry wilderness lover. The coniferous mountain forests of the Kaibab Plateau are themselves worth the trip—broken by grassy meadows and painted with summer wildflowers, populated by often-seen elk and mule deer, and dappled with aspens that turn yellow and red in the fall and burst out of the otherwise uniform dark green like solitary flames. But it is a long trip, and you need to be prepared for a land of scant services and the simple, contemplative pleasures of nature in the raw.

## Getting There

Although it's only an average of about 10 miles across the canyon from the South to North Rims for a hawk, raven, or condor, it's a 215-mile, five-hour drive for those of us who are primarily earthbound. The long route north is something to behold, moving through a corner of Navajoland, past the towering Vermilion Cliffs, and deep into the high forests of the Kaibab Plateau. AZ-67 from Jacob Lake to the North Rim typically closes to vehicles late November-May. In the winter, it's not uncommon for cross-country skiers and snowshoe hikers to take to the closed and snow-covered highway, heading with their own power toward the canyon and the North Kaibab Trail.

Between the hotel, restaurant, and gas station at Jacob Lake on the Kaibab Plateau and the entrance to Grand Canyon National Park on the North Rim, there's not much more than high-mountain scenery. But in case you forget anything before venturing into this relative wilderness, you can always stop at the well-stocked **North Rim Country Store** (AZ-67, mile marker 605, 928/638-2383, www.northrimcountrystore.com, 7:30am-7pm daily mid-May-early Nov.), about 43 miles along AZ-67 from Jacob Lake. The store has just about anything you'll need, from snacks to gas to camping supplies. There's also a small auto shop here in case you're having car troubles or catch a flat that you can't fix

yourself. The store closes for winter, as does the whole region, around the beginning of November.

The **Trans Canyon Shuttle** (928/638-2820, www.trans-canyonshuttle.com, $90 one-way, reservations required) makes a daily round-trip excursion between the North and South Rims, departing the North Rim at 7am and arriving at the South Rim at 11:30am. The shuttle then leaves the South Rim at 1:30pm and arrives back at the North Rim at 6:30pm.

To get from the Grand Canyon Lodge—the park's only accommodations on the North Rim—to the North Kaibab Trailhead, take the **hikers shuttle** ($7 for first person, $4 for each additional person), which leaves the lodge twice daily first thing in the morning. Tickets must be purchased the day before at the lodge.

If you paid your park entrance fee at the South Rim, this will be honored at the North as long as you go within seven days. If not, you'll have to pay again. A North Rim edition of the park's helpful newspaper *The Pocket Map* is passed out at the North Rim entrance.

## Driving Tours
### Cape Royal Scenic Drive

You can reach Point Imperial and several other lookout spots on the Cape Royal Scenic Drive, one of the most scenic, dramatic roads in the state. From the lodge to Cape Royal, it's about 30 miles round-trip on a paved road that wends through the mixed conifer and aspen forests of the **Walhalla Plateau.** There are plenty of chances for wildlife-spotting, plus short trails to viewpoints offering breathtaking views of the canyon off to the east and even as far as Navajoland. Plan to spend at least half a day, and take food and water. Go to **Point Imperial** first, reached by a 3-mile side road at the beginning of the Cape Royal Road. The best way to do it would be to leave the lodge just before sunrise, watch the show from Point Imperial, and then hit the scenic drive for the rest of the day, stopping often. Along the way, **Vista Encantadora** (Charming View) provides just that, rising above Nanokoweap Creek. Just beyond is **Roosevelt Point,** where you can hike the easy 0.2-mile loop trail to a view worthy of the man who saved the Grand Canyon. When you finally reach the point of the drive, **Cape Royal** at 7,865 feet, you'll walk out on a 0.6-mile round-trip paved trail for an expansive and unbounded view of the canyon—one of the best, from which, on a clear day, you can spot the South Rim's Desert View Watchtower way across the gorge, and the river far below. Along the short trail you'll pass the rock arch called **Angel's Window.**

## Sights
### ★ Grand Canyon Lodge

Even if you aren't staying at the **Grand Canyon Lodge** (www.grandcanyonlodgenorth.com), a rustic log-and-stone structure built in 1927-1928 and perched on the edge of the rim at the end of the highway, don't make the trip to the North Rim without going into its warm Sun Room to view the canyon through the huge picture windows. You may want to sink into one of the comfortable couches and stare for hours. At sunset, head out to the Adirondack chairs on the lodge's back patio and watch the sun sink over the canyon; everybody's quiet, hushed in reverence, bundled up in jackets and sweaters. Right near the door leading out to the patio, check out sculptor Peter Jepson's charming life-size bronze of **Brighty,** a famous canyon burro and star of the 1953 children's book *Brighty of the Grand Canyon* by Marguerite Henry. A display nearby tells Brighty's story, and they say if you rub his bronze nose you'll have good luck. The book, along with a movie based on the story, is available at gift shops and bookstores on both the North and South Rims.

### Viewpoints

There are three developed viewpoints at the North Rim, each of them offering a slightly different look at the canyon. **Bright Angel Point,** about a half-mile round-trip walk outside the lodge's back door, looks over Bright Angel Canyon with a view of Roaring Springs, the source of Bright Angel Creek and fresh water for the North Rim and inner canyon; **Point Imperial,** at 8,803 feet the highest point on the North Rim, probably has the best all-around view of the canyon; and **Cape Royal,** a 23-mile one-way drive across the Walhalla Plateau, looks toward the South Rim.

## Recreation
### Hiking

It's significantly cooler on the high, forested North Rim than it is on the South, making hiking, especially summer hiking below the rim, much less of a chore. There are a few easy rim trails to choose from and several tough but unforgettable day hikes into the canyon along the North Kaibab Trail.

Easy trails lead to and from all the developed scenic overlooks on the rim, their trailheads accessible and well marked. *The Pocket Map* has a comprehensive listing of the area's trails and where to pick them up. The four-mile round-trip **Transept Trail** is an easy hike through the forest from the Grand Canyon Lodge to the campground. It has a few nice views and is a good introduction to the North Rim.

### Uncle Jim Trail

**Distance:** 5 miles round-trip
**Duration:** 3 hours
**Elevation gain:** about 200 feet
**Effort:** easy
**Trailhead:** North Kaibab Trail parking lot, 3 miles north of Grand Canyon Lodge on the main park entrance road

Take this easy, flat trail through the forest to watch backpackers winding their way down the North Kaibab Trail's twisting switchbacks and maybe see a mule train or two along the way.

The **Uncle Jim Trail** winds through old stands of spruce and fir, sprinkled with quaking aspen, to Uncle Jim Point, where you can let out your best roar into the tributary known as Roaring Springs Canyon.

### Widforss Trail

**Distance:** 10 miles round-trip
**Duration:** 5-6 hours
**Elevation gain:** negligible
**Effort:** easy
**Trailhead:** 4 miles north of Grand Canyon Lodge; look for the sign

Named for the 1930s canyon painter Gunnar Widforss, the mostly flat and easy **Widforss Trail** leads along the rim of the side canyon called Transept Canyon and through ponderosa pine, fir, and spruce forest, with a few stands of aspen mixed in, for five miles to Widforss Point, where you can stare across the great chasm and rest before heading back.

For a shorter hike, pick up the free guide to the Widforss Trail at the trailhead or the visitors center. It proposes a five-mile round-trip hike on the first half of the trail, and includes a map and information on the natural and human history of the North Rim.

### North Kaibab Trail

**Distance:** varies; 9.4 miles to Roaring Springs
**Duration:** a few hours to overnight
**Elevation gain:** 5,961 feet from Phantom Ranch
**Effort:** moderate to difficult
**Trailhead:** North Kaibab Trail parking area

The **North Kaibab Trail** starts out among the coniferous heights of the North Rim. The forest surrounding the trail soon dries out and becomes a red-rock desert, the trail cut into the rock face of the cliffs and twisting down improbable routes hard against the cliffs, with nothing but your sanity keeping you away from the gorge. This is the only North Rim route down into the inner canyon and to the Colorado River. Sooner than you realize, the walls close in, and you are deep in the canyon, the trees on the rim just green blurs now. A good introduction to this corridor trail and ancient native route is the short, 1.5-mile round-trip jog down to the **Coconino Overlook,** from which, on a clear day, you can see the San Francisco Peaks and the South Rim. A four-mile round-trip hike down will get you to **Supai Tunnel,** blasted out of the red rock in the 1930s by the Civilian Conservation Corps. A little more than a mile onward you'll reach **The Bridge in the Redwall** (5.5 miles round-trip), built in 1966 after a flood ruined this portion of the trail. For a tough, all-day hike that will likely have you sore but smiling the next morning, take the North Kaibab roughly five miles down to **Roaring Springs,** the source of life-giving Bright Angel Creek. The springs fall headlong out of the cliffside and spray mist and rainbows into the hot air. Just remember, you also have to go five miles back up. Start hiking early, and take plenty of water.

The North Kaibab Trailhead is a few miles north of the Grand Canyon Lodge, the park's only accommodations on the North Rim. To get from the lodge to the trailhead, take the **hiker's shuttle** (first person $7, each additional person $4), which leaves every morning from the lodge at 5:30am and 6am. Tickets must be purchased 24 hours before at the lodge.

### North Rim Mule Rides

The mules at the North Rim all work for **Canyon Trail Rides** (435/679-8665, www.canyonrides.com, May 15-Oct. 15), the park's northside trail-riding concessionaire. Guides will take you and your friendly mule on a one-hour rimside ride ($45) or a three-hour ride to Uncle Jim's Point ($90). You can also take a mule down into the canyon along the North Kaibab Trail to the Supai Tunnel (three hours, $90). Kids have to be at least 7 years old for the one-hour ride, and at least 10 for the three-hour rides. There's a 220-pound weight limit. Call ahead for a reservation if this is something you're set on doing. You might be able to hop on last-minute, though probably not in June, which is the busiest time at the North Rim.

## Food

The **Grand Canyon Lodge Dining Room** (928/638-2611, www.grandcanyonlodgenorth.com, 6:30am-10am, 11:30am-2:30pm, and 4:30pm-9:30pm daily mid-May-mid-Oct., reservations required for dinner, $10-30) serves breakfast, lunch, dinner, and a buffet every day during the too-brief North Rim season. The lodge's historic dining room is a great place to be, with its high log-mansion ceilings, exposed pinewood vigas, local-stone walls, and floor-to-ceiling windows framing the canyon, and the food is pretty good, too. For breakfast they have excellent omelets and breakfast burritos, along with hiker-friendly options like oatmeal and granola. Lunch and dinner feature regionally sourced

and inspired creations such as elk chili, Lee's Ferry trout, and venison meat loaf. There are quite a few vegetarian options here as well. Every night in season the lodge also offers a buffet in the main auditorium, and you can take your plate out to the veranda and gaze at the canyon while you eat.

The only other option within 50 miles of the park is the **Kaibab Lodge Restaurant** (928/638-2389, www.kaibablodge.com, breakfast, lunch, and dinner daily mid-May-early Nov., $10-15), about 18 miles north of the Grand Canyon Lodge. Here they serve hearty comfort fare perfect for the high, cool country. The knotty-pine dining room feels like a throwback to the days of summer camps and family lodges, and the food is homemade and flavorful: burgers, ribs, steaks, hot and cold sandwiches, big breakfasts, beer and wine. Vegetarian options are limited to a few pasta dishes and a garden burger.

along the Transept Trail

## Accommodations

Built in the late 1930s after the original lodge burned down, the ★ **Grand Canyon Lodge** (928/638-2611 or 888/297-2757, www.grandcanyonlodgenorth.com, mid-May-mid-Oct., $132 rooms, $143-219 cabins) is the only hotel on the North Rim. The rustic but comfortable log-and-stone lodge has a large central lobby, high-ceilinged dining room, deli, saloon, gift shop, general store, and gas station. There are several small, comfortable lodge rooms and dozens of cabins scattered around the property, each with a bathroom and most with a gas-powered fireplace that makes things cozy on a cold night. The lodge is open mid-May-mid-October. You must book far in advance (at least six months), though there are sometimes cancellations allowing for a last-minute booking.

The **Kaibab Lodge** (928/638-2389, www.kaibablodge.com, mid-May-early Nov., $95-185) is a small gathering of rustic, cozy cabins (some more rustic

than others) on the edge of a meadow, tucked behind the tree line along AZ-67, about five miles north of the park. You can rent cabins of varying sizes and enjoy the lounge, gift shop, and warm fireplace in the lobby. The lodge closes in early November. Book 3-6 months in advance if you want to stay here in summer. A small room with a bed and bathroom is included in the $95 "hiker's special" here, which is a great option if you can nab a reservation. There are no TVs and no cell service.

The main oasis on the Kaibab Plateau is the **Jacob Lake Inn** (junction of U.S. 89A and Rte. 67, 928/643-7232, www.jacoblake.com, $126-144 rooms, $94-144 cabins, restaurant 6:30am-9pm daily), about 42 miles from the park entrance. It features rustic cabins as well as motel-style rooms, alongside a bakery, gift shop, small general store, and gas station, and **restaurant** (6:30am-9pm daily, $8-15) with excellent homemade bread and soups.

## Camping

The in-park **North Rim Campground** (877/444-6777, www.recreation.gov, reservation only, May 15-Oct. 31, $18-25) has basic camping spots near the rim, with showers and a coin-operated laundry. About 25 miles south of Jacob Lake and about 7 miles north of the park entrance on AZ-67 is the **DeMotte Campground** (May-Oct., $18), operated by the U.S. Forest Service. It has 38 sites with tables and cooking grills, toilets, and drinking water. Tents, trailers, and motor homes are allowed, but there are no utility hookups or dump stations available. Reservations must be made three days ahead between September 7 and March 21.

**Kaibab Camper Village** (AZ 67, just south of Jacob Lake, 928/643-7804 or 800/525-0924, www.kaibabcampervillage.com, May 14-Oct. 15) has full-hookup sites ($37) and basic tent sites ($18). The village also has cabins ($85)

and offers fire pits, tables, bathrooms, and coin-operated showers.

# The Inner Canyon

Inside the canyon is a strange desert, red and green, pink and rocky. It's those sheer rock walls, tight and claustrophobic in the interior's narrowest slots, that make this place a different world altogether. A large part of a canyon-crossing hike takes place in Bright Angel Canyon along Bright Angel Creek. As you hike along the trail beside the creek, greenery and the cool rushing water clash with the silent heat washing off the cliffs on your other side.

On any given night there are only a few hundred visitors sleeping below the rim—at either Phantom Ranch, a Mary Colter-designed lodge near the mouth of Bright Angel Canyon, or at three campgrounds along the corridor trails. Until a few decades ago, visiting the inner canyon was something of a free-for-all, but these days access to the interior is strictly controlled; you have to purchase a permit ($10, plus $8 pp per night), and they're not always easy to get—each year the park receives 30,000 requests for backcountry permits and issues only 13,000.

No matter which trail you use, there's no avoiding an arduous, leg- and spirit-punishing hike there and back if you really want to see the inner canyon. It's not easy, no matter who you are, but it is worth it; it's a true accomplishment, a hard walk you'll never forget.

## Exploring the Inner Canyon

If you want to be one of the small minority of canyon visitors to spend some quality time below the rim, stay at least one full day and night in the inner canyon. Even hikers in excellent shape find that they are sore after trekking down to the river, Phantom Ranch, and beyond. A rim-to-rim hike, either from the south or from the north, pretty much requires at

cabins at the Grand Canyon Lodge

least a day of rest below the rim. The ideal inner canyon trip lasts three days and two nights: one day hiking in, one day of rest, and one day to hike out.

River trips range from three days up to three weeks and often include a hike down one of the corridor trails to the river. Depending on how long you want to spend on the river, plan far, far in advance, and consider making the river trip your only major activity on that particular canyon visit. Combining too much strenuous, mind-blowing, and life-changing activity into one trip tends to water down the entire experience.

### Permits and Reservations

The earlier you apply for a permit, the better, but you can't apply for one prior to the first of the month four months before your proposed trip date. The easiest way to get a permit is to go to the **park's website** (www.nps.gov/grca), print out a backcountry permit request form, fill it out, and then fax it first thing in the morning on the date in question—for example, if you want to hike in October, you would **fax** (928/638-2125) your request May 20-June 1. Have patience; on the first day of the month the fax number is usually busy throughout the day—keep trying. On the permit request form you'll indicate where you plan to stay. If you are camping, the permit is your reservation, but if you want to stay at Phantom Ranch, you must get separate reservations, and that is often a close-to-impossible task. For more information on obtaining a backcountry permit, call the **South Rim Backcountry Information Center** (928/638-7875, 8am-5pm daily).

### Guides

You certainly don't need a guide to take a classic backpacking trip into the Grand Canyon along one of the corridor trails. The National Park Service makes it a relatively simple process to plan and complete such a memorable expedition, and, while hikers die below the rim pretty much every year, the more popular regions of the inner canyon are as safe as can be expected in a vast wilderness. Then again, having some friendly, knowledgeable, and undoubtedly badass canyonlander plan and implement every detail of your trip sure couldn't hurt. Indeed, it would probably make the whole expedition infinitely more enjoyable. As long as you're willing to pay for it—and it is never cheap—hiring a guide is an especially good idea if you want to go places where few tourists and casual hikers dwell.

There are more than 20 companies authorized, through a guide permit issued by the National Park Service, to take trips below the rim. If your guide does not have such a permit, do not follow him or her into the Grand Canyon. For an up-to-date list, go to www.nps.gov/grca.

The **Grand Canyon Field Institute** (928/638-2481, www.grandcanyon.org, $450-995), which is operated by the nonprofit Grand Canyon Association, offers

several three- to five-day guided backpacking trips to various points inside the canyon, including trips designed specifically for women, for beginners, and for those interested in the canyon's natural history. Operating out of Flagstaff, **Four Season Guides** (1051 S. Milton Rd., 928/779-6224, www.fsguides.com, $799-1,450) offers more than a dozen different backpacking trips below the rim, from a three-day frolic to Indian Garden to a weeklong, 45-mile expedition on some of the canyon's lesser-known trails. The experienced and friendly guides tend to inspire a level of strength and ambition that you might not reach otherwise. These are the guys to call if you want to experience the lonely, out-of-the-way depths of the canyon but don't want to needlessly risk your life doing it alone.

## Hiking
### Into the Inner Canyon
Although there are lesser-known routes into and through the canyon, most hikers stick to the corridor trails—Bright Angel, South Kaibab, and North Kaibab. A classic Grand Canyon backpacking journey begins at either the Bright Angel Trailhead or the South Kaibab Trailhead on the South Rim. Consider going up the one you don't use going down, mostly for variety's sake. Via the Bright Angel Trail, it's a 9.5-mile hike to the Bright Angel Campground, which is just a short walk from the Colorado River and also from Phantom Ranch. Ideally, spend at least two days—the hike-in day and one full day after that—and two nights in the Phantom Ranch area, hiking up the North Kaibab a short way to see the narrow and close walls, talking to the rangers, sitting on the beach watching the river-trippers float by, and losing yourself to the calm, quiet soul of the wilderness.

When it's time to leave the oasis that is Bright Angel Campground and Phantom Ranch, a question arises: Should you rise headlong to the rim (7 miles up on the South Kaibab or 9.5 miles up on the

Bright Angel Canyon

Bright Angel) or move on leisurely to the next oasis? Those inclined to choose the latter should stay an extra night below the rim at the campground at **Indian Garden,** a green and lush spot about 4.5 miles up the Bright Angel Trail from the Bright Angel Campground. The small campground is primitive but charming, and the area around it is populated by deer and other creatures. After setting up camp and resting a bit, head out on the flat, 3-mile round-trip hike to Plateau Point and a spectacular view of the canyon and river, especially at sunset. When you wake up beneath the shady trees at Indian Garden, you face a mere 4.9-mile hike to the rim.

From the **North Rim,** the **North Kaibab** is the only trail to the river and Phantom Ranch.

### Rim to Rim

For an epic, **23.9-mile** rim-to-rim hike, you can choose, as long as the season permits, to start either on the north or south. Starting from the South Rim, you may want to go down the **Bright Angel Trail** to see beautiful Indian Garden; then again, the **South Kaibab Trail** provides a faster, more direct route to the river. If you start from the north, you may want to come out of the canyon via the South Kaibab; it is shorter and faster, and at that point you are probably going to want to take the path of least resistance. Remember though, while it's shorter, the South Kaibab is a good deal steeper than the Bright Angel, and there is no water available.

No matter who you are or what trail you prefer, the hike out of the Grand Canyon is, at several points, a brutal trudge. It's even worse with 30-40 pounds of stuff you don't really need on your back. Try to take only the essentials to keep your pack weight down. The best rim-to-rim hikes include at least one full day at Phantom Ranch or the Bright Angel Campground. You could do the hike without a permit with a bit of pre-planning: Reserve a room on the North Rim and hike there from the South Rim in one day. Then after a day of rest and another night, hike back to the South Rim in one day.

No matter how you do it, when you finally gain the final rim after a cross-canyon hike, a profound sense of accomplishment washes away at least half the fatigue. The other half typically hangs around for a week or so.

### Day Hikes Around Phantom Ranch

Some people prefer to spend their time in the canyon recovering from the hard walk or mule ride that brought them there, and a day spent cooling your feet in Bright Angel Creek or drinking beer in the cantina is not a day wasted. However, if you want to do some exploring around Phantom Ranch, there are a few popular day hikes from which to choose. When you arrive, the friendly rangers will usually tell you, unsolicited, all about these hikes and provide detailed directions. If

you want to get deeper out in the bush and far from other hikers, ask one of the rangers to recommend a lesser-known route.

### River Trail

**Distance:** 1.5 miles round-trip
**Duration:** 1-2 hours
**Elevation gain:** negligible
**Effort:** easy

This rather short hike is along the precipitous River Trail, high above the Colorado just south of Phantom Ranch. The Civilian Conservation Corps blasted this skinny cliffside trail out of the rock walls in the 1930s to provide a link between the Bright Angel and the South Kaibab Trails. Heading out from Phantom, it's about a 1.5-mile loop that takes you across two suspension bridges and high above the river. It's an easy walk with fantastic views, and is a good way to get your sore legs stretched and moving again. And you are likely to see a bighorn sheep's cute little face poking out from the rocks and shadows on the steep cliffs.

### Clear Creek to Phantom Overlook

**Distance:** about 1.5 miles
**Duration:** 1-2 hours
**Elevation gain:** 826 feet
**Effort:** easy to moderate
**Trailhead:** about 0.25 mile north of Phantom Ranch on the North Kaibab Trail

Another popular CCC-built trail near Phantom, the 1.5-mile **Clear Creek Loop** takes you high above the river to Phantom Overlook, where there's an old stone bench and excellent views of the canyon and Phantom Ranch below. The rangers seem to recommend this hike the most, but, while it's not tough, it can be a little steep and rugged, especially if you're exhausted and sore. The views are, ultimately, well worth the pain.

### Ribbon Falls

**Distance:** 11 miles round-trip
**Duration:** 5-6 hours to all day

riding mules into the canyon

**Elevation gain:** 1,174 feet

**Effort:** easy to moderate

**Trailhead:** look for the sign 5.5 miles north of Phantom Ranch on the North Kaibab Trail

If you hiked in from the South Rim and you have a long, approximately 11-mile round-trip day hike in you, head north on the North Kaibab Trail from Phantom Ranch to beautiful **Ribbon Falls,** a mossy, cool-water oasis just off the hot, dusty trail. The falls are indeed a ribbon of cold water falling hard off the rock cliffs, and you can scramble up the slickrock and through the green creekside jungle and stand beneath the shower. This hike will also give you a chance to see the eerie, claustrophobic "Box," one of the strangest and most exhilarating stretches of the North Kaibab.

## Mule Rides

For generations, these famous mules have been dexterously picking along the canyon's skinny trails, loaded with packs and people. Even the Brady Bunch rode them,

so they come highly recommended. A descent into the canyon on the back of a friendly mule—with an often taciturn cowboy-type leading the train—can be an unforgettable experience, but don't assume because you're riding and not walking that you won't be sore in the morning. One night at Phantom Ranch, meals included, and a ride down on a mule costs $588 per person or $1,378 for two. Two nights at Phantom, meals, and a mule ride costs $838 per person or $1,229 for two. For reservations call 888/297-2757 or visit www.grandcanyonlodges.com. You can make a reservation up to 13 months in advance, and you really should do it as soon as you know your plans. There's a 225-pound weight restriction.

## River Trips

People who have been inside the Grand Canyon often have one of two reactions—either they can't wait to return, or they swear never to return. This is doubly true of those intrepid souls who ride the great river, braving white-water roller coasters while looking forward to a star-filled evening—dry, and full of gourmet camp food—camping on a white beach deep in the gorge. To boat the Colorado, one of the last explored regions of North America, is one of the most exciting and potentially life-changing trips the West has to offer.

Because of this well-known truth, trips are neither cheap nor easy to book. Rafting season in the canyon runs April-October, and there are myriad trips to choose from—from a 3-day long-weekend ride to a 21-day full-canyon epic. An Upper Canyon trip will take you from River Mile 0 at Lee's Ferry through the canyon to Phantom Ranch, while a Lower Canyon trip begins at Phantom, requiring a hike down the Bright Angel Trail with your gear on your back. Furthermore, you can choose between a motorized pontoon boat, as some three-quarters of rafters do, a paddleboat, a kayak, or some other combination. It all depends on what you want and what you can afford.

If you are considering taking a river trip, the best place to start is the website of the **Grand Canyon River Outfitters Association** (www.gcroa.org), a nonprofit group of about 16 licensed river outfitters, all of them monitored and approved by the National Park Service, each with a good safety record and relatively similar rates. Expect to pay about $1,400 per person for a three-day motor trip, $2,600 per person for a six-day motor trip, $2,000 per person for a six-day oar trip, and up to $4,000 per person for a 13-day oar trip. Your guide takes care of all the permits you need to spend nights below the rim. After you decide what kind of trip you want, the website links to the individual outfitters for booking. Most of the companies offer trips lasting between 3 and 18 days and have a variety of boat styles. It's a good idea to choose two or three companies, call them up, and talk to someone live. You'll be putting your life in their hands, so you want to make sure that you like the spirit of the company. Also consider the size of the group. These river trips are social; you'll be spending a lot of time with your fellow boaters. Talk to a company representative about previous trips so you can get a gauge of what kind of people, and how many, you'll be floating with.

If you are one of the majority of river explorers who can't wait to get back on the water once you've landed at the final port, remember that the National Park Service enforces a strict limit of one trip per year per person

## Food and Accommodations

Designed by Mary Colter for the Fred Harvey Company in 1922, ★ **Phantom Ranch** (888/297-2757, www.grandcanyonlodges.com, dormitory $51 pp, two-person cabin $149, $13 each additional person), the only non-camping accommodations inside the canyon, is a shady, peaceful place that you're likely to miss

and yearn for once you've visited and left it behind. Perhaps Phantom's strong draw is less about its intrinsic pleasures and more about it being the only sign of civilization in a deep wilderness that can feel like the end of the world, especially after a 17-mile hike in from the North Rim. It would probably be an inviting place even if you could get there without hiking into the canyon, and it's all the better because you cannot.

Phantom has several rustic, air-conditioned cabins and dormitories, one for men and one for women, both offering restrooms with showers. The lodge's center point is the **Phantom Ranch Canteen,** a welcoming, air-conditioned, beer- and lemonade-selling sight for anyone who has just descended one of the trails. The Canteen offers two meals per day—breakfast, made up of eggs, pancakes, and thick slices of bacon ($22.50), and dinner, with a choice of steak ($45), stew ($28), or vegetarian ($28). The cantina also offers a box lunch ($13) with a bagel, fruit, and salty snacks. Reservations for meals are also difficult to come by.

Most nights and afternoons, a ranger based at Phantom Ranch will give a talk on some aspect of canyon lore, history, or science. These events are always interesting and well attended, even in the 110°F heat of summer.

Phantom is located near the mouth of Bright Angel Canyon, within a few yards of clear, babbling Bright Angel Creek, and shaded by large cottonwoods planted in the 1930s by the Civilian Conservation Corps. There are several day hikes within easy reach, and the Colorado River and the two awesome suspension bridges that link one bank to the other are only about 0.25 mile from the lodge.

In 2017, Phantom Ranch **reservations** changed to a **lottery system.** You have to enter the lottery between the 1st and 25th of the month 15 months prior to your proposed trip. You'll be notified at least 14 months before your trip if you won a stay. Go to www.grandcanyonlodges.

# Lee's Ferry: River Mile 0

**Lee's Ferry** (www.nps.gov/glca) is the only spot in hundreds of miles where you can drive down to the Colorado River. Located in the Glen Canyon National Recreation Area, Lee's Ferry provides the dividing line between the upper and lower states of the Colorado River's watershed, making it "river mile 0," the gateway and crossroads to both the upper and lower Colorado, and the place where its annual flows are measured and recorded. It's also the starting point for river-trippers who venture into the Grand Canyon atop the Colorado every year. It's a popular fishing spot, though the trout have been introduced and were not native to the warm muddy flow before the dam at Glen Canyon changed the Colorado's character. For guides, gear, and any other information about the area, try **Lee's Ferry Anglers** (928/355-2261 or 800/962-9755, www.leesferry.com, 6am-9pm daily), located at the Cliff Dweller's Lodge.

This lonely spot is named for a man who occupied the area rather briefly in the early 1870s, Mormon outlaw John D. Lee, who was exiled here after his participation in the infamous Mountain Meadows Massacre in Utah. He didn't stay long, escaping as a fugitive before his capture and execution. One of Lee's wives, Emma Lee, ended up running the ferry more than Lee ever did. The Lee family operated a small ranch and orchard near the crossing, the remnants of which can still be seen on a self-guided tour of the **Lonely Dell Ranch Historic Site.** There's a nice **campground** ($16, no hookups, no reservations), a ranger station, and a launch ramp.

## Food and Accommodations

**Cliff Dweller's Lodge** (928/355-2261 or 800/962-9755, www.cliffdwellerslodge.com, $80-100) offers charming, rustic-but-comfortable rooms with satellite television, and the restaurant serves good breakfasts, lunches, and dinners ($10-25), everything from fajitas and ribs to falafel and halibut. They also serve beer and wine, which you can sip on the little patio at what seems like the end of the world. There's a gas station too.

The **Lee's Ferry Lodge at Vermilion Cliffs** (US-89A near Marble Canyon, 928/355-2231 or 800/451-2231, www.leesferrylodge.com, $65) has romantic little rooms in a rock-built structure that blends into the tremendous background. A delicious restaurant (daily breakfast, lunch, and dinner, $10-25) serves hearty fare like hand-cut steaks and ribs, as well as a diverse selection of beer.

## Getting There

Lee's Ferry is located in the vast, empty regions along the road between the South and North Rims, about 60 miles from the North Rim. Just after crossing over **Navajo Bridge** at Marble Canyon, along **US-89A,** turn on **Lee's Ferry Road.** The river is about seven miles along the road from the Navajo Bridge Visitors Center.

---

com/lodging/phantom-ranch/lottery for more details.

## Camping

There are three developed campgrounds in the inner canyon: **Cottonwood Campground,** about 7 miles from the North Rim along the North Kaibab Trail; **Bright Angel Campground,** along the creek of the same name near Phantom Ranch; and **Indian Garden,** about 4.5 miles from the South Rim along the Bright Angel Trail. To stay overnight at any of these campgrounds you must obtain a permit from the **South Rim Backcountry Information Center** (928/638-7875, $10 plus $8 pp per night). All three campgrounds offer restrooms, a freshwater spigot, picnic tables, and food storage bins to keep the critters out. There are no showers or other amenities.

The best campground in the inner canyon is Bright Angel, a shady, cottonwood-lined setting along cool Bright

Angel Creek. Because of its easy proximity to Phantom Ranch, campers can make use of the Phantom Ranch Canteen, even eating meals there if they can get a reservation, and can attend the ranger talks offered at the lodge. There's nothing quite like sitting on the grassy banks beside your campsite and cooling your worn feet in the creek.

# Grand Canyon West

Since the Hualapai Tribe's Skywalk opened in 2007, the remote Grand Canyon West has become a busy tourist attraction. The Skywalk is about two hours of dirt-road driving from the Hualapai Reservation's capital, Peach Springs, located along Route 66 east of Kingman. If you want to experience Grand Canyon West during your trip to Grand Canyon National Park, remember that it is about 250 miles from the South Rim and will take at least an extra two days. Along the way, you can drive on the longest remaining portion of Route 66 and, if you have a few days on top of that, hike down into Havasupai Canyon and see its famous, fantastical waterfalls.

## Getting There

The best way to get to **Grand Canyon West** from the South Rim is to take I-40 to the Ash Fork exit and then drive west on Route 66. Starting at Ash Fork and heading west to Peach Springs, the longest remaining portion of Route 66 moves through **Seligman,** a small roadside town that's caught in the heyday of the Mother Road. The route through Seligman, which stands up to a stop and a walk around if you have the time, is popular with nostalgic motorcyclists, and there are a few eateries and tourist-style stores in town. Once you reach Peach Springs, take Antares Road for 25 miles, head right on Pearce Ferry Road for 3 miles, and then turn east onto

Phantom Ranch cabins

Diamond Bar Road for 21 miles, 14 of it on dirt. Diamond Bar Road ends at the only entrance to Grand Canyon West. The 49-mile trip takes about two hours. For park-and-ride reservations, call 702/260-6506.

To reach **Havasupai Canyon,** turn north on Highway 18 just before Peach Springs and drive 60 miles north to a parking area at Hualapai Hilltop. From there it's an eight-mile hike in to Supai Village and the lodge, and another two miles to the campground. The trail is moderate and leads through a sandy wash with overhanging canyon walls. For the first two miles or so, rocky, moderately technical switchbacks lead to the canyon floor. Then it's easy and beautiful the rest of the way. If you don't want to hike in, you can arrange to **rent a horse** (928/448-2121, 928/448-2174, or 928/448-2180, www.havasupaitribe.com, $120 round-trip to lodge, $150 round-trip to campground), or even hire a **helicopter** (623/516-2790, $85 pp one-way).

**Hualapai Reservation's Skywalk** is only 125 miles from Las Vegas (about a 2.5-hour drive), so it makes sense to include this remote side trip if you're headed to the South Rim from Vegas anyway. To reach Grand Canyon West from Las Vegas, take US-93 out of the city, heading south for about 65 miles to mile marker 42, where you'll see the Dolan Springs/Meadview City/Pearce Ferry exit. Turn north onto Pearce Ferry Road. About 30 miles in, turn east on Diamond Bar Road. Then it's about 20 miles, 7 or so miles of it unpaved, to Grand Canyon West.

## Havasupai Indian Reservation

Havasu Creek is heavy with lime, which turns the water an almost tropical blue-green. It passes below the weathered red walls of the western Grand Canyon, home these many centuries to the Havasupai (Havasu 'Baaja), the "people of the blue-green water."

The creek falls through the canyon on its way to join the Colorado River, passing briefly by the ramshackle, inner-canyon village of Supai, where it is not unusual to see horses running free in the dusty streets, where reggae plays all day through some community speaker, and where the supply helicopter alights and then hops out again every 10 minutes or so in a field across from the post office. Then, about two miles on from the village, the creek plunges 120 feet into a misty turquoise pool. It does it again after another mile, but not before passing peacefully through a cottonwood-shaded campground.

Thousands of people from all over the world visit **Havasupai** (928/448-2121, http://theofficialhavasupaitribe.com, entry fee $50 plus $10 environmental fee) every year just to see these blue-green waterfalls, to swim in their pools, and to see one of the remotest hometowns in America. The trip is all the more enticing and memorable because it's rather an expedition, or near to it. Still, there are those who return year after year, as if going home.

As of 2017, the tribe was no longer taking reservations on its website. It is reportedly difficult to obtain a permit to visit the waterfalls, much more difficult than it was just a few years ago. If you want to go, you must call the tribe and talk to them personally, and it's a good idea to do so at least a year before your trip.

### Planning Your Visit

A visit to Havasupai takes some planning. It's unbearably hot in the deep summer, when you can't hike except in the early morning; the best months to visit are September-October and April-June. If you aren't a backpacker, you can hire a **pack horse** ($242 round-trip) or take the **helicopter** ($85 one-way). A popular way to visit is to hike in and take the helicopter out. It's a five-minute thrill ride through the canyon to the rim, and the helipad is only about 50 yards from the trailhead parking lot. The tribe requires a reservation to visit Supai and the falls, and they are not easy to come by.

Most visitors stay the night at one of the motels along Historic Route 66 before hiking in. Get an early start, especially during the summer. It's a **60-mile drive** to the trailhead at Hualapai Hill from Route 66. The closest hotel is the **Hualapai Lodge** (900 Route 66, 928/769-2230 or 928/769-2636, www.grandcanyonwest.com, $150-170) in Peach Springs, about 7 miles west of Highway 18, which leads to the trailhead. You'll find cheaper accommodations in **Seligman,** about 30 miles east.

The **eight-mile one-way hike** to the village of Supai from Hualapai Hilltop is one of the easier treks into the Grand Canyon. A few miles of switchbacks lead to a sandy bottomland, where you're surrounded by eroded humps of seemingly melted, pockmarked sandstone. This is not Grand Canyon National Park: You'll know that for sure when you see the trash along the trail. It doesn't ruin the hike, but it nearly breaks the spell. When you reach the village, you'll see the twin rock spires, called Wii'Gliva, that tower over the little farms and homes of Supai.

### The Waterfalls

What used to be Navajo Falls, just down the trail from the village, was destroyed in a 2008 flash flood. Now there's a wider set of falls and a big pool that sits below a flood-eroded hill. Perhaps the most famous of the canyon's falls, **Havasu Falls** comes on you all of a sudden as you get closer to the campground. Few hikers refuse to toss their packs aside and strip to their swimming suits when they see Havasu Falls for the first time. The other major waterfall, **Mooney Falls,** is another mile down the trail, through the campground. It's not easy to reach the pool below; it requires a careful walk down a narrow rock-hewn trail with chain handles, but most reasonably dexterous people can handle it. **Beaver Falls,** somewhat underwhelming by comparison, is another two miles toward the river, which is seven miles from the campground.

### Food and Accommodations

The **Havasupai Lodge** (928/448-2111, up to four people $145) has air-conditioning and private baths. The village also has a small café that serves decent breakfast, lunch, and dinner, and a general store. Most visitors pack in and stay at the primitive campground (first-come, first-served, $25) not far from the main waterfall, which is another 1.5 miles from the village.

## Hualapai Indian Reservation

Although Peach Springs is the capital of the Hualapai (WALL-uh-pie) Reservation, there's not much there but a lodge and a few scattered houses. The real attractions are up on the West Rim about 50 miles and two hours away. Peach Springs makes an obvious base for a visit to the West Rim, which has several

# The Hualapai

Before the 1850s, northwestern Arizona's small Hualapai Nation didn't really exist. It was the federal government's idea to group together 13 autonomous bands of Yuman-speaking Pai Indians, who had lived on the high dry plains near Grand Canyon's western reaches for eons, as the "People of the Tall Pines."

Before the colonial clampdown and the Hualapai Wars of the 1860s, the Pai bands were independent, though they "followed common rules for marriage and land use, spoke variations of one language, and shared social structures, kin networks, cultural practices, environmental niches, and so on," according to Jeffrey Shepherd's *We Are an Indian Nation: A History of the Hualapai People*, which the scholar spent 10 years researching and writing.

The U.S. Army nearly wiped out the bands during the land wars of the 1860s, and the internment of the survivors almost finished the job. But the bands persisted, and in 1883 the government established the million-acre Hualapai Reservation, with its capital at Peach Springs. Then it spent the next 100 years or so trying to take it away from them for the benefit of Anglo ranchers, the railroad, and the National Park Service.

These days the Hualapai Nation, though still impoverished, is a worldwide brand—Grand Canyon West. How did this happen?

The small, isolated tribe has always been willing to take economic risks, one of the many ways, as Shepherd argues, that the Hualapai have twisted colonial objectives for their own survival. A few years ago they partnered with Las Vegas entrepreneur David Jin and built the Hualapai Skywalk, a 70-foot-long glass walkway hanging from the Grand Canyon's western rim. Now you can't walk two steps along the Vegas strip without a tour guide offering to drive you to one of the most isolated sections of Arizona.

Throughout their relatively short history as a nation, the Hualapai have consistently tried to make their windy and dry reservation economically viable, sometimes with the assistance of the government but often in direct contradiction to its goals. For generations they were cattle ranchers, but they could never get enough water to make it pay. They successfully sued the Santa Fe Railroad over an important reservation spring in a landmark case for indigenous rights. For a time in the 1980s they even hesitantly explored allowing uranium mining on their reservation. Now, they have bet their future on tourism.

lookout points, the famous Skywalk, and a kitschy Old West-style tourist attraction called Hualapai Ranch. The tribe's **Hualapai River Runners** (928/769-2219) will take you on a day trip on the river, and there are several all-inclusive package tours to choose from. Check out the **tribe's website** (www.grandcanyonwest.com) for more information.

## Tour Packages

To visit Grand Canyon West, the Hualapai require you to purchase one of the rather overpriced **Legacy Packages** ($50-83 pp), and only the more expensive Gold and VIP packages include the Skywalk. The lesser packages allow you to ride a shuttle from **Eagle Point,** where the Skywalk juts out, to **Guano Point,** a nice view of the western canyon, and **Hualapai Ranch,** where fake cowboys will entertain you with Old West clichés, take you on a ride in a wagon, or lead a horseback ride in a corral or to the canyon rim ($10-75). You can stay the night in one of the ranch's rustic cabins ($100). A couple of the packages include a meal, or you can add one for $15 per person. You can also add the Skywalk to your package for $22 if you get up there and decide you really have to try it. Frankly, the packages that don't include the Skywalk are definitely not worth the price or the drive. The views from the South and North Rims are much more dramatic and memorable, and cost only $30.

## The Skywalk

**The Skywalk** (928/769-2636, www.grandcanyonwest.com, $75) is as much an art installation as it is a tourist attraction. A horseshoe-shaped glass and steel platform jutting out 70 feet from the canyon rim, it appears futuristic surrounded by the rugged, remote western canyon. It's something to see for sure, but is it worth the long drive and the high price tag? Not really. If you have time for an off-the-beaten-path portion of your canyon trip, it's better to go to the North Rim and stand out on Bright Angel Point—you'll get a somewhat similar impression, and it's cheaper. There is something of a thrill ride feel to the Skywalk, however. Some people can't handle it: They walk out a few steps, look down through the glass at the canyon 4,000 feet below, and head for (seemingly) more solid ground. It's all perfectly safe, but it doesn't feel that way if you are subject to vertigo. Another drawback of this site is that they won't let you take your camera out on the Skywalk. If you want a record of this adventure, you have to buy a "professional" photo taken by somebody else. You have to store all your possessions, including your camera, in a locker before stepping out on the glass, with covers on your shoes.

## Recreation

Though the Skywalk may not be worth the high price of admission and the long drive to reach it, the Hualapai offer one adventure that is worth the steep price tag: the canyon's only **one-day river rafting experience** (928/769-2636, www.grandcanyonwest.com, May-Oct., $450 pp). It generally takes up to a year of planning and several days of roughing it to ride the river and the rapids through the inner gorge, making a Colorado River adventure something that the average tourist isn't likely to try. Not so in Grand Canyon West. For about $450 per

The Skywalk is 4,000 feet above the canyon.

person, Hualapai river guides will pick you up in a van early in the morning at the Hualapai Lodge in Peach Springs and drive you to the Colorado via the rough Diamond Creek Road, where you'll float downstream in a motorboat over roiling white-water rapids and smooth and tranquil stretches. You'll stop for lunch on a beach and take a short hike through a watery side canyon to beautiful Travertine Falls. At the end of the trip, a helicopter picks you out of the canyon and drops you on the rim near the Skywalk. It's expensive, yes, but if you want to ride the river without a lot of preplanning and camping, this is the way to do it. Along the way the Hualapai guides tell stories about this end of the Grand Canyon, sprinkled with tribal history and lore.

You can drive to the river's edge yourself along the 19-mile **Diamond Creek Road** through a dry, scrubby landscape scattered with cacti. The road provides the only easy access to the river's edge between Lee's Ferry, not far from the North Rim, and Pearce Ferry, near Lake Mead. The route is best negotiated in a high-clearance SUV; they say you can do it in a regular sedan, but you have to cross Diamond Creek six times as the dirt road winds down through Peach Springs Canyon, dropping some 3,400 feet from its beginning at Peach Springs on Route 66. The creek is susceptible to flash floods during the summer and winter rainy seasons, so call ahead to check **road conditions** (928/769-2230). At the end of the road, where Diamond Creek marries the Colorado, there's a sandy beach by an enchanting, lush oasis, and, of course, there's that big river rolling by.

## Food and Accommodations

The **Hualapai Lodge** (900 Route 66, 928/769-2230 or 928/769-2636, www.grandcanyonwest.com, $150-170) in Peach Springs has a small heated saltwater pool, an exercise room, a gift shop, 57 comfortable, newish rooms with soft beds, cable, free wireless Internet access, and train tracks right out the back door. The lodge is a good place to stay the night before hiking into Havasupai, as it's only about seven miles west of the turnoff to Hualapai Hill and the trailhead.

The lodge's restaurant, **Diamond Creek** (6am-9pm daily, $10-15), serves American and Native American dishes. They offer a heaping plate of delicious spaghetti if you're carbo-loading for a big hike to Havasupai; the Hualapai taco (similar to the Navajo taco, with beans and meat piled high on a fluffy slab of fry bread) and the Hualapai stew (with luscious sirloin tips and vegetables swimming in a delicious, hearty broth) are both recommended. They also have a few vegetarian choices, good chili, and pizza.

More food and lodging options are available in **Kingman** and **Seligman** along Old Route 66.

# Los Angeles

With palm trees lining sunny boulevards, surfers riding the deep-blue Pacific, and unending Hollywood glitz, Los Angeles is the California that lives in our imaginations.

SAN FRANCISCO

Mono Lake

Nevada California

Yosemite National Park

230 mi/370 km 3.5 hrs

250 mi/400 km 5.5 hrs

Sequoia and Kings Canyon National Park

Death Valley National Park

300 mi/485 km 6 hrs

SAN LUIS OBISPO

LAS VEGAS

200 mi/320 km 3.5 hrs

270mi/435km 5 hrs

LOS ANGELES

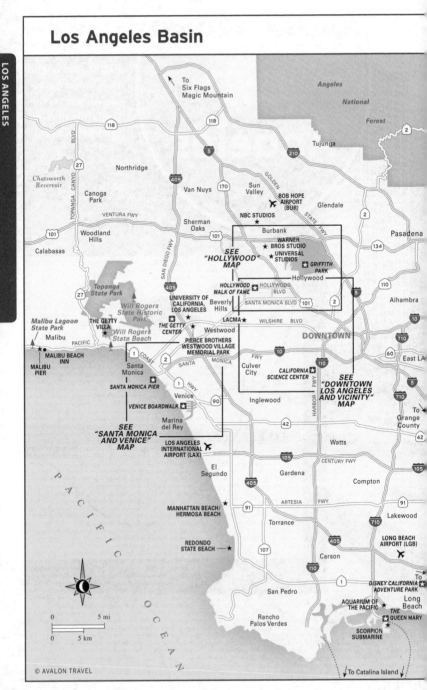

# Los Angeles Basin

To Six Flags Magic Mountain

Angeles National Forest

Chatsworth Reservoir

Northridge

Canoga Park

Woodland Hills

Calabasas

Topanga State Park

Malibu Lagoon State Park

Malibu

MALIBU BEACH INN

MALIBU PIER

Van Nuys

Sun Valley

Sherman Oaks

BOB HOPE AIRPORT (BUR)

Glendale

Pasadena

NBC STUDIOS

Burbank

WARNER BROS STUDIO

UNIVERSAL STUDIOS

*SEE "HOLLYWOOD" MAP*

GRIFFITH PARK

Hollywood

HOLLYWOOD WALK OF FAME

HOLLYWOOD BLVD

SANTA MONICA BLVD

Alhambra

UNIVERSITY OF CALIFORNIA, LOS ANGELES

Beverly Hills

THE GETTY VILLA

Will Rogers State Historic Park

THE GETTY CENTER

Will Rogers State Beach

LACMA

WILSHIRE BLVD

DOWNTOWN

Westwood

PIERCE BROTHERS WESTWOOD VILLAGE MEMORIAL PARK

Santa Monica

SANTA MONICA PIER

VENICE BOARDWALK

Marina del Rey

*SEE "SANTA MONICA AND VENICE" MAP*

Culver City

CALIFORNIA SCIENCE CENTER

*SEE "DOWNTOWN LOS ANGELES AND VICINITY" MAP*

East LA

To Orange County

Inglewood

LOS ANGELES INTERNATIONAL AIRPORT (LAX)

El Segundo

Gardena

Watts

CENTURY FWY

Venice

MANHATTAN BEACH/ HERMOSA BEACH

Torrance

ARTESIA FWY

Compton

Lakewood

REDONDO STATE BEACH

Carson

LONG BEACH AIRPORT (LGB)

San Pedro

Rancho Palos Verdes

PACIFIC OCEAN

0   5 mi
0   5 km

DISNEY CALIFORNIA ADVENTURE PARK

AQUARIUM OF THE PACIFIC

Long Beach

THE QUEEN MARY

SCORPION SUBMARINE

To Catalina Island

# Highlights

★ **California Science Center:** Come to see the retired Space Shuttle *Endeavour* and the accompanying exhibit. Stay for displays on the world's ecosystems and humanity's amazing technological innovations (page 271).

★ **Griffith Park:** This large urban park in the Santa Monica Mountains is home to the iconic Hollywood sign and the Griffith Observatory (page 272).

★ **Hollywood Walk of Fame:** Walk all over your favorite stars—they're embedded in the ground beneath your feet (page 273).

★ **The Getty Center:** The art collections alone would make this sprawling museum complex worth a visit. The soaring architecture, beautiful grounds, and remarkable views of the skyline make it a must. And except for paid parking, it's entirely free (page 279).

★ **Santa Monica Pier:** Ride the Scrambler, take in the view from the solar-powered Ferris wheel, or dine on a hot dog on a stick at this 100-year-old amusement park by the sea (page 280).

★ **Venice Boardwalk:** It's hard not to be amused when walking down this paved coastal path in L.A.'s most

free-spirited beach community, crowded with street performers, bodybuilders, and self-identified freaks (page 281).

★ **Disney California Adventure Park:** Tour a Disneyfied version of the Golden State, which includes the Pixar-inspired Cars Land (page 309).

★ **The *Queen Mary:*** Take a tour, spend the evening, or stay the night on this huge art deco ocean liner docked in the Long Beach Harbor. Decide for yourself whether it's truly haunted (page 315).

It's true that the Pacific Ocean warms to a swimmable temperature here, there are palm trees, and stars are embedded in the sidewalks on Hollywood Boulevard.

But celebrities don't crowd every sidewalk signing autographs, and movies aren't filming on every corner. Instead, L.A. combines the glitz, crowds, and speed of the big city with an easier, friendlier feel in its suburbs. Power shoppers pound the sparkling pavement lining the ultra-urban city streets. Visitors can catch a premiere at the Chinese Theatre, try their feet on a surfboard at Huntington Beach, and view the prehistoric relics at the La Brea Tar Pits. For visitors who want a deeper look into the Los Angeles Basin, excellent museums dot the landscape, as do theaters, comedy clubs, and live-music venues. L.A. boasts the best nightlife in California, with options that appeal to star-watchers, hard-core dancers, and cutting-edge music lovers alike.

In Orange County lies the single most recognizable tourist attraction in California: Disneyland. Even the most jaded local residents tend to soften at the bright colors, cheerful music, sweet smells, and sense of fun that permeate the House of Mouse.

# Getting to Los Angeles

## From San Francisco
### The Coastal Route

The **Pacific Coast Highway (CA-1)** from Los Angeles to San Francisco is one of America's iconic drives. This coastal route has a lot to see and do, but it's not the fastest route between the two cities. It runs almost **500 miles** and can easily take **eight hours** or longer, depending on traffic. It's worth the extra time to experience the gorgeous coastal scenery, which includes Monterey, Big Sur, and Santa Barbara. The highway is long, narrow, and winding; in winter, rockslides and mudslides may close the road entirely. Always check **Caltrans** (www.dot.ca.gov) for highway traffic conditions before starting your journey.

From San Francisco, take **CA-1 South** down the coast through the towns of Half Moon Bay, Santa Cruz, and Monterey. The section of **CA-1 South** that you don't want to miss is the 96-mile winding drive along the coastline of **Big Sur,** which takes 2.5 hours or longer. (For a quicker route, you can take **US-101 South** out of the city; you save roughly an hour, but miss the most scenic drives along the coast).

After Big Sur, in San Luis Obispo, **CA-1 South** merges with **US-101 South.** At Pismo Beach, **US-101 South** heads inland for 60 miles before returning to the coast 35 miles northwest of Santa Barbara. **US-101 South** follows the coast through Santa Barbara and Ventura for 72 miles until Oxnard, where it heads inland to detour around the Santa Monica Mountains and dip into Los Angeles after 60 miles. **CA-1 South** splits off **US-101 South** in Oxnard for a more scenic drive of the coast, continuing 43 miles through Malibu before hitting Santa Monica, where you can take a 13-mile drive on **I-10 East** to downtown Los Angeles.

### Stopping in San Luis Obispo

It's easier to enjoy the drive by dividing it up over two days and spending a night somewhere along the coast. Right off both CA-1 and US-101, the city of **San Luis Obispo** is close to halfway between the two cities, which makes it an ideal place to stop. It takes three hours to make the 201-mile drive from Los Angeles if traffic isn't bad. The additional 232 miles to San Francisco takes four hours or more. An affordable motel right off the highway is the **Peach Tree Inn** (2001 Monterey St.,

## Best Hotels

★ **Ace Hotel:** This downtown hotel has a lot going for it, including a stunning on-site theater that hosts major entertainment events and a rooftop bar and pool that show off the L.A. skyline (page 300).

★ **Freehand Los Angeles:** This hip complex is one part hostel, three parts boutique hotel (page 299)

★ **Hotel Normandie:** This historic hotel in Koreatown gets extra points for having the city's best throwback burger joint and its most forward-looking bar in the same building (page 301).

★ **Magic Castle Hotel:** Next door to the acclaimed magic club, this hotel spoils its guests with great customer service, free snacks, and a pool open at all hours (page 302).

★ **Élan Hotel:** Here you'll find comfortable rooms at moderate prices, a rarity at the intersection of ritzy Beverly Hills and glitzy Hollywood (page 303).

★ **Hotel Erwin:** This eclectic hotel is feet from the raucous Venice Boardwalk. Take in the madness from the hotel's rooftop bar (page 305).

800/227-6396, http://peachtreeinn.com, $89-299). For a wilder experience, stay at popular tourist attraction **The Madonna Inn** (10 Madonna Rd., 805/543-3000, www.madonnainn.com, $209-489), which offers the **Gold Rush Steak House** for dinner and the **Copper Café & Pastry Shop** for breakfast. **Novo** (726 Higuera St., 805/543-3986, www.novorestaurant.com, 11am-9pm Sun.-Thurs., 11am-1am Fri.-Sat., $18-37) has a truly international menu and outdoor dining on decks overlooking San Luis Obispo Creek. For something fast, the **Firestone Grill** (1001 Higuera St., 805/783-1001, www.firestonegrill.com, 11am-10pm Sun.-Wed., 11am-11pm Thurs.-Sat., $5-22) is known for its tasty tri-tip sandwich. For complete information on San Luis Obispo, see page 354.

### The Interior Route

A faster but much less interesting driving route is **I-5** from Los Angeles to San Francisco. It takes about **six hours** if the traffic is cooperating. On holiday weekends, the drive time can increase to 10 hours. Take **I-80 East** out of San Francisco, crossing the Bay Bridge into the East Bay suburbs. Then hop onto **I-580 East** for 63 miles. Not long after

the outer suburb of Livermore, connect with **I-5 South,** which you will follow for the next 292 miles. I-5 crosses the **Tejon Pass** over the Tehachapi Mountains in the section of the highway nicknamed **the Grapevine,** which can close in winter due to snow and ice (and sometimes in summer due to wildfires). November-March, tule fog (thick, ground-level fog) can also seriously impede driving conditions and reduce visibility to a crawl. After crossing the Grapevine, you will enter the outer edge of the Los Angeles metro area. From I-5, take **CA-170 South** for 9.5 miles, then connect to **US-101 South** and continue into the city center. Always check **Caltrans** (www.dot.ca.gov) for highway traffic conditions before starting your journey.

### From Yosemite

Getting from Yosemite National Park to Los Angeles involves driving about **300 miles** (roughly **six hours**) along two of the state's biggest highways. It's best to head out of the park's **South entrance** and get on **CA-41 South** toward Fresno. After 62 miles, you'll reach Fresno, where you should get on **CA-99 South.** Stay on this major highway for 132 miles until it becomes **I-5 South,** which you'll stay on

# Restaurants

★ **B.S. Taqueria:** Chef Ray Garcia updates the tacos with clam and lardo creations at this wonderful, causal downtown joint (page 293).

★ **Kagaya:** This Japanese restaurant is acclaimed for its thinly sliced *shabu-shabu* (page 293).

★ **Cassell's Hamburgers:** This resurrected L.A. staple does a great hamburger and an even better potato salad (page 294).

★ **Yuca's:** Not many taquerias win a prestigious James Beard Award; this Los Feliz eatery did (page 294).

★ **Taix French Restaurant:** This Echo Park institution serves elegant French cuisine in an Old World setting (page 294).

★ **The Griddle Café:** Industry insiders meet at this Hollywood restaurant for breakfast creations like red velvet pancakes (page 297).

★ **AOC:** Small plates of California cuisine pair perfectly with selections from an extensive wine list and creative cocktails at this Beverly Hills hot spot (page 298).

★ **C&O Trattoria:** Fill up on delicious Italian fare at this longtime favorite in Marina del Rey (page 298).

★ **Neptune's Net:** The crispy shrimp tacos and pitchers of beer at this casual coast-side eatery hit the spot after a long day in the surf (page 299).

---

for over 60 more miles. From I-5, take **CA-170 South** for 9.5 miles, then connect to **US-101 South** and continue into the city center.

## From Las Vegas

Multilane highways ensure that the **270-mile, five-hour** drive from Las Vegas to Los Angeles is smooth, if not especially visually appealing. From Las Vegas, take **I-15 South** for about 220 miles. In the San Bernardino area, turn off onto **I-210 West,** which you'll take for 27 miles before continuing on **I-605 South.** Continue for 5.5 miles, then get on **I-10 West.** Take it for about 12 miles to **US-101 North** and continue into the city center.

## From the Grand Canyon

It's roughly **500 miles** from the Grand Canyon's South Rim to Los Angeles, a grueling **eight-hour** drive through an empty, hard landscape without too much respite save the usual interstate fare. If you are at the popular South Rim of the Grand Canyon, head out of the park on

**US-180 East** and then take **AZ-64 South** for about 50 miles until it reaches the pleasant Southwest town of Williams. At Williams, catch **I-40 West,** which starts off as a scenic drive through a pine tree-dotted landscape before becoming more barren and crowded with trucks. The most exciting part of the drive is crossing the Colorado River at the California-Arizona border.

You'll have clocked about 320 miles on I-40 West when it enters Barstow and becomes **I-15 South.** Beware the increasing traffic as you head toward Los Angeles on I-15 for about 66 miles. In the San Bernardino area, turn off onto **I-210 West,** which you'll take for 27 miles before continuing on **I-605 South.** Continue for 5.5 miles, then get on **I-10 West.** Take it for about 12 miles to **US-101 North** and continue into the city center.

### Stopping in Needles

The Mojave Desert town of Needles is on the Colorado River, at the border of California, Arizona, and Nevada. It's

## Stretch Your Legs

Do you see a giant golf ball teed up in the desert off I-40? You're not hallucinating. It's called the **Golf Ball House** (Grand Canyon-Los Angeles Drive, east of the Alamo Rd. I-40 exit, Yucca, AZ). The orb with the 40-foot diameter was intended to be the Dinosphere, a nightclub and restaurant. That development failed, so today it's a private residence and surreal photo-op.

three hours and 45 minutes from the Grand Canyon's South Rim and four hours and 15 minutes from Los Angeles. Translation: It's a good overnight spot for the long drive between the Grand Canyon and Los Angeles.

Relax after a long day of driving at the **Best Western Colorado River Inn** (2371 W. Broadway, 760/326-4552, www.bestwestern.com, $100-160). It has rooms equipped with a fridge and satellite TV. Even better, there's an outdoor pool, spa, and sauna. A complimentary hot breakfast at adjacent Juicy's River Café is included with your stay. The **Rio del Sol Inn** (1111 Pashard St., 760/326-5660, http://riodelsolinn.com, $77-116) has an outdoor swimming pool, hot tub, and steam room along with guest laundry.

**Juicy's River Café** (2411 W. Broadway, 760/326-2233, www.juicysrivercafe.com, 5:30am-10pm Sun.-Thurs., 5:30am-10:30pm Fri.-Sat. summer, 5:30am-9:30pm Sun.-Thurs., 5:30am-10:30pm Fri.-Sat. winter, $9-24) dishes out a diverse menu from very early until relatively late. This includes breakfast (eggs Benedict, omelets), lunch (wraps, salads, sandwiches), and dinner (steaks, ribs, pasta, seafood). They also have an acclaimed Bloody Mary made from a secret recipe. The awesomely and appropriately named **Munchy's** (829 Front St., 760/326-1000, 6:30am-6pm Mon.-Fri., 6:30am-3pm Sat., $5-10) satisfies Mexican food cravings with tacos and burritos.

### By Air, Train, or Bus

L.A. is one of the most airport-dense metropolitan areas in the country. **Los Angeles International Airport** (LAX, 1 World Way, Los Angeles, 310/646-5252, www.lawa.org) has the most flights, which makes it the most crowded of the L.A. airports, with the longest security and check-in lines. If you can find a way around flying into LAX, do so. One option is to fly into other local airports, including **Hollywood Burbank Airport** (BUR, 2627 N. Hollywood Way, Burbank, 818/840-8840, http://hollywoodburbankairport.com) and **Long Beach Airport** (LGB, 4100 Donald Douglas Dr., Long Beach, 562/570-2600, www.lgb.org). It may be a slightly longer drive to your final destination, but it can be well worth it. If you use LAX, arrive a minimum of two hours ahead of your domestic flight time, three hours on busy holidays.

For train travel, **Amtrak** (800/872-7245, www.amtrak.com) has an active rail hub in Los Angeles. Most trains come in to **Union Station** (800 N. Alameda St., 323/466-3876), which is owned by the Los Angeles Metropolitan Transportation Authority (MTA, www.metro.net). The *Coast Starlight* train connects the San Francisco Bay Area with Los Angeles. Union Station also acts as a hub for the **Metro** (www.metro.net, one ride $1.75, day pass $7), which includes both the subway system and a network of buses throughout the L.A. metropolitan area. You can pay on board a bus if you have exact change. Otherwise, purchase a ticket or a day pass from the ticket vending machines at all Metro Rail Stations.

Some buses run 24 hours. The Metro Rail lines start running as early as 4:30am and don't stop until as late as 1:30am. See Metro's website (www.metro.net) for route maps, timetables, and fare details.

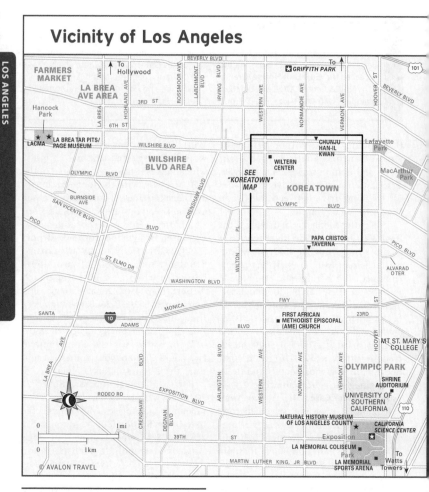

## Vicinity of Los Angeles

FARMERS MARKET

To Hollywood

LA BREA AVE AREA

GRIFFITH PARK

To 101

Hancock Park

LA BREA TAR PITS/ PAGE MUSEUM

LACMA

3RD ST

6TH ST

WILSHIRE BLVD

WILSHIRE BLVD AREA

OLYMPIC BLVD

BURNSIDE AVE

SAN VICENTE BLVD

PICO

BLVD

ST. ELMO DR

WASHINGTON BLVD

SEE "KOREATOWN" MAP

CHUNJU HAN-IL KWAN

Lafayette Park

WILTERN CENTER

KOREATOWN

MacArthur Park

OLYMPIC BLVD

PAPA CRISTOS TAVERNA

PICO BLVD

ALVARADO TER

SANTA MONICA

ADAMS

FWY

23RD

FIRST AFRICAN METHODIST EPISCOPAL (AME) CHURCH

BLVD

MT ST. MARY'S COLLEGE

OLYMPIC PARK

SHRINE AUDITORIUM

UNIVERSITY OF SOUTHERN CALIFORNIA

RODEO RD

EXPOSITION BLVD

NATURAL HISTORY MUSEUM OF LOS ANGELES COUNTY

CALIFORNIA SCIENCE CENTER

Exposition Park

LA MEMORIAL COLISEUM

0  1mi

0  1km

© AVALON TRAVEL

39TH ST

MARTIN LUTHER KING, JR BLVD

LA MEMORIAL SPORTS ARENA

To Watts Towers

# Sights

The only problem you'll have with the sights of Los Angeles and its surrounding towns is finding a way to see enough of them to satisfy you. You'll find museums, streets, ancient art, and modern production studios ready to welcome you throughout the sprawling cityscape.

## Downtown and Vicinity

Downtown Los Angeles is experiencing serious renewal with streets of new restaurants, new bars, new hotels, and new attractions, including The Broad museum. The initials "DTLA" (which stands for downtown Los Angeles) can be found everywhere: from the sides of buildings to Internet hashtags.

## El Pueblo de Los Angeles Historical Monument

For a city that is famously berated for lacking a sense of its own past, **El Pueblo de Los Angeles Historical Monument** (Olvera St. between Spring St. and Alameda St., 213/485-6855, tours 213/628-1274, http://elpueblo.lacity.org,

# Two Days in Los Angeles

Los Angeles is notoriously sprawling, but in a couple of days, it is possible to get a serious dose of culture and a few hours on the beach.

### Day 1

Start your morning with coffee and avocado toast at downtown's **Verve Coffee.** Then browse through the aisles of books at **The Last Bookstore,** including the book art on the 2nd floor. Spend the rest of the morning taking in the sprawling **Los Angeles County Museum of Art,** known as LACMA.

When hunger strikes, head downtown again for some tasty tacos at **B.S. Taqueria.** With your belly full, take a trip to the **California Science Center** to see the Space Shuttle *Endeavour.*

Before the sun drops into the Pacific, rush to the **Ace Hotel's Rooftop Bar** for a fine view of the city's skyline at sunset. Head downstairs for dinner at **L.A. Chapter,** a hip restaurant on the hotel's ground level. End your evening by taking in a movie or a band at a unique venue: the **Hollywood Forever Cemetery.** Or catch an up-and-coming music act at **The Echo and Echoplex.**

### Day 2

Start your beach day at **Cora's Coffee Shoppe** in Santa Monica, a local favorite with a lovely patio. Then walk off that food by taking a half-mile stroll to the **Santa Monica Pier,** where you can ride a Ferris wheel or a roller coaster right over the ocean.

From there, hop in your car and head up the coast toward Malibu. If the waves

The Getty Center

are breaking, rent a board and wetsuit from the **Malibu Surf Shack** and paddle out into the peeling waves of **Malibu's Surfrider Beach.** Or drive another 20 minutes to **Leo Carrillo State Park,** where you can explore tide pools and coastal caves a world away from urban L.A.

Continue up the coast a few more miles to **Neptune's Net** for lunch. This informal restaurant right on the Pacific Coast Highway has wonderful shrimp tacos topped with pineapple slaw.

Returning south, detour to the **Venice Boardwalk,** where you can be entertained by street performers, bodybuilders, and skateboarders carving the on-the-beach skate park. Finish up with a fine Italian meal and a glass of wine at the **C&O Trattoria,** not far from the Venice Pier.

visitors center 9am-4pm daily) is a veritable crash course in history. Just a short distance from where Spanish colonists first settled in 1781, the park's 44 acres contain 27 buildings dating 1818-1926.

Facing a central courtyard, the oldest church in the city, **Our Lady Queen of the Angels,** still hosts a steady stream of baptisms and other services. On the southern

end of the courtyard stands a cluster of historic buildings, the most prominent being Pico House, a hotel built in 1869-1870. The restored **Old Plaza Firehouse** (10am-3pm Tues.-Sun.) dates to 1884 and exhibits firefighting memorabilia from the late 19th and early 20th centuries. On Main Street, **Sepulveda House** (10am-3pm Tues.-Sun.) serves as the Pueblo's

# Downtown Los Angeles

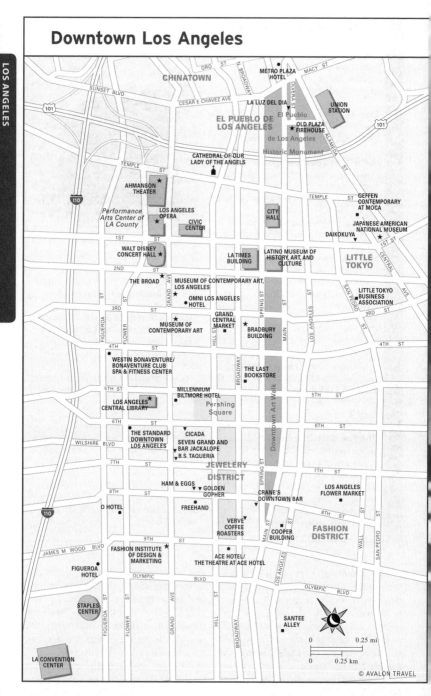

© AVALON TRAVEL

visitors center and features period furniture dating to 1887.

Off the central square is **Olvera Street,** an open-air market packed with mariachis, clothing shops, crafts stalls, and taquerias. Hidden in the midst of this tourist market is the **Avila Adobe** (9am-4pm daily), a squat adobe structure said to be the oldest standing house in Los Angeles. The home now functions as a museum detailing the lifestyle of the Mexican ranchero culture that thrived here before the Mexican-American War.

Free 50-minute docent-led **tours** (213/628-1274, www.lasangelitas.org, 10am, 11am, and noon Tues.-Sat.) start at the Las Angelitas del Pueblo office, next to the Old Plaza Firehouse on the southeast end of the plaza. Some of the best times to visit are during festive annual celebrations like the Blessing of the Animals, around Easter, and, of course, Cinco de Mayo.

### Cathedral of Our Lady of the Angels

Standing on a hillside next to the Hollywood Freeway (U.S. 101), the colossal concrete **Cathedral of Our Lady of the Angels** (555 W. Temple St., 213/680-5200, www.olacathedral.org, 6:30am-6pm Mon.-Fri., 9am-6pm Sat., 7am-6pm Sun., free tours 1pm Mon.-Fri., parking $4-20) is the third-largest cathedral in the world. Every aspect of Spanish architect Rafael Moneo's design is monumental: the 25-ton bronze doors, 27,000 square feet of clerestory windows of translucent alabaster, and the 156-foot-high campanile topped with a 25-foot-tall cross.

### Union Station

When **Union Station** (800 N. Alameda St., Amtrak 800/872-7245, www.union-stationla.com, 4am-1am daily) opened in 1939, 1.5 million people supposedly passed through its doors in the first three days, all wanting to witness what is now considered one of the last of the nation's great rail stations. Its elegant mixture of Spanish mission and modern styles—incorporating vaulted arches, marble floors, and a 135-foot clock tower—harkens back to a more glamorous era of transportation. The hub for the city's commuter rail network, including L.A.'s first modern subway line, is also a vision of the future: It's slated to be a major hub of the planned California High-Speed Rail System. Two-hour tours of the station's art and architecture happen 10:30am-12:30pm on the second Sunday of the month.

### MOCA

The **Museum of Contemporary Art, Los Angeles** (MOCA, 250 S. Grand Ave., 213/626-6222, www.moca.org, 11am-6pm Mon., Wed., and Fri., 11am-8pm Thurs., 11am-5pm Sat.-Sun., $15 adults, $10 seniors, $8 students, children under 12 free) is where you'll see an array of artwork created between 1940 and yesterday afternoon. Highlights include pop art and abstract expressionism from Europe and the United States. Temporary exhibits have displayed the work of Andy Warhol and British artist-turned-Oscar-winning filmmaker Steve McQueen. MOCA has two other locations: The **Geffen Contemporary at MOCA** (152 N. Central Ave., www.moca.org, 11am-5pm Mon. and Fri., 11am-8pm Thurs., 11am-6pm Sat.-Sun.) is a former police car warehouse turned hangar-like gallery, while the **MOCA Pacific Design Center** (8687 Melrose Ave., West Hollywood, 11am-5pm Tues.-Fri., 11am-6pm Sat.-Sun., free) showcases architecture and design.

### The Broad

After opening in 2015, **The Broad** (221 S. Grand Ave., 213/232-6200, www.thebroad.org, 11am-5pm Tues.-Wed., 11am-8pm Thurs.-Fri., 10am-8pm Sat., 10am-6pm Sun., free but advance reservations required through website) is already a downtown landmark due to its unique honeycombed architecture, impressive contemporary art collection, and free admission. The two floors of gallery space dig into the 2,000 works donated by philanthropists Eli and Edythe Broad. The collection includes pieces by modern masters including Jean-Michel Basquiat, Jeff Koons, and Cindy Sherman.

## Downtown Art Walk

The dramatic sculptures and fountains adorning two blocks on **Hope Street** (300-500 Hope St.) include Alexander Calder's enormous *Four Arches* (1974) beside the Bank of America Plaza and Nancy Graves's whimsical *Sequi* (1986) near the Wells Fargo Center. A free, self-guided, public **Downtown Art Walk** (213/617-4929, http://downtownartwalk. org, hours vary but usually noon-10pm on the second Thursday of each month) centers predominantly on the galleries bounded by Spring, Main, 2nd, and 9th Streets, but also spreads out to the Calder and Graves pieces on Hope Street. **Historic Core Mural Tours** and **Building on History Tours** are other options.

## Grand Central Market

In operation since 1917, the **Grand Central Market** (317 S. Broadway, 213/624-2378, www.grandcentralsquare.com, 8am-6pm Sun.-Wed., 8am-9pm Thurs.-Sat.) houses dozens of food vendors including a falafel stand, a gourmet ice cream booth, and the popular Tacos Tumbras a Tomas, which is known for its giant carnitas tacos. Most vendors advertise with bright neon signs. A $10 or more purchase and validation will get you an hour's free parking at the **garage** (308 S. Hill St.). The market also hosts events including live music and game nights. Right across the street is **Angel's Flight** (https://angelsflight.org), the world's shortest railway, which was featured in the 2016 film *La La Land*.

## Bradbury Building

One of several historic L.A. structures featured in the movies *Chinatown* (1974), *Blade Runner* (1982), and *The Artist* (2011), the 1893 **Bradbury Building** (304 S. Broadway, lobby 9am-5pm daily) is an office building that wows filmmakers with its light-filled Victorian court that includes wrought-iron staircases, marble stairs, and open-cage elevators. On Saturday mornings, the 2.5-hour, docent-led **Historic Downtown Walking Tour** (213/623-2489, www.laconservancy. org, 10am Sat., reservations required, $15 adults, $10 children 17 and under), run by the Los Angeles Conservancy, takes visitors through downtown to sights including the Bradbury Building.

## Japanese American National Museum

The **Japanese American National Museum** (100 N. Central Ave., 213/625-0414, www.janm.org, 11am-5pm Tues.-Wed. and Fri.-Sun., noon-8pm Thurs., $12 adults, $6 students and seniors, children under 5 free) focuses on the experiences of Japanese people coming to and living in the United States, particularly California. This museum shows the Japanese American experience in vivid detail, with photos and artifacts telling much of the story.

## Fashion Institute of Design and Marketing

The **Fashion Institute of Design and Marketing Museum and Galleries** (FIDM, 919 S. Grand Ave., Ste. 250, 213/623-5821, http://fidmmuseum.org, 10am-5pm Tues.-Sat., free) are open to the public, giving costume buffs and clotheshorses a window into high fashion and Hollywood costume design. FIDM pulls from its collection of more than 10,000 costumes and textiles to create exhibits based on style, era, movie genre, and whatever else the curators dream up. Parking is available in the underground garage for a fee. When you enter the building, tell the folks at the security desk that you're headed for the museum. A small but fun museum

# Watts Towers

The quirky Watts Towers tower over the surrounding neighborhood.

With almost 100-foot-tall steel towers decorated with bottles, pottery, seashells, and tile, the **Watts Towers** (1727 E. 107th St., 213/847-4646, www.wattstowers. us, tours 11am-3pm Thurs.-Fri., 10:30am-3pm Sat., noon-3pm Sun., $7 adults, $3 seniors and children 13-17, children under 13 free) is outsider art on a grand scale. Italian immigrant Simon Rodia spent 33 years building the impressive landscape of spires, walls, birdbaths, and a gazebo without help. The whole structure is meant to resemble a ship stuffed with Rodia's memories. An informative half-hour guided tour is available. Because it's just feet from I-105 and minutes from I-405, a tour of Watts Towers makes a nice break from Los Angeles' crowded freeways.

shop offers student work, unique accessories, and more.

### Natural History Museum of Los Angeles County

If you'd like your kids to have some fun with an educational purpose, take them to the **Natural History Museum of Los Angeles County** (900 Exposition Blvd., 213/763-3466, www.nhm.org, 9:30am-5pm daily, $12 adults, $9 students and seniors, $5 children, parking $10 cash only). This huge museum features many amazing galleries; some are transformed into examples of mammal habitats, while others display artifacts of various peoples indigenous to the Western Hemisphere. The Discovery Center welcomes children with a wide array of live animals and insects, plus hands-on displays that let kids learn by touching as well as looking. Admission to the Butterfly Pavilion and special exhibits costs extra.

### ★ California Science Center

The **California Science Center** (700 Exposition Park Dr., 323/724-3623, www.californiasciencecenter.org, 10am-5pm daily, admission free, parking $10) focuses on the notable achievements and gathered knowledge of humankind. There are many interactive exhibits here, including one that lets visitors "lift" a giant truck off the ground. The Ecosystems section showcases 11 different natural environments, such as a living kelp forest and a polar ice wall.

One major reason people come to the California Science Center is to view the last of NASA's space shuttles, the

*Endeavour.* The 132-foot-long shuttle hangs on display in a pavilion and eventually will be shown in its launch position. To see the shuttle exhibit, reserve a timed entry by calling (213/744-2019) or going online (www.californiasciencecenter.org).

Many people also come to the California Science Center for the **IMAX theater** (213/744-2019; $8.50 adults, $6.25 seniors, teens, and students, $5.25 children), which shows educational films on its tremendous seven-story screen. Your IMAX ticket also gets you onto the rideable attractions of the Science Court.

## Los Feliz and Silver Lake

East of Hollywood and northwest of downtown, Los Feliz ("loss FEEL-is") is home to an eclectic mix of retired professionals, Armenian immigrants, and movie-industry hipsters lured by the bohemian vibe, midcentury modern architecture, and the neighborhood's proximity to Griffith Park.

## ★ Griffith Park

**Griffith Park** (Los Feliz Blvd., Zoo Dr., or Griffith Park Blvd., 323/913-4688, www.laparks.org, 5am-10:30pm daily, free) is the country's largest municipal park with an urban wilderness area. Griffith Park has also played host to many production companies over the years, with its land and buildings providing backdrops for many major films. Scenes from *Rebel Without a Cause* were filmed here, as were parts of the first two *Back to the Future* movies.

If you love the night skies, visit the **Griffith Observatory** (2800 E. Observatory Rd., 213/473-0800, www.griffithobservatory.org, noon-10pm Tues.-Fri., 10am-10pm Sat.-Sun., free), where free telescopes are available and experienced demonstrators help visitors gaze at the stars. Or take in a film about the earth or sky in the aluminum-domed **Samuel Oschin Planetarium** (www.griffithobservatory.org for showtimes, $3-7).

Griffith Observatory

If you prefer a more structured park experience, try the **L.A. Zoo and Botanical Gardens** (5333 Zoo Dr., 323/644-4200, www.lazoo.org, 10am-5pm daily, $20 adults, $17 seniors, $15 children, parking free), where you can view elephants, rhinos, and gorillas. If the weather is poor, step inside **The Autry National Center of the American West** (4700 Western Heritage Way, 323/667-2000, www.theautry.org, 10am-4pm Tues.-Fri., 10am-5pm Sat.-Sun., $14 adults, $10 students and seniors, $6 children), which showcases artifacts of the American West.

Kids love riding the trains of the operating miniature railroad at both the **Travel Town Railroad** (5200 Zoo Dr., 323/662-9678, www.griffithparktrainrides.com, 10am-3:15pm Mon.-Fri., 10am-4:45pm Sat.-Sun. summer, 10am-3:15pm Mon.-Fri., 10am-4:15pm Sat.-Sun. winter, $2.75), which runs the perimeter of the **Travel Town Museum** (5200 Zoo Dr., 323/662-5874, www.traveltown.org, 10am-5pm Mon.-Fri.,

10am-6pm Sat.-Sun. summer, 10am-4pm Mon.-Fri., 10am-6pm Sat.-Sun. winter, free), and the **Griffith Park & Southern Railroad** (4730 Crystal Springs Rd., www.griffithparktrainrides.com, 10am-4:45pm Mon.-Fri., 10am-5pm Sat.-Sun. summer, 10am-4:15pm Mon.-Fri., 10am-4:30pm Sat.-Sun. winter, $2.75 adults and children, $2.25 seniors), which takes riders on a one-mile track.

The **Hollywood Sign** sits on Mount Lee, which is part of the park and indelibly part of the mystique of Hollywood. A strenuous five-mile hike will lead you to an overlook just above and behind the sign. To get there, drive to the top of Beachwood Drive, park, and follow the **Hollyridge Trail.**

## Hollywood

You won't find blocks of movie studios in Hollywood, and few stars walk its streets except on premiere evenings. But still, if you've ever had a soft spot for Hollywood glamour or American camp, come and check out the crowds and bustle of downtown Tinseltown (and be aware that no local would *ever* call it that). Hollywood is also famous for its street corners. While the most stuff sits at Hollywood and Highland, the best-known corner is certainly Hollywood and Vine.

### ★ Hollywood Walk of Fame

One of the most recognizable facets of Hollywood is its star-studded **Walk of Fame** (Hollywood Blvd. from La Brea Ave. to Vine St., www.walkoffame.com). This area, portrayed in countless movies, contains more than 2,500 five-pointed stars honoring both real people and fictional characters that have contributed significantly to the entertainment industry and the Hollywood legend. Each pink star is set in a charcoal-colored square and has its honoree's name in bronze. Eight stars were laid in August 1958 to demonstrate what the walk would look like. Legal battles delayed the actual construction until February 1960, and the

# Hollywood

walk was dedicated in November 1960. At each of the four corners of Hollywood and Vine is a moon that honors the three Apollo 11 astronauts: Neil Armstrong, Michael Collins, and Edwin E. "Buzz" Aldrin Jr. At the edges of the Walk of Fame, you'll find blank stars waiting to be filled by up-and-comers making their mark on Tinseltown.

The complete walk is about 3.5 miles. You'll be looking down at the stars, so watch out for other pedestrians crowding the sidewalks in this visitor-dense area. Careful reading of the information on the Walk of Fame website (www.walkoffame. com) should help you find every star you need to see.

### Hollywood Wax Museum

It immortalizes your favorite stars, all right. If you want to see the Hollywood heavyweights all dressed up in costume and completely unable to run away, visit the **Hollywood Wax Museum** (6767 Hollywood Blvd., 323/462-5991, www. hollywoodwaxmuseum.com, 9am-midnight Sun.-Thurs., 9am-1am Fri.-Sat., $23 adults, $13 children 4-11, children under 4 free). The exhibits are re-creations of the sets of all sorts of films, and as you pass through, you'll be right in the action (if staring at eerie, life-size wax likenesses of real people can be called action). You can even get a glimpse of stars on the red carpet at an awards show-style set. Save a dollar by purchasing a ticket online.

### TCL Chinese Theatre

You can't miss the **TCL Chinese Theatre** (6925 Hollywood Blvd., 323/461-3331, www.tclchinesetheatres.com) on Hollywood Boulevard. With its elaborate 90-foot-tall Chinese temple gateway and unending crowd of visitors, the Chinese Theatre may be the most visited and recognizable movie theater in the world. Along with the throngs of tourists out front, there are usually elaborately costumed movie characters, from Captain Jack Sparrow to Spider-Man,

shaking hands with fans and posing for pictures (for a fee). Inside the courtyard, you'll find handprints and footprints of legendary Hollywood stars. Stop and admire the bells, dogs, and other artifacts in the courtyard; most are the genuine article, imported from China by special permit in the 1920s.

The studios hold premieres here all the time. Check the website for showtimes and ticket information. The Chinese Theatre has only one screen, but seats over 1,000 people per showing. Daily 20-minute tours (323/463-9576 or tours@ chinesetheatres.com for tickets, $18 adults, $14 seniors, $6 children) featuring anecdotes about the fabled theater are available with a reservation. While you're welcome to crowd the sidewalk to try to catch a glimpse of the stars at a premiere, most of these are private events.

### Egyptian Theater

Built under the auspices of the legendary Sid Grauman, the **Egyptian Theater** (6712 Hollywood Blvd., 323/466-3456, www. americancinemathequecalendar.com, $12 adults, $10 students and seniors) was the first of the grandiose movie houses in Hollywood proper and a follower of those in downtown Los Angeles. King Tut's tomb had been discovered in 1922, and the glorified Egyptian styling of the theater followed the trend for all things Egyptian that came after. The massive courtyard and the stage both boast columns and sphinxes. The first movie to premiere here was *Robin Hood*, in 1922.

Today, get tickets to an array of old-time films, film festivals, and double features, or take a morning tour to get a glimpse of the history of this magnificent theater. Expect to pay $5-20 for parking in one of the nearby lots.

### Hollywood Forever Cemetery

The final resting place of such Hollywood legends as Rudolph Valentino, Marion Davies, Douglas Fairbanks, and Johnny Ramone, the **Hollywood Forever**

# Film Festivals

Home of Hollywood and many of the world's most famous movie stars, Los Angeles is an ideal place to go to the movies. It's even better when you can attend a film festival.

There seems to be an endless array of film festivals in the Los Angeles area. Co-founded by actor Danny Glover, the **Pan African Film and Arts Festival** (310/337-4737, www.paff.org) takes place in February and highlights the works of people of African descent from all over the world.

Movies often debut at the **Los Angeles Film Festival** (866/345-6337, www.filmindependent.org). The LAFF happens in June and includes the screening of 100 films.

**Outfest** (213/480-7088, www.outfest. org) is the oldest continuous film festival in Los Angeles, and it highlights LBGT-oriented movies in July.

The **Downtown Film Festival L.A.** (www.dtffla.com), which also happens in July, is for filmgoers who enjoy under-the-radar indie cinema.

The **Sundance Next Fest** (www.sundance.org/next) is a worthy addition to the L.A. film scene. This unique summer fest in August includes movie premieres and concerts by musical acts.

The nonprofit American Film Institute plays some of the biggest pictures of the year at its November **AFI Fest** (866/234-3378, www.afi.com). Come to see what are sure to be some of the year's most talked-about movies.

**Cemetery** (6000 Santa Monica Blvd., 323/469-1181, www.hollywoodforever. com, 8:30am-5:30pm daily summer, 8:30am-5pm daily winter) has received a dramatic makeover and now offers live funeral webcasts. During the summer, the cemetery screens films and holds concerts by national touring acts on its Fairbanks Lawn and in its Masonic Lodge. Visit the website for a list of upcoming events.

## Paramount Studios

**Paramount Studios** (5515 Melrose Ave., 323/956-1777, www.paramountstudiotour.com, tours $58-178) is the only major movie studio still operating in Hollywood proper. The wrought-iron gates that greet visitors were erected to deter adoring Rudolph Valentino fans in the 1920s. Tours ranging 2-4.5 hours are available. Visit the website or call the studio for tour information.

## Mulholland Drive

As you drive north out of central Hollywood into the residential part of the neighborhood, you will find folks on street corners hawking maps of stars'

homes on **Mulholland Drive** (entrance west of U.S. 101 via Barham Blvd. exit) and its surrounding neighborhoods. Whether you choose to pay up to $10 for a photocopied sheet of dubious information is up to you. What's certain is that you can drive the famed road yourself. When you reach the ridge, you'll see why so many of the wealthy make their homes here. From the ridgeline, on clear days you can see down into the Los Angeles Basin and the coast to the west, and the fertile land of the San Fernando Valley to the east. Whether you care about movie-star homes or not, the view itself is worth the trip, especially if it has rained recently and the smog is down.

## Universal Studios Hollywood

The longtime Hollywood-centric alternative to Disneyland is the **Universal Studios Hollywood** (100 Universal City Plaza, Los Angeles, 800/864-8377, www. universalstudios.com, hours vary, $105-116) theme park. (Save up to $10 by getting tickets online.) Kids adore this park, which puts them right into the action of their favorite movies. Flee the carnivorous dinosaurs of *Jurassic Park*, take a rafting adventure on the pseudo-set of *Waterworld*, quiver in terror of an ancient curse in *Revenge of the Mummy*, or explore the magic of Hogwarts Castle in the *Wizarding World of Harry Potter*. You can also experience the shape-shifting Transformers in a ride based on the movies and the Hasbro toy.

If you're more interested in how the movies are made than the rides made from them, take the Studio Tour with a recorded Jimmy Fallon as host. You'll get an extreme close-up of the sets of major blockbuster films like *War of the Worlds*. Better yet, get tickets at the Audiences Unlimited Ticket Booth and be part of the studio audience of TV shows currently taping. Serious movie buffs can get a VIP pass for $329; a six-hour tour takes you onto working sound stages and into the current prop warehouse.

## La Brea, Fairfax, and Miracle Mile

Lined with fabric emporiums, antiques dealers, and contemporary furniture design shops, Beverly Boulevard and La Brea Avenue north of Wilshire Boulevard are increasingly trendy haunts for interior decorators. Along bustling and pedestrian-friendly Fairfax Avenue, kosher bakeries and signs in Hebrew announce the presence of the neighborhood's sizable Jewish population. Around the corner on 3rd Street, The Original Farmers Market is one of L.A.'s historic gathering places. And farther south, Wilshire Boulevard is home to some of the city's many museums, including the Los Angeles County Museum of Art.

### La Brea Tar Pits

Nothing can stop the smell of the **La Brea Tar Pits,** where untold thousands of animals became trapped in the sticky tar and met their ancient fate. Paved paths lead around the most accessible pits, while others (mostly those that are in active excavation) are accessible by guided tour only. If what interests you most are the fossilized contents, head for the beautiful **La Brea Tar Pits Museum** (5801 Wilshire Blvd., 213/763-3499, www.tar-pits.org, 9:30am-5pm daily, $12 adults, $9 students and seniors, $5 children, parking $10). The museum's reasonably small size and easy-to-understand interpretive signs make it great for kids. Genuine mammoths died and were fossilized in the tar pits, as were the tiniest of mice and about a zillion dire wolves. For a closer look at how the fossils were buried, get tickets to one of the **Excavator Tours** (noon, 1pm, 2pm, and 3pm daily, free with museum ticket), which are available online.

### Los Angeles County Museum of Art

Travelers who desperately need a break from the endless, shiny, and mindless entertainments of L.A. can find respite and solace in the **Los Angeles County Museum of Art** (5905 Wilshire Blvd., 323/857-6000, www.lacma.org, 11am-5pm Mon.-Tues. and Thurs., 11am-8pm Fri., 10am-7pm Sat.-Sun., $15 adults, $10 seniors and students with ID, children under 17 free), the largest art museum in the western United States. Better known to its friends as LACMA, this museum complex prides itself on a diverse array of collections and exhibitions of art from around the world, from ancient to modern. With nine full-size buildings filled with galleries, don't expect to get through the whole thing in an hour, or even a full day. You'll see all forms of art, from classic painting and sculpture to all sorts of decorative arts (that is, ceramics, jewelry, metalwork, and more). All major cultural groups are represented, so you can check out Islamic, Southeast Asian, European, and Californian art, plus more. Specialties of LACMA include Japanese art and artifacts in the beautifully designed Pavilion for Japanese Art, and the costumes and textiles of the Doris Stein Research Center. Several galleries of LACMA West are dedicated to arts and crafts for children. Perhaps best of all, some of the world's most prestigious traveling exhibitions come to LACMA.

The 120,000 objects at LACMA include pieces by Andy Warhol, David Hockney, and Roy Lichtenstein. Head outdoors for Chris Burden's *Urban Light*, a forest of street lamps, and Michael Heizer's *Levitated Mass*, a giant boulder displayed above a sunken walkway. Moving the rock to its current home was such a feat that it is documented in the 2013 film *Levitated Mass*.

### Farmers Market

Begun in 1934 as a tailgate co-op for a handful of fruit farmers, **The Original Farmers Market** (6333 W. 3rd St., 323/933-9211 or 866/993-9211, www. farmersmarketla.com, 9am-9pm Mon.-Fri., 9am-8pm Sat., 10am-7pm Sun.) remains a favorite locale for shopping and people-watching. Along with the adjacent shopping center, The Grove, there are now more than 30 restaurants and 50 shops hawking everything from hot sauce to stickers. Annual events include free summer concerts every Friday.

## Beverly Hills and West Hollywood

Although the truly wealthy live above Hollywood on Mulholland Drive, in Bel Air, or on the beach in Malibu, there's still plenty of money floating around Beverly Hills. Some of the world's best and most expensive shops line its streets. You'll also find plenty of high-end culture in this area, which bleeds into West L.A.

### Sunset Strip

The **Sunset Strip** really is part of Sunset Boulevard—specifically the part that runs 1.5 miles through West Hollywood from the edge of Hollywood to the Beverly Hills city limits. The Strip exemplifies all that's grandiose and tacky about the L.A. entertainment industry. You'll also find many of the Strip's

La Brea Tar Pits

legendary rock clubs, such as **The Roxy** and the **Whisky a Go Go** and the infamous after-hours hangout the **Rainbow Bar & Grill.** Over several decades, up-and-coming rock acts first made their names on the Strip and lived at the "Riot Hyatt."

## Westwood

Designed around the campus of UCLA and the Westwood Village commercial district, this community situated between Santa Monica and Beverly Hills won national recognition in the 1930s as a model of innovative suburban planning.

### University of California, Los Angeles

From its original quad of 10 buildings, the campus of the **University of California, Los Angeles** (UCLA, bounded by Hilgard Ave., Sunset Blvd., Le Conte Ave., and Gayley Ave., tours available at https://connect.admission.ucla.edu/portal/tours, www.ucla.edu) has become the largest in the University of California

system, with more than 400 buildings set on and around 419 beautifully kept acres. Today its facilities include one of the top medical centers in the country, a library of more than eight million volumes, and renowned performance venues, including **Royce Hall** and **Schoenberg Hall.**

### ★ The Getty Center

Located on a hilltop above the mansions of Brentwood and the 405 freeway, **The Getty Center** (1200 Sepulveda Blvd., 310/440-7300, www.getty.edu, 10am-5:30pm Sun. and Tues.-Thurs., 10am-9pm Fri.-Sat. summer, 10am-5:30pm Sun. and Tues.-Fri., 10am-9pm Sat. winter, admission free, parking $15) is famous for art and culture in Los Angeles. Donated by the family of J. Paul Getty to the people of Los Angeles, this museum features European art, sculpture, manuscripts, and European and American photos. The magnificent works are set in fabulous modern buildings with soaring architecture, and you're guaranteed to find something beautiful to catch your eye and feed your imagination. The spacious galleries have comfy sofas to let you sit back and take in the paintings and drawings. There are frequent temporary exhibitions on diverse subjects. Take a stroll outdoors to admire the sculpture collections on the lawns as well as the exterior architecture.

On a clear day, the views from The Getty, which sweep from downtown L.A. clear west to the Pacific, are remarkable. But the museum pavilions themselves are also stunning. Richard Meier's striking design is multi-textured, with exterior grids of metal and unfinished Italian travertine marble. The blockish buildings have fountains, glass windows several stories high, and an open plan that permits intimate vistas of the city below. A stroll through the gardens is a must.

### Pierce Brothers Westwood Village Memorial Park

The **Pierce Brothers Westwood Village Memorial Park** (1218 Glendon Ave.,

310/474-1579, www.dignitymemorial. com, 8am-6pm daily) is the final resting place of some of the world's most popular entertainers and musicians. Under the shadows of the towering high-rises of Wilshire Boulevard, this small cemetery is the home of **Marilyn Monroe's crypt** (frequently decorated with lipstick marks), as well as Rat Packer **Dean Martin,** author **Truman Capote,** eclectic musician **Frank Zappa,** and the stars of *The Odd Couple,* **Walter Matthau** and **Jack Lemmon.**

## Santa Monica, Venice, and Malibu

Some of the most famous and most expensive real estate in the world sits on this stretch of sand and earth. Of the communities that call the northern coast of L.A. County home, the focal points are Malibu to the north, Santa Monica, and Venice to the south.

### ★ Santa Monica Pier

For the ultimate in SoCal beach kitsch, you can't miss the **Santa Monica Pier** (Ocean Ave. at Colorado Ave., 310/458-8901, www.santamonicapier.org, hours vary). As you walk the rather long stretch of concrete out over the water, you'll see an amazing array of carnival-style food stands, an arcade, a small amusement park, a trapeze school, and restaurants leading out to the fishing area at the tip of the pier. There's even an aquarium under the pier. The main attraction is **Pacific Park** (310/260-8744, www.pacpark.com, hours vary, $5-10 per ride, all-ride pass $16-30, parking $6-15). This park features a roller coaster, a Scrambler, and the world's first solar-powered Ferris wheel. Several rides are geared for the younger set, and a 20-game midway offers fun for all ages. Free **historic walking**

**From top to bottom:** The Sunset Strip's Rainbow Bar & Grill; The Getty Center's cactus garden; unique architecture in Venice Beach.

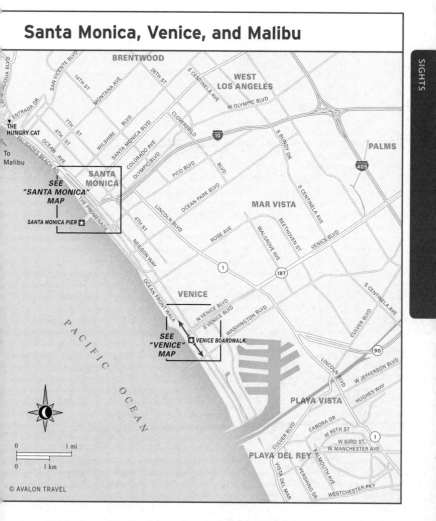

# Santa Monica, Venice, and Malibu

BRENTWOOD

WEST
LOS ANGELES

PALMS

THE
HUNGRY CAT

To
Malibu

SANTA
MONICA

SEE
"SANTA MONICA"
MAP

SANTA MONICA PIER ★

THE PROMENADE

MAR VISTA

VENICE

SEE
"VENICE"
MAP

VENICE BOARDWALK

PACIFIC OCEAN

PLAYA VISTA

PLAYA DEL REY

0        1 mi

0        1 km

© AVALON TRAVEL

tours (11am-noon Sat.-Sun.) leave from the Pier Shop.

## ★ Venice Boardwalk

If the Santa Monica Pier doesn't provide you with enough chaos and kitsch, head on down to the **Venice Boardwalk** (Ocean Front Walk at Venice Blvd., 310/396-6764, www.venicebeach.com) for a nearly unlimited supply of both year-round. As you shamble down the tourist-laden path, you'll pass an astonishing array of tacky souvenir stores, tattoo and piercing parlors, walk-up food stands, and more. On the beach side of the path, dozens of artists create sculptures and hawk their wares. This area has more than its share of L.A.'s colorful characters, including some who perform for tips. The beach side includes the famous **Muscle Beach** (2 blocks north of Venice Blvd., www.musclebeach.net), an easily distinguishable chunk of sand filled with modern workout equipment and encircled by a

# Santa Monica

© AVALON TRAVEL

barrier, and the **Venice Skate Park** (1500 Ocean Front Walk, 310/650-3255, www. veniceskatepark.com), where skaters get some serious air.

## Venice Canals

Take a sedate walk along the paths of the **Venice Canals** (bounded by Washington Blvd., Strongs Dr., S. Venice Blvd., and Ocean Ave.), where locals take a stroll or walk their dogs (Venice is a very dog-oriented town), and enjoy the serenity and

peace of the quiet waterways. The home gardens and city-maintained landscaping add a lush layer of greenery to the narrow canals. These paths get you deep into the neighborhood and close to the impressive 20th-century Southern California architecture of Venice.

## Malibu Pier

One of Malibu's few sights besides the sand and surf, the **Malibu Pier** (23000 Pacific Coast Hwy., http://malibupier.

# Venice

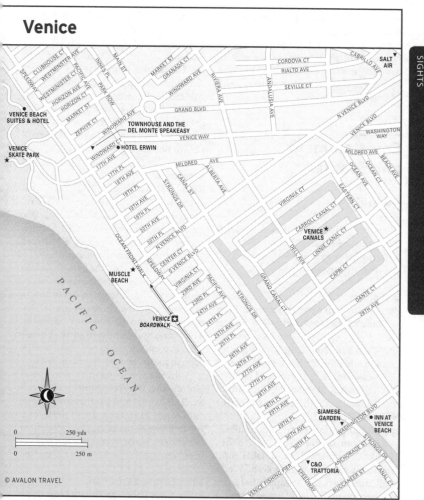

© AVALON TRAVEL

com, 6:30am-sunset daily) gets busy in the summer and lonely in the winter, when only die-hard surfers ply the adjacent three-point break and a few anglers brave the chilly solitude. Interpretive signs describe the history of Malibu amid the food stands and sport-fishing and whale-watching charters. A surf museum is planned in the near future. If you'd prefer to hit the waves yourself, you can rent boards and other beach toys.

## The Getty Villa

Even driving up to **The Getty Villa** (17985 Pacific Coast Hwy., Pacific Palisades, 310/440-7300, www.getty.edu, 10am-5pm Sun.-Mon. and Wed.-Fri., 10am-9pm Sat. summer, 10am-5pm Wed.-Mon. winter, reservations required, admission free, parking $15) on its Roman-inspired stone driveway will send your mind back to ancient times. The two-floor villa is modeled after a Roman country house that was buried by the AD 79 eruption of Mount Vesuvius. The architecture and surrounding gardens are a fitting environment for the 1,200 works of art inside, including intact statues and jewelry from the ancient Greeks, Romans, and Etruscans. Tickets are free, but require advance reservations.

# Entertainment and Events

## Nightlife

### Bars

Whatever your taste in bars, whether it tends toward hipster dives, old-school watering holes, or beautiful lounges, L.A. can offer its version.

### Downtown

For a money dive bar experience, head to **Crane's Downtown Bar** (810 S. Spring St., 323/787-7966, 5pm-2am Mon.-Thurs., 4pm-2am Fri., 2pm-2am Sat.-Sun.), located inside a former bank vault. There's the occasional DJ spinning and comedy on the second Monday of the month. Next door inside the basement of the NCT Building is the Peking Tavern, if you get hungry for creative dumplings.

At **Seven Grand** (512 W. 7th St., 213/614-0736, http://213hospitality.com/sevengrandla/, 4pm-2am Sun.-Wed., 3pm-2am Thurs.-Sat.), dapper bartenders steer you to the right fermented grain mash—commonly referred to as whiskey. Enjoy it while playing pool, watching live music, or sitting under deer heads mounted on the walls. Deep inside Seven Grand, the exclusive 18-seat **Bar Jackalope** (7pm-2am Sun.-Thurs.) zeroes in on Japanese whiskies.

Under a sign touting breakfast foods, the unassuming **Ham & Eggs Tavern** (433 W. 8th St., http://hamandeggstavern.com, 5pm-midnight Mon.-Thurs., 5pm-2am Fri.-Sat.) serves can beers and wine in one room and hosts music acts next door.

The tiny stage has hosted larger-than-expected acts including Nick Waterhouse, The Gooch Palms, and Avi Buffalo.

It may not be as hip as it once was, but **The Golden Gopher** (417 W. 8th St., 213/614-8001, http://213hospitality.com/goldengopher, 5pm-2am daily) jumpstarted downtown nightlife. It's still a great place to enjoy a drink, with a smoking patio and a liquor store on the premises for bottles to go.

### Koreatown

**R Bar** (3331 W. 8th St., 213/387-7227, 7pm-2am Mon.-Tues., 5pm-2am Wed.-Fri., 11am-2am Sat.-Sun.) doesn't look like much from the outside except a dingy corner building with a gold "R" affixed to it. But inside this speakeasy (the password can be found on the bar's Facebook page or on their Twitter page) oozes debauched gothic Victorian decor and a range of events including live music, DJs, storytellers, and karaoke on Wednesday, Thursday, and Sunday nights. There's good beer on tap, cocktails, and a weekly brunch touted by *L.A. Weekly* as well.

A hidden bar within the Hotel Normandie, **The Walker Inn** (3612 W. 6th St., 213/263-2709, www.thewalkerinnla.com, 6pm-2am Tues.-Sun.) delivers a cocktail tasting menu curated by talented bartenders. Make an advance reservation to ensure you will be one of just 27 guests.

### Silver Lake and Echo Park

In hip Silver Lake, **The Thirsty Crow** (2939 W. Sunset Blvd., 323/661-6007, www.thirstycrowbar.com, 5pm-2am Mon.-Sat., 2pm-2am Sun.) is a neighborhood bar with 100 different kinds of whiskey, including over 60 small-batch bourbons and a friendly happy hour (5pm-8pm Mon.-Fri., 2pm-8pm Sat.-Sun.).

Echo Park's beer lovers flock to the **Sunset Beer Company** (1498 W. Sunset Blvd., 213/481-2337, www.sunsetbeercompany.com, store hours noon-11pm Mon.-Thurs., noon-midnight Fri.-Sat., noon-10pm Sun.; bar hours 4pm-11pm

Mon.-Thurs., 1pm-midnight Fri.-Sat., 1pm-10pm Sun.), an intimate space well-stocked with the latest craft brews from California and beyond. Sip your suds inside over board games or books or outside on a smoker's patio.

### Beverly Hills and West Hollywood

Hit the **Rainbow Bar & Grill** (9015 W. Sunset Blvd., 310/278-4232, www.rainbowbarandgrill.com, 11am-2am daily, cover charge varies) to see an amazing myriad of rock-and-roll memorabilia and get a taste of music history. A group of musicians known as the "Hollywood Vampires," which included Alice Cooper, Keith Moon, John Lennon, Ringo Starr, Harry Nilsson, and Micky Dolenz, congregated here in the 1970s. Today, rockers still drop in after playing shows in the neighborhood. The crowds trickle in as the sun goes down; by the time the shows let out at the nearby Roxy and Whisky a Go Go, your chances of finding a booth diminish significantly. The back rooms also open up late, for dancing, drinking, and smoking (*sh!*). To the surprise of some diners, the hallowed haven also serves a tasty cheeseburger, available until 2am.

They say that Courtney Love used to dance at **Jumbo's Clown Room** (5153 Hollywood Blvd., 323/666-1187, http://jumbos.com, 4pm-2am daily), a one-of-a-kind dive bar with a blood-red interior and a circus theme. They also say David Lynch was inspired to write a section of his film *Blue Velvet* after a visit here.

Located in the Sunset Tower Hotel, **The Tower Bar** (8358 Sunset Blvd., 323/654-7100, www.sunsettowerhotel.com, 6pm-11pm Sun.-Thurs., 6pm-11:30pm Fri.-Sat.) offers a glimpse of old Hollywood. Mobster Bugsy Siegel once had an apartment here. Today, it has walnut-paneled walls, a fireplace, and dim lighting so that celebrities can keep their cool.

Across from the Chateau Marmont, **The Den on Sunset** (8226 W. Sunset Blvd., 323/656-0336, www.thedenonsunset.com, 5pm-2am Mon.-Fri., 3pm-2am Sat., 10am-2am Sun.) has an outside fire pit, while inside there is a collection of board games including Rock 'Em, Sock 'Em Robots. Some nights have DJs and karaoke.

### Santa Monica, Venice, and Malibu

In Venice beach, head to the **Townhouse and the Del Monte Speakeasy** (52 Windward Ave., Venice Beach, 310/392-4040, www.townhousevenice.com, 5pm-2am Mon.-Thurs., 2pm-2am Fri., noon-2am Sat.-Sun.). Upstairs, enjoy the candlelit tables and pool table of the oldest bar in Venice. Downstairs, the speakeasy is a cellar space that hosts jazz bands, DJs, and comedians.

**Casa del Mar Lobby Lounge** (1910 Ocean Way, Santa Monica, 310/581-5533, www.hotelcasadelmar.com, 3pm-midnight Sun.-Thurs., 3pm-1:30am Fri.-Sat.) is a dramatic real-life sandcastle on Santa Monica State Beach. Enjoy beautiful ocean views, glittering mosaics, marble floors, romantic piano music, and perhaps the most elegant cocktails in the city.

Also in Santa Monica, **Ye Olde King's Head** (116 Santa Monica Blvd., Santa Monica, 310/451-1402, www.yeoldekingshead.com, 10am-2am daily) is a British pub, restaurant, and gift shop that stretches down a long half block. Crowds of imbibing patrons visit from far and near.

### Clubs

Which of the many dance and nightclubs in the L.A. area is the hottest, hippest, or most popular with the stars this week? Ask the locals or check the alternative weekly papers when you arrive. Clubs get crowded on weekend nights, and bouncers take joy in allowing only the chicest hipsters into the sacred spaces beyond the doors. Being young and beautiful helps, of course, as does being dressed in the latest designer fashions.

For those in the know, **Karma Lounge** (3954 Beverly Blvd., 213/375-7141, http://karmaloungela.com, 5pm-1am Tues.-Thurs., 5pm-2am Fri.-Sat., 10am-9pm Sun.) in Koreatown is a worthy stop for drinks or dancing. Burlesque shows alternate with frequent DJs who spin everything from industrial to Latin. They also serve small plates if you need some fuel.

Dance to world-famous DJs under pulsating lights, falling confetti, or floating bubbles at **Create** (6021 Hollywood Blvd., 323/463-3331, http://sbe.com, 10pm-close Fri.-Sat.). You may catch Kaskade or Afrojack on the turntables at this weekend-only dance club.

The **Three Clubs Cocktail Lounge** (1123 Vine St., Hollywood, 323/462-6441, www.threeclubs.com, 5pm-2am daily, no cover) acts both as a locals' watering hole and a reasonably priced nightclub catering mostly to the collegiate set. Expect to find the dance floor of the rear club crowded and sweaty, with modern dance mixes blaring out over the crush of writhing bodies. Two bars serve up drinks to the masses, and drinks are cheaper here than in the hotter spots. Three Clubs has no decent parking, so you may have to walk several blocks along Hollywood Boulevard long after dark. Bring friends along for safety.

### Gay and Lesbian

Sleek, glamorous, and candlelit, **The Abbey Food and Bar** (692 N. Robertson Blvd., West Hollywood, 310/289-8410, www.theabbeyweho.com, 11am-2am Mon.-Thurs., 10am-2am Fri., 9am-2am Sat.-Sun.) is a popular bar with a great outdoor patio and pillow-strewn private cabanas, all of which are usually jam-packed. Savvy bartenders mix 22 different specialty martinis in flavors that include chocolate banana and Creamsicle.

Every Thursday night, **Avalon Hollywood** (1735 Vine St., Hollywood, 323/462-8900, http://avalonhollywood.com, 10pm-3am Thurs., 9:30pm-5am Fri., 9:30pm-8am Sat.) hosts **TigerHeat,** which is said to be the West Coast's largest gay event. Lady GaGa, Britney Spears, and Elton John have made appearances in the club.

An alternative to glammed-up West Hollywood bars, Silver Lake's **Akbar** (4356 Sunset Blvd., 323/665-6810, www.akbarsilverlake.com, 4pm-2am daily) pulls in a gay-friendly crowd with its cozy Moroccan-themed decor, neighborhood vibe, and friendly, unpretentious bartenders.

### Live Music

The clubs on the Sunset Strip incubated some of the biggest rock acts of all time. The **Whisky a Go Go** (8901 Sunset Blvd., West Hollywood, 310/652-4202, www.whiskyagogo.com, cover from $10) helped launch The Doors, Mötley Crüe, and Guns N' Roses. Truth be told, it doesn't draw many big names anymore, even though go-go dancers still gyrate on either side of the stage at times. Most nights you'll get a lineup of new bands, sometimes including as many as seven on Tuesday's "Ultimate Jam Night."

Almost next door, **The Roxy Theatre** (9009 Sunset Blvd., West Hollywood, 310/278-9457, www.theroxy.com, cover charge varies) opened in 1973 with a Neil Young performance. Bob Marley, Patti Smith, and Bruce Springsteen have all recorded live albums here since then. Today, it's still relevant, with acts like J. Roddy Walston and The Business. The big black-box theater has an open dance floor, comfy-ish booths (if you can get one), and bare-bones food service. Street parking is nearly nonexistent, and nearby lots will cost $5-15 or more, so think about public transit or a cab. For one of the best after-hours parties on the Strip, try to get into **On the Rox,** located directly above The Roxy. Or stagger next door to the **Rainbow Bar & Grill** (9015 Sunset Blvd., West Hollywood, 310/278-4232, www.rainbowbarandgrill.com, 11am-2am daily).

It's not on the Strip, but **The Troubadour** (9081 Santa Monica Blvd., West Hollywood, 310/276-1158, www.troubadour.com, ticket prices vary) is just as big and bad as its brethren. Over its more than 50 years, Bob Dylan jammed here, Tom Waits was discovered, and Billy Joel opened for somebody else. Countless A-listers have recorded songs in and even about The Troubadour. Buy tickets online; tickets are available at the on-site box office only on the day of the show—unless it's sold out.

With less history under its belt, **The Echo and Echoplex** (1822 W. Sunset Blvd., Echo Park, 213/413-8200, www.spacelandpresents.com) hosts a lot of up-and-coming indie acts, along with the occasional big act (TV on the Radio) and some impressive coups, including a performance by the Rolling Stones in 2013.

**The Theatre at Ace Hotel** (929 Broadway, 213/623-3233, http://www.acehotel.com/losangeles/theatre) has already hosted big acts like Coldplay. The restored 1,600-seat movie theater from the 1920s features more than just rock shows, including lectures, film festivals, and dance productions.

Proclaimed the city's best music venue by the *L.A. Weekly*, **The Fonda Theatre** (6126 Hollywood Blvd., 323/464-6269, www.fondatheatre.com) can accommodate 1,200 people, which is pretty intimate if you're there for a concert by the Rolling Stones, Radiohead, or Lorde.

## Comedy

L.A.'s live comedy scene is second only to Manhattan's. More than a dozen major live comedy clubs make their home in the smog belt. Pick your favorite, sit back, and laugh (or groan) the night away.

Located on the Strip, **The Comedy Store** (8433 Sunset Blvd., West Hollywood, 323/650-6268, www.thecomedystore.com, age 21 and older, $15-20) is owned by comedian Pauly Shore's mother, Mitzi. You'll find a show going on at The Store every night of the week;

most start at 9pm or later; check the online calendar. In each of three rooms, you'll find a showcase with more than a dozen stand-ups all performing one after another, leaving space for possible celebrity drop-ins. Steve Martin, Whoopi Goldberg, and Yakov Smirnoff got their start here. Buy tickets online for bigger shows, or at the door for shows that don't sell out. Open mics are at 10pm on Sunday.

Will Ferrell, Kristen Wiig, Lisa Kudrow, and Will Forte are alumni of **The Groundlings Theatre and School** (7307 Melrose Ave., 323/934-4747, www.groundlings.com, prices vary). Get tickets to take in some sketch comedy by up-and-coming talents.

## The Arts
### Theater

Even with all the hoopla over film in L.A., there's still plenty of room for live theatrical entertainment in and around Tinseltown.

In addition to the Academy Awards, the **Dolby Theatre** (6801 Hollywood Blvd., 323/308-6300, www.dolbytheatre.com, box office 10am-5pm Mon.-Sat., 10am-4pm Sun.) hosts various live performances, from ballet to shows from music legends like Bob Dylan. Of course, all shows utilize the theater's state-of-the-art Dolby sound system. Half-hour **tours** (on the half hour 10:30am-4pm daily, $23 adults, $18 seniors and children) that include a view of an Oscar statuette are available daily.

The **Ford Theater** (2580 Cahuenga Blvd. E., 323/461-3673, www.fordamphitheater.org, box office noon-5pm Tues.-Sun. and 2 hours before evening performances, ticket prices vary) takes advantage of Hollywood's temperate climate to bring the shows outdoors in summer. Every sort of theatrical event imaginable can find a stage at the Ford, from jazz, folk, world music, hip-hop, and dance to spoken word.

The **Ahmanson Theater** (135 N.

Grand Ave., 213/628-2772, www.center-theatregroup.org, box office noon-6pm Tues.-Sun. and 2 hours before performances, ticket prices vary) specializes in big Broadway-style productions. You might see a grandiose musical, a heart-wrenching drama, or a gut-busting comedy. Expect to find the titles of classic shows alongside new hits on the schedule. With hundreds of seats (all of them expensive), there's usually enough room to provide entertainment, even for last-minute visitors.

The intimate **Kirk Douglas Theatre** (9820 Washington Blvd., Culver City, 213/628-2772, www.centertheatregroup.org) hosts world premieres and edgy productions like David Mamet's *Race*.

Well-known television actors, including Jason Alexander and Neil Patrick Harris, frequently act in the productions at the **Geffen Playhouse** (10886 Le Conte Ave., 310/208-5454, http://geffenplayhouse.org, ticket prices vary). Some shows developed here move on to Broadway.

## Classical Music
Although L.A. is better known for its rock than its classical music offerings, you can still find plenty of high-culture concerts as well. The **Los Angeles Opera** (135 N. Grand Ave., 213/972-8001, www.laopera.org, box office 10am-6pm Tues.-Sat., prices vary) has only existed since 1986 but has grown to become one of the largest opera companies in the United States, gaining national recognition. The dazzling performances are held in the Dorothy Chandler Pavilion at the Music Center of Los Angeles County. Grammy-winning singer Placido Domingo has been the opera's general director since 2003.

Better known to its friends as the L.A. Phil, the **Los Angeles Philharmonic** (111 S. Grand Ave., 323/850-2000 or 323/850-2000, www.laphil.com, prices vary) performs primarily at the **Walt Disney Concert Hall** (111 S. Grand Ave.).

Concerts can range from classics by famed composers like Tchaikovsky, Bach, and Beethoven to the world music of Asha Bhosle or jazz by Bobby McFerrin. Guest performers are often the modern virtuosos of classical music.

With its art deco band shell set against canyon chaparral, the **Hollywood Bowl** (2301 N. Highland Ave., 323/850-2000, www.hollywoodbowl.com, box office noon-6pm Tues.-Sun.) has long been a romantic setting for outdoor summer concerts by the L.A. Philharmonic and other artists. It also hosts some rock and pop acts.

The **Los Angeles Doctors Symphony Orchestra** (310/259-9604, http://ladso.org, prices vary) has been performing regularly since its inception in 1953. Many, though not all, of the musicians are members of the medical profession. They play everything from Mozart to Schubert.

## Cinema
Crowds throng the streets to see stars tromp down the red carpets for premieres at the **Chinese Theatre** (6925 Hollywood Blvd., 323/461-3331, www.tclchinesetheatres.com) and the **Egyptian Theater** (6712 Hollywood Blvd., 323/466-3456, www.americancinemathequecalendar.com, $12 adults, $10 students and seniors).

The current favorite movie house for star sightings is the **ArcLight Hollywood Cinema** (6360 W. Sunset Blvd., Hollywood, 323/464-1478, www.arclight-cinemas.com), where 21-and-older-only screenings allow patrons include beer and wine on sale. Expect the best visual and sound technologies, all-reserved seating, and the updated geodesic Cinerama Dome theater. Make reservations in advance and ask for parking validation for a discount at the adjacent parking structure.

For eclectic films and events beyond the multiplex, seek out **The Cinefamily at the Silent Movie Theatre** (611 N. Fairfax

Ave., 323/655-2510, www.cinefamily.org). Its 14 weekly screenings unearth eclectic, little-seen gems.

Acclaimed filmmaker and movie enthusiast Quentin Tarantino owns and programs the **New Beverly Cinema** (7165 Beverly Blvd., 323/938-4038, www.thenewbev.com). The slate of 35-millimeter films include spaghetti westerns, horror films, classics, and selections from the filmmaker's personal collection.

# Shopping

## Downtown and Vicinity

Lovers of the written word should not miss **The Last Bookstore** (453 S. Spring St., 213/488-0599, http://lastbookstorela.com, 10am-10pm Mon.-Thurs., 10am-11pm Fri.-Sat., 10am-9pm Sun.). The 22,000 square feet of new and used books include several art pieces and a tunnel made of books, as well as a space devoted to L.A. writers. A full slate of events includes concerts and author readings.

Anyone can come and stroll the narrow aisles of the world-famous **L.A. Flower District** (700 block of Wall St., 213/622-1966, www.laflowerdistrict.com, 8am-noon Mon. and Wed., 6am-noon Tues. and Thurs., 8am-2pm Fri., 6am-2pm Sat., admission $1-2), where just about every kind of cut flower, potted plant, and exotic species can be purchased. One caution: While the flower market itself is safe for visitors, the area to the south is not. Don't wander the neighborhood on foot.

A mix of modern art galleries and fun, touristy gift shops line the 900 block of **Chung King Road** (http://chungkingroad.wordpress.com/galleries), a one-block stretch of Chinatown. Interior decorators often browse the eclectic selection. It can be quiet during the day, but it comes alive during art-opening evenings.

Located in the Fashion District, **Santee Alley** (between Santee St. and Maple Ave. from Olympic Blvd. to 12th St., www.thesanteealley.com, 9:30am-6pm daily) is a bustling outdoor marketplace crammed in an alley. This is the place for deals on everything from dresses to bathing suits to suitcases to cellphone cases.

## Los Feliz and Silver Lake

Artsy, hip boutiques, cafés, and restaurants line **Sunset Junction** (Sunset Blvd. from Santa Monica Blvd. to Maltman Ave.), a colorful stretch of Sunset Boulevard concentrated around where Sunset meets Santa Monica Boulevard (or, rather, where Santa Monica Boulevard ends). Weekend mornings bring floods of neighborhood locals down from the hills. This strip is also home to the **Silver Lake Certified Farmers Market** (323/661-7771, 2pm-7:30pm Tues., 9am-1pm Sat.).

The fiercely independent **Skylight Books** (1818 N. Vermont Ave., 323/660-1175, www.skylightbooks.com, 10am-10pm daily) in Los Feliz features alternative literature, literary fiction, Los Angeles-themed books, and an extensive film section. It hosts frequent author events and sells signed books.

## Hollywood

The **Hollywood and Highland Center** (6801 Hollywood Blvd., 323/467-6412 or 323/817-0200, www.hollywoodandhighland.com, 10am-10pm Mon.-Sat., 10am-7pm Sun.) flaunts outlandish architecture that's modeled after the set of the 1916 film *Intolerance*. Stroll amid the more than 70 retail stores and 25 eateries that surround the open-air Babylon Court. Save yourself stress and park in the center's lot ($2 for up to 2 hours with validation).

Encompassing an entire city block and two floors, **Amoeba Music** (6400 Sunset Blvd., 323/245-6400, www.amoeba.com, 10:30am-11pm Mon.-Sat., 11am-10pm Sun.) is the world's largest independent music store. This is the place in L.A. to find that rare record or used CD.

## La Brea, Fairfax, and Miracle Mile

The stretch of charming and eclectic shops on **West 3rd Street** (between Fairfax Ave. and La Cienega Blvd.) encompasses one-of-a-kind clothing boutiques, home stores, and bath-and-body shops. At one end you'll find The Original Farmers Market and The Grove shopping center; at the other, the Beverly Center.

## Beverly Hills and West Hollywood

Big spenders browse the three-block stretch of luxury stores on **Rodeo Drive** (www.rodeodrive-bh.com) in Beverly Hills. Among the upscale retailers are **Chanel** (400 N. Rodeo Dr., 310/278-5500, www.chanel.com, 10am-6pm Mon.-Sat., noon-5pm Sun.), **Tiffany's** (210 N. Rodeo Dr., 310/273-8880, www.tiffany.com, 10am-7pm Mon.-Sat., 11am-5pm Sun.), and **Frette** (445 N. Rodeo Dr., 310/273-8540, www.frette.com, 10am-6pm Mon.-Sat., noon-5pm Sun.). The Rodeo Drive Walk of Style salutes fashion and entertainment icons with sidewalk plaques.

**Melrose Avenue** (between San Vicente Blvd. and La Brea Ave.) is really two shopping districts. High-end fashion and design showrooms dominate the western end, near La Cienega Boulevard; head east past Fairfax Avenue for tattoo parlors and used clothing.

For vintage castoffs, check out **Decades** (8214 Melrose Ave., 323/655-1960, www.decadesinc.com, 11am-6pm Mon.-Sat., noon-5pm Sun.), while **Ron Robinson at Fred Segal** (8118 Melrose Ave., 323/651-1935, www.ronrobinson.com, 10am-7pm Mon.-Sat., noon-6pm Sun.) is a deluxe department store that has everything from the ridiculously trendy to the severely tasteful.

On the strip of Sunset Boulevard famous for nightlife, indie bookstore **Book Soup** (8818 Sunset Blvd., 310/659-3110, www.booksoup.com, 9am-10pm

Shop for deals on Santee Alley.

Mon.-Sat., 9am-7pm Sun.) crams every nook and cranny of its space, which includes a strong film section.

# Sports and Recreation

You'll find an endless array of ways to get outside and have fun in the L.A. area. Among the most popular recreation options are those that get you out onto the beach or into the Pacific Ocean.

## Beaches

Southern California has a seemingly endless stretch of public beaches with lots of visitor amenities, such as snack bars, boardwalks, showers, beach toy rental shacks, surf schools, and permanent sports courts. However, you won't always find clean, clear water to swim in, since pollution is a major issue on the L.A. coast, and water temperatures cool off significantly when you dive into the surf.

### Leo Carrillo State Park

Just 28 miles north of Santa Monica on the Pacific Coast Highway, **Leo Carrillo State Park** (35000 W. Pacific Coast Hwy., Malibu, 310/457-8143, www.parks.ca.gov, 8am-10pm daily, $12 per vehicle) feels like a Central Coast beach even though it's right outside the Los Angeles city limits. Explore the park's natural coastal features, including tide pools and caves. A point break offshore draws surfers when the right swell hits. Dogs are also allowed on a beach at the northern end of the park.

### Zuma Beach

**Zuma Beach** (30000 Pacific Coast Hwy., Malibu, 19 miles north of Santa Monica, surf report 310/457-9701, http://beaches.lacounty.gov, sunrise-sunset daily, parking $3-12.50) is a popular surf and boogie-boarding break, complete with a nice big stretch of clean white sand that fills up fast on summer weekends. Grab a spot on the west side of the Pacific Coast Highway (CA-1) for free parking, or pay for one of the more than 2,000 spots in the beach parking lot. Zuma has all the amenities you need for a full day out at the beach, from restrooms and showers to a kid-friendly snack bar and a beachside boardwalk.

### Malibu Beach

Amid the sea of mansions fronting the beach, **Malibu Lagoon State Beach** (23200 Pacific Coast Hwy., 310/457-8143, www.parks.ca.gov, 8am-sunset daily, $12 per vehicle) and its ancillary **Malibu Surfrider Beach** offer public access to this great northern L.A. location. Running alongside the **Malibu Pier** (23000 Pacific Coast Hwy., www.malibu-pier.com), this pretty stretch of sugar-like sand offers a wealth of activities as well as pure California relaxation. It's likely to get crowded quickly in the summer, so get here early for a parking spot.

### Santa Monica State Beach

**Santa Monica State Beach** (Pacific Coast Hwy., 310/458-8300, www.smgov.net, parking from $7) lines the water-side edge of town. For 3.5 miles, the fine sand gets raked daily beneath the sun that shines over the beach more than 300 days each year. Enjoy the warm sunshine, take a dip in the endless waves, stroll along the boardwalk, or look for dolphins frolicking in the surf. The best people-watching runs south of the pier area and on toward Venice Beach. For more elbow room, head north of the pier to the less populated end of the beach.

## Surfing

The northern section of Los Angeles has some of the region's best surf breaks including County Line, which is on the L.A.-Ventura county line, and Zuma, a series of beach breaks along the beach of the same name. But L.A.'s premier surf spot is Malibu, one of the world's most famous waves. This is where the 1960s surf culture took hold, thanks to legends like Miki Dora, an iconic Malibu-based surfer. The southern section of L.A. County's coastline offers places to surf, but not with the same quality as the breaks around Malibu.

If you've left your board at home, run to the **Malibu Surf Shack** (22935 Pacific Coast Hwy., 310/456-8508, www.malibusurfshack.com, 10am-6pm daily, surfboards $25 per hour, $30-40 per day, wetsuits $10-15) to rent a board. It's walking distance to the break.

**Learn to Surf LA** (641 Westminster Ave., Ste. 5, Venice, 310/663-2479, www.learntosurfla.com, $130-380) has lessons on the beach near the Santa Monica Pier (near lifeguard tower no. 18), Manhattan Beach's 45th Street lifeguard tower, and Venice Beach's Navy Street lifeguard tower. Each lesson lasts almost two hours and includes all equipment (you'll get a full wetsuit in addition to a board), shore instruction and practice, and plenty of time in the water. Intermediate and advanced surfers can also find great fun with this school, which has advanced instructors capable of helping you improve your skills.

## Spectator Sports

Los Angeles went from having no NFL teams to being home to the **Los Angeles Rams** (www.therams.com) and **Los Angeles Chargers** (www.chargers.com) in 2017. They will begin playing in the **Los Angeles Stadium** at Hollywood Park in 2020. Until then, the Rams suit up at **Los Angeles Memorial Park** (www.lacoliseum.com), while the Chargers hit the field at the **StubHub Center** (www.stubhubcenter.com) in nearby Carson.

The **L.A. Kings** (http://kings.nhl.com) are no joke now after winning the Stanley Cup in 2012 and 2014. They play lightning-fast NHL ice hockey in downtown L.A. at the **Staples Center** (1111 S. Figueroa St., 213/742-7100, www.staplescenter.com).

The **Los Angeles Lakers** (www.nba.com/lakers) play at the **Staples Center** (1111 S. Figueroa St., 213/742-7100, www.staplescenter.com), along with the often-overlooked **L.A. Clippers** (www.nba.com/clippers), who are now rising in stature.

The **Los Angeles Dodgers** (http://los-angeles.dodgers.mlb.com) play often and well at **Dodger Stadium** (1000 Elysian Park Ave., www.dodgers.com).

# Food

Whatever kind of food you prefer, from fresh sushi to Armenian, you can probably find it in a cool little hole-in-the-wall somewhere in L.A. Local recommendations often make for the best dining experiences, but even just walking down the right street can yield a tasty meal.

## Downtown and Vicinity

Sure, you can find plenty of bland tourist-friendly restaurants serving American and Americanized food in the downtown area, but why would you, when one of downtown L.A.'s greatest strengths is its ethnic diversity and the great range of cuisine that goes along with it? An endless array of fabulous holes-in-the-wall awaits you. Getting local recommendations is the best way to find the current hot spots. The food stalls at the **Grand Central Market** (317 S. Broadway, 213/624-2378, www.grand-centralsquare.com, 8am-6pm Sun.-Wed., 8am-9pm Thurs.-Sat.) are also fun options.

### Classic American
The house specialty at **Langer's Delicatessen and Restaurant** (704 S. Alvarado St., 213/483-8050, www.langersdeli.com, 8am-4pm Mon.-Sat., $12-25), operating continuously since 1947, is a hot pastrami sandwich that some say is the best in the world (yes, that includes New York City). The hot and cold dishes in the traditional Jewish deli style, a vast breakfast menu, and plenty of desserts (noodle kugel, anyone?) will satisfy any appetite level. It's still California, so you can get fresh avocado on your tongue sandwich if you really want to. You can also order in advance and pick up your meal curbside.

### Mexican
Chef Ray Garcia puts some twists on the typical taqueria at his ★ **B.S. Taqueria** (514 W. 7th St., 213/622-3744, http://bstaqueria.com, 11:30am-10pm Mon.-Thurs., 11:30am-11pm Fri., 5pm-11pm Sat., 5pm-10pm Sun., $3-15). The menu is heavy on tacos including the famed lardo and clams version, but also includes heartier fare like carne asada. The interior is bright and lively, serving cocktails and craft beer. Make sure to finish with the churros and their spicy melted chocolate dipping sauce.

**La Luz del Dia** (1 W. Olvera St., 213/628-7495, www.luzdeldia.com, 11am-3:30pm Mon., 10am-8pm Tues.-Thurs., 10am-9pm Fri.-Sat., 8:30am-9pm Sun.,

$7-10) has been dishing up simple, spicy cafeteria-style Mexican food since 1959. The handmade-to-order tortillas are worth snacking on.

### Italian
It seems odd to name a high-end restaurant after a decidedly low-end bug, but that's what the owners of **Cicada Restaurant** (617 S. Olive St., 213/488-9488, www.cicadarestaurant.com, 5:30pm-9pm Tues.-Sat., $24-42) did. Set in the 1920s Oviatt building, decorated in high French art deco style, the beautiful restaurant glitters with original Lalique glass panels—check out the elevator doors. There's a palatial dining room for large parties and balcony seating for intimate duos. The cuisine fuses Italian concepts with California ingredients, techniques, and presentations. Save room for dessert.

### Japanese
Even L.A. denizens who've eaten in Japan come back to ★ **Kagaya** (418 E. 2nd St., 213/617-1016, 6pm-10:30pm Tues.-Sat., 6pm-10pm Sun., $40-128) again and again. They also make reservations in advance, because the dining room is small and the quality of the food makes it popular even on weeknights. The *shabu-shabu* (paper-thin slices of beef and vegetables) is but one course in a meal that includes several appetizers, *udon* noodles, and dessert. You can pay a premium for Wagyu beef if you choose, but the king crab legs in season are part of the regular price of dinner. Sit at the counter to watch your food prepared before your eyes.

Busy, noisy **Daikokuya** (327 E. 1st St., 213/626-1680, www.daikoku-ten.com, 11am-midnight Mon.-Thurs., 11am-1am Fri.-Sat., 11am-11pm Sun., under $10) is among the best ramen places in Little Tokyo, hailed by Pulitzer Prize-winning food writer Jonathan Gold. The steaming bowls of hearty pork broth and noodles satisfy even the brawniest appetite.

### Coffee and Tea

Santa Cruz chain **Verve Coffee** (883 Spring St., 213/455-5991, www.vervecoffee.com, 7am-7pm Mon.-Fri., 7am-8pm Sat.-Sun.) feels right at home in DTLA, with a high-tech industrial setting and a small deck shaded with a canopy of tangled vines.

## Koreatown

Three miles west of downtown, densely populated Koreatown has scores of great restaurants.

### Classic American

Old-school gem ★ **Cassell's Hamburgers** (3600 W. 6th St., 213/387-5502, www.cassellsburgers.com, Sun.-Thurs. 7am-11pm, Fri.-Sat. 7am-2pm, $6-12) has served its famous burgers since 1948. While the original location closed in 2012, it's reopened and modernized inside the Hotel Normandie. The burger is a thing of greasy beauty, still cooked up on the original crossfire broiler, while the can't-miss potato salad has a slight horseradish kick. Just feet from a rotating pie case, a bar serves up craft beers and cocktails.

### Gastropub

As its name makes clear, **Beer Belly** (532 S. Western Ave., 213/387-2337, www.beerbellyla.com, Sun.-Tues. 11:30am-11pm, Wed.-Thurs. 11:30am-midnight, Fri.-Sat. 11:30am-1am, $9-21) is not for people who are watching their weight. Order a California craft beer for fortification as you try to take down the quadruple-decker grilled cheese sandwich with smoked bacon and maple syrup. Finish the meal with a deep-fried Pop-Tart—and vow to eat nothing but salads for the rest of the week.

### Korean

**Chunju Han-il Kwan** (3450 W. 6th St., 213/480-1799, 8am-11pm Mon.-Sat., 11am-10pm Sun., $10-15) is a casual restaurant in a strip mall with gas burners on the tables that caters primarily to the Korean expat community. You won't find English menus, but helpful waitstaff can guide you through your order. If your server says a dish is spicy, she means it. The menu is eclectic: You can get a hot dog, octopus, fish soup, kimchi, Korean stew (thickened with American cheese), and much more.

### Greek

Originally a Greek import company in the 1960s, **Papa Cristos Taverna** (2771 W. Pico Blvd., 323/737-2970, www.papacristos.com, 9:30am-3pm Tues., 9:30am-8pm Wed.-Sat., 9am-4pm Sun., $7-20) still supplies the local Greek community with hard-to-come-by delicacies, which also become ingredients in the cuisine at the Taverna, from the salads to the kebabs to the baba ghanoush.

## Los Feliz, Silver Lake, and Echo Park

### Mexican

Not every taco stand wins awards from the James Beard Foundation. ★ **Yuca's** (2056 Hillhurst Ave., 323/662-1214, www.yucasla.com, 11am-8pm Mon.-Sat., $5) received the honor in 2005, confirming what Los Feliz locals have known for decades: This shack serves truly memorable (and cheap) tacos and burritos. Vegetarians beware: Even the beans are made with pork fat.

### French

The ★ **Taix French Restaurant** (1911 W. Sunset Blvd., 213/484-1265, http://taixfrench.com, 11:30am-10pm Mon.-Thurs., 11:30am-11pm Fri., noon-11pm Sat., noon-10pm Sun., $13-34) has been serving superb French cuisine in a dimly lit Old World setting in Echo Park since 1927. The menu includes nightly dishes like roast chicken and frog legs Provençal as well as recurring weekly soups and entrées. Enjoy live music or comedy during your dinner at the on-site **321 Lounge**.

## Follow That Food Truck!

Some of the city's best culinary creations are being served out of food trucks. Gourmet chefs can follow their dreams with little overhead, and the result is some of the L.A. food scene's most blogged-about bites. The annual **LA Street Food Fest** (http://lastreetfoodfest.com) celebrates the rise of this foodie phenomenon.

Websites including **Find LA Food Trucks** (www.findlafoodtrucks.com) and **Roaming Hunger** (http://roaminghunger.com) have sprung up to help you find some of your roving favorites.

Food truck favorite **Kogi BBQ** (twitter @kogibbq, http://kogibbq.com) is still going strong, serving a Mexican-Korean hybrid menu that includes kimchi quesadillas and short-rib tacos.

The owner of **The Grilled Cheese Truck** (twitter @grlldcheesetruk, www.thegrilledcheesetruck.com) was inspired to start a truck selling grilled cheeses after he entered the Annual Grilled Cheese Invitational at the Rose Bowl and realized how many people loved this basic sandwich. His famous item is the cheesy mac and rib, which has barbecued pork tucked into the grilled cheese.

For East Coast meets West Coast fare, search for **Cousins Maine Lobster** (twitter @CMLobster, http://cousinsmainelobster.com), serving lobster rolls and crustacean-stuffed quesadillas.

Happy hunting!

**FOOD**

### BREAKFAST

A small, colorful eatery in a Silver Lake strip mall, **Trois Familia** (3510 Sunset Blvd., 323/725-7800, www.troisfamilia.com, 9am-2pm daily, $7-15) is helmed by three chefs fusing French, Mexican, and California cuisines to produce tasty and creative breakfasts and lunches. Examples include chorizo crepes and a rich breakfast burrito with French ham, caramelized onions, and truffle salt.

## Hollywood

Hollywood has just as many tasty treats tucked away in strip malls as other areas of Los Angeles. If you want to rub elbows with rock stars, you're likely to find yourself at a big, slightly raunchy bar and grill. For a chance at glimpsing stars of the silver screen, look for upscale California cuisine or perhaps a high-end sushi bar. If all you need is tasty sustenance, you can choose from a range of restaurants.

### Classic American

Lit up like a Las Vegas show club into the wee hours of the morning, **Pink's Famous Hot Dogs** (709 N. La Brea Ave., 323/931-4223, www.pinkshollywood.com, 9:30am-2am Sun.-Thurs., 9:30am-3am Fri.-Sat., $3.50-7) is hot dog heaven. Frankophiles have been lining up at this roadside stand for variations on a sausage in a bun that range from the basic chili dog to the more elaborate Martha Stewart Dog since 1939.

### Gastropub

A playful California take on British pub food, **The Pikey** (7617 Sunset Blvd., 323/850-5400, www.thepikeyla.com, 11:45am-2am Mon.-Fri., 10:30am-2am Sat.-Sun., $15-32) has a sense of humor. Case in point: One of its cocktails is named the Divine Brown for the prostitute that actor Hugh Grant was caught with on this same city block back in 1995. The dinner menu is divided into small plates and large plates. The buttery burger with cheddar and Worcestershire aioli is a highlight. It can get loud and crowded at dinnertime.

### Italian

The warm but clamorous dining room at **Pizzeria Mozza** (641 N. Highland Ave., 323/297-0101, www.pizzeriamozza.com, noon-midnight daily, $11-29) has

## Koreatown

been packed since chef Nancy Silverton opened the doors. The wood-fired oven turns out rustic, blistered pizzas with luxurious toppings. Reservations are tough to get, but bar seats are available for walk-ins. They also have an outpost in Newport Beach and farther away in Singapore.

### Brazilian

Need food really, really, *really* late? **Bossa Nova** (7181 W. Sunset Blvd., 323/436-7999, www.bossanovafood. com, 11am-3:30am Sun.-Wed., 11am-4am Thurs.-Sat., $10-20) can hook you up. A big menu of inexpensive entrées can satisfy any appetite from lunch to way past dinnertime. Some of the dishes bear the spicy flavors of the owners' home country of Brazil, but you'll also find pasta, salads, and pizzas. There are two other locations: one at 685 N. Robertson Blvd. (310/657-5070, 11am-11:30pm Mon.-Thurs., 11am-3:30am Fri.-Sat., 11am-midnight Sun.) and one in West L.A. at 10982 W. Pico Blvd. (310/441-0404, 11am-1am Sun.-Thurs., 11am-3:30am Fri.-Sat.). Bossa also delivers.

## Breakfast

If you're a flapjack fan, plan on breakfast at ★ **The Griddle Café** (7916 Sunset Blvd., 323/874-0377, www.thegriddlecafe.com, 7am-4pm Mon.-Fri., 8am-4pm Sat.-Sun., $11-30). This hectic, loud breakfast joint serves up creations like a Red Velvet pancake and a pancake with brown sugar-baked bananas. Those who prefer savory to sweet can opt for delicious breakfast tacos or a cobb omelet. The Director's Guild of America is next door, so you may spot a celebrity *auteur*.

## La Brea, Fairfax, and Miracle Mile
### California Cuisine

Pairing meat and potatoes with a retro-clubby dining room, **Jar** (8225 Beverly Blvd., 323/655-6566, www.thejar.com, 5:30pm-close Tues.-Sun., $21-49) puts a Southern California spin on the traditional steak house. Meats and grilled fishes are served à la carte with your choice of sauce, and the side orders serve two. Jar is also known for its Sunday brunch; try the lobster Benedict. On Sunday, you can order a fried chicken plate, while Tuesday nights feature lobster.

### Deli

Midnight snackers unhinge their jaws on the hulking corned beef sandwiches at **Canter's Deli** (419 N. Fairfax Ave., 323/651-2030, www.cantersdeli.com, 24 hours daily, $12-18), in the heart of the Jewish Fairfax district. This venerable 24-hour deli also boasts its share of star sightings, so watch for noshing rock stars in the wee hours of the morning.

## Beverly Hills and West Hollywood

Between Beverly Hills and West L.A. you'll find an eclectic choice of restaurants. Unsurprisingly, Beverly Hills

---

**From top to bottom:** B.S. Taqueria; Cassell's Hamburgers; Taix French Restaurant.

tends toward high-end eateries serving European and haute California cuisine. On the other hand, West L.A. boasts a wide array of international restaurants. You'll have to try a few to pick your favorites, since every local has their own take on the area's best eats.

## Italian

If you're looking for upscale Italian cuisine in a classy environment, enjoy lunch or dinner at **Il Pastaio Restaurant** (400 N. Canon Dr., Beverly Hills, 310/205-5444, www.giacominodrago.com, 11:30am-11pm Mon.-Thurs., 11:30am-midnight Fri.-Sat., 11:30am-10pm Sun., $13-45). The bright dining room offers a sunny luncheon experience, and the white tablecloths and shiny glassware lend an elegance to dinner, served late even on weeknights. Il Pastaio offers a wide variety of salads, risotto, and pasta dishes. The blue-painted bar offers a tasteful selection of California and Italian vintages.

## Seafood

With a roof that resembles a giant ray gliding through the sea, **Connie and Ted's** (8171 Santa Monica Blvd., 323/848-2722, www.connieandteds.com, 4pm-10pm Mon.-Tues., 11:30am-10pm Wed.-Thurs., 11:30am-11pm Fri., 10am-11pm Sat., 10am-10pm Sun., $12-44) brings the fruit of the sea to West Hollywood. The menu is inspired by New England clam shacks, oyster bars, and fish houses and includes a raw bar of oysters and clams. A West Coast influence creeps in on items like the smoked albacore starter, lobster rolls, and a Mexican shrimp dish.

## Tapas

★ **AOC** (8700 W. 3rd St., 310/859-9859, www.aocwinebar.com, 11:30am-10pm Mon., 11:30am-11pm Tues.-Fri., 10am-11pm Sat., 10am-10pm Sun., $14-88) is wildly popular for three reasons: breakfast, lunch, and dinner. Breakfast is served until 3pm and includes fried chicken and cornmeal waffles along with

house-made corned beef hash. Lunch features focaccia sandwiches, salads, and plate lunches. At dinner, you can go small (foccacias or salads) or big (roasted fish or meats). Sample from an acclaimed wine list and creative cocktails.

## Santa Monica, Venice, and Malibu

Yes, there's lots of junky beach food to be found in Santa Monica and Venice Beach, but there is also an amazing number of gems hiding in these towns.

### Contemporary

Don't be fooled by the unpretentious exterior of **Cora's Coffee Shoppe** (1802 Ocean Ave., Santa Monica, 310/451-9562, www.corascoffee.com, 7am-3pm Sun.-Mon., 7am-10pm Tues.-Sat., $7-18). The small, exquisite restaurant inside is a locals' secret hiding in plain sight, serving breakfast, lunch, and dinner to diners who are more than willing to pack into the tiny spaces, including the two tiny marble-topped tables and miniature marble counter inside, and a small patio area screened by venerable bougainvillea. The chefs use high-end and sometimes organic ingredients to create typical breakfast and lunch dishes with a touch of the unexpected, including a hamburger salad and a BLT with a smear of goat cheese. The dinner menu includes short rib tacos and all kinds of burgers (including turkey and veggie).

### Italian

The ★ **C&O Trattoria** (31 Washington Blvd., Marina del Rey, 310/823-9491, www.candorestaurants.com, 11:30am-10pm Sun.-Thurs., 11:30am-11pm Fri.-Sat., $13-23) manages to live up to its hype and then some. Sit outside in the big outdoor dining room, enjoying the mild weather and the soft pastel frescoes on the exterior walls surrounding the courtyard. C&O is known for its self-described gargantuan portions, which are best shared family-style. Start off with the addictive little garlic rolls. Your attentive but not overzealous server can help you choose from the creative pasta list; the rigatoni al forno is a standout. While C&O has a nice wine list, it's worth trying out the house chianti, where you get to serve yourself on an honor system.

## Caribbean

**Cha Cha Chicken** (1906 Ocean Ave., Santa Monica, 310/581-1684, www. chachachicken.com, 11am-10pm Mon.-Fri., 10am-10pm Sat.-Sun., $7-12) looks just like it sounds: It's a slightly decrepit but brightly painted shack a short walk from the Santa Monica Pier and the Third Street Promenade. The palm tree-strewn patio is the perfect atmosphere to enjoy the Caribbean dishes that come from the fragrant kitchen. The jerk dishes bring a tangy sweetness to the table, while the *ropa vieja* heats up the place. Quaff an imported Jamaican soda or a seasonal *agua fresca* with your meal, since Cha Cha Chicken doesn't have a liquor license.

## Seafood

Situated on the Malibu coastline adjacent to the County Line surf break, ★ **Neptune's Net** (42505 Pacific Coast Hwy., Malibu, 310/457-3095, www.neptunesnet.com, 10:30am-8pm Mon.-Thurs., 10:30am-9pm Fri., 10am-8pm Sat.-Sun. summer, 10:30am-7pm Mon.-Thurs., 10:30am-8pm Fri., 10am-7pm Sat.-Sun. winter, $11-30) catches all kinds of seafood to serve to hungry diners. You'll often find sandy and salt-encrusted local surfers satisfying their enormous appetites after hours out on the waves, or bikers downing a beer after a ride on the twisting highway. One of the Net's most satisfying options is the shrimp tacos: crispy fried shrimp on tortillas topped with a pineapple salsa. The large menu includes a seemingly endless variety of other combinations, à la carte options, and side dishes.

**Salt Air** (1616 Abbot Kinney Blvd., Venice Beach, 310/396-9333, www.saltairvenice.com, 10am-3pm and 5pm-10pm Sun., 11am-3pm and 5pm-10pm Mon.-Tues., 11am-3pm and 5pm-11pm Wed.-Fri., 10am-3pm and 5pm-11pm Sat., $16-43) is a seafood restaurant with a busy bar. Everyone gets a plate of tasty corn fritters stuffed with cheddar cheese and a dollop of molasses butter to start. The raw bar has oysters from both coasts, while the dinner menu highlights seafood, including slow-cooked cod, seared trout, and olive oil-poached salmon.

# Accommodations

From the cheapest roach-ridden shack motels to the most chichi Beverly Hills hotel, Los Angeles has an endless variety of lodgings to suit every taste and budget.

## Downtown and Vicinity

If you want to stay overnight in downtown L.A., plan to pay for the privilege. Most hostelries are high-rise towers catering more to businesspeople than the leisure set. Still, if you need a room near the heart of L.A. for less than a month's mortgage, you can find one if you look hard enough. Once you get into the Jewelry District and farther south toward the Flower Market, the neighborhood goes from high-end to sketchy to downright terrifying. If you need a truly cheap room, avoid these areas and head instead to the San Fernando Valley.

### Under $150

A testament to the DTLA renaissance, ★ **Freehand Los Angeles** (416 W. 8th St., 213/612-0021, www.freehandhotels.com/los-angeles, $55-229) has taken up shop in the old Commercial Exchange Building. The hip 226-room complex splits the difference between hotel and hostel with 167 private rooms and 59 shared rooms with bunk beds. There's much on-site including a communal lobby with bar, a coffee counter, a home goods store, the Israeli

American restaurant **The Exchange,** and the rooftop bar Broken Shaker with an adjacent pool.

Imagine staying at a cute B&B only a mile from the towering skyscrapers. The **Inn at 657** (657 and 663 W. 23rd St., 213/741-2200, www.patsysinn657.com, $140-220) is two side-by-side buildings with one-bedroom guest accommodations and two-bedroom suites, each individually decorated. You'll find a comfortable bed in a room scattered with lovely fabrics and pretty antiques. Each morning, you'll head downstairs for a full breakfast. The inn has a massage therapist on retainer, Wi-Fi, and laundry service.

### $150-250

The ★ **Ace Hotel** (929 Broadway, 213/623-3233, www.acehotel.com/los-angeles, $199-650) is one of the hippest places to stay in downtown. You can enjoy an evening's entertainment without venturing off the hotel's grounds. The property's 1,600-seat theater hosts the Sundance Next Fest and music performances by big indie acts like Slowdive and Belle and Sebastian. DJs spin poolside at the rooftop bar on the 14th floor, with the downtown skyline as a backdrop. Downstairs, dine at the trendy **L.A. Chapter** (213/235-9660, 7am-3:30pm and 5:30pm-11pm daily, $17-28). The guest rooms, converted from the former offices of the United Artists film studio, feel like arty studio apartments, with concrete ceilings and exposed concrete floors. Some rooms have private terraces; all have Internet radios.

### Over $250

For a taste of true L.A. style, get a room at the **Omni Los Angeles at California Plaza** (251 S. Olive St., 213/617-3300, www.omnihotels.com, $276-542). From the grand exterior to the elegant lobby and on up to your guest room, the stylish decor, lovely accents, and plush amenities will

crispy shrimp tacos at Neptune's Net

make you feel rich, if only for one night. Business travelers can request a room complete with a fax machine and copier, while families can enjoy suites with adjoining rooms specially decorated for children. On-site meals are available at the **Noé Restaurant** (213/356-4100, 5pm-10pm Sun.-Thurs., 5pm-11pm Fri.-Sat.) and the **Grand Café** (213/617-3300, ext. 4155, 6:30am-3pm Mon.-Fri., 7am-3pm Sat.-Sun.). Take a swim in the lap pool, work out in the fitness room, or relax at the spa.

**The Standard** (550 S. Flower St., 213/892-8080, www.standardhotels.com, $260-1,500) is a mecca for the see-and-be-seen crowd. From its upside-down sign to the minimal aesthetic in the guest rooms, the hotel gives off an ironic-chic vibe. If you're sharing a room, be aware that the shower is only separated from the rest of the room by clear glass. On-site amenities include a gym, a barbershop, and a restaurant open 24-7. The rooftop bar, seen in the 2005 film *Kiss Kiss, Bang Bang*, features spectacular views of the L.A. cityscape.

If you're yearning to stay someplace with a movie history, book a room at the **Westin Bonaventure Hotel and Suites** (404 S. Figueroa St., 213/624-1000, www.starwoodhotels.com, $379-2,500). The climactic scene of the Clint Eastwood thriller *In the Line of Fire* was filmed in one of the unusual elevators in the glass-enclosed, four leaf clover-shaped high-rise building. This hotel complex has every single thing you'd ever need: shops, restaurants, a day spa, and a concierge. Views range from innocuous street scenes to panoramic cityscapes. The **Bona Vista Lounge** (213/612-4743, 5pm-1am daily) slowly rotates through 360 degrees at the top of the building.

The **Tuck Hotel** (820 S. Spring St., 213/947-3815, www.tuckhotel.com, $229-309) is located in a sliver of a building between South Spring Street and South Main Street. It used to house a brothel, but now is home to a small boutique hotel with a lobby bar and restaurant below the rooms. The black walls in the units make it easy to sleep in, while smart TVs and Bluetooth speakers provide entertainment and a soundtrack during your stay.

## Koreatown
### $150-250
★ **Hotel Normandie** (605 S. Normandie Ave., 800/617-4071, www.hotelnormandiela.com, $159-359) has been welcoming guests to Koreatown since opening in 1926, including British author Malcom Lowry, who completed his novel *Under the Volcano* here in the 1930s. Today the building has anything you'd want, including clean rooms, showers with superb water pressure, complimentary continental breakfasts, and complimentary wine in the afternoon. The high-ceilinged lobby leads to the bars at the **Normandie Club** and the exclusive **Walker Inn** with its world, as well as the classic **Cassell's Hamburgers,** gussied-up for modern diners.

### Over $250

A block away from the Hotel Normandie, **The Line** (3515 Wilshire Blvd., 213/381-7411, www.thelinehotel.com/los-angeles/, $259-550) is a 1960s hotel spruced up for the modern age. The rooms have floor to ceiling windows, and the restaurants are run by famed chef Roy Choi. There's also a 1980s-throwback bar on-site called Break Room 86.

## Hollywood

If you're star-struck, a serious partier, or a rock music aficionado, you'll want to stay the night within staggering distance of the hottest clubs or the hippest music venues. You might find yourself sleeping in the same room where Axl Rose once vomited or David Lee Roth broke all the furniture.

### Under $150

OK, the exterior doesn't look like much, but at the **USA Hostels—Hollywood** (1624 Schrader Blvd., 323/462-3777 or 800/524-6783, www.usahostels.com, dorm $56-59, private room $150), it's what's inside that counts. It still offers the same great prices you'll find at more bare-bones hostels, but you can choose between dorm rooms and private guest rooms. Even the larger dorm rooms have baths attached. (You'll also find several common baths in the hallways, helping to diminish the morning shower rush.) The daily all-you-can-make pancake breakfast is included, along with all the coffee or tea you can drink. Add free barbecue nights on Monday, Wednesday, and Friday, and you've got a great start on seriously diminished food costs for your trip. This smaller hostel also fosters a sense of community among its visitors, with walking tours, a beach shuttle, and free comedy nights.

Hollywood motel rooms for around $100? They exist at the **Hollywood Downtowner Inn** (5601 Hollywood Blvd., 323/464-7191, www.hollywooddowntowner.com, $99-199). Just 1.5 miles from sights such as TCL Chinese Theatre and the Griffith Observatory, this 33-room motel offers basic amenities, including a courtyard pool, complimentary hot breakfast, and, maybe most important, free parking.

### $150-250

Named for the world-renowned magic club next door, the ★ **Magic Castle Hotel** (7025 Franklin Ave., 323/851-0800, www.magiccastlehotel.com, $204-399) boasts the best customer service of any L.A.-area hostelry. Sparkling light guest rooms with cushy white comforters and spare, clean decor offer a haven of tranquility. A courtyard pool invites lounging day and night. All suites have their own kitchens, and all guests can enjoy unlimited free snacks (sodas, candy, salted goodies). Enjoy the little luxurious touches, such as high-end coffee, baked goodies in the free continental breakfast, plushy robes, and nightly turndown service. But the most notable perks are free tickets to the exclusive **Magic Castle** (7001 Franklin Ave., 323/851-3313, www.magiccastle.com), although there is a door charge.

The **Hollywood Celebrity Hotel** (1775 Orchid Ave., 323/850-6464 or 800/222-7017, www.hotelcelebrity.com, $169-250) is a nice budget motel that aspires to Hollywood's famed luxury. Guest rooms have mini fridges for leftovers; some have kitchens as well. In the morning, come down to the lobby for a complimentary continental breakfast. Leave your car in the gated, off-street parking lot for just $10 per night, which is a deal.

For film lovers or star seekers, the location of the **Hollywood Orchid Suites** (1753 Orchid Ave., 323/874-9678 or 800/537-3052, www.orchidsuites.com, $179-239) couldn't be better: It's in the Hollywood and Highland Center, right behind the Chinese Theatre and around the corner from the Walk of Fame. Inexpensive parking and proximity to public transit are a bonus. Guest rooms are actually suites; all but the juniors have full kitchens. Don't expect luxury, although you'll get a coffeemaker and free Wi-Fi. The rectangular pool offers cool refreshment after a long day of stalking Brad or Angie.

## Beverly Hills and West Hollywood

If you want to dive headfirst into the lap of luxury, stay in Beverly Hills. Choose wisely and save your pennies to see how the 1 percent lives. West Hollywood, which serves as L.A.'s gay mecca, offers a wider range of accommodations, including budget options, chain motels, and unique upscale hotels.

### $150-250

Comfortable and quiet, the ★ **Élan Hotel** (8435 Beverly Blvd., 323/658-6663, www. elanhotel.com, $145-239) has a great location where Beverly Hills and West Hollywood meet. With its friendly staff, this unassuming hotel makes a fine base for exploring Hollywood attractions and the Sunset Strip. The understated rooms are decorated with soothing abstract art. All have mini fridges, coffeemakers, flat-screen TVs; many rooms have small balconies or porches for a breath of fresh air. A complimentary continental breakfast is served every morning.

The affordable **Hotel Beverly Terrace** (469 N. Doheny Dr., Beverly Hills, 310/274-8141 or 800/842-6401, www. hotelbeverlyterrace.com, $220-260) is a spruced-up, retro-cool motor hotel that enjoys a great spot on the border of Beverly Hills and West Hollywood. Lounge in the sun in the garden courtyard or on the rooftop sundeck. In the morning, enjoy a complimentary continental breakfast. The on-site **Cafe Amici** (310/858-0271, 7am-10pm daily) can satisfy your Italian food cravings.

### Over $250

The **Beverly Wilshire** (9500 Wilshire Blvd., Beverly Hills, 310/275-5200, www. fourseasons.com, $800-2,000) is the most famous of all the neighborhood's grand hotels. Even the plainest guest rooms feature exquisite appointments such as 55-inch plasma TVs, elegant linens, and attractive artwork. The presidential suite resembles a European palace, complete with Corinthian columns. Enjoy the in-house spa, a dining room, room service, and every other service you could imagine, and you might consider a stay here worth the expense.

In West Hollywood, the **Sunset Tower Hotel** (8358 Sunset Blvd., West Hollywood, 323/654-7100, www.sunsettowerhotel.com, $345-3,000) has a gorgeous art deco exterior and a fully renovated modern interior. Guest accommodations range from smallish guest rooms with smooth linens and attractive appointments up to luxurious suites with panoramic views and limestone baths. All guest rooms include flat-screen TVs, 24-hour room service, and free Wi-Fi.

With architecture like a French castle, **Chateau Marmont** (8221 Sunset Blvd., West Hollywood, 323/656-1010 or 800/242-8328, www.chateaumarmont. com, $450-6,000) looks out on the city from a perch above the Sunset Strip. It has long attracted the in crowd, from Garbo to Leo. It is also where writers from F. Scott Fitzgerald to Hunter S. Thompson have holed up to produce work. The design is eccentric and eclectic, from vintage 1940s suites to Bauhaus bungalows. The hotel was front and center in Sofia Coppola's 2010 film *Somewhere*.

## Santa Monica, Venice, and Malibu

The best place to stay in Los Angeles is down by the beach. It's ironic that you can camp in a park for $25 in exclusive Malibu or pay over $1,000 for a resort room in "working-class" Santa Monica. Whichever you choose, you'll get some of the best atmosphere in town.

### Under $150

The huge **HI-Santa Monica** (1436 2nd St.,

Santa Monica, 310/393-9913, www.hilo-sangeles.org, dorm beds $40-71, private rooms $140-230) offers 260 beds right in the thick of downtown Santa Monica, within walking distance of the pier, the Third Street Promenade, and good restaurants. This ritzy hostel offers tons of amenities for the price, including a computer room, a TV room, a movie room, excursions, wheelchair access, sheets with the bed price, and even a complimentary continental breakfast every morning. The local public transit system runs right outside the door.

### $150-250

While it's about a 30-minute drive from Santa Monica, the **Hyatt Regency Los Angeles International Airport** (6225 W. Century Blvd., 424/702-1234, https://losangelesairport.regency.hyatt.com/en/hotel/home.html, $229-449) makes an ideal first or last stop in the city. The 580 rooms all have 55-inch HD TVs and soundproof windows. But the property really excels at unexpected amenities including an on-site market open 24 hours a day and a resident dog named Sir Hyatt who is available for petting from travelers who left their own furry friends at home. There's also a bar, a restaurant that serves cuisine inspired by L.A. neighborhoods, an exercise room with views of the LAX runways, a shuttle to the terminals, and a pool deck with cabanas and fire pits.

The surprisingly lovely and affordable **Venice Beach Suites & Hotel** (1305 Ocean Front Walk, 310/396-4559 or 888/877-7602, www.venicebeachsuites.com, $229-349) sits right on the beach, but it's far enough from the boardwalk to acquire a touch of peace and quiet. You can also stroll over to Washington Boulevard to grab a meal or a cup of coffee. Inside, the guest rooms and suites all have full kitchens so you can cook for yourself, which is perfect for budget-conscious travelers. The decor is cuter than that of an average motel; you might find exposed brick walls

the Élan Hotel

and polished hardwood floors. Check the website for weeklong rental deals.

## Over $250

There's probably no hotel that is a better reflection of Venice's edgy attitude than ★ **Hotel Erwin** (1697 Pacific Ave., 800/786-7789, www.hotelerwin.com, $289-530), just feet from the boardwalk. Graffiti art adorns the outside wall and some of its rooms; all have balconies and playful decor including lamps resembling the barbells used by the weightlifters at nearby Muscle Beach. Sitting atop the hotel is **High,** a rooftop bar that allows you to take in all the action of the bustling boardwalk while sipping a cocktail. The staff is laid-back, genial, and accommodating.

For a charming hotel experience only a block from the ever-energetic Venice Boardwalk, stay at the **Inn at Venice Beach** (327 Washington Blvd., 310/821-2557 or 800/828-0688, www.innatvenicebeach.com, $250-450). The charming orange-and-brown exterior, complete with a lovely bricked interior courtyard-cum-café, makes all guests feel welcome. Common spaces are decorated in a post-modern blocky style, while the guest rooms pop with brilliant yellows and vibrant accents. The two-story boutique hotel offers 45 guest rooms, and its location on Washington Boulevard makes it a perfect base from which to enjoy the best restaurants of Venice. Start each day with a complimentary continental breakfast, either in the dining room or outside in the Courtyard Café. There's complimentary Wi-Fi throughout.

One of this area's best-known resort hotels is **Shutters on the Beach** (1 Pico Blvd., Santa Monica, 310/458-0030, www.shuttersonthebeach.com, $795-1,165). You'll pay handsomely for the privilege of laying your head on one of Shutters' hallowed pillows. On the other hand, the gorgeous airy guest rooms will make you feel like you're home, or at least staying at the home you'd have if you could hire a famous designer to decorate for you. Even the most modest guest rooms have comfortable beds, white linens, plasma TVs, and oversize bathtubs. Head down to the famed lobby for a drink and people-watching. Get a reservation for the elegant **One Pico** (310/587-1717, 11:30am-2:30pm and 6pm-10pm Mon.-Fri., 10am-3pm and 6pm-10pm Sat.-Sun.) or grab a more casual meal at beachside **Coast** (310/587-1717, 7am-9pm daily).

If you've got silly amounts of cash to spare, stay at the **Malibu Beach Inn** (22878 Pacific Coast Hwy., Malibu, 310/456-6444 or 800/462-5428, www.malibubeachinn.com, $679-1,459), an ocean-side villa on an exclusive stretch of sand known as "Billionaire's Beach." Expect all the best furnishings and amenities. Your guest room will be done in rare woods, gleaming stone, and the most stylish modern linens and accents. A high-definition TV, plush robes, and comfy beds tempt some visitors to stay inside, but equally tempting are the

balconies with their own entertainment in the form of endless surf, glorious sunsets, and balmy breezes (every room has an ocean view). Enjoy delicious cuisine at the airy, elegant, on-site **Carbon Beach Club** (310/456-6444, 7am-10pm daily).

# Transportation and Services

## Air

L.A. is one of the most commercial airport-dense metropolitan areas in the country. Wherever you're coming from and whichever part of L.A. you're headed for, you can get there by air. **Los Angeles International Airport** (1 World Way, Los Angeles, 855/463-5252, www.lawa.org), known as LAX, has the most flights to and from the most destinations of any area airport. LAX is also the most crowded of the L.A. airports, with the longest security and check-in lines. If you can find a way around flying into LAX, do so.

One option is to fly into other airports in the area, including **Hollywood Burbank Airport** (BUR, 2627 N. Hollywood Way, Burbank, 818/840-8840, http://hollywoodburbankairport.com) and the **Long Beach Airport** (LGB, 4100 Donald Douglas Dr., Long Beach, 562/570-2600, www.lgb.org). It may be a slightly longer drive to your final destination, but it can be well worth it. If you must use LAX, arrive a minimum of two hours ahead of your domestic flight time for your flight out, and consider three hours on busy holidays.

## Train

**Amtrak** (800/872-7245, www.amtrak.com) has an active rail hub in Los Angeles. Most trains come in to **Union Station** (800 N. Alameda St., 213/683-6875, www.unionstationla.com, 4am-1am daily), which has been owned by the Los Angeles Metropolitan Transportation Authority (MTA, www.metro.net) since 2011. From Union Station, which also acts as a Metro hub, take Metro Rail to various parts of Los Angeles. Against fairly significant odds in the region that invented car culture, Los Angeles has created a functional and useful public transit system.

## Car

Los Angeles is crisscrossed with freeways, providing numerous yet congested access points into the city. From the north and south, I-5 provides the most direct access to downtown L.A. From I-5, U.S. 101 south leads directly into Hollywood; from here, Santa Monica Boulevard can take you west to Beverly Hills. Connecting from I-5 to I-210 will take you east to Pasadena. The best way to reach Santa Monica, Venice, and Malibu is via CA-1, also known as the Pacific Coast Highway. I-10 can get you there from the east, but it will be a long, tedious, and trafficked drive. I-710, which runs north-south, is known as the Long Beach Freeway. Along the coast, the Pacific Coast Highway (CA-1) can get you from one beach town to the next.

### Parking

Parking in Los Angeles can be as much of a bear as driving. And it can cost you quite a lot of money. You will find parking lots and structures included with many hotel rooms, but parking on the street can be difficult or impossible, parking lots in sketchy areas (like the Flower and Jewelry Districts) can be dangerous, and parking structures at popular attractions can be expensive. Beach parking on summer weekends is the worst, but on weekdays and in the off-season, you can occasionally find a decent space down near the beach for a reasonable rate.

### Metro

The **Metro** (323/466-3876, www.metro.net, cash fare $1.75, day pass $7) runs both the subway Metro Rail system and a network of buses throughout the L.A. metropolitan area. Pay on board a bus if you have exact change. Otherwise, purchase a ticket or a day pass from the ticket vending machines at all Metro Rail stations.

Some buses run 24 hours. The Metro Rail lines start running as early as 4:30am and don't stop until as late as 1:30am. See the website (www.metro.net) for route maps, timetables, and fare details.

### Taxis and Ride Shares

Taxis aren't cheap, but they're quick, easy, and numerous. And in some cases, when you add up gas and parking fees, you'll find that the cab ride isn't that much more expensive than driving yourself.

To call a cab, try **Yellow Cab** (424/222-2222, www.layellowcab.com, L.A., LAX, Beverly Hills, Hollywood) or **City Cab** (888/713-5240, www.lacitycab.com, San Fernando Valley, Hollywood, and LAX), which now has a small fleet of green, environmentally friendly vehicles. Or check out www.taxicabsla.org for a complete list of providers and phone numbers.

Another option is to download a ride-sharing app on your smartphone. Both **Lyft** (www.lyft.com) and **Uber** (www.uber.com) are available all over the city.

### Tourist Information

The **Hollywood Los Angeles Visitor Information Center** (6801 Hollywood Blvd., 323/467-6412, www.discoverlosangeles.com, 9am-10pm Mon.-Sat., 10am-7pm Sun.) is adjacent to a Metro station and includes a self-serve kiosk where you can purchase discount tickets to area attractions. There are additional self-serve centers at the Los Angeles Convention Center, the Port of Los Angeles (Berth 93), and the California Science Center.

### Medical Services

For medical assistance, **LAC & USC Medical Center** (2051 Marengo St., 323/409-1000, http://dhs.lacounty.gov/ wps/portal/dhs/lacusc/) can fix you up no matter what's wrong with you, or visit the emergency room at the **Long Beach Memorial Medical Center** (2801 Atlantic Ave., Long Beach, 562/933-2000, www.memorialcare.org).

---

# Disneyland Resort

The "Happiest Place on Earth" lures millions of visitors of all ages each year with promises of fun and fantasy. During high seasons, waves of humanity flow through **Disneyland** (1313 N. Harbor Blvd., Anaheim, 714/781-4623, http://disneyland.disney.go.com, 9am-midnight daily, $97-124, Hopper Ticket $166-185), moving slowly from land to land and ride to ride. The park is well set up to handle the often-immense crowds. Despite the undeniable cheese factor, even the most cynical and jaded resident Californians can't quite keep their cantankerous scowls once they're ensconced inside Uncle Walt's dream. It really *is* a happy place.

### Getting There

The nearest airport to Disneyland, serving all of Orange County, is **John Wayne Airport** (SNA, 18601 Airport Way, Santa Ana, 949/252-5200, www.ocair.com). It's much easier to fly into and out of John Wayne than LAX, though it can be more expensive. John Wayne's terminal has plenty of rental car agencies, as well as many shuttle services that can get you where you need to go—especially to the House of Mouse.

If you have to fly into LAX for scheduling or budget reasons, catch a shuttle straight from the airport to your Disneyland hotel. Among the many companies offering and arranging such transportation, the one with the best name is **MouseSavers** (www.mousesavers.com). Working with various shuttle and van companies, MouseSavers can get you a ride in a van or a bus from LAX or John

Wayne to your destination at or near Disneyland.

Disneyland is on Disneyland Drive in Anaheim and is most accessible from I-5 South where it crosses Ball Road (stay in the left three lanes for parking). The parking lot (1313 S. Disneyland Dr.) costs $20.

If you're coming to the park from elsewhere in Southern California, consider leaving the car (avoiding the parking fees) and taking public transit instead. **Anaheim Resort Transit** (ART, 1280 Anaheim Blvd., Anaheim, 714/563-5287, www.rideart.org, $5.50 adults, $2 children) can take you to and from the Amtrak station and all around central Anaheim. Buy passes via the website or at conveniently located kiosks.

## Orientation

The Disneyland Resort is a massive kingdom that stretches from **Harbor Boulevard** on the east to **Walnut Street** on the west and from **Ball Road** to the north to **Katella Avenue** to the south. It includes two amusement parks, three hotels, and an outdoor shopping and entertainment complex. The Disneyland-affiliated hotels (Disneyland Hotel, Paradise Pier Hotel, and Disney's Grand Californian) all cluster on the western side of the complex, between Walnut Street and **Disneyland Drive (West Street).** The area between Disneyland Drive and Harbor Boulevard is shared by **Disneyland** in the northern section and **Disney California Adventure Park** in the southern section, with **Downtown Disney** between them in the central-west section. There is no admission fee for Downtown Disney. You can reach the amusement park entrances via Downtown Disney (although visitors going to Disneyland or Disney California Adventure Park should park in the paid lots, rather than the Downtown Disney self-park lot, which is only free for the first three hours) or from the walk-in entrance (for those taking public transportation or being dropped off) on Harbor Boulevard. There are also trams from the parking lot to the entrance.

Your first stop inside the park should be one of the information kiosks near the front entrance gates. Get a map, a schedule of the day's events, and the inside scoop on what's going on in the park during your visit.

### Tickets

There are as many varied ticket prices and plans as there are themes in the park. A single-day theme park ticket will run from $97 to $124. A variety of other combinations and passes are available online (http://disneyland.disney.go.com).

To buy tickets, go to one of the many kiosks in the central gathering spot that serves as the main entrance to both Disneyland and Disney California Adventure Park. Bring your credit card, since a day at Disney is not cheap. After you've got tickets in hand (or if you've bought them online ahead of time), proceed to the turnstiles for the main park. You'll see the Disneyland Railroad terminal and the large grassy hill with the flowers planted to resemble Mickey's famous face. Pass through the turnstiles and head under the railroad trestle to get to Main Street and the park center. You can exit and reenter the park on the days for which your tickets are valid.

The already expensive regular one-day Disneyland ticket doesn't include Disney California Adventure Park. If you're interested in checking out Disney California Adventure Park as well as Disneyland, your best bet is to buy a **Park Hopper pass** ($172-185 adults, $166-178 children 3-9), which lets you move back and forth between the two parks at will for a slight discount. If you're planning to spend several days touring the Houses of Mouse, buy multiday passes in advance online to save a few more bucks per day. It'll help you feel better about the cash you'll spend on junk food, giant silly hats, stuffed animals, and an endless array of Disney apparel.

**Fastpasses** are free with park admission and might seem like magic after a while. The newest and most popular rides offer Fastpass kiosks near the entrances. Feed your ticket into one of the machines and it will spit out both your ticket and a Fastpass with your specified time to take the ride. Come back during your window and enter the always-much-shorter Fastpass line, designated by a sign at the entrance. If you're with a crowd, be sure you all get your Fastpasses at the same time, so you all get the same time window to ride. It's possible to claim three Fastpasses at a time. Once you've used up your initial allotment, you can visit a Fastpass kiosk to reload.

### Rides

In **New Orleans Square,** the favorite ride is the **Pirates of the Caribbean.** Beginning in the dim swamp, which can be seen from the Blue Bayou Restaurant, the ride's classic scenes inside have been revamped to tie in more closely to the movies. Lines for Pirates can get long, so grab a Fastpass if you don't want to wait. Pirates is suitable for younger children as well as teens and adults.

For a taste of truly classic Disney, line up in the graveyard for a tour of the **Haunted Mansion.** The sedate motion makes the Haunted Mansion suitable for younger children, but the ghosts and ghoulies that amuse adults can be intense for kids.

**Adventureland** sits next to the New Orleans Square area. **Indiana Jones Adventure** is arguably one of the best rides in all of Disneyland, and the details make it stunning. This one isn't the best for tiny tots, but the big kids love it. Everyone might want a Fastpass for the endlessly popular attraction.

In **Frontierland,** take a ride on a Wild West train on the **Big Thunder Mountain Railroad,** an older roller coaster that whisks passengers on a brief but fun thrill ride through a "dangerous, decrepit" mountain's mineshafts.

**Fantasyland** rides tend to cater to the younger set. For many Disneyphiles, **"it's a small world"** is the ultimate expression of Uncle Walt's dream, and toddlers adore this ride. Older kids might prefer **Mr. Toad's Wild Ride.** The wacky scenery ranges from a sedate library to the gates of hell. If it's a faster thrill you're seeking, head for the **Matterhorn Bobsleds.** You'll board a sled-style coaster car to plunge down a Swiss mountain on a twisted track that takes you past rivers, glaciers, and the Abominable Snowman.

The best thrill ride of the main park sits inside **Tomorrowland. Space Mountain** is a fast roller coaster that whizzes through the dark. Despite its age, Space Mountain remains one of the more popular rides in the park. Get a Fastpass to avoid long lines.

In 2019, a highly anticipated section of the park inspired by **Star Wars** opens.

## ★ Disney California Adventure Park

**Disney California Adventure Park** (http://disneyland.disney.go.com, 8am-10pm daily, ticket prices vary, one-day $99 children over 9, $93 children 3-9, one-day Park Hopper ticket for entry to both parks $172-185 adults, $166-178 children 3-9) celebrates much of what makes California special. If Disney is your only stop on this trip, but you'd like to get a sense of the state as a whole, this park can give you a little taste.

Disney California Adventure Park is divided into themed areas. You'll find two information booths just inside the main park entrance, one off to the left as you walk through the turnstile and one at the opening to Sunshine Plaza.

### Rides

**Monsters, Inc. Mike & Sully to the Rescue!** invites guests into the action of the movie of the same name. You'll help the heroes as they chase the intrepid Boo. This ride jostles you around but is suitable for smaller kids as well as bigger ones.

# Here at Disney, We Have a Few Rules

Think that anything goes at the Happiest Place on Earth? Think again. Uncle Walt had distinct ideas about what his dream theme park would look like, and that vision extended to the dress and manners of his guests. When the park opened in 1955, among the many other restrictions, no man sporting facial hair was allowed into Disneyland. The rules on dress and coiffure have relaxed since the opening, but you still need to mind your manners when you enter the Magic Kingdom.

• Adults may not wear costumes of any kind except on Halloween.

• No shirt, no shoes, no Disneyland.

• If you must use the F word, do it quietly. If staff members catch you cussing or cursing in a way that disturbs others, you can be asked to desist or leave.

• The happiest of happiness is strictly prohibited inside the Magic Kingdom. If you're caught having sex on park grounds, not only will you be thrown out, you'll also be banned from Disneyland for life (at least that's the rumor).

• Ditto for any illicit substances.

Get a sample of the world of tiny insects on **It's Tough to Be a Bug!** This big-group, 3-D, multisensory ride offers fun for little kids and adults alike. You'll fly through the air, scuttle through the grass, and get a good idea of what life is like on six little legs.

For the littlest adventurers, **Flik's Fun Fair** offers almost half a dozen rides geared toward toddlers and little children. They can ride pint-size hot-air balloons known as Flik's Flyers, climb aboard a bug-themed train, or run around under a gigantic faucet to cool down after hours of hot fun.

**Paradise Pier** mimics the Santa Monica Pier, with thrill rides and an old-fashioned midway. **California Screamin'** is a high-tech roller coaster designed after the classic wooden coasters of carnivals past. This extra-long ride includes drops, twists, a full loop, and plenty of time and screaming fun. California Screamin' has a four-foot height requirement and is just as popular with nostalgic adults as with kids. **Toy Story Midway Mania!** magnifies the midway mayhem as passengers of all ages take aim at targets in a 4-D ride inspired by Disney-Pixar's *Toy Story*.

In **Condor Flats, Soarin' Over California** is a combination ride and show that puts you and dozens of other guests on the world's biggest "glider" and sets you off over the hills and valleys of California. Get Disney's version of a wilderness experience at **Grizzly Peak.** Enjoy a white-water raft ride through a landscape inspired by the Sierra Nevada foothills on the **Grizzly River Run.**

**Cars Land** was inspired by the hit 2006 film *Cars.* Float on larger-than-life tires on the **Luigi's Flying Tires** ride or be serenaded by Mater as you ride in a tractor on **Mater's Junkyard Jamboree.** The **Radiator Springs Racers** finds six-person vehicles passing locations and characters from *Cars* before culminating in a real-life race with a car of other park visitors.

## Parades and Shows

Watch your favorite Pixar characters come to life in the **Pixar Play Parade.** Other regular shows are **Disney Junior— Live on Stage!** and **Disney's Aladdin—A Musical Spectacular.** Both of these shows hark back to favorite children's activities and movies. Check your park guide and *Time Guide* for more information about live shows.

## Food

### Disneyland

One of the few things the Mouse doesn't do too well is haute cuisine. For a truly

# Alternatives to the Mouse

## Universal Studios Hollywood

The longtime Hollywood-centric alternative to Disneyland is the **Universal Studios Hollywood** (100 Universal City Plaza, Los Angeles, 800/864-8377, www.universalstudios.com, hours vary, $105-116, parking $10-15) theme park. Kids adore this park, which puts them right into the action of their favorite movies. Flee the carnivorous dinosaurs of *Jurassic Park*, take a rafting adventure on the pseudo-set of *Waterworld*, or quiver in terror of an ancient curse in *Revenge of the Mummy*. If you're more interested in how the movies are made than the rides made from them, take the **Studio Tour.** You'll get an extreme close-up of the sets of major blockbuster films like *War of the Worlds*. Better yet, be part of the studio audience of TV shows currently taping by getting tickets at the Audiences Unlimited Ticket Booth. If you're a serious movie buff, consider buying a **VIP pass**—you'll get a six-hour tour that takes you onto working sound stages, into the current prop warehouse, and through a variety of working build shops that service movies and programs currently filming.

## Six Flags Magic Mountain

**Six Flags Magic Mountain** (Magic Mountain Parkway, Valencia, 661/255-4100, www.sixflags.com, hours vary, $85 adults, $60 children) provides good fun for the whole family. Magic Mountain has long been the extreme alternative to the Mouse, offering a wide array of thrill rides. You'll need a strong stomach to deal with the g-forces of the major-league roller coasters and the death-defying drops, including the Lex Luthor: Drop of Doom, where you plummet 400 feet at speeds up to 85 mph. For the younger set, plenty of rides offer a less intense but equally fun amusement-park experience. Both littler and bigger kids enjoy interacting with the classic Warner Bros. characters, especially in Bugs Bunny World, and a kids' show features Bugs Bunny, Donald Duck, and more. Other than that, Magic Mountain has little in the way of staged entertainment—this park is all about the rides. The park is divided into areas, just like most other major theme parks; get a map at the entrance to help you maneuver around and pick your favorite rides.

## Knott's Berry Farm

For a taste of history along with some ultramodern thrill rides and plenty of cooling waterslides, head for **Knott's Berry Farm** (8039 Beach Blvd., Buena Park, 714/220-5200, www.knotts.com, hours vary, $75 adults, $45 children, parking $15). From the tall landmark GhostRider wooden coaster to the 30-story vertical-drop ride to the screaming Silver Bullet suspended coaster, Knott's supplies excitement to even the most hard-core ride lover. For the younger crowd, Camp Snoopy offers an array of pint-size rides and attractions, plus Snoopy and all the characters they love from the *Peanuts* comics and TV shows.

In the heat of the summer, many park visitors adjourn from the coasters to **Knott's Soak City** (www.soakcityoc.com, hours vary daily Memorial Day-Labor Day, adults $48, children $37, parking $15-20), a full-size water park with 22 rides, a kid pool and water playground, and plenty of space to enjoy the O.C. sunshine.

Convenient to the parks, **Knott's Berry Farm Resort Hotel** (7675 Crescent Ave., Buena Park, 714/995-1111, www.knotts.com, $145-215) is a high-rise resort with a pool and spa, a fitness center, and several on-site restaurants.

---

good or healthy meal, get a hand stamp and go outside the park. But if you're stuck inside and you absolutely need sustenance, you can get it. The best areas of the park to grab a bite are Main Street, New Orleans, and Frontierland, but you can find at least a snack almost anywhere in the park.

For a sit-down restaurant meal inside the park, make reservations in advance for a table at the **Blue Bayou Restaurant** (New Orleans Square, 714/781-3463, $55-59). The best part about this restaurant is its setting in the dimly lit swamp overlooking the Pirates of the Caribbean ride. Appropriately, the Bayou has Cajunish cuisine and a reputation for being haunted. You will get large portions, and tasty desserts make a fine finish to your meal. Watch your silverware, though; the alleged ghosts in this restaurant like to mess around with diners' tableware.

If you need to grab a quicker bite, *don't* do it at the French Market restaurant in the New Orleans area. It sells what appears to be day-old (or more) food from the Bayou that has been sitting under heat lamps for a good long time.

### Disney California Adventure Park

If you need a snack break in Disney California Adventure Park, you'll find most of the food clustered in the Golden State area. For a Mexican feast, try **Cocina Cucamonga Mexican Grill** ($15). For more traditional American fare, enjoy the food at the **Pacific Wharf Cafe** ($15) or the **Taste Pilots' Grill** ($15).

Unlike Disneyland proper, in Disney California Adventure Park, responsible adults can quash their thirst with a variety of alcoholic beverages. If you're just dying for a cold beer, get one at **Bayside Brews.** Or, if you love the endless array of high-quality wines produced in the Golden State, head for the **Mendocino Terrace,** where you can learn the basics of wine creation and production. Have a glass and a pseudo-Italian meal at the sit-down **Wine Country Trattoria at the Golden Vine Winery** (714/781-3463, $15-36).

### Downtown Disney

Downtown Disney is outside the amusement parks and offers additional dining options. National chains like **House of Blues** (1530 S. Disneyland Dr., Anaheim, 714/778-2583, www.houseofblues.com, 11am-midnight daily, $15-30) and

**Rainforest Café** (1515 S. Disneyland Dr., Anaheim, 714/772-0413, www.rainforestcafe.com, 8am-11pm Sun.-Thurs., 8am-midnight Fri.-Sat., $11-30) serve typical menu staples like sandwiches, burgers, pasta, and steak and seafood entrées, with House of Blues putting a Southern spin on these items and adding live-music shows, while kid-friendly Rainforest Café puts on tropical touches like coconut and mango. **ESPN Zone** (1545 Disneyland Dr., Anaheim, 714/300-3776, www.espnzone.com, 11am-midnight daily, $11-26) has similar offerings with a "sports bar on steroids" restaurant concept.

There are also more individual restaurants, but even these feel a little like chains. The most distinctive of them, **Ralph Brennan's Jazz Kitchen** (1590 S. Disneyland Dr., Anaheim, 714/776-5200, www.rbjazzkitchen.com, 11am-11pm Mon.-Sat., 10am-3pm and 4pm-11pm Sun., $8-37), is meant to replicate the experience of eating in New Orleans's French Quarter. The Cajun menu hits all the staples, including jambalaya, beignets, and various blackened meats and seafood.

The Patina Restaurant Group runs **Catal Restaurant** (1580 Disneyland Dr., Anaheim, 714/774-4442, www.patina-group.com, 8am-11am and 5pm-9pm daily, $19-41), with Mediterranean fare; **Naples Ristorante** (1550 Disneyland Dr., Anaheim, 714/776-6200, www.patina-group.com, 8am-10pm daily, $15-46) for Italian food; and **Tortilla Jo's** (1510 Disneyland Dr., Anaheim, 714/535-5000, www.patinagroup.com, 11am-10pm Sun.-Thurs., 11am-11pm Fri.-Sat., $15-21) for Mexican food.

Finally, **La Brea Bakery** (1556 Disneyland Dr., Anaheim, 714/490-0233, www.labreabakery.com, 11am-11pm Mon.-Fri., 9am-11pm Sat.-Sun., $15-35) is the Disney outpost of an L.A. favorite. This bakery, founded by Nancy Silverton, supplies numerous markets and restaurants with crusty European-style loaves.

The morning scones, sandwiches, and fancy cookies are superb.

## Accommodations

The best way to get fully Disney-fied is to stay at one of the park's hotels.

### Disney Hotels

For the most iconic Disney resort experience, you must stay at the **Disneyland Hotel** (1150 Magic Way, Anaheim, 714/778-6600, http://disneyland.disney.go.com, $460-1,016). This nearly 1,000-room high-rise monument to brand-specific family entertainment has everything a vacationing Brady-esque bunch could want: themed swimming pools, themed play areas, and even character-themed rooms that allow the kids to fully immerse themselves in the Mouse experience. Adults and families on a budget can also get rooms with either a king or two queen beds and more traditional motel fabrics and appointments. The monorail stops inside the hotel, offering guests the easiest way into the park proper without having to deal with parking or even walking.

It's easy to find the **Paradise Pier Hotel** (1717 S. Disneyland Dr., Anaheim, 714/999-0990, http://disneyland.disney.go.com, $344-952); it's that high-rise thing just outside Disney California Adventure Park. This hotel boasts what passes for affordable lodgings within walking distance of the parks. Rooms are cute, colorful, and clean; many have two doubles or queens to accommodate families or couples traveling together on a tighter budget. You'll find a (possibly refreshing) lack of Mickeys in the standard guest accommodations at the Paradise, which has the feel of a beach resort motel. After a day of wandering the park, relax by the rooftop pool.

**Disney's Grand Californian Hotel and Spa** (1600 S. Disneyland Dr., Anaheim, 714/635-2300, http://disneyland.disney.go.com, $417-1,477) is inside Disney California Adventure Park, attempting to mimic the famous Ahwahnee Lodge in Yosemite. While it doesn't quite succeed (much of what makes the Ahwahnee so great is its views), the big-beam construction and soaring common spaces do feel reminiscent of a great luxury lodge. The hotel is surrounded by gardens and has restaurants, a day spa, and shops attached on the ground floor; it can also get you right out into Downtown Disney and thence to the parks proper. Rooms here offer more luxury than the other Disney resorts, with dark woods and faux-craftsman details creating an attractive atmosphere. Get anything from a standard room that sleeps two up to spacious family suites with bunk beds that can easily handle six people. As with all Disney resorts, you can purchase tickets and a meal plan along with your hotel room (in fact, if you book via the website, they'll try to force you to do it that way).

### Outside the Parks

The massive park complex is ringed with motels, both popular chains and more interesting independents. **The Anabella** (1030 W. Katella Ave., Anaheim, 714/905-1050 or 800/863-4888, www.anabella-hotel.com, $332-662) offers a touch of class along with a three-block walk to the parks. The elegant marble-clad lobby seems like it belongs closer to Downtown L.A. than Downtown Disney. A decent restaurant, two pools, a whirlpool tub, and a fitness center are on-site. You can get limited room service at The Anabella, and you can leave your car in the hotel's parking lot to avoid the expense of parking at Disneyland.

Within walking distance is the **Desert Palms Hotel & Suites** (631 W. Katella Ave., Anaheim, 888/788-0466, www.desertpalmshotel.com, $250-415). The pool and spa provide fun for children and adults alike, and the many amenities make travelers comfortable. Guests with more discretionary income can choose from a number of suites, some designed to delight children and others aimed at couples on a romantic getaway. There are even condo-style accommodations with kitchens.

Away from the Disneyland complex and surrounding area, the accommodations in Orange County run to chain motels with little character or distinctiveness, but the good news is that you can find a decent room for a reasonable price.

The **Hyatt Regency Orange County** (11999 Harbor Blvd., Garden Grove, 714/750-1234, http://orangecounty.hyatt. com, $129-289) in Garden Grove is about 1.5 miles (10 minutes' drive on Harbor Blvd.) south of the park. The family-friendly suites have separate bedrooms with bunk beds and fun decor geared toward younger guests. Enjoy a cocktail in the sun-drenched atrium, or grab a chaise lounge by the pool or take a refreshing dip.

### Services

Each park has information booths near the park entrance. On the website for **Visit Anaheim** (http://visitanaheim.org), you can plan a trip to the area in advance by looking at the upcoming events and suggested itineraries or by downloading the travel guide.

If you need to stow your bags or hit the restroom before plunging into the fray, banks of lockers and restrooms sit in the main entrance area. If mobility is a problem, consider renting a **stroller, wheelchair,** or **scooter.** Ask for directions to the rental counter when you enter the park.

Disneyland offers its own minor medical facilities, which can dispense first aid for scrapes, cuts, and mild heat exhaustion. They can also call an ambulance if something nastier has occurred. The **West Anaheim Medical Center** (3033 W. Orange Ave., Anaheim, 714/827-3000, www.westanaheimmedctr.com) is a full-service hospital with an emergency room.

# Long Beach and Orange County Beaches

The Los Angeles coastline continues beyond the city limits, passing the Palos Verdes Peninsula and stretching farther south to Long Beach, where haunted ships and sunny coasts await.

The Orange County coast begins at Huntington Beach and stretches south across a collection of sunny, scenic beach towns (Newport Beach, Laguna Beach, and Dana Point) until ending at San Juan Capistrano. The surf here is world-renowned. If you've ever seen a surf magazine or surf movie, you've seen surfers ripping Orange County breaks like Salt Creek and Trestles.

## Long Beach

Long Beach has several worthy attractions befitting its size, including the historic and possibly haunted *Queen Mary* ocean liner and the Aquarium of the Pacific. Long Beach Harbor is also one of the best places to catch a boat ride out to Catalina Island, about 22 miles from shore.

### Getting There

Long Beach is about 25 miles directly south of downtown Los Angeles. Head down **I-5 South** for two miles and then merge onto **I-710 South** toward Long Beach. Stay on the roadway for 17 miles, then turn off on Exit 1C for the downtown area and the aquarium.

Long Beach is just 20 miles from Disneyland Resort. Take **CA-22 West** from Disneyland for 12 miles. The roadway turns into Long Beach's East 7th Street, with will take you to the Long Beach city center.

While you can get to the coast easily enough from LAX, the **Long Beach Airport** (LGB, 4100 Donald Douglas Dr., 562/570-2600, www.lgb.org) is both closer to Long Beach and less crowded than LAX.

## Sights
### ★ The *Queen Mary*
The major visitor attraction of Long Beach is **The *Queen Mary*** (1126 Queens Hwy., 877/342-0738, www.queenmary. com, 10am-6pm daily, adults $27-34, children $17.50-24.50, parking $15), one of the most famous ships ever to ply the high seas. This great ship, once a magnificent pleasure-cruise liner, now sits at permanent anchor in Long Beach Harbor. The *Queen Mary* acts as a **hotel** (877/342-0742, $99-389), a museum, and an entertainment center with several restaurants and bars. Book a stateroom and stay aboard, come for dinner, or just buy a regular ticket and take a self-guided tour. The museum exhibits describe the history of the ship, which took its maiden voyage in 1936, with special emphasis on its tour of duty as a troop transport during World War II.

It's not just the extensive museum and the attractive hotel that make the *Queen Mary* well known today. The ship is also one of the most famously haunted places in California. Over its decades of service, a number of people lost their lives aboard the *Queen Mary*. Rumors say several of these unfortunate souls have remained on the ship since their tragic deaths. If you're most interested in the ghost stories of the *Queen Mary*, book a spot on the **Paranormal Ship Walk** (www.queenmary. com, $44), which takes you to the hottest haunted spots; **Dining with the Spirits** (7pm Fri.-Sat., includes three-course dinner, $134), a combination dinner and two-hour haunted tour; or **Paranormal Investigation** (www.queenmary.com, $79), for serious ghost hunters.

The *Queen Mary* **Passport** ($27 adults, $17.50 children 4-11) includes a self-guided audio tour, a look at the vessel's historical exhibits, a viewing of a film showing in the 4-D theater, and admission to the Ghosts and Legends Tour.

The **First Class Passport** ($34 adults, $24.50 children 4-11) includes all of the *Queen Mary* Passport attractions along with a ticket to your choice of the Glory Days Historical Tour or the Haunted Encounters Tour.

The *Queen Mary* offers a large paid parking lot near the ship's berth. You'll walk from the parking area up to a square with a ticket booth and several shops and a snack bar. Purchase your general-admission ticket to get on board the ship. It's also a good idea to buy any guided tour tickets at this point. Night tours can fill up in advance, so call ahead to reserve a spot.

### Aquarium of the Pacific
The **Aquarium of the Pacific** (100 Aquarium Way, 562/590-3100, www. aquariumofpacific.org, 9am-6pm daily, $30 adults, $27 seniors, $18 children) hosts animals and plant life native to the Pacific Ocean, from the local residents of SoCal's sea up to the northern Pacific and down to the tropics. While the big, modern building isn't much to look at from the outside, it's what's inside that's beautiful—sea stars, urchins, and rays in the touch-friendly tanks, and a Shark Lagoon where you can pet a few of the more than 150 sharks that live here.

## Food
Combining elegance, fine continental-California cuisine, and great ghost stories, **Sir Winston's Restaurant and Lounge** (1126 Queens Hwy., 562/499-1657, www.queenmary.com, 5pm-9pm Tues.-Thurs., 5pm-10pm Fri.-Sat., $30-78) floats gently on board the *Queen Mary*. For the most beautiful dining experience, request a window table and make reservations for sunset. Dress in your finest; Sir Winston's requests that diners adhere to their semiformal dress code.

A locals' favorite down where the shops and cafés cluster, **Natraj Cuisine of India** (5262 E. 2nd St., 562/930-0930, www.na-trajlongbeach.com, 11am-2:30pm and 5pm-10pm Mon.-Thurs., 11am-2:30pm

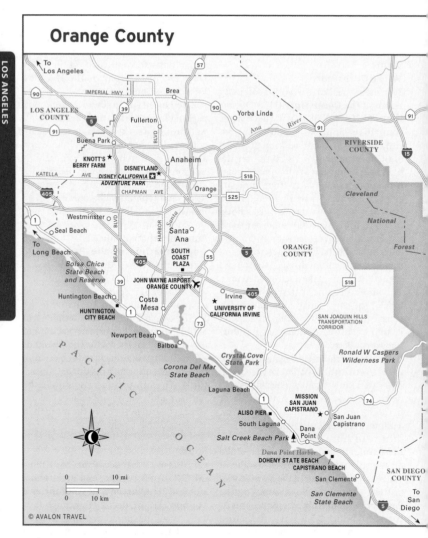

# Orange County

© AVALON TRAVEL

and 5pm-11pm Fri., 11am-11pm Sat., 11am-9:30pm Sun., $12-20) offers good food for reasonable prices. Come by for the all-you-can-eat lunch buffet Monday-Saturday to sample a variety of properly spiced meat and vegetarian dishes created in classic Indian tradition.

## Accommodations

**The Varden** (335 Pacific Ave., 562/432-8950, www.thevardenhotel.com, $149-199) offers the type of tiny, clean, and modern rooms you'd expect to find in Europe. If you don't mind your bath being a foot or two from your bed, the sleek little rooms in this hotel, which dates back to 1929, are a great deal. The oldest operating hotel in Long Beach, it is named after an eccentric circus performer named Dolly Varden, who is rumored to have hoarded jewels on the premises. The staff is friendly and helpful, and coffee, ice, and fresh fruit are available to guests 24 hours a day. It's also one block from Pine Street, which is lined with restaurants and bars.

Looking for something completely different? At **Dockside Boat and Bed** (Dock 5A, Rainbow Harbor, 562/436-3111 or 800/436-2574, www.boatandbed.com, $200-350, overnight parking $24, unless you get the $10 discount parking pass from Dockside), you won't get a regular old hotel room, you'll get one of four yachts. The yachts run 38-54 feet and can sleep four or more people each ($25 pp after the first 2). Amenities include TVs with DVD players, stereos, kitchen facilities, wet bars, and ample seating. The boats are in walking distance from the harbor's restaurants and the aquarium. Don't expect to take your floating accommodations out for a spin; these yachts are permanent residents of Rainbow Harbor.

### Information and Services
For information, maps, brochures, and advice about Long Beach and the surrounding areas, visit the **Long Beach Convention and Visitors Bureau** (301 E. Ocean Blvd., Ste. 1900, 562/436-3645, www.visitlongbeach.com, 8am-5pm Mon.-Fri.).

## Huntington Beach
This Orange County beach town is known for its longtime association with surfing and surf culture, beginning when Hawaiian legend Duke Kahanamoku first rode waves here back in 1922. Surfers still ride the surf on either side of the **Huntington Beach Pier,** a large concrete pier that offers fine views of the beach scene on both sides. Across the Pacific Coast Highway, Huntington Beach's Main Street is full of restaurants, bars, and shops, including lots of surf shops.

### Getting There
It can take just 45 minutes to get to Huntington Beach from central Los Angeles. Take **I-5 South** out of downtown

for nine miles. Then get on **I-605 South** for 11 miles before merging onto **I-405 South.** Take the Seal Beach Boulevard exit from I-405 and turn left on Seal Beach Boulevard. After 2.5 miles, turn left on the **Pacific Coast Highway,** which you'll take for eight miles to Huntington Beach.

Huntington Beach is one of the closest beaches to Disneyland, just 16 miles away. From Disneyland, get on **CA-22 West** for four miles and then turn on the Beach Boulevard exit. Take Beach Boulevard (CA-39) for eight miles to Huntington Beach.

The beach route between Long Beach and Huntington Beach is the **Pacific Coast Highway (CA-1).** Take it south out of Long Beach for 9.6 miles to reach Huntington Beach. If it's a crowded beach weekend, hop on **CA-22 East** to reach **I-405 South.** Continue for 6.8 miles to the CA-39/Beach Boulevard exit and follow the road to the beach.

### Beaches
**Huntington City Beach** (Pacific Coast Hwy. from Beach Blvd. to Seapoint St., beach headquarters 103 Pacific Coast Hwy., 714/536-5281, www.huntington-beachca.gov, beach 5am-10pm daily, office 8am-5pm Mon.-Fri.) runs the length of the south end of town, petering out toward the oil industry facilities at the north end. This famous beach hosts major sporting events such as the U.S. Open of Surfing and the X Games. But even the average beachgoer can enjoy all sorts of activities on a daily basis, from sunbathing to beach volleyball, surfing to skim-boarding. There's a cement walkway for biking, in-line skating, jogging, and walking. Plus, you'll find a dog-friendly section at the north end of the beach where dogs can be let off-leash.

### Food
**The Black Trumpet Bistro** (18344 Beach Blvd., 714/842-1122, www.theblacktrumpetbistro.com, 11:30am-10pm Tues.-Fri.,

4pm-10pm Sat., 4pm-9pm Sun., $12-23) has paintings of jazz legends adorning the walls. The owner wants to represent Mediterranean cuisine from tapas to more substantial entrées. His endeavor has caused The Black Trumpet to be proclaimed one of Huntington Beach's best restaurants by the *OC Weekly*.

For a quick bite to eat, stop off at the **Bodhi Tree Vegetarian Cafe** (501 Main St., Ste. E, 714/969-9500, www.bodhitreehb.com, 11am-10pm Mon. and Wed.-Sun., $6-10) for vegetarian soups, salads, and sandwiches. **Sugar Shack Café** (213 Main St., 714/536-0355, www.hbsugarshack.com, 6am-2pm Mon.-Tues and Thurs.-Fri., 6am-8pm Wed., 6am-3pm Sat.-Sun., $7-10) is a great place for breakfast, serving omelets and breakfast burritos.

## Accommodations

The 17-room **Sun 'N Sands Motel** (1102 Pacific Coast Hwy., 714/536-2543, www.sunnsands.com, $249-399) is a tiny place where you can expect the standard motel room, but the main attraction is across the treacherous Pacific Coast Highway: long, sweet Huntington Beach. Be careful crossing the highway to get to the sand. Find a traffic light and a crosswalk rather than risking life and limb for the minor convenience of jaywalking.

For something more upscale, book a room at the **Shorebreak Hotel** (500 Pacific Coast Hwy., 714/861-4470, www.shorebreakhotel.com, $329-749). Some rooms have private balconies looking out over the beach and pier. Everyone can enjoy the hotel's on-site restaurant, fitness center, and courtyard with fire pits.

## Information and Services

Get assistance at the **Huntington Beach Marketing and Visitors Bureau** (301 Main St., Ste. 208, 714/969-3492 or 800/729-6232, www.surfcityusa.com, 9am-5pm Mon.-Fri.), which also has a visitor information kiosk (Pacific Coast Hwy. and Main St., hours vary). Huntington Beach

the *Queen Mary* in Long Beach

has a **post office** (316 Olive Ave., 714/536-4973, www.usps.com, 9am-5pm Mon.-Fri.) and the **Huntington Beach Hospital** (17772 Beach Blvd., 714/843-5000, www.hbhospital.org).

## Newport Beach

Affluent Newport Beach is known for its beaches, harbor, and The Wedge, a notorious bodysurfing and body-boarding wave.

### Getting There

It takes less than an hour to drive the 40 miles between the L.A. city center and Newport Beach. Disneyland is even closer, just 26 miles. From either starting point, take **I-5 South** and then merge onto **CA-55 South,** which leads the remaining 10 miles into town. From Huntington Beach, Newport Beach is just a five miles' drive on the **Pacific Coast Highway (CA-1).**

### Beaches

Most of the activity in **Newport Beach**

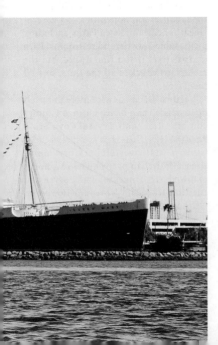

(www.visitnewportbeach.com) centers around Newport Pier (McFadden Pl.) and Main Street on the Balboa Peninsula. This 10-mile stretch of sand is popular for fishing, swimming, surfing, and other ocean activities. On the east end of Balboa Peninsula, **The Wedge** is the world's most famous bodysurfing spot. On south swells, the wave jacks up off the adjacent rock jetty and creates monsters up to 30 feet high that break almost right on the beach. Beginners should stay out of the water and enjoy the spectacle from the sand.

### Food

For something French, colorful **Pescadou Bistro** (3325 Newport Blvd., 949/675-6990, www.pescadoubistro.com, 5:30pm-9pm Tues.-Sun., $21-36) fills the bill. Meanwhile, **Eat Chow** (211 62nd St., 949/423-7080, www.eatchownow.com, 8am-9pm Mon.-Thurs., 8am-10pm Fri., 7am-10pm Sat., 7am-9pm Sun., $9-18) is a local favorite, with items like breakfast *carnitas* tacos and braised short rib burritos.

Expect a line outside **Cappy's Café & Cantina** (5930 W. Coast Hwy., 949/646-4202, 6am-3pm Thurs.-Tues., 6am-8pm Wed., $10-20), a low-slung building that has served breakfast and lunch since 1957. Cappy's serves expand-your-waistband items including a 20-ounce porterhouse steak and eggs and a knockwurst and eggs dish. Enjoy the fare while mellowing out in a beachy atmosphere with plenty of colorful murals.

### Accommodations

South of downtown Newport Beach, the **Crystal Cove Beach Cottages** (35 Crystal Cove, 949/376-6200, https://crystalcove.org, reservations 800/444-7275 or www.reservecalifornia.com, dorms $36-108, cottages $179-251) give anyone the opportunity to experience life right on the Southern California sand. Some of the cabins are individual rentals that you can have all to yourself. The dorm cottages offer by-the-room accommodations for solo travelers (linens included; room doors lock). None of the cottages have TVs or any type of digital entertainment. And all the cottages include a common refrigerator and microwave, but no full kitchen, so plan to eat out, perhaps at the adjacent **Beachcomber Cafe** (15 Crystal Cove, 949/376-6900, www.thebeachcombercafe.com, 7am-9:30pm daily, $18-37), where items like breakfast *chilaquiles* and crab-stuffed salmon are served.

## Laguna Beach Area

Laguna Beach stands apart from other Orange County beach communities with its long-running arts scene, touted fine-dining restaurants, tide-pool-pocked coastline jammed between sandy beaches, and clear ocean water that beckons snorkelers and divers underwater.

### Getting There

Laguna Beach is just 50 miles from central Los Angeles, although the highway traffic may make the drive feel a lot longer. Take **I-5 South** for 37 miles and then get on **CA-133 South** for 9.5 miles into town.

If I-5 is jammed up, there's an **alternate route,** but it involves a **toll road,** CA-73, that requires electronic payment. You can register an account or pay a one-time fee online at www.thetollroads.com. From **I-5 South,** merge onto **I-605 South,** following it for 11 miles. Then take **I-405 South** for 14 miles. From there, take **CA-73 South** for 11 miles. Exit on **CA-133** (Laguna Canyon Rd.) and take a right to drive a few miles into Laguna Beach.

The drive from Disneyland to Laguna Beach is only 30 minutes without traffic. Just take **I-5 South** for 13 miles and then get on **CA-133 South** for 10 miles. Laguna Beach is an 11-mile drive south of Newport Beach on the **Pacific Coast Highway (CA-1).**

## Mission San Juan Capistrano

**Mission San Juan Capistrano** (26801 Ortega Hwy., 949/234-1300, www.missionsjc.com, 9am-5pm daily, $9 adults, $8 seniors, $6 children 4-11, children under 4 free), in the lovely little town of San Juan Capistrano, has a beautiful Catholic church and extensive gardens and grounds. In late fall and early spring, monarch butterflies flutter about in the flower gardens and out by the fountain in the courtyard. Inside the original church, artifacts from the early time of the mission tell the story of its rise and fall, as does an audio tour available in the museum.

### Beaches

**Heisler Park** and **Main Beach Park** (Pacific Coast Hwy., Laguna Beach, www.lagunabeachinfo.com) offer protected waterways, with tide pools and plenty of water-based playground equipment. The two parks are connected, so you can walk from one to the other. If you're into scuba diving, there are several reefs right off the beach. You'll find all the facilities and amenities you need at Heisler and Main Beach Parks, including picnic tables, lawns, and restrooms. Park on the street if you find a spot, but the meters get checked all the time, so feed them well.

Laguna Beach has a lot more undeveloped space than other Orange County communities, and **Crystal Cove State Park** (8471 N. Coast Hwy., 949/494-3539, www.crystalcovestatepark.org, 6am-sunset daily, $15 per vehicle) just north of town has 3.2 miles of lightly developed coastline with sandy coves and tide pools. Offshore is the Crystal Cove Underwater Park, which has several snorkeling and diving sites. The park also includes a 2,400-acre inland section with unpaved roads and trails that are open to hikers, bikers, and horseback riders.

At the southern tip of the O.C., Dana Point has a harbor (34551 Puerto Pl., 949/923-2280, www.ocparks.com) that has become a recreation marina that draws locals and visitors from all around. It also has several beaches nearby. One of the prettiest is **Capistrano Beach** (35005 Beach Rd., 949/923-2280 or 949/923-2283, www.ocparks.com, 6am-10pm daily, parking $1-2 per hour). You'll find a metered parking lot adjacent to the beach, plus showers and restrooms available.

Also in Dana Point, **Doheny State Beach** (25300 Dana Point Harbor Dr., 949/496-6172, www.parks.ca.gov, 6am-10pm daily, $15) is popular with surfers and anglers. The northern end of Doheny has a lawn along with volleyball courts, while the southern side has a popular campground with 121 campsites.

Visit **Salt Creek Beach** (33333 S. Pacific Coast Hwy., 949/923-2280, www.ocparks. com, 5am-midnight daily, parking $1 per hour) for a renowned surf break and a great place to spend a day in the sun.

## Food

**Carmelita's Kitchen De Mexico** (217 Broadway, 949/715-7829, www.carmel-itaskdm.com, 11am-10pm Mon.-Fri., 9am-9pm Sat.-Sun. $14-28) is a popular local favorite serving upscale Mexican cuisine. The open kitchen puts out terrific entrées including *tampiqueña* (marinated skirt steak) and a seafood trio platter with a lobster enchilada, shrimp taco, and crab relleno. Carmelita's also does some twists on the classic margarita, with cilantro-cucumber and strawberry-jalapeño versions.

**Watermarc** (448 S. Coast Hwy., 949/376-6272, http://watermarcrest-aurant.com, 11am-10pm Mon.-Thurs., 8am-11pm Fri.-Sat., 8am-10pm Sun., small plates $8-18, entrées $29-37), run by executive chef Marc Cohen, focuses on its "grazing plates," from filet mignon potpie to smoked bacon-wrapped dates. The two-story restaurant also has exceptional cocktails. Happy hour (4pm-6pm daily) offers burgers at half price, while all drinks and appetizers are $2 off.

For a casual meal, visit **The Stand** (238 Thalia St., 949/494-8101, www.thestand-naturalfoods.com, 7am-8pm daily summer, 7am-7pm daily winter, $7-11), a shack that has lovingly served up vegan food for more than 40 years. Order at the window and dine on the small outdoor porch or take your meal a couple of blocks to the beach.

At **Sapphire Laguna** (1200 S. Coast Hwy., 949/715-9888, www.sapphirellc. com, 11am-10:30pm Mon.-Fri., 9am-10:30pm Sat.-Sun., $24-37), Chef Azmin Ghahreman knows no national boundaries. His international seasonal cuisine might include a Greek octopus salad, Moroccan couscous, a half *jidori* chicken, or Hawaiian-style steamed mahi-mahi.

**South of Nick's** (110 N. El Camino Real, San Clemente, 949/481-4545, www. nickrestaurants.com, 11am-10pm Mon.-Thurs., 11am-11pm Fri.-Sat., 10am-10pm Sun., $10-38) offers a menu with an upscale Mexican twist. The bar keeps up with the kitchen's creativity by serving up regular margaritas as well as coconut and cucumber versions.

## Accommodations

Perched on a bluff over Laguna Beach's Main Beach, **The Inn at Laguna Beach** (211 N. Pacific Coast Hwy., 800/544-4479, $289-1,074) is the ideal place to stay for an upscale beach vacation. Half of its rooms face the ocean, and a majority of those have balconies to take in the salt air and sound of the sea. Hit up the inn's beach valet for complimentary beach umbrellas, chairs, and towels. After time on Main Beach, retire to the inn's brick pool deck with its pool and hot tub, or head up to the rooftop terrace and warm up by the fire pit.

The **Laguna Beach House** (475 N. Pacific Coast Hwy., 800/297-0007, www. thelagunabeachhouse.com, $299-559) is a casual, surfing-obsessed motel geared toward wave riders and surf-culture aficionados, with killer decor (including a surfboard shaped by the owner) in each

# Side Trip to Catalina Island

You can see Catalina from the shore of Long Beach on a clear day, but for a better view, you've got to get onto the island. The port town of Avalon welcomes visitors with Mediterranean-inspired hotels, restaurants, and shops. But the main draw of Catalina lies outside the walls of its buildings. Catalina beckons hikers, horseback riders, ecotourists, and, most of all, water lovers.

The **Catalina Casino** (1 Casino Way, 310/510-7428, www.visitcatalinaisland.com) is a round, white art deco building, opened in 1929 not for gambling but as a community gathering place. Today, it hosts diverse activities, including the Catalina Island Jazz Festival. Stroll through the serene **Wrigley Memorial and Botanical Garden** (Avalon Canyon Rd., 1.5 miles west of town, 310/510-2897, www.catalinaconservancy.org, 8am-5pm daily, $7 adults, $5 seniors and veterans with ID, $3 children 5-12 and students with ID, children under 5 and active military and their families free) in the hills above Avalon.

Outdoor recreation is the main draw. Swim or snorkel at the **Avalon Underwater Park** (Casino Point). A protected section at the north end of town offers access to a reef with plentiful sea life, including bright orange garibaldi fish. Out at the deeper edge of the park, nearly half a dozen wrecked ships await exploration. For a guided snorkel or scuba tour, visit **Catalina Snorkel & Scuba** (310/510-8558, www.catalinasnorkelscuba.com). If you need snorkeling gear, hit up **Wet Spot Rentals** (310/510-2229, www.catalinakayaks.com, snorkel gear $10 per hour, $20 per day).

**Descanso Beach Ocean Sports/ Catalina Island Kayak & Snorkel** (310/510-1226, www.kayakcatalinaisland.com, half-day to full-day $40-72) offers several kayak tours to different parts of

Catalina Casino

the island. **Jeep Eco-Tours** (310/510-2595, www.catalinaconservancy.org, chartered half-day $549 for up to 6 people, chartered full-day $889, nonchartered 2-hour tour $70-109 pp) will take you out into the wilderness to see bison, wild horses, and plant species unique to the island.

The best dining option is **The Lobster Trap** (128 Catalina St., 310/510-8585, www.catalinalobstertrap.com, 11am-late daily, $14-44), which serves up its namesake crustacean in various forms, along with other seafood.

## Getting There

The **Catalina Express** (310/519-1212, www.catalinaexpress.com, round-trip $74.50-76.50 adults, $68-70 seniors, $59-61 children 2-11, $5 children under 2, $7 bicycles and surfboards) offers multiple ferry trips every day, even in the off-season. During the summer, you can depart from Long Beach, San Pedro, or Dana Point. Bring your bike, your luggage, and your camping gear aboard for the hour-long ride.

of its 36 rooms and a daily surf report written up on a chalkboard in the lobby. The U-shaped structure surrounds a pool deck with pool, hot tub, and fire pit. Before hitting the waves, enjoy a complimentary breakfast parfait and coffee put out in the lobby.

The **Blue Lantern Inn** (34343 Street of the Blue Lantern, Dana Point, 800/950-1236, www.bluelanterninn. com, $210-585) crowns the bluffs over the Dana Point Harbor. This attractive contemporary inn offers beachfront elegance in 29 rooms boasting soothing colors, charming appointments, and lush amenities, including a spa tub in every bath, gas fireplaces, and honest-to-goodness free drinks in the mini fridge; some feature patios or balconies with impressive views of the harbor and the Pacific. The inn also offers complimentary bike usage, a hot breakfast, and an afternoon wine-and-appetizers spread.

Stay in a historic and stunning Spanish colonial villa at the **Beachcomber Inn** (533 Avenida Victoria, San Clemente, 949/492-5457, $280-415). The 10 standard villas and two deluxe villas all come with porches, full kitchens, and full views of the ocean, the beach, and the pier.

## Getting Around

The **Orange County Transportation Authority** (OCTA, 714/636-7433, www. octa.net, one trip $2, day pass $5) runs buses along the O.C. coast. The appropriately numbered **Route 1** bus runs right along the Pacific Coast Highway (CA-1) from Long Beach down to San Clemente and back. Other routes can get you to and from inland O.C. destinations, including Anaheim. Regular bus fares are payable in cash on the bus with exact change. You can also buy a day pass from the bus driver.

The one true highway on the O.C. coast is the **Pacific Coast Highway,** often called "PCH" for short and officially designated **CA-1.** You can get to PCH from **I-405** near Seal Beach, or catch **I-710** to Long Beach and then drive south from there. From Disneyland, take **I-5** to **CA-55,** which takes you into Newport Beach. If you stay on I-5 going south, you'll eventually find yourself in San Juan Capistrano.

**Parking** along the beaches of the O.C. on a sunny summer day has been compared to one of Dante's circles of hell. You're far better off staying near the beach and walking out to your perfect spot in the sand. Other options include public transit and paid parking.

# Pacific Coast Highway

**N**ever far from the cool blue ocean, PCH twists and turns through charming coastal cities and surf towns. It's one of the world's best coastal drives.

SAN FRANCISCO

HALF MOON BAY

SANTA CRUZ

MONTEREY

CARMEL

BIG SUR

300 mi/480 km
6 hrs

SAN SIMEON

CAMBRIA

SAN LUIS OBISPO

MORRO BAY

SANTA BARBARA

VENTURA

LOS ANGELES

Yosemite National Park

Mono Lake

Nevada
California

Sequoia and Kings Canyon National Park

Death Valley National Park

# Pacific Coast Highway

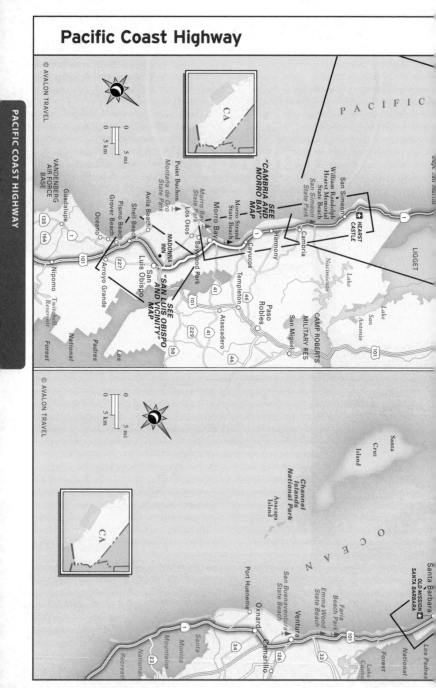

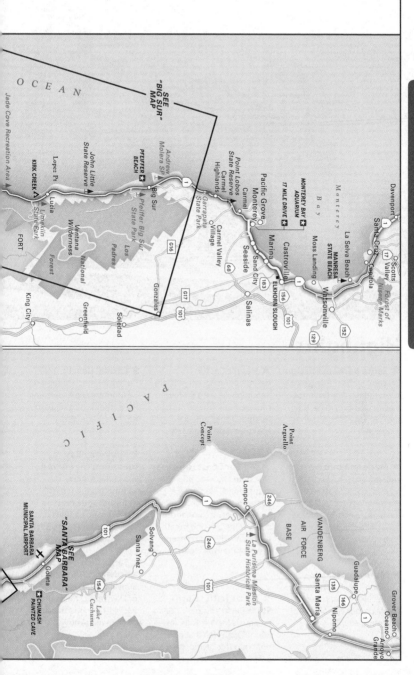

OCEAN

"SEE BIG SUR" MAP

Jade Cove Recreation Area

John Little State Reserve

Andrew Molera SP

PFEIFFER BEACH

Lopez Pt.

KIRK CREEK

Lucia

Limekiln State Park

FORT

Pfeiffer Big Sur State Park

Big Sur

Ventana Wilderness

Los Padres National Forest

G16

G17

Gonzales

Greenfield

Soledad

101

King City

Salinas

Carmel Highlands

Point Lobos State Reserve

Garrapata State Park

Carmel Valley Village

Pacific Grove

Monterey

MONTEREY BAY AQUARIUM

17 MILE DRIVE

Carmel

Seaside

Sand City

68

183

ELKHORN/SLOUGH

156

Marina

Castroville

Moss Landing

Monterey Bay

La Selva Beach

MANRESA STATE BEACH

Watsonville

1

129

152

Davenport

Santa Cruz

Scotts Valley

Forest of Nisene Marks

17

Capitola

P A C I F I C

Point Concept

Point Arguello

Lompoc

246

246

VANDENBERG AIR FORCE BASE

La Purisima Mission State Historical Park

Santa Maria

135

166

Guadalupe

Nipomo

1

Grover Beach

Oceano

Arroyo Grande

SANTA BARBARA MUNICIPAL AIRPORT

"SEE SANTA BARBARA" MAP

Goleta

101

Solvang

Santa Ynez

154

Lake Cachuma

CHUMASH PAINTED CAVE

101

# Highlights

★ **Santa Barbara Mission:** Graceful architecture, serene surroundings, and an informative museum make this the "Queen of the Missions" (page 342).

★ **Madonna Inn:** Overrun with pink kitsch, this flamboyant roadside attraction is a unique place to stop for the night, a meal, a photo-op—or even just to gawk (page 354).

★ **Morro Rock:** The 576-foot-high "Gibraltar of the Pacific" towers over the scenic harbor city of Morro Bay (page 360).

★ **Hearst Castle:** Newspaper magnate William Randolph Hearst's 56-bedroom estate is the closest thing that the United States has to a castle (page 370).

★ **Big Sur Coast Highway:** One of the most scenic drives in the world, Big Sur's CA-1 passes redwood forests and crystal-clear streams and rivers while offering breathtaking, nearly ever-present views of the coast (page 375).

★ **Julia Pfeiffer Burns State Park:** This park's claim to fame is McWay Falls, an 80-foot waterfall that pours right into the Pacific (page 375).

★ **Carmel Beach:** This is the finest stretch of sand on the Monterey Peninsula and one of the best beaches in the state (page 387).

★ **Monterey Bay Aquarium:** The first of its kind in the country, this mammoth aquarium still astonishes with a vast array of sea life and exhibits on the local ecosystem (page 395).

★ **Santa Cruz Beach Boardwalk:** With thrill rides, carnival games, and retro-cool live music, this is the best old-time boardwalk in the state (page 405).

**T**his is the edge of California—the edge of the continent—where it dramatically meets the sea.

The route itself is sometimes a highway, sometimes a city street, and often a slow, winding roadway. It all begins with Ventura and Santa Barbara, two coastal cities that enjoy the near-perfect Southern California climate without the sprawl of nearby Los Angeles. Following the coastline's contours up past Point Conception, the roadway is dotted with the communities of San Luis Obispo, Morro Bay, and Cambria. These unassuming towns make ideal stops for road-trippers, especially those who want to explore some of the state's best beaches. Head out on a kayak or try your hand at surfing. Cambria also boasts one of California's most popular attractions: opulent Hearst Castle.

Big Sur is the standout section of the drive along PCH. The roadway perches between steep coastal mountains and the Pacific and snakes through groves of redwood trees, passing by beaches, waterfalls, and state parks along the way. North of Big Sur, the highway straightens, heading into the Monterey Peninsula. There you'll find Carmel with its stunning white-sand beach, exclusive Pebble Beach, the old-fashioned Victorian buildings of Pacific Grove, and the cannery town turned tourist magnet Monterey. The north end of the Monterey Bay is the location of the quirky surf town Santa Cruz. Enjoy the mild but worthwhile thrills of the Santa Cruz Beach Boardwalk, a seaside amusement park that has been operating since 1907.

The final leg up the coast from Santa Cruz to San Francisco has plenty of wide-open space. Its coastal terraces are punctuated by surprisingly undeveloped towns like Half Moon Bay. These are ideal places to indulge in some hiking, surfing, or kayaking before returning to the urban atmosphere of San Francisco.

## Driving PCH

The drive from **Los Angeles** to **San Francisco** on the **Pacific Coast Highway (CA-1)** is **roughly 500 miles.** This can take eight hours or longer depending on traffic (and you should expect traffic, especially as you enter or leave the Los Angeles and San Francisco metropolitan areas). While you can drive straight through in one day, it's worth planning on spending two days so that you can slow down and make some stops along the way. Some of California's best attractions (**Santa Barbara Mission, Hearst Castle, Monterey Bay Aquarium**) are along this route, not to mention its best beaches and scenery. Of course, the route can also be driven in the opposite direction, from San Francisco to Los Angeles, if that works better for your road trip.

The pleasant city of **San Luis Obispo,** halfway between the two cities, is right on CA-1 and US-101, making it a good place to stop for the night. It is a little closer to Los Angeles; expect the 201-mile drive from the city to take three hours if traffic isn't bad. The drive up to San Francisco is 232 miles and will take about four hours or more. The coastal towns of **Morro Bay** (15 miles north of San Luis Obispo) and **Cambria** (30 miles north of San Luis Obispo) on CA-1 are also fine places to lay your head.

# Ventura

Ventura is short for San Buenaventura, which means "city of good fortune." There is much that is good about Ventura, including its weather (daytime temperatures average 70°F), consistent waves for surfers, and a historic downtown that includes a restored mission. Downtown Ventura is compact and easy to walk around; it is three blocks from the beach and still feels somehow unfettered

# Two Days Along the Pacific Coast

A handful of the California coast's best attractions can be enjoyed on a two-day trip up the Pacific Coast Highway from Los Angeles to San Francisco.

## Day 1

Take US-101 out of Los Angeles 1.5 hours north to the scenic coastal city of **Santa Barbara.** History lovers should stop at the **Santa Barbara Mission,** while architecture aficionados will want to see the striking Spanish colonial **Santa Barbara County Courthouse.** After walking around one or both of the attractions, head to **State Street** for a Southern-meets-Southern California lunch at the **Tupelo Junction Café** or sit down for a salad at local favorite **Opal.**

Continue up US-101 for two hours to the Central Coast towns of **San Luis Obispo, Morro Bay,** and **Cambria.** If you are into quirky attractions, stop at the **Madonna Inn,** a kitschy hotel complex dating to 1958. If natural landmarks are more your thing, take the brief detour off the highway at Morro Bay to see the 576-foot **Morro Rock** towering over a scenic fishing harbor. Or if you want to see California's version of a castle, continue 45 minutes north of San Luis Obispo to **Hearst Castle** in Cambria. Just make sure you secure a reservation for one of the tours.

San Luis Obispo, Morro Bay, and Cambria are also ideal places to spend the evening. Budget travelers can choose San Luis Obispo's **Peach Tree Inn** or Cambria's **Bridge Street Inn-HI Cambria.** For something completely different, book the rock-walled "Caveman Room" at San Luis Obispo's **Madonna Inn.**

## Day 2

Wherever you stay, head to **Frankie & Lola's** in Morro Bay for a fine breakfast and coffee. You're now fortified for the morning drive up through **Big Sur,** a highlight of any Pacific Coast drive. After 2.5 hours driving north on **CA-1,** you'll reach **Julia Pfeiffer Burns State Park,** a worthwhile stop for its view of 80-foot **McWay Falls** spilling into the ocean. The overlook is accessible by a short walk (just over 0.5 mile round-trip). Stop for lunch at **Nepenthe,** a restaurant with tasty burgers and stellar views of the coast.

Continue north on **CA-1,** stopping for the breathtaking views and photo-ops like **Bixby Bride.** It's an hour and 15 minutes' drive to your next stop in Monterey. At the **Monterey Bay Aquarium,** you'll see everything from jellyfish to sharks behind glass. Or take an hour-long **kayaking or paddling tour** of Monterey Bay, where you can get fairly close to harbor seals, sea lions, and sea otters.

From Monterey, continue along **CA-1** for another two hours to **Half Moon Bay** for a sunset seafood dinner at **Sam's Chowder House.** From Half Moon Bay, it's just a 45 minutes' drive to **San Francisco.**

by "progress," with buildings that date to the 1800s (a long time by California standards).

In recent years, the city has encouraged the growth of an impressive arts community and a thriving restaurant scene. A few blocks from Main Street is Surfer's Point, a coastal area also known as C Street. A ribbon of pavement by the ocean, the Omer Rains Bike Trail almost always hosts a collection of walkers, runners, and cyclists. Farther away, Ventura Harbor has a cluster of restaurants, bars, and hotels located around the harbor, which is the gateway to the nearby Channel Islands National Park.

## Getting There

There are several ways to get from Los Angeles up to Ventura. The drive should take just 1-1.5 hours unless you get ensnared in L.A.'s notorious freeway traffic. Check the Los Angeles Department of Transportation's live traffic information website (http://trafficinfo.lacity.org) before heading out of the city.

The most direct route is **US-101 North** from central Los Angeles. After 60 miles (an hour and 15 minutes without traffic), you'll reach the exits for Ventura. The more scenic route is **CA-1 North** from Santa Monica. You'll pass Malibu and some surprisingly undeveloped coastal areas before merging onto US-101 North at Oxnard. It is about 10 miles longer than the **US-101 North** route, but adds 20-30 minutes to your drive, depending on traffic.

To get to Ventura from **Los Angeles International Airport** (LAX, 1 World Way, Los Angeles, 855/463-5252, www.lawa.org), contact the **Ventura County Airporter** (805/650-6600, www.venturashuttle.com, $35 one-way, $65 round-trip). The small and efficient **Oxnard Airport** (2889 W. 5th St., 805/947-6804, www.iflyoxnard.com) has no scheduled flights but welcomes private aircraft and hosts rental car agencies.

The nearest **Greyhound bus station** is in Oxnard, but the *Pacific Surfliner* by **Amtrak** (800/872-7245, www.amtrak.com) still stops in Ventura (Harbor Blvd. and Figueroa St.) several times each day in both directions on its runs between San Diego and San Luis Obispo.

## Sights
### Main Street

The seven-block section of Ventura's **Main Street** (Main St. between Ventura Ave. and Fir St.) combines the best of the city's past and present. Important cultural and historic sites include Mission San Buenaventura, the missionary Junípero Serra's ninth California mission; and the Ortega Adobe, where the Ortega Chile Packing Company originated. But Main Street is not stuck in the past; it's also home to stylish restaurants like the Watermark on Main, clothing boutique Le Monde Emporium, and the brick-and-mortar store for the popular online surf-culture retailer WetSand.

### Mission San Buenaventura

Referred to as the "mission by the sea," **Mission San Buenaventura** (211 E. Main St., 805/643-4318, www.san-buenaventuramission.org, self-guided tours 10am-5pm Sun.-Fri., 9am-5pm Sat., $4 adults, $3 seniors, $1 children) is right on Ventura's Main Street and just blocks from the beach. It is just one of six missions that was personally dedicated by Junípero Serra, the founder of California's mission system.

A seven-mile-long aqueduct was built to bring water to the mission from the Ventura River. Because of its abundant water supply, Mission San Buenaventura became known for its lush orchards and gardens.

Today, the mission is a peaceful remnant of California's past. Beautiful high ceilings and walls are decorated with paintings of Jesus at various Stations of the Cross, depicting the series of events before the Crucifixion. A one-room museum on the grounds displays the church's original doors and a collection of indigenous Chumash artifacts. Between the museum and the church is a scenic garden with a tile fountain, an old olive press, and a shrine.

### C Street

The **California Street** area (on the coast from the end of Figueroa St. to the end of California St.), or **C Street,** hosted the world's first pro surfing event: 1965's Noseriding International. Today, extending 0.75 mile from Surfer's Point Park to the cove beside Ventura Pier, it's Ventura's recreation hub. Lines of white water streaming off the point entice surfers and stand-up paddleboarders, while old long-boarders relive their glory days catching waves that can continue for 0.75 mile. You might see pro surfers like Ventura local Dane Reynolds out ripping apart the waves or practicing aerials. It's worth a visit even if you don't surf. The vibrant coastal scene includes the Promenade walkway, which

# Ventura and Vicinity

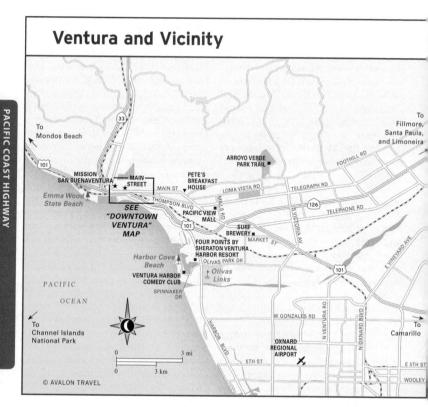

bustles with joggers and power walkers, and the popular Omer Rains Bike Trail. Facilities include an outdoor shower, restrooms, and a picnic area. Parking can be challenging: There's a free lot that fills up quickly as well as a paid lot ($2 per day).

## Entertainment and Events
### Bars and Clubs

Filling multiple rooms in a house dating back to 1912, **The Tavern** (211 E. Santa Clara St., 805/643-3264, http://tavernordie.com, 5pm-2am Mon.-Sat., 10am-2am Sun.) is quite a bar. Inside on a weekend night there may be two bands playing in two different rooms. If you're more interested in conversation, head for the room to the left upon entering, which has a fireplace and a couch, or opt for the large outdoor deck out back. While sipping your spirits, be on the lookout for a spirit: They say The Tavern is haunted by the ghost of a young girl who died here in the late 1800s. Entertainment includes DJs, karaoke, and live music.

Located in an industrial park southeast of downtown Ventura, **Surf Brewery** (4561 Market St., Ste. A, 805/644-2739, www.surfbrewery.com, 4pm-9pm Tues.-Thurs., 1pm-9pm Fri., noon-9pm Sat., noon-7pm Sun.) is the place to go for a pint of Mondo's Blonde Ale, County Line Rye Pale Ale, or Oil Piers Porter. There's live music 6pm-8pm on Saturday.

By the end of the evening, a lot of people end up at dive bar **Sans Souci Cocktail Lounge** (21 S. Chestnut St., 805/643-4539, 2pm-2am daily), which stays open late. The small interior, with red-couch seating, can get a bit claustrophobic on crowded nights; escape to the

# Downtown Ventura

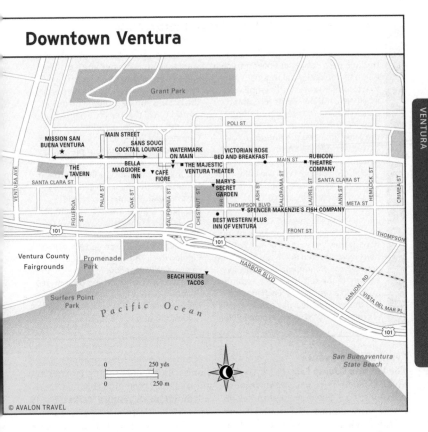

semi-covered courtyard out front before it fills up with drinkers and smokers.

## Live Music

**The Majestic Ventura Theater** (26 S. Chestnut St., 805/653-0721, www.venturatheater.net, box office 11am-6pm Tues.-Fri.) gets a variety of pretty big national acts, including music icons Alice Cooper and more recent acts like Insane Clown Posse. The 1,200-seat Mission-style theater opened in 1928 as a movie house; decades later it was converted into a concert venue. The old chandeliers still hang in the auditorium, and other remnants of the 1920s decor remain.

## Performing Arts

The **Rubicon Theatre Company** (1006 E. Main St., 805/667-2900, www.rubicontheatre.org) stages plays in a 186-seat venue that was once a church. Expect classics like Thornton Wilder's *Our Town* as well as new works; there is usually one wholly original show each season. One of Rubicon's original plays, *Daddy Long Legs*, landed on the London stage. Rubicon has also begun performing some plays in Spanish with English subtitles.

Owned by two comedy pros, the **Ventura Harbor Comedy Club** (1559 Spinnaker Dr., Ste. 205, 805/644-1500, http://venturaharborcomedyclub.com, shows Thurs. 8pm, Fri. 8pm and 10pm, Sat. 7pm and 9pm, Sun. 9pm, $15) hosts heavy hitters like Ron White and Bobcat Goldthwaite. They also have open-mike nights.

# El Camino Real: The King's Highway

As you drive US-101 from Ventura up through Paso Robles and beyond, you'll begin to notice signs along the road that look like a shepherd's crook with a bell on it and the words "El Camino Real." The signs are peppered along a nearly 600-mile route in California. At the same time that the American colonies were rebelling against England, a handful of Spaniards and Mexicans were establishing outposts up the California coast. In 1769, a fortress and the first mission were established in San Diego. A footpath called El Camino Real, meaning "the king's highway," was created to connect each of the subsequent missions as they were constructed. The missions were situated in areas where large populations of indigenous people lived and where the soil was fertile enough to sustain a settlement. Each mission was designed to be a day's travel from the next, all linked by El Camino Real.

As time progressed and more missions were built, the path became a roadway wide enough to accommodate horses and wagons. It was not, however, until the last mission was completed in Sonoma in 1823 that the little pathway became a major road. Ultimately, El Camino Real linked all 21 of California's missions, pueblos, and four presidios, from San Diego to Sonoma. In 1904 the El Camino Real Association was formed to preserve and maintain California's historic road. The first commemorative bell was placed in 1906 in front of the Old Plaza Church in downtown Los Angeles, and by 1915 approximately 158 bells had been installed along El Camino Real. The bells were made of cast iron, which encouraged theft, and the number of original bells plummeted to about 75. New bells made of concrete were installed in 1974. US-101 loosely follows this original footpath.

## Festivals and Events

The **Ventura County Fair** (10 W. Harbor Blvd., 805/648-3376, www.venturacountyfair.org) goes down every summer on the Ventura County Fairgrounds, next to the city's main coastal recreation area. Expect the usual attractions: a Ferris wheel, cotton candy, and livestock exhibits.

While it began as a chamber music festival, the **Ventura Music Festival** (805/648-3146, www.venturamusicfestival.org) has expanded to include jazz and crossover artists such as Sérgio Mendes. It takes place at the end of April and early May.

## Shopping

**Main Street** in downtown Ventura is home to a surprising number of unique local and specialty stores and has managed to retain a sense of individuality.

**Downtown Ventura County's Farmers Market** (Santa Clara St. and Palm St., www.vccfarmersmarkets.com,

8:30am-noon Sat.) has produce stands along with vendors selling tamales and pot stickers. If you miss that one, there's still the **Midtown Ventura Market** (Pacific View Mall, West Parking Lot, 3301 N. Main St., www.vccfarmersmarkets.com, 9am-1pm Wed.) on Wednesday.

The **Pacific View Mall** (3301 E. Main St., 805/642-5530, www.shoppacificview.com, 10am-9pm Mon.-Sat., 11am-7pm Sun.) features 140 brand-name stores and restaurants. Farther south are the **Camarillo Premium Outlets** (740 E. Ventura Blvd., off Los Posas Ave., Camarillo, 805/445-8520, www.premiumoutlets.com, 10am-9pm Mon.-Sat., 10am-8pm Sun., holiday hours vary), with 160 stores peddling reduced-price merchandise.

## Beaches
### San Buenaventura State Beach
**San Buenaventura State Beach** (San Pedro St., off US-101, 805/968-1033, www.parks.ca.gov, dawn-dusk daily, day

use $10) has an impressive two miles of beach, dunes, and ocean. It also includes the 1,600-foot Ventura Pier, home to Eric Ericsson's Seafood Restaurant and Beach House Tacos. The historic pier was built way back in 1872. This is a safer place to swim than some area beaches because it doesn't get the breakers that roll into the nearby point. Cyclists can take advantage of trails connecting with other nearby beaches, and sports enthusiasts converge on the beach for occasional triathlons and volleyball tournaments. Facilities include a snack bar, an equipment rental shop, and an essential for the 21st-century beach bum: Wi-Fi, although to pick up the signal, you need to be within about 200 feet of the lifeguard tower.

### Emma Wood State Beach

**Emma Wood State Beach** (W. Main St. and Park Access Rd., 805/968-1033, www.parks.ca.gov, dawn-dusk daily, day use $10) borders the estuary north of the Ventura River, and it includes the remnants of a World War II artillery site. There are no facilities, but a few minutes' walk leads to the campgrounds (reservations required mid-May-Labor Day, first-come, first-served winter), one for RVs and one group camp. At the far eastern side of the parking lot is a small path leading out to the beach that goes under the train tracks. To the right are views up the coast to the Rincon. It's a great spot for windsurfing, as the winds come off Rincon Point just up from the mouth of the Ventura River to create ideal windy conditions. There's a 0.5-mile trail leading through the reeds and underbrush at the far end of the parking lot; although you can hear the surf and the highway, you can't see anything, and you'll feel like you're on safari until you reach the beach where the Ventura River ends.

### Harbor Cove Beach

Families flock to **Harbor Cove Beach** (1900 Spinnaker Dr., dawn-dusk daily, free), located directly across from the Channel Islands Visitors Center at the end of Spinnaker Drive. The harbor's breakwaters provide children and less confident swimmers with relative safety from the ocean currents. In addition, it's a great place to try your hand at stand-up paddleboarding. There's plenty of free parking, lifeguards during peak seasons, restrooms, and foot showers.

## Sports and Recreation
### Surfing

Ventura is definitely a surf town. The series of point breaks referred to as California Street, **C Street** for short, is the best place for consistent right breaks. There are three distinct zones along this mile-long stretch of beach. At the point is the Pipe, with some pretty fast short breaks. Moving down the beach is Stables, which continues with the right breaks with an even low shoulder, and then C Street, breaking both right and left. The waves get mushier and easier for beginners the closer you get to Ventura Pier. There is a paid parking lot right in front of the break across the street from the Ventura County Fairgrounds (10 W. Harbor Blvd.).

Long-boarders and beginners should head to **Mondos Beach** (six miles north of town) for soft peeling waves. It's a little north of town toward Santa Barbara; take US-101 north to the State Beaches exit. Then head 3.5 miles north on the Pacific Coast Highway. Park in the dirt lot on the right side of PCH.

If you just need gear, swing by **Seaward Surf and Sport** (1082 S. Seaward Ave., 805/648-4742, www.seawardsurf.com, 9am-7pm daily, surfboard rental $15-50), which is the place to buy or rent almost anything for the water, including body boards and wetsuits. It's half a block from the beach, so you can head straight to the water. **Ventura Surf Shop** (88 E. Thompson Blvd., 805/643-1062, www.venturasurfshop.com, 9am-6pm Mon.-Sat., 9am-5pm Sun., board rental $30 per day, wetsuit $20 per day) rents out surfboards, wetsuits, body boards, and a couple of stand-up paddleboards.

**Ventura Surf School** (461 W. Channel Islands Blvd., 805/218-1484, www.venturasurfschool.com, private two-hour lesson $125, two or more $80 pp) can also teach you to surf, and they offer a week-long surf camp and kids-only classes. Beginner lessons are at Mondos Beach (six miles north of town).

### Whale-Watching

December-March is the ideal time to see Pacific gray whales pass through the channel off the coast of Ventura. Late June-late August has the narrow window for both blue and humpback whales as they feed offshore near the islands. **Island Packers Cruises** (1691 Spinnaker Dr., Ste. 105B, 805/642-1393, www.islandpackers.com, $38-68 adults, $34-62 seniors, $28-55 children) has operated whale-watching cruises for years and is the most experienced. It also runs harbor cruises with a variety of options, including dinner cruises and group charters. Most whale-watching trips last about three hours. Remember that whale watching is weather-dependent, so cancellations can occur.

### Cycling

The eight-mile-long paved **Omer Rains Bike Trail** runs along Ventura's beachfront from San Buenaventura State Beach past the Ventura Pier and Surfer's Point to Emma Wood State Beach. The **Ventura River Trail** (Main St. and Peking St., www.cityofventura.net) follows the Ventura River inland from Main Street just over six miles one-way, ending at Foster Park. From here it joins the **Ojai Trail,** a two-lane bike path that follows CA-33 into Ojai (16 miles one-way).

If you want to pedal it, **Wheel Fun Rentals** (850 Harbor Blvd., 805/765-5795, www.wheelfunrentals.com, 9am-sunset daily summer, 9am-sunset Fri.-Sun. and holidays winter, bike rentals $10-35 per hour) rents out beach cruisers, surreys,

mountain bikes, and low-riding chopper bikes. The **Ventura Bike Depot** (239 W. Main St., 805/652-1114, http://venturabikedepot.com, 9am-5pm Mon.-Fri., 8:30am-5pm Sat.-Sun., bike rentals $15-30 per hour) rents out mountain bikes, road bikes, hybrid bikes, beach cruisers, and surreys for two-hour, four-hour, and all-day stints.

## Food
### Seafood

Housed in a building that resembles a boat, ★ **Spencer Makenzie's Fish Company** (806 E. Thompson Blvd., 805/643-8226, www.spencermakenzies.com, 11am-9pm Sun.-Thurs., 10:30am-9pm Fri-Sat., $5-12.50) is known for its giant fish tacos, a tasty fusion of Japanese and Mexican flavors. The sushi-grade fish is hand-dipped in tempura batter and then fried, while the white sauce, cabbage, and cilantro are traditional Baja ingredients. Choose from the array of homegrown sauces along the counter to add splashes of sweet and heat.

### Mexican

In a prime spot on the Ventura Pier, ★ **Beach House Tacos** (668 Harbor Blvd., 805/648-3177, 11am-8:30pm Mon.-Thurs., 11am-9pm Fri., 8:30am-9pm Sat., 8:30am-8:30pm Sun., $2.25-7.25) doesn't coast on its enviable location. Creative ingredients include soy ginger lime cream sauce-soaked ahi and fish tacos with fruit salsa. Beginners can try "The Combo," a lump of grilled meat (chicken, carne asada, or pork) topped with melted cheese, grilled pasilla chiles, zucchini, and carrots. Order at the counter and dine in an enclosed seating section on the pier. Expect long lines on summer weekends.

### Italian

Bolstered by a popular wood bar, **Café Fiore** (66 California St., 805/653-1266, www.cafefioreventura.com,

# ☝ Side Trip to the Channel Islands

Inspiration Point on Anacapa Island

## Channel Islands National Park

(805/658-5720, www.nps.gov/chis) sweeps visitors back to a time when the California coastline was undeveloped and virtually pristine. Due to its remote location, Channel Islands National Park is only accessible by boat or plane, placing it in the top 20 least crowded national parks. It's worth a detour even if just for a day.

The best islands to visit are also the two closest to the mainland: Santa Cruz Island and Anacapa Island. The largest and most hospitable of the islands, **Santa Cruz** is also by far the most popular island to visit. It has more buildings and a campground near Scorpion Bay where you can pitch a tent and store your food in metal lockers. Its main draws are amazing sea caves that can be explored by kayak. Other activities include hiking and snorkeling opportunities.

**Anacapa** is wilder and more barren than nearby Santa Cruz. Anacapa actually comprises three islets, together 5 miles long and 0.25 mile wide, with a land area totaling just one square mile. There's a two-mile trail system, a small visitors center, and a campground. Hiking trails offer stunning views. If you have seen a photo of the Channel Islands on a calendar or a postcard, it's most likely the spectacular view from Inspiration Point. From this high vantage point on the west end of the

island, Middle Anacapa Island and West Anacapa Island rise out of the ocean like a giant sea serpent's spine. Another iconic sight is Arch Rock, a 40-foot-high rock window off the islet's eastern tip.

## Getting There

Get to Santa Cruz Island or Anacapa Island by hopping aboard a boat run by **Island Packers Cruises** (1691 Spinnaker Dr., Ste. 105B, Ventura Harbor, 805/642-1393, www.islandpackers.com). Even the boat ride out to the islands is an adventure, with porpoises frequently racing beside the boats. In addition to trips to the islands, Island Packers hosts wildlife cruises, whale-watching tours, and Ventura Harbor dinner cruises. Trips to Anacapa and Santa Cruz are offered 5-7 days a week year-round. The most common landing at **Santa Cruz** (daily Apr.-Oct., Tues. and Fri.-Sun. Nov.-Mar., $59 adults, $54 seniors, $41 children 3-12) is Scorpion Cove, with a crossing time of 90 minutes. Trips to **Anacapa** (daily year-round, $59 adults, $54 seniors, $41 children 3-12) take an average of 45 minutes. Keep a close eye on the weather as your trip approaches, as weather and ocean conditions can change quickly. In case of inclement weather, call Island Packers the morning of your journey to confirm your trip.

11:30am-10pm Mon.-Thurs., 11:30am-11pm Fri.-Sat., 11:30am-9pm Sun., $16-32) is a hot spot for Ventura professionals grabbing a cocktail or meal after work. The food includes Italian favorites like cioppino and osso buco, served in a sleek, high-ceilinged room decorated with furnishings that recall the interior of a Cost Plus World Market. Expect to wait a while for service on crowded nights and during happy hour.

### Breakfast

Most mornings you'll have to wait to get inside the popular **Pete's Breakfast House** (2055 E. Main St., 805/648-1130, www.petesbreakfasthouse.com, 7am-2pm daily, $5-12). Pete's fresh-squeezed orange juice, biscuits made daily, strawberry jam made in-house, pancakes, and omelets make it worth the wait. But the homemade corned beef hash and eggs are the real stars, inspiring breakfast lovers to drive all the way up from Los Angeles to spend the morning at Pete's.

## Accommodations
### Under $150

The **Bella Maggiore Inn** (67 S. California St., 805/652-0277, www.bellamaggiore-inn.com, $75-175) has not changed its prices since 2001, making it a great place to stay for budget travelers. The inn has a great location a few blocks from the beach and just a block off Ventura's Main Street. Some of the guest rooms are no larger than a college dorm room, but there is a lobby with couches, Italian chandeliers, a piano, and a fireplace. Even better is the courtyard with a fountain and a dining area surrounded by vines. There's free overnight parking behind the building.

### $150-250

If you are traveling to Channel Islands National Park out of Ventura Harbor, the ★ **Four Points by Sheraton Ventura Harbor Resort** (1050 Schooner Dr., 805/658-1212, www.fourpoints.com, $150-285) is a great place to lay your head before an early-morning boat ride or to relax after a few days of camping on the islands. The guest rooms are clean and comfortable, with balconies and patios. With a gym, a tennis court, a pool, and a basketball court, there is a wide array of recreational opportunities available at the resort. For folks who have hiked all over the Channel Islands, Four Points has a hot tub in a glass dome to ease your aching muscles.

## Information and Services

The **Ventura Visitors Center** (101 California St., 800/333-2989, www.ventura-usa.com, 9am-5pm Mon.-Sat., 10am-4pm Sun. summer, 9am-4pm Mon.-Sat., 10am-4pm Sun. winter) occupies a big space in downtown Ventura and offers a lot of information, including a historical walking tour guide of the city.

**Community Memorial Hospital** (147 N. Brent St., 805/652-5011, www.cmhshealth.org) has the only emergency room in the area. Police services are the **City of Ventura Police Department** (1425 Dowell Dr., 805/339-4400); in case of emergency, call 911 immediately.

## Getting Around

Travel Ventura in a cab by calling **Gold Coast Cab** (805/444-6969, www.goldcoastcab.com). Both Uber (www.uber.com) and Lyft (www.lyft.com) operate in Ventura, so download one of the apps on your smartphone if interested.

# Santa Barbara

It's been called the American Riviera, with sun-drenched beaches reminiscent of the Mediterranean coast. In truth, Santa Barbara is all California. It's one of the state's most picturesque cities, with a plethora of palm trees and chic residents.

It's famous for its Spanish colonial revival architecture. After a 1925 earthquake, the city rebuilt itself in the style of the Santa Barbara Mission, arguably the most beautiful of the California missions, with white stucco surfaces, red-tiled roofs, arches, and courtyards.

Nestled between the Pacific Ocean and the mountains, its wide roads, warm sandy beaches, and challenging mountain trails inspire physical activity and healthy living. Along the waterfront, a paved path allows anyone on two feet, two wheels, or anything else that moves to enjoy the coastline alongside grassy areas with palm trees gently swaying in the breeze. Several weekly area farmers markets make healthy produce abundant and accessible.

## Getting There

From Ventura, drive 28 miles on **US-101 North** to Santa Barbara. It's a quick drive unless there is a traffic jam, which is often the case on Friday afternoons and evenings as L.A. locals head north to escape the city. Check the Ventura County Transportation Commission website (www.goventura.org) for current highway conditions.

To reach Santa Barbara by air, fly into **Santa Barbara Municipal Airport** (SBA, 500 Fowler Rd., 805/683-4011, www.santabarbaraca.gov). A number of major commercial airlines fly into Santa Barbara, including United, Alaska, Frontier, US Airways, and American.

A more beautiful and peaceful way to get to Santa Barbara is by train with **Amtrak** (800/872-7245, www.amtrak.com). The *Coast Starlight* stops at the centrally located train station (209 State St.) daily in each direction on its way between Seattle and Los Angeles. The *Pacific Surfliner* makes up to 10 stops daily on its route between San Luis Obispo and San Diego. If you're traveling by bus, your destination is the **Greyhound Bus Station** (224 Chapala St., 805/965-7551, www.greyhound.com) near the Amtrak station.

## Sights
### State Street

Although **State Street** runs through different sections of Santa Barbara, the roadway through 12 blocks downtown is the heart of the city. With wide brick sidewalks on either side shaded by palm trees and decorated with flowers that give it a tropical feel, State Street is perfect for an afternoon stroll. Clothing stores, restaurants, and bars line the street along with popular attractions that include the Santa Barbara Museum of Art and the Granada Theatre.

### Stearns Wharf

Stretching 2,250 feet into the harbor, **Stearns Wharf** (State St. and Cabrillo Blvd., www.stearnswharf.org, parking $2.50 per hour, first 1.5 hours free with validation) was the longest deep-water pier between Los Angeles and San Francisco at the time of its construction by lumberman John P. Stearns in 1872. It has weathered many natural disasters, including storms and fires; a restaurant fire in 1973 caused its closure for almost nine years. Today it hosts seaside tourist favorites like fish-and-chips eateries, candy stores, and gift shops. It's also home to the **Ty Warner Sea Center** (211 Stearns Wharf, 805/962-2526, www.sbnature.org, 10am-5pm daily, multi-museum passes $8.50 adults, $7.50 seniors and teens, $6 children), operated by the Museum of Natural History, with many interactive exhibits, such as a live shark touch pool and a 1,500-gallon surge tank filled with sea stars, urchins, and limpets.

### Santa Barbara Museum of Natural History

Continuing the outdoors theme that pervades Santa Barbara, the **Santa Barbara Museum of Natural History** (2559 Puesta del Sol, 805/682-4711, www.sbnature.org, 10am-5pm daily, $12 adults, $8 seniors and teens, $7 children) has exhibits to delight visitors of all ages. Inside, visit the large galleries that display stories of

# Santa Barbara

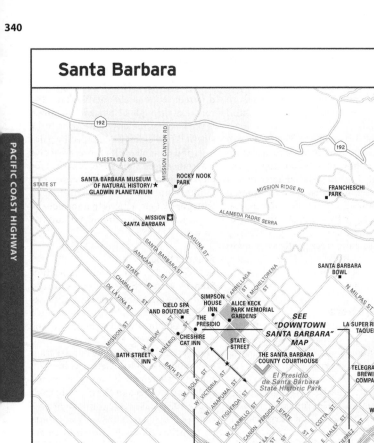
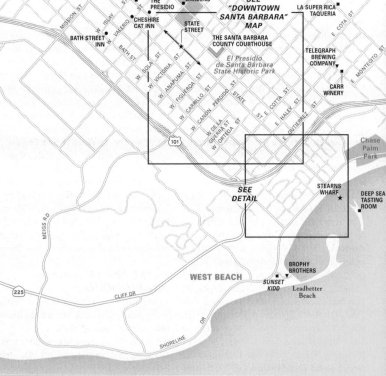

192

PUESTA DEL SOL RD

MISSION CANYON RD

STATE ST

SANTA BARBARA MUSEUM
OF NATURAL HISTORY/ ★
GLADWIN PLANETARIUM

ROCKY NOOK
PARK

192

MISSION RIDGE RD

FRANCHESCHI
PARK

MISSION
SANTA BARBARA

ALAMEDA PADRE SERRA

LAGUNA ST

SANTA BARBARA ST

ANACAPA ST

STATE ST

CHAPALA ST

DE LA VINA ST

MISSION ST

SANTA BARBARA
BOWL

N MILPAS ST

E ARRELLAGA ST

E MICHELTORENA ST

CIELO SPA
AND BOUTIQUE

SIMPSON
HOUSE
INN

ALICE KECK
PARK MEMORIAL
GARDENS

THE
PRESIDIO

SEE
"DOWNTOWN
SANTA BARBARA"
MAP

LA SUPER RICA
TAQUERIA

E COTA ST

CHESHIRE
CAT INN

BATH STREET
INN

W VALERIO ST

W ISLAY ST

BATH ST

STATE
STREET

THE SANTA BARBARA
COUNTY COURTHOUSE

El Presidio
de Santa Barbara
State Historic Park

TELEGRAPH
BREWING
COMPANY

E MONTECITO ST

CARR
WINERY

W SOLA ST

W VICTORIA ST

W ANAPUMA ST

W FIGUEROA ST

W CARRILLO ST

W CANON PERDIDO ST

STATE ST

E COTA ST

E HALEY ST

E GUTIERREZ ST

W DE LA
GUERRA ST

W ORTEGA ST

101

SEE
DETAIL

Chase
Palm
Park

STEARNS
WHARF

DEEP SEA
TASTING
ROOM

MEIGS RD

225

WEST BEACH

CLIFF DR

SUNSET
KIDD

BROPHY
BROTHERS

Leadbetter
Beach

SHORELINE DR

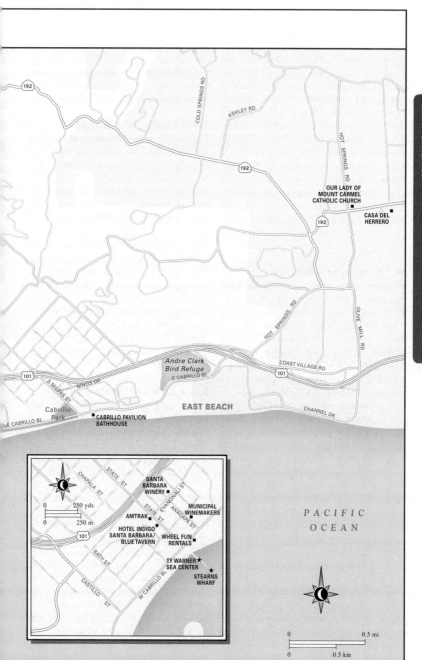

192

ASHLEY RD

COLD SPRINGS RD

HOT SPRINGS RD

192

**OUR LADY OF MOUNT CARMEL CATHOLIC CHURCH**

**CASA DEL HERRERO**

192

HOT SPRINGS RD

OLIVE MILL RD

*Andre Clark Bird Refuge*

COAST VILLAGE RD

101

101

S MILPAS ST

NINOS DR

E CABRILLO BL

Cabrillo Park

E CABRILLO BL

**EAST BEACH**

CHANNEL DR

**CABRILLO PAVILION BATHHOUSE**

CHAPALA ST

STATE ST

**SANTA BARBARA WINERY**

EYANONALI ST

ANACAPA ST

0 250 yds
0 250 m

**MUNICIPAL WINEMAKERS**

**AMTRAK**

STATE ST

**HOTEL INDIGO SANTA BARBARA/ BLUE TAVERN**

101

**WHEEL FUN RENTALS**

BATH ST

**TY WARNER SEA CENTER**

**STEARNS WHARF**

CASTILLO ST

W CABRILLO BL

PACIFIC OCEAN

0 0.5 mi
0 0.5 km

the life and times of insects, mammals, birds, and dinosaurs. Of particular interest is a display showcasing the remains of a pygmy mammoth specimen that was found on the nearby Channel Islands. Learn a little about the human history of the Santa Barbara area at the Chumash exhibit. Head outdoors to circle the immense skeleton of a blue whale, and to hike the Mission Creek Nature Trail. If you're interested in the nature of worlds other than this one, go into the **Gladwin Planetarium** ($4 with paid admission) and wander the Astronomy Center exhibits. The planetarium hosts shows portraying the moon and stars, plus monthly Star Parties and special events throughout the year.

### ★ Santa Barbara Mission

It's easy to see why the **Santa Barbara Mission** (2201 Laguna St., 805/682-4713, www.santabarbaramission.org, 9am-4:30pm daily, self-guided tours 9am-4:15pm day after Labor Day-July 2, 9am-5:15pm July 3-Labor Day, $9 adults, $7 seniors, $4 children, children under 5 free; docent-guided tours $13 adults, $11 seniors, $8 children, children under 4 free) is referred to as the "Queen of the Missions." Larger, more beautiful, and more impressive than many of the 20 other missions, it's second to none for its art displays and graceful architecture, all of which are complemented by the serene local climate and scenery. Unlike many of the California missions, the church at Santa Barbara remained in use after the secularization of the mission chain in the 19th century. When you visit, you'll find the collection of buildings, artwork, and even the ruins of the water system in better shape than at the other missions. The self-guided tour includes a walk through the mission's striking courtyard, with its blooming flowers and towering palm trees, and entrance to the mission museum, which has, among other displays, a photo of the church after a 1925

earthquake toppled its towers, as well as a collection of Chumash artifacts. The original purpose of the mission was to convert the indigenous Chumash people to Christianity. The mission's cemetery is the final resting place of more than 4,000 Chumash people.

### Santa Barbara Museum of Art

The two-floor **Santa Barbara Museum of Art** (1130 State St., 805/963-4364, www.sbma.net, 11am-5pm Tues.-Wed. and Fri.-Sun., Thurs., $10 adults, $6 children, children 6 and under free) has an impressive art collection that would make some larger cities envious. Wander the spacious, well-curated museum and take in some paintings from the museum's collection of Monets, the largest collection of the French impressionist's paintings in the West. The museum also has ancient works like a bronze head of Alexander from Roman times and a collection of Asian artifacts, including a 17th- or 18th-century Tibetan prayer wheel. There are interesting temporary exhibitions on display as well.

### Santa Barbara County Courthouse

If only all government buildings could be as striking as the **Santa Barbara County Courthouse** (1100 Anacapa St., 805/962-6464, http://sbcourthouse.org, docent-led tours 10:30am-4:45pm Mon.-Fri., 2pm Sat.-Sun., free). Constructed in 1929 after the devastating 1925 earthquake, the courthouse, which comprises four buildings covering a full city block, is one of the city's finest examples of Mediterranean architecture. The interior's high ceilings, tile floors, ornate chandeliers, and art-adorned walls give it the feel of a California mission. The old Board of Supervisors room is impressive, with 6,700 square feet of murals depicting the county's history and its resources. Also visit El Mirador, the clock tower, an 85-foot-high open deck that provides great views of the towering Santa Ynez Mountains and the Pacific

Ocean, with the city's red-tiled roofs in the foreground.

## Wineries

The wines of Santa Barbara County have been receiving favorable reviews in the national media. The area is known predominantly for wines made from pinot noir and chardonnay grapes, but with the diversity of microclimates, there are over 50 grape varietals grown here.

Not all wine tasting happens in vineyards. On the **Urban Wine Trail** (www.urbanwinetrailsb.com), you can sample some of the county's best wines without even seeing a vine.

The oldest winery in the county, **Santa Barbara Winery** (202 Anacapa St., 805/963-3633, www.sbwinery.com, 10am-6pm Sun.-Thurs., 10am-7pm Fri.-Sat.) started in 1962. The chardonnay is delightful and truly expresses a Santa Barbara character with its bright citrus notes. Other varieties include pinot noir, sangiovese, and sauvignon blanc.

**Municipal Winemakers** (22 Anacapa St., 805/931-6864, www.municipalwinemakers.com, 11am-8pm Sun.-Wed., 11am-11pm Thurs.-Sat., tasting $12) is in an unpretentious small space with an even smaller deck. Inside are rough wood ceilings and plain walls, with a four-top table and standing room at the bar. The offerings are Rhône-style wines, including grenache, syrah, and a sparkling shiraz.

**Carr Winery** (414 N. Salsipuedes St., 805/965-7985, www.carrwinery.com, 11am-9pm Mon.-Sat., 11am-6pm Sun., tasting $12-15) focuses on small lots of syrah, grenache, cabernet franc, and pinot noir. The tasting room is in a World War II Quonset hut, with a bar up front and tables in the back. The wine bar hosts live music 6pm-8pm every Friday night.

Nothing improves a great glass of

**From top to bottom:** State Street; the Santa Barbara County Courthouse; the Simpson House Inn.

# Downtown Santa Barbara

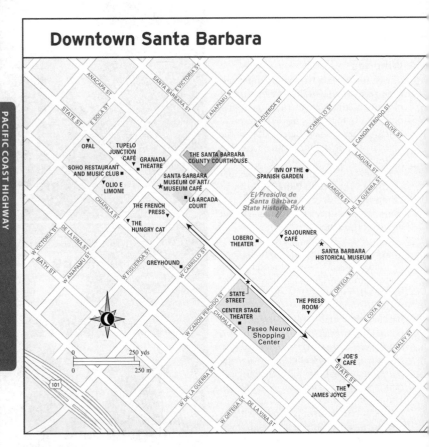

wine like a great view. The **Deep Sea Wine Tasting Room** (217 Stearns Wharf, 805/618-1185, www.conwayfamilywines. com, noon-7pm Sun.-Thurs., noon-8pm Fri.-Sat., tasting $8-20) takes advantage of this fact with a location right on Stearns Wharf, offering views of the harbor, the shoreline, and the distant Channel Islands. Sample Conway Family Wines, including the popular signature Deep Sea Red, a blend of five grapes that are mostly syrah.

## Entertainment and Events

A wealthy town with close ties to cosmopolitan Los Angeles, Santa Barbara offers visitors a wealth of live cultural displays, from a symphony and opera to a near-endless parade of festivals. The students of UCSB add zest to the town's after-dark scene.

## Bars and Clubs

The proximity of the University of California to downtown Santa Barbara guarantees a livelier nighttime scene than you'll find elsewhere on the Central Coast. Bars cluster on State Street and beyond, and plenty of hip clubs dot the landscape.

The best place to start an evening out on the town is at **Joe's Café** (536 State St., 805/966-4638, www.joescafesb.com, 7:30am-11pm daily), a steak house and bar known for the stiffest drinks in town. Don't expect a fancy cocktail menu; just go with the classics in this historic establishment and its throwback feel, with checkered tablecloths, a tin-paneled ceiling, and framed black-and-white photos of mostly old men adorning the walls.

A half block off State Street, **The Press Room** (15 E. Ortega St., 805/963-8121, 11am-2am daily) calls itself both an "untraditional English pub" and the "unofficial British Consulate since 1995." The long, narrow room with red walls distinguishes itself from nearby State Street bars by being a place where you can actually have a conversation while enjoying a pint of Bass, Boddingtons, or the lesser-known Bombardier. It has a great jukebox playing punk and indie music.

For a traditional Irish bar experience in downtown Santa Barbara, head to **The James Joyce** (513 State St., 805/962-2688, www.sbjamesjoyce.com, 11am-2am daily). Peanut shells litter the floor as locals sip Guinness at the bar or play competitive games of darts in the backroom. The James Joyce has live entertainment six days a week.

**Telegraph Brewing Company** (418 N. Salsipuedes St., 805/963-5018, www.telegraphbrewing.com, tasting room 2pm-10pm Fri., noon-10pm Sat., noon-7pm Sun.) is located in a renovated World War II-era Quonset hut. Up to 10 taps pour tastes of small-batch beers, including the flagship California Ale, Stock Porter, and Cerveza de Fiesta, a pilsner-style lager, and the experimental Telegraph Obscura beers.

## Live Music

A great place to take in a concert during the warm summer and fall months is the **Santa Barbara Bowl** (1122 N. Milpas St., 805/962-7411, www.sbbowl.com, box office hours 11am-6pm Mon.-Fri.), which has hosted concerts by artists such as Bob Dylan, Arcade Fire, Lorde, Lana Del Rey, and local girl Katy Perry. Built in 1936, it's the largest outdoor amphitheater in the county. The seats on the left side have the best views of the city below.

Founded in 1873, the **Lobero Theater** (33 E. Canon Perdido St., 805/963-0761, www.lobero.org) is the oldest continuously operating theater in the state. While it used to host entertainers like Tallulah Bankhead and Bela Lugosi, it now welcomes jazz acts like Pat Metheny and Dianne Reeves along with indie rock darlings like Jenny Lewis and salsa-funk outfit Ozomatli. The medium-size theater has only one level, and it's filled with cushy red velvet seats, perfect for a music-filled night out on the town.

Located in an upstairs suite, **Soho** (1221 State St., Ste. 205, 805/962-7776, www.sohosb.com, from 5pm daily) has hosted big-time touring acts that include Jimmy Cliff, Real Estate, and Built to Spill. It has live music seven nights a week. With its brick walls, Soho is going for a sophisticated New York City-type atmosphere.

## Classical Music

The **Santa Barbara Symphony** (Granada Theatre, 1214 State St., 805/898-9386, tickets 805/899-2222, www.thesymphony.org) aspires to compete with its brethren in Los Angeles and San Francisco. The symphony orchestra puts on seasons that pay homage to the great composers, plus the works of lesser-known talented artists. Whether you prefer Mozart or Mahler, you can listen to it at the concert hall at the Granada Theatre. Every seat has a great view of the stage, and the acoustics were designed with music in mind, making for an overall great symphony experience.

**Opera Santa Barbara** (805/898-3890, www.operasb.com) focuses on the classics and little-known works of the Italian masters, staging operas such as *Aida, Don Pasquale,* and *Madame Butterfly* at the Granada Theatre.

## Dance

The **Center Stage Theater** (751 Paseo Nuevo, 805/963-0408, www.centerstagetheater.org) focuses on dance, including ballet and modern performances. A handful of local groups, including the Lit Moon Theatre and Out of the Box Theater Company, have also made the Center Stage their home, staging everything from plays with a formerly incarcerated cast to improv comedy.

### Festivals and Events

Painters use Mission Plaza as their canvas at the **I Madonnari Italian Street Painting Festival** (805/964-4710, www.imadonnarifestival.com, late May, free), inspired by a similar event in Grazie di Curtatone, Italy. Participants and their sponsors buy sections of the street, with proceeds benefiting the nonprofit Children's Creative Project.

**Fiesta** (various venues in Santa Barbara, 805/962-8101, www.oldspanishdays-fiesta.org, Aug., some events free), or Old Spanish Days, is Santa Barbara's biggest annual festival. Since 1924, it has paid tribute to the city's Spanish and Mexican heritage with parades, live music, horse shows, bull riding, and the erection of public marketplaces known as *mercados*. During Fiesta, hotel rooms become near impossible to find, with rare vacancies filled at premium rates.

The longest day of the year gets its due at the annual **Solstice Parade** (805/965-3396, www.solsticeparade.com, late June, free). A line of extravagantly dressed participants and colorful floats proceeds nine blocks down State Street and three blocks down West Micheltorena Street before ending in Alameda Park.

The 11-day **Santa Barbara International Film Festival** (various venues, 805/963-0023, http://sbiff.org, Jan.-Feb.) showcases over 200 films and includes 20 world premieres, drawing big Hollywood players like Quentin Tarantino, Jennifer Lawrence, Daniel Day-Lewis, Amy Adams, and Ben Affleck.

## Shopping

In Santa Barbara, even the malls and shopping districts are visually interesting. They are all outdoor malls, fun for hanging out. From end to end, the busy main drag **State Street** hosts an unbelievable array of chain stores, plus a few independent boutiques for variety. You'll find lots of lovely women's apparel and plenty of housewares.

Explore the **Paseo Nuevo Shopping Center** (651 Paseo Nuevo, 805/963-7147, www.paseonuevoshopping.com, 10am-9pm Mon.-Fri., 10am-8pm Sat., 11am-6pm Sun.), a series of pathways off State Street that have clothing stores, including Nordstrom and Macy's, along with chain eateries like Chipotle and California Pizza Kitchen. Also right off State Street is **La Arcada Court** (1114 State St., 805/966-6634, www.laarcadasantabarbara.com), a collection of shops, restaurants, specialty stores, and art galleries. Along the tile-lined walkways, playful humanlike sculptures appear in front of some of the shops.

## Beaches

There's nothing easier than finding a beach in Santa Barbara. Just follow State Street to its end, and you'll be at the coast.

### East Beach

Named because it is east of Stearns Wharf, **East Beach** (1400 Cabrillo Blvd., 805/564-5418, www.santabarbaraca.gov, sunrise-10pm daily) is all soft sand and wide beach, with a dozen volleyball nets in the sand close to the zoo. If you look closely you can see the giraffes and lions. It has all the amenities a sun worshipper could need: a full beach house, a snack bar, a play area for children, and a path for cycling and in-line skating. The beachfront has picnic facilities and a full-service restaurant at the East Beach Grill. The **Cabrillo Pavilion Bathhouse** (1119 E. Cabrillo Blvd.), built in 1927, offers showers, lockers, a weight room, one rentable beach wheelchair, and volleyball rentals.

## West Beach

On the west side of Stearns Wharf, **West Beach** (Cabrillo Blvd. and Chapala St., between Stearns Wharf and the harbor, 805/897-1982, www.santabarbaraca.gov, sunrise-10pm daily) has 11 acres of picturesque sand for sunbathing, swimming, kayaking, windsurfing, and beach volleyball. There are also large palm trees, a wide walkway, and a bike path, making it a popular spot. Outrigger canoes also launch from this beach.

## Leadbetter Beach

Considered by many to be the best beach in Santa Barbara, **Leadbetter Beach** (Shoreline Dr. and Loma Alta Dr., 805/564-5418, www.santabarbaraca. gov, sunrise-10pm daily) divides the area's south-facing beaches from the west-facing ones. It's a long, flat beach with a large grassy area. Sheer cliffs rise from the sand, and trees dot the point. The beach, which is also bounded by the harbor and the breakwater, is ideal for swimming because it's fairly well protected, unlike the other flat beaches.

Many catamaran sailors and windsurfers launch from this beach, and you'll occasionally see surfers riding the waves. The grassy picnic areas have barbecue sites that can be reserved for more privacy, but otherwise there is a lot of room. There are restrooms, a small restaurant, and outdoor showers.

## Arroyo Burro Beach

To the north of town, **Arroyo Burro Beach** (Cliff Dr., 805/568-2461, www.sbparks. org, 8am-sunset daily), also known as Hendry's, is a favorite for locals and dog owners. To the right as you face the water, past Arroyo Burro Slough, dogs are allowed off-leash to dash across the packed sand and frolic and fetch out in the gentle surf. Arroyo Burro is rockier than the downtown beaches, making it less pleasant for games and sunbathing. But the rocks and shells make for great beachcombing, and you might find it

slightly less crowded on sunny weekend days. You'll find a snack bar, restrooms, outdoor showers, and a medium-size paid parking lot. At peak times, when the parking lot is full, there's nowhere else to park.

## Sports and Recreation

With the year-round balmy weather, it's nearly impossible to resist the temptation to get outside and do something energetic and fun in Santa Barbara. From golf to sea kayaking, you've got plenty of options for recreation.

### Hiking

The two-mile hike up to **Inspiration Point** (4 miles round-trip, moderate-strenuous) gives you access to the best vistas of the city, the ocean, and the Channel Islands. The uphill hike starts out paved, then becomes a dirt road, and then a trail. To reach the trailhead from the Santa Barbara Mission, head up Mission Canyon Road. At the stop sign, take a right onto Foothill Road. Take a left at the next stop sign on Mission Canyon Road, and stay left at the fork onto Tunnel Road. Continue down Tunnel Road to the end, where there is a parking area.

Starting from the same spot, **Seven Falls** (3 miles round-trip, easy) begins as a hike but becomes a scramble up a creek bed to its namesake attraction, where bowls of rock hold pools of water. It's a good place to cool off on a hot day. Follow the paved road at the end of Tunnel Road; it's gated and locked against vehicle traffic but is accessible to hikers. After 0.75 mile, continue on the Tunnel Trail. When the trail dips down by the creek, head upstream. The hike requires some boulder-hopping and mild rock climbing.

### Cycling

There are plenty of cycling opportunities in Santa Barbara, from flat leisurely pedals by the water to climbs up into the foothills. An option for Santa Barbara cycling information is **Traffic Solutions**

(805/963-7283, www.trafficsolutions. info). Visit the website to obtain a copy of the free Santa Barbara County bike map.

If you'd rather be pedaling the dirt rather than the pavement, Santa Barbara's mountainous and hilly terrain makes for good mountain biking. **Velo Pro Cyclery** (http://velopro.com) provides a fine introduction to the area's mountain biking resources. **Elings Park** (1298 Las Positas Rd., 805/569-5611, www.elingspark.org, 7am-sunset daily) has single-track trails for beginners and intermediates. Just a few minutes from downtown Santa Barbara, it's perfect for a quick, no-hassle ride.

If you need to rent a bike, **Wheel Fun Rentals** (23 E. Cabrillo Blvd. and 22 State St., 805/966-2282, 9am-sunset daily summer, 9am-sunset Fri.-Sun. and holidays winter, www.wheelfunrentals.com) has two locations. Rent a surrey bike or a beach cruiser for an easy ride by the coast, or rent a road bike to head up into the foothills.

## Surfing

During the summer months, the Channel Islands block the south swells and keep them from reaching the Santa Barbara coastline. During fall and winter, the big north and northwest swells wrap around Point Conception, offering some of the best waves in the area and transforming places like Rincon in nearby Carpinteria into legendary surf breaks.

Beginners should head to **Leadbetter Point** (Shoreline Park, just north of the Santa Barbara Harbor), a slow, mushy wave that's also perfect for long-boarders. For a bit more of a challenge, paddle out to the barrels at **Sandspit** (Santa Barbara Harbor). The harbor's breakwater creates hollow right breaks for adventurous surfers only. Be careful, though: Sandspit's backwash has been known to toss surfers onto the breakwater.

Known as the "Queen of the Coast," **Rincon** (US-101 at Bates Rd., on the Ventura County-Santa Barbara County line) is considered California's best right point break, with long waves that hold up for as long as 300 yards. If it's firing, you'll also most likely be sharing Rincon with lots of other surfers. You might even see revered three-time world champion surfer Tom Curren in the lineup. Rincon truly comes alive during the winter months when the large winter swells roll into the area.

Looking for surfing lessons? Check out the **Santa Barbara Surf School** (805/708-9878, www.santabarbarasurfschool.com). The instructors have decades of surfing experience and pride themselves on getting beginners up and riding in a single lesson. **Surf Happens** (805/966-3613, http://surfhappens.com) has private and group lessons for beginning to advanced surfers.

## Kayaking and Stand-Up Paddleboarding

You can see Santa Barbara Harbor and the bay under your own power by kayak or stand-up paddleboard. A number of rental and touring companies offer lessons, guided paddles, and good advice for exploring the region. **Channel Islands Outfitters** (117B Harbor Way, 805/899-4825, www.channelislandso. com, 10am-5pm daily) rents out kayaks and paddleboards and also offers kayak tours of Santa Barbara Harbor and stand-up paddleboard tours of Goleta Point.

## Sailing

Hop aboard the *Sunset Kidd* (125 Harbor Way, 805/962-8222, www.sunsetkidd. com, from $40) for a two-hour morning or afternoon cruise, or opt for the romantic sunset cocktail cruise.

## Whale-Watching

With its proximity to the feeding grounds of blue and humpback whales, Santa Barbara is one of the best spots in the state to go whale-watching. **Condor Express** (301 W. Cabrillo Blvd., 805/882-0088, www.condorexpress.com) offers cruises to the Channel Islands to see the big cetaceans feed (blue and humpback whales in summer; gray whales in winter).

## Golf

It might not get the most press of the many golf destinations in California, but with its year-round mild weather and resort atmosphere, Santa Barbara is a great place to play a few holes. There's everything from a popular municipal course to championship courses with views of the ocean from the greens.

The **Sandpiper** (7925 Hollister Ave., 805/968-1541, www.sandpipergolf.com, $150-195, cart $25) boasts some of the most amazing views you'll find in Santa Barbara. The view of the Pacific Ocean is so great because it's right there, and on several holes your ball is in danger of falling into the world's largest water trap. And hey, there's a great championship-rated 74.5, par-72, 18-hole golf course out there on that picturesque beach too. Take advantage of the pro shop and the on-site restaurant.

**Santa Barbara Golf Club** (3500 McCaw Ave., 805/687-7087, www.playsantabarbara.com, 6am-7pm daily Mar.-May and Sept.-Oct., 6am-8pm daily June-Aug., 6am-5pm daily Nov.-Feb., greens fees $52) is an 18-hole, par-70 course with views of the foothills and the sea.

## Spas

Folks who can afford to live in Santa Barbara tend to be able to afford many of the finer things in life, including massages, facials, and luxe skin treatments. You'll find a wide array of day spas and medical spas in town.

If you prefer a natural spa experience, book a treatment at **Le Reve** (21 W. Gutierrez St., 805/564-2977, www.le-reve.com). Using biodynamic skin care products and pure essential oils, Le Reve makes good on its advertising that bills it as an "aromatherapy spa." Choose from an original array of body treatments, massage, hand and foot pampering, facials, and various aesthetic treatments.

**Cielo Spa and Boutique** (1725 State St., Ste. C, 805/687-8979, www.cielospasb.com) prides itself on its warm, nurturing environment. Step inside and admire the scents, soft lighting, and the natural New Agey decor. Contemplate the colorful live orchids, feel soothed by the flickering candlelight, and get lost in the tranquil atmosphere.

## Food

### California Cuisine

**Opal** (1325 State St., 805/966-9676, http://opalrestaurantandbar.com, 11:30am-2:30pm and 5pm-10pm Mon.-Thurs., 11:30am-2:30pm and 5pm-11pm Fri.-Sat., 5pm-10pm Sun., $13-29) is a comfortable but lively local favorite. As a matter of fact, the menu points out local favorites, including the pesto-sautéed bay scallop salad and the chili-crusted filet mignon. In addition to its eclectic offerings, most with an Asian twist, the stylish eatery serves up gourmet pizzas from a wood-burning oven and fine cocktails from a small bar. A quieter side room with rotating art is ideal for a more romantic meal.

### Seafood

It takes something special to make Santa Barbara residents take notice of a seafood restaurant, and **Brophy Brothers** (119 Harbor Way, 805/966-4418, www.brophybros.com, 11:30am-10pm Mon.-Fri., 9:30am-10pm Sat.-Sun., $10-22) has it. Look for a small list of fresh fish done up California style with upscale preparations. The delectable menu goes heavy on locally caught seafood. With a prime location looking out over the masts of the sailboats in the harbor, it's no surprise that Brophy Brothers gets crowded at both lunch and dinner, especially on weekends in the summer. There's also a location in Ventura Harbor.

# ◈ Side Trip to Solvang

Founded in 1911 as a Danish retreat, Solvang makes a fun side trip. It's ripe with Scandinavian heritage as well as a theme-park atmosphere not lacking in kitsch. In the 1950s, far earlier than other themed communities, Solvang decided to promote itself via a focus on Danish architecture, food, and style, which still holds a certain charm over 60 years later. You'll still hear the muted strains of Danish spoken on occasion, and you'll notice storks displayed above many of the stores in town as a traditional symbol of good luck.

Solvang draws nearly two million visitors each year. During peak summer times and holidays, people clog the brick sidewalks. Try to visit during the off-season, when meandering the lovely shops can still be enjoyed. It's at its best in the fall and early spring when the hills are verdant green and the trees in town are beautiful.

The **Elverhøj Museum** (1624 Elverhoj Way, 805/686-1211, www.elverhoj.org, 11am-4pm Wed.-Sun., $5 donation) features exhibits of traditional folk art from Denmark, including paper-cutting and lace-making, wood clogs, and the rustic tools used to create them. It also offers a comprehensive history of the area with nostalgic photos of the early settlers.

The small **Hans Christian Andersen Museum** (1680 Mission Dr., 805/688-2052, www.solvangca.com, 10am-5pm daily, free) chronicles his life, work, and impact on literature. Displays include first editions of his books from the 1830s in Danish and English.

Contact the **Solvang Visitor Information Center** (1639 Copenhagen Dr., 805/688-6144, www.solvangusa.com) for more advice on a Solvang visit.

## Getting There

If you're heading from Santa Barbara north to Solvang, you have two choices. You can drive the back route, **CA-154,** also known as the **San Marcos Pass Road,** and arrive in Solvang in about **30 minutes.** This is a two-lane road, with only a few places to pass slower drivers, but it has some stunning views of the coast as you climb into the hills. You pass **Cachuma Lake,** then turn west on **CA-246** to Solvang. The other option is to take **US-101,** which affords plenty of coastal driving before you head north into the **Gaviota Pass** to reach Solvang. This route takes longer, about **45 minutes.** Known as **Mission Drive** in town, CA-246 connects both to US-101 and CA-154, which connects to Santa Barbara in the south and US-101 farther north.

## Mexican

Looking for authentic Mexican food? ★ **La Super-Rica Taqueria** (622 N. Milpas St., 805/963-4940, 11am-9pm Sun.-Thurs., 11am-9:30pm Sat.-Sun., $5) can hook you up. Just be prepared to stand in line with dozens of locals and even commuters from Los Angeles and the occasional Hollywood celeb. All agree that La Super-Rica has some of the best down-home Mexican cuisine in all of SoCal. This was Julia Child's favorite taco stand, and it has been reviewed by the *New York Times.* The corn tortillas are made fresh for every order, the meat is slow cooked and seasoned to perfection, and the house special is a grilled pork-stuffed pasilla chile pepper. Vegetarians can choose from a few delicious meat-free dishes, including the *rajas,* a standout with sautéed strips of pasilla peppers, sautéed onions, melted cheese, and herbs on a bed of two fresh corn tortillas. There's no need for ambience; the taqueria feels like a beach shack.

## Italian

If you want a superb Italian meal and a sophisticated dining experience, ★ **Olio e Limone** (11 W. Victoria St., Ste. 17, 805/899-2699, www.olioelimone.com, 11:30am-2pm and 5pm-close Mon.-Sat.,

5pm-close Sun., $18-37) is the place to go in Santa Barbara. Chef Alberto Morello is a Sicily native who opened Olio e Limone in 1999. You'll be impressed by the artistic presentation of the dishes, which include homemade pasta. The duck ravioli with creamy porcini mushroom sauce is easy to rave about. The adjacent **Olio Pizzeria** (11 W. Victoria St., Ste. 21, 805/899-2699, 11:30am-close daily, $15-20) is a more casual affair, focusing on brick-oven pizzas. They also have a detailed menu of antipasti with salamis, cheeses, and breads.

### Breakfast

The ★ **Tupelo Junction Café** (1218 State St., 805/899-3100, www.tupelojunction. com, 8am-2pm Mon., 8am-2pm and 5pm-8pm Tues.-Sun., $14-22) serves breakfast, lunch, and dinner, but it is the breakfast that shouldn't be missed. At this Southern-meets-Southern California restaurant, your juice or mimosa will be served in a mason jar. The collision between cuisines continues on the morning menu, which includes a breakfast wrap with Southern elements like andouille sausage mixed into a Mexican breakfast burrito with a tasty avocado salsa. Don't miss the half biscuit covered in spicy red sausage gravy. Despite all the Southern charm, the sleek interior will remind you that you're in Santa Barbara.

### Coffee

A long, narrow coffee shop right on State Street, **The French Press** (1101 State St., 805/963-2721, 6am-7pm Mon.-Fri., 7am-7pm Sat.-Sun.) is lined with hipsters and couples getting caffeinated and using the free Wi-Fi. As its name suggests, the popular café serves individually prepared French press coffee and espresso along with other beverages that'll leave your body buzzing. Also on the drink menu is the Magic Bowl, which mixes steamed milk, chamomile, and honey. There's a small seating area out front and another out back on Figueroa Street, as well as a second location (528 Anacapa St.).

### Markets

It's no surprise that Santa Barbara has two weekly farmers markets: **Saturday morning** (Santa Barbara and Cota St., 805/962-5354, www.sbfarmersmarket.org, 8:30am-1pm Sat.) and **Tuesday afternoon** (500-600 blocks of State St., 805/962-5354, www.sbfarmersmarket.org, 4pm-7:30pm Tues. summer, 3pm-6:30pm Tues. winter).

Want to pick up some humanely raised meat, gourmet cheese, organic produce, or fair trade coffee beans? If so, the **Santa Barbara Public Market** (38 W. Victoria St., 805/770-7702, http://sbpublicmarket.com, 7am-10:30pm Mon.-Thurs., 7am-11pm Fri.-Sat., 8am-10pm Sun.) is the place in downtown. The multi-vendor facility is Santa Barbara's take on San Francisco's Ferry Building Marketplace and Napa's Oxbow Public Market.

## Accommodations

If you want a plush beachside room in Santa Barbara, be prepared to pay for it. Almost all of Santa Barbara's hotels charge premium rates, but there are a few charming and reasonably priced accommodations near downtown and other attractions.

### $150-250

Part of an international boutique hotel chain, ★ **Hotel Indigo Santa Barbara** (121 State St., 805/966-6586, www.indigosantabarbara.com, $189-289) opened in 2012. While the guest rooms are not spacious, they are artfully designed, clean, and modern. Expect sleek, compact guest rooms with hardwood floors. The European-style collapsible glass shower wall is located right in front of the toilet. Some guest rooms also have small outdoor patios. The hotel's hallways are essentially art galleries showcasing a rotating group of regional and local artists. The hotel is in a great location, one block from the beach and two blocks from Santa Barbara's downtown, although it's also near the train station, so expect to hear the occasional train roll by.

Reasonably priced, **The Presidio** (1620 State St., 805/963-1355, www.presidiosb.com, $150-250) is close to the action. Its 16 guest rooms are clean and have been recently renovated. Second-floor guest rooms have vaulted ceilings, and every guest room has Wi-Fi and TVs with HBO. Other assets include the friendly staff, a sundeck, and a fleet of beach cruisers for motel guests.

The **Bath Street Inn** (1720 Bath St., 805/682-9680, www.bathstreetinn.com, $200-300) specializes in small-town charm and hospitality. It is large for a B&B, with eight guest rooms in the Queen Anne-style main house and another four in the more modern summer house. Each room has its own unique color scheme and style, some with traditional floral Victorian decor, others with elegant stripes. Some guest rooms have king beds, others have queens, and several have two-person whirlpool tubs. Despite the vintage trappings, you can expect a few modern amenities, including free Wi-Fi. But the inn has not entered the DVD era yet. All guest rooms have a TV and a VCR, and the common area has an extensive collection of movies on videotape. Early each morning, a sumptuous home-cooked breakfast is served downstairs.

### Over $250

If you're willing to pay a premium rate for your room, the **Cheshire Cat Inn** (36 W. Valerio St., 805/569-1610, www.cheshire-cat.com, $236-490) can provide you with true luxury B&B accommodations. Each room has an *Alice in Wonderland* name, but the decor doesn't really match the theme: Instead of whimsical and childish, you'll find comfortable Victorian elegance. Guest rooms are spread through two Victorian homes, the coach house, and two private cottages. Some suites feel like well-appointed apartments complete with a dining room table, a soaking tub, and a bookshelf stocked with a

few hardbacks. Relax in the evening in the spacious octagonal outdoor spa, or order a massage in the privacy of your own room. Each morning, come downstairs and enjoy breakfast.

For a taste of Santa Barbara's upscale side, stay at the **Inn of the Spanish Garden** (915 Garden St., 805/564-4700, www.spanishgardeninn.com, $369-700). This small boutique hotel gets it right from the first glimpse; the building has the white-washed adobe exterior, red-tiled roof, arched doorways, and wooden balconies characteristic of its historic Presidio neighborhood. Courtyards seem filled with lush greenery and tiled fountains, while the swimming pool promises relief from the heat. The pleasing setup of this luxury hotel definitely has something to do with the two owners' urban planning backgrounds. Inside, guest rooms and suites whisper luxury with their white linens, earth-toned accents, and rich, dark wooden furniture. Enjoy the benefits of your own gas fireplace, sitting area, balcony or patio, fridge, and minibar. The complimentary continental breakfast includes fresh-baked quiches and fruit smoothies on request.

The ★ **Canary Hotel** (31 W. Carrillo St., 805/884-0300, www.canarysantabarbara.com, $295-675) is stylish, playful, and right downtown. Worth splurging on, the elegant guest rooms have wooden floors, extremely comfortable canopied beds, and giant flat-screen TVs, along with unexpected amenities such as a pair of binoculars for sightseeing and bird-watching and a giant candle to set the mood for romantic evenings. While it may be difficult to leave such comforts, the hotel has a rooftop pool and a lounge on its 6th floor that offer stunning views of the Santa Ynez Mountains and the red-tiled roofs of the beautiful city.

The historic ★ **Simpson House Inn** (121 E. Arrellaga St., 805/963-7067, www.simpsonhouseinn.com, $329-569) is a wonderful place to spend an evening or two. The main house, constructed in

## ♦ Side Trip to La Purisima Mission

The **La Purisima Mission State Park** (2295 Purisima Rd., Lompoc, 805/733-3713, www.lapurisimamission.org, 9am-5pm daily, vehicles $6, seniors $5) is the best way to experience what life was like at a California mission, unless you figure out how to build a time machine. Founded in 1787, La Purisima Mission is the most extensively restored mission in California. Docents and staff members offer a glimpse of mission-era life, demonstrating candle-making, blacksmithing, and leatherwork, among other endeavors. The state park also has 20 miles of hiking trails and a shiny new **visitors center** (11am-3pm Mon., 10am-4pm Tues.-Sun.).

### Getting There

To reach La Purisima Mission State Park, take **Exit 140A** from **US-101** in **Buellton.** Travel west on **CA-246** for **18 miles** until you see the La Purisima Mission Golf Course. After that landmark, take a right on **Purisima Road** and drive 1 mile to the park entrance.

1874, is a historic landmark that withstood the 1925 earthquake. Stay inside one of the main building's six ornately decorated guest rooms or opt for one of the four guest rooms in the reconstructed carriage house. There are also four garden cottages. Whichever you choose, you will be treated to comfortable beds and a flat-screen TV with modern features that include Netflix, YouTube, and Pandora Radio access. The service is first-rate, and the staff is happy to help you get restaurant reservations or will deliver popcorn to your room if you opt to stay in with a movie. In the morning, dine on a vegetarian breakfast in the main house's dining room or in your own room. The grounds include one acre of English gardens with fragrant flowers, gurgling fountains, fruit trees, chairs, tables, and the oldest English oak tree in Southern California.

### Information and Services

The **Santa Barbara Conference and Visitors Bureau** (500 E. Montecito St., 805/966-9222, www.santabarbaraca.com, 8am-5pm Mon.-Fri.) maintains an informative website and visitors center. The **Outdoor Santa Barbara Visitors Center** (1 Garden St., 805/965-3021, 9am-5pm Mon.-Sat., 10am-5pm Sun.) provides information about Channel Islands National Park, the Channel Islands National Marine Sanctuary, the Los Padres National Forest, and the city of Santa Barbara.

Look for the *Santa Barbara News Press* (www.newspress.com) in shops, on newsstands, and in your hotel. It has information about entertainment, events, and attractions. The local free weekly, the *Santa Barbara Independent* (www.independent.com), has a comprehensive events calendar.

**Cottage Hospital** (400 W. Pueblo St., 805/682-7111) is the only hospital in town and has the only emergency room.

### Getting Around

Santa Barbara has its own local transit authority. The **MTD Santa Barbara** (805/963-3364, www.sbmtd.gov, regular fare $1.75, waterfront service $0.50) runs the local buses, the Waterfront Shuttle, and the Downtown-Waterfront line. Have exact change to pay your fare when boarding the bus or shuttle; if you're going to change buses, ask the driver for a free transfer pass. Parking can be challenging, especially at the beach on sunny weekends. Expect to pay a premium for a good-to-mediocre parking spot, or to walk for several blocks. If possible, leave your car elsewhere and take the public shuttle from downtown to the beach. To get to the **Santa Ynez Valley** and other **local wine regions,** take **CA-154** east of Santa Barbara.

# San Luis Obispo

Eleven miles inland from the coast, San Luis Obispo (SLO) is a worthy home base to explore nearby Montaña de Oro State Park and Morro Bay. Founded in 1772 by Junípero Serra, SLO is one of California's oldest communities. Despite this, the presence of the nearby California Polytechnic State University (Cal Poly) gives the small city a youthful, vibrant feel.

Higuera Street is a one-way, three-lane street lined with restaurants, clothing stores, and bars. Half a block away, restaurant decks are perched over the small San Luis Obispo Creek, a critical habitat for migrating steelhead. In front of the Mission San Luis Obispo de Tolosa is a plaza overlooking the creek with grassy lawn sections, plenty of benches, and a fountain with sculptures of bears, a fish, and one of the area's first human residents.

## Getting There

San Luis Obispo is 95 miles north of Santa Barbara via **US-101,** a drive that usually takes a little more than 90 minutes. Both CA-1 and US-101 run through San Luis Obispo, merging on the north side of town. From the south, take the CA-1/US-101-combined freeway into town.

**Amtrak** (800/872-7245, www.amtrak.com) has a San Luis Obispo station (1011 Railroad Ave.); the *Coast Starlight* train stops here once daily in each direction on its way between Seattle and Los Angeles, and SLO is also the northern terminus of the *Pacific Surfliner*, with several departures daily on its route to San Diego. There are scheduled flights from Los Angeles, San Francisco, and Phoenix to the **San Luis Obispo County Regional Airport** (SBP, 901 Airport Dr., 805/781-5205).

**Greyhound** (805/238-1242, www.greyhound.com) travels along US-101 and

stops at **San Luis Obispo Transit Center** (800 Pine St.). Buses managed by the **San Luis Obispo Regional Transit Authority** (805/781-4472, www.slorta.com) can offer transportation within the county. There are various weekday and weekend routes. A door-to-door public transit system, **Dial-A-Ride** (805/226-4242, www.slorta.org), operates within the city limits. Call by noon the day before your desired ride.

## Sights
### Mission San Luis Obispo de Tolosa

The **Mission San Luis Obispo de Tolosa** (751 Palm St., 805/781-8220, www.missionsanluisobispo.org, 9am-5pm daily summer, 9am-4pm daily winter) was founded by the missionary Junípero Serra in 1772; it's the fifth mission in the chain of 21 California missions. The church is long and narrow, with exposed wooden beams on the ceiling. On the grounds is a small **museum** (805/543-6850, donation $3) with artifacts from the indigenous Chumash people and exhibits on the mission and the Spanish missionaries. A garden and the Mission Plaza are a nice place to spend the afternoon on a warm day.

### Higuera Street

Similar to Santa Barbara's State Street, San Luis Obispo's **Higuera Street** is the heart of the city. For seven blocks, the one-way street is lined with restaurants, bars, gift shops, and lots of women's clothing stores. The clean sidewalks are perfect for a stroll under a canopy of ficus, carrot wood, and Victorian box trees.

### ★ Madonna Inn

The **Madonna Inn Resort & Spa** (100 Madonna Rd., 805/543-3000, www.madonnainn.com) is truly one of a kind. It's considered a pilgrimage site for lovers of all-American kitsch, but it wasn't planned that way. When Alex and Phyllis Madonna opened the inn

# Downtown San Luis Obispo

MILL ST

OSOS ST

SANTA ROSA ST

PALM ST

MORRO ST

KOBERL AT BLUE ▼

COURT ST

FIRESTONE GRILL

■ PALM THEATRE

CHORRO ST

MONTEREY ST

★ SAN LUIS OBISPO CHAMBER OF COMMERCE VISITOR'S CENTER

ROSE ALY

BROAD ST

★ MISSION SAN LUIS OBISPO DE TOLOSA

LUNA RED ▼

HIGUERA ST

GRANADA HOTEL & BISTRO ▼

*Mission*

*Plaza*

MARSH ST

OSOS ST

CREEKSIDE BREWING COMPANY ▼

FROG & PEACH PUB ▼

BLACK SHEEP

NOVO ▼

BUBBLEGUM ▼ ALLEY

★ MOTHER'S TAVERN

GARDEN ALY

GARDEN ST

PACIFIC ST

BIG SKY ▼ CAFE

BROAD ST

0     100 yds

0     100 m

NIPOMO ST

PISMO ST

© AVALON TRAVEL

in 1958, they wanted it to be different from a typical motel, and they made each guest room special. It started with 12 guest rooms; today, there are 110 unique guest rooms, each decorated wildly differently to suit the diverse tastes of the road-trippers who converge on the area. The creative names given to each over the years suggest what you will find inside: The Yahoo, Love Nest, Old Mill, Kona Rock, Irish Hills, Cloud Nine, Just Heaven, Hearts & Flowers, Rock Bottom, Austrian Suite, Caveman Room, Daisy Mae, Safari Room, Jungle

Rock, and Bridal Falls. Then there is the famous men's restroom downstairs; the urinal is built out of rock and a waterfall flushes it. Men routinely stand guard so that their mothers, sisters, wives, and female friends can go in to gawk at the unusual feature.

Obviously, the rooms are for overnight guests, but there is still a lot to take in if you pull over for a peek. The **Copper Café & Pastry Shop** has copper-plated tables and a copper-plated circular bar, while the **Gold Rush Steak House** is a garish explosion of giant fake flowers and rose-colored furniture. It might remind you of a room in your grandmother's home on steroids.

### Bubblegum Alley

**Bubblegum Alley** (Higuera St. between Broad St. and Garden St.) is a 70-foot-long alleyway whose walls are covered in pieces of already chewed gum. The newly chewed chunks are bright green, red, yellow, and so on, while the older pieces have turned a darker color. Some people have called this oddity an "eyesore," while others have touted it as one of the city's "special attractions." Regardless, Bubblegum Alley, which is rumored to have started as early as the late 1950s, is here to stay. Even after firefighters blasted the alleyway with water hoses in 1985, another layer of gum appeared a little later.

## Entertainment and Events
### Bars and Clubs

As a college town, San Luis Obispo offers plenty of bars in the downtown area. A popular spot with the college students is **Mother's Tavern** (725 Higuera St., 805/541-8733, www.motherstavern.com, 11am-2am Mon.-Sat., 10am-2am Sun.), with two-for-one drink nights, karaoke evenings, and weekend dance parties. Across the street is another popular drinking establishment called the **Frog & Peach Pub** (728 Higuera St., 805/595-3764, http://frogandpeachpub.com, noon-2am daily). It has live music almost nightly, along with a deck out back.

The **Black Sheep Bar & Grill** (1117 Chorro St., 805/544-7433, www.black-sheepslo.com, 11am-2am daily) has a cozy pub feel on uncrowded nights. This brick-walled, wood-floored tavern has a fireplace and a back patio. It also serves a burger basted in a Guinness beer reduction sauce.

Just a block off Higuera Street but a world away from the college bars there, **McCarthy's Irish Pub** (600 Marsh St., 805/544-0268, 8am-2am daily) is a dark, low-slung bar with loud music, friendly locals, and a shuffleboard table. Order up a draft Guinness, Smithwick's, or Magners Irish cider and get ready to make some new friends.

### Live Music

**SLO Brew** (736 Higuera St., 805-543-1843, www.slobrew.com, 11:30am-midnight Sun.-Mon., 11:30am-2am Tues.-Sat.) is a brewpub that hosts local music acts. East of San Luis Obispo, the **Pozo Saloon** (90 W. Pozo Rd., Pozo, 805/438-4225, www.pozosaloon.com) is a historic watering hole dating back to 1858. It somehow pulls in acts like Willie Nelson, Wiz Khalifa, Snoop Dogg, and the Black Crowes to perform on its outdoor stage.

### Festivals and Events

The **San Luis Obispo Farmers Market** (Higuera St. between Osos St. and Nipomo St., www.slocountyfarmers.org, http://downtownslo.com, 6pm-9pm Thurs.) is a true phenomenon. One of the largest farmers markets in the state, this weekly gathering has the goods of 70 farmers and lots of live music.

Every March, the **San Luis Obispo International Film Festival** (805/546-3456, http://slofilmfest.org) screens a range of films at the city's Palm Theatre (817 Palm St.) and Fremont Theatre (1035 Monterey St.) along with other venues around the county, including Paso Robles and Avila Beach. The five-day fest draws film folks like Josh Brolin and Jeff Bridges.

## Sports and Recreation
### Hiking

Just north of San Luis Obispo, the 1,546-foot-high **Bishop Peak** (trailheads at the end of Highland Dr. and off Patricia Dr., 805/781-7300, www.slocity.org) is the city's natural treasure. A four-mile round-trip hike to the rocky crown of Bishop Peak offers commanding views of San Luis Obispo and the surrounding area. Named by Spanish missionaries who thought the mountain resembled a bishop's hat, Bishop Peak is the tallest of the *morros*, or "Nine Sisters," a chain of nine volcanic peaks stretching from San Luis Obispo up to Morro Bay. In addition to the fine views, Bishop Peak teems with wildlife, especially birds that float on the mountain's thermals. The hour-long hike passes through a forest, past Volkswagen Beetle-size boulders, and into a series of exposed switchbacks. Bring water!

## Food

San Luis Obispo restaurants take advantage of their location near farms and wineries. The big college presence means that even the higher-end establishments keep things casual.

### Contemporary

**Novo** (726 Higuera St., 805/543-3986, www.novorestaurant.com, 11am-9pm Sun.-Thurs., 11am-1am Fri.-Sat., $18-37) has a collection of decks overlooking San Luis Obispo Creek for dining and drinking. Novo serves tapas, including fresh shrimp avocado spring rolls and full-on entrées like grilled lamb chops. International flavors creep into the menu on items like pork *carnitas sopes*, Thai curries, and a stir-fried noodle dish.

Celebrity chef Rachael Ray has approved **Big Sky Café** (1121 Broad St., 805/545-5401, www.bigskycafe.com, 8am-9pm Sun.-Thurs., 8am-10pm Fri.-Sat., $15-26). It's known for healthy vegetarian entrées, but there are plenty of options for carnivores.

### Burgers and Steaks

The ★ **Firestone Grill** (1001 Higuera St., 805/783-1001, www.firestonegrill.com, 11am-10pm Sun.-Wed., 11am-11pm Thurs.-Sat., $5-22) creates a masterpiece of meat in its tender and tasty tri-tip sandwich. Locals swear by it. Brought to you by the same folks behind Cambria's Main Street Grill, the Firestone Grill also serves pork ribs, burgers, and salads.

**Eureka!Burger** (1141 Chorro St., 805/903-1141, www.eurekaburger.com, Sun.-Mon. 11am-11pm, Tues.-Sat. 11am-midnight, $9-23) is a small chain that focuses on gourmet burgers and craft beers. This popular two-story restaurant has some unique takes on the American classic, including a fig marmalade burger and a jalapeño egg burger. The meat is juicy, tasty, and cooked to order. They also have a range of microbrews on tap, including Scrimshaw, Racer 5, and Stone Pale Ale.

A trip to the Madonna Inn is always worthwhile. Its over-the-top dining room, the **Gold Rush Steak House** (100 Madonna Rd., 805/784-2433, www.madonnainn.com, 5pm-10pm daily, $25-98), serves steaks of the filet mignon, New York, and top sirloin varieties. If you are not feeling like red meat, they also have Australian lobster tail and Cayucos abalone.

## Accommodations
### $100-150

A superb value, the ★ **Peach Tree Inn** (2001 Monterey St., 800/227-6396, http://peachtreeinn.com, $89-299) has nice guest rooms, friendly staff, and a complimentary breakfast. The finest guest rooms at the Peach Tree are the Creekside Rooms, each with its own brick patio. Next to the lobby is a large common room with a back deck and rocking chairs to enjoy San Luis Obispo's frequently pleasant weather. The Peach Tree is located on the Old SLO Trolley route and is an easy one-mile walk to San Luis Obispo's downtown.

### $150-250

If you want to feel like you're spending the night in a cave, on safari, or on a showboat, stay at the ★ **Madonna Inn** (100 Madonna Rd., 805/543-3000, www.madonnainn.com, $209-489). An under-hyped asset on Madonna Inn's 2,200 acres is its deck with a large heated pool, two hot tubs, a poolside bar, and a view of an artificial cascade tumbling down the hillside.

The **La Cuesta Inn** (2074 Monterey St., 805/543-2777, www.lacuestainn.com, $139-229) has reasonably priced guest rooms right near US-101. All guest rooms have microwaves and fridges. This independently owned hotel has a small heated kidney-shaped pool and a hot tub. In the morning, a deluxe continental breakfast is served; coffee and juice are available in the lobby at any hour.

For a rejuvenating stay in a natural setting, head to ★ **Sycamore Mineral Springs Resort** (1215 Avila Beach Dr., 805/595-7302, www.sycamoresprings.com, $179-339), located in a tranquil canyon nine miles from San Luis Obispo. Amenities on the grounds include a yoga dome, a labyrinth, a wellness center, a restaurant, and sulfur mineral springs, which can be enjoyed in hillside hot tubs. The Bob Jones Trail offers a paved two-mile walkway that connects the resort to Avila Beach. Lodging options range from cozy guest rooms to a two-story guesthouse with three bedrooms and three baths. Up on stilts, the West Meadows Suites include a living room with a gas fireplace and a bedroom with a four-poster king bed. The back decks have large soaking tubs that can be filled with fresh mineral water.

### $250 and Up

The **Granada Hotel & Bistro** (1126 Morro St., 805/544-9100, www.granadahotelandbistro.com, $279-579) is a 17-room boutique hotel located just half a block off Higuera Street. The 1920s hotel has been renovated and modernized, with exposed brick walls, steel-frame windows, and hardwood floors. Most guest rooms also have fireplaces. On the 2nd floor is a comfortable indoor and outdoor lounge area.

## Information and Services

Visitor information can be obtained at the **San Luis Obispo Chamber of**

the view from Bishop Peak

Commerce Visitors Center (895 Monterey St., 805/786-2673, www.slochamber.org, 10am-5pm Sun.-Wed., 10am-7pm Thurs.-Sat.). San Luis Obispo has its own daily newspaper, *The Tribune* (www.sanluisobispo.com), and its own free weekly newspaper, the *New Times* (www.newtimesslo.com).

There are two branches of the **post office** (893 Marsh St., 805/543-5353; 1655 Dalidio Dr., 805/543-2605).

San Luis Obispo is home to two hospitals: **Sierra Vista Regional Medical Center** (1010 Murray Ave., 805/546-7600, www.sierravistaregional.com) and **French Hospital Medical Center** (1911 Johnson Ave., 805/543-5353, www.frenchmedicalcenter.org).

## Getting Around
The regional bus system, the **RTA** (805/541-2228, www.slorta.org), connects San Luis Obispo, Morro Bay, Cayucos, Cambria, and San Simeon. Fares range $1.50-3.

# Morro Bay

The picturesque fishing village of Morro Bay is dominated by Morro Rock, a 576-foot-high volcanic plug that looms over the harbor. In 1542, Juan Rodríguez Cabrillo, the first European explorer to navigate the California coast, named the landmark Morro Rock, because he thought it appeared to resemble a moor's turban.

With a view of the rock, the small city's Embarcadero is a string of tourist shops, restaurants, and hotels strung along Morro Bay, a large estuary that includes the harbor, the Morro Bay State Marine Recreational Management Area, and the Morro Bay State Marine Reserve. Uphill from the water, more restaurants, bars, and stores are located in Morro Bay's Olde Towne section.

With natural attractions that include the stunning Montaña de Oro State Park just miles from town and with a nice waterfront focus, Morro Bay is a worthy destination or detour for a weekend, even though a lot of the area's lodgings fill up during high-season weekends.

## Getting There
In San Luis Obispo, US-101 heads east over the mountains toward Paso Robles. San Luis Obispo's Santa Rosa Street becomes CA-1 North and continues along the coast. To get to Morro Bay, take **CA-1 North** for 13 miles from San Luis Obispo. Take the **Morro Bay Boulevard** exit into town.

There is no direct bus service to Morro Bay, although **Greyhound** (805/238-1242, www.greyhound.com) travels along US-101 and stops at **San Luis Obispo Transit Center** (800 Pine St., San Luis Obispo). From there you'll need to connect with **San Luis Obispo Regional Transit Authority** (805/781-4472, www.slorta.org) buses to get to Morro Bay. There are various weekday and weekend routes. A door-to-door public transit system,

# Nine Sisters

The ancient volcanic peaks known as the **Nine Sisters of the Morros** extend from the prominent 576-foot **Morro Rock** of Morro Bay 14 miles south to the 775-foot **Islay Hill,** which is located in the city of San Luis Obispo. The Nine Sisters' highest peak is the 1,546-foot **Bishop Peak.** The top por-tion is a part of the 360-acre Bishop Peak Natural Reserve and is a popular spot for hikers and rock climbers. The Nine Sisters also make for unique animal and plant habitats. Morro Rock is a nest-ing place for peregrine falcons, while **Hollister Peak** hosts a colony of black-shouldered kites.

**Dial-A-Ride** (805/226-4242, www.slorta. org), operates within the city limits. Call by noon the day before your desired ride.

## Sights
### ★ Morro Rock
It would be difficult to come to the town of Morro Bay and not see **Morro Rock** (www.slostateparks.com). The 576-foot-high volcanic plug, which has been called the "Gibraltar of the Pacific," dominates the town's scenery, whether you are walking along the bayside Embarcadero or beachcombing on the sandy coastline just north of the promi-nent geologic feature. The rock was an island until the 1930s, when a road was built connecting it to the mainland. The area around the rock is accessible, but the rock itself is off-limits because it is home to a group of endangered per-egrine falcons. Indeed, a multitude of birds always seems to be swirling around the rock they call home.

### Montaña de Oro State Park
**Montaña de Oro State Park** (Pecho Rd., 7 miles south of Los Osos, 805/528-0513, www.parks.ca.gov) is for those seeking a serious nature fix on the Central Coast. This sprawling 8,000-acre park with 7 miles of coastline has coves, tide pools, sand dunes, and al-most 50 miles of hiking trails. A great way to get a feel for the park's immense size is to hike up the 2-mile **Valencia Peak Trail** (4 miles round-trip). In springtime the sides of the trail are decorated with blooming wildflowers, and the 1,347-foot-high summit of-fers commanding views of Montaña de Oro's pocked coastline and Morro Rock jutting out in the distance.

For a feel of the coast, park right in front of **Spooner's Cove** and walk out on its wide, coarse-grained beach. On the cove's north end, Islay Creek drains into the ocean. There's also a picturesque arch across the creek in the rock face on the north side. The **Spooner Ranch House Museum** informs visitors about early in-habitants of the park's land, the Spooner family. There are also displays about the area's plants, mountain lions, and raptors in the small facility.

### Morro Bay State Park
**Morro Bay State Park** (Morro Bay State Park Rd., 805/772-7434, www.parks. ca.gov) is not a typical state park. It has hiking trails, a campground, and recre-ational opportunities, but this park also has its own natural history museum, a golf course, and a marina. Just south of town, the park is situated on the shores of Morro Bay. One way to get a feel for the park is to hike the **Black Hill Trail** (three miles round-trip).

A unique aspect of Morro Bay State Park is the **Morro Bay Museum of Natural History** (Morro Bay State Park Rd., 805/772-2694, www.parks.ca.gov, 10am-5pm daily, $3 adults, children under 12 free). Small but informative, the museum has displays that explain the habitats of the Central Coast and some interactive exhibits for kids. An observation deck hanging off the museum allows for a great view of Morro Bay. Beside the museum is a garden that shows how the area's original inhabitants, the Chumash people, utilized the region's plants.

Play a round of golf at the **Morro Bay State Park Golf Course** (201 State Park Rd., 805/782-8060, www.slocountyparks.com, $43 Mon.-Fri., $48 Sat.-Sun.), or head out on the water in a kayak, a canoe, or a stand-up paddleboard rented from the **Kayak Shack** (10 State Park Rd., 805/772-8796, www.morrobaykayakrental.com, 9am-5pm daily summer, 9am-4pm Fri.-Sun. winter, kayaks $14-18 per hour, canoes $18 per hour, stand-up paddleboards $16 per hour).

## Entertainment and Events
### Bars
Down on the Embarcadero, **The Libertine Pub** (801 Embarcadero, 805/772-0700, http://libertinebrewing.com, 11am-10pm Mon.-Thurs., 11am-11pm Fri.-Sat., 10am-10pm Sun.) is the place for the discerning beer drinker, with 20 rotating craft beers on tap and a selection of over 80 bottled beers. One of the beers on tap will always be a sour. You can also order craft cocktails (a basil bourbon drink that counts marmalade as one of its ingredients) and pub food (including clams, burgers, and *moules frites*). The bartenders also act as DJs, playing selections from the Libertine's stash of vinyl.

**Legends Bar** (899 Main St., 805/772-2525, 11am-2am daily) has a red pool table and a giant moose head poking out from behind the bar. Grab a drink and look at the framed historical photos covering the walls.

### Festivals and Events
Strong winds kick up on the Central Coast in the spring. The **Morro Bay Kite Festival** (805/772-0113, www.morrobaykitefestival.org) takes advantage of

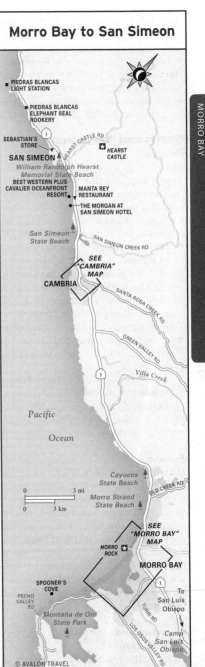

**Morro Bay to San Simeon**

these gales with pro kite fliers twirling and flipping their kites in the sky. The festival also offers kite-flying lessons.

For over 30 years, the **Morro Bay Harbor Festival** (800/366-6043, www.mbhf.com, Oct.) has showcased the best of the region, including wines, seafood, live music, and a clam chowder contest.

## Sports and Recreation
### Beaches
There are several beaches in and around Morro Bay. Popular with surfers and beachcombers, **Morro Rock Beach** (west end of Embarcadero, 805/772-6200, www.morro-bay.ca.us) lies within the city limits, just north of Morro Rock. The **Morro Bay Sandspit** (www.parks.ca.gov) is a four-mile-long line of dunes and beach that separates Morro Bay from the ocean. The northernmost mile is within city limits, while the southern portion is located in Montaña de Oro State Park. You can access this area by walking in from the state park or by paddling across Morro Harbor to the land south of the harbor mouth.

Just north of town is **Morro Strand State Beach** (CA-1, 805/772-8812, www.parks.ca.gov). The three-mile strand of sand is popular with anglers, windsurfers, and kite fliers.

### Surfing
**Morro Rock Beach** (west end of Embarcadero, 805/772-6200, www.morro-bay.ca.us) has a consistent beach break. It's a unique experience to be able to stare up at a giant rock while waiting for waves. **Wavelengths Surf Shop** (998 Embarcadero, 805/772-3904, 9:30am-6pm daily, board rental $20 per day, wetsuit $10 per day), on the Embarcadero on the way to the beach, rents out boards and wetsuits.

### Kayaking and Stand-Up Paddleboarding
Paddling the protected scenic waters of Morro Bay, whether you're in a kayak or on a stand-up paddleboard (SUP), is a great way to see wildlife up close. You might see otters lazily backstroking in the estuary or clouds of birds gliding just above the surface of the water.

Paddle over the **Morro Bay Sandspit,** a finger of dunes located in the northern section of Montaña de Oro State Park that separates the bay from the ocean. Then beach your vessel and climb over the dunes to the mostly isolated beach on the ocean side. Parts of the dunes can be closed to protect the snowy plover. Away from the harbor area, the estuary can be shallow; plan your paddling at high tide to avoid too much portaging.

**Kayak Horizons** (551 Embarcadero, 805/772-6444, www.kayakhorizons.com, 9am-5pm daily) rents kayaks ($12-22 per hour) and paddleboards ($12 per hour) and hosts a three-hour paddle around the estuary ($59). In Morro Bay State Park, you can secure a canoe or kayak from **A Kayak Shack** (10 State Park Rd., 805/772-8796, www.morrobaykayakrental.com, 9am-5pm daily summer, 9am-4pm Fri.-Sun. winter, kayaks $14-18 per hour, canoes $18 per hour, stand-up paddleboards $16 per hour).

### Boat Tours
**Sub Sea Tours** (699 Embarcadero, 805/772-9463, www.subseatours.com, $14 adults, $11 seniors and students, $7 children) is like snorkeling without getting wet. The yellow 27-foot semi-submersible vessel has a cabin outfitted with windows below the water. The 45-minute tour takes you around the harbor in search of wildlife. Expect to see sea lions sunning on a floating dock and sea otters playing in the water. At a much-touted secret spot, fish congregate for feeding. You'll typically see smelt, appearing like silver splinters, but may also catch a glimpse of salmon, lingcod, perch, and sunfish. Kids will love it. Sub Sea Tours also schedules 2- to 3.5-hour **whale-watching excursions** ($40 adults, $35 seniors and students, $30 children

MORRO BAY

# Morro Bay

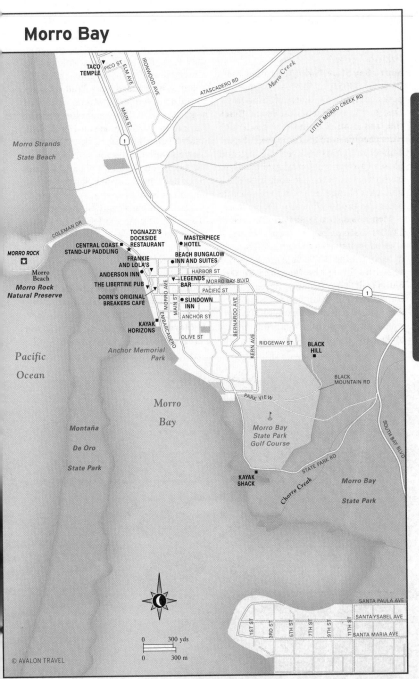

TACO
TEMPLE
PICO ST
ELM AVE
MAIN ST
IRONWOOD AVE
ATASCADERO RD
Morro Creek
LITTLE MORRO CREEK RD
1
*Morro Strands*
*State Beach*
COLEMAN DR
TOGNAZZI'S
DOCKSIDE
RESTAURANT
MASTERPIECE
HOTEL
CENTRAL COAST
STAND-UP PADDLING
FRANKIE
AND LOLA'S
BEACH BUNGALOW
INN AND SUITES
MORRO ROCK
ANDERSON INN
THE LIBERTINE PUB
HARBOR ST
LEGENDS
BAR
MORRO BAY BLVD
*Morro*
*Beach*
*Morro Rock*
*Natural Preserve*
DORN'S ORIGINAL
BREAKERS CAFÉ
PACIFIC ST
SUNDOWN
INN
MORRO AVE
MAIN ST
EMBARCADERO
ANCHOR ST
BERNARDO AVE
KAYAK
HORIZONS
OLIVE ST
KERN AVE
RIDGEWAY ST
BLACK
HILL
*Anchor Memorial*
*Park*
BLACK
MOUNTAIN RD
*Pacific*
*Ocean*
*Morro*
*Bay*
PARK VIEW
SOUTH BAY BLVD
*Montaña*
*De Oro*
*State Park*
*Morro Bay*
*State Park*
*Golf Course*
KAYAK
SHACK
STATE PARK RD
*Morro Bay*
*Chorro Creek*
*State Park*
1
SANTA PAULA AVE
SANTA YSABEL AVE
1ST ST
3RD ST
5TH ST
7TH ST
9TH ST
11TH ST
SANTA MARIA AVE

0        300 yds
0        300 m

© AVALON TRAVEL

under 12) to see California gray whales and humpback whales.

## Hiking

**Morro Bay State Park** (Morro Bay State Park Rd., 805/772-7434, www.slostateparks.com) has 13 miles of hiking trails. One of the most popular is the **Black Hill Trail** (3 miles round-trip, moderate), which begins from the campground road. This climb gains 600 vertical feet and passes through chaparral and eucalyptus on the way to the 640-foot-high Black Hill, part of the same system of volcanic plugs that produced nearby Morro Rock.

**Montaña de Oro State Park** (Pecho Rd., 7 miles south of Los Osos, 805/528-0513, www.slostateparks.com) has almost 50 miles of hiking trails. Take in the park's coastline along the **Montaña de Oro Bluffs Trail** (4 miles round-trip, easy). The trailhead begins about 100 yards south of the visitors center and campground entrance and runs along a marine terrace to the park's southern boundary. Starting at the parking area just south of the visitors center, **Valencia Peak Trail** (4 miles round-trip, moderate) leads to its namesake 1,347-foot-high peak, which offers a nice view of the coastline spread out below. The **Hazard Peak Trail** (6 miles round-trip, moderate-strenuous) starts at Pecho Valley Road and climbs to the summit of 1,076-foot Hazard Peak, with unobstructed 360-degree views. The **Islay Canyon Trail** (6 miles round-trip, moderate) takes you through the park's inland creek beds and canyons. Starting at the bottom of Islay Creek Canyon, this wide dirt path is popular with birders because of the 25-40 different bird species that frequent the area.

## Bird-Watching

Morro Bay is one of California's great birding spots. **Morro Bay State Park** is home to a **heron rookery,** located just north of the Museum of Natural History. At **Morro Rock,** you'll see endangered peregrine falcons, ever-present gulls,

Montaña de Oro State Park

and the occasional canyon wren. On the northwest end of **Morro Bay State Park Marina** (off State Park Dr.), birders can spot loons, grebes, brants, and ducks; you may also see American pipits and Nelson's sparrows. The cypress trees host roosting black-crowned night herons. The **Morro Coast Audubon Society** (805/772-1991, www.morrocoastaudubon.org) conducts birding field trips to local hot spots; check the website for information on upcoming field trips.

## Food
### Seafood

Seafood is the way to go when dining in the fishing village of Morro Bay. An unassuming fish house with views of the fishing boats and the bay, ★ **Tognazzini's Dockside Restaurant** (1245 Embarcadero, 805/772-8100, www.morrobaydockside.com, 11am-9pm daily, $18-27) has an extensive seafood menu as well as art depicting sultry mermaids hanging on the wall. Entrées include albacore kebabs and

wild salmon in a unique tequila marinade. Oyster lovers can't go wrong with Dockside's barbecued appetizer, which features the shellfish swimming in garlic butter studded with scallions. Behind the main restaurant is the **Dockside Too Fish Market** (10am-7pm Sun.-Thurs., 10am-8pm Fri.-Sat. summer, 10am-6pm Sun.-Thurs., 10am-8pm Fri.-Sat. winter), a local favorite with beer, seafood, and live music.

Located on a hill above the Embarcadero, **Dorn's Original Breakers Café** (801 Market Ave., 805/772-4415, www.dornscafe.com, 7am-9pm daily, $13-44) offers a great view of Morro Rock from its dining room. It has been family-owned and operated since 1942. Dinner begins with bread and a dish of garlic, olive oil, vinegar, and cheese. The large menu of seafood and steak includes fresh daily specials like snapper, petrale sole, salmon, and halibut from local waters.

### Mexican

People worship the crab cake and fish tacos at ★ **Taco Temple** (2680 N. Main St., 805/772-4965, 11am-9pm daily, $7-22, cash only). Housed in a big multicolored building east of CA-1, where colorful surfboards hang on the walls, this is not the standard taqueria. The California take on classic Mexican dishes includes sweet potato enchiladas and tacos filled with soft-shell crab or calamari. The tacos are served like salads, with the meat and greens piled on tortillas. The chips and salsa are terrific.

### Breakfast and Brunch

★ **Frankie & Lola's** (1154 Front St., 805/771-9306, www.frankieandlolas.com, 6:30am-2pm Sun.-Wed., 6:30am-2pm and 5pm-8pm Thurs.-Sat., $4-13) does breakfast right. Creative savory dishes include the fried green tomato Benedict topped with creole hollandaise sauce and tasty, colorful *chilaquiles* with red chorizo, avocado, and tomatillo salsa. Lunch focuses on salads and sandwiches, while dinner is a little heartier, with options like bacon-wrapped meatloaf or chorizo-stuffed chicken.

On the road toward Montaña de Oro State Park, **Celia's Garden Café** (1188 Los Osos Valley Rd., Los Osos, 805/528-5711, http://celiasgardencafe.com, 7:30am-2pm Mon.-Fri., 7:30am-2:30pm Sat.-Sun., $9-12) is an ideal place to fuel up for a day of hiking. Fill up on a pork chop and eggs or the chicken-fried steak. Other options include omelets, Benedicts, and hotcakes. Located in a plant nursery, the café has an indoor dining room and a dog-friendly outdoor patio.

## Accommodations
### Under $150
The **Sundown Inn** (640 Main St., 805/772-3229 or 800/696-6928, http://sundown-inn.com, $139-209) is a well-priced motel within walking distance of Morro Bay's downtown and waterfront areas. Guest rooms have fridges, microwaves, and—here's something different—coin-operated vibrating beds.

The ★ **Masterpiece Hotel** (1206 Main St., 805/772-5633, www.masterpiecehotel.com, $130-300) is a great place to stay for art enthusiasts and lovers of quirky motels. Each guest room is decorated with framed prints from master painters, and the hallways also have prints of paintings by Henri Matisse, Vincent Van Gogh, and Norman Rockwell. There's also a large indoor spa pool decorated like a Roman bathhouse that further differentiates this motel from other cookie-cutter lodging options.

### $150-250
Built in 1939, the bright ★ **Beach Bungalow Inn and Suites** (1050 Morro Ave., 805/772-9700, www.morrobay-beachbungalow.com, $159-309) has been extensively renovated. The 12 clean, spacious, and modern guest rooms have hardwood floors, local art on the walls, and flat-screen TVs. Eleven of the guest rooms have gas fireplaces. Family suites accommodate four people, while king deluxe suites have full kitchens. Two bicycles are available for cruising around town. Guests receive a voucher for a meal at a local restaurant (including Frankie & Lola's, The Hungry Fishermen, Mi Casa, Giovanni's Fish Market, or Stax Wine Bar).

### Over $250
The family-run **Anderson Inn** (897 Embarcadero, 866/950-3434 www.andersoninnmorrobay.com, $269-419) is an eight-room boutique hotel located right on Morro Bay's busy Embarcadero. Three of the guest rooms are perched right over the estuary with stunning views of the nearby rock. Those premium guest rooms also include fireplaces and jetted tubs.

## Camping
Located a couple of miles outside downtown Morro Bay, the **Morro Bay State Park Campground** (Morro Bay State Park Rd., 800/444-7275, www.parks.ca.gov, tents $35, RVs $50) has 140 campsites, many shaded by eucalyptus and pine trees; right across the street is the Morro Bay estuary. Six miles southwest of Morro Bay, **Montaña de Oro State Park** (Pecho Rd., 7 miles south of Los Osos, 800/444-7275, www.parks.ca.gov, $25) has more primitive camping facilities. There are walk-in environmental campsites and a primitive campground behind the Spooner Ranch House that has pit toilets.

## Information and Services
The **Morro Bay Chamber Visitors Center** (255 Morro Bay Blvd., 800/231-0592, www.morrobay.org, 9am-5pm daily) has a vast array of printed material, including maps.

To access the **post office** (898 Napa Ave., 805/772-0839), you'll need to leave the Embarcadero area and head uptown.

In an emergency, dial **911**. The local police are the **Morro Bay Police Department** (870 Morro Bay Blvd.,

805/772-6225). **French Hospital Medical Center** (1911 Johnson Ave., San Luis Obispo, 805/543-5353, www.frenchmedicalcenter.org) is the closest hospital.

## Getting Around

The **Morro Bay Trolley** (595 Harbor Way, 805/772-2744, 11am-5pm Mon., 11am-7pm Fri.-Sat., 11am-6pm Sun., Memorial Day-Oct., $1 per ride over age 12, $0.50 ages 5-12) operates three routes. The **Waterfront Route** runs the length of the Embarcadero, including out to Morro Rock. The **Downtown Route** runs through the downtown (as in uptown) area all the way out to Morro Bay State Park. The **North Morro Bay Route** runs from uptown through the northern part of Morro Bay, north of the rock, along CA-1. An all-day pass (not a bad idea if you plan on seeing a lot of sights) is $3.

---

# Cambria

Cambria, originally known as Slabtown, retains nothing of its original if uninspired moniker. Divided into east and west villages, it is a charming area of low storefronts, easily walkable with moss-covered pine trees as a backdrop. When it comes to this area, there is only one true sight. Cambria owes much of its prosperity to the immense tourist trap on the hill: Hearst Castle. Once you're through with the castle tours, a few attractions in the lower elevations beckon as well. Typically you'll see visitors meandering in and out of the local stores, browsing art galleries, or combing Moonstone Beach for souvenir moonstone rocks. The really great thing about Cambria is that, aside from the gas stations, you won't find any chain stores in town, and Cambrians, and most visitors, like it that way.

## Getting There

Cambria is located 21 miles north of Morro Bay, directly along **CA-1**, and is only accessible by this road, whether you're coming from the north or the south. Cambria is not accessible by public transit, so if you are planning to use the town as a base to explore the area, a car will be necessary.

## Sights and Beaches
### Nitt Witt Ridge

While William Randolph Hearst built one of the most expensive homes ever seen in California, local eccentric Arthur Harold Beal (a.k.a. Captain Nit Wit or Der Tinkerpaw) got busy building the cheapest "castle" he could. **Nitt Witt Ridge** (881 Hillcrest Dr., 805/927-2690, tours by appointment) is the result of five decades of scavenging trash and using it as building supplies to create a multistory home like no other on the coast. The rambling structure is made of abalone shells, used car rims, and toilet seats, among other found materials. It's weird, it's funky, it's fun. Make an appointment with owners Michael and Stacey O'Malley to tour the property.

Known for its namesake, a shimmering gemstone littering the shore, **Moonstone Beach** (Moonstone Beach Dr.) is a scenic pebbly slice of coastline with craggy rocks offshore. Huts constructed from driftwood can be found on some sections of the beach, and there is plenty more than just moonstones to find washed up on the shoreline. There is also a wooden boardwalk that runs along the top of the bluffs above the beach to take in the scenery and watch moonstone collectors with buckets wander below in the tideline. Access is at Leffingwell Landing, Moonstone Beach Drive, and Santa Rosa Creek.

## Nightlife

If touring Hearst Castle leaves you thirsty for a beer, Cambria has a few different options. **Mozzi's** (2262 Main St., 805/927-4767, http://mozzissaloon.com, 1pm-midnight Mon.-Wed., 1pm-2am Thurs.-Fri., 11am-2am Sat., 11am-midnight Sun.) is a classic old California saloon. Old artifacts

# Cambria

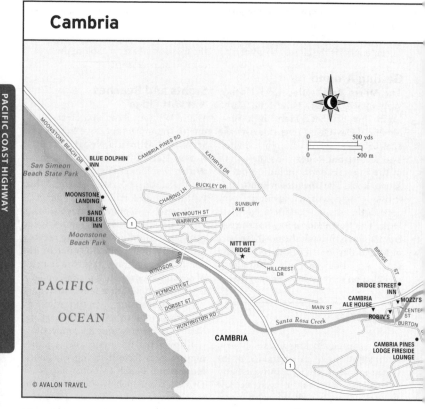

like lanterns and farm equipment hang from the ceiling above the long redwood bar, jukebox, and pool tables in this historic watering hole. On Tuesday, well drinks and draft beers are just $2. Friday nights feature karaoke, while Mozzi's hosts live music on Saturday nights.

**Cambria Pines Lodge Fireside Lounge** (Cambria Pines Lodge, 2905 Burton Dr., 805/927-4200, www.cambriapineslodge. com, 2pm-midnight daily) has live music nightly, performed on a stage to the right of a big stone fireplace. Enjoy a cocktail, beer, or wine seated at one of the couches or small tables.

## Food

The ★ **Main Street Grill** (603 Main St., 805/927-3194, www.firestonegrill.com,

11am-9pm daily June-Aug., 11am-8pm daily Sept.-May, $4-23) is a popular eatery housed in a cavernous building located on the way into Cambria. The tri-tip steak sandwich (tri-tip drenched in barbecue sauce and placed on a French roll dipped in butter) is the favorite, even though the ABC burger, with avocado, bacon, and cheese topping the meat, puts most burger joints to shame.

If the smell of the salt air on Moonstone Beach leaves you longing for a seafood dinner, head for the ★ **Sea Chest Oyster Bar** (6216 Moonstone Beach Dr., 805/927-4514, 5:30pm-9pm Mon.-Sat., $20-30, cash only). No reservations are accepted, so expect a long line out the door at opening time, and prepare to get here early (or wait a long while) for one of the window-side tables. The wait is worth it. The restaurant is located in a wooden cottage with great ocean views. Framed photographs on the walls and books on bookshelves add to the homey feel of the place. Sit at the bar to watch the cooks prepare the impressive dishes like halibut, salmon, and cioppino, which is served in the pot it was cooked in. The menu of oyster and clam appetizers includes terrific calamari strips and the indulgent Devils on Horseback, a decadent dish of sautéed oysters drenched in wine, garlic, and butter and topped with crispy bacon on two slabs of toast. Yum!

The eclectic menu at **Robin's** (4095 Burton Dr., 805/927-5007, www.robinsrestaurant.com, 11am-9:30pm Sun.-Thurs., 11am-10pm Fri.-Sat., $20-34) has cuisine from around the world, including Thailand (tofu pad Thai, Thai green chicken), India (a selection of curries, tandoori chicken), the Mediterranean (meze plate), Mexico (lobster enchiladas), and the old U.S. of A. (flatiron steak, burgers). What makes it so impressive is that Robin's does it all so well. Start with the signature salmon bisque or the grilled naan pizzette of the day. The menu also has a number of vegetarian and gluten-free dishes. Expect fine service from a staff that's proud of its product.

## Accommodations
### Under $150
Located next to a church, the ★ **Bridge Street Inn-HI Cambria** (4314 Bridge St., 805/215-0724, www.bridgestreetinncambria.com, $28-78) used to be the pastor's house. Now it's a clean, cozy hostel with a dorm room and four private rooms. The kitchen has a collection of cast-iron kitchenware, and there's a volleyball court out front. Part of Bridge Street's appeal is its enthusiastic young owner, Brandon Follett, who sometimes books live bands to play at the hostel. Even if there's no band scheduled to play, it doesn't take much to entice Brandon to grab his acoustic guitar and play an eclectic song for his guests.

### $150-250
A pebble's throw from Moonstone Beach, the ★ **Sand Pebbles Inn** (6252 Moonstone Beach Dr., 805/927-5600, www.cambriainns.com, $194-314) is a two-story gray building where most guest rooms have glimpses of the ocean through bay windows. The clean, tastefully decorated guest rooms have comfortable beds, mini fridges, and microwaves. The six guest rooms facing west have full ocean views, while the bottom three have patios. Expect amenities such as welcome cookies, a better-than-average continental breakfast, coffee and tea served in the lobby, and a lending library of DVDs. Owned by the same family, the adults-only **Blue Dolphin Inn** (6470 Moonstone Beach Dr., 805/927-3300, www.cambriainns.com, $259-400) is more upscale than its neighbor. The six full ocean-view rooms come with fireplaces, Keurig coffeemakers, robes, and slippers. Breakfast is delivered to your room every morning.

**Moonstone Landing** (6240 Moonstone Beach Dr., 805/927-0012, www.moonstonelanding.com, $150-315) provides inexpensive partial-view guest rooms with the decor and amenities of a midtier chain motel as well as oceanfront luxury guest rooms featuring porches with ocean views, soaking tubs, and gas fireplaces.

## Information and Services
The **Cambria Chamber of Commerce** (767 Main St., 805/927-3624, www.cambriachamber.org, 9am-5pm Mon.-Fri., noon-4pm Sat.-Sun.) is probably the best resource for information on the area. It also provides a free annual publication that lists many of the stores, restaurants, and lodgings. Pick up a trail guide for additional hikes and walks. The **Cambria Public Library** (900 Main St., 805/927-4336, 10am-5pm Tues.-Fri., 11am-4pm Sat.) offers additional information and

local history, including a map for a self-guided historical walking tour.

Cambria is served by three medical facilities: **Twin Cities Hospital** (1100 Las Tablas Rd., Templeton, 805/434-3500, www.twincitieshospital.com), in Templeton, 25 miles inland, and **Sierra Vista Regional Medical Center** (1010 Murray St., San Luis Obispo, 805/546-7600, www.sierravistaregional.com) and **French Hospital Medical Center** (1911 Johnson Ave., San Luis Obispo, 805/543-5353, www.frenchmedicalcenter.org), both in San Luis Obispo, 37 miles south.

## Getting Around

The regional bus system, the **RTA** (805/541-2228, www.slorta.org), connects San Luis Obispo, Morro Bay, Cayucos, Cambria, and San Simeon. Fares range $1.25-2.50.

# San Simeon

From Cambria, San Simeon is seven miles north along **CA-1.** Its biggest attraction, Hearst Castle, quite frankly, *is* San Simeon. The town grew up around it to support the overwhelming needs and never-ending construction of its megalomaniacal owner.

## Sights
### ★ Hearst Castle

There's nothing else in California quite like **Hearst Castle** (CA-1 and Hearst Castle Rd., 800/444-4445, www.hearstcastle.org, tours 9am-3:20pm daily). Newspaper magnate William Randolph Hearst conceived the idea of a grand mansion in the Mediterranean style on land his parents bought along the central California coast. He hired Julia Morgan, the first female civil engineering graduate from the University of California,

**From top to bottom:** Moonstone Beach boardwalk; Main Street Grill; Sea Chest Oyster Bar.

Berkeley, to design and build the house for him. She did a brilliant job with every detail, despite the ever-changing wishes of her employer. By way of decoration, Hearst assisted in the relocation of hundreds of European medieval and Renaissance antiquities, from tiny tchotchkes to whole gilded ceilings. Hearst also adored exotic animals, and he created one of the largest private zoos in the nation on his thousands of Central Coast acres. Most of the zoo is gone now, but you still see the occasional zebra grazing peacefully along CA-1 south of the castle, heralding the exotic nature of Hearst Castle ahead.

The visitors center is a lavish affair with a gift shop, a restaurant, a café, a ticket booth, and a movie theater. The film *Hearst Castle—Building the Dream* gives an overview of the construction and history of the marvelous edifice, as well as William Randolph Hearst's empire. After buying your ticket, board the shuttle that takes you up the hill to your tour. No private cars are allowed on the roads up to the castle. There are four tours to choose from, each focusing on different spaces and aspects of the castle.

## Tours

Expect to walk for at least an hour on whichever tour you choose, and to climb up and down many stairs. Even the most jaded traveler can't help but be amazed by the beauty and opulence that drips from every room in the house. Lovers of European art and antiques will want to stay forever.

The **Grand Rooms Museum Tour** (45 minutes, 106 stairs, 0.6 mile, $25 adults, $12 children under 12) is recommended for first-time visitors. It begins in the castle's assembly room, which is draped in Flemish tapestries, before heading into the dining room, the billiard room, and the impressive movie theater, where you'll watch a few old Hearst newsreels. The guide then lets you loose to take in the swimming pools: the indoor pool, decorated in gold and blue, and the stunning outdoor Neptune Pool.

For a further glimpse into Hearst's personal life, take the **Upstairs Suites Tour** (45 minutes, 273 stairs, 0.75 mile, $25 adults, $12 children under 12). Among the highlights are a stop within Hearst's private suite and a visit to his library, which holds over 4,000 books and 150 ancient Greek vases. At the end of this tour, you can explore the grounds, including the Neptune Pool, on your own.

Epicureans should opt for the **Cottages & Kitchen Tour** (45 minutes, 176 stairs, 0.75 mile, $25 adults, $12 children under 12). You visit the wine cellar first, where there are still bottles of wine, gin, rum, beer, and vermouth along the walls. (After a visit here, actor David Niven once said that "the wine flowed like glue.") Then take in the ornate guest cottages Casa Del Monte and Casa del Mar, where Hearst spent the final two years of his life. The tour concludes in the massive castle kitchen, before leaving you to explore the grounds on your own.

The seasonal **Evening Museum Tour** (100 minutes, 308 stairs, 0.75 mile, $36 adults, $18 children under 12) is only given in spring and fall. Volunteers dress in 1930s fashions and welcome guests as if they are arriving at one of Hearst's legendary parties.

Buy tour tickets at least a few days in advance, and even farther ahead on summer weekends. Wheelchair-accessible Grand Rooms and Evening Tours are available for visitors with limited mobility. Strollers are not permitted. The restrooms and food concessions are all in the visitors center. No food, drink, or chewing gum is allowed on any tour.

## Piedras Blancas Light Station

First illuminated in 1875, the **Piedras Blancas Light Station** (tours meet at the Piedras Blancas Motel, 1.5 miles north of the light station on CA-1, 805/927-7361, www.piedrasblancas.gov, tours 9:45am-11:45am Mon.-Sat., June 15-Aug. 31,

9:45am-11:45am Tues., Thurs., and Sat. Sept. 1-June 14, $10 adults, $5 children 6-17, children under 6 free) and its adjacent grounds can be accessed on a two-hour tour. The name Piedras Blancas means "white rocks" in Spanish. In 1948 a nearby earthquake caused a crack in the lighthouse tower and the removal of a first-order Fresnel lens, which was replaced with an automatic aero beacon. Since 2001 the lighthouse has been run by the federal Bureau of Land Management.

### Piedras Blancas Elephant Seal Rookery

Stopping at the **Piedras Blancas Elephant Seal Rookery** (CA-1, 7 miles north of San Simeon, 805/924-1628, www.elephant-seal.org, free) is like watching a nature documentary in real time. On this sliver of beach, up to 17,000 elephant seals rest, breed, give birth, or fight one another to mate. The rookery is right along CA-1: Turn into the large gravel parking lot and follow the boardwalks north or south to viewing areas where informative plaques give background on the elephant seals; volunteer docents are available to answer questions (10am-4pm daily). The beaches themselves are off-limits to humans; they're covered in the large marine mammals.

### William Randolph Hearst Memorial State Beach

Down the hill from Hearst Castle is **William Randolph Hearst Memorial State Beach** (750 Hearst Castle Rd., 805/927-2020, www.parks.ca.gov, 8am-8pm daily), with kelp-strewn sand along a protected cove. The 795-foot-long pier is great for fishing and strolling, and the **Coastal Discovery Center** (805/927-2145, 11am-5pm Thurs.-Sun., free), run by California State Parks and the Monterey Bay National Marine Sanctuary, warrants a stop. It focuses on local natural history and culture, with exhibits on shipwrecks, a display on elephant seals, and an interactive tide pool.

This beach offers a protected cove that's ideal for kayaking. You may see sea otters, seals, and sea lions while paddling. Located right on the beach, **Sea For Yourself Kayak Outfitters** (805/927-1787, http://kayakcambria.com, 10am-4pm daily mid-June-early Sept., call for times mid-Sept.-early June, single kayak $10 per hour, double kayak $20 per hour, stand-up paddleboard $15 per hour) rents equipment and offers two- to three-hour kayak tours of San Simeon Cove ($50 pp).

### Food

The best spot to fuel up for a Hearst Castle tour is easily ★ **Sebastian's Store** (442 Slo San Simeon Rd., 805/927-3307, 11am-4pm daily, $7-12). Housed alongside the Hearst Ranch Winery tasting room and the tiny San Simeon post office, this small eatery showcases tender, juicy beef from nearby Hearst Ranch in burgers, French dips, and unique creations like the Hot Beef Ortega Melt. This is a popular place, and the sandwiches take a few minutes to prepare, so don't stop in right before your scheduled Hearst Castle tour.

An unassuming steak and seafood restaurant attached to San Simeon's Quality Inn, the family-owned **Manta Rey Restaurant** (9240 Castillo Dr., 805/924-1032, www.mantareyrestaurant.com, 5pm-9pm daily, $20-50) pleasantly surprises with its artfully done and tasty seafood dishes. Items like salmon, oysters, and sea bass come from nearby Morro Bay when in season. A good place to start is with Manta Rey's oysters Rockefeller appetizer, a rich mix of baked oyster, bacon, cheese, and spinach in an oyster shell. Try the perfectly breaded sand dabs in a creamy basil and sherry sauce, also often caught fresh in nearby Morro Bay.

### Accommodations

San Simeon has a small strip of hotels on either side of the highway south of Hearst Castle. There are more accommodations in Cambria, just five miles away.

The **Best Western Plus Cavalier Oceanfront Resort** (9415 Hearst Dr., 805/927-4688, www.cavalierresort.com, $240-400) occupies a prime piece of real estate in San Simeon on a bluff above the ocean just south of Pico Creek. The highest-priced rooms are oceanfront offerings with wood-burning fireplaces, soaking tubs, and private patios. The grounds include a pool, an exercise room, a day spa, and a restaurant.

One of San Simeon's best lodging options, **The Morgan at San Simeon Hotel** (9135 Hearst Dr., 800/451-9900, www.hotel-morgan.com, $149-299) is named for Hearst Castle architect Julia Morgan, paying tribute to her with reproductions of her architectural drawings in all the guest rooms. The rooms are clean and well appointed, and some have partial ocean views; eight rooms come with soaking tubs and gas fireplaces. The Morgan also has a wind-sheltered pool and deck. A complimentary continental breakfast is served every morning.

### information and Services

Located in the Cavalier Plaza Shopping Center, the **San Simeon Chamber of Commerce** (250 San Simeon Ave., Ste. 3A, 805/927-3500, http://sansimeon-chamber.org, 805/927-3500, 10am-4pm daily) has visitor information. Its website covers accommodations, restaurants, recreation, attractions, events, and the region's history.

San Simeon has a cool old **post office** (440 Slo San Simeon Rd., 805/927-4156), located in the same historic building as the Hearst Ranch Winery tasting room and Sebastian's Store.

San Simeon is served by three medical facilities that are each about 45 minutes away: **Twin Cities Hospital** (1100 Las Tablas Rd., Templeton, 805/434-3500, www.twincitieshospital.com), **Sierra Vista Regional Medical Center** (1010 Murray St., San Luis Obispo, 805/546-7600, www.sierravistaregional.com), and **French Hospital Medical Center** (1911 Johnson Ave., San Luis Obispo, 805/543-5353, www.frenchmedicalcenter.org).

### Getting Around

The regional bus system, the **RTA** (805/541-2228, www.slorta.org), connects San Luis Obispo, Morro Bay, Cayucos, Cambria, and San Simeon. Fares range $1.25-2.50.

# Big Sur

Big Sur welcomes many types of visitors. Nature-lovers come to camp and hike the pristine wilderness areas, to don thick wetsuits and surf often-deserted beaches, and even to hunt for jade in rocky coves. On the other hand, some of the wealthiest people from California and beyond visit to relax at unbelievably upscale hotels and spas with dazzling views of the ocean. Whether you prefer a low-cost camping trip or a luxury resort, Big Sur offers its beauty and charm to all. Part of that charm is Big Sur's determination to remain peacefully apart from the Information Age; this means that your cell phone may not work in many parts of Big Sur.

### Getting There

Big Sur can only be reached via **CA-1.** The drive from San Simeon into Big Sur is where the Pacific Coast Highway gets really interesting, twisting and turning along with the coastline. Big Sur is not a town but rather the name for the lightly developed coastline stretching from San Simeon to Carmel. The largest concentration of businesses is located within the Big Sur Valley, 61 miles north of San Simeon.

The drive from San Simeon to the Big Sur Valley usually takes around **1.5 hours,** but it can be slow going, especially if you are behind an RV. You may want to stop every few miles to snap a photo of the stunning coastline. If traffic is backing up behind you, pull into a turnout to

# Big Sur

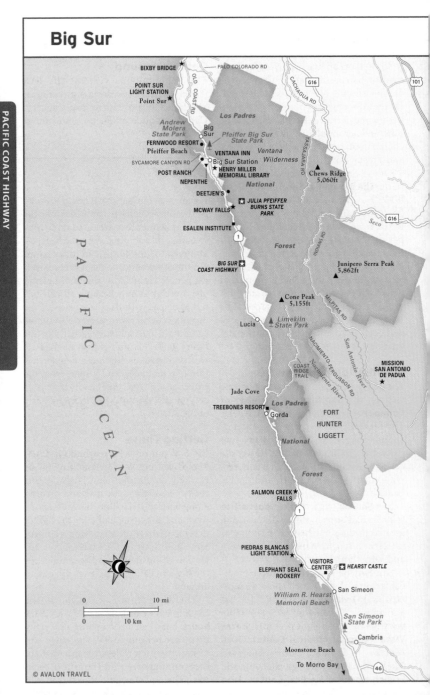

BIXBY BRIDGE

PALO COLORADO RD

G16

101

POINT SUR
LIGHT STATION
Point Sur

OLD COAST RD

CACHAGUA RD

Los Padres

Andrew
Molera
State Park

Big
Sur

Pfeiffer Big Sur
State Park

FERNWOOD RESORT
Pfeiffer Beach

Ventana
Wilderness

TASSAJARA RD

VENTANA INN

SYCAMORE CANYON RD

Big Sur Station
HENRY MILLER
MEMORIAL LIBRARY

Chews Ridge
5,060ft

POST RANCH

NEPENTHE

National

DEETJEN'S

JULIA PFEIFFER
BURNS STATE
PARK

G16

MCWAY FALLS

Seco

ESALEN INSTITUTE

1

Forest

INDIANS RD

Junipero Serra Peak
5,862ft

BIG SUR
COAST HIGHWAY

Cone Peak
5,155ft

MILPITAS RD

PACIFIC

Lucia

Limekiln
State Park

NACIMIENTO-FERGUSSON RD

San Antonio River

MISSION
SAN ANTONIO
DE PADUA

OCEAN

COAST
RIDGE
TRAIL

Nacimiento River

Jade Cove

TREEBONES RESORT
Gorda

Los Padres

FORT
HUNTER
LIGGETT

National

Forest

SALMON CREEK
FALLS

1

PIEDRAS BLANCAS
LIGHT STATION

VISITORS
CENTER

HEARST CASTLE

ELEPHANT SEAL
ROOKERY

William R. Hearst
Memorial Beach

San Simeon

San Simeon
State Park

0          10 mi

0      10 km

Cambria

Moonstone Beach

To Morro Bay

46

© AVALON TRAVEL

let other cars pass; the local drivers can be impatient with tourist traffic.

CA-1 can have one or both lanes closed at times, especially in the winter months when rockslides occur. The 2016 winter made the highway through Big Sur impassable due to a bridge failure and a massive landslide. Check the **Caltrans** website (www.dot.ca.gov) or the *Big Sur California Blog* (www.thebigsurblog.com) for current road conditions. Also, the *Big Sur Kate Blog* (https://bigsurkate.blog) is run by a Big Sur local and is one of the best places to look for information when fires, storms, and road closures plague Big Sur.

## Sights
### ★ Big Sur Coast Highway
The **Big Sur Coast Highway,** a 90-mile stretch of CA-1, is quite simply one of the most picturesque roads in the country. A two-lane road, CA-1 twists and turns with Big Sur's jagged coastline, running along precipitous cliffs and rocky beaches, through dense redwood forest, over historic bridges, and past innumerable parks. In the winter, you might spot migrating whales offshore spouting fountains of air and water, while spring finds yucca plants feathering the hillsides and wildflowers coloring the landscape. Construction on this stretch of road was completed in the 1930s, connecting Cambria to Carmel. You can start out at either of these towns and spend a whole day making your way to the other end of the road. The road has plenty of wide turnouts set into picturesque cliffs to make it easy to stop to admire the glittering ocean and stunning wooded cliffs running right out to the water. There can be frequent highway delays due to road construction.

### Salmon Creek Falls
One of the southern portion of Big Sur's best natural attractions is **Salmon Creek Falls** (8 miles south of Gorda or 3.5 miles north of Ragged Point on CA-1, 831/385-5434, www.fs.usda.gov). Flowing year-round, a pair of waterfalls pour down rocks over 100 feet high, and their streams join halfway down. To get a great perspective of the falls, take an easy 10-minute walk from the highway over a primitive trail littered with rocks. The unmarked parking area is a pullout in the middle of a hairpin turn on CA-1.

### ★ Julia Pfeiffer Burns State Park
Postcard-perfect views can be attained at **Julia Pfeiffer Burns State Park** (CA-1, 37 miles north of Ragged Point, 831/667-2315, www.parks.ca.gov, day use half hour before sunrise-half hour after sunset, day use $10). Photo ops are available from the **Overlook Trail,** runing only 0.66 mile round-trip, along a level, wheelchair-friendly boardwalk. Stroll under CA-1, past the Pelton wheelhouse, and out to the observation deck to view the stunning view of **McWay Falls.** The 80-foot-high waterfall cascades year-round off a cliff and onto the beach of a remote cove, where the water wets the sand and trickles out into the sea. The water of the cove gleams bright cerulean blue against the off-white sand of the beach; it looks more like the South Pacific than California. Anyone with an ounce of love for the ocean will want to build a hut right there beside the waterfall. But you can't. In fact, the reason you look down on a pristine and empty stretch of sand is that there's no way down to the cove that is even remotely safe.

If you're up for a longer hike after taking in the falls, go back the other way to pick up the **Ewoldsen Trail** (4.5 miles round-trip, moderate-strenuous). This hike takes you past the park's biggest redwoods on the way to a ridgeline that offers great views of the coastline.

### Henry Miller Memorial Library
A number of authors have done time in Big Sur, soaking in the remote wilderness and sea air to gather inspiration for their

work. Henry Miller lived and wrote in Big Sur for 18 years, and his 1957 novel *Big Sur and the Oranges of Hieronymus Bosch* describes his time here. Today, the **Henry Miller Memorial Library** (CA-1, 0.25 mile north of Deetjen's Big Sur Inn, 831/667-2574, www.henrymiller.org, 11am-6pm daily) celebrates the life and work of Miller and his brethren in this quirky community center, museum, coffee shop, and gathering place. What you won't find is a typical lending library or slicked-up museum. Instead, inside is a well-curated bookstore featuring the works of Miller as well as other authors like Jack Kerouac and Richard Brautigan, along with a crew of employees who are always worth striking up a conversation with. Over the last few years, the library has become an important arts and music center for the Central Coast. During the summer months, the library hosts an international short film series every Thursday night. Throughout the year, there are poetry readings, live music performances, film screenings, and more. Check the website for upcoming events.

### Big Sur Station

**Big Sur Station** (CA-1, 0.33 mile south of Pfeiffer Big Sur State Park, 831/667-2315, 9am-4pm daily) offers maps and brochures for all the major parks and trails of Big Sur, plus a minimal bookshop. This is also where the trailhead for the popular backcountry **Pine Ridge Trail** is located. You can get a **free backcountry fire permit** as well as pay for Pine Ridge Trailhead parking here.

### Pfeiffer Big Sur State Park

The most developed park in Big Sur is **Pfeiffer Big Sur State Park** (CA-1, 0.25 mile north of Big Sur Station, 831/667-2315, www.parks.ca.gov, day use half hour before sunrise-half hour after sunset, day use $10). It's got the Big Sur Lodge, a restaurant and café, a shop, an amphitheater, a somewhat incongruous softball field, plenty of hiking-only trails,

Pfeiffer Beach

and lovely redwood-shaded campsites. This park isn't situated by the beach; it's up in the coastal redwoods forest, with a network of roads that can be driven or biked up into the trees and along the Big Sur River.

Pfeiffer Big Sur has the tiny **Ernest Ewoldsen Memorial Nature Center,** which features stuffed examples of local wildlife. It's open seasonally; call the park for days and hours. The historic **Homestead Cabin,** located off the Big Sur Gorge Trail, was once the home of part of the Pfeiffer family—the first European immigrants to settle in Big Sur.

No bikes or horses are allowed on trails in this park, which makes it quite peaceful for hikers. For a starter walk, take the **Nature Trail** (0.7 mile round-trip), an easy self-guided stroll that imparts information about local vegetation.

Need to cool off after hiking? Scramble out to the undeveloped **Big Sur River Gorge,** where the river slows and creates pools that are great for swimming. Relax and enjoy the water, but don't try to dive here. The undeveloped trail to the gorge can be found at the eastern end of the campground.

### Pfeiffer Beach

Big Sur has plenty of striking meetings of land and sea, but **Pfeiffer Beach** (end of Sycamore Canyon Rd., http:// campone.com, 9am-8pm daily, $10) is one of the coastline's most picturesque spots. This frequently windswept beach has two looming rock formations right where the beach meets the surf, and both of these rocks have holes that look like doorways, allowing waves and sunlight to pass through.

For newcomers, getting to Pfeiffer Beach is a bit tricky. Heading south on CA-1 from Big Sur Station, take the second paved right turn. Motorists (no motor homes) must then travel down a narrow, windy, two-mile-long road before reaching the entrance booth and the beach's parking lot. It's part of the adventure. The road can get backed up during peak summer hours, so opt for an early morning or off-hour visit instead. Note that the beach can be incredibly windy at times.

### Andrew Molera State Park

At 4,800 acres, **Andrew Molera State Park** (CA-1, 4.5 miles north of Pfeiffer Big Sur State Park, 831/667-2315, www.parks. ca.gov, day use half hour before sunrise-half hour after sunset, day use $10) is a great place to immerse yourself in Big Sur's coastal beauty and rugged history.

Today, the **Cooper Cabin,** which is off the Trail Camp Beach Trail, is a remnant from the park's past. The redwood structure, built in 1861, is the oldest building standing on the Big Sur coast. The **Molera Ranch House Museum** (831/667-2956, http://bigsurhistory.org, 11am-3pm Sat. summer) displays stories of the life and times of Big Sur's human pioneers and artists as well as the wildlife and plants of the region. Take the road toward

the horse tours to get to the ranch house. Next to the ranch house is the **Ventana Wildlife Society's Big Sur Discovery Center** (831/624-1202, www.ventanaws.org, 10am-4pm Sat.-Sun. Memorial Day-Labor Day). This is the place to learn about the successful reintroduction of the California condor to the region.

The park has numerous hiking trails that run down to the beach and up into the forest along the river. Many trails are open to cycling and horseback riding as well. Most of the park trails lie to the west of the highway. The beach is a 1-mile walk down the easy, multiuse **Trail Camp Beach Trail.** From there, climb out on the **Headlands Trail,** a 0.25-mile loop, for a beautiful view from the headlands of the Big Sur River emptying into the sea. For an even longer and more difficult trek up the mountains and down to the beach, take the 8-mile **Ridge Trail and Panorama Trail Loop.** It offers a serious day hike and fine views of the coast by connecting the **Ridge Trail,** the **Panorama Trail,** and the **Bluffs Trails** to the park's **Creamery Meadow.**

### Point Sur Light Station

Sitting lonely and isolated out on its cliff, the **Point Sur Light Station** (CA-1, 0.25 mile north of Point Sur Naval Facility, 831/625-4419, www.pointsur.org, 10am and 2pm Wed. and Sat., 10am Sun. Apr.-Sept., 1pm Wed., 10am Sat.-Sun., Oct.-Mar., $12 adults, $5 children) crowns the 361-foot-high volcanic rock Point Sur, keeping watch over ships navigating near the rocky waters of Big Sur. It's the only complete 19th-century light station in California that you can visit, and even here access is severely limited. First lit in 1889, this now fully automated light station still provides navigational aid to ships off the coast; families stopped living and working in the tiny stone-built compound in 1974. But is the lighthouse truly uninhabited? Take one of the moonlight tours (call for information) to learn

about the haunted history of the light station buildings.

You can't make a reservation for a Point Sur tour, so you should just show up and park your car off CA-1 on the west side by the farm gate. Your guide will meet you there and lead you up the paved road 0.5 mile to the light station. Once there, you'll climb the stairs up to the light, explore the restored keepers' homes and service buildings, and walk out to the cliff edge. Expect to see a great variety of flora and fauna, with brilliant wildflowers in the spring and gray whales in the winter, and flocks of pelicans flying in formation at any time of year. Dress in layers; it can be sunny and hot or foggy and cold, winter or summertime, and sometimes both on the same tour! Tours last three hours and require more than a mile of walking, with a bit of slope, and more than 100 stairs. If you need special assistance for your tour or have questions about accessibility, call 831/649-2836 as far in advance as possible of your visit to make arrangements.

### Bixby Bridge

You'll probably recognize the **Bixby Bridge** (CA-1, 8.25 miles north of Andrew Molera State Park) when you come upon it on CA-1 in Big Sur. The picturesque cement, open-spandrel arched bridge is one of the most photographed bridges in the nation, and it has been used in countless car commercials over the years. The bridge was built in the early 1930s as part of the massive government works project that completed CA-1 through the Big Sur area, connecting the road from the north end of California to the south. Today, you can pull out at the north of the bridge to take photos or just look out at the attractive span and Bixby Creek flowing into the Pacific far below. Get another great view of the bridge by driving a few hundred feet down the dirt Old Coast Road, which is located on the bridge's northeast side.

# Best Big Sur Day Hikes

For adventurous hikers, the **Cone Peak Trail** (4 miles round-trip, strenuous) offers serious rewards for those willing to find its out-of-the-way trailhead. At 5,150 feet, Cone Peak is a rocky lump on an impressive flank of the Santa Lucia Mountains, and it has the distinction of being the second-highest peak in the Big Sur area. The two-mile ascent from the trailhead rises 1,355 feet without much shade, so bring water. At the summit of Cone Peak are a closed fire lookout hut and, most importantly, a sensational 360-degree view. Look west, as the steep mountain range drops from over 5,000 feet to sea level in less than three miles. To the east, you can see the Salinas Valley and, on clear days, the Sierra Nevada.

Getting to the **Cone Peak Trailhead** is a big part of the adventure. It is located on the mountainous and unpaved **Cone Peak Road,** which is usually closed November-May. You can call the **U.S. Forest Service Monterey Ranger District Station** (831/385-5434, www.fs.usda.gov) to check if the road is open. To reach the trailhead, drive 10 miles north of Gorda on CA-1 until you reach Nacimiento-Fergusson Road on the right. Drive up the paved but steep road for 7 miles to its crest; there you will see dirt roads departing to your left and right. Take a left onto Cone Peak Road and follow it for almost 5.5 miles. Look for a trail sign and small area to park your vehicle on the left.

Easier to find is the **Ewoldsen Trail** (4.5 miles round-trip, moderate-strenuous) in **Julia Pfeiffer Burns State Park** (CA-1, 37 miles north of Ragged Point, 831/667-2315, www.parks.ca.gov, day use half hour before sunrise-half hour after sunset, day use $10). This trek takes you through McWay Canyon, where you'll see the creek and surrounding lush greenery as you walk. Some of Big Sur's finest redwoods are located here. Then you'll loop away from the water and climb up into the hills. One part of the trail is perched on a ridgeline, where there is little vegetation growing on the steep hillside below. This is the site of a 1983 landslide that closed the highway below for a whole year. Bring water, as this hike can take several hours.

For a coastal hike, take the **Ridge Trail and Panorama Trail Loop** (8 miles round-trip, moderate-strenuous) at **Andrew Molera State Park** (CA-1, 4.5 miles north of Pfeiffer Big Sur State Park, 831/667-2315, www.parks.ca.gov, day use half hour before sunrise-half hour after sunset, day use $10). You'll start at the parking lot on the Creamery Meadow Beach Trail, then make a left onto the long and fairly steep **Ridge Trail** to get a sense of the local ecosystem. Then turn right onto the **Panorama Trail,** which runs down to the coastal scrublands. From the **Panorama Trail,** you can take a short spur called the **Spring Trail** out to a secluded beach. The **Panorama Trail** turns into the **Bluffs Trail,** which takes you back to Creamery Meadow, on the last leg.

## Sports and Recreation
### Hiking

The main reason to come to Big Sur is to get out of your vehicle and hike its beaches and forests. There are lots of hiking opportunities, from short walks under a canopy of redwood trees to multiday backpacking trips into Big Sur's wilderness interior.

### Horseback Riding

You can take a guided horseback ride into the forests or out onto the beaches of Andrew Molera State Park with **Molera Horseback Tours** (831/625-5486, http://molerahorsebacktours.com, Apr.-Nov., $48-84). Tours of 1-2.5 hours depart each day starting at 9am, 11am, 1pm, and 3:30pm. Call ahead to guarantee your spot, or call to book a private guided

# California Condors

With wings spanning 10 feet from tip to tip, the California condors soaring over the Big Sur coastline are some of the area's most impressive natural treasures. But, in 1987, there was only one bird left in the wild, which was taken into captivity as part of a captive breeding program. The condors' population had plummeted due to its susceptibility to lead poisoning along with deaths caused by electric power lines, habitat loss, and being shot by indiscriminate humans.

Now the reintroduction of the high-flying California condor, the largest flying bird in North America, to Big Sur and the Central Coast is truly one of conservation's greatest success stories. In 1997, the Monterey County-based nonprofit Ventana Wildlife Society (VWS) began releasing the giant birds back into the wild. Currently, over 60 wild condors soar above Big Sur and the surrounding area,

and in 2006, a pair of condors were found nesting in the hollowed-out section of a redwood tree.

The species' recovery in the Big Sur area means that you might be able to spot a California condor flying overhead while visiting the rugged coastal region. Look for a tracking tag on the condor's wing to determine that you are actually looking at a California condor and not just a big turkey vulture. Or take a two-hour tour with the **Ventana Wildlife Society** (831/455-9514, second Sun. every month, $50 pp), which uses radio telemetry to track the released birds. Or visit the **VWS Discovery Center** (Andrew Molera State Park, CA-1, 22 miles south of Carmel, 831/624-1202, www.ventanaws.org, 10am-4pm Sat.-Sun. Memorial Day-Labor Day), where there's an exhibit that details the near extinction of the condor and the attempts to restore the population.

ride. Each ride takes you from the modest corral area along multiuse trails through forests or meadows, or along the Big Sur River, and down to Molera Beach. You'll guide your horse along the solid sands as you admire the beauty of the wild Pacific Ocean.

Molera Horseback Tours are suitable for children over age six and riders of all ability levels; you'll be matched to the right horse for you. All but one of the rides go down to the beach. Tours can be seasonal, so call ahead if you want to ride in the fall or winter.

### Bird-Watching

Many visitors come to Big Sur just to see the birds. The Big Sur coast is home to innumerable species, from the tiniest bushtits up to grand pelicans and beyond. The most famous avian residents of this area are no doubt the rare and endangered California condors. Once upon a time, condors were all but extinct, with only a few left alive in captivity and conservationists struggling to

help them breed. Today, more than 60 birds soar above the trails and beaches of Big Sur. You might even see one swooping down low over your car as you drive down CA-1!

The **Ventana Wildlife Society** (VWS, www.ventanaws.org) watches over many of the endangered and protected avian species in Big Sur. As part of its mission to raise awareness of the condors and many other birds, the VWS offers bird-watching expeditions. Check the website for schedules and prices.

### Spas

**Spa Alila** (48123 CA-1, 800/628-6500, www.ventanainn.com, 10am-7pm daily, massages $175-615) offers a large menu of spa treatments to both hotel guests and visitors. You'll love the serene atmosphere of the treatment and waiting areas. Greenery and weathered wood create a unique space that helps to put you in a tranquil state of mind, ready for your body to follow your mind into a state of relaxation. Indulge in a soothing massage, purifying body treatment, or rejuvenating or beautifying facial. Take your spa experience a step further in true Big Sur fashion with an astrological reading, essence portrait, or a jade stone massage. If you're a hotel guest, you can choose to have your spa treatment in the comfort of your own room or out on your private deck.

Just across the highway from the Ventana, the **Post Ranch Inn's Spa** (47900 CA-1, 831/667-2200, www.postranchinn. com, 10am-7pm daily, massages $165-495) is another high-end resort spa, only open to those who are staying the night at the spendy resort. Shaded by redwoods, the relaxing spa offers massages and facials along with more unique treatments, including Big Sur jade stone therapy and craniosacral therapy.

## Entertainment and Events
### Live Music
Over the last few years, Big Sur has become an unexpected hotbed for big music concerts. More than just a place to down a beer and observe the local characters, **Fernwood Bar & Grill** (CA-1, 831/667-2422, www.fernwoodbigsur.com, 11am-11pm Sun.-Thurs., 11am-1am Fri.-Sat.) also has live music. Most of the big-name acts swing through Big Sur in the summer and fall. Even when Big Sur isn't hosting nationally known touring bands, Fernwood has a wide range of regional acts on Saturday nights. You might hear country, folk, or even indie rock from the small stage. Most live music happens on weekends, especially Saturday nights, starting at 9:30pm.

Down the road, the **Henry Miller Memorial Library** (0.25 mile north of Deetjen's Big Sur Inn, 831/667-2574, www.henrymiller.org) has had some internationally known acts perform on its stage, including Arcade Fire, TV on the Radio, and the Fleet Foxes, who typically fill far bigger venues but are now transitioning to more intimate

shows. Check the website for upcoming events.

### Bars
The primary watering hole in Big Sur is **Fernwood Bar & Grill** (CA-1, 831/667-2422, www.fernwoodbigsur.com, 11am-11pm Sun.-Thurs., 11am-1am Fri.-Sat.). Enjoy a beer or cocktail inside or out back on a deck under the redwoods.

The newest place to grab a beer in Big Sur is the **Big Sur Taphouse** (47250 CA-1, 831/667-2225, www.bigsurtaphouse.com, noon-10pm Mon.-Thurs., noon-midnight Fri., 10am-midnight Sat., 10am-10pm Sun.). The Taphouse has 10 rotating beers on tap, with a heavy emphasis on West Coast microbrews. They also serve better-than-average bar food, including tacos and pork sliders.

### Festivals and Events
Each year, the Pacific Valley School hosts the fund-raising **Big Sur Jade Festival** (831/241-1154, www.bigsurjadeco.com, Oct.). Come out to see the artists, craftspeople, jewelry makers, and rock hunters displaying their wares in the early fall. The school is located across CA-1 from Sand Dollar Beach. Munch snacks as your feet tap to the live music playing as part of the festival. Check the website for the exact dates and information about this year's festival.

Throughout the summer months, Big Sur cultural mecca the **Henry Miller Memorial Library** (0.25 mile north of Deetjen's Big Sur Inn, 831/667-2574, www.henrymiller.org) hosts the **Big Sur International Short Film Screening Series,** where free films from all over the globe are shown every Thursday night.

The **Big Sur Marathon** (831/625-6226, www.bsim.org, Apr.), touted as one of the world's best, is a 26.2-mile running race from Big Sur Station to Carmel. Enjoy the rare opportunity to experience the stunning Big Sur coastline without any traffic.

## Food

As you traverse the famed CA-1 through Big Sur, you'll quickly realize that a ready meal isn't something to take for granted. You'll see no In-N-Out Burgers, Starbucks, or Safeways lining the road here. While you can find groceries, they tend to appear in small markets attached to motels. Pick up staple supplies in Cambria or Carmel before you enter the area if you don't plan to leave again for a few days, to avoid paying premium prices at the mini-marts.

### Casual Dining

One of Big Sur's most popular attractions is ★ **Nepenthe** (48510 CA-1, 831/667-2345, www.nepenthe.com, 11:30am-10pm daily, $17-50), a restaurant on the site where Rita Hayworth and Orson Welles owned a cabin until 1947. The deck offers views on par with those you might attain on one of Big Sur's great hikes. At sunset, order up a basket of fries with Nepenthe's signature Ambrosia dipping sauce and wash them down with a potent South Coast margarita. For dinner there is glazed duck and an eight-ounce filet mignon, but the best bet is the restaurant's most popular item: the Ambrosia burger, a ground steak burger drenched in that tasty Ambrosia sauce.

The **Fernwood Bar & Grill** (CA-1, 831/667-2129, www.fernwoodbigsur.com, 11am-10pm daily, $10-25) at Fernwood Resort looks and feels like a grill in the woods ought to. Even in the middle of the afternoon, the aging, wood-paneled interior is dimly lit and strewn with casual tables and chairs. Walk up to the counter to order tacos, burgers, or pizzas, then on to the bar to grab a soda or a beer.

The **Big Sur Bakery** (47540 CA-1, 831/667-0520, www.bigsurbakery.com, 8am-3:30pm Mon., 8am-9pm Tues.-Sun., $18-32) might sound like a casual, walk-up eating establishment, and the bakery part of it is. You can stop in from 8am every day to grab a fresh-baked scone, a homemade jelly donut, or a flaky croissant sandwich to save for lunch later on. But on the dining room side, an elegant surprise awaits diners who've spent the day hiking the redwoods and strolling the beaches. Make reservations or you might miss out on the creative wood-fired pizzas, wood-grilled meats, and seafood. At brunch, they serve the unique wood-fired bacon and three-egg breakfast pizza.

Easing into the day is easy at ★ **Deetjen's** (48865 CA-1, 831/667-2378, www.deetjens.com, 8am-noon and 6pm-9pm Mon.-Fri., 8am-12:30pm and 6pm-9pm Sat.-Sun., $10-32). Among fanciful knickknacks and cabinets displaying fine china, fill up on Deetjen's popular eggs Benedict dishes or the equally worthy Deetjen's dip, a turkey and avocado sandwich that comes with hollandaise dipping sauce. In the evening, things get darker and more romantic as entrées, including the spicy seafood paella and a roasted, smoked bacon-wrapped pork tenderloin, are served to your candlelit table. The locals know Deetjen's for its breakfast, and it is an almost required experience for visitors to the area.

If it's a warm afternoon, get a table on the sunny back deck of the **Big Sur River Inn Restaurant** (46840 CA-1, 831/667-2700, www.bigsurriverinn.com, 8am-9pm daily, $15-40). On summer Sundays, bands perform on the crowded deck, and you can take your libation out back to one of the chairs situated right in the middle of the cool Big Sur River. This restaurant serves sandwiches, burgers, and fish-and-chips for lunch along with steak, ribs, and seafood at dinner. The bar is known for its popular spicy Bloody Mary cocktails.

A cozy, rural-modern eatery, the **Big Sur Roadhouse** (47080 CA-1, 831/667-2370, www.glenoaksbigsur.com, 8am-2:30pm daily, $10-16) was featured as a location in the 2016 independent film *Always Shine*. Currently doing just breakfast and lunch, the roadhouse serves up recommended items including tacos, a pulled pork sandwich, and *chilaquiles*, a traditional Mexican breakfast dish.

### Fine Dining

You don't need to be a guest at the gorgeous Ventana to enjoy a fine gourmet dinner at **The Sur House** (CA-1, 831/667-4242, www.ventanainn.com, 7:30am-10:30am, 11:30am-4:30pm, and 6pm-close daily, four-course dinner tasting menu $80). The spacious dining room boasts a warm wood fire, an open kitchen, and comfortable banquettes with plenty of throw pillows to lounge against as you peruse the menu. Request a table outside to enjoy stunning views with your meal. The inside dining room has great views from the bay windows too, along with pristine white tablecloths and pretty light wooden furniture. Even in such a setting, the real star at this restaurant is the cuisine. Chef Paul Corsentino has upped the quality of the menu, which at times has wild boar and Monterey sardine courses. You can choose an à la carte main course entrée or go for the Chef's Taste of the Season ($90) or the Vegetarian Tasting Menu ($80).

The **Sierra Mar** (47900 CA-1, 831/667-2800, www.postranchinn.com, 12:15pm-3pm and 5:30pm-9pm daily, lunch $65, dinner $120-175 pp) restaurant at the Post Ranch Inn offers a decadent four-course prix fixe dinner menu ($125) every night). There's also a less formal three-course lunch every day. With floor-to-ceiling glass windows overlooking the plunging ridgeline and the Pacific below, it's a good idea to schedule dinner during sunset. The daily menu rotates, but courses have included farm-raised abalone in brown butter and a succulent short rib and beef tenderloin duo.

### Markets

With no supermarkets or chain mini-marts in the entire Big Sur region, the local markets do a booming business. The best of these is the **Big Sur Deli** (47520 CA-1, 831/667-2225, www.bigsurdeli. com, 7am-8pm daily, $5-8), which offers basic goods. It is also the spot to grab a sandwich or burrito to bring on a picnic or take back to your campsite. Also good is the **River Inn Big Sur General Store** (46840 CA-1, 831/667-2700, 7am-8pm daily, $10), which has basic snacks as well as a burrito and fruit smoothie bar.

## Accommodations
### Under $150

Your guest room at **Deetjen's Big Sur Inn** (48865 CA-1, 831/667-2378, www. Deetjen's.com, $105-270) will be unique, still decorated with the art and collectibles chosen and arranged by Grandpa Deetjen many moons ago. The inn prides itself on its rustic historic construction, so expect thin weathered walls, funky cabin construction, no outdoor locks on the doors, and an altogether one-of-a-kind experience. Five rooms have shared baths, but you can request a room with private bath when you make reservations. Deetjen's prefers to offer a serene environment, and to that end does not permit children under 12 unless you rent both rooms of a two-room building. Deetjen's has no TVs or stereos, no phones in guest rooms, and no cell phone service. One of the primary sources of entertainment is the rooms' guest journals, which have occupied the evenings of many who have stayed here for years. Decide for yourself whether this sounds terrifying or wonderful.

### $150-250

Along CA-1 in the valley of Big Sur, you'll find a couple of small motels. One of the more popular of these is the **Fernwood Resort** (CA-1, 831/667-2422, www.fernwoodbigsur.com, motel rooms $155-200, cabins $250). The low cluster of buildings includes a 12-room motel, a small convenience store, a restaurant, and a bar that is a gathering place for locals and a frequent host of live music. The motel units are located on either side of the restaurant-bar-convenience store. The nicely priced units start at a simple queen bedroom and go up to a queen bedroom with a fireplace and a two-person hot tub on an outdoor back deck. Down near the Big Sur River, the cabins have fully equipped kitchens with refrigerator. The cabins are a good deal for larger groups of 2-6 people.

## Over $250

Filled with creative touches and thoughtful amenities, ★ **Glen Oaks Big Sur** (47080 CA-1, 831/667-2105, www.glenoaksbigsur.com, $275-650) offers the region's best lodging for the price. Its 16 motor-lodge units bring the motor lodge into the new millennium with heated stone bathroom floors, in-room yoga mats, spacious two-person showers, and gas fireplaces that double as art pieces. These combine seamlessly with the motor lodge's longtime adobe walls and wood rafters. For those who would rather spend an evening in a stand-alone structure, Glen Oaks has two cottages in the oak trees and eight cabins in an impressive redwood grove by the Big Sur River. The cabins are clean with a modern rustic feel and have kitchenettes along with outdoor fire pits that are already set up with kindling and firewood. All guests have access to two on-site beaches situated on scenic sections of the Big Sur River.

The best part about staying at the **Big Sur Lodge** (47225 CA-1, 800/424-4787, www.bigsurlodge.com, $255-476), inside Pfeiffer Big Sur State Park, is that you can leave your room and hit the trail. In the early 1900s, the park was a resort owned by the pioneering Pfeiffer family. Though the amenities have been updated, the Big Sur Lodge still evokes the classic woodsy vacation cabin. Set in the redwood forest along an array of paths and small roads, the rustic rooms feature quilts, understated decor, and simple but clean baths. One option sleeps six, and others have kitchenettes. Stock your kitchenette at the on-site grocery store or eat at the lodge's restaurant or café. The lodge has

a swimming pool for the sunny summer and fall days.

One of Big Sur's two luxury resorts, **Ventana Inn & Spa** (48123 CA-1, 831/667-2331, www.ventanainn.com, $600-2,000) is a place where the panoramic views begin on the way to the parking lot. Picture home-baked pastries, fresh yogurt, in-season fruit, and organic coffee that can be delivered to your room in the morning or eaten in the restaurant. And that's just the beginning of an unbelievable day at the Ventana. Next, don your plush spa robe and rubber slippers and head for the Japanese bathhouse. Choose from two bathhouses, one at each end of the property. Both are clothing-optional and gender segregated, and the upper house has glass and open-air windows that let you look out to the ocean. Two swimming pools offer a cooler hydro-respite from your busy life; the lower pool is clothing-optional, and the upper pool perches on a high spot for enthralling views. Even daily complimentary yoga classes can be yours for the asking.

Even though a night at **Post Ranch Inn** (47900 CA-1, 831/667-2200 or 888/524-4787, www.postranchinn.com, $925-2,585) can total more than some people's monthly paycheck, an evening staring at the smear of stars over the vast blue Pacific from one of the stainless steel hot soaking tubs on the deck of the Post Ranch's ocean-facing rooms can temporarily cause all of life's worries to ebb away. Though it may be difficult to leave the resort's well-appointed units, it is a singular experience to soak in the Infinity Jade Pool, an ocean-facing warm pool made from chunks of the green ornamental stone.

On a 1,200-foot-high ridgeline, all the rooms at this luxury resort have striking views, whether it's of the ocean or the jagged peaks of the nearby Ventana Wilderness. The units also blend in well with the natural environment, including the seven tree houses, which are perched 10 feet off the ground. A night at Post

Ranch also includes an impressive breakfast with made-to-order omelets and French toast as well as a spread of pastries, fruit, and yogurt served in the Sierra Mar restaurant with its stellar ocean views.

## Camping

Many visitors to Big Sur want to experience the unspoiled beauty of the landscape daily. To accommodate true outdoors lovers, many of the parks and lodges have overnight campgrounds. You'll find all types of camping, from full-service, RV-accessible areas to environmental tent campsites to wilderness backpacking. You can camp in a state park or out behind one of the small resort motels near a restaurant and a store and possibly the cool, refreshing Big Sur River. Pick the option that best suits you and your family's needs.

In summer months, especially on weekends, campers without reservations coming to Big Sur are frequently turned away from the full campgrounds. A backup option for the desperate is to try and secure one of the 12 first-come, first-served tent campsites at **Bottcher's Gap** (11 miles south of Carmel's Rio Rd., take Palo Colorado Rd. 8 miles inland, 805/434-1996, http://campone. com, $15). There are few amenities and it can get hot up here, but at 2,100 feet, the camp has some good views of the Big Sur backcountry.

### Treebones Resort

For the ultimate high-end California green lodging-cum-camping experience, book a yurt (a circular structure made with a wood frame covered by cloth) at the **Treebones Resort** (71895 CA-1, 877/424-4787, www.treebonesresort. com). The yurts ($320-420) at Treebones tend to be spacious and charming, with polished wood floors, queen beds, seating areas, and outdoor decks for lounging. There are also five walk-in campsites ($95 for 2 people, breakfast and use of the facilities included). For a truly different experience, camp in the human nest ($175), a bundle of wood off the ground outfitted with a futon mattress, or the Twig Hut ($215). In the central lodge, you'll find hot showers and usually clean restroom facilities. There is also a heated pool with an ocean view and a hot tub on the grounds. Being away from any real town, Treebones has a couple of on-site dining options: the Wild Coast Restaurant and the Wild Coast Sushi Bar.

### Plaskett Creek Campground

**Plaskett Creek Campground** (CA-1, 60 miles north of San Luis Obispo, 805/434-1996, www.recreation.gov, $35) is located right across the highway from Sand Dollar Beach. The sites are in a grassy area under Monterey pine and cypress trees. There are picnic tables and a campfire ring with a grill at every site along with a flush toilet and drinking water in the campground.

### Kirk Creek Campground

A popular U.S. Forest Service campground on the south coast of Big Sur, **Kirk Creek Campground** (CA-1, 65 miles north of San Luis Obispo, 805/434-1996, www.recreation.gov, $35) has a great location on a bluff above the ocean. Right across the highway is the trailhead for the Vicente Flat Trail and the scenic mountain Nacimiento-Fergusson Road. The sites have picnic tables and campfire rings with grills, while the grounds have toilets and drinking water.

### Julia Pfeiffer Burns State Park

**Julia Pfeiffer Burns State Park** (CA-1, 37 miles north of Ragged Point, 831/667-2315 or 800/444-7275, www.parks. ca.gov, www.reservecalifornia.com, $30) has two walk-in environmental campsites perched over the ocean behind the stunning McWay Waterfall. It's a short 0.33-mile walk to these two sites, which have fire pits, picnic tables, and a shared pit toilet, but there is no running water. Obviously these two sites book up far in advance, particularly in the summer months, but it is worth checking with the state park to see if there have been any cancellations. Also, you will need to check in at Pfeiffer Big Sur State Park, which is 12 miles north on CA-1.

## Pfeiffer Big Sur State Park

The biggest and most developed campground in Big Sur is at **Pfeiffer Big Sur State Park** (CA-1, 0.25 mile north of Big Sur Station, 800/444-7275, www.reserve-california.com, standard campsite $35, riverside campsite $50). With 170 individual sites, each of which can take two vehicles and eight people or an RV (maximum 32 feet, trailer maximum 27 feet, dump station on-site), there's enough room for almost everybody, except during a crowded summer weekend. During those times, a grocery store and laundry facilities operate within the campground for those who don't want to hike down to the lodge, and plenty of flush toilets and hot showers are scattered throughout the campground. In the evenings, walk down to the Campfire Center for entertaining and educational programs. Pfeiffer Big Sur fills up fast in the summertime, especially on weekends. Reservations are recommended.

## Fernwood Resort

The **Fernwood Resort** (47200 CA-1, 0.5 mile north of Pfeiffer Big Sur State Park, 831/667-2422, www.fernwoodbigsur. com, tent site $60, campsite with electric hookup $80, tent cabin $110, adventure tent $150) offers a range of camping options. There are 66 campsites located around the Big Sur River, some with electric hookups for RVs. Fernwood also has tent cabins, which are small canvas-constructed spaces with room for four in a double and two twins. You can pull your car right up to the back of your cabin. Bring your own linens or sleeping bags, pillows, and towels to make up the inside of your tent cabin. Splitting the difference between camping and a motel room are the rustic "Adventure Tents," canvas tents draped over a solid floor whose biggest comfort are the fully made queen beds and electricity courtesy of an extension cord run into the tent. All camping options have easy access to the river, where you can swim, inner tube, and hike. Hot showers and restrooms are a short walk away. Also, you will be stumbling distance from Big Sur's most popular watering hole, the Fernwood Bar.

## Andrew Molera State Park

**Andrew Molera State Park** (CA-1, 5 miles north of Pfeiffer Big Sur State Park, 831/667-2315, www.parks.ca.gov, $25) offers 24 walk-in, tent-only campsites located 0.25-0.5 mile from the parking lot via a level, well-maintained trail. You'll pitch your tent at a pretty meadow near the Big Sur River, in a site that includes a picnic table and a fire ring. No reservations are taken, so come early in summertime to get one of the prime spots under a tree. While you're camping, look for bobcats, foxes, deer, raccoons (stow your food securely!), and any number of birds. From the camping area, it's an easy one-mile hike to the beach.

## Information and Services

The **Big Sur Chamber of Commerce**'s website (www.bigsurcalifornia.org) includes up-to-date information about hikes as well as links to lodging and restaurants. The closest thing to a visitors center is the **Big Sur Station** (0.3 mile south of Pfeiffer Big Sur State Park, 831/667-2315, 9am-4pm daily), which has information on the backcountry. Pick up the *Big Sur Guide,* a publication of the Big Sur Chamber of Commerce with a map and guide to local businesses.

Your **cell phone** may not work anywhere in Big Sur, but especially out in the undeveloped reaches of forest and on CA-1 away from the valley. The **Big Sur Health Center** (46896 CA-1, Big Sur, 831/667-2580, 10am-1pm and 2pm-5pm

Mon.-Fri.) can take care of minor medical needs and provides an ambulance service and limited emergency care. The nearest full-service hospital is the **Community Hospital of the Monterey Peninsula** (23625 Holman Hwy., Monterey, 831/624-5311, www.chomp.org).

## Getting Around

It is difficult to get around Big Sur without a car. However, on Saturday-Sunday from Memorial Day weekend to Labor Day, **Monterey-Salinas Transit** (888/678-2871, www.mst.org, $3.50) runs a bus route through Big Sur that stops at Nepenthe, the Big Sur River Inn, and Andrew Molera State Park as it heads to Carmel and Monterey. Check the website for times.

# Carmel

Formerly a Bohemian enclave where local poets George Sterling and Robinson Jeffers hung out with literary heavyweights including Jack London and Mary Austin, Carmel is now a popular vacation spot for the well moneyed, the artistic, and the romantic. People come to enjoy the small coastal town's almost European charm: strolling its sidewalks and peering in the windows of upscale shops and art galleries, which showcase the work of sculptors, plein air painters, and photographers. Among the galleries are some of the region's most revered restaurants. The main thoroughfare, Ocean Avenue, slopes down to Carmel Beach, one of the finest on the Monterey Peninsula.

The old-world charms of Carmel can make it a little confusing for drivers. Because there are no addresses, locations are sometimes given via directions, for example: on 7th between San Carlos and Dolores, or the northwest corner of Ocean Avenue. You get used to it. The town is compact, laid out on a plain grid system, so you're better off getting out

of your car and walking anyway. Expect to share everything from Carmel's sidewalks to its restaurants with our furry canine friends; Carmel is very pro-pup.

## Getting There

From the Big Sur Valley to Carmel is just **32 miles,** but most likely you will spend **45 minutes** or more on the drive up **CA-1,** which still twists and turns with the coastline. From CA-1, take **Ocean Avenue** into downtown Carmel. A more expensive but also more scenic route is via Pebble Beach's **17-Mile Drive** from the north.

CA-1 can have one or both lanes closed at times, especially in the winter months when rockslides occur. Check the **Caltrans** website (www.dot.ca.gov).

## Sights
### ★ Carmel Beach

Found at the end of Carmel's Ocean Avenue, **Carmel Beach** (Ocean Ave., 831/620-2000, http://ci.carmel.ca.us/carmel/) is one of the Monterey Bay region's best beaches. Under a bluff dotted with twisted skeletal cypress trees, it's a long white sandy beach that borders a usually clear blue-green Pacific. In the distance to the south, Point Lobos juts out from the land like a pointing finger, while just north of the beach, the golf courses, green as billiard table felt, cloak the grounds of nearby Pebble Beach.

Like most of Carmel, Carmel Beach is dog-friendly; on any given day, all sorts of canines fetch, sniff, and run on the white sand. For surfers, Carmel Beach is one of the Monterey area's most consistent breaks. It's also the site of the annual Sunshine Freestyle Surfabout, the only surf contest in Monterey County.

### Carmel Mission

**San Carlos Borromeo de Carmelo Mission** (3080 Rio Rd., 831/624-1271, www.carmelmission.org, 9:30am-7pm daily May-Sept., 9:30am-5pm daily

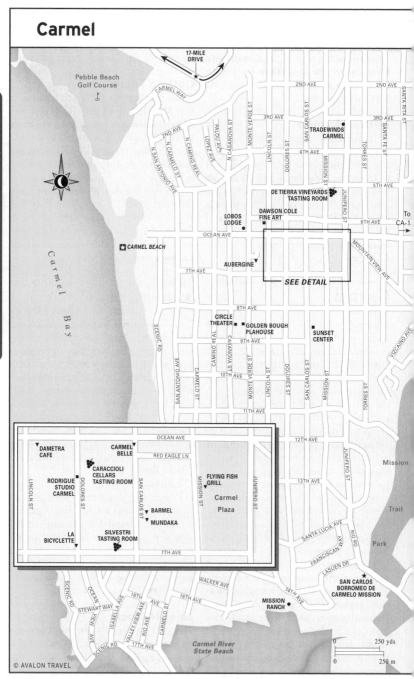

# Carmel

Sept.-May, $9.50 adults, $7 seniors, $5 children, children 6 and under free) was Father Junípero Serra's personal favorite among his California mission churches. He lived, worked, and eventually died here, and visitors today can see a replica of his cell. A working Catholic parish remains part of the complex, so be respectful when taking the self-guided tour. The rambling buildings and courtyard gardens show some wear, but enough restoration work has gone into the church and living quarters to make them attractive and eminently visitable. The Carmel Mission has a small memorial museum in a building off the second courtyard, but don't make the mistake of thinking that this small and outdated space is the only historical display. In fact, the "museum" runs through many of the buildings, showing a small slice of the lives of the 18th- and 19th-century friars. The highlight of the complex is the church with its gilded altar front, its shrine to the Virgin Mary, the grave of Junípero Serra, and an ancillary chapel dedicated to his memory. Round out your visit by walking out into the gardens to admire the flowers and fountains and to read the grave markers in the small cemetery.

### Point Lobos State Reserve

Said to be the inspiration behind the setting of Robert Louis Stevenson's *Treasure Island*, **Point Lobos State Reserve** (CA-1, 3 miles south of Carmel, 831/624-4909, www.parks.ca.gov and www.pointlobos. org, 8am-7pm daily spring-fall, 8am-half hour after sunset daily winter, $10 per vehicle) is a wonderland of coves, hills, and jumbled rocks. The reserve's Cypress Grove Trail winds through a forest of antler-like Monterey cypress trees that are cloaked in a striking red algae. Point Lobos also offers a lesson on the region's fishing history in the **Whaler's Cabin** (9am-5pm daily, staff permitting), a small wooden structure that was built by Chinese fishermen in the 1850s. Half of the reserve is underwater, open for scuba

divers who want to explore the 70-foot-high kelp forests located just offshore. The parking lots in Point Lobos tend to fill up on crowded weekends, but the reserve allows people to park on nearby CA-1 and walk in to visit the park during these times.

### 17-Mile Drive

Located between Carmel and Pacific Grove, the gated community of **Pebble Beach** lays claim to some of the Monterey Peninsula's best coastal views—and highest-priced real estate, both represented in the collection of high-end resorts, restaurants, spas, and golf courses, along the **17-Mile Drive.** Because the stunning scenery is also a precious commodity, a toll ($10.25 per vehicle) is charged to use the road. The good news is that when you pay the fee at the gatehouse, you receive a map of the drive that describes the parks and sights that you will pass along the winding coastal road: the much-photographed Lone Cypress, the beaches of Spanish Bay, and Pebble Beach's golf course, resort, and housing complex. (You can also be reimbursed if you spend over $35 at one of Pebble Beach's restaurants.) You can get from one end of the 17-Mile Drive to the other in 20 minutes, but go slowly and stop often to enjoy the natural beauty of the area (and get your money's worth). There are plenty of turnouts where you can stop to take photos of the iconic cypress trees and stunning coastline. Traveling the **17-Mile Drive** by bike means you don't have to pay the $10 vehicle admission fee. Expect fairly flat terrain with lots of twists and turns, and a ride that runs about 17 miles.

### Wineries

The town of Carmel now has 13 wine-tasting rooms in its downtown area, even though the vineyards are in the nearby Carmel Valley or Santa Lucia Highlands. Visit the Carmel Chamber of Commerce website (www.carmelcalifornia.org) for

a downloadable map of Carmel's tasting rooms.

In the sleek **Caraccioli Cellars Tasting Room** (Dolores St. between Ocean Ave. and 7th Ave., 831/622-7722, www.caracciolicellars.com, 2pm-7pm Mon.-Thurs., 11am-10pm Fri.-Sat., 11am-7pm Sun., tasting $20), taste wines made from pinot noir and chardonnay grapes. They also pour a brut and a brut rosé that you can enjoy on the wooden slab bar.

The family-owned **De Tierra Vineyards Tasting Room** (Mission St. and 5th Ave., 831/622-9704, www.detierra.com, 2pm-8pm Tues.-Thurs., noon-9pm Fri.-Sat., noon-8pm Sun. summer, 2pm-6pm Tues.-Thurs., noon-8pm Fri.-Sun. winter, tasting $10-15) has a range of wines including rosé, syrah, merlot, chardonnay, red blend, Riesling, and pinot noir. The chalkboard behind the counter has a cheese and chocolate plate menu.

Grammy award-winning composer Alan Silvestri has scored everything from the TV series *CHiPs* to *Forrest Gump* to the music in the new *Cosmos*. He also makes wines in Carmel Valley, which can be sampled in the **Silvestri Tasting Room** (7th Ave. between Dolores St. and San Carlos St., 831/625-0111, www.silvestrivineyards.com, noon-7pm daily, tasting $10-15).

Just a block away, **Scheid Vineyards Tasting Room** (San Carlos and 7th Ave., 831/626-9463, www.scheidvineyards.com, noon-7pm Sun.-Thurs., noon-8pm Fri.-Sat., tasting $10) pours 39 tasty varietals from the winery's Salinas Valley vineyards. It's worth a stop.

## Entertainment and Events

### Bars and Clubs

**Barmel** (San Carlos St. between Ocean Ave. and 7th Ave., 831/626-2095,

**From top to bottom:** Carmel Beach; Point Lobos State Reserve; a mansion alongside Pebble Beach's 17-Mile Drive

2pm-2am Mon.-Fri., 1pm-2am Sat.-Sun.) has entertainment seven nights a week, including DJs, local bands, and touring bands. The live music side of the equation happens 7pm-9pm Thursday-Saturday, while a DJ follows the band on Friday and Saturday.

## Live Music

Classical music aficionados will appreciate the dulcet tones of the musicians who perform for **Chamber Music Monterey Bay** (831/625-2212, www.chambermusicmontereybay.org). This society brings talented ensembles and soloists from around the world to perform on the lovely Central Coast in Carmel's **Sunset Center** (San Carlos St. at 9th Ave.). One night you might find a local string quartet, and another you'll get to see and hear a chamber ensemble. (String quartets definitely rule the small stage and intimate theater.) Far from banning young music fans, Chamber Music Monterey Bay reserves up-front seats at all its shows for children and their adult companions.

The **Sunset Center** (San Carlos St. at 9th Ave., 831/620-2048, www.sunsetcenter.org) is a state-of-the-art performing center with over 700 seats that hosts a true range of events and artistic endeavors, including rock shows, dance recitals, classical music concerts, and theater performances. Recent performers have included Dwight Yoakam, Shemeika Copeland, and Neil Sedaka.

## Theater

Despite its small size, Carmel has a handful of live theater groups. In a town that defines itself by its love of art, the theater arts don't get left out. The **Pacific Repertory Theater** (831/622-0100, www.pacrep.org, $15-39 adults, $15-28 seniors, $10-15 students, teachers, and military, $7.50 children) is the only professional theater company on the Monterey-Carmel Peninsula. Its shows go up all over the region, most often in the **Golden Bough Playhouse** (Monte Verde St. and 8th Ave.), the company's home theater. Other regular venues include the **Forest Theater** (Mountain View Ave. and Santa Rita St.) and the **Circle Theater** (Casanova St. between 8th Ave. and 9th Ave.) within the Golden Bough complex. The company puts on dramas, comedies, and musicals both new and classic. You might see a work of Shakespeare or a modern classic like *Mamma Mia!*

## Festivals and Events

In a town famed for art galleries, one of the biggest events of the year is the **Carmel Art Festival** (Devendorf Park, Mission St., www.carmelartfestivalcalifornia.org, May). This four-day event celebrates visual arts in all media with shows by internationally acclaimed artists at galleries, parks, and other venues all across town. For a more classical experience, one of the most prestigious festivals in Northern California is the **Carmel Bach Festival** (www.bachfestival.org). For 15 days each July, Carmel and its surrounding towns host dozens of classical concerts. Naturally the works of J. S. Bach are featured, but you can also hear renditions of Mozart, Vivaldi, Handel, and other heavyweights of Bach's era. The **Carmel International Film Festival** (http://carmelfilmfest.com, Oct.) lures movie debuts and movie stars to Carmel in October. In addition to movies, the fest has parties, art events, and music performances.

## Shopping

One way to sample Carmel's art scene is to take part in its monthly **Carmel Art Walk** (www.carmelartwalk.com, 5pm-8pm second Sat. of the month), a self-guided tour of the town's artist-controlled galleries. Enjoy art, talk to the artists, sip wine, and listen to live music.

It is easy to spend an afternoon poking into galleries. The **Joaquin Turner Gallery** (Dolores St. between 5th Ave. and 6th Ave., 831/869-5564, www.joaquinturnergallery.com, 11am-5pm

Wed.-Mon., Tues. by appointment) has paintings that nod to the works of early 20th-century Monterey Peninsula artists, while **Steven Whyte Sculpture Gallery** (Dolores St. between 5th Ave. and 6th Ave., 831/620-1917, www.stevenwhytestudio.com, 9:30am-4pm Mon. and Wed.-Thurs., 9:30am-5pm Fri., 10am-5pm Sat., 10:30am-4pm Sun.) is where you can watch the artist creating amazing life-sized sculptures in his open studio.

When your head starts spinning from all the art, head to **Carmel Plaza** (Ocean Ave. and Mission St., 831/624-1385, www.carmelplaza.com, 10am-6pm Mon.-Sat., 11am-5pm Sun.), which offers lots of ways to part with your money. This outdoor mall has luxury fashion shops like Tiffany & Co. as well as the hip clothing chain Anthropologie. But don't miss locally owned establishment **The Cheese Store** (831/625-2272, 10am-6pm Mon.-Sat., 11am-5:30pm Sun.), which sells delicacies like cave-aged gruyère that you can pair with a local wine.

## Sports and Recreation
### Golf
There's no place for golfing quite like Pebble Beach, just north of Carmel. Golf has been a major pastime here since the late 19th century; today, avid golfers come from around the world to tee off inside the gated community. You can play courses trodden by the likes of Tiger Woods and Jack Nicholson, pause a moment before you putt to take in the sight of the stunning Pacific Ocean, and pay $300 or more for a single round of golf.

One of the Pebble Beach Resort courses, the 18-hole, par-72 **Spyglass Hill** (1700 17-Mile Dr., 800/877-0597, www.pebblebeach.com, $395) gets its name from the Robert Louis Stevenson novel *Treasure Island*. Don't be fooled—the holes on this beautiful course may be named for characters in an adventure novel, but that doesn't mean they're easy. Spyglass Hill boasts some of the most

challenging play in this golf course-laden region. Expect a few bogeys, and tee off from the championship level at your own ego's risk.

Though it's not managed by the same company, the famed 18-hole, par-72 **Poppy Hills Golf Course** (3200 Lopez Rd., 831/250-1819, www.poppyhillsgolf.com, $225) shares amenities with Pebble Beach golf courses. Expect the same level of care and devotion to the maintenance of the course and your experience as a player.

### Surfing
**Carmel Beach** has some of the area's most consistent beach breaks. Contact **Carmel Surf Lessons** (831/915-4065, www.carmelsurflessons.com, private lessons $200, group lessons $100 pp) if you want to try to learn to surf at Carmel Beach. To rent a board, head to Monterey's **Sunshine Freestyle Surf & Sport** (443 Lighthouse Ave., Monterey, 831/375-5015, www.sunshinefreestyle.com, 10am-6pm Mon.-Sat., 11am-5pm Sun., surfboard rental $30 per day, wetsuit $15 per day).

## Food
### American
In the open section of an indoor mall, ★ **Carmel Belle** (Doud Craft Studios, Ocean Ave. and San Carlos St., 831/624-1600, www.carmelbelle.com, 8am-5pm Mon.-Tues., 8am-8pm Wed.-Sun., $6-15) is a little eatery with a big attention to detail. Creative breakfast fare includes an open-face breakfast sandwich featuring a slab of toasted bread topped with a poached egg and wedges of fresh avocado. Meanwhile, its slow-cooked Berkshire pork sandwich with red onion-currant chutney is a perfect example of savory meets sweet. Dinners (Wed.-Sun. only) feature a choice of two main items and three side items.

### Fine Dining
**Aubergine** (Monte Verde St. at 7th Ave., 831/624-8578, www.auberginecarmel.com, 6pm-9:30pm daily, $150) has

been racking up accolades including coveted awards from the James Beard Foundation. Settle in for an eight-course tasting menu (which may include the elusive abalone) and enjoy selections from the impressive 2,500-bottle wine cellar.

### Seafood

The **Flying Fish Grill** (Mission St. between Ocean Ave. and 7th Ave., 831/625-1962, http://flyingfishgrill.com, 5pm-10pm daily, $21-36) serves Japanese-style seafood with a California twist in the Carmel Plaza open-air shopping mall. Entrées include rare peppered ahi and black bean halibut. You might even be able to score a market-priced meal of Monterey abalone. Whatever you order, you'll dine in a dimly lit, wood-walled establishment.

### Mexican

**Cultura Comida y Bebida** (Dolores St. between 5th Ave. and 6th Ave., 831/250-7005, www.culturacarmel.com, 5:30pm-midnight Mon.-Fri., 10:30am-midnight Sat.-Sun., $18-28) satisfies with superb upscale Mexican cuisine. Be adventurous and try the *chapulines* (toasted grasshoppers) appetizer or skip ahead to rellenostyle abalone. The restaurant's large Mezcal menu offers the smoky spirit in cocktails or one-ounce pours. The latenight menu (10pm-midnight daily) includes $2 street tacos.

### Sushi

★ **Akaoni** (Mission St. and 6th Ave., 831/620-1516, 5:30pm-8:30pm Mon.-Sat., $7-40) is a superb hole-in-the-wall sushi restaurant. Sit at the bar or one of the few tables if you can get in. The menu includes tempura-fried oysters, soft shell crab rolls, and a *unagi donburi* (eel bowl). The live Monterey spot prawn is the freshest seafood you'll ever eat, and the daily specials include items flown in from Japan.

### Italian

On paper, **Vesuvio** (6th Ave. and Junipero St., 831/625-1766, http://chefpepe.com/restaurants/vesuvio, 4pm-11pm daily, $16-32) is an Italian restaurant with dishes like cannelloni, gnocchi, and wood-oven pizzas, but technically there's a lot more going on. There's a popular rooftop bar with fire pits, heat lamps, and love seats. There's also a great eight-ounce burger topped with bunches of caramelized onions, oozing cambozola cheese, and a chipotle aioli on a house-made mini sub roll. It can be ordered as a "Grown-up Happy Meal" with fries and a well cocktail or glass of wine.

### Mediterranean

While **Dametra Café** (Ocean Ave. at Lincoln St., 831/622-7766, www.dametra-cafe.com, 11am-11pm daily, $11-27) has a wide-ranging international menu that includes an all-American cheeseburger and Italian dishes like spaghetti alla bolognese, it's best to go with the lively restaurant's signature Mediterranean food. The Greek chicken kebab entrée is a revelation with two chicken-and-vegetable kebabs drizzled with a distinct aioli sauce over yellow rice and a Greek salad. The owner and his staff have been known to serenade evening diners.

## Accommodations
### $150-250

The Bavarian-inspired, locally owned **Hofsas House** (San Carlos St. between 3rd Ave. and 4th Ave., 800/221-2548, www.hofsashouse.com, $150-400) offers surprisingly spacious rooms in a quiet semi-residential neighborhood within easy walking distance of downtown Carmel. Family suites include two bedrooms and two baths. Ocean-view rooms have patios or balconies looking out over the town of Carmel toward the serene Pacific. The property also has a heated swimming pool, a sauna, and continental breakfast for guests.

Just two blocks from the beach, the **Lamp Lighter Inn** (Ocean Ave. and Camino Real, 831/624-7372 or

888/375-0770, www.carmellamplighter.com, $225-425) has 11 rooms located in five blue and white cottages. The units have a comfortable, beachy decor befitting their location. The cottages encircle a courtyard area with two fire pits, perfect for hanging out with old friends or making new ones. Guests are treated to an afternoon wine and cheese reception and a morning continental breakfast that they can enjoy in the courtyard. This is a pet-friendly property, and two of the units even have fenced-in backyards.

### Over $250

Touted by *Architectural Digest*, **Tradewinds Carmel** (Mission St. and 3rd Ave., 831/624-2776, www.tradewinds-carmel.com, $250-550) brings a touch of the Far East to California. Inspired by the initial proprietor's time spent in Japan, the 28 serene hotel rooms are decorated with Asian antiques and live orchids. Outside, the grounds feature a water fountain that passes through bamboo shoots and horsetails along with a Buddha meditation garden, where an oversize Buddha head overlooks a trio of cascading pools. A stay comes with a continental breakfast that includes French pastries and fruit.

Feel like a Hearst—or a Ghirardelli—with a stay at ★ **La Playa Carmel** (Camino Real at 8th Ave., 831/293-6100 or 800/582-8900, www.laplayahotel.com, $399-800). The initial structure here was a mansion built for the Ghirardellis, California's first family of chocolate, by a renowned landscape painter in 1905. An extensive remodel in 2012 retained many of the features from the earlier era, including its dark-wood bar and the stained-glass window alongside its tiled staircase, both influenced by nearby Carmel Mission. Half of the 75 rooms look out on Carmel Beach. The grounds are worthy of exploration, from the heated outdoor pool to the courtyard with its oversized

chessboard and pieces. For a $35 amenity fee, you can enjoy a champagne breakfast with made-to-order omelets and waffles, an afternoon wine reception, and an evening dessert.

### Information and Services

You'll find the **Carmel Visitor Center** (Carmel Plaza, 2nd Fl., Ocean Ave. between Junipero St. and Mission St., 831/624-2522, www.carmelchamber.org, 10am-6pm Mon.-Sat., 11am-5pm Sun.) right in the middle of downtown. For more information about the town and current events, pick up a copy of the weekly *Carmel Pine Cone* (www.pinecone-archive.com), the local newspaper.

The nearest major medical center is the **Community Hospital of the Monterey Peninsula** (23625 Holman Hwy., Monterey, 831/624-5311, www.chomp.org).

### Getting Around

As you read the addresses in Carmel and begin to explore the neighborhoods, you'll realize something interesting. There are **no street addresses.** Years ago, Carmel residents voted not to enact door-to-door mail delivery, thus there is no need for numeric addresses on buildings. You have to pay close attention to the **street names** and the **block** you're on. Just to make things even more fun, street signs can be difficult to see in the mature foliage, and a dearth of streetlights can make them nearly impossible to find at night. Luckily, there are GPS systems in our cars and phones these days.

---

# Monterey

Monterey has a past as a fishing town. Native Americans were the first to fish the bay, and fishing became an industry with the arrival of European settlers in the 19th century. Author John Steinbeck immortalized this unglamorous industry in his novel *Cannery Row*. Its blue-collar past is still evident in its architecture, even though the cannery workers have been replaced by tourists.

Monterey is the "big city" on the well-populated southern tip of the wide-mouthed Monterey Bay. There are two main sections of Monterey: the old downtown area and "New Monterey," which includes Cannery Row and the Monterey Bay Aquarium. The old downtown is situated around Alvarado Street and includes the historic adobes that make up Monterey State Historic Park. New Monterey bustles with tourists during the summer. The canneries are long gone, and today the Row is packed with businesses, including the must-see Monterey Bay Aquarium, seafood restaurants, shops, galleries, and wine-tasting rooms. The aquarium is constantly packed with visitors, especially on summer weekends. One way to get from one section to the other is to walk the Monterey Bay Coastal Recreation Trail, a paved path that runs right along a stretch of coastline.

## Getting There

Monterey can be reached from Carmel by driving 4.5 miles north on **CA-1.** Take Exit 399B for **Munras Avenue,** which leads to downtown Monterey. Both **Greyhound** (3 Station Pl., Salinas, 831/424-4418, www.greyhound.com, 5am-11:30pm daily) and the **Amtrak** *Pacific Surfliner* (800/872-7245, www.amtrak.com) stop in nearby Salinas. From there, you can rely on **Monterey-Salinas Transit** (MSRT, 888/678-2871, www.mst.org, $1.50-2.50) to reach Monterey.

## Sights
### Cannery Row

**Cannery Row** (www.canneryrow.com) did once look and feel as John Steinbeck described it in his famed novel of the same name. In the 1930s and 1940s, fishing boats offloaded their catches straight into the huge warehouse-like cannery buildings. Low-wage workers processed the fish and put it into cans, ready to ship across the country and around the world. But overfishing took its toll, and by the late 1950s, Cannery Row was deserted; some buildings even fell into the ocean.

A slow renaissance began in the 1960s, driven by new interest in preserving the historical integrity of the area, as well as a few savvy entrepreneurs who understood the value of beachfront property. Today, what was once a workingman's wharf is now an enclave of boutique hotels, big seafood restaurants, and souvenir stores selling T-shirts adorned with sea otters. Cannery Row is anchored at one end by the aquarium and runs for several blocks that include a beach; it then leads to the Monterey Harbor area.

### ★ Monterey Bay Aquarium

The first aquarium of its kind in the country, the **Monterey Bay Aquarium** (886 Cannery Row, 831/648-4800, www.montereybayaquarium.org, 10am-5pm daily, $50 adults, $40 seniors and students, $30 children) is still unique in many ways. From the beginning, the aquarium's mission has been conservation, and they're not shy about it. Many of the animals in the aquarium's tanks were rescued, and those that survive may eventually be returned to the wild. All the exhibits you'll see in this mammoth complex contain only local sea life.

The aquarium displays a dazzling array of species. When you come to visit, a good first step is to look up the feeding schedules for the tanks you're most interested in. The critters always put on the best show at feeding time, and it's smart to show up several minutes in advance of feeding to get a good spot near the glass. Check the website for current feeding times.

The living, breathing **Kelp Forest** is just like the kelp beds outside in the bay, except this one is 28 feet tall. Between the swaying strands of kelp, leopard sharks glide over the aquarium floor, and warty sea cucumbers and starfish adorn rocks.

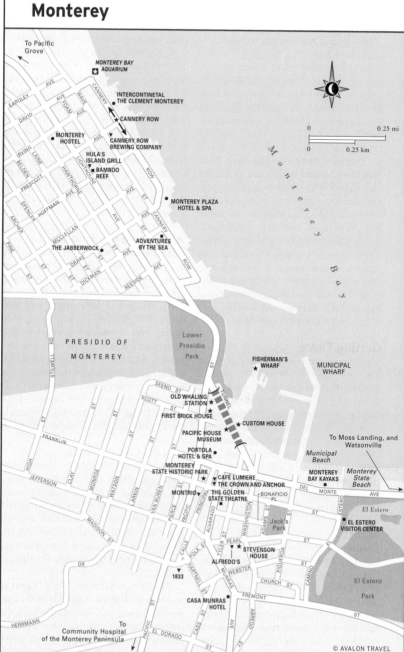

# Monterey

To Pacific Grove

MONTEREY BAY AQUARIUM

INTERCONTINETAL THE CLEMENT MONTEREY

CANNERY ROW

MONTEREY HOSTEL

CANNERY ROW BREWING COMPANY

HULA'S ISLAND GRILL

BAMBOO REEF

MONTEREY PLAZA HOTEL & SPA

THE JABBERWOCK

ADVENTURES BY THE SEA

EARDLEY AVE

DAVID

FOAM AVE

WAVE

CANNERY

IRVING

LAINE

BELDEN

PRESCOTT

HOFFMAN

SPENCER

ARCHER

PINE ST

DRAKE

DICKMAN

REESIDE AVE

LIGHTHOUSE

HAWTHORNE

MCCLELLAN

ROW

Monterey Bay

0        0.25 mi
0        0.25 km

PRESIDIO OF MONTEREY

Lower Presidio Park

FISHERMAN'S WHARF

MUNICIPAL WHARF

STILWELL RD

SEENO ST

SCOTT ST

FRANKLIN

OLD WHALING STATION

FIRST BRICK HOUSE

PACIFIC HOUSE MUSEUM

CUSTOM HOUSE

PORTOLA HOTEL & SPA

MONTEREY STATE HISTORIC PARK

CAFÉ LUMIERE

THE CROWN AND ANCHOR

MONTRIO

THE GOLDEN STATE THEATRE

To Moss Landing, and Watsonville

Municipal Beach

MONTEREY BAY KAYAKS

Monterey State Beach

BONAFICIO PL

DEL MONTE AVE

El Estero

EL ESTERO VISITOR CENTER

HIGH

JEFFERSON

CLAY

MONROE

WATSON

LARKIN

VAN BUREN

PIERCE

PACIFIC

PRINCIPAL

ALVARADO

CALLE

POLK ST

TYLER

WEBSTER

STEVENSON HOUSE

PEARL

ALFREDO'S

1833

ADAMS

WASHINGTON

Jack's Park

FIGUEROA

CAMINO

ESTERO

CHURCH ST

El Estero Park

MADISON ST

DR

HARTNELL

MUNRAS

FREMONT

CASA MUNRAS HOTEL

ABREGO

HERRMANN

PACIFIC

EL DORADO

CASS ST

AVE

To Community Hospital of the Monterey Peninsula

© AVALON TRAVEL

# Steinbeck

John Ernst Steinbeck was born and grew up in Salinas, then a tiny, isolated agricultural community, in 1902. He somehow managed to escape life as a farmer, a sardine fisherman, or a fish canner and ended up living the glamorous life of a writer for his too-short 66 years.

Steinbeck's experiences in the Salinas Valley farming community and in the fishing town of Monterey informed many of his novels. The best known of these is *Cannery Row*, but *Tortilla Flat* is also set in working-class Monterey (though no one knows exactly where the fictional Tortilla Flat neighborhood was supposed to be). The Pulitzer Prize-winning novel *The Grapes of Wrath* takes more of its inspiration from the Salinas Valley. Steinbeck used the valley as a model for farming in the Dust Bowl—the wretched, impoverished time during the Great Depression.

Steinbeck was fascinated by the plight of working men and women; his novels and stories depict ordinary folks going through tough and terrible times. Steinbeck lived and worked through the Great Depression, and thus it's not surprising that many of his stories don't feature Hollywood happy endings. Steinbeck was a realist in almost all of his novels, portraying the good, the bad, and the ugly of human life and society. His work gained almost immediate respect: In addition to his Pulitzer Prize, Steinbeck also won the Nobel Prize for Literature in 1962. Almost every American high school student from the 1950s onward has read at least one of Steinbeck's novels or short stories; his body of work forms part of the enduring American literary canon.

As the birthplace of California's most illustrious literary son, Salinas became famous for inspiring his work. You'll find a variety of Steinbeck maps online (www.mtycounty.com) that offer self-guided tours of the regions made famous by his various novels. Steinbeck's name is taken in vain all over now-commercial Cannery Row—even the cheesy Wax Museum tries to draw customers in by claiming kinship with the legendary author. More serious Steinbeck fans prefer the **National Steinbeck Center** (1 Main St., Salinas, 831/796-3833, www.steinbeck.org, 10am-5pm daily, $13 adults, $10 seniors and students, $7 children 6-17, children under 6 free) and the **Steinbeck House** (132 Central Ave., Salinas, 831/424-2735, www.steinbeckhouse.com, restaurant 11:30am-2pm Tues.-Sat., gift shop 11am-3pm Tues.-Sat.), both in the still-agricultural town of Salinas. And if the museums aren't enough, plan to be in Monterey County in early August for the annual **Steinbeck Festival** (www.steinbeck.org), a big shindig put on by the Steinbeck Center to celebrate the great man's life and works in fine style.

Try to time your visit for the feeding times here, too, when the fish in the tank put on quite a show.

The deep-water tank in the **Open Sea** exhibit area always draws a crowd. Inside its depths, hammerhead sharks and an enormous odd-looking sunfish coexist. The aquarium has even had one of the ocean's most notorious predators in this tank: the great white shark. The aquarium has great whites infrequently, but if one is on display, it's definitely worth looking at this sleek and amazing fish up close.

The **Wild About Otters** exhibit gives visitors a personal view of rescued otters. The adorable, furry marine mammals come right up to the glass to interact with curious children and enchanted adults. Another of the aquarium's most popular exhibits is its **Jellies** display, which illuminates delicate crystal jellies and the comet-like lion's mane jellyfish.

The aquarium is a wildly popular weekend destination. Especially in the summer, the crowds can be forbidding. Weekdays can be less crushing (though you'll run into school groups during much of the year), and the off-season is almost always a better time to visit. The

**MONTEREY BAY AQUARIUM**

aquarium has facilities for wheelchair access to almost all exhibits.

### Monterey State Historic Park

**Monterey State Historic Park** (831/649-2907, www.parks.ca.gov, hours vary seasonally, check website for current hours, free) pays homage to the long and colorful history of the city of Monterey. This busy port town acted as the capital of California when it was under Spanish rule, and then later when it became part of the United States. Today, this park provides a peek into Monterey as it was in the middle of the 19th century when it was a busy place filled with dockworkers, fishermen, bureaucrats, and soldiers. And yet it blends into the modern town of Monterey as well: Modern stores, galleries, and restaurants sit next to adobe structures dating from the 1800s.

It's tough to see everything in just one visit to Old Monterey. If you only have time for one spot, make it the **Custom House** (20 Custom House Plaza, hours vary seasonally, free). Built in 1827, it's California State Historic Landmark No. 1 and the oldest government building still standing in the state. Wander the adobe building, check out the artifacts on display, looking out the upstairs window toward the sea. Also on the plaza is the **Pacific House Museum** (hours vary seasonally, check website for current hours, free). The 1st floor shows a range of Monterey's history from the Native Californians to the American Period, while the 2nd floor has a plethora of Native American artifacts.

The other buildings in the park were built mostly with adobe and/or brick between 1834 and 1847. These include the **Casa del Oro** (210 Oliver St., 831/649-3364, 11am-3pm Thurs.-Sun.); the **First Brick House** (hours vary seasonally, check website for current hours, free); the

**From top to bottom:** Monterey Bay Aquarium; the Custom House in Monterey State Historic Park; Asilomar State Beach in Pacific Grove.

**Larkin House** (464 Calle Principal, available for private tours); and the **Stevenson House** (530 Houston St., hours vary seasonally, free), once a temporary residence of author Robert Louis Stevenson. The Old Whaling Station and the Sherman Quarters are not open to public.

One-hour **guided tours** (usually 10:30am, 12:30pm, and 2pm, $5) start at the Pacific House, offering a good introduction to the park.

## Asilomar State Beach

Popular **Asilomar State Beach** (Exit 68 West from CA-1, turn left on Sunset Dr., Pacific Grove, 831/646-6440, www.parks. ca.gov, 8am-8pm daily) draws beachgoers, walkers, and surfers. Located in nearby Pacific Grove, the beach itself is a narrow one-mile strip of coastline with a boardwalk trail on the dunes behind it. You can keep walking on the trail into nearby Pebble Beach, an easy, cost-free way to get a taste of that exclusive community.

Adjacent to the state beach is the **Asilomar Conference Grounds** (888/635-5310, www.visitasilomar.com), a cluster of meeting rooms and accommodations designed by Hearst Castle architect Julia Morgan. Take one of four self-guided tours of the grounds that focus on the living dunes, the coast trail, the forest, and Julia Morgan's architecture.

## Entertainment and Events
### Live Music

Downtown Monterey's historic **Golden State Theatre** (417 Alvarado St., 831/649-1070, www.goldenstatetheatre.com) hosts live music, speaker series, and other arts events. The theater dates back to 1926 and was designed to look like a Moorish castle. Performers in its ornate main room have included music legends like Patti Smith and Arlo Guthrie and newer acts like the Fleet Foxes.

### Bars and Clubs

Descending down into **The Crown and Anchor** (150 W. Franklin St., 831/649-6496, www.crownandanchor.net, 11am-1:30am daily) feels a bit like entering a ship's hold. Along with the maritime theme, The Crown and Anchor serves up 20 international beers on tap. Sip indoors or on the popular outdoor patio. They also have good pub fare, including cottage pies and curries.

Another good bet for a beer or cocktail is the **Cannery Row Brewing Company** (95 Prescott Ave., 831/643-2722, www.canneryrowbrewingcompany.com, 11am-11pm Sun.-Thurs., 11am-midnight Fri.-Sat.), just a block up from bustling Cannery Row. They pour 75 beers on tap, ranging from hefeweizens to barleywine. Expect good happy-hour deals on food and beer 3pm-6pm.

A distinct stone building just a couple blocks off Alvarado Street, **Alfredo's** (266 Pearl St., 831/375-0655, 10am-midnight Sun.-Thurs., 10am-2am Fri.-Sat., cash only) is a cozy dive bar with dim lighting, a gas fireplace, cheap drinks, and a good jukebox.

The **Alvarado Street Brewery & Grill** (426 Alvarado St., 831/655-2337, www.alvaradostreetbrewery.com, 11:30am-10pm Sun.-Wed., 11:30am-11pm Thurs.-Sat., $7-27) is a 10-barrel brewpub focusing on West Coast and Belgian-inspired ales. They serve snacks alongside the suds, including flatbread and pork belly poutine. Sit inside the massive 5,000-square-foot space (a former theater), or on the enclosed patio out front.

### Festivals and Events

The Monterey region hosts numerous festivals and special events each year. Whether your pleasure is fine food or funky music, you'll probably be able to plan a trip around some sort of multiday festival with dozens of events and performances scheduled during Monterey's busy year.

One of the biggest music festivals in California is the **Monterey Jazz Festival** (Monterey County Fairgrounds, 2004

Fairground Rd., 831/373-3366, www. montereyjazzfestival.org, Sept.). As the site of the longest-running jazz festival on earth, Monterey attracts 500 artists from around the world to play on its eight stages. Held each September at the Monterey County Fairgrounds, this long weekend of amazing music can leave you happy for the whole year. Recent acts to grace the Monterey Jazz Festival's stages include Herbie Hancock, Booker T. Jones, and The Roots.

In keeping with the Central Coast's obsession with food and wine, the annual **Monterey Wine Festival** (Custom House Plaza, 360/693-6023, www.montereywine.com, June) celebrates wine with a generous helping of food on the side. The wine festival is also incongruously home to the West Coast Chowder Competition. This festival offers the perfect opportunity to introduce yourself to Monterey and Carmel wineries, many of

which have not yet hit the "big time" in major wine magazines.

## Sports and Recreation

Monterey Bay is the premier Northern California locale for a number of water sports, especially scuba diving.

### Scuba Diving

Any native Northern Californian knows that there's only one really great place in the region to get certified in scuba diving—Monterey Bay. Even if you go to a dive school up in the Bay Area, they'll take you down to Monterey for your open-water dive. Accordingly, dozens of dive schools cluster in and around the town of Monterey.

A local's favorite, **Bamboo Reef** (614 Lighthouse Ave., 831/372-1685, www. bambooreef.com, 9am-6pm Mon.-Fri., 7am-6pm Sat.-Sun.) offers scuba lessons and rents equipment just a few blocks

the Monterey Jazz Festival

## Sea Sanctuary

Monterey Bay is in a federally protected marine area known as **Monterey Bay National Marine Sanctuary** (MBNMS, https://montereybay.noaa.gov). Designated a sanctuary in 1992, the protected waters stretch far past the confines of Monterey Bay to a northern boundary seven miles north of the Golden Gate Bridge and a southern boundary at Cambria in San Luis Obispo County.

MBNMS holds many marine treasures, including the Monterey Bay Submarine Canyon, right offshore of the fishing village of Moss Landing. The canyon is similar in size to the Grand Canyon and has a rim-to-floor depth of 5,577 feet. In 2009, MBNMS expanded to include another fascinating underwater geographical feature: the Davidson Seamount. Located 80 miles southwest of Monterey, the undersea mountain rises an impressive 7,480 feet, yet its summit is still 4,101 feet below the ocean's surface.

The sanctuary was created for resource protection, education, public use, and research. The MBNMS is the reason so many marine research facilities, including the Long Marine Laboratory, the Monterey Bay Marine Laboratory, and the Moss Landing Marine Laboratories, dot the Monterey Bay's shoreline.

from popular dive spots, including Breakwater Cove.

The **Aquarius Dive Shop** (2040 Del Monte Ave., 831/375-1933, www.aquariusdivers.com, 9am-6pm Mon.-Thurs., 9am-7pm Fri., 7am-7pm Sat., 7am-6pm Sun.) offers everything you need to go diving out in Monterey Bay, including air and nitrox fills, equipment rental, certification courses, and help booking a trip on a local dive boat. Aquarius works with five boats to create great trips for divers of all interests and ability levels. Call or check the website for current local dive conditions as well.

### Kayaking and Stand-Up Paddleboarding

Relatively protected Monterey Bay is one of the best places on the California coast to head offshore in a kayak or stand-up paddleboard. The Monterey Peninsula protects paddlers from some ocean swells, and you can frequently see sea otters, harbor seals, and other marine life.

**Adventures by the Sea** (299 Cannery Row; 685 Cannery Row; 32 Cannery Row; 210 Alvarado St., 831/372-1807, www.adventuresbythesea.com, 9am-8pm daily summer, 9am-5pm daily winter, 2.5-hour kayak tours $60 pp, kayak rentals $30 per day, SUP rentals $30 for 2 hours) has a whopping four locations in Monterey. Come by to rent kayaks or stand-up paddleboards, or join a 2.5-hour kayaking tour of the area.

Right on Monterey Beach, **Monterey Bay Kayaks** (693 Del Monte Ave.,

831/373-5357, www.montereybaykayaks.com, 9am-7pm daily summer, 9am-6pm daily fall, 9am-5pm daily winter, tours $55-150 pp, kayak rentals $30-50 per day, SUP rentals $75 per day) specializes in tours of central Monterey; it also rents a range of kayaks and SUPs. There's also a branch up in Moss Landing on the Elkhorn Slough.

### Whale-Watching

Whales pass quite near the shores of Monterey year-round. While you can sometimes even see them from the beaches, any number of boats can take you out for a closer look at the great beasts as they travel along their own special routes north and south. The area hosts many humpbacks, blue whales, and gray whales, plus the occasional killer whale, minke whale, fin whale, and pod of dolphins. Most tours last 2-3 hours and leave from Fisherman's Wharf, which is easy to get to and has ample parking.

**Monterey Bay Whale Watch** (84 Fisherman's Wharf, 831/375-4658, www.montereybaywhalewatch.com) leaves right from an easy-to-find red building on Fisherman's Wharf and runs tours in every season (call or check the website for schedules). You must make a reservation in advance, even for regularly scheduled tours. Afternoon tours are available. **Princess Monterey Whale Watching** (96 Fisherman's Wharf, 831/372-2203, www.montereywhalewatching.com) prides itself on its knowledgeable marine biologist guides and its comfortable, spacious cruising vessels.

### Hiking

If you want to explore Monterey's coastline without the possibility of getting wet, head out on the **Monterey Bay Coastal Recreation Trail** (www.monterey.org). The 18-mile paved path stretches from Pacific Grove to the south all the way to the northern Monterey County town of Castroville. The best section is from Monterey Harbor down to Pacific Grove's Lovers Point Park.

## Food

The organic and sustainable food movements have caught hold on the Central Coast. The **Monterey Bay Seafood Watch program** (www.montereybayaquarium.org) is the definitive resource for sustainable seafood, while inland, the Salinas Valley hosts a number of organic farms.

### Seafood

Located in nearby Pacific Grove, ★ **Passionfish** (701 Lighthouse Ave., Pacific Grove, 831/655-3311, www.passionfish.net, 5pm-9pm Sun.-Thurs., 5pm-10pm Fri.-Sat., $26) is one of the region's most highly regarded seafood restaurants. One reason is that this long-time restaurant sources its ingredients from sustainable farms and fisheries. Another reason is the delectable menu that changes daily, which may feature ocean-dwelling delicacies like sea scallops in a tomato truffle butter or rockfish in a black pepper rum sauce.

For a South Pacific spin on seafood, head to ★ **Hula's Island Grill** (622 Lighthouse Ave., 831/655-4852, www.hulastiki.com, 4pm-9:30pm Sun.-Mon., 11:30am-9:30pm Tues.-Thurs., 11:30am-10pm Fri.-Sat., $13-25). With surfing movies playing on the TVs and tasty tiki drinks, it's a fun place to hang out. In addition to fresh fish and a range of tacos, the menu has land-based fare like Jamaican jerk chicken. Hula's also has one of Monterey's best **happy hours** (4pm-6pm Sun.-Mon., 2pm-9:30pm Tues., 2pm-6pm Wed.-Sat.), with superb cocktails and not-the-usual-suspects appetizers (ceviche, edamame).

**The Poke Lab** (475 Alvarado St., 831/200-3474, www.thepokelab.com, 11am-8pm Mon.-Sat., $10-20) gives raw fish salads the Chipotle treatment. Custom make your own bowl with raw seafood or veggies over rice or salad. It's hard to beat The Poke Lab's namesake bowl with spicy tuna, ahi tuna, salmon, and avocado as the core ingredients. The place is so successful that it already has a food truck in case you can't make it to the downtown Monterey location.

### Classic

Inside an old brick firehouse, ★ **Montrio** (414 Calle Principal, 831/648-8880, www. montrio.com, 4:30pm-close daily, $16-29) is a long-running leader in elegantly casual Monterey dining. The menu boasts a wide range of small bites and appetizers alongside meat and seafood entrées and inspired cocktails. Belt busters like the 40-ounce rib eye steak are available for heartier appetites.

Locals consider **Melville Tavern** (484 Washington St., 831/643-9525, www. melvilletav.com, 11am-9pm Mon.-Fri., 10:30am-9pm Sat.-Sun., $12-19) an open secret. The fish tacos appetizer is a tasty meal for light appetites, while most of the menu is devoted to heartier fare like a green chile cheeseburger. Its $3 beer of the week and $6 wine of the week are great deals, while the weekend brunches including egg curry tacos and stellar huevos rancheros make Melville an under-rated brunch spot.

### Coffee

Connected to the Osio Cinemas, Monterey's art-house movie theater, **Café Lumiere** (365 Calle Principal, 831/920-2451, http://cafelumieremonterey.com, 7am-10pm daily) is where Monterey's old Sicilian anglers hang out in the morning while sipping coffee drinks and munching on pastries. Lumiere has daily lunch specials that tend to be a good deal for their price. It also has tempting baked goods. This coffee shop offers free Wi-Fi to its customers.

### Markets

Located in an old railroad station adjacent to the Monterey Bay Coastal Recreation Trail, **The Wharf Marketplace** (290 Figueroa St., 831/649-1116, www. thewharfmarketplace.com, 9am-7pm Mon.-Sat., 9am-6pm Sun.) touts itself as being the place to buy the "bounty of the county." This means local produce and fresh seafood. The marketplace café also serves breakfast (breakfast sandwiches, quiches) and lunch (salads, sandwiches, *pizzetas*).

The primary farmers market in the county, the **Monterey Farmers Market** (Alvarado St. between Del Monte Ave. and Pearl St., www.oldmonterey.org, 4pm-8pm Tues. summer, 4pm-7pm Tues. winter) takes over downtown Monterey with fresh produce vendors, restaurant stalls, jewelry booths, and live music every Tuesday late afternoon.

## Accommodations
### Under $150

The **Monterey Hostel** (778 Hawthorne St., 831/649-0375, http://montereyhostel.org, bunk $57, private room $139, family room with 5 beds $179) offers inexpensive accommodations within walking distance of the major attractions of Monterey. This hostel has a men's dorm, women's dorm, private rooms, a family room, and a coed dorm with 16 beds. There's no laundry facility on-site, but there are full-enclosure bike lockers. The hostel has some unexpected perks, including a free pancake breakfast every morning and an ice cream social on Sunday. Linens are included with your bed, and there are comfy, casual common spaces with couches and musical instruments. And then there's the location—you can walk to the aquarium and Cannery Row, stroll the Monterey Bay Coastal Trail, or drive over to Carmel to see a different set of sights.

### $150-250

Call in advance to get a room at **The Jabberwock** (598 Laine St., 831/372-4777, www.jabberwockinn.com, $219-459), a favorite with frequent visitors to Monterey. This Alice in

Wonderland-themed B&B is both whimsical and elegant. Some rooms have fireplaces and hot tubs. Take advantage of the daily wine and appetizer reception in the afternoon. They also do a chef-prepared breakfast in the morning. Though located up a steep hill, The Jabberwock is within walking distance of Cannery Row and all its adjacent attractions.

Accommodations are available at the 107-acre **Asilomar Conference Grounds** (804 Crocker Ave., Pacific Grove, 831/372-8016, www.visitasilomar.com, $200-280) in Pacific Grove. Options include historic rooms and family cottages, some designed by architect Julia Morgan, some with views of nearby Asilomar Beach. There are no TVs or telephones, an incentive to get you outdoors.

### Over $250
Hear the squawks of seagulls and barks of seals at the ★ **Spindrift Inn** (652 Cannery Row, 831/646-8900, www. spindriftinn.com, $239-719), a boutique hotel towering above the golden sand and green waters of McAbee Beach. This 45-room establishment has been called the country's most romantic hotel with good reason. Most of the hardwood-floored rooms have fireplaces and full or half canopy beds. The friendly staff serves up a wine and cheese reception 4:30pm-6pm and delivers a complimentary continental breakfast in the morning. The only problem is that you'll never want to leave.

The name of the ★ **Monterey Bay Inn** (242 Cannery Row, 831/373-6242 or 800/424-6242, www.montereybayinn. com, $250-600) is generic but the setting is not. Located between San Carlos Beach and Cannery Row, the boutique hotel's oceanfront rooms have private balconies that allow guests to peer right down on the waters of the bay. The in-room binoculars are handy to spot diving cormorants, bobbing harbor seals, and playful otters. The hotel's rooftop hot tub offers another vantage point. Enjoy a continental breakfast delivered to your room in the morning and tasty cookies in the evening.

## Camping
The campground at the 50-acre **Veterans Memorial Park** (Via Del Rey and Veterans Dr., 831/646-3865, www.monterey.org, $30) is a little-known secret. A mile up a hill from downtown Monterey are 40 first-come, first-served campsites with bay views.

## Information and Services
In Monterey, the **El Estero Visitors Center** (401 Camino El Estero, 888/221-1010, www.seemonterey.com, 9am-6pm Mon.-Sat., 9am-5pm Sun. summer, 9am-5pm daily winter) is the local outlet of the Monterey County Convention and Visitors Bureau. A few miles from downtown, the **Monterey Peninsula Chamber of Commerce** (243 El Dorado St., Ste. 200, 831/648-5350, www.montereychamber. com, 9am-5pm Mon.-Fri.) can also provide helpful information.

The local daily newspaper is the *Monterey County Herald* (www.montereyherald.com). The free weekly *Monterey County Weekly* (www.montereycountyweekly.com) has a comprehensive listing of the area's arts and entertainment events.

The **Monterey Post Office** (565 Hartnell St., 831/372-4063, www.usps. com, 8:30am-5pm Mon.-Fri., 10am-2pm Sat.) is a couple of blocks from downtown. The **Community Hospital of the Monterey Peninsula** (23625 Holman Hwy., 831/624-5311, www.chomp.org) provides emergency services.

## Getting Around
Once in Monterey, take advantage of the free **WAVE** bus (Waterfront Area Visitor Express, 831/899-2555, www.monterey. org, 10am-8pm daily Memorial Day-Labor Day) that loops between downtown Monterey and the aquarium. Also, **Monterey-Salinas Transit** (888/678-2871,

www.mst.org, $1.50-2.50) has routes through Monterey.

# Santa Cruz

There's no place like Santa Cruz. Even in the left-leaning Bay Area, you won't find another town that has embraced cultural experimentation, radical philosophies, and progressive politics quite like this little beach city, which has made out-there ideas into a kind of municipal cultural statement. Everyone does their own thing: Surfers ride the waves, nudists laze on the beaches, tree-huggers wander the redwood forests, tattooed and pierced punks wander the main drag, and families walk their dogs along West Cliff Drive.

Most visitors come to Santa Cruz to hit the Boardwalk and the beaches. Locals and UC Santa Cruz students tend to hang downtown on Pacific Avenue and stroll on West Cliff. The east side of town has fewer attractions for visitors but offers a vibrant surf scene situated around Pleasure Point.

## Getting There

In light traffic, Santa Cruz is **45 minutes** north of Monterey on **CA-1.** The problem is that the highway goes from four lanes to two lanes a few miles south of Moss Landing, which causes traffic to slow. North of Monterey 27.5 miles, CA-1 has a section called **"the fishhook,"** where **accidents** regularly occur. Consider taking the **Soquel Avenue** or **Morrissey Boulevard** exits to miss this mess.

## Sights

### ★ Santa Cruz Beach Boardwalk

The **Santa Cruz Beach Boardwalk** (400 Beach St., 831/423-5590, www.beach-boardwalk.com, daily Memorial Day-Labor Day, Sat.-Sun. and holidays Labor Day-Nov. and Dec. 26-Memorial Day, check website for hours, individual rides $4-7, all-day pass $37, parking $6-15), or

just "the Boardwalk" as it's called by the locals, has a rare appeal that beckons to young children, too-cool teenagers, and adults of all ages.

The amusement park rambles along each side of the south end of the Boardwalk; entry is free, but you must buy either per-ride tickets or an unlimited ride wristband. The Giant Dipper is an old-school wooden roller coaster that opened back in 1924 and is still giving riders a thrill after all this time. The Double Shot shoots riders up a 125-foot tower with great views of the bay or inland Santa Cruz before freefalling straight down. In summertime, a log ride cools down guests hot from hours of tromping around. The Boardwalk also offers several toddler and little-kid rides.

At the other end of the Boardwalk, avid gamesters choose between the lure of prizes from the traditional midway games and the large arcade. Throw baseballs at things, try your arm at skee ball, or take a pass at a classic or newer video game. The traditional carousel even has a brass ring you (or your children) can try to grab.

During the summer, the Boardwalk puts on free Friday-night concerts on the beach featuring retro acts like hair metal band Great White and 1980s New Wave band The Fixx. See the website for a complete schedule of upcoming acts.

### Santa Cruz Mission State Historic Park

Believe it or not, weird and funky Santa Cruz started out as a mission town. **Santa Cruz Mission State Historic Park** (School St., off Mission St. and Emmett St., 831/425-5849, www.parks.ca.gov, 10am-4pm Mon. and Thurs.-Sat., noon-4pm Sun.) was one of the later California missions, dedicated in 1791. Today, the attractive white building with its classic red-tiled roof welcomes parishioners to the active Holy Cross church and fourth-grade students from around the Bay Area to the historic museum areas of the old

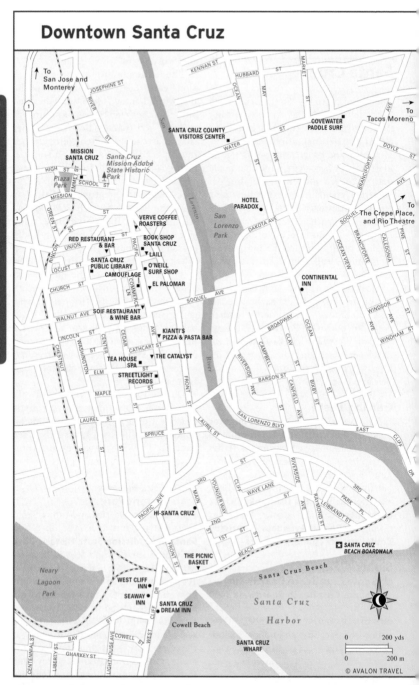

# Downtown Santa Cruz

To San Jose and Monterey

KENNAN ST

JOSEPHINE ST

HUBBARD ST

MARKET ST

To Tacos Moreno

COVEWATER PADDLE SURF

DOYLE ST

SANTA CRUZ COUNTY VISITORS CENTER

WATER ST

BRANCIFORTE AVE

MISSION SANTA CRUZ

Santa Cruz Mission Adobe State Historic Park

HIGH ST

SCHOOL ST

Plaza Park

EMMET ST

MISSION ST

GREEN ST

RINCON ST

San Lorenzo River

VERVE COFFEE ROASTERS

RED RESTAURANT & BAR

SANTA CRUZ PUBLIC LIBRARY

CAMOUFLAGE

BOOK SHOP SANTA CRUZ

LAILI

O'NEILL SURF SHOP

EL PALOMAR

PACIFIC AVE

CEDAR ST

COMMERCE LN

HOTEL PARADOX

San Lorenzo Park

DAKOTA AVE

To The Crepe Place, and Rio Theatre

BRANCIFORTE

CALEDONIA

PINE ST

OCEAN VIEW

SOQUEL

CONTINENTAL INN

LOCUST ST

UNION ST

CHURCH ST

WALNUT AVE

SOIF RESTAURANT & WINE BAR

SOQUEL AVE

LINCOLN ST

WASHINGTON ST

CHESTNUT ST

CENTER ST

CATHCART ST

KIANTI'S PIZZA & PASTA BAR

TEA HOUSE SPA

THE CATALYST

STREETLIGHT RECORDS

ELM ST

FRONT ST

MAPLE ST

BROADWAY

CAMPBELL ST

CLAY ST

OCEAN ST

WINDSOR ST

WINDHAM ST

RIVERSIDE AVE

BARSON ST

CANFIELD AVE

BIXBY ST

LAUREL ST

SPRUCE ST

LAUREL ST

SAN LORENZO BLVD

EAST CLIFF DR

3RD ST

YOUNGER WAY

CLIFF ST

WAVE LANE

RIVERSIDE AVE

RAYMOND ST

LEIBRANDT ST

PARK PL

3RD ST

PACIFIC AVE

MAIN ST

HI-SANTA CRUZ

2ND ST

1ST ST

BEACH ST

FRONT ST

THE PICNIC BASKET

SANTA CRUZ BEACH BOARDWALK

Neary Lagoon Park

WEST CLIFF INN

SEAWAY INN

SANTA CRUZ DREAM INN

Santa Cruz Beach

Santa Cruz Harbor

Cowell Beach

CENTENNIAL ST

LIBERTY ST

BAY ST

GHARKEY ST

COWELL ST

LIGHTHOUSE AVE

WEST CLIFF DR

SANTA CRUZ WHARF

0       200 yds

0       200 m

© AVALON TRAVEL

## Surf City

There's a plaque outside the Santa Cruz Surfing Museum that explains how three Hawaiian princes introduced surfing to California in 1885. Apparently, they rode redwood planks from a nearby lumber mill on waves at the mouth of the San Lorenzo River in Santa Cruz.

While Santa Cruz's claim as the birthplace of surfing on the mainland is not disputed, the popular surfing town calling itself "Surf City" has raised the hackles of Southern California's Huntington Beach, which also likes to have its tourist T-shirts adorned with "Surf City." In 2006,

Huntington Beach was awarded exclusive use of the title "Surf City" by the U.S. Patent and Trademark Office and went after Santa Cruz beachwear stores that sold T-shirts with the words "Santa Cruz" and "Surf City."

Despite Huntington Beach's aggressive legal action, the residents of Santa Cruz might have the last laugh. In 2009, *Surfer* magazine proclaimed that Santa Cruz is "The Real Surf City, USA" in a piece about the top 10 surf towns. To Huntington Beach's chagrin, it didn't even make the magazine's top 10 list.

mission. In fact, the building you can visit today, like many others in the mission chain, is not the original complex built by the Spanish fathers in the 18th century. Instead it's a replica that was built in the 1930s. One exhibit relates the story of the local Ohlone and Yokuts people.

### Long Marine Laboratory

While the Monterey Bay Aquarium down the road in Monterey provides the best look into the nearby bay, the **Long Marine Laboratory** (100 Shaffer Rd., 831/459-3800, http://seymour-center.ucsc.edu, 10am-5pm Tues.-Sun., $8 adults, $6 seniors and children) is a worthwhile stop for people interested in sea creatures and marine issues. Your visit will be to the **Seymour Marine Discovery Center,** the part of the lab that's open to the public. You'll be greeted outside the door by a full blue whale skeleton that's lit up at night. Inside, instead of a standard aquarium setup, you'll find a marine laboratory similar to those used by scientists elsewhere in the complex. The aquariums showcase fascinating creatures, including monkey-face eels and speckled sand dabs, while displays highlight environmental issues like shark finning. Kids particularly love the touch tanks, while

curious adults enjoy checking out the seasonal tank that contains the wildlife that's swimming around outside in the bay *right now*. Tours run each day at 11am, 1pm, 2pm, and 3pm; sign up an hour in advance to get a slot.

### Santa Cruz Surfing Museum

Just feet away from Santa Cruz's best-known surf spot, Steamer Lane, the tiny **Santa Cruz Surfing Museum** (1701 W. Cliff Dr., 831/420-6289, www.cityof-santacruz.com, 10am-5pm Thurs.-Tues. July 4-Labor Day, noon-4pm Thurs.-Mon., day after Labor Day-July 3, donation) is housed within a still-operating lighthouse. First opened in 1986, it is the world's first museum dedicated to the water sport. Run by the Santa Cruz Surfing Club Preservation Society, the one-room museum has pictures of Santa Cruz's surfing culture from the 1930s to the present. One haunting display on shark attacks includes a local surfboard with bite marks from a great white shark.

### Entertainment and Events
#### Bars and Clubs

Lovers of libations should grab a drink at **Red Restaurant & Bar** (200 Locust St., 831/425-1913, http://redrestaurantand-bar.com, 5pm-1:30am daily), located upstairs in the historic Santa Cruz Hotel

Building. Creative cocktails include signature creations like the Jean Grey, a mix of house-infused Earl Grey organic gin, lemon, and simple syrup. They also have a nice selection of craft beers and Belgian beers on tap. With its dark wood paneling and burgundy bar stools, Red feels like an old speakeasy. It also serves a comprehensive late-night menu until 1am for those who need some food to soak up their alcohol.

**The Crepe Place** (1134 Soquel Ave., 831/429-6994, http://thecrepeplace.com, 11am-midnight Mon.-Thurs., 11am-1am Fri., 9am-midnight Sat.-Sun.) has recently emerged as a hangout for the hipster crowd, who are drawn in by the high-profile indie rock acts and popular Bay Area bands that perform in its intimate front room. They also have outdoor seating and a comprehensive menu of creative crepes.

### Live Music

**The Catalyst** (1011 Pacific Ave., 831/429-4135, www.catalystclub.com), right downtown on Pacific Avenue, hosts a variety of reggae, rap, and punk acts from Snoop Dogg to FIDLAR. The main concert hall is a standing-room-only space, while the balconies offer seating. Meanwhile, the remodeled Atrium is now an attached mid-size venue that attracts indie rock and punk acts.

The **Crow's Nest** (2218 E. Cliff Dr., 831/476-4560, www.crowsnest-santa-cruz.com, free-$10) is a venue for all kinds of live music acts. Rock, soul, and funk bands typically play Wednesday-Saturday. Sundays are live comedy evenings, and Tuesdays are reggae jam nights.

A former 1940s movie house, the **Rio Theatre** (1205 Soquel Ave., 831/423-8209, www.riotheatre.com) has been hosting everything from film festivals to performances by national touring acts from Judy Collins to Built to Spill. Check the theater's website for a full list of upcoming events.

### Theater

The nonprofit **Santa Cruz Shakespeare** (831/640-6399, www.santacruzshakespeare.com) was formed so residents could get their Elizabethan theater fix. Productions are staged at the Audrey Stanley Grove in **DeLaveaga Park** (501 Upper Park Rd.).

## Shopping

For a small city, Santa Cruz has a bustling downtown, centered on Pacific Avenue. The quirky performance artists on the sidewalk might make you think you're in Berkeley or San Francisco. It's a good idea to park in one of the structures a block or two off Pacific Avenue and walk from there. Among the worthy downtown shops are **Book Shop Santa Cruz** (1520 Pacific Ave., 831/423-0900, www.bookshopsantacruz.com, 9am-10pm Sun.-Thurs., 9am-11pm Fri.-Sat.); **O'Neill Surf Shop** (110 Cooper St., 831/469-4377, www.oneill.com, 10am-9pm Sun.-Thurs., 10am-10pm Fri.-Sat.); **Camouflage** (1329 Pacific Ave., 831/423-7613, www.shop-camouflage.com, 10am-10pm Mon.-Sat., 10am-8pm Sun.), which is an independent, family-owned, and women-friendly adult store; and **Streetlight Records** (939 Pacific Ave., 888/648-9201, www.streetlightrecords.com, noon-8pm Sun.-Mon., 11am-9pm Tues.-Thurs., 11am-10pm Fri.-Sat.).

## Sports and Recreation
### Beaches

At the tip of the West Side, **Natural Bridges State Beach** (2531 W. Cliff Dr., 831/423-4609, www.parks.ca.gov, 8am-sunset daily, $10) used to have three coastal arches right offshore. Even though there is only one arch remaining, this picturesque state park has a beach that doesn't stretch wide, but falls back deep, crossed by a creek that feeds out into the sea. Hardy sun-worshippers brave the breezes, bringing out their beach blankets, umbrellas, and sunscreen on rare sunny days (usually in late spring and fall). Back from the beach, a wooded picnic area has tables and grills for small and larger parties. Even farther back, the park has a monarch butterfly preserve, where the migrating insects take over the eucalyptus grove during the fall and winter months.

At **Cowell's Beach** (350 W. Cliff Dr.), lots of beginning surfers have ridden their first waves. This West Side beach sits right at a crook in the coastline that joins with underwater features to create a reliable small break that lures new surfers by the dozens.

At the south end of Santa Cruz, down by the harbor, beachgoers flock to **Seabright Beach** (E. Cliff Dr. at Seabright Ave., 831/427-4868, www.santacruzstateparks.org, 6am-10pm daily, free) all summer long. This miles-long stretch of sand, protected by the cliffs from the worst of the winds, is a favorite retreat for sunbathers and loungers. While there's little in the way of snack bars, permanent volleyball courts, or facilities, you can still have a great time at Seabright.

### Surfing

The coastline of Santa Cruz has more than its share of great surf breaks. The water is cold, demanding full wetsuits year-round, and the shoreline is rough and rocky. But that doesn't deter the hordes of locals who ply the waves every day they can.

The best place for beginners is **Cowell's** (stairs at W. Cliff Dr. and Cowell's Beach). The waves rarely get huge here, so they provide long, mellow rides, perfect for surfers just getting their balance. Because the Cowell's break is acknowledged as the newbie spot, the often-sizable crowd tends to be polite to newcomers and visitors.

Visitors who know their surfing lore will want to surf the more famous spots along the Santa Cruz shore. **Pleasure Point** (between 32nd Ave. and 41st Ave.) encompasses a number of different breaks. You may have heard of **The Hook** (steps at 41st Ave.), a well-known experienced long-boarder's paradise. But don't mistake The Hook for a beginner's break; the locals feel protective of the waves here and aren't always friendly toward inexperienced newcomers.

The most famous break in all of Santa Cruz can also be the most hostile to newcomers. **Steamer Lane** (W. Cliff Dr. between Cowell's and the Lighthouse) has a fiercely protective crew of locals. But if you're experienced and there's a swell coming in, Steamer Lane can have some of the best waves on the California coast.

Yes, you can learn to surf in Santa Cruz despite the distinct local flavor at some of the breaks. Check out either **Club Ed** (831/464-0177, www.club-ed.com, beginner group lesson $90 pp) or the **Richard Schmidt School Inc.** (849 Almar Ave., 831/423-0928, www.richardschmidt.com, 2-hour class $90 pp) to sign up for lessons. Who knows, maybe one day the locals will mistake you for one of their own.

### Stand-Up Paddleboarding

The latest water-sports craze has definitely hit Santa Cruz. Stand-up paddleboarders vie for waves with surfers at Pleasure Point and can also be found in the Santa Cruz waters with less wave action. **Covewater Paddle Surf** (726 Water St., 831/600-7230, www.covewatersup.com, 2-hour lesson $70) conducts beginner stand-up paddleboarding (SUP) classes in the relatively calm waters of the Santa Cruz Harbor. They also rent SUPs for $30 a day.

### Hiking and Bicycling

To walk or cycle where the locals do, just head out to **West Cliff Drive.** This winding street with a full-fledged sidewalk trail running its length on the ocean side is the town's favorite walking, dog-walking, jogging, skating, scootering, and biking route. You can start at Natural Bridges (the west end of W. Cliff Dr.) and go for miles. The *To Honor Surfing* statue is several miles down the road, along with plenty of fabulous views.

## Spas

It's hard to beat a soak in some hot water after a day of surfing Santa Cruz's breaks or walking the city's vibrant downtown area. The **Tea House Spa** (112 Elm St., 831/426-9700, www.teahousespa.com, 11am-midnight daily, $16-27 per hour pp) is half a block off Pacific Avenue and offers private hot tubs with a view of a bamboo garden. It's not a fancy facility, but the tubs will warm you up and mellow you out.

# Food
## Afghan

**Laili** (101 B Cooper St., 831/423-4545, http://lailirestaurant.com, 11:30am-2:30pm and 5pm-close Tues.-Sun., $10-28) is in a sleek, modern building with an open kitchen and marbled bar that oozes style. This Afghan restaurant's cuisine complements the space with artfully prepared dishes, from a cilantro Caesar salad to bolani, a vegan flatbread. Meals begin with a serving of naan bread the size of a plate and some dipping sauce. From there, the filet mignon kebab, which is three tender pieces of meat with dipping sauces, is exceptional.

## Mexican

Santa Cruz has some great taquerias, but **Tacos Moreno** (1053 Water St., 831/429-6095, 11am-8pm daily, $6-11) may be the best. Around lunch, locals line up outside the nondescript eatery. Tacos Moreno serves just the basics: burritos, tacos, quesadillas, and beverages to wash them down. The standout item is the al pastor burrito supreme with crispy barbecued pork, cheese, sour cream, and guacamole, among other savory ingredients.

**El Palomar** (1336 Pacific Ave., 831/425-7575, http://elpalomarsantacruz.com, 11am-9pm Mon.-Wed., 11am-10pm Thurs., 11am-10:30pm Fri., 10am-10:30pm Sat., 10am-9pm Sun., $13-27)

is located in the dining room of an old luxury hotel. Enjoy shrimp enchiladas or chicken mole while mariachi bands rove around and play to diners. Owner Jose's special appetizer ($17) can be a light meal for two, though don't forget to try El Palomar's tasty guacamole. The informal taco bar is great for a quick bite and drink. It also has a happy hour (3pm-6pm Mon.-Fri.).

## Japanese

South of downtown, ★ **Akira** (1222 Soquel Ave., 831/600-7093, http://akirasantacruz.com, 11am-11pm daily, special rolls $10-17) is a modern sushi bar with some interesting creations. Some of the rolls employ unconventional ingredients like skirt steak, Sriracha sauce, and spicy truffled shoestring yams. There are also more traditional rolls, all served up at the sushi bar or your table. This being Santa Cruz, skateboard art decorates the restaurant. Stop by happy hour (4pm-6pm and 9:30pm-10:30pm daily) to snack on appetizers and enjoy beer, sake, or wine.

## Pizza

An untold number of surfers have stopped into ★ **Pleasure Pizza** (4000 Portola Dr., 831/475-4002, http://pleasurepizzasc.com, 11am-9pm daily, slices $3-6) for a slice after catching waves at nearby Pleasure Point or The Hook. This unassuming slice shack is just a couple of blocks from the beach. The large, tasty slices are served on paper plates in a somewhat dingy building decorated with old surf memorabilia. Legend Jay Moriarity once worked here, as immortalized in the 2012 film *Chasing Mavericks*. On Tuesday, slices of cheese pizza go for just $2. There is also a **downtown location** (1415 Pacific Ave., 831/600-7859, 11am-10pm Sun.-Wed., 11am-12:30am Thurs.-Sat.).

**Kianti's Pizza & Pasta Bar** (1100 Pacific Ave., 831/469-4400, www.kiantis.com, 11am-10pm Mon.-Fri., 10am-10pm

Sat.-Sun., $13-21) draws in crowds with individual and family-size servings of pastas, pizzas, and salads. Toppings range from traditional Italian ingredients to more creative options (like avocado and tortilla chips). People are also drawn in by the full bar and outdoor seating area right on bustling Pacific Avenue.

## Casual Eats

Just feet from the corndog-slinging Santa Cruz Boardwalk is a casual eatery that prides itself on its simple menu that utilizes locally sourced, tasty goodness: **The Picnic Basket** (125 Beach St., 831/427-9946, http://thepicnicbasketsc. com, 7am-9pm daily, $3-9). Its attention to detail shines through, even if it is on a deceptively simple turkey, cheese, and avocado sandwich. Other options include breakfast items, salads, mac and cheese, and even local beer and wine. Dine inside or out front, where you can take in the sounds of the bustling boardwalk.

## Coffee

**Verve Coffee Roasters** (1540 Pacific Ave., 831/475-7776, www.vervecoffee-roasters.com, 6am-8pm daily) offers a hip, open space with lots of windows at the eastern edge of Pacific Avenue. Verve roasts its own beans in the nearby Seabright neighborhood. After ordering your coffee drink at the counter, look for a seat in this frequently crowded coffee shop.

## Accommodations
### Under $150

Staying at a hostel in Santa Cruz just feels right. And the **Hostelling International Santa Cruz Hostel at the Carmelita Cottages** (321 Main St., 831/423-8304, www.hi-santacruz.org, dorm beds $31, private rooms $71-155) offers the area's only real budget lodging. These historic renovated cottages are just two blocks from the Santa Cruz Boardwalk. It's clean, cheap, friendly, and also close to Cowell's Beach. The big, homey kitchen

is open for guest use and might even hide extra free food in its cupboards. Expect all the usual hostel amenities, a garden out back, an outdoor deck, free linens, laundry facilities, and a free Internet kiosk. The private rooms are a real deal due to their size and cleanliness. One drawback: The hostel is closed to guests 11am-5pm, when it becomes a city park. Guests are allowed to leave their luggage inside or in outdoor lockers. Also of note: the unenforced curfew.

The ★ **Seaway Inn** (176 W. Cliff Dr., 831/471-9004, www.seawayinn.com, $107-274) offers a night's stay in a great location across from Cowell's Beach. The rooms are clean but not fancy, and the bathrooms are small. All have a shared patio or deck with chairs. The 18 units in the main building boast of TVs with DVD players along with microwaves and mini fridges. Family suites can accommodate up to five adults. Add in a complimentary breakfast with make-your-own waffles and a friendly staff, and you have a good place to stay without breaking the bank. They also operate a nearby building with five studio apartments, each with a full kitchen. Pets are welcome in all units with a $15 fee.

### $150-250

The ★ **West Cliff Inn** (174 W. Cliff Dr., 831/457-2200, www.westcliffinn.com, $209-429) is a gleaming white mansion topping the hill above Cowell's Beach and the Boardwalk. This three-story historic landmark was constructed back in 1877, the first of the "Millionaires' Row" residences. Since that time, it's been a nurses' headquarters and auto court before becoming the elegant inn it is now in 2007. The nine rooms in the main house have stunning white-marble bathrooms, and some have oversized soaking tubs. The more moderately priced and pet-friendly "Little Beach Bungalow" is behind the main house. All guests can fill up on an afternoon wine and appetizer hour and a morning breakfast buffet. The inn's veranda and 2nd-floor balcony provide wonderful views.

### Over $250

The ★ **Santa Cruz Dream Inn** (175 W. Cliff Dr., 831/426-4330, www.dream-innsantacruz.com, $250-600) is in a location that cannot be beat. Perched over Cowell's Beach and the Santa Cruz Wharf, the Dream Inn has 165 rooms, all with striking ocean views and either a private balcony or a shared common patio. The rooms have a retro-chic feel that matches perfectly with the vibrant colors of the nearby Santa Cruz Boardwalk. On a sunny day, it would be difficult to ever leave the Dream Inn's sundeck, which is located right on Cowell's Beach. You can take in the action of surfers, stand-up paddleboarders, and volleyball players from the comforts of the deck's heated swimming pool or large multi-person hot tub. Or you could just relax on a couch or reclining chair while sipping a cocktail from the poolside bar.

The large pool deck at the **Hotel Paradox** (611 Ocean St., 831/425-7100, www.hotelparadox.com, $329-469) is the new boutique hotel's best asset. Take advantage of Santa Cruz's sunshine with the tempting pool and large hot tub that can accommodate a dozen or more. Waiters from the hotel restaurant Solaire deliver cocktails and food to those enjoying the deck. The rooms are clean and modern with flat-screen TVs and Keurig coffeemakers. Opt for a unit on the ground floor with a small outdoor deck area or choose a room higher up with a view of the pool action.

### Information and Services

While it can be fun to explore Santa Cruz just by using your innate sense of direction and the bizarre, those who want a bit more structure to their travels can hit the **Santa Cruz County Visitors Center** (303 Water St., Ste. 100, 800/833-3494, www.santacruz.org, 9am-4pm Mon.-Fri., 11am-3pm Sat.-Sun.) for maps, advice, and information.

The daily **Santa Cruz Sentinel** (www.santacruzsentinel.com) offers local news plus up-to-date entertainment information. The free weekly newspaper **Good Times** (www.gtweekly.com) is also filled with upcoming events.

You can get your mail on at the **post office** (850 Front St., 831/426-0144, www.usps.com, 9am-5pm Mon.-Fri.) in downtown Santa Cruz. Medical treatment is available at **Dominican Hospital** (1555 Soquel Ave., 831/462-7700, www.dignityhealth.org).

### Getting Around

Visitors planning to drive or bike around Santa Cruz should get a good map, either before they arrive or at the visitors center in town. Navigating the winding, occasionally broken-up streets of this oddly shaped town isn't for the faint of heart. **CA-1,** which becomes **Mission Street** on the West Side, acts as the main artery through Santa Cruz and down to **Capitola, Soquel, Aptos,** and coastal points farther south. You'll find that CA-1 at the interchange to **CA-17,** and sometimes several miles to the south, is a parking lot most of the time. No, you probably haven't come upon a major accident or a special event; it's just like that a lot of the time.

In town, the buses are run by the **Santa Cruz METRO** (831/425-8600 www.scmtd.com, $2 per ride adults, passes available). With routes running all around Santa Cruz County, you can probably find a way to get nearly anywhere you'd want to go on the METRO.

# Half Moon Bay

To this day, the coastal city of Half Moon Bay retains its character as an "ag" (agricultural) town. The locals all know each

# Half Moon Bay

GARDEN DELI CAFE ▼

HALF MOON BAY FEED AND FUEL

MILL ST

N MAIN ST

JOHNSTON ST

ABODE

KELLY ST

To Pacifica and San Francisco

SAM'S CHOWDER HOUSE

BEACH HOUSE AT HALF MOON BAY

BACH DANCING AND DYNAMITE SOCIETY

Mavericks Beach

Mavericks Break

Dunes Beach

Venice Beach

Arroyo de en Medio

Frenchmans Creek

FRENCHMANS CREEK RD

Apanolio Creek

Corinda Los Trancos

CABRILLO HWY N

SAN MATEO RD

To San Mateo

Pilarcitos Creek

Francis Beach

Half Moon Bay State Beach

KELLY ST

SEE DETAIL

MIRAMONTES ST

MONTE VISTA LN

OLD THYME INN

POPLAR ST

MAIN ST

HIGGINS PURISIMA RD

Arroyo Creek

Wave Crest Open Space

REDONDO BEACH RD

Half Moon Bay Golf Links

MIRAMONTES RD

RITZ-CARLTON HALF MOON BAY

Arroyo Cañada Verde

0          1 mi
0          1 km

© AVALON TRAVEL

other, even though the majority of residents commute "over the hill" to more lucrative peninsula and Silicon Valley jobs. For those who farm in the area, strawberries, artichokes, and Brussels sprouts are the biggest crops, along with flowers, pumpkins, and Christmas trees, making the coast the place to come for holiday festivities. Half Moon Bay enjoys a beautiful natural setting and earns significant income from tourism, especially during the world-famous Pumpkin Festival each October.

Some people know Half Moon Bay

for Maverick's, a monster wave that can rise to 80 feet off nearby Pillar Point during the winter months. Maverick's is one of the world's most renowned surf spots and has been chronicled in the 2004 surf documentary *Riding Giants* and the 2012 feature film *Chasing Mavericks*.

## Getting There

It takes about **one hour** to make the **49-mile** drive from Santa Cruz to Half Moon Bay on **CA-1.** You may want to stop at a beach or a produce stand in the tiny town of **Pescadero**; Half Moon Bay is **18 miles** north of it.

## Beaches

The beaches of Half Moon Bay draw visitors from over the hill and farther afield all year long. As with most of the North Pacific region, summer can be a chilly, foggy time on the beaches. For the best beach weather, plan your Half Moon Bay trip for September-October. **Half Moon Bay State Beach** (650/726-8819, www.parks.ca.gov, 8am-sunset daily, parking $10 per day) encompasses three discrete beaches stretching four miles down the coast, each with its own access point and parking lot. **Francis Beach** (95 Kelly Ave.) has the most developed amenities, including a good-size campground (800/444-7275, www.reservecalifornia.com, $35) with grassy areas to pitch tents and enjoy picnics, a visitors center, and indoor hot showers. **Venice Beach** (Venice Blvd., off CA-1) offers outdoor showers

and flush toilets. **Dunes Beach** (Young Ave., off CA-1) is the southernmost major beach in the chain and the least developed.

At the end of West Point Avenue in Princeton, a long stretch of beach wraps around the edge of the Pillar Point Marsh. This is the launch pad for surfers paddling out to tackle the famous **Mavericks Break** (Pillar Point Marsh parking lot, past Pillar Point Harbor). Formed by unique underwater topography, the waves at Mavericks are some of the biggest rideable waves in the continental United States.

## Entertainment and Events

The biggest annual event in this small agricultural town is the **Half Moon Bay Art & Pumpkin Festival** (www.miramarevents.com). Every October, nearly 250,000 people trek to Half Moon Bay to pay homage to the big orange squash. The festival includes live music, food, artists' booths, contests, activities for kids, an

pumpkin patch ready for annual Half Moon Bay Art & Pumpkin Festival

adults lounge area, and a parade. Perhaps the best-publicized event is the pumpkin weigh-off, which takes place before the festivities begin.

Half Moon Bay boasts one of the best jazz venues in the Bay Area. Since it opened in 1964, the **Bach Dancing and Dynamite Society** (311 Mirada Rd., 650/726-4143, www.bachddsoc. org) has been a hangout for bohemians and jazz aficionados, hosting the biggest names in jazz, including Bill Evans, Dizzy Gillespie, Etta James, and Duke Ellington. Not only is the music fantastic, but the venue, the Douglas Beach House, can't be beat.

## Shopping
Strolling Main Street is another reason folks come to Half Moon Bay. A holdover from the town's agricultural roots is **Half Moon Bay Feed and Fuel** (331 Main St., 650/726-4814, http://halfmoonbay-feedandfuel.com, 8:30am-6pm Mon.-Fri., 9am-5pm Sat., 10am-4pm Sun.). In

addition to animal feed, the store sells home goods, gardening supplies, plants, clothing, and gifts.

To see what Half Moon Bay does best, drop by the **Coastside Farmer's Market** (225 Cabrillo Hwy., 650/726-4895, www. coastsidefarmersmarket.org, 9am-1pm Sat. May-Dec.). There is plenty of local meat, bread, produce, pottery, art, and even wool skeins, spun and dyed by hand. Local bands are always at the market, and there is plenty of street food.

## Sports and Recreation
### Hiking
There are plenty of great trails around Half Moon Bay. A local favorite is **Purisima Creek Redwoods** (4.4 miles up Higgins Canyon Rd., 650/619-1200, www. openspace.org, dawn-half hour after sunset daily). There are a multitude of trails in this 4,711-acre preserve, and many ascend to Skyline Boulevard for an elevation gain of 1,700 feet. You can take a leisurely stroll through the redwoods, complete with dripping ferns, flowering dogwood, and wood sorrel, along Purisima Creek Trail (3.9 miles, easy to strenuous), until it turns steep and eventually takes you to its literally breathtaking Skyline terminus. If you don't want to crest the ridge of the Santa Cruz Mountains, choose the Harkins Ridge Trail (6 miles, moderate), which rises out of the canyon shortly past the trailhead. You'll hike through redwoods, then oaks and chaparral, and back again into firs, pines, and redwoods as you gain 800 feet in elevation over 2.5 miles. To make a loop, cut down Craig Britton Trail, which meets Purisima Creek Trail.

The most popular trail in Half Moon Bay is the **Coastside Trail** (www.parks. ca.gov). Extending five miles from Miramar Beach to Poplar Beach, this flat, paved trail follows the coast and is filled with joggers, dog walkers, and bikes. There are a multitude of beach-access points along the way, and if you want to go downtown, jump off at Kelly Avenue and take it across CA-1 to the heart of Half Moon Bay.

### Fishing

For a sedate ocean adventure, take a winter whale-watching cruise or a shallow-water rockfish fishing trip on board the *Queen of Hearts* (Pillar Point Harbor, 510/581-2628, www.fishingboat.com, reservations recommended, $85-99). Whale-watching trips (Jan.-Apr.) cost a bit less than fishing trips on the *Queen of Hearts*. Deep-sea fishing for albacore and salmon (if the season isn't canceled) makes for a more energetic day out on the Pacific, although motion-sickness medication is recommended.

### Kayaking and Stand-Up Paddleboarding

One of the coolest ways to see the coast is from the deck of a sea kayak or stand-up paddleboard. Many tours with the **Half Moon Bay Kayaking Company** (Pillar Point Harbor, 650/773-6101, www.hmbkayak.com, 9am-5pm Wed.-Mon., kayak rental $75-150 per day, SUP rental $75 per day, tours $75-150) require no previous kayaking experience. For an easy first paddle, try the Pillar Point tour, the full-moon tour, or the sunset paddle.

### Food

Twenty miles south of Half Moon Bay in the blink-and-you-missed-it town of Pescadero, ★ **Duarte's Tavern** (202 Stage Rd., Pescadero, 650/879-0464, www.duartestavern.com, 7am-8pm daily, $13-25) has been honored by the James Beard Foundation as "An American Classic." Once you walk through the doors, you'll see why. The rambling building features sloping floors and age-darkened wooden walls. The food is good, the service friendly, and the coffee plentiful. And while almost everybody comes to Duarte's for a bowl of artichoke soup or a slice of olallieberry pie, it's really the atmosphere that's the biggest draw. Locals of all stripes, including farmers,

farmhands, ranchers, and park rangers, sit shoulder to shoulder with travelers sharing conversation and a bite to eat, particularly in the dimly lit bar but also in the dining room or at the old-fashioned lunch counter.

The quality of food in Half Moon Bay itself also is superb. For seafood, go to ★ **Sam's Chowder House** (4210 N. Cabrillo Hwy., 650/712-0245, www.samschowderhouse.com, 11:30am-9pm Mon.-Thurs., 11:30am-9:30pm Fri., 11am-9:30pm Sat., 11am-9pm Sun., $12-35), a fusion of an East Coast chowder and lobster shack with West Coast sensibilities and a view of the Pacific. The lobster clambake for two is a splurge, but it's an excellent introduction to Sam's seafood-heavy menu. Armed with a lobster cracker, bib, and wet nap, attempt to finish the starting bowl of clam chowder followed by a tasty mound that includes a whole lobster, clams, mussels, potatoes, and a spicy andouille sausage. Many other diners opt for the buttery lobster roll.

Good bread is the secret weapon of great sandwiches at the **Garden Deli Café** (356 Main St., 650/726-9507, www.sanbenitohouse.com, 10am-5pm daily, $6.60), located in the historic San Benito House. Basic sandwiches like turkey, roast beef, and ham taste better lying between slabs of tasty homemade bread. Get your sandwich to go or eat in the adjacent courtyard.

### Accommodations

Twenty miles south of Half Moon Bay near the tiny town of Pescadero, the **Pigeon Point Lighthouse Hostel** (210 Pigeon Point Rd., at CA-1, 650/879-0633, www.norcalhostels.org/pigeon, dorm beds $30, private rooms $82) has simple but comfortable accommodations, both private and dorm-style. Amenities include three kitchens, free Wi-Fi, a fire pit, and beach access. But the best amenity of all is the cliff-top hot tub ($8 per half hour).

The stunning **Ritz-Carlton Half Moon Bay** (1 Miramontes Point Rd.,

650/712-7000, www.ritzcarlton.com, $750-4,000) resembles a Scottish castle transported to the California coast. Surrounding the luxury hotel are two emerald-green golf courses perched above the Pacific. The sprawling grounds are dotted with always-lit fire pits and chairs to take in the marvelous ocean views. Right out front is Half Moon Bay Coastside Trail, where you can hike for up to seven miles. The hotel also has a spa, restaurant, two fitness rooms, a pool, tennis courts, and a basketball court. Inside, guests enjoy the finest of modern amenities. Baths have marble floors and marble countertops, while many of the upscale guest rooms overlook the sea. The superb staff seems to be as excited to be here as you are.

The ★ **Beach House at Half Moon Bay** (4100 N. Cabrillo Hwy., 650/712-0220 or 800/315-9366, www.beach-house.com, $285-485) is situated in an ideal location a few feet from Pillar Point Harbor and the popular Coastside Trail. All the rooms, which are multilevel lofts, have a private patio or balcony to take in the bobbing sailboats and the groaning foghorn. On fog-shrouded days, the Beach House has in-room real wood-burning fireplaces and an outdoor hot tub and heated pool on the pool deck to warm up with. They also serve a continental breakfast in the mornings.

## Information and Services

Visitor information, including maps, brochures, and a schedule of events, can be found at the **Half Moon Bay Chamber of Commerce** (235 Main St., 650/726-8380, www.visithalfmoonbay.org, 9am-5pm Mon.-Fri., 10am-3pm Sat.-Sun.), located in the red house just after you turn on Main Street from CA-92.

The *Half Moon Bay Review* (www.hmbreview.com) is published weekly and provides the best information about live local entertainment.

The **post office** (500 Stone Pine Rd., 650/726-4015, www.usps.com, 9:30am-5pm Mon.-Fri., 9:30am-noon Sat.) is off Main Street before the bridge heading south. **Cell phones** work fine in the town of Half Moon Bay, but coverage can be spotty up in the hills above town and out on the undeveloped coastline and beaches along CA-1.

There is a 24-hour emergency room at the **Seton Coastside Hospital** (600 Marine Blvd., Moss Beach, 650/563-7100, https://setoncoastside.verity.org). For non-urgent care, the **Coastside Clinic** (Shoreline Station, Ste. 100A, 225 S. CA-1, Half Moon Bay, 650/573-3941, www.smchealth.org) is just north of the intersection of Kelly Avenue and CA-1.

## Getting Around

**Parking** in downtown Half Moon Bay is an easy proposition except during the **Pumpkin Festival in October,** when it becomes a nightmare of epic proportions. Your best bet is to stay in town with your car safely stowed in a hotel parking lot before the festival.

# Getting There

## Getting to San Francisco
### By Air

San Francisco's major airport is **San Francisco International Airport** (SFO, US-101, 650/821-8211 or 800/435-9736, www.flysfo.com), located approximately 13 miles south of the city center, near the town of Millbrae. Plan to arrive at the airport up to three hours before your flight leaves. Airport lines, especially on weekends and holidays, are notoriously long, and planes can be grounded due to fog.

To avoid the SFO crowds, consider booking a flight into one of the Bay Area's less crowded airports. **Oakland International Airport** (OAK, 1 Airport Dr., Oakland, 510/563-3300, www.oaklandairport.com) serves the East Bay with access to San Francisco via the Bay Bridge and commuter trains. **Mineta San José Airport** (SJC, 1701 Airport Blvd., San Jose, 408/392-3600, www.flysanjose.com) is 45 miles south of San Francisco. These airports are quite a bit smaller than SFO, but service is frequent from many U.S. destinations.

Several public and private transportation options can get you into San Francisco. **Bay Area Rapid Transit** (BART, 415/989-2278, www.bart.gov, one-way ticket to any downtown station $8.95) connects directly with SFO's international terminal, providing a simple and relatively fast (under one hour) trip to downtown San Francisco. The BART station is an easy walk or a free shuttle ride from any point in the airport. BART trains also connect Oakland Airport to the city of San Francisco. Both BART and **Caltrain** (800/660-4287, www.caltrain.com, tickets $3.75-13.75) connect Mineta San José Airport to San Francisco. To access Caltrain from the airport, you must first take BART to the Millbrae stop, where the two lines meet. This station is designed for folks jumping from one line to the other. Caltrain tickets vary in price depending on your destination.

**Shuttle vans** are another cost-effective option for door-to-door service, although these make several stops along the way. From the airport to downtown San Francisco, the average one-way fare is $17-25 per person. Shuttle vans congregate on the second level of SFO above the baggage claim area for domestic flights, and on the third level for international flights. Advance reservations guarantee a seat, but these aren't required and don't necessarily speed the process. Some companies to try include **Quake City Shuttle** (415/255-4899, www.quakecityshuttle.com) and **SuperShuttle** (800/258-3826, www.supershuttle.com).

For **taxis,** the average fare to downtown San Francisco is around $40. Use your cell phone to access ride-sharing services **Lyft** (www.lyft.com) or **Uber** (www.uber.com), which charge $29-85 for a ride from the airport to downtown.

### By Train

Several long-distance **Amtrak** (800/872-7245, www.amtrak.com) trains rumble through California daily. There are eight train routes that serve the region: The *California Zephyr* runs from Chicago and Denver to Emeryville; the *Coast Starlight* travels down the West Coast from Seattle and Portland as far as Los Angeles; the *Pacific Surfliner* will get you to the Central Coast. There is no train depot in San Francisco; the closest station is in Emeryville (5885 Horton St.) in the East Bay. Fortunately, comfortable coach buses ferry travelers to and from the Emeryville Amtrak station with many stops in downtown San Francisco.

### By Bus

An affordable way to get around California is on **Greyhound** (800/231-2222, www.greyhound.com). The San Francisco Station (200 Folsom St., 415/495-1569) is a hub for Greyhound bus lines. They also have stations all along the coast from Crescent City down to San Diego. Greyhound routes generally follow the major highways, traveling US-101. Most counties and municipalities have bus service with routes to outlying areas. Another option is **Megabus** (http://us.megabus.com), which has stops in San Francisco and San Jose.

How about going to sleep in San Francisco and waking up in Los Angeles? That's the idea behind **Cabin** (www.ridecabin.com), a charter bus with sleeping pods that leaves from San Francisco's Bayside Lot (1 Bryant St.) at 11pm and arrives at 7am at Santa Monica's Palisades Park (Palisades Park at Ocean Ave. and Arizona Ave.).

## Getting to Los Angeles
### By Air

The greater Los Angeles area is thick with airports. **Los Angeles International Airport** (LAX, 1 World Way, 855/872-7245, www.lawa.org) serves the region and is located about 10 miles south of the city of Santa Monica. If you're coming in from another country or from across the continent, you're likely to find your flight coming into this endlessly crowded hub. If you're flying home from LAX, plan plenty of time to get through security and the check-in lines, up to three hours for a domestic flight on a holiday weekend.

To miss the major crowds, consider flying into one of the many suburban airports. Just 20 miles north of downtown Los Angeles is **Hollywood Burbank Airport** (BUR, 2627 N. Hollywood Way, Burbank, 818/840-8840, http://hollywoodburbankairport.com) in Burbank. **John Wayne Airport** (SNA, 18601 Airport Way, Santa Ana, 949/252-5200, www.ocair.com) serves Disneyland perfectly, and **Long Beach Airport** (LGB, 4100 Donald Douglas Dr., Long Beach, 562/570-2600, www.lgb.org) is convenient to the beaches. **Ontario Airport** (ONT, 2500-2900 E. Airport Dr., Ontario, 909/544-5300, www.flyontario.com) is farther out but a good option for travelers planning to divide their time between Los Angeles, Palm Springs, and the deserts.

From LAX, free shuttle buses provide service to **Metro Rail** (323/466-3876, www.metro.net, $1.75), accessible at the Green Line Aviation Station. Metro Rail trains connect Long Beach, Hollywood, North Hollywood, downtown Los Angeles, and Pasadena. Passengers should wait under the blue "LAX Shuttle Airline Connection" signs outside the lower-level terminals and board the "G" shuttle. Passengers may also take the "C" shuttle to the **Metro Bus Center** (323/466-3876, www.metro.net), which connects to city buses that serve the entire L.A. area. Information about bus service is provided via telephones on the Information Display Board inside each terminal.

Shuttle services are also available if you want to share a ride. **Prime Time Shuttle** (800/733-8267, www.primetimeshuttle. com) and **SuperShuttle** (800/258-3826, www.supershuttle.com) are authorized to serve the entire Los Angeles area from LAX. These vans can be found on the lower arrivals deck in front of each terminal, under the orange "Shared Ride Vans" signs. Average fares for two people are about $32 to downtown Los Angeles, $34 to West Hollywood, and $30 to Santa Monica.

**Taxis** can be found on the lower arrivals level islands in front of each terminal, below the yellow "Taxi" signs. Only licensed taxis are allowed into the airport; they have standard rates of about $40 to downtown and $30 to West Los Angeles. Use your cell phone to access ride-sharing services **Lyft** (www.lyft.com) or **Uber** (www.uber.com), which charge $27-99 for a ride from LAX to downtown.

## By Train
**Amtrak** (800/872-7245, www.amtrak. com) travels to Los Angeles. The main stop is **Union Station** (800 N. Alameda St., www.unionstationla.com), though there are other stops in **Glendale** (400 W. Cerritos Ave.), **Anaheim** (2626 E. Katella Ave.), and **Santa Ana** (1000 E. Santa Ana Blvd.). Both of the train's classic *Coast Starlight* (Seattle to Los Angeles) and *Pacific Surfliner* (San Luis Obispo to San Diego) routes stop in Los Angeles. In addition, the *Sunset Limited* (New Orleans to Los Angeles) and *Southwest Chief* (Chicago to Los Angeles) bring out-of-state visitors to the city.

## By Bus
**Greyhound** (800/231-2222, www.greyhound.com) provides cheap transportation to Los Angeles and many of the surrounding communities. There's the **Los Angeles Station** (1716 E. 7th St., 213/629-8401) along with other stations including **Long Beach** (1498 Long Beach Blvd., 562/218-3011), **North Hollywood** (11239 Magnolia Blvd., 818/761-5119), and **Anaheim** (2626 E. Katella Ave., 714/999-1256). **Megabus** (http://us.megabus.com) provides another inexpensive bus seat to Los Angeles.

**Cabin** (www.ridecabin.com) allows you to sleep on a charter bus with sleeping pods that leaves Santa Monica's Palisades Park (Palisades Park at Ocean Ave. and Arizona Ave.) at 11pm and arrives at 7am in San Francisco's Bayside Lot (1 Bryant St.).

## Getting to Las Vegas
### By Air
**McCarran International Airport** (LAS, 5757 Wayne Newton Blvd., 702/261-5211, www.mccarran.com) is the airport for Las Vegas. The big airlines (Delta, American Airlines, United) fly into Las Vegas, but many smaller airlines (Allegiant, Spirit, Volaris) sometimes offer better deals. Vision Airlines flies into the significantly less crowded **North**

**Las Vegas Airport** (VGT, 2730 Airport Dr., 702/261-3801, www.vgt.aero).

The Las Vegas Strip and its hotels are just three miles from the airport. Ten taxicab companies pick up from the airport, including the **Desert Cab Company** (702/386-9102, www.desertcabinc.com). The three-mile ride will cost around $15. Shuttles are also an option. **SuperShuttle** (800/258-3826, www.supershuttle.com) and **Airline Shuttle Corp.** (702/444-1234, www.airlineshuttlecorp.com) pick up at the airport. Of course, this is Las Vegas, so a limo service is not out of the question. **Las Vegas Limousines** (702/888-4848, www.lasvegaslimo.com) can get you from the airport to where you need to be in style. Ride-sharing services **Lyft** (www.lyft.com) and **Uber** (www.uber.com) can pick you up at McCarran International Airport, but only from the parking garage, not the terminals.

### By Train

Believe it or not, there is no **Amtrak** (800/872-7245, www.amtrak.com) train stop in Las Vegas. But passengers who take the train to Kingman, Arizona, can catch an Amtrak shuttle bus to the **Las Vegas Curbside Bus Stop** (6675 Gilespie St.). In addition, Amtrak reserves a number of seats on Greyhound buses from Los Angeles to Las Vegas, which can be booked through Amtrak.

### By Bus

**Greyhound** (800/231-2222, www.greyhound.com) and **Megabus** (http://us.megabus.com) both have buses traveling to Las Vegas. Like the casinos, the **Greyhound Bus Station** (200 S. Main St., 702/384-9561) is open 24-7.

# Road Rules

In California, scenic coastal routes such as CA-1 and US-101 are often destinations in themselves. **CA-1,** also known as the Pacific Coast Highway, follows the North Coast from Leggett to San Luis Obispo on the Central Coast and points south. Running parallel and intertwining with CA-1 for much of its length, **US-101** stretches north-south from Crescent City on the North Coast through the Central Coast, meeting CA-1 in San Luis Obispo.

**CA-120** from San Francisco to Yosemite National Park starts off going through nondescript Central Valley towns, but the road really becomes scenic as it climbs up into the foothills of the Sierra Nevada. From the town of Groveland to the entrance to the park, it is a nice drive with occasional mountain vistas and worthwhile stops like Rainbow Pool on the Tuolumne River. If it's summer or fall, you can take CA-120 across the park and over Tioga Pass. It is one of California's best mountain drives.

Uncrowded **US-395,** on the route between Yosemite and Las Vegas, skirts the dramatic eastern Sierra. Desert highways **I-95** and **I-40** connect California with neighboring states Nevada and Arizona, respectively.

## Car and RV Rental

Most car-rental companies are located at each of the major California airports. To reserve a car in advance, contact **Budget Rent A Car** (U.S. 800/218-7992, outside U.S. 800/472-3325, www.budget.com), **Dollar Rent A Car** (800/800-5252, www.dollar.com), **Enterprise** (855/266-9289, www.enterprise.com), or **Hertz** (U.S. and Canada 800/654-3131, international 800/654-3001, www.hertz.com).

To rent a car, drivers in California must be at least 21 years of age and have a valid driver's license. California law also requires that all vehicles carry liability insurance. You can purchase insurance with your rental car, but it generally costs an additional $10 per day, which can add up quickly. Most private auto insurance will also cover rental cars. Before buying rental insurance, check your car insurance policy to see if rental-car coverage is included.

The **average cost** of a rental car is $50 per day or $210 per week; however, rates vary greatly based on the time of year and distance traveled. Weekend and summer rentals cost significantly more. Generally, it is more expensive to rent from car rental agencies at an airport. To avoid excessive rates, first plan travel to areas where a car is not required, then rent a car from an agency branch in town to further explore more rural areas. Rental agencies occasionally allow vehicle drop-off at a different location from where it was picked up for an additional fee.

Another option is to rent an **RV.** You won't have to worry about camping or lodging options, and many facilities, particularly farther north, accommodate RVs. However, RVs are difficult to maneuver and park, limiting your access to metropolitan areas. They are also expensive, both in terms of gas and the rental rates. Rates during the summer average $1,300 per week and $570 for three days, the standard minimal rental. **Cruise America** (800/671-8042, www.cruiseamerica.com) has branches in San Mateo (just south of San Francisco), San Jose, San Luis Obispo, Los Angeles, Burbank, and Costa Mesa. **El Monte RV** (800/337-2214, www.elmonterv.com) operates out of San Francisco, Santa Cruz, Los Angeles, and Newport Beach.

**Jucy Rentals** (U.S. 800/650-4180, U.K. 0808 234 7261, Canada 1844 261 0376, Germany 0800 181 7169, www.jucyrentals.com) rents minivans with pop-up tops. These colorful vehicles are smaller and easier to manage than large RVs, but still come equipped with a fridge, a gas cooker, a sink, a DVD player, and two double beds. Rental locations are in San Francisco, Los Angeles, and Las Vegas.

## Road Conditions

Road closures are not uncommon in winter. CA-1 along the coast can shut down due to flooding or landslides. I-5 through the Central Valley can close or be subject to hazardous driving conditions resulting from tule fog, which can reduce visibility to only a few feet.

Traffic jams, accidents, mudslides, fires, and snow can affect interstates and local highways at any time. Before heading out on your adventure, check road conditions online with the state highways department, **Caltrans** (www.dot.ca.gov).

## Roadside Assistance

In an emergency, **dial 911** from any phone. The American Automobile Association, better known as **AAA** (800/222-4357, www.aaa.com), offers roadside assistance—free to members; others pay a fee.

Be aware of your car's maintenance needs while on the road. The most frequent maintenance needs result from **summer heat.** If the car gets hot or overheats, stop for a while to cool it off. Never open the radiator cap if the engine is steaming. After the engine cools, squeeze the top radiator hose to see if there's any pressure in it; if there isn't, it's safe to open. Never pour water into a hot radiator because it could crack the engine block. If you start to smell rubber, your tires are overheating, and that's a good way to have a blowout. Stop and let them cool off. During **winter** in the high country around Yosemite, a can of silicone lubricant such as WD-40 will unfreeze door locks, dry off humid wiring, and keep your hinges in shape.

## Parking

Parking is at a premium in big cities. Most hotels within San Francisco, Los Angeles, and Las Vegas will charge guests $50 or more per night for parking. Remove any valuables from your vehicle for the evening, because some hotel valets just park your car in an adjacent public parking deck. Many attractions charge visitors an admission fee *and* a parking fee. For instance, Disneyland charges a $20 parking fee.

Parking is strictly regulated at the national parks. At Yosemite and the Grand Canyon, **park entrance fees** include entry and parking for up to seven days. Visitors are encouraged to park their cars at the outer edges of the parks and use the extensive network of **free shuttles** to get around the parks.

## International Drivers Licenses

If you are visiting the United States from another country, you need to secure an International Driving Permit from your home country before coming to the United States. It can't be obtained once you're here. You must also bring your government-issued driving permit.

Visitors from outside the United States should check the driving rules of the states they will visit at www.usa.gov/Topics/Motor-Vehicles.shtml. Among the most important rules is that traffic runs on the right side of the road in the United States. Note that both California and Nevada have bans on using handheld cell phones while driving. If you get caught, expect to pay a hefty fine.

## Maps and Visitor information

When visiting **California,** rely on **local, regional,** and **national park visitors centers,** which are usually staffed by rangers or volunteers who feel passion and pride for their locale. The **Golden State Welcome Centers** (www.visitcalifornia.com) scattered throughout the state are less useful, but can be a good place to pick up maps and brochures. The state's **California Travel and Tourism Commission** (916/444-4429, www.visitcalifornia.com) also provides helpful and free tips, information, and downloadable maps and guides.

The website **Travel Nevada** (www.travelnevada.com) has downloadable visitor guides, including the US-95 Adventure. The **Arizona Office of Tourism** (www.visitarizona.com) also offers a free downloadable state map online.

The American Automobile Association, better known as **AAA** (www.aaa.com), offers free maps to its members. The **Thomas Guide Road Atlas** (866/896-6277, www.mapbooks4u.com) is a reliable and detailed map and road guide and a great insurance policy against getting lost. Almost all gas stations and drugstores sell maps.

California and Nevada are in the Pacific time zone (PST and PDT) and observe daylight saving time March-November. Arizona is in the Mountain time zone (MST), and only the Navajo Nation observes daylight saving time.

# Visas and Officialdom

## Passports and Visas

Visiting from another country, you must have a **valid passport** and a **visa** to enter the United States. If you hold a current passport from one of the following countries, you may qualify for the **Visa Waiver Program:** Andorra, Australia, Austria, Belgium, Brunei, Chile, Czech Republic, Denmark, Estonia, Finland, France, Germany, Greece, Hungary, Iceland, Ireland, Italy, Japan, Latvia, Liechtenstein, Lithuania, Luxembourg, Malta, Monaco, the Netherlands, New Zealand, Norway, Portugal, San Marino, Singapore, Slovakia, Slovenia, South Korea, Spain, Sweden, Switzerland, Taiwan, and the United Kingdom. To qualify, you must apply online with the Electronic System for Travel Authorization at www.cbp.gov and hold a **return plane or cruise ticket** to your country of origin dated less than **90 days** from your date of entry. Holders of Canadian passports don't need visas or visa waivers.

In most other countries, the local U.S. embassy should be able to provide a **tourist visa.** The application fee for a visa is US$160, although you will have to pay an issuance fee as well. While a visa may be processed in as little as 24 hours on request, plan for at least a couple of weeks, as there can be unexpected delays, particularly during the busy summer season (June-Aug.). For information, visit http://travel.state.gov.

## Consulates

San Francisco and Los Angeles are home to consulates from many countries around the globe. If you should lose your passport or find yourself in some other trouble while visiting California, contact your country's offices for assistance. The website of the **U.S. State Department** (www.state.gov) lists the websites for all foreign embassies and consulates in the United States. A representative will be able to direct you to the nearest embassy or consulate.

The **British Consulate** (www.gov.uk) has California offices in **San Francisco** (1 Sansome St., Ste. 850, 415/617-1300) and **Los Angeles** (2029 Century Park E., Ste. 1350, 310/789-0031). The Los Angeles office also represents Nevada and Arizona.

The **Australian Consulate** has offices in **Los Angeles** (2029 Century Park E., 310/229-2300, www.losangeles.consulate. gov.au) and **San Francisco** (575 Market St., Ste. 1800, 415/644-3260, www.usa. embassy.gov.au).

The **Consulate General of Canada** has an office in **San Francisco** (580 California St., 14th Fl., 415/834-3180) and **Los Angeles** (550 S. Hope St., 9th Fl., 213/346-2700).

## Customs

Before you enter the United States from another country by sea or by air, you'll be required to fill out a customs form. Check with the U.S. embassy in your country or the **Customs and Border Protection** website (www.cbp.gov) for an updated list of items you must declare.

If you require medication administered by injection, you must pack your syringes in a checked bag; syringes are not permitted in carry-ons coming into the United States. Also, pack documentation describing your need for any narcotic medications you've brought with you. Failure to produce documentation for narcotics on request can result in severe penalties in the United States.

If you're driving into California along I-5 or another major highway, prepare to stop at **Agricultural Inspection Stations** a few miles inside the state line. You don't need to present a passport, a visa, or even a driver's license; instead, you must be prepared to present all your fruits and vegetables. California's largest economic sector is agriculture, and a number of the major crops grown here are sensitive to pests and diseases. In an effort to prevent known pests from entering the state and endangering crops, travelers are asked to identify all produce they're carrying in from other states or from Mexico. If you've got produce, especially homegrown or from a farm stand, it could be infected by a known problem pest or disease. Expect it to be confiscated on the spot.

You'll also be asked about fruits and veggies on your U.S. Customs form, which you'll be asked to fill out on the airplane or ship before you reach the United States.

# Travel Tips

## Conduct and Customs

The legal **drinking age** everywhere in the United States is 21. Expect to have your ID checked if you look under age 30, especially in bars and clubs, but also in restaurants and wineries. California bars and clubs that serve alcohol close at 2am; you'll find the occasional after-hours nightspot in San Francisco.

**Smoking** has been banned in many places throughout California. Don't expect to find a smoking section in any restaurant or an ashtray in any bar. Smoking is illegal in all bars and clubs, but your new favorite watering hole might have an outdoor patio where smokers can huddle. Taking the ban one step further, many hotels, motels, and inns throughout

California are strictly nonsmoking, and you'll be subject to fees of hundreds of dollars if your room smells of smoke when you leave. There's no smoking in any public building, and even some parks don't allow cigarettes. There's often good reason for this; the fire danger is extreme in the summer, and one carelessly thrown butt can cause a catastrophe.

In 2016, the state of California officially legalized **recreational marijuana.** That said, don't light up that joint in public just yet. Though it is technically legal to use, share, or possess cannabis, there will not be any legal stores open where you can purchase pot until 2018. In addition, the drug is still illegal under federal law, setting up a possible legal fight between the federal and state governments.

## Money

California, Nevada, and Arizona use the **U.S. dollar ($).** Most businesses also accept the **major credit cards** Visa, MasterCard, Discover, and American Express. ATM and debit cards work at many stores and restaurants, and ATMs are available throughout the region.

You can **change currency** at any international airport in California and at McCarran International Airport in Las Vegas. Currency exchange points also crop up in downtown San Francisco and at some of the major business hotels in urban areas.

### ATMs

As with anywhere, traveling with a huge amount of cash is not recommended, which may make frequent trips to the bank necessary. Fortunately, most destinations have at least one major bank. Bank of America and Wells Fargo have a large presence throughout California. **Banking hours** tend to be 8am-5pm Monday-Friday, 9am-noon Saturday. Never count on a bank being open on Sunday or on federal holidays. If you need cash when the banks are closed,

there is generally a **24-hour ATM** available. Furthermore, many cash-only businesses have an ATM on-site for those who don't have enough cash ready in their wallets. The unfortunate downside to this convenience is a fee of $2-4 per transaction. This also applies to ATMs at banks at which you don't have an account.

### Tax

**California sales tax** varies by city and county, but the base rate is 7.25 percent. All goods are taxable with the exception of food not eaten on the premises. For example, your bill at a restaurant will include tax, but your bill at a grocery store will not. The hotel tax is another unexpected added expense to traveling in California. Most cities have enacted a **hotel room tax** largely to make up for budget shortfalls. As you would expect, these taxes are higher in areas more popular with visitors.

**Nevada sales tax** is 6.85 percent and can reach up to 8.1 percent, depending where you are. **Arizona sales tax** is 5.6 percent but can reach as high as 10.7 percent, depending on the municipality.

### Tipping

Tipping is expected and appreciated, and a **15 percent tip** for **restaurants** is the norm. When ordering in bars, tip the bartender or waitstaff $1 per drink. Cafés and coffee shops often have tip jars out. There is no consensus on what is appropriate when purchasing a $3 beverage. Often $0.50 is enough, depending on the quality and service. For **taxis,** plan to tip **15-20 percent** of the fare, or simply round up the cost to the nearest dollar.

## Traveling Without Reservations

During the busy summer months, accommodations can be hard to come by. If you find yourself without reservations in one of the cities, many online travel services, including **www.hotels.com,** can set you up with a last-minute room. Download the superb **HotelTonight** (www.hoteltonight.com) app on your smartphone for great last-minute deals on hotel stays.

It's also not unusual for national park lodgings and campgrounds to be full during high season. It may be possible to find a last-minute campsite at one of the nearby national forests. The **Stanislaus National Forest** (www.fs.usda. gov/stanislaus) and the **Sierra National Forest** (www.fs.usda.gov/sierra) surround Yosemite, while the **Kaibab National Forest** (www.fs.usda.gov/kaibab) is near the Grand Canyon.

Discount hotel chain **Super 8** (800/454-3213, www.wyndhamho-tels.com/super-8) has locations in Los Angeles, San Francisco, Las Vegas, and Williams, Arizona, gateway to the Grand Canyon. Slightly more upscale, **La Quinta** (800/753-3757, www.lq.com) has hotels in California and Las Vegas.

## Communications and Media

**Cell phone reception** is good except in places far from any large town. Likewise, you can find **Internet access** just about anywhere. The bigger cities are well wired, but even in small towns you can log on either at a library or in a café with a computer in the back. Be prepared to pay a per-minute usage fee or purchase a drink. The desert regions of Arizona and Nevada have limited or nonexistent cell phone reception, but Las Vegas is a good place to retrieve voicemails if you've missed incoming calls.

The main newspapers in California are the *San Francisco Chronicle* (www. sfchronicle.com) and the *Los Angeles Times* (www.latimes.com). The big daily paper in Las Vegas is the *Las Vegas Sun* (www.lasvegassun.com). Each major city also has a free weekly newspaper that has comprehensive arts and events coverage. Of course, there are other regional papers that may offer some international news in addition to the local color. As for radio, there are some news stations on the FM dial, and in most regions you can count on finding a **National Public Radio** (NPR, www.npr.org) affiliate. While they will all offer some NPR news coverage, some will be more geared toward music and local concerns.

Because of the area's size both geographically and in terms of population, you will have to contend with multiple **telephone area codes.** The 800 or 866 area codes are **toll-free numbers.** Any time you are dialing out of the area, you must dial a 1 plus the area code followed by the seven-digit number.

To **mail** a letter, find a blue post office box, which are found on the main streets of any town. Postage rates vary by destination. You can purchase stamps at the local post office, where you can also mail packages. Stamps can also be bought at some ATMs and online at www.usps. com, which can also give you the location and hours of the nearest post office. Post offices are generally open Monday-Friday, with limited hours on Saturday. They are always closed on Sunday and federal holidays.

## Accessibility

Most California attractions, hotels, and restaurants are accessible for **travelers with disabilities.** State law requires that public transportation must accommodate travelers with disabilities. Public spaces and businesses must have adequate facilities with equal access. This includes national parks and historic structures, many of which have been refitted with ramps and wider doors. Many hiking trails are also accessible to wheelchairs, and most campgrounds designate specific campsites that meet the Americans with Disabilities Act standards. The state of California also provides a free telephone TDD-to-voice relay service; just dial 711.

If you are traveling with a disability, there are many resources to help you plan your trip. **Access Northern California** (http://accessnca.org) is a non-profit organization that offers general travel tips, including recommendations on accommodations, parks and trails, transportation, and travel equipment. **Gimp-on-the-Go** (www.gimponthego. com) is another travel resource. The message board on the **American Foundation for the Blind** (www.afb.org) website is a good forum to discuss travel strategies for the visually impaired. For a comprehensive guide to wheelchair-accessible beaches, rivers, and shorelines from Santa Cruz to Marin County, including the East Bay and Wine Country, contact the **California Coastal Conservancy** (510/286-1015, www.scc.ca.gov), which publishes a free and downloadable guide. **Wheelchair Getaways** (800/642-2042, www.wheelchairgetaways.com) in San Francisco (800/638-1912), Los Angeles (800/638-1912), and Las Vegas (888/824-7413) rent wheelchair-accessible vans and offer pickup and drop-off service from airports ($100-300). Likewise, **Avis Access** (888/879-4273, www.avis.com) rents cars, scooters, and other products to make traveling with a disability easier; click on the "Services" link on its website.

The **Las Vegas Convention and Visitor's Authority** (www.lasvegas.com) provides for information on the assistance available in Las Vegas. **Grand Canyon National Park** operates wheelchair-accessible park shuttles and the park's website (www.nps.gov/grca) has a downloadable accessibility guide.

## Traveling with Children

Many spots in California are ideal destinations for families with children of all ages. Amusement parks, interactive museums, zoos, parks, beaches, and playgrounds all make for family-friendly fun. On the other hand, there are a few spots in the Golden State that beckon more to adults than to children. Frankly, there aren't many family activities in Wine Country. This adult playground is all about alcoholic beverages and high-end dining. In fact, before you book a room at a B&B that you expect to share with your kids, check to be sure that the inn can accommodate extra people in the guest rooms and whether they allow guests under age 16.

## Senior Travelers

Senior discounts are available nearly every place you go, including restaurants, golf courses, major attractions, and even some hotels. The minimum age ranges 50-65. Ask about discounts and be prepared to produce ID if you look younger than your years. You can often get additional discounts on rental cars, hotels, and tour packages as a member of **AARP** (888/687-2277, www.aarp.org). If you're not a member, its website can also offer helpful travel tips and advice. **Elderhostel** (800/454-5768, www.road-scholar.org) is another great resource for senior travelers. Dedicated to providing educational opportunities for older travelers, Elderhostel provides package trips to beautiful and interesting destinations. Called "Educational Adventures," these trips are generally 3-9 days long and emphasize nature, history, art, and music. **Senior Discounts Las Vegas** (http://seniordiscountslasvegas.com) has an online directory of businesses with senior discounts.

## Gay and Lesbian Travelers

The Golden State is a golden place for gay travel. As with much of the country, the farther you venture into rural and agricultural regions, the less likely you are to experience liberal attitudes and acceptance. The **International Gay and Lesbian Travel Association** (www.iglta.org) has a directory of gay- and lesbian-friendly tour operators, accommodations, and destinations.

**San Francisco** has the biggest and arguably best **Gay Pride Festival** (www.sf-pride.org) in the nation, usually held on the last weekend in June. Year-round, the **Castro District** offers fun of all kinds, from theater to clubs to shopping, mostly targeted at gay men but with a few places sprinkled in for lesbians. If the Castro is your primary destination, you can even find a place to stay in the middle of the action. South of San Francisco on the Pacific Coast, **Santa Cruz** is known for its lesbian-friendly culture. In **Los Angeles, West Hollywood** has its own upscale gay culture, where clubs are havens of the see-and-be-seen crowd.

Gay and lesbian travelers may find Arizona less welcoming, but **Las Vegas** has some gay-friendly fixtures, whether it's the glamorous entertainers on stage or the **Fruit Loop,** a cluster of gay bars along Paradise Road, north of the airport.

# Health and Safety

## Medical Services

For an emergency anywhere in California, Nevada, or Arizona, **dial 911.** Inside hotels and resorts, check your emergency number as soon as you get to your guest room. In urban and suburban areas, full-service hospitals and medical centers abound, but in more remote regions, help can be more than an hour away.

## Wilderness Safety

If you're planning a **backcountry expedition,** follow all rules and guidelines for obtaining **wilderness permits** and for self-registration at trailheads. These are for your safety, letting the rangers know roughly where you plan to be and when to expect you back. National park and state park visitors centers can advise in more detail on any health or wilderness alerts in the area. It is also advisable to let someone outside your party know your route and expected date of return.

Being out in the elements can present its own set of challenges. Despite California's relatively mild climate, **heat exhaustion** and **heatstroke** can affect anyone during the hot summer months, particularly during a long strenuous hike

in the sun. Common symptoms include nausea, lightheadedness, headache, or muscle cramps. **Dehydration** and loss of electrolytes are the common causes of heat exhaustion. The risks are even higher in the desert regions of Arizona and Nevada. If you or anyone in your group develops any of these symptoms, get out of the sun immediately, stop all physical activity, and drink plenty of water. Heat exhaustion can be severe, and if untreated can lead to heatstroke, in which the body's core temperature reaches 105°F. Fainting, seizures, confusion, and rapid heartbeat and breathing can indicate the situation has moved beyond heat exhaustion. If you suspect this, call 911 immediately.

Similar precautions hold true for **hypothermia,** which is caused by prolonged exposure to cold water or weather. For many in California, this can happen on a hike or backpacking trip without sufficient rain gear, or by staying too long in the ocean or another cold body of water without a wetsuit. Symptoms include shivering, weak pulse, drowsiness, confusion, slurred speech, or stumbling. To treat hypothermia, immediately remove wet clothing, cover the person with blankets, and feed him or her hot liquids. If symptoms don't improve, call 911.

**Ticks** live in many of the forests and grasslands throughout California, except at higher elevations. Tick season generally runs late fall-early summer. If you are hiking through brushy areas, wear pants and long-sleeve shirts. Ticks like to crawl to warm moist places (armpits are a favorite) on their host. If a tick is engorged, it can be difficult to remove. There are two main types of ticks found in California: dog ticks and deer ticks. Dog ticks are larger, brown, and have a gold spot on their backs, while deer ticks are small, tear-shaped, and black. Deer ticks are known to carry Lyme disease. While Lyme disease is relatively rare in California, it is very serious. If you get bitten by a deer tick and the bite leaves a red ring, seek medical attention. Lyme disease can be successfully treated with early rounds of antibiotics.

There is only one major variety of plant in California that can cause an adverse reaction in humans if you touch the leaves or stems: **poison oak,** a common shrub that inhabits forests throughout the state. Poison oak has a characteristic three-leaf configuration, with scalloped leaves that are shiny green in the spring and then turn yellow, orange, and red in late summer-fall. In fall, the leaves drop, leaving a cluster of innocuous-looking branches. The oil in poison oak is present year-round in both the leaves and branches. Your best protection is to wear long sleeves and long pants when hiking, no matter how hot it is. A product called Tecnu is available at most California drugstores; slather it on before you go hiking to protect yourself from poison oak. If your skin comes into contact with poison oak, expect a nasty rash known for its itchiness and irritation. Poison oak is also extremely transferable, so avoid touching your eyes, face, or other parts of your body to prevent spreading the rash. Calamine lotion can help, and in extreme cases a doctor can administer cortisone to help decrease the inflammation.

## Wildlife

Many places are still wild in California, making it important to use precautions with regard to wildlife. While California no longer has any grizzly bears, **black bears** thrive and are often seen in the mountains foraging for food in the spring, summer, and fall. Black bears certainly don't have the size or reputation of grizzlies, but there is good reason to exercise caution. Never get between a bear and her cub, and if a bear sees you, identify yourself as human by waving your hands above your head, speaking in a calm voice, and backing away slowly. If a bear charges, do not run. One of the best precautions against an unwanted bear encounter is to keep a clean camp; store all food in airtight, bear-proof containers, and strictly follow any guidelines given by the park or rangers.

Even more common than bears are **mountain lions,** which can be found in the Coast Range as well as in grasslands and forests. Because of their solitary nature, it is unlikely you will see one, even on long trips in the backcountry. Still, there are a couple things to remember. If you come across a kill, probably a large partly eaten deer, leave immediately. And if you see a mountain lion and it sees you, identify yourself as human, making your body appear as big as possible, just as with a bear. And remember: Never run. As with any cat, large or small, running triggers its hunting instincts. If a mountain lion should attack, fight back; cats don't like to get hurt.

The other treacherous critter in the backcountry is the **rattlesnake.** They can be found in summer in generally hot and dry areas from the coast to the Sierra Nevada. When hiking in this type of terrain (many parks will indicate if rattlesnakes are a problem in the area), keep your eyes on the ground and an ear out for the telltale rattle. Snakes like to warn you to keep away. The only time this is not the case is with baby rattlesnakes that have not yet developed their rattles. Unfortunately, they have developed their fangs and venom, which is particularly potent. Should you get bitten, get immediate medical help.

While mountain lions and rattlesnakes also exist in the Grand Canyon area, it is wild deer, elk, and, believe it or not, rock squirrels that have caused visitors to the park the most harm. Squirrel bites are actually the most common wildlife-inflicted injury in the area.

## Crime

In both rural and urban areas, **theft** can be a problem. Don't leave any valuables in the car. If you must, place them out of sight, either in a locked glove box or in the trunk. Don't leave your wallet, camera, or other expensive items accessible to others, for example, in a backpack or purse. Keep them on your person at all times if possible.

Take some **basic precautions** and pay attention to your surroundings, just as you would in any unfamiliar place. Carry your car keys in your hand when walking out to your car. Don't sit in your parked car in a lonely parking lot at night; just get in, turn on the engine, and drive away. When you're walking down a city street, be alert and keep an eye on your surroundings and on anyone who might be following you. Certain **urban neighborhoods** are best avoided at night. If you find yourself in these areas after dark, call a taxi to avoid walking blocks and blocks to get to your car or waiting for public transportation. In case of a theft or any other emergency, **call 911.**

# Internet Resources

Spend some time on the Internet before your trip to find out about current conditions in the areas you are visiting. You also may be able to find out about some places to visit that you never knew existed.

### Caltrans (California Department of Transportation)
**www.dot.ca.gov**
Check Caltrans for state map and highway information before planning a coastal road trip.

### Arizona Department of Transportation
**www.azdot.gov**
For information about the conditions of Arizona's roadways, visit this site.

### Nevada Department of Transportation
**www.nevadadot.com**
Nevada Department of Transportation's website has a map detailing current road conditions.

### Visit California
**www.visitcalifornia.com**
Before your visit, visit the official tourism site of the state of California.

### California Outdoor and Recreational Information
**www.caoutdoors.com**
This recreation-focused website includes links to maps, local newspapers, festivals, and events as well as a wide variety of recreational activities throughout the state.

### California State Parks
**www.parks.ca.gov**
The official website lists hours, accessibility, activities, camping areas, fees, and more information for all parks in the state system.

### SFGate
**www.sfgate.com**
This website affiliated with the *San Francisco Chronicle* offers information on activities, festivals, and events in the city by the bay.

### SF Weekly
**www.sfweekly.com**
This website for one of the city's weekly alternative papers has a strong arts and entertainment emphasis.

### LA Weekly
**www.laweekly.com**
One of the best alternative weeklies out there, the *LA Weekly* has superb arts, music, and food coverage.

### LATourist
**www.latourist.com**
This informative tourism website is dedicated to the City of Angels.

### Los Angeles Convention and Visitors Bureau
**www.discoverlosangeles.com**
It's the official website of the Los Angeles Convention and Visitors Bureau.

### Disneyland
**http:/disneyland.disney.go.com**
Find information on all things Disney.

### Yosemite National Park
**www.nps.gov/yose**
The park's website has lots of great information for trip planning, including an overview of park features, a write-up on trails, and the latest road conditions.

### Grand Canyon National Park
**www.nps.gov/grca**
The park's website has lots of great information for trip planning including an overview of park features, a write-up on trails, and the latest road conditions.

### Las Vegas
**www.lasvegas.com**
"The only official website of Las Vegas" has hotel deals, show deals, and a downloadable visitors guide.

# Index

# LIST OF MAPS

# PHOTO CREDITS

# MOON NATIONAL PARKS

**ACADIA**
NATIONAL PARK
HILARY NANGLE

**ARCHES &
CANYONLANDS**
NATIONAL PARKS
W.C. MCRAE, JUDY JEWELL

**BANFF**
NATIONAL PARK
ANDREW HEMPSTEAD

**DEATH VALLEY**
NATIONAL PARK
JENNA BLOUGH

**GLACIER**
NATIONAL PARK
BECKY LOMAX

**GRAND
CANYON**
KATHLEEN BRYANT

**GREAT SMOKY
MOUNTAINS**
NATIONAL PARK
JASON FRYE

**MOUNT RUSHMORE
& THE BLACK HILLS**
Including the Badlands
LAURAL A. BIDWELL

**ROCKY MOUNTAIN**
NATIONAL PARK
ERIN ENGLISH

## In these books:

- Full coverage of gateway cities and towns
- Itineraries from one day to multiple weeks
- Advice on where to stay (or camp) in and around the parks